The Practical

Perfect for the tourist in Japan or student of Japanese, this handy pocket-size dictionary contains over 8,000 entries, selected and compiled with an emphasis on usefulness and naturalness of expression. For those concerned about their less-than-perfect pronunciation, all entries appear in both romanized Japanese and Japanese writing—thus the user need only point to be understood.

NOAH S. BRANNEN, who holds a doctorate degree in Far Eastern languages and literature from the University of Michigan, recently retired as professor at International Christian University in Tokyo. Among his numerous writings are *Everyday Japanese* and *Japanese by the Total Method*.

THE PRACTICAL
ENGLISH-JAPANESE
DICTIONARY

by Noah S. Brannen

New York · WEATHERHILL · *Tokyo*

First edition, 1991
Third printing, 1993

Published by Weatherhill, Inc., of New York and Tokyo, with editorial offices
at 420 Madison Avenue, 15th Floor, New York, N.Y. 10017. Protected by
copyright under the terms of the International Copyright Union; all rights
reserved. Printed in the U.S.A.

Library of Congress Cataloging in Publication Data: Brannen,
Noah S. / The practical English-Japanese dictionary. / 1. English
language—Dictionaries—Japanese. 2. Japanese language—Text-
books for foreign speakers. I. Title. / PL679.B72   1983
423′.956 / 83–6933 / ISBN 0–8348–0187–6

This book is dedicated to
my daughter Sharon
with all my love

Contents

Preface

Like many non-Japanese residing in Japan, when I prepare myself for an event such as a trip in a taxi to an unfamiliar place or an appointment with the doctor, I have to consult English-Japanese dictionaries to supplement my vocabulary. In most instances, however, I find my search frustrated by the very sources I hoped would solve my problems. Either their viewpoint is strangely alien, the vocabulary not meeting my needs, or the appropriateness in terms of context and time is not specified for the equivalents given. Another vexation is their choice of the stiff and impersonal, polite style when rendering sample sentences in Japanese. Add to these the fact that their grammatical notation is from the point of view of English, which is no help to one who wants to know more about Japanese, and it's easy to see why I find it hard to believe they were written for non-Japanese.

Similar problems are encountered in romanized English-Japanese dictionaries, although most of these are more in the nature of phrase books prepared for tourists and necessarily limited. The greater part of these inadequacies, I believe, stem from the fact that these dictionaries were prepared by people whose native language is not English. To my knowledge, no comprehensive romanized English-Japanese dictionary has yet been compiled by a native speaker of English. This dictionary aims to fill this gap.

The strength of this point of departure is that it represents the fruits of a native speaker's search for the right way to say something originally thought up in English. All entries were selected with sensitivity to the needs of adult resident aliens, students of Japanese, and visitors to Japan. In many, a number of Japanese equivalents are presented, each in terms of its appropriateness. The user is thus spared the dilemma of choosing from among the many equivalents for, for example, the English word "president" and advised that the appropriate term to use when referring to a club president is *kaichō*. In such entries the equivalent whose usage is closest to the English appears first and is followed by those equivalents that require explanation or focusing.

Illustrations come directly from my own and other people's experiences of living in Japan and are presented in the most commonly used colloquial Japanese. Polite and/or honorific forms of

Preface

certain phrases, however, are included for those situations when their use is recommended. In every instance, careful attention has been given to the naturalness and effectiveness of both the English entries and the Japanese equivalents and illustrations. For example, even though the Japanese verb meaning "betray" is illustrated with the English sentence "She betrayed me," the Japanese equivalent, were it to be translated, is the passive "I was betrayed by her," which is more natural to the Japanese.

Priority is given to nouns in this dictionary because they are the building blocks of language. If you can name a thing you have the basis for communicating a thought about it. Additionally, in Japanese, many nouns can become verbs by simply suffixing the verb *suru* ([to] do); for example, the noun *benkyō* (study) with the addition of *suru* becomes the verb *benkyō-suru* ([to] study). In all verb (and adjective) entries, basic stems are clearly indicated. By following the instructions provided, you can attach various endings to these stems to specify tense, mood, and different levels of formality. Most verb entries also feature one or more illustrations in a variety of tenses to show how the verb can be conjugated to meet a given situation.

A special feature of this dictionary is the inclusion of particles in verb entries. Particles are words with functions similar to the prepositions in the English phrases "to be contrary *to*" and "to agree *with*." A particle specifies the relationship of a noun and the final predicate in a Japanese sentence—for example, whether the noun to which a particle is attached is the object or the location of the action of the verbal predicate. They also function in complex sentences to show relationships between clauses, such as sequence, cause and effect, subordination, and so on.

To further aid the user, included are a capsule guide to Japanese grammar and simple sentence structure, conjugation tables, and instructions for pronunciation.

Needless to say, numerous colleagues and friends have contributed to the making of this dictionary. Especially do I want to thank Takashi Kawawa, Sachiko Nakazawa, Shinji Takahashi, Hideo Takahashi, Tomoo Yamada, Charles de Rolf, James Wada, Keiko Wada, Deborah Urich, Sydney Ward, Sarah Ward, Akito Miyamoto, James Frederick, and Katsuhisa Yamaguchi. All of us pray that this little dictionary will have a small part to play in fostering deeper and more meaningful exchange between West and East in the years ahead. In addition, I want to say thanks to Meredith Weatherby, who suggested the project, and to the staff of Weatherhill.

Japanese Grammar Basics

The Parts of Speech

Nouns. Japanese nouns present few problems. They have no gender and, in most cases, no plural suffix. So the Japanese word for school, *gakkō*, can mean either one or several schools, depending on its context. Japanese nouns can be classified into ten categories:

ORDINARY NOUNS. Native Japanese nouns, nouns derived from Chinese (distinguished from native Japanese nouns by certain phonetic characteristics), and nouns borrowed from Western languages constitute the body of ordinary nouns.

HONORIFIC NOUNS. In polite-style and honorific-style speech, ordinary nouns are turned into honorific nouns by attaching prefixes or suffixes; for example, the honorific form of *isha* (doctor) is *o-isha-san*; that of *cha* (tea), *o-cha*; and that of *Yamamoto* (a person's last name), *Yamamoto-san*. In plain-style speech many ordinary nouns, especially the names for things connected with daily living, take the honorific prefix *o*.

INTERROGATIVE NOUNS AND INDEFINITE NOUNS. Interrogative nouns, such as *dore* (which), are made indefinite by suffixing the interrogative particle *ka* (for a discussion of particles see page xiv).

Interrogative Noun	Indefinite Noun
dore (which)	*doreka* (whichever)
dare (who)	*dareka* (someone)
doko (where)	*dokoka* (somewhere)
itsu (when)	*itsuka* (sometime)
dō (how)	*dōka* (somehow)

PRONOUNS. There are no special forms for nominative and objective cases like the English I/me and he/him. Pronouns, however, take plural suffixes.

Singular	Plural
watashi (I/me)	*watashi-tachi* (we/us)
anata (you)	*anata-gata* (you all)

Japanese Grammar Basics

kare (he/him)	*kare-ra* (they/them, masculine)
kanojo (she/her)	*kanojo-tachi* (they/them, feminine)
kore (this)	*kore-ra* (these)
sore (that)	*sore-ra* (those)
are (that, distant)	*are-ra* (those, distant)

There is a wide variety of alternate forms of personal pronouns, ranging from extremely polite to vulgar regional variations and, when referring to oneself, numerous masculine and feminine terms. The list given above, however, will suffice for the purposes of standard, polite speech. In conversation, personal pronouns, especially the equivalents for "you," are used sparingly, and the equivalent for "I" is frequently omitted.

TIME NOUNS. Time nouns are nouns that designate time, time interval, or seasons. They may have attached to them certain time-noun affixes that mean "each," "every," "about," "around," and so forth. An example of the usage of a time noun can be found on page xvi.

NUMERALS. There are two sets of numerals: one is derived from Chinese; the other, native Japanese, only extends to ten.

	Chinese-Derived Numerals	Native Japanese Numerals
1	*ichi*	*hitotsu*
2	*ni*	*futatsu*
3	*san*	*mittsu*
4	*shi/yon*	*yottsu*
5	*go*	*itsutsu*
6	*roku*	*muttsu*
7	*shichi/nana*	*nanatsu*
8	*hachi*	*yattsu*
9	*ku/kyū*	*kokonotsu*
10	*jū*	*tō*

For numerals beyond ten, combinations of Chinese-derived numerals are used; for example, *jūichi* (11), *jūni* (12), *nijūsan* (23), *sanjūyon* (34), *hyaku* (100), *gohyaku* (500), and so on.

COUNTER NOUNS. When counting objects up to ten in number, native Japanese numerals are used; for quantities greater than ten, Chinese-derived numerals are used, except in cases where there is a special counter (a combination of a Japanese- or Chinese-derived numeral and a classifier). The use of special counters in Japanese is similar to the English-speaker's practice of counting cattle by head and shoes in pairs. Many classifiers are included in this dictionary, and a handy listing of twenty common ones appears in Appendix 1.

PLURAL NOUNS. This category refers to the small number of nouns that have traditional plural forms made by reduplicating the singular form—nouns such as *ieie* (houses), *yamayama* (mountains), and *hitobito* (people). Even though plural nouns such as these exist, their standard, singular form, without reduplication, can also function as a plural as with the majority of Japanese nouns.

PLACE NAMES. Special suffixes are attached to the names of towns, prefectures, and other places; for example, *Kantō-mura* (Kanto Village), *Mitaka-shi* (Mitaka City), *Yasukuni-jinja* (Yasukuni Shrine), *Miyake-jima* (Miyake Island), *Fuji-san* (Mount Fuji), and so on.

COPULAR NOUNS. In traditional Japanese grammars this category of nouns has been called by a number of names, including adjectival verb. Two features distinguish these nouns as a category by themselves: (1) the English meaning of most such nouns is usually carried by an adjective in English, for example, *jōzu [na]* (skillful), and (2) unlike all other nouns, copular nouns take the particle *na* instead of *no* when they come before another noun and modify it, for example, *jōzu na hito* (a skillful person).

Verbs. Verbs do not have an infinitive form; for example, the verb *taberu* (eat) does not mean "to eat." Rather, it can mean "I eat," "you eat," "he/she/it eats," "we eat," "you (all) eat," or "they eat," depending on its context.

A Japanese verb is composed of a stem and an ending. In this dictionary, a dot appears in regular verb entries to separate the stem from the ending. For example, the verb *taberu* appears as *tabe·ru*, in which case the ending is *ru* and the stem *tabe*.

There are two major classes of Japanese verbs, the class in which the stem ends in a vowel and the class in which the stem ends in a consonant. It is important to recognize this distinction when attaching suffixes. To conjugate a verb whose stem ends in a vowel, all one need do is substitute a new ending for the ending of the dictionary form of the verb; for example, substituting *ta* for *ru* in *tabe·ru* (eat) yields the past indicative *tabeta* (ate). The procedure for conjugating a verb whose stem ends in a consonant is more complicated because of the assimilation of sounds. For instance, to substitute the past-tense ending *ta* for *u* in *yom·u* (read), it must be altered to *da* to accommodate the final *m* of the stem, and, in turn, the *m* is altered to *n* to accommodate the new form of the ending, yielding *yonda*.

The verbs *suru* (do) and *kuru* (come) are irregular verbs. In other words, they cannot be classified in either of the two major classes just described. These two verbs and verb compounds consisting of a noun plus *suru* are indicated with the abbreviation "irr." For a guide to verb conjugation, see Tables 1, 2, 3, and 4 on pages xxi–xl.

Adjectives. In Japanese, adjectives are made up of a stem and the ending *i* and are declined. This means that various endings—*-ku, -kute, -katta, -kattara, -kereba*, and so on—are attached to the stem of an adjective, which is separated from the ending by a dot. That adjectives have a tense may be difficult to grasp, but one soon learns to compare this concept with English expressions like "I am busy," "I was busy," and "I will be busy," where the adjective plus the auxiliary verbs can be thought of as the present, past, and future of the adjective "busy." For a guide to adjective conjugation, see Table 5 on page xli.

Copula. The word *desu* (plain: *da*) is here referred to as the copula. In Japanese grammar, the copula is not a verb, neither is it an adjective; but, like the verb and adjective, the copula is conjugated. Often it is translated as "is." The copula functions in a basic sentence type (see pages xvi–xviii) to make statements like "I am a man," "I was a boy," and "This isn't my book." For a guide to the conjugation of the copula, see Table 5 on page xli.

Adverbs. Adverbs in Japanese, as in English, are essentially manner expressions describing either how or to what extent an action takes place. Adverbs are not declined, so the form that appears in this dictionary can be used as it appears. Some adverbs are made from adjective stems by suffixing *-ku*; for example, the adjective *yasashi·i* (gentle) provides the stem for the adverb *yasashiku* (gently). A large number of adverbs are formed from copular nouns by adding the manner particle *ni*, as in *jōzu ni* (skillfully), and from time nouns, also using the manner particle *ni*, as in *shichiji ni* (at seven o'clock), *getsuyōbi ni* (on Monday).

Particles. Particles are words, usually of one syllable, that function somewhat like English prepositions. However, unlike prepositions, they come in a wider variety and are positioned after a phrase rather than before it. There are also particles that end sentences—the emphatic *yo*, *ne*, and *sa*, the feminine *wa*, the masculine *zo*, and so on. Interrogative sentences end with the particle *ka*, and an indecisive utterance may be finished off by a woman with *kashira* or by a man with *kana*, both of which mean "I wonder."

Japanese Grammar Basics

More difficult to use are particles that "mark" the function of the noun they follow. Typical of such particles are *kara* (from) and *e* (to), which mark, respectively, the direction from which and to which a movement is made: *Amerika kara Nihon e kimashita* (I came from America to Japan). In this dictionary, certain verb entries are preceded by the notation of one or two of the particles that may appear with nouns in a sentence with that particular verb. In the following list of particles, selected particles are followed by the notation used to indicate them in such verb entries.

Particle	Function of Preceding Noun	Approximate English Equivalent
de (loc *de*)	location	at/in
de	instrument	with
de	cause	because of
e	direction	to
ga	subject	
ga (obj *ga*)	object	
kara	direction	from
made	direction	up to
ni (compl *ni*)	complement (completes the verb)	
ni (ind-obj *ni*)	indirect object	to
ni	direction	to
ni	manner	-ly
ni (loc *ni*)	location	at/in
ni	agent	by
ni	time	in/on
no	possessive	of
o (obj *o*)	direct object	
o (loc *o*)	location	in/through
to (compl *to*)	complement (completes the verb)	
to (comp *to*)	companion; accompaniment	with
to	manner	-ly
wa	topic (of sentence, subject of verb acting as topic, or object acting as topic)	

Japanese Grammar Basics

It may be helpful to think of a Japanese sentence as a string of beads, each bead representing a noun marked with a particle. The following sentence demonstrates how particles can mark the function of nouns with respect to the verbal predicate:

Jūhachi-nichi **ni** (time) *watashi* **wa** (subject acting as topic) *Shinjuku* **de** (location) *Satō-san* **to** (companion) *sono eiga* **o** (object) *bideo* **de** (instrument) *mita* (verbal predicate).

On the eighteenth (time) I (subject acting as topic) in Shinjuku (location) with Mr. Sato (companion) that movie (object) on videotape (instrument) saw (verbal predicate).

On the eighteenth I saw that movie on videotape in Shinjuku with Mr. Sato.

Simple Sentence Structure

Statements. For many people, the simple description of an English sentence as consisting of a subject and a predicate suffices; still others may think of a sentence as basically a noun phrase and a verb phrase. In either case, an English sentence is generally thought of as having a verb. In Japanese, however, two of the three basic types of sentences do not contain a verb. Furthermore, as is obvious in the discussion on particles, Japanese sentences that do feature a verb do not easily divide into subject and predicate.

The three basic types of sentences and their subtypes are presented in the following table. Described are a total of seven affirmative and seven negative statements that can serve as models for the construction of innumerable, useful statements in Japanese. Polite forms of the predicates are given in parentheses. Affirmative predicates precede negative predicates and are separated by a solidus.

	Subject	Predicate
Type A-1	noun + *wa*	noun + copula
	Kore wa	*gakkō da.*
		(*gakkō desu.*)
		is a school.
		gakkō ja nai.
		(*gakkō ja arimasen.*)
	This	is not a school.

Japanese Grammar Basics

Type A-2	noun + *wa*		copular noun + copula
	Kare wa		*jōzu da.* / *jōzu ja nai.* (*jōzu desu.* / *jōzu ja arimasen.*)
	He		is skillful. / is not skillful.
Type B	noun + *wa*		adjective
	Sore wa		*takai.* / *takaku nai.* (*takai desu.* / *takaku arimasen.*)
	That		is expensive. / is not expensive.
Type C-1	noun + *wa* (or *ga*)		intransitive verb
	Kare wa		*hataraku.* / *hatarakanai.* (*hatarakimasu.* / *hatarakimasen.*)
	He		works. / does not work.
	Subject	Complement	Predicate
Type C-2	noun + *wa* (or *ga*)	noun + *ni*	intransitive verb
	Kare wa	*byōki ni*	*naru.* / *naranai.* (*narimasu.* / *narimasen.*)
	He	sick	becomes. / does not become.
	(He becomes sick. / He doesn't become sick.)		
	Subject	Object	Predicate
Type C-3	noun + *wa* (or *ga*)	noun + *o*	transitive verb
	Kare wa	*pan o*	*taberu.* / *tabenai.* (*tabemasu.* / *tabemasen.*)
	He	bread	eats. / does not eat.

(He eats bread. / He
doesn't eat bread.)

	Subject	Indirect Object	Object	Predicate
Type C-4	noun + *wa* (or *ga*)	noun + *ni*	noun + *o*	transitive verb
	Kare wa	*kodomo ni*	*Ei-go o*	*oshieru.* / *oshienai.* (*oshie-masu.* / *oshie-masen.*)
	He	to children	English	teaches. / doesn't teach.

(He teaches English to children. / He doesn't teach English to children.)

For statements of type A (1, 2) and type B, the simple patterns given will probably suffice in many situations. If you wish to expand upon these first two types, you may do so by expanding the nouns into noun phrases, or, in type B sentences, the adjectives into adjectival phrases. For example:

Kore wa **watashi no gakkō** *desu.*   This is **my school.**
Sore wa **totemo takai.**   That is **very expensive.**

Type C (1, 2) sentences represent sentences whose verbal predicates take neither an object nor an indirect object. In this dictionary, verbs that may take an object are preceded by "obj *o*"; verbs that may take both an indirect object and an object, by "ind-obj *ni*, obj *o*"; and verbs that may take a complement (as in type C-2), by "compl *ni*." Expansion of type C (3, 4) sentences presents many more possibilities (and complications) involving the use of other particles. An example of such an expanded sentence is given on page xix. Depending upon the verb, nouns (marked by particles indicating direction, manner, instrument, agent, and so on) may be added to a sentence. However, in everyday conversation, sentences do not usually contain more than three or four such nouns.

To make a statement negative, simply change the predicate into its negative form according to Tables 1–5 on pages xxi–xli.

Questions. To turn a type A, B, or C statement into a question,

Japanese Grammar Basics

simply add the interrogative particle *ka* to the end of the polite form of the predicate. Negative questions are formed in exactly the same way; that is, simply add the interrogative particle *ka* to the polite form of the negative predicate.

Type A-1   *Kore wa gakkō desu ka?* Is this a school?
              Kore wa gakkō ja arimasen ka? Isn't this a school?

Type A-2   *Kare wa jōzu desu ka?* Is he skillful?
              Kare wa jōzu ja arimasen ka? Isn't he skillful?

Type B   *Sore wa takai desu ka?* Is that expensive?
              Sore wa takaku arimasen ka? Isn't that expensive?

Type C-1   *Kare wa hatarakimasu ka?* Does he work?
              Kare wa hatarakimasen ka? Doesn't he work?

Type C-2   *Kare wa byōki ni narimasu ka?* Does (will) he become sick?
              Kare wa byōki ni narimasen ka? Doesn't (won't) he become sick?

Type C-3   *Kare wa pan o tabemasu ka?* Does he eat bread?
              Kare wa pan o tabemasen ka? Doesn't he eat bread?

Type C-4   *Kare wa kodomo ni Ei-go o oshiemasu ka?* Does he teach English to children?
              Kare wa kodomo ni Ei-go o oshiemasen ka? Doesn't he teach English to children?

Be careful not to misunderstand *hai* (yes) and *iie* (no) answers to negative questions. A *hai* answer to a negative question means in essence "Yes, what you said is correct," and *iie*, "No, what you said is incorrect." For example:

     Question: *Kare wa pan o tabemasen ka?*
                 Doesn't he eat bread?
     Answer: *Hai. Kare wa pan o tabemasen.*
                 Yes [what you said is correct].
                 He doesn't eat bread.
     Answer: *Iie. Kare wa pan o tabemasu.*
                 No [what you said is incorrect].
                 He eats bread.

Conversation and Styles of Speech

In conversation use short, uncomplicated sentences. With the addition of the question operation, twenty-eight basic sentences are already at your disposal. Add nouns and particles to indicate time, location, instrument, and so on as you would add beads to a string, but remember to put the predicate last. Pronounce each syllable deliberately—never slighting a syllable—and be especially careful of the correct pronunciation of vowels. Speak with a steady rhythm so that your speech sounds something like the rat-a-tat-tat of a drum or machine-gun fire. Avoid the types of rises and falls that are characteristic of English speech. You may pause for breath after a particle. Sentence subjects can be omitted in conversation, especially in conversations between two people: one rarely says *anata* (you) and avoids using *watashi* (I or me) unless a sentence would be ambiguous without them.

The everyday, conversational style used throughout the dictionary may be referred to as the plain style, in contrast to the polite and honorific styles. In brief, these three speech styles can be characterized as follows:

Plain. Plain style refers specifically to the form of the predicate. In other words, plain-style speech does *not* use the polite forms *desu* and *-masu*. There are other characteristics of plain-style speech as well as distinctions in plain-style men's and women's speech that are beyond the scope of this discussion. In this dictionary, all type B and type C statements are given in plain stlye.

Polite. Polite speech is characterized by the usage of the polite form of the predicate, that is, speech using type A and type B sentences ending in *desu* or some form of *desu* (*deshita, ja arimasen, deshō*) and type C sentences with verbs ending in *-masu* or some form of *-masu* (*-mashita, -masen, -mashō*). The polite style of speech is the most appropriate form for impersonal or formal situations, for business, or when talking with strangers. All type A sentences in this dictionary are given in polite style. Questions in all sentence types appear in polite style because it is more courteous.

Honorific. Honorific speech is characterized in great part by (1) honorific prefixes and suffixes on nouns; (2) special verbs that are considered to be either "humble," showing one's humility, or "exalted," showing deference to another; (3) honorific affixes attached to verbs and adjectives, and an honorific form of the copula; and (4) the polite *-masu* ending on verbs. Honorific speech is often heard by non-Japanese because the Japanese frequently address guests and foreigners in this style. One should not attempt to use this style of speech, however, before having acquired considerable fluency. In this dictionary, a few honorific expressions have been included where it was considered that they were appropriate for usage by non-Japanese.

Conjugation Tables

The following tables show representative examples for conjugating the two classes of regular verbs, the irregular verbs *suru* (do) and *kuru* (come), adjectives, and the copula *desu*. Included are all endings in current use as well as most possible combinations of endings. To use tables 1 and 2, simply substitute the stem of a given verb for those in the appropriate table. However, when using table 2, keep in mind that the final consonant of the stem often changes when combined with certain endings due to the assimilation of sounds. In addition, there are a few semantic restrictions on verb formation. For example, regular verbs that are already potential in meaning do not take the potential endings, those that are already passive in meaning do not take the passive endings, and those already causative in meaning do not take the causative endings. Throughout these tables, accent marks have been omitted because the accent varies depending on the word that is substituted.

Table 1. Regular Verb with Stem Ending in a Vowel

Affirmative forms appear above negative forms. Polite forms, where such forms are in use, are given in parentheses.

	Indicative	Potential	Passive
Non-Past, Habitual, Future	*tabe·ru* (*tabe·masu*) eats	*tabe·rareru* (*tabe·raremasu*) can eat	*tabe·rareru* (*tabe·raremasu*) is eaten
	tabe·nai (*tabe·masen*) doesn't eat	*tabe·rarenai* (*tabe·rarema-sen*) cannot eat	*tabe·rarenai* (*tabe·raremasen*) isn't eaten
Past	*tabe·ta* (*tabe·mashita*) ate	*tabe·rareta* (*tabe·rarema-shita*) was able to eat	*tabe·rareta* (*tabe·rarema-shita*) was eaten
	tabe·nakatta (*tabe·masen*	*tabe·rarena-katta*	*tabe·rarenakatta* (*tabe·raremasen*

Conjugation Tables

	Indicative	Potential	Passive
	deshita) didn't eat	(*tabe·raremasen* *deshita*) wasn't able to eat	*deshita*) wasn't eaten
Presumptive, Hortative, Probable- Future	*tabe·yō* (*tabe·mashō*) let's (or probably will) eat	*tabe·rareru darō* (*tabe·rareru de- shō*) probably can eat	*tabe·rareru darō* (*tabe·rareru de- shō*) probably is (or will be) eaten
	tabe·nai darō (*tabe·nai de- shō*) probably won't eat	*tabe·rarenai da- rō* (*tabe·rarenai deshō*) probably can- not eat	*tabe rarenai·darō* (*tabe·rarenai deshō*) probably isn't (or won't be) eaten
Conditional	*tabe·tara* if one eats	*tabe·raretara* if one can eat	*tabe·raretara* if (it) is eaten
	tabe·nakattara if one doesn't eat	*tabe·rarena- kattara* if one cannot eat	*tabe·rarena- kattara* if (it) isn't eaten
Provisional	*tabe·reba* providing one eats	*tabe·rarereba* providing one can eat	*tabe·rarereba* providing (it) is eaten
	tabe·nakereba providing one doesn't eat	*tabe·rarenake- reba* providing one cannot eat	*tabe·rarenake- reba* providing (it) isn't eaten
Alternative	*tabe·tari* alternating be- tween eating and . . .	*tabe·raretari* alternating be- tween being able to eat and . . .	*tabe·raretari* alternating be- tween being eaten and . . .
	tabe·nakattari alternating be- tween not eating and . . .	*tabe·rarenakat- tari* alternating be- tween not being able to eat and . . .	*tabe·rarenakat- tari* alternating be- tween not being eaten and . . .

Conjugation Tables

	Indicative	Potential	Passive
Gerund	*tabe·te* eating	*tabe·rarete* being able to eat	*tabe·rarete* being eaten
	tabe·naide without eating	*tabe·rarenaide* not being able to eat	*tabe·rarenaide* not being eaten
Correlative	*tabe·nagara* while eating		*tabe·rarenagara* while being eaten
Imperative (The form given in brackets is preferred in most situations.)	*tabe·ro* (*tabe·nasai*) [*tabe·te kuda-sai*] eat (it) *tabe·ru na* [*tabe·naide kudasai*] don't eat (it)		

	Causative	Causative-Passive	Desiderative (Indicative)
Non-Past, Habitual, Future	*tabe·saseru* (*tabe·sasema-su*) causes (or al-lows) to eat	*tabe·saserareru* (*tabe·saserarema-su*) is caused to eat	*tabe·tai* (*tabe·tai desu*) (I) want to eat
	tabe·sasenai (*tabe·sasema-sen*) doesn't cause (or allow) to eat	*tabe·saserarenai* (*tabe·saserarema-sen*) isn't caused to eat	*tabe·taku nai* (*tabe·taku ari-masen*) (I) don't want to eat
Past	*tabe·saseta* (*tabe·sasema-shita*)	*tabe·saserareta* (*tabe·saserarema-shita*)	*tabe·takatta* (*tabe·takatta desu*)

Conjugation Tables

	Causative	Causative-Passive	Desiderative (Indicative)
	caused (or allowed) to eat	was caused to eat	(I) wanted to eat
	tabe·sasena-katta (tabe·sasema-sen deshita) didn't cause (or allow) to eat	tabe·saserarena-katta (tabe·saserarema-sen deshita) wasn't caused to eat	tabe·taku naka-tta (tabe·taku arima-sen deshita) (I) didn't want to eat
Presumptive, Hortative, Probable-Future	tabe·saseru darō (tabe·saseru deshō) probably will cause (or allow) to eat	tabe·saserareru darō (tabe·saserareru deshō) probably will be caused to eat	tabe·tai darō (tabe·tai deshō) probably wants to eat
	tabe·sasenai darō (tabe·sasenai deshō) probably won't cause (or allow) to eat	tabe·saserarenai darō (tabe·saserarenai deshō) probably won't be caused to eat	tabe·taku nai darō (tabe·taku nai deshō) probably doesn't want to eat
Conditional	tabe·sasetara if one causes (or allows) to eat	tabe·saseraretara if one is caused to eat	tabe·takattara if one wants to eat
	tabe·sasena-kattara if one doesn't cause (or allow) to eat	tabe·saserarena-kattara if one is not caused to eat	tabe·taku na-kattara if one doesn't want to eat
Provisional	tabe·sasereba providing one causes (or allows) to eat	tabe·saserareba providing one is caused to eat	tabe·takereba providing one wants to eat

Conjugation Tables

	Causative	Causative-Passive	Desiderative (indicative)
	tabe·sasena-kereba providing one doesn't cause (or allow) to eat	*tabe·saserarena-kereba* providing one is not caused to eat	*tabe·taku na-kereba* providing one doesn't want to eat
Alternative	*tabe·sasetari* alternating between causing (or allowing) to eat and ...	*tabe·saseraretari* alternating between being caused to eat and ...	*tabe·takattari* alternating between wanting to eat and ...
	tabe·sasena-kattari alternating between not causing (or allowing) to eat and ...	*tabe·saserárena-kattari* alternating between not being caused to eat and ...	*tabe·taku na-kattari* alternating between not wanting to eat and ...
Gerund	*tabe·sasete* causing to eat	*tabe·saserarete* being caused to eat	*tabe·takute* wanting to eat
	tabe·sasenaide not causing to eat	*tabe·saserarenai-de* not being caused to eat	*tabe·taku nakute* not wanting to eat
Correlative	*tabe·sasena-gara* while causing to eat	*tabe·saserare-nagara* while being caused to eat	

Conjugation Tables

Table 2. Regular Verb with Stem Ending in a Consonant*

Affirmative forms appear above negative forms. Polite forms, where such forms are in use, are given in parentheses.

	Indicative	Potential	Passive
Non-Past, Habitual, Future	yom·u (yom·imasu) reads	yom·eru (yom·emasu) can read	yom·areru (yom·aremasu) is read
	yom·anai (yom·imasen) doesn't read	yom·enai (yom·emasen) cannot read	yom·arenai (yom·aremasen) isn't read
Past	yon·da (yom·imashita) read	yom·eta (yom·emashita) was able to read	yom·areta (yom·aremashita) was read
	yom·anakatta (yom·imasen deshita) didn't read	yom·enakatta (yom·emasen (deshita)) couldn't read	yom·arenakatta (yom·aremasen deshita) wasn't read
Presumptive, Hortative, Probable-Future	yom·ō (yom·imashō) let's (or probably will) read	yom·eru darō (yom·eru deshō) probably can read	yom·areru darō (yom·areru deshō) probably is (or will be) read
	yom·anai darō (yom·anai deshō) probably won't read	yom·enai darō (yom·enai deshō) probably can-not read	yom·arenai darō (yom·arenai deshō) probably isn't (or won't be) read
Conditional	yon·dara if one reads	yom·etara if one can read	yom·aretara if (it) is read
	yom·anakat-tara if one doesn't read	yom·enakattara if one cannot read	yom·arenakatta-ra if (it) isn't read
Provisional	yom·eba providing one reads	yom·ereba providing one can read	yom·arereba providing (it) is read

Conjugation Tables

	Indicative	Potential	Passive
	yom·anakereba providing one doesn't read	*yom·enakereba* providing one cannot read	*yom·arenakereba* providing (it) isn't read
Alternative	*yon·dari* alternating between reading and . . .	*yom·etari* alternating between being able to read and . . .	*yom·aretari* alternating between being read and . . .
	yom·anakattari alternating between not reading and . . .	*yom·enakattari* alternating between not being able to read and . . .	*yom·arenakattari* alternating between not being read and . . .
Gerund	*yon·de* reading	*yom·ete* being able to read	*yom·arete* being read
	yom·anaide without reading	*yom·enaide* not being able to read	*yom·arenaide* not being read
Correlative	*yom·inagara* while reading		*yom·arenagara* while being read
Imperative (The form given in brackets is preferred in most situations.)	*yom·e* (*yom·inasai*) [*yon·de kudasai*] read (it)		
	yom·u na [*yom·anaide kudasai*] don't read (it)		

Conjugation Tables

	Causative	Causative-Passive	Desiderative (Indicative)
Non-Past	yom·aseru (yom·asemasu) causes (or allows) to read	yom·as[er]areru (yom·as[er]are-masu) is caused to read	yom·itai (yom·itai desu) (I) want to read
	yom·asenai (yom·asema-sen) doesn't cause (or allow) to read	yom·as[er]arenai (yom·as[er]are-masen) isn't caused to read	yom·itaku nai (yom·itaku ari-masen) (I) don't want to read
Past	yom·aseta (yom·asema-shita) caused (or allowed) to read	yom·as[er]areta (yom·as[er]are-mashita) was caused to read	yom·itakatta (yom·itakatta desu) (I) wanted to read
Presumptive, Hortative, Probable-Future	yom·asenakat-ta (yom·asemasen deshita) didn't cause (or allow) to read	yom·as[er]arena-katta (yom·as[er]are-masen deshita) wasn't caused to read	yom·itaku na-katta (yom·itaku ari-masen deshita) (I) didn't want to read
	yom·aseru darō (yom·aseru deshō) probably will cause (or allow) to read	yom·as[er]areru darō (yom·as[er]areru deshō) probably will be caused to read	yom·itai darō (yom·itai deshō) probably wants to read
	yom·asenai darō (yom·asenai deshō) probably won't cause (or allow) to read	yom·as[er]arenai darō (yom·as[er]arenai deshō) probably won't be caused to read	yom·itaku nai darō (yom·itaku nai deshō) probably doesn't want to read

Conjugation Tables

	Causative	Causative-Passive	Desiderative (Indicative)
Conditional	*yom·asetara* if one causes (or allows) to read	*yom·as[er]aretara* if one is caused to read	*yom·itakattara* if one wants to read
	yom·asena-kattara if one doesn't cause (or allow) to read	*yom·as[er]arena-kattara* if one is not caused to read	*yom·itaku na-kattara* if one doesn't want to read
Provisional	*yom·asereba* providing one causes (or allows) to read	*yom·as[er]arereba* providing one is caused to read	*yom·itakereba* providing one wants to read
	yom·asena-kereba providing one doesn't cause (or allow) to read	*yom·as[er]arena-kereba* providing one is not caused to read	*yom·itaku na-kereba* providing one doesn't want to read
Alternative	*yom·asetari* alternating between causing (or allowing) to read and . . .	*yom·as[er]aretari* alternating between being caused to read and . . .	*yom·itakattari* alternating between wanting to read and . . .
	yom·asena-kattari alternating between not causing (or allowing) to read and . . .	*yom·as[er]arena-kattari* alternating between not being caused to read and . . .	*yom·itaku na-kattari* alternating between not wanting to read and . . .
Gerund	*yom·asete* causing to read	*yom·as[er]arete* being caused to read	*yom·itakute* wanting to read
	yom·asenaide	*yom·as[er]are-*	*yom·itaku*

Conjugation Tables

	Causative	Causative-Passive	Desiderative (Indicative)
	not causing to read	*naide* not being caused to read	*nakute* not wanting to read
Correlative	*yom·asenagara* while causing read	*yom·as[er]arena-gara* while being caused to read	

* In addition to the type of verb represented by *yomu* in this table, there are eight other types of regular verbs that have stems ending in consonants. Before conjugating such verbs, compare their stems with the stems of the verbs listed below and follow the examples for changing the stem's final consonant and/or the initial consonant of the suffix, observing the following three rules:

1. Use the stem in the Negative column to form the Passive, Causative, and Causative-Passive.

2. Use the stem in the Past column to form the Conditional, Alternative, and Gerund.

3. Use the stem in the Indicative column to form all other inflections.

Indicative (Non-Past; Habitual; Future)	Negative	Past
yom·u read	*yom·anai* doesn't read	*yon·da* read
asob·u play	*asob·anai* doesn't play	*ason·da* played
shin·u die	*shin·anai* doesn't die	*shin·da* died
oyog·u swim	*oyog·anai* doesn't swim	*oyoi·da* swam

Conjugation Tables

Indicative (Non-Past; Habitual; Future)	Negative	Past
*ak·u** open	*ak·anai* doesn't open	*ai·ta* opened
suwar·u sit	*suwar·anai* doesn't sit	*suwat·ta* sat
mots·u† hold	*mot·anai* doesn't hold	*mot·ta* held
ka·u† buy	*kaw·anai* doesn't buy	*kat·ta* bought
hanas·u† talk	*hanas·anai* doesn't talk	*hanashi·ta* talked

* The verb *ik·u* (go) is an exception: *iku/ikanai/itta*.
† All verbs whose dictionary form ends in two successive vowels are conjugated as consonant-ending verbs.
† Stems of these verbs change irregularly as follows:

Presumptive:	*mot·ō*	
Provisional:	*mot·eba*	
Correlative:	*mochi·nagara*	*hanashi·nagara*
Imperative:	*mot·e*	
Potential:	*mot·eru*	
Desiderative:	*mochi·tai*	*hanash·itai*
Polite:	*mochi·imasu*	*hanash·imasu*

Conjugation Tables

Table 3. Irregular Verb *Suru* (do)

In this table, the stem is not separated from the ending. Affirmative forms appear above negative forms. Polite forms, where such forms are used, are given in parentheses.

	Indicative	Potential	Passive
Non-Past, Habitual, Future	*suru* (*shimasu*) does	*dekiru* (*dekimasu*) can	*sareru* (*saremasu*) is done
	shinai (*shimasen*) doesn't do	*dekinai* (*dekimasen*) cannot do	*sarenai* (*saremasen*) isn't done
Past	*shita* (*shimashita*) did	*dekita* (*dekimashita*) could do	*sareta* (*saremashita*) was done
	shinakatta (*shimasen deshita*) didn't do	*dekinakatta* (*dekimasen deshita*) couldn't do	*sarenakatta* (*saremasen deshita*) wasn't done
Presumptive, Hortative, Probable-Future	*shiyō* (*shimashō*) let's (or probably will) do	*dekiru darō* (*dekiru deshō*) probably can do	*sareru darō* (*sareru deshō*) probably is (or will be) done
	shinai darō (*shinai deshō*) probably won't do	*dekinai darō* (*dekinai deshō*) probably cannot do	*sarenai darō* (*sarenai deshō*) probably isn't (or won't be) done
Conditional	*shitara* if one does	*dekitara* if one can	*saretara* if (it) is done
	shinakattara if one doesn't do	*dekinakattara* if one cannot do	*sarenakattara* if (it) isn't done
Provisional	*sureba* providing one does	*dekireba* providing one can	*sarereba* providing (it) is done

Conjugation Tables

	Indicative	Potential	Passive
	shinakereba providing one does not do	*dekinakereba* providing one cannot	*sarenakereba* providing (it) isn't done
Alternative	*shitari* alternating between doing and . . .	*dekitari* alternating between being able and . . .	*saretari* alternating between being done and . . .
	shinakattari alternating between not doing and . . .	*dekinakattari* alternating between not being able and . . .	*sarenakattari* alternating between not being done and . . .
Gerund	*shite* doing	*dekite* being able	*sarete* being done
	shinakute without doing	*dekinakute* without being able	*sarenakute* without being done
Correlative	*shinagara* while doing		*sarenagara* while being done
Imperative (The form given in brackets is preferred in most situations.)	*shiro* (*shinasai*) [*shite kudasai*] do (it) *suru na* [*shinaide kudasai*] don't (do it)		

	Causative	Causative-Passive	Desiderative (Indicative)
Non-Past, Habitual,	*saseru* (*sasemasu*)	*saserareru* (*saseraremasu*)	*shitai* (*shitai desu*)

Conjugation Tables

	Causative	Causative-Passive	Desiderative (Indicative)
Future	causes (or allows) to do	is caused to do	(I) want to do
	sasenai (*sasemasen*) doesn't cause (or allow) to do	*saserarenai* (*saseraremasen*) isn't caused to do	*shitaku nai* (*shitaku arimasen*) (I) don't want to do
Past	*saseta* (*sasemashita*) caused (or allowed) to do	*saserareta* (*saserarema shita*) was caused to do	*shitakatta* (*shitakatta desu*) (I) wanted to do
	sasenakatta (*sasemasen deshita*) didn't cause (or allow) to do	*saserarenakatta* (*saseraremasen deshita*) wasn't caused to do	*shitaku nakatta* (*shitaku arimasen deshita*) (I) didn't want to do
Presumptive, Hortative, Probable-Future	*saseru darō* (*saseru deshō*) probably will cause (or allow) to do	*saserareru darō* (*saserareru deshō*) probably will be caused to do	*shitai darō* (*shitai deshō*) probably wants to do
	sasenai darō (*sasenai deshō*) probably won't cause (or allow) to do	*saserarenai darō* (*saserarenai deshō*) probably won't be caused to do	*shitaku nai darō* (*shitaku nai deshō*) probably doesn't want to do
Conditional	*sasetara* if one causes (or allows) to do	*saseraretara* if one is caused to do	*shitakattara* if one wants to do
	sasenakattara if one doesn't cause (or allow) to do	*saserarenakattara* if one is not caused to do	*shitaku nakattara* if one doesn't want to do

Conjugation Tables

	Causative	Causative-Passive	Desiderative (Indicative)
Provisional	*sasereba* providing one causes (or allows) to do	*saserarereba* providing one is caused to do	*shitakereba* providing one wants to do
	sasenakereba providing one doesn't cause (or allow) to do	*saserarenakereba* providing one is not caused to do	*shitaku nakereba* providing one doesn't want to do
Alternative	*sasetari* alternating between causing (or allowing) to do and ...	*saseraretari* alternating between being caused to do and ...	*shitakattari* alternating between wanting to do and ...
	sasenakattari alternating between not causing (or allowing) to do and ...	*saserarenakattari* alternating between not being caused to do and ...	*shitaku nakattari* alternating between not wanting to do and ...
Gerund	*sasete* causing to do	*saserarete* being caused to do	*shitakute* wanting to do
	sasenaide not causing to do	*saserarenaide* not being caused to do	*shitaku nakute* without wanting to do
Correlative	*sasenagara* while causing to do	*saserarenagara* while being caused to do	

Conjugation Tables

Table 4. Irregular Verb *Kuru* (come)

In this table, the stem is not separated from the ending. Affirmative forms appear above negative forms. Polite forms, where such forms are used, are given in parentheses.

	Indicative	Potential	Passive
Non-Past, Habitual, Future	*kuru* (*kimasu*) comes	*ko[ra]reru* (*ko[ra]remasu*) can come	*korareru* (*koraremasu*) adversely affected by (someone's) coming
	konai (*kimasen*) doesn't come	*ko[ra]renai* (*ko[ra]remasen*) cannot come	
Past	*kita* (*kimashita*) came	*ko[ra]reta* (*ko[ra]remashita*) could come	*korareta* (*koraremashita*) adversely affected by (someone's) having come
	konakatta (*kimasen deshita*) didn't come	*ko[ra]renakatta* (*ko[ra]remasen deshita*) couldn't come	*korarenakatta* (*koraremasen deshita*) adversely affected by (someone's) not having come
Presumptive, Hortative, Probable-Future	*koyō* (*kimashō*) let's (or probably will) come	*ko[ra]reru darō* (*ko[ra]reru deshō*) probably can come	*korareru darō* (*korareru deshō*) adversely affected by (someone's) probably coming
	konai darō (*konai deshō*) probably won't come	*ko[ra]renai darō* (*ko[ra]renai deshō*)	

Conjugation Tables

	Indicative	Potential	Passive
		probably cannot come	
Conditional	*kitara* if one comes	*ko[ra]retara* if one can come	*koraretara* if adversely affected by (someone's) coming
	konakattara if one doesn't come	*ko[ra]renakattara* if one cannot come	
Provisional	*kureba* providing one comes	*ko[ra]rereba* providing one can come	
	konakereba providing one doesn't come	*ko[ra]renakereba* providing one cannot come	
Alternative	*kitari* alternating between coming and . . .	*ko[ra]retari* alternating between being able to come and . . .	*koraretari* alternating between being adversely affected by (someone's) coming and . . .
	konakattari alternating between not coming and . . .	*ko[ra]renakattari* alternating between not being able to come and . . .	*korarenakattari* alternating between being adversely affected by (someone's) not coming and . . .
Gerund	*kite* coming	*ko[ra]rete* being able to come	*korarete* being adversely affected by (someone's) coming

Conjugation Tables

	Indicative	Potential	Passive
	konakute without coming	*ko[ra]renakute* without being able to come	
Correlative	*kinagara* while coming		
Imperative (The form given in brackets is preferred in most situations.)	*koi* (*kinasai*) [*kite kudasai*] come		
	kuru na [*konaide kudasai*] don't come		

	Causative	Causative-Passive	Desiderative (Indicative)
Non-Past, Habitual, Future	*kosaseru* (*kosasemasu*) causes (or allows) to come	*kosaserareru* (*kosaseraremasu*) is caused to come	*kitai* (*kitai desu*) (I) want to come
	kosasenai (*kosasemasen*) doesn't cause (or allow) to come	*kosaserarenai* (*kosaseraremasen*) isn't caused to come	*kitaku nai* (*kitaku arimasen*) (I) don't want to come
Past	*kosaseta* (*kosasemashita*) caused (or allowed) to come	*kosaserareta* (*kosaseraremashita*) was caused to come	*kitakatta* (*kitakatta desu*) (I) wanted to come

Conjugation Tables

	Causative	Causative-Passive	Desiderative (Indicative)
	kosasenakatta (*kosasemasen deshita*) didn't cause (or allow) to come	*kosaserarena-katta* (*kosaserarema-sen deshita*) wasn't caused to come	*kitaku nakatta* (*kitaku arimasen deshita*) (I) didn't want to come
Presumptive, Hortative, Probable-Future	*kosaseru darō* (*kosaseru deshō*) probably will cause (or allow) to come	*kosaserareru darō* (*kosaserareru deshō*) probably will be caused to come	*kitai darō* (*kitai deshō*) probably wants to come
	kosasenai darō (*kosasenai deshō*) probably won't cause (or allow) to come	*kosaserarenai darō* (*kosaserarenai deshō*) probably won't be caused to come	*kitaku nai darō* (*kitaku nai deshō*) probably doesn't want to come
	kosasetara if one causes (or allows) to come	*kosaseraretara* if one is caused to come	*kitakattara* if one wants to come
Conditional	*kosasenaka-ttara* if one doesn't cause (or allow) some-one to come	*kosaserarenaka-ttara* if one is not caused to come	*kitaku nakattara* if one doesn't want to come
Provisional	*kosasereba* providing one causes (or allows) to come	*kosaserarereba* providing one is caused to come	*kitakereba* providing one wants to come
	kosasenakere-ba providing one	*kosaserarena-kereba* providing one is	*kitaku nakereba* providing one doesn't want

Conjugation Tables

	Causative	Causative-Passive	Desiderative (Indicative)
	doesn't cause (or allow) to come	not caused to come	to come
Alternative	*kosasetari* alternating between causing (or allowing) to come and . . .	*kosaseraretari* alternating between being caused to come and . . .	*kitakattari* alternating between wanting to come and . . .
	kosasenaka-ttari alternating between not causing (or allowing) to come and . . .	*kosaserarena-kattari* alternating between not being caused to come and . . .	*kitaku nakattari* alternating between not wanting to come and . . .
Gerund	*kosasete* causing to come	*kosaserarete* being caused to come	*kitakute* wanting to come
	kosasenaide not causing to come	*kosaserarenaide* not being caused to come	*kitaku nakute* without wanting to come

	Causative	Causative-Passive
Correlative	*kosasenagara* while causing to come	*kosaserarenagara* while being caused to come

Conjugation Tables

Table 5. Adjective and Copula

Affirmative forms appear above negative forms. Polite forms, where such forms are in use, are given in parentheses.

	Adjective (Indicative)	Copula (Indicative)
Non-Past, Habitual, Future	*aka·i* (*aka·i desu*) (is) red	*da* (*desu*) is
	aka·ku nai (*aka·ku arimasen*) (is) not red	*ja nai* (*ja arimasen*) is not
Past	*aka·katta* (*aka·katta desu*) (was) red	*datta* (*deshita*) was
	aka·ku nakatta (*aka·ku arimasen deshita*) (was) not red	*ja nakatta* (*ja arimasen deshita*) was not
Presumptive, Probable-Future	*aka·i darō* (*aka·i deshō*) probably is red	*darō* (*deshō*) probably is
	aka·ku nai darō (*aka·ku nai deshō*) probably isn't red	*ja nai darō* (*ja arimasen deshō*) probably is not
Conditional	*aka·kattara* if red	*dattara, nara* (*deshitara*) if (it) is
	aka·ku nakattara if not red	*ja nakattara* (*ja nakattara*) if (it) is not
Provisional	*aka·kereba* providing (it) is red *aka·ku nakereba* providing (it) is not red	*nara(ba)* providing (it) is *ja nakereba* (*ja nakereba*) providing (it) is not
Gerund	*aka·kute* being red *aka·ku nakute* not being red	*de* being *ja nakute* not being

Pronunciation Guide

For the speaker of English, Japanese is not especially difficult to pronounce. As is often pointed out, the pronunciation of Japanese vowels is very close to that of Italian vowels, and, with very few exceptions, consonants correspond to similar consonants in English. The Japanese themselves, however, do not think in terms of consonant and vowel; rather, they conceive of a syllable as a distinct and indivisible unit formed either of a single vowel or a consonant followed by a vowel, for example *a, su, to*, and so on. There are exceptions to this consonant-plus-vowel rule. One is a series of syllables that, when romanized, feature a *y* immediately after a consonant as in *kya, myu*, and *ryo*. Another is the series *cha, chi, cho, chu*. A further complication is the occurrence of the double and triple consonants *kk, mm, nn, pp, ss, ssh, tch, tt*, and *tts*. These can be understood by thinking of them as "long" consonants (as in long vowels) that are sounded twice as long as their corresponding, single-element counterparts. An example in English of such a long consonant is the *kk* in book*k*eeper. In addition, some syllables feature an *n* after a vowel as in *kan* (tin can). While this too may seem to be an exception, to the Japanese, *kan* is comprised of the two syllables *ka* and *n, n* being the only consonant that functions as a syllable by itself.

The mind-set of the Japanese toward the syllabic nature of their language is partly responsible for the staccato delivery of Japanese. This delivery strikes the English speaker as quite different from the large intonation contours and relatively melodic delivery that characterize English. To further enhance this effect, when pronouncing individual words and speaking in complete sentences, the Japanese do not stress any particular part of a word or a sentence but keep a steady rhythm and a relatively even tone. (However, see the sections below on word-accent and intonation.)

The following is a listing of the majority of Japanese syllables with guides (where possible) to their pronunciation in American English. Not included are those composed of consonants and long vowels, the pronunciation of which can be inferred from the examples given in this basic list.

Pronunciation Guide

a	as in m*a*ma	*ho*	as in *ho*pe
ā	as in r*ah*	*hya*	(pronounce as one syllable*)
ba	as in *bo*b		
be	as in *be*d	*hyo*	(pronounce as one syllable*)
bi	as in *bee*t		
bo	as in *boa*t	*hyu*	as in *hue*
bu	as in *boo*t	*i*	as in *ea*t†
bya	(pronounce as one syllable*)	*ī/ii*	as in ma*chi*ne
		ja	as in *jo*t
byo	(pronounce as one syllable*)	*je*	as in *je*t
		ji	as in *jee*p
byu	as in *beau*ty	*jo*	as in *jo*ke
cha	as in *cha*-cha	*ju*	as in *ju*te
chi	as in *chea*p	*ka*	as in *co*t
cho	as in *cho*re	*ke*	as in *ke*pt
chu	as in *chew*	*ki*	as in *kee*p
da	as in *do*t	*ko*	as in *co*coa
de	as in *de*bt	*ku*	as in *coo*p
di	as in *dee*p	*kya*	(pronounce as one syllable*)
do	as in *do*se		
e	as in b*e*t	*kyo*	(pronounce as one syllable*)
ē/ei	as in *e*dge		
fa	as in *fo*x	*kyu*	as in *cu*te
fe	as in *fe*tch	*ma*	as in m*a*ma
fi	as in *fee*t	*me*	as in *me*t
fo	as in *fo*lk	*mi*	as in *mee*k
fu	somewhat as the *foo* in *foo*t, but without the upper front teeth touching the bottom lip	*mo*	as in *mo*at
		mu	as in *moo*t
		mya	(pronounce as one syllable*)
ga	as in *go*t		
ge	as in *ge*t	*myo*	(pronounce as one syllable*)
gi	as in *gee*se		
go	as in *goa*t	*myu*	as in *mu*sic
gu	as in *goo*f	*n/n'*	as in si*ng*
gya	(pronounce as one syllable*)	*na*	as in *no*t
		ne	as in *ne*t
gyo	(pronounce as one syllable*)	*ni*	as in *nea*t
		no	as in *no*
gyu	(pronounce as one syllable*)	*nu*	as in *noo*se
		nya	(pronounce as one syllable*)
ha	as in *ho*t		
he	as in *he*ck	*nyo*	(pronounce as one syllable*)
hi	as in *hea*t	*nyu*	as in *new*

Pronunciation Guide

ō	as in nose	sa	as in sot
o	as in note	se	as in set
pa	as in papa	sha	as in shock
pe	as in pet	she	as in chef
pi	as in peep	shi	as in sheet
po	as in pope	sho	as in showoff
pu	as in poot	shu	as in shoot
pya	(pronounce as one syllable*)	so	as in soap
		su	as in soup
pyo	(pronounce as one syllable*)	ta	as in tot
		te	as in test
pyu	as in pupa	ti	as in teach
ra	[Syllables beginning with r often present problems	to	as in tote
		tsu	as in cats
re	to the non-Japanese.	u	as in toot†
ri	Try to make the r sound	ū	as in sue
ro	like the dd in Eddy or	wa	as in watt
ru	the tt in Betty.]	ya	as in yacht
rya	(pronounce as one syllable*)	yo	as in yoke
		yu	as in youth
ryo	(pronounce as one syllable*)	za	as in zazen
		ze	as in zest
ryu	(pronounce as one syllable*)	zo	as in zoology
		zu	as in zoot suit

* No English equivalent.
† The vowels i and u are often unvoiced (or whispered) under certain conditions, such as their occurrence between two unvoiced consonants and at the end of a word. For example, in the two sentences that follow, the unvoiced vowels appear in brackets: Kono h[i]to wa K[i]shimoto-san to issho ni k[i]ta (This person came with Mr. Kishimoto); S[u]kiyaki ga s[u]ki des[u] (I like sukiyaki).

Word-Accent

In this dictionary, word-accent, or more correctly, high and low pitch on words, is indicated in the romanized entries with the symbol ('). This symbol indicates that the syllable immediately following the symbol is to be pronounced at a lower pitch than the syllable preceding it. When pronouncing a word by itself (not in a sentence), use two pitches, high and low: high for all syllables preceding the symbol, and low for the *one* syllable immediately following, after which the high pitch is resumed. For example:

Pronunciation Guide

flannel	*fura'nneru*	*fura⌐n neru*
flirt	*fuzake'ru*	*fuzake\ru*

Avoid adding stress to the syllable preceding ('). In Japanese accent, it is the *tone*, not stress, that is significant. Note that the word-accent may change under the influence of surrounding words.

Intonation

Intonation is characteristic of all speech; one cannot speak without intonation. Some sentence intonation patterns (four, in Japanese) are basic; others are peripheral, such as polite intonation, intonation to indicate cajoling or sarcasm, and so forth. The intonation at the end of a sentence signals that the speaker is making a statement, question, and so on. Four basic sentence-ending intonation patterns of Japanese are (1) falling (↘) from level 2 to level 1, marking the end of a sentence; (2) rising (↗) to level 2 at the end of the sentence, indicating a question or emphasis; (3) level (→), indicating that the statement is not finished; and (4) an abrupt rising or falling (↑↓), indicating excitement, anger, intense concern, fear, and so forth. For example:

Pattern 1	*Ho'n desu.* ↘	It is a book.
Pattern 2	*Ho'n desu ka?* ↗	Is it a book?
Pattern 3	*Ma'do o a' kete* →	Open the window and ...
Pattern 4	*Ka' ji da.* ↓	Fire!

Intonation affects word-accent and vice versa, as you will note in the sample expressions in this dictionary.

Abbreviations and Symbols

abbr	abbreviation or abbreviated form
adj	adjective, i.e., a word that takes the adjective endings shown in Table 5, page xli
adv	adverb or adverbial expression
Anat	Anatomy
Astron	Astronomy
attr	attributive, i.e., a word or phrase that can precede a noun to modify it

Abbreviations and Symbols

Bank	Banking
Biol	Biology
Bot	Botany
Budd	Buddhism
Cath	Roman Catholicism
caus	causative verb form
Chr	Christianity
coll	colloquial
comp *to* (v/irr)	verb that may take a companion marked by the particle *to*, e.g., **Dare to** *ikimashita ka?* **With whom** did you go?
compl *ni* (v/irr)	verb that may take a complement marked by the particle *ni*, e.g., *Ashita* **tenki ni** *naru deshō*. Tomorrow will be **a nice day.**
Elec	Electricity
fem	feminine
Geom	Geometry
Gram	Grammar
idiom	word or expression that does not conform to standard Japanese word classes such as noun, verb, etc.
ind-obj *ni* (v/irr)	verb that may take an indirect object marked by the particle *ni*, e.g., **Watashi ni** *sore o kudasai.* Give that **to me.**
irr	irregular verb or irregular verb construction, see Tables 3 and 4, pp. xxxii–xl, for conjugation
J	Japanese or Japanese-style
Lab	Laboratory
Leg	Legal term
lit	literally
loc *de* (v/irr)	verb that may take a location marked with the particle *de*, e.g., *Kare wa* **koko de** *hataraku.* He works **here.**
loc *ni* (v/irr)	verb that may take a location marked with the particle *ni*, e.g., *Watashi wa ichinichi* **koko ni** *iru.* I'll be **here** all day.
loc *o* (v/irr)	verb that may take a location marked with the particle *o*, e.g., *Kono basu wa* **Mitaka-eki o** *tōrimasu ka?* Does this bus go **to Mitaka Station?**
masc	masculine
Math	Mathematics
Mech	Mechanical

Abbreviations and Symbols

neg	negative predicate
obj *ga* (v/irr)	verb that may take an object marked with the particle *ga*, e.g., **Nihon-go** *ga wakarimasu ka?* Do you understand **Japanese?**
obj *o* (v/irr)	verb that may take a direct object marked with the particle *o*, e.g., **Biru** o *nomimasen ka?* Would you like a **beer?**
pass	passive verb form
pot	potential verb form
Prot	Protestantism
R.R.	railroad
Tech	Technical term
US	United States of America
v	regular verb, see Table 1 or 2, pages xxi–xxxi, for conjugation
W	Western (European and/or American) or Western-style
[ ]	may be omitted depending on context
·(*ru, u, i*)	point in a verb or adjective where the break between stem and ending occurs
;	or
,	and
ʾ	pitch change: the following syllable is lower in pitch

The Practical English-Japanese Dictionary

A

a *see* one; certain

A.B. (academie degree) *see* Bachelor of Arts

abacus *soroban* 算盤

abalone *a'wabi* 鮑

abandon obj *o* (v) **1** give up; desist *yame·ru* 止める abandon a project *keikaku o yameru* 計画を止める **2** give up forever *sute·ru* 捨てる abandon all hope *arayu'ru nozomi o sute·ru* あらゆる望みを捨てる **3** desert *misute·ru* 見捨てる He abandoned his children. *Ka're wa kodomo o misute'ta.* 彼は子供を見捨てた. **4** renounce (irr) *hō'ki-suru* 放棄する abandon one's claim/right *ke'nri o hō'ki-suru* 権利を放棄する

abandonment (renunciation) *hō'ki* 放棄

abbot (Budd) *sō'jō* 僧正

abbreviate obj *o* (irr) **1** *tanshuku-suru* 短縮する abbreviate a long report *naga'i repō'to o tanshuku-suru* 長いレポートを短縮する **2** abbreviate to... ... *to ryaku's·u* ...と略す

abbreviated (pass) be abbreviated to... ... *to ryakusare·'ru* ...と略される In Japan, "Los Angeles" is abbreviated to "Los." *Niho'n de wa Rosanze'rusu wa "Ro'su" to ryakusa'reie iru.* 日本ではロサンゼルスは「ロス」と略されている. ——(attr) *ryaku'shita* 略した abbreviated form *ryaku'shita katachi* 略した形

abbreviation **1** truncation *tanshuku* 短縮 **2** omission *shōryaku* 省略

abdomen *onaka* お腹; (Anat) *fuku'bu* 腹部

abduct obj *o* (irr) *yūkai-suru* 誘拐する abduct a person *hito o yūkai-suru* 人を誘拐する

abduction *yūkai* 誘拐 an abduction case *yūkai ji'ken* 誘拐事件

abductor *yūka'ihan* 誘拐犯

ability **1** capability *nō'ryoku* 能力 intellectual ability *chiteki nō'-ryoku* 知的能力 **2** competence *jitsuryoku* 実力 She has ability in English. *Ka'nojo wa Ei-go no jitsuryoku ga a'ru.* 彼女は英語の実力がある. **3** talent *sainō* 才能 a person of ability *sainō no a'ru hito* 才能のある人

able (to) obj *ga* (v) *deki·'ru* できる Are you able to do that? *Ana'ta ni sore ga dekima'su ka?* あなたにそれができますか. Are you able to go early in the morning? *A'sa ha'yaku iku koto ga deki'run desu ka?* 朝早く行くことができるんですか. ——(attr) **1** *yo'ku deki'ru* よくできる an able person *yo'ku deki'ru hito'* よくできる人 **2** powerful *chikara no a'ru* 力のある an able person

3

chikara no a'ru hito' 力のある人 *see also* potential verb form in tables 1–4, pp. xxi–xl.

abnormal 1 unnatural *fushi'zen [na/ni]* 不自然[な/に] abnormal behavior *fushi'zen na kōdō* 不自然な行動 It looks abnormal. *Fushi'zen ni mie'ru.* 不自然にみえる. 2 unusual *ijō [no/na]* 異常 [の/な] There was nothing abnormal. *Ijō ga na'katta.* 異常がなかった.

abolish obj *o* (irr) *haishi-suru* 廃止する abolish capital punishment *shikei o haishi-suru* 死刑を廃止する

abolition *haishi* 廃止

abort 1 obj *o* (irr) *datai-suru* 堕胎する abort a baby to protect the mother *botai o ho'go-suru tame, a'kachan o datai-suru* 母体を保護 するため赤ちゃんを堕胎する 2 (irr) *shippai-suru* 失敗する That plan aborted. *Sono keikaku wa shippai-shita.* その計画は失敗した.

abortion 1 miscarriage *ryū'zan* 流産 2 (surgical) *datai* 堕胎

about 1 *ya'ku* 約 about fifty years *ya'ku gojūnen* 約50年 2 *-kurai* 位; *-gurai* ぐらい about ten people *jūnin-gu'rai* 10人ぐらい 3 (time) *-koro* 頃; *-goro* ごろ about ten o'clock *jūji-go'ro* 10時ごろ about that time *sono ko'ro* その頃 4 concerning ... *ni tsuite* ... について I want to talk about that. *Sore ni tsu'ite hanashita'i.* そ れについて話したい.

about to ... *tokoro' desu* ...ところです I am about to leave now. *I'ma dekakeru tokoro'desu.* 今出かけるところです.

above [... *no*] *ue'[ni]* [... の]上[に] above the clouds *ku'mo no ue'* 雲の上 Hang the picture above the piano. *E' o piano no ue'ni ka'-kete kudasa'i.* 絵をピアノの上に掛けて下さい.

abroad *ka'igai* 海外 traveling abroad *kaigai ryokō* 海外旅行; studying abroad *ryūgaku* 留学

abscess *haremono* はれもの

absence *kesseki* 欠席

absent obj *o* (irr) be absent *kesseki-suru* 欠席する I'm going to be absent from the meeting tomorrow. *Ashita no ka'igi o kesseki-suru.* 明日の会議を欠席する.

absent-minded *bon'ya'ri* ぼんやり

absent-mindedly *bon'ya'ri to* ぼんやりと

absolute *zettai [no]* 絶対[の] absolute zero *zettai re'ido* 絶対零度

absolutely 1 *zettai ni* 絶対に absolutely necessary *zettai ni hitsuyō* 絶対に必要 2 absolutely ... not *zenzen* (＋neg) 全然 I absolutely could not do it. *Sore ga zenzen deki'nakatta.* それが全然できなか った.

absorb obj *o* (irr) *kyūshū-suru* 吸収する absorb moisture from the air *kū'ki kara su'ibun o kyūshū-suru* 空気から水分を吸収する ——(idiom) absorb well *kyūshū ga i'i* 吸収がいい

absorption *kyūshū* 吸収

abstain obj *o* (v) *hikae′·ru* 控える The doctor told me to abstain from alcohol. *Isha′ ni sake o hikae′ru yō ni iwareta*. 医者に酒を控えるように言われた.

abstention (from voting) *kiken* 棄権

abstract *yōyaku* 要約 an abstract of a paper (treatise) *rombun no yōyaku* 論文の要約 ——(attr) not concrete *chūshōteki* [na] 抽象的[な] That professor's lectures are hard to understand because they're too abstract. *Sono sense′i no hanashi′wa chūshōteki-su′gite, rikai-shiniku′i*. その先生の話は抽象的すぎて理解しにくい. —— obj *o* (v) *to′r·u* 取る abstract iron from ore *kōseki kara te′tsu o to′ru* 鉱石から鉄を取る

absurd (adj) *baka-rashi′·i* ばからしい

abundance 1 *yutaka′sa* 豊かさ 2 *taryō* 多量

abundant *yu′taka* [na] 豊か[な] abundant harvest *yu′taka na shūkaku* 豊かな収穫 ——(attr) *ryō′ no ō′i* 量の多い a harvest more abundant than last year's *kyo′nen yori ryō′ no ō′i shūkaku* 去年より量の多い収穫 ——(idiom) be abundant *ryō′ ga ō′·i* 量が多い This year's harvest was more abundant than last year's. *Kotoshi no shūkaku wa kyo′nen yori ryō′ go ō′katta*. 今年の収穫は去年より量が多かった.

abundantly *taryō ni* 多量に

abuse *ran′yō* 濫用——obj *o* (v) 1 speak ill of *nonoshi′r·u* ののしる 2 (misuse) (irr) *ran′yō-suru* 濫用する A ruler should not abuse power. *Tōchisha wa ke′nryoku o ran′yō-shite wa nara′nai*. 統治者は権力を濫用してはならない. 3 injure; mistreat (irr) *ko′kushi-suru* 酷使する abuse one's eyes *me′ o ko′kushi-suru* 目を酷使する; (irr) *gyakutai-suru* 虐待する The number of parents who abuse their children is increasing. *Kodomo o gyakutai-suru oya′ ga fu′ete iru*. 子供を虐待する親がふえacている.

AC, A.C., a.c. *see* alternating current

academic an academic *gakusha* 学者 ——(attr) *gakumonteki* [na] 学問的[な] an academic discussion *gakumonteki na gi′ron* 学問的な議論; *gaku′mon no* 学問の academic freedom *gaku′mon no jiyū* 学問の自由

accent 1 *a′kusento* アクセント 2 regional pronunciation *namari′* なまり You have no accent. *Ana′ta wa namari′ga na′i*. あなたはなまりがない.

accept obj *o* (v) 1 *ukeire·ru* 受け入れる That person does not easily accept new ideas. *Ano′ hito wa atarashi′i kanga′e o nakanaka ukeirena′i*. あの人は新しい考えをなかなか受け入れない 2 assent to (irr) *shōdaku-suru* 承諾する accept a proposal *teian o shōdaku-suru* 提案を承諾する 3 receive *uke′·ru* 受ける Please accept this. *Dō′zo kore o u′kete kudasa′i*. どうぞこれを受けて下さい. 4 undertake *hikiuke′·ru* 引き受ける Will you accept this work? *Kono* *shigoto o hikiu'kete kudasaima'su ka?* この仕事を引き受けて下さいますか.

acceptance *shōdaku* 承諾

accident *ji'ko* 事故 car accident *jidōsha ji'ko* 自動車事故 There's been an accident! *Ji'ko da!* 事故だ.

accidental *gūzen [no]* 偶然[の]

accidentally *ayama'tte* 誤って I accidentally put the car into reverse. *Ayama'tte kuruma o ba'kku-sasete shima'tta.* 誤って車をバックさせてしまった.

accommodations *se'tsubi* 設備 What kind of accommodations does the hotel have? *Ho'teru ni wa do'nna se'tsubi ga arima'su ka?* ホテルにはどんな設備がありますか.

accompany 1 ind-obj *ni* (v) *tsukia'·u* 付き合う Won't you accompany me? *Tsukia'tte kuremase'n ka?* 付き合ってくれませんか. 2 *...to issho' ni iku* ...と一緒に行く I accompanied him to Kyushu. *Ka're to issho ni Kyū'shū ni itta.* 彼と一緒に九州に行った.

accomplish obj *o* (v) *nashitoge'·ru* なし遂げる He gave his life to accomplish the project. *Ka're wa isshō o sasagete, sono ji'gyō o nashito'geta.* 彼は一生をささげて,その事業をなし遂げた.; *hatas·u* 果たす accomplish one's aim *mokuteki o hatasu* 目的を果たす

according to   *...ni yoru to* [...*sō desu*] ...によると [...*そうです*] According to the radio, tomorrow will be fair. *Ra'jio ni yoru to, ashita' wa te'nki ni na'ru sō desu.* ラジオによると,明日は天気になるそうです.

account 1 bank account *ginkō kō'za* 銀行口座 open a bank account *ginkō ni kō'za o hira'ku* 銀行に口座を開く   2 bank savings account (ordinary) *futsū yo'kin* 普通預金; (term) *teiki yo'kin* 定期預金   3 charge account *tsuke'* 付け a charge customer *tsuke' no kyaku* 付けの客   4 checking account *tō'za yo'kin* 当座預金   5 expense account *kōsa'ihi* 交際費; *hitsuyō ke'ihi* 必要経費   6 postal savings account (ordinary) *tsūjō cho'kin* 通常貯金; (term) *teigaku cho'kin* 定額貯金

accountant *kaikei'shi* 会計士; *ke'iri tantō'sha* 経理担当者

accounting 1 *kaike'igaku* 会計学   2 (department) *ke'iri [-ka]* 経理[課]

accounts (finances) *kaikei* 会計; *ke'iri* 経理

accumulate obj *o* (v) *tsum·u* 積む accumulate wealth *to'mi o tsumu* 富を積む; *atsume'·ru* 集める How did I accumulate so much junk! *Dō' shite konna ni takusan no garakuta o atsume'tan deshō!* どうしてこんなにたくさんのがらくたを集めたんでしょう.   ――(v) *tamar·u* たまる It's surprising how much dust accumulates in the corners of the room. *Hokori wa odoro'ku hodo heya' no sumi ni tamaru.* 埃は驚くほど部屋の隅にたまる.

accurate *seikaku [na]* 正確[な] an accurate watch *seikaku na tokei*

正確な時計 Is this watch accurate? *Kono tokei wa seikaku de'su ka?* この時計は正確ですか.

accusation 1 imputation *iigakari* 言いがかり 2 indictment *kokuhatsu* 告発

accuse ind-obj *ni*, obj *o* (irr) *kokuhatsu-suru* 告発する ——(idiom) impute *iigakari o tsuke'·ru* 言いがかりをつける

accustomed compl *ni* (v) become accustomed *nare'·ru* 慣れる Have you become accustomed to Japan? *Niho'n ni wa mō' narema'shita ka?* 日本にはもう慣れましたか.

ace (card) *e'su* エース

ache *itami'* 痛み ——(v) *ita'm·u* 痛む Does it ache? *Itamima'su ka?* 痛みますか.

achieve obj *o* (irr) *tassei-suru* 達成する achieve one's purpose *mokuteki o tassei-suru* 目的を達成する In 1991 Japan will achieve a 10%increase in its GNP. *Sen-kyū' hyaku-kyūjū-ichi'-nen ni Niho'n wa juppā' sento no kokumin sōseisan zō'ka o tassei-su'ru deshō.* 1991年に日本は, 10%の国民総生産増加を達成するでしょう.

acid *sa'n* 酸 sulfuric acid *ryūsan* 硫酸

acidic (sour) (adj) *suppa'·i* すっぱい

acknowledge obj *o* (v) (irr) *shōnin-suru* 承認する acknowledge a fact *ji' jitsu o shōnin-suru* 事実を承認する; *mitome·ru* 認める acknowledge a mistake *ayamari' o mitomeru* 誤りを認める

acknowledgment *shōnin* 承認; *shōchi* 承知

acne *ni'kibi* にきび

acorn *do'nguri* どんぐり

acquaintance *shiriai* 知り合い an old acquaintance *fu'ruku kara no shiriai* 古くからの知り合い

acquire obj *o* (irr) *kakutoku-suru* 獲得する acquire rights (to) [...no] *ke'nri o kakutoku-suru* [...の] 権利を獲得する; *e'·ru* 得る acquire wealth (fame; knowledge) *za'isan* [*me'iyo; chishiki*] *o e'ru* 財産[名誉; 知識]を得る

acquisition *kakutoku* 獲得

across *mukō* 向こう across the street *michi no mukō'* 道の向こう

act 1 of a play *maku* 幕 It is now the third act. *I'ma sammaku-me' desu.* 今三幕目です. 2 action *jikkō* 実行 ——(irr) act in a play *shutsuen-suru* 出演する ——obj *o* (irr) act on *jikkō-suru* 実行する act on an agreement *keiyaku o jikkō-suru* 契約を実行する

active loc *de* (irr) *katsuyaku-suru* 活躍する He was active in the strike. *Sono suto' de ka're wa mottomo katsuyaku-shita.* そのストで彼は最も活躍した. ——(attr) *katsudōteki* [*na*] 活動的[な] an active person *katsudōteki na hito'* 活動的な人

activity *katsudō* 活動 extracurricular activity *kagai ka'tsudō* 課外活動

actor 1 (in traditional dramas) *yakusha* 役者 2 (in modern dramas) *haiyū* 俳優; (screen) *eiga ha′iyū* 映画俳優

actress *joyū* 女優 *see also* actor

actually *jissai [ni]* 実際[に] Do you actually think so? *Jissai ni sō omoima′su ka?* 実際にそう思いますか.

acupuncture *hari [chi′ryō]* 鍼[治療] I'd like to have acupuncture. *Hari chi′ryō o uketa′i.* 鍼治療を受けたい.

acute *kyūsei [no]* 急性[の] acute pneumonia *kyūsei ha′ien* 急性肺炎

A.D. (in the Christian era) *seireki* 西暦; *ki′gen* 紀元

adapt compl *ni* (irr) *tekiō-suru* 適応する adapt to one's environment *kankyō ni tekiō-suru* 環境に適応する

adaptation *tekiō* 適応

add ind-obj *ni*, obj *o* (v) 1 *tas·u* 足す add water *mizu o tasu* 水を足す 2 append *kuwae·ru* 加える add an index *sakuin o kuwaeru* 索引を加える 3 supplement (irr) *tsuika-suru* 追加する Please add this data to the report. *Repō′to ni kono shi′ryō o tsuika-shinasa′i.* レポートにこの資料を追加しなさい.

addition 1 (Math) *tashi′zan* 足し算 2 addendum *tsuika* 追加 3 addition to a building *zōchiku* 増築 ——(adv) in addition *sono ue′* その上

address *jū′sho* 住所 Tell me your address, please. *Jū′sho o oshiete kudasa′i.* 住所を教えて下さい. Would you write the address on this letter, please? *Kono tegami ni jū′sho o ka′ite kudasaimase′n ka?* この手紙に住所を書いて下さいませんか.; *atesaki* 宛先 Write the address clearly, please. *Atesaki o hakki′ri ka′ite kudasa′i.* 宛先をはっきり書いて下さい.

addressee *uketorinin* 受取人

adhesive tape *bansōkō* ばんそうこう

adjective *keiyō′shi* 形容詞

adjust obj *o* (irr) *chōsetsu-suru* 調節する adjust the height of a stool *isu no ta′kasa o chōsetsu-suru* 椅子の高さを調節する

adjustment *chōsei* 調整; *chōsetsu* 調節

administer obj *o* (irr) *ka′nri-suru* 管理する administer a school *gakkō o ka′nri-suru* 学校を管理する

administration 1 act of administering *ka′nri* 管理 2 (school) *gyōsei [bu]* 行政[部] 3 (government office) *ka′nchō* 官庁

administrator *ka′nrisha* 管理者

admirable 1 splendid *mi′goto [na]* みごと[な] an admirable victory *mi′goto na shō′ri* みごとな勝利 2 worthy of admiration *kanshin [na]* 感心[な] One of her admirable traits is that she never bad-mouths people. *Hito′ no waru′kuchi o iwanai koto′ wa ka′nojo no kanshin na tokoro′ desu.* 人の悪口を言わないことは彼女の感心なところです.

admiral   *kaigun ta'ishō* 海軍大将

admiration   *kanshin* 感心

admire   compl *ni* (irr) *kanshin-suru* 感心する I admire her patience. *Ka'nojo no ninta'iryoku ni kanshin-suru.* 彼女の忍耐力に感心する.

admission (to a theater, etc.) *nyūjō* 入場 admission ticket *nyūjō'ken* 入場券

admit   obj *o* (v) **1** recognize *mitome·ru* 認める I admit that I was mistaken. *Watashi ga machiga'tte ita koto' o mitomeru.* 私が間違っていたことを認める. **2** allow to enter *ire·ru* 入れる I was admitted through the back gate. *Uramon kara irete moratta.* 裏門から入れてもらった.

adolescence   **1** teens *jū'dai* 十代 **2** minority *mise'inen* 未成年 **3** puberty *shishu'nki* 思春期

adolescent   **1** (female) *shō'jo* 少女 **2** (male) *shōnen* 少年

adopt   obj *o* (irr) *sa'iyō-suru* 採用する ——(idiom) adopt a child (girl) *yō'jo ni suru* 養女にする; (boy) *yōshi ni suru* 養子にする

adopted child   **1** (daughter) *yō'jo* 養女 **2** (son) *yōshi* 養子

adult   *otona* 大人; *seijin* 成人

adultery   *kantsū* 姦通 ——(irr) commit adultery *kantsū-suru* 姦通する

advance (v) *susum·u* 進む How far did you advance? *Do'ko made susumima'shita ka?* どこまで進みましたか. ——(adv) in advance *arakajime* あらかじめ Let me say in advance that ... *Arakajime itte okima'su ga...* あらかじめ言っておきますが...

advantage   *toku'* 得 It would be to your advantage to buy it. *Sore o katta hō' ga toku' desu.* それを買った方が得です. ——obj *o* (irr) take advantage of *riyō-suru* 利用する He takes advantage of people. *Ka're wa hito' o riyō-suru.* 彼は人を利用する.

advantageous   *yū'ri* [*na*] 有利[な] advantageous position *yū'ri na tachiba* 有利な立場

Advent (Chr)   *Kōri'nsetsu* 降臨節

adventure   *bōken* 冒険

adventurous   *bōkenteki* [*na*] 冒険的[な]; *bōkenzuki* [*na*] 冒険好き[な]

adverb   *fukushi* 副詞

advertise   obj *o* (irr) *senden-suru* 宣伝する ——(idiom) *kōkoku o da's·u* 広告を出す advertise in a newspaper *shimbun ni kōkoku o da'sù* 新聞に広告を出す

advertisement   *kōkoku* 広告

advice   *jogen* 助言 seek advice from a person *hito' ni jogen o motomeru* 人に助言を求める; *chūi* 注意 advice to travelers *ryokō'sha e no chūi* 旅行者への注意; *chūkoku* 忠告 seek advice *chūkoku o motome·ru* 忠告を求める

advise   obj *o* (irr) *jogen-suru* 助言する; *chū'i-suru* 注意する

adviser 1 *ko'mon* 顧問 technical adviser *gijutsu ko'mon* 技術顧問 2 counselor *sōda'n-yaku* 相談役

aerogram *kōkū-sho'kan* 航空書簡

aesthetic *biteki* [na] 美的[な]

aesthetics *bi'gaku* 美学

affair 1 event *ji'ken* 事件 a big affair *daiji'ken* 大事件 2 love affair *jō'ji* 情事

affection *aijō* 愛情

affirm obj *o* (irr) *dangen-suru* 断言する He affirmed that it was a fact. *Sore wa ji'jitsu da to ka're wa dange'n-shita*. それは事実だと彼は断言した.

affirmation *dangen* 断言

affluence *yūfuku* 裕福

affluent *yūfuku* [na] 裕福[な] an affluent life *yū fuku na kurashi* 裕福な暮らし

afford (idiom) *kau yoyū ga a'r·u* 買う余裕がある I can't afford it. *Sore o kau yoyū ga na'i*. それを買う余裕がない.

Afghan 1 (language) *Afuganisutan-go* アフガニスタン語 2 (person) *Afuganisuta'njin* アフガニスタン人 ——(attr) *Afuganisutan no* アフガニスタンの

Afghanistan *Afugani'sutan* アフガニスタン

afraid (adj) *kowa'i* 怖い Are you afraid? *Kowa'i desu ka?* 怖いですか. I'm not afraid. *Watashi wa ko'waku na'i* 私は怖くない. Don't be afraid. *Kowagarana'ide kudasa'i*. 怖がらないで下さい.

Africa *Afurika* アフリカ

after [no] *a'to de* [の]後で I'll see you after class. *Ku'rasu no a'to de aimashō'*. クラスの後で会いましょう.; ... *kara* ... から Let's go after we eat. *Ta'bete kara ikimashō'*. 食べてから行きましょう.

after all 1 as expected *yaha'ri* やはり 2 in the end *kekkyoku* 結局

after a while *shiba'raku shite'* [*kara*] しばらくして[から]

aftereffect (sickness) *kōi'shō* 後遺症

afternoon (P.M.) *go'go* 午後 at two o'clock in the afternoon *go'go ni'ji ni* 午後二時に this afternoon *kyō' no go'go* 今日の午後 tomorrow afternoon *asu no go'go* あすの午後 yesterday afternoon *kinō no go'go* きのうの午後

after the hour *-sugi* すぎ ten minutes after the hour of ten *jū'ji juppu'n-sugi* 十時十分すぎ

afterward *sore kara* それから Afterward, what shall we do? *Sore kara dō' shimashō wa o'*. それからどうしましょうか.

again 1 *mata'* また I'll phone again. *Mata' denwa-suru*. また電話する. 2 once again *mō ichido* もう一度 Please say it again. *Mō ichido itte' kudasa'i*. もう一度言って下さい. 3 anew *arata'mete*

あらためて Let me ask again. *Arata′mete o-kiki shima′su.* あらた
めてお聞きします.

against 1 be against compl *ni* (irr) *hantai-suru* 反対する They were
against our proposal. *Ka′rera wa wata′shi-tachi no teian ni hantai-
shita.* 彼らは私たちの提案に反対した. 2 leaning on compl *ni* (v)
motare′·ru もたれる I sat with my back against the wall. *Kabe ni
mota′rete suwa′tta.* 壁にもたれてすわった.

age *toshi* 年 I have a daughter just your age. *Watashi wa ana′ta
to onaji nen no musume′ ga iru.* 私はあなたと同じ年の娘がいる.;
nenrei 年齢 Write your age here. *Koko ni nenrei o ka′ite kudasa′i.*
ここに年齢を書いて下さい. ——(idiom) grow old (animate sub-
ject) *toshi o to′r·u* 年をとる; (inanimate subject) *fu′ruku nar·u* 古
くなる

agency *dairi′ten* 代理店

agenda *gi′ji* 議事

agent *dairinin* 代理人

aggression 1 *kōgeki* 攻撃 2 (military) *shinryaku* 侵略

aggressive 1 enterprising *sekkyokuteki [na]* 積極的[な] He is an
aggressive salesman. *Ka′re wa sekkyokuteki na sērusu′man desu.*
彼は積極的なセールスマンです. 2 belligerent (military) *shinryaku
[teki na]* 侵略[的な] an aggressive policy *shinryaku seisaku* 侵略政
策 3 *kōgekiteki [na]* 攻撃的[な] In a meeting he always takes an
aggressive stance. *Ka′re wa kaigi no sekijō de i′tsumo kōgekiteki
na taido o to′ru.* 彼は会議の席上でいつも攻撃的な態度をとる.

aggressively *kōgekiteki ni* 攻撃的に; *shinryakuteki ni* 侵略的に;
sekkyokuteki ni 積極的に You must act more aggressively. *Ana′ta
wa mo′tto sekkyokuteki ni yarana′kute wa nara′nai.* あなたはもっ
と積極的にやらなくてはならない.

ago *ma′e* 前 a year ago *ichinen ma′e* 一年前 ——(adv) awhile
ago *sa′kki* さっき ——(idiom) a long time ago *mukashi* 昔

agree compl *ni* (irr) *sansei-suru* 賛成する I agree. *Sansei-shima′su.*
賛成します. ——(pot) *sansei-deki′·ru* 賛成できる I cannot agree
with that opinion. *Sono i′ken ni sansei-deki′nai.* その意見に賛成
できない. ——comp *to* (irr) *itchi-suru* 一致する My ideas agree
with his. *Watashi no kanga′e wa ka′re no to itchi-suru.* 私の考え
は彼のと一致する.

agreement *sansei* 賛成; *itchi* 一致

agriculture *nō′gyō* 農業

ahead *saki [ni]* 先[に] The interchange is up ahead. *I′ntā wa kono
saki ni a′ru.* インターはこの先にある. ——compl *ni* (v) be ahead
(in a competition) *ka′tte i·ru* 勝っている Which (team) is ahead?
Do′tchi ga ka′tte imasu ka? どっちが勝っていますか. ——(idiom)
Go ahead. *Dō′zo o-saki ni.* どうぞお先に.

aid 1 *ho′jo* 補助 2 (financial) *e′njo* 援助 I received aid from the

Japan Foundation. *Kokusai Kōryū Kikin ni e'njo o moratta.* 国際
交流基金に援助をもらった． ——obj *o* (irr) 1 *ho'jo-suru* 補助する
2 give financial assistance *e'njo-suru* 援助する

aim (purpose) *mokuhyō* 目標

aim at obj *o* (v) *nera·u* ねらう

air 1 *kū'ki* 空気 breathe fresh air *shinsen na kū'ki o suu* 新鮮な空
気を吸う 2 for tires *e'a* エア Put in some air, please. *E'a o irete
kudasa'i.* エアを入れて下さい． ——obj *o* (v) air out *ho's·u* 干す
It's sunny today, so please air the bedding. *Kyō' wa te'nki ga i'i
kara, futon o ho'shite kudasa'i.* 今日は天気がいいからふとんを干
して下さい．

air base *kūgun ki'chi* 空軍基地

air conditioned 1 (cool) *reibō ka'mbi [no]* 冷房完備[の] 2 (warm
& cool) *rei-da'mbō [no]* 冷暖房[の] completely air conditioned
kanzen rei-da'mbō [no] 完全冷暖房[の]

air conditioner *eakon* エアコン; *kū'rā* クーラー automobile air
conditioner *kā e'akon* カーエアコン

air conditioning *reibō* 冷房; *reibō-sō'chi* 冷房装置

air force *kūgun* 空軍

air letter see aerogram

airline *kōkū-ga'isha* 航空会社; domestic airline *kokunai kō'kū* 国
内航空

airmail *kōkū'bin* 航空便

airplane *hikō'ki* 飛行機

airport *kūkō* 空港 domestic airport *kokunai kū'kō* 国内空港 international airport *kokusai kū'kō* 国際空港; airfield *hikōjō* 飛行場

airsickness *hikōki-yoi* 飛行機酔い

aisle *tsū'ro* 通路

alarm clock *mezamashi-do'kei* 目ざまし時計

album (photo/record) *arubamu* アルバム

alcohol *arukōru* アルコール

alcoholic (person) *arukōru izon-shō [ka'nja]* アルコール依存症[患
者]

alcoholic drink *sake* 酒

alcoholism *arukōru izon-shō* アルコール依存症

alert *kibin [na]* 機敏[な] He is alert. *Ka're wa kibin na hito' desu.*
彼は機敏な人です． ——(idiom) *nukeme ga na'i* 抜け目がない She
is alert to any opportunity to make money. *Ka'nojo wa kanemō'ke
no tame' nara, do'nna kikai ni mo nukeme ga na'i.* 彼女は金もうけ
のためなら，どんな機会にも抜け目がない．

algebra *daisū'* 代数

Algeria *Aruje'ria* アルジェリア

Algerian (person) *Arujeria'jin* アルジェリア人 ——(attr) *Arujeria
no* アルジェリアの

alien (foreigner) *gaijin* 外人; *gaikoku' jin* 外国人 alien registration certificate *gaikoku' jin tōroku shōmeisho* 外国人登録証明書

alike *onaji yō* [na] 同じよう[な] These two (things) are alike. *Kono futatsu' wa onaji yō' desu.* この二つは同じようです.

alimony *bekkyo fujo'ryō* 別居扶助料

alive (v) *i'kite i·ru* 生きている Is it alive? *I'kite imasu ka?* 生きていますか.

all (every) **1** *su'bete* [no] すべて[の] All the crops were ruined because of a drought. *Hideri de saku'motsu wa su'bete dame' ni natta.* 日照りで作物はすべてだめになった. **2** everyone *minasan* 皆さん; *minna'* みんな Let's all go! *Minna' de ikimashō'!* みんなで行きましょう. **3** everything *ze'mbu* 全部 Use it all, please. *Ze'mbu tsukatte kudasa'i.* 全部使って下さい.

allergic *arerugi-sei no* アレルギー性の; *are'rugi no* アレルギーの

allergy *are'rugi* アレルギー

alley *ura-dō'ri* 裏通り

alligator *wa'ni* わに alligator skin *wani-gawa'* わに皮

allotment *wariate* 割り当て; *buntan* 分担

allow ind-obj *ni*, obj *o* (v) *yuru's·u* 許す I can't allow that. *Sore o yuru'su koto' wa deki'nai.* それを許すことはできない. ——caus -sase·ru させる Allow me to think it over, please. *Kangaesa'sete kudasa'i.* 考えさせて下さい.

allowance **1** stipend *kyū' yo* 給与 **2** personal/household allowance *kozu'kai* こづかい

all right *daijō'bu* [na] 大丈夫[な] I'm all right (free from harm). *Watashi wa daijō'bu desu.* 私は大丈夫です. ——(idiom) If it's all right (with you) ... *Sashitsukae na'kereba ...* さしつかえなければ...

allspice *ōrusupa'isu* オールスパイス

ally *mikata* 味方; (nation) *dōme'ikoku* 同盟国

almond *āmo'ndo* アーモンド

almost *hoto'ndo* ほとんど It's almost impossible. *Hoto'ndo fuka'nō desu.* ほとんど不可能です. My money is almost all gone. *Okane wa hotondo nakuna'tta.* お金はほとんどなくなった. I'm almost finished. *Hoto'ndo owarima'shita.* ほとんど終わりました.

alone *hito'ri* 一人 Are you alone? *O-hito'ri desu ka?* お一人ですか. ——(adv) *hito'ri de* 一人で I went alone. *Hito'ri de itta.* 一人で行った.

along ...*ni sotte* ...に沿って Modern hotels have been built along the old highway. *Kyūka'idō ni sotte, modan na ho'teru ga ta'tte kite iru.* 旧街道に沿ってモダンなホテルが建ってきている.

alongside (of) ...*ni sotte* ...に沿って They walked alongside the river. *Ka'rera wa kawa' ni sotte aru'ita.* 彼らは川に沿って歩いた.

aloud *ko'e o da'shite* 声を出して Read aloud, please. *Ko'e o da'-shite yo'nde kudasa'i.* 声を出して読んで下さい.

already *mō* もう Is it already done? *Mō' dekima'shita ka?* もうできましたか.

also *mata'* また He is a scholar, and he is also a poet. *Ka're wa gakusha de mo ari, mata' shijin de' mo aru.* 彼は学者でもあり、また詩人でもある.; ... *mo* ... も Give me that also. *Sore mo kudasa'i.* それも下さい.

altar *saidan* 祭壇

alter obj *o* (v) 1 adjust *nao's·u* 直す alter the size (of a suit) [*sū'tsu no*] *sa'izu o nao'su* [スーツの]サイズを直す 2 change *kae·ru* 変える alter one's lifestyle *seikatsu yō'shiki o kaeru* 生活様式を変える

alternate obj *o* (irr) *kōtai-suru* 交替する On long-distance truck runs two drivers alternate every four hours. *Chōkyo'ri tora'kku wa futa'ri no untenshu ga yojikan-go'to ni kōtai-shite iku.* 長距離トラックは二人の運転手が四時間ごとに交替していく.

alternate between *-tari ... -tari suru* たり...たりする The weather in spring alternates between clear and cloudy. *Ha'ru no te'nki wa ha' retari kumo'ttari suru.* 春の天気は、晴れたり曇ったりする.

alternately *kawaru-ga'waru* [*ni*] かわるがわる[に]; *kō'go ni* 交互に

alternating current (AC, A.C., a.c.) *kōryū* 交流

altitude *ta'kasa* 高さ; (Tech) *kō'do* 高度; high altitude (location) *kō'sho* 高所

alto (voice) *a'ruto* アルト

aluminum *aruminyū'mu* アルミニウム

alumna; alumnus 1 *sotsugyō'sei* 卒業生 2 alumni/alumnae organization *dōsō'kai* 同窓会

always *i'tsu mo* いつも I always go on Thursday. *I'tsu mo mokuyō'bi ni iku.* いつも木曜日に行く. I'll always love you. *I'tsu made mo a'i-shite iru.* いつまでも愛している·

A.M. (academic degree) *see* Master of Arts

A.M. (morning) *go'zen* 午前 I woke up at ten A.M. *Go'zen jū' ji ni o'kita.* 午前十時に起きた.

amateur *shi'rōto* しろうと; *amachua* アマチュア

amaze obj *o* (v) *odoroka's·u* 驚かす

ambassador *ta'ishi* 大使

ambiguous *aimai* [*na*] あいまい[な] He gave an ambiguous answer. *Ka're wa aimai na henji' o shita.* 彼はあいまいな返事をした.

ambition *ya'shin* 野心

ambitious *yashinteki* [*na*] 野心的[な] ——(idiom) be ambitious *taishi o idak·u* 大志を抱く

ambulance *kyūkyū'sha* 救急車

amendment (to a motion) *shūse'i-an* 修正案

America *Amerika* アメリカ

American (person) *Amerika' jin* アメリカ人 ——(attr) *Amerika no* アメリカの

amiable *aisō no i'·i* 愛想のいい an amiable person *aisō no i'i hito'* 愛想のいい人

ammonia *ammonia* アンモニア

ammunition *dan'yaku* 弾薬

among ... *no na'ka de* ...の中で Among my friends, he is the closest. *Tomodachi no na'ka de ka're ga ichiban shitashi'i.* 友達の中で彼が一番親しい.

amount **1** (quantity) *ryō* 量 **2** total amount *gōkei* 合計 ——compl *ni* (v) amount to [*ni*] *na'r·u* [に]なる How much does it amount to? *I'kura ni narima'su ka?* いくらになりますか.

amusement *goraku* 娯楽 What do you do for amusement? *Goraku ni na'ni o shima'su ka?* 娯楽に何をしますか.; *asobi* 遊び It's just for amusement. *Ta'da no asobi de'su.* ただの遊びです.

amusement park *yūe'nchi* 遊園地

amusing (adj) *omoshiro'·i* 面白い an amusing game *omoshiro'i ge'mu* 面白いゲーム She told a joke, but it wasn't very amusing. *Ka'nojo wa jōdan o itta ga, amari omoshiro'roku na'katta.* 彼女は冗談を言ったが, あまり面白くなかった.

analysis *bunseki* 分析

analyze obj *o* (irr) *bunseki-suru* 分析する

anatomy **1** structure of an organism *kaibō* 解剖 **2** (study of) *kaibō'gaku* 解剖学

ancestor *se'nzo* 先祖

anchor *ikari* 錨

ancient (adj) *furu'·i* 古い ancient period (of history) *furu'i jidai* 古い時代; *ko'dai* 古代

ancient times *mukashi* 昔

and **1** ... *to* と apples and oranges *ringo to ore'nji* りんごとオレンジ **2** ... *shi* し I wrote a letter and telephoned as well. *Tegami mo ka'ita shi, denwa mo ka'keta.* 手紙も書いたし, 電話もかけた. **3** ... *-te* [*-de*] て[で] I ate and went to bed. *Watashi wa ta'bete nema'shita.* 私は食べて寝ました.   **4** (inclusive) ... *ya* ... *na'do* や ... *na'do* books and notebooks and so forth *ho'n ya nō'to na'do* 本やノートなど

and so forth *na'do-na'do* などなど

and then *soshite* そして

anemia *hinketsu* 貧血; *hinketsu-shō* 貧血症

anesthesia *masui* 麻酔 general anesthesia *zenshin ma'sui* 全身麻酔 local anesthesia *kyokubu ma'sui* 局部麻酔

anesthetic *masui* 麻酔; *masu'i-yaku* 麻酔薬

angel *te'nshi* 天使

anger *ikari* 怒り ——obj *o* (caus) *okorase'·ru* 怒らせる; *okora'·su* 怒らす Don't make him angry. *Ka're o okorasa'naide.* 彼を怒らさないで.

angle   *ka'kudo* 角度

angry   (attr) *oko'tta* 怒った an angry expression *oko'tta kao* 怒っ
た顔 ——ind-obj *ni*, obj *o* (v) become angry *oko'r·u* 怒る Please
don't be angry at me. *Watashi o okora'naide kudasa'i.* 私を怒ら
ないで下さい. ——(idiom) become angry *hara'ga ta'ts·u* 腹が立
つ I'm angry. *Hara' ga ta'tte iru.* 腹が立っている.

animal   *dōbutsu* 動物

ankle   *ashiku'bi* 足首

annex   *bekkan* 別館 ——obj *o* (irr) *gappei-suru* 合併する

anniversary   *kine'mbi* 記念日 wedding anniversary *kekkon kine'mbi*
結婚記念日

announce   obj *o* (irr) *happyō-suru* 発表する

announcement   1 report *happyō* 発表 2 information *o-shirase* お知
らせ

annoying   (adj) *urusa'·i* うるさい That child is really annoying!
Ano' ko wa totemo urusa'i! あの子はとてもうるさい. You're annoying me! *Urusa'i!* うるさい.

annual   *maitoshi no* 毎年の; *ne'n ni ikka'i no* 年に一回の

annually   *maitoshi* 毎年; *ne'n ni ikka'i* 年に一回

another   1 *hoka no* ほかの Do you have another color? *Hoka no
iro'ga arima'su ka?* ほかの色がありますか. 2 one more *mō hito'-
tsu [no]* もう一つ[の] Give me another one, please. *Mō hito'tsu
kudasa'i.* もう一つ下さい.

answer   *henji* 返事; *kota'e* 答え ——obj *o* (irr) *henji'-suru* 返事
する answer by letter *tegami de henji'-suru* 手紙で返事する ——
compl *ni* (v) *kotae'·ru* 答える answer a question *shitsumon ni kotae'ru* 質問に答える

ant   *ari* 蟻

antarctic   *nankyoku* 南極

anthropology   *jinru'igaku* 人類学

antibiotic   *kōseibu'sshitsu* 抗生物質

anticipate   (idiom) *tanoshimi' ni suru* 楽しみにする Everyone's
anticipating the party. *Minna' ga pā'ti o tanoshimi' ni shite iru.*
みんながパーティーを楽しみにしている.

antidote   *gedoku-zai* 解毒剤

antihistamine   *kōhisitami'n-zai* 抗ヒスタミン剤

antique   (object) *kottōhin* 骨董品

antiseptic   (substance) *bōfū'-zai* 防腐剤

antisocial   *shakō-gi'rai no* 社交ぎらいの

antonym   *hantaigo* 反対語

anxiety   *shimpai* 心配

anxious   be anxious obj *o* (irr) *shimpai-suru* 心配する I was
anxious for his safety. *Ka're no ampi o shimpai-shita.* 彼の安否
を心配した.

any *do're* [de] *mo* どれ[で]も Any will do. *Do're de mo i'i.* どれで もいい. ——(idiom) not even one … *mo na i* …もない There aren't any (lit., not even one). *Hitotsu mo na'i.* 一つもない. I don't have any money (lit., not even one yen). *Okane wa ichi-en mo na'i.* お金は一円もない.

anyhow *to'nikaku* とにかく; *na'nishiro* 何しろ We'll have to try anyhow. *Na'nishiro yatte mi'nakute wa nara'nai.* 何しろやってみ なくてはならない.

any kind of *do'nna … demo* どんな … でも Any kind of drink is OK. *Do'nna nomi'mono de'mo i'i.* どんな飲み物でも いい.

anyone *da're* [de] *mo* だれ[で]も Anyone can do it. *Da're demo deki'ru.* だれでもできる.

anyplace *do'ko demo* どこでも Will anyplace do? *Do'ko demo i'i desu ka?* どこでもいいですか.

anything *na'n demo* 何でも Anything will do. *Na'n demo i'i.* 何で もいい.

anytime *i'tsu demo* いつでも Come anytime. *I'tsu demo ki'te ku-dasa'i.* いつでも来て下さい.

anyway *to'nikaku* とにかく Anyway, it's better to try. *To'nikaku yatte mi'ta hō' ga i'i.* とにかくやってみた方がいい.

anywhere *do'ko ni …* [de] *mo* どこに…[で]も I didn't go any-where. *Do'ko ni mo ikana'katta.* どこにも行かなかった.

apart (v) be apart *hana're te i·ru* 離れている My children are two years apart. *Watashi no kodomo wa ni'sai toshi ga hana'rete iru.* 私の子どもは二歳年が離れている. ——(idiom) fall/come apart *barabara ni na'r·u* ばらばらになる It came apart. *Barabara ni na'tta.* ばらばらになった.

apartment 1 *apā'to* アパート 2 condominium *ma'nshon* マンシ ョン

apathetic *muka'ndō* [na] 無感動[な] Young people nowadays are apathetic toward everything. *Saikin no waka'mono wa arayuru mono' ni ta'ishite muka'ndō na ta'ido o shime'su.* 最近の若者はあ らゆる物に対して無感動な態度を示す.

apathy *muka'ndō* 無感動

aphrodisiac *biyaku* 媚薬

apologize ind-obj *ni*, obj *o* (v) *ayama'r·u* 謝る; *wabi·ru* 詫びる apologize to one's teacher for being rude *sense'i ni bure'i o wabiru* 先生に無礼を詫びる

apology *wabi* 詫び I have no words of apology. *O-wabi no shiyō mo arimase'n.* お詫びのしようもありません.

appeal 1 supplication *o-negai* お願い; *utta'e* 訴え 2 (Leg) *kō'so* 控訴 ——obj *o* (v) *utta'e·ru* 訴える The President appealed to the people for support of his SDI program. *Daitō'ryō wa kokumin* *ni SDI kō′sō o shi′ji-shite kudasa′i to utta′eta.* 大統領は国民に SDI 構想を支持して下さいと訴えた.

appear (v) *araware′-ru* 現れる ——(idiom) have semblace of ... [no] *yō′* [na] ...[の]よう[な] She appears to be sick. *Ka′nojo wa byōki no yō′ desu.* 彼女は病気のようです.

appearance (countenance; look; condition) *yōsu* 様子 What was his appearance like? *Ka′re wa do′nna yōsu de′shita ka?* 彼はどんな様子でしたか.

appendectomy *mōchō shu′jutsu* 盲腸手術; (Tech) *chūsui se′tsujo* 虫垂切除

appendicitis *mōchō′en* 盲腸炎; (Tech) *chūsu′ien* 虫垂炎

appendix 1 (Anat) *mō′chō* 盲腸; (Tech) *chūsui* 虫垂 2 of a book *furoku* 付録

appetite *shokuyoku* 食欲 I have no appetite. *Shokuyoku ga na′i.* 食欲がない.

applaud obj *o* (irr) *ha′kushu-suru* 拍手する

applause *ha′kushu* 拍手

apple *ringo* りんご

appliance *ki′gu* 器具

application 1 request *mōshikomi* 申し込み; *shinsei* 申請 2 practical application *ōyō* 応用

applied *ōyō-* 応用 applied linguistics *ōyō-gengo′gaku* 応用言語学 applied science *ōyō-ka′gaku* 応用科学

apply obj *o* (v) 1 request *mōshikom·u* 申し込む Did you apply for a job? *Shūshoku o moshikomima′shita ka?* 就職を申し込みましたか. 2 put to use (irr) *ōyō-suru* 応用する apply basic grammatical patterns *kiso bu′nkei o ōyō-suru* 基礎文型を応用する 3 put on *tsuke′-ru* 付ける Apply this salve. *Kono nuri-gu′suri o tsu′kete kudasa′i.* この塗り薬を付けて下さい.

appoint obj *o* (irr) *nimmei-suru* 任命する ——(pass) *nimmei-sare′-ru* 任命される She was appointed professor. *Ka′nojo wa kyōju ni nimmei-sa′reta.* 彼女は教授に任命された.

appointment *nimmei* 任命; *yakusoku* 約束 I have an appointment at 3:00. *Sa′nji ni yakusoku ga a′ru.* 三時に約束がある.

appreciate obj *o* (irr) *ka′nsha-suru* 感謝する; *kanshō-suru* 鑑賞する He cannot appreciate English poetry. *Ka′re ni wa Eishi wa kanshō-deki′nai.* 彼には英詩は鑑賞できない. ——(idiom) I appreciate your kindness. *Go-shinsetsu o ariga′tō gozaima′su.* ご親切をありがとうございます.

appreciation *ka′nsha* 感謝 They were full of appreciation. *Ka′rera wa ka′nsha no kimochi de ippai de′shita.* 彼らは感謝の気持ちでいっぱいでした. ——ind-obj *ni* (irr) show appreciation *ka′nsha-suru* 感謝する show one's appreciation to one's parents *ryō′shin ni ka′nsha-suru* 両親に感謝する

approach (v) *chikazuk·u* 近づく The ship approached land. *Fu'ne ga riku ni chikazu'ita.* 船が陸に近づいた. That person is easy to approach. *Ano' hito wa chikazuki-yasu'i desu.* あの人は近づきやすいです.

appropriate *tekisetsu* [*na*] 適切[な] What is the most appropriate way to implement this project? *Kono keikaku o jitsugen-suru motto'mo tekisetsu na hōhō wa na'n desu ka?* この計画を実現する最も適切な方法は何ですか. ——obj *o* (irr) *jūtō-suru* 充当する The government has not yet decided what percentage of the national budget to appropriate to defense. *Se'ifu wa raine'ndo no kokka yo'san no nan-pā'sento o bōe'ihi ni jūtō-suru ka wa ma'da ketteishite ina'i.* 政府は来年度の国家予算の何%を防衛費に充当するかはまだ決定していない.

approval 1 consent *shōnin* 承認 This needs the boss's approval. *Kore wa shachō no shōnin ga i'ru.* これは社長の承認がいる. 2 permission *kyo'ka* 許可 Approval was granted. *Kyo'ka ga o'rita.* 許可がおりた. 3 adoption of a motion *kaketsu* 可決 4 concurrence of opinion *sansei* 賛成

approve of compl *ni* (irr) *sansei-suru* 賛成する Did you approve of that? *Sore ni sansei-shima'shita ka?* それに賛成しましたか.

approximately *see* about

apricot *anzu* あんず dried apricots *hoshi a'nzu* 干しあんず

April *shigatsu'* 四月 April 4 *shigatsu yokka* 四月四日

aquarium 1 *suizo'kukan* 水族館 2 (home) *yōgyo'bachi* 養魚ばち

Aquarius *Mizugame-za* 水瓶座

Arab *Arabia' jin* アラビア人

Arabia *Arabia* アラビア

Arabian *see* Arab; Arabic

Arabic (language) *Arabia-go* アラビア語 ——(attr) *Arabia no* アラビアの

arbitrary *katte'* [*na*] 勝手[な] Without listening to everyone's opinions, the chairman made an arbitrary decision. *Minna' no i'ken o kika'zu ni, ii'nchō wa katte' na ketsuron o da'shita.* みんなの意見を聞かずに. 委員長は勝手な結論を出した.

arbitrate obj *o* (irr) *chūkai-suru* 仲介する ——(idiom) *aida ni ta'ts·u* 間に立つ

arbitration *chūkai* 仲介

archaeologist *kōkoga'kusha* 考古学者

archaeology *kōko'gaku* 考古学

archery 1 (J) *kyū'dō* 弓道 2 (W) *a'cheri* アーチェリー

architect *kenchikuka* 建築家

architectural firm *kenchiku-ga'isha* 建築会社; *sekkeijimu'sho* 設計事務所

architecture 1 (design and construction) *kenchiku* 建築 2 architectronics *kenchiku'gaku* 建築学

Arctic (the) *Hokkyoku* 北極

area (measure of a bounded region) *me'nseki* 面積

Argentina *Aruze'nchin* アルゼンチン

Argentine (person) *Aruzenchi'njin* アルゼンチン人 ——(attr) *Aruze'nchin no* アルゼンチンの

argue obj *o* (irr) *gi'ron-suru* 議論する; *kenka-suru* けんかする

argument 1 dispute; debate *ronsō* 論争 2 quarrel *kenka* けんか

Aries *Ohitsuji-za* 牡羊座

aristocracy 1 *ki'zoku* 貴族 2 (system of government) *kizoku se'iji* 貴族政治

aristocrat *ki'zoku* 貴族

arithmetic *sansū* 算数

arm (Anat) *ude'* 腕

armaments *gu'mbi* 軍備

Armenia *Arumenia* アルメニア

Armenian 1 (language) *Arumenia-go* アルメニア語 2 (person) *Arumenia'jin* アルメニア人 ——(attr) *Arumenia no* アルメニアの

armor *yoroi* 鎧

armpit *waki-no'-shita* 腋の下

army *riku'gun* 陸軍; *gu'ntai* 軍隊 enlist in the army *gu'ntai ni ha'iru* 軍隊に入る

aroma *kaori* 香り

around in the vicinity of ... *no hen* [*ni*] ... の辺[に] around here *kono hen* この辺; ... *no mawari* [*ni*] ... のまわり[に] around the (outside of the) house *ie' no mawari* 家のまわり ——(idiom) 1 around the corner *ka'do o magatta tokoro'* 角をまがった所 2 turn around *ushiro o muk·u* 後ろを向く Turn around, please. *U-shiro o muite kudasa'i.* 後ろを向いて下さい。 3 (wrap) around *guruguru* [*to*] [*mak·u*] ぐるぐる[と][巻く] He has a bandage wrapped around his arm. *Ka·re wa ude' ni hōtai o guruguru ma'ite iru.* 彼は腕に包帯をぐるぐる巻いている。

arrange obj *o* (v) 1 put in order *soroe'·ru* そろえる 2 straighten up (irr) *se'iri-suru* 整理する 3 prepare (irr) *ju'mbi-suru* 準備する 4 arrange (flowers) [*hana' o*] *ike'·ru* [花を]生ける

arranged marriage *miai ke'kkon* 見合結婚

arrangement (preparation) *ju'mbi* 準備

arrest *ta'iho* 逮捕 ——obj *o* (irr) *ta'iho-suru* 逮捕する ——(pass) *ta'iho-sare·ru* 逮捕される She was arrested. *Ka'nojo wa ta'iho-sareta.* 彼女は逮捕された。

arrival *tōchaku* 到着 arrival time *tōchaku ji'kan* 到着時間

arrive (v) *tsu'k·u* 着く What time does he arrive? *Ka're wa na'nji ni tsukima'su ka?* 彼は何時に着きますか。

arrow 1 *ya* 矢 2 (symbol) *yaji′rushi* 矢印

art 1 *geijutsu* 芸術 a work of art *geijutsu′-hin* 芸術品 2 fine arts *bi′jutsu* 美術 classical art *koten bi′jutsu* 古典美術 modern art *gendai bi′jutsu* 現代美術 folk art *mingei* 民芸

artery (Anat) *dōmyaku* 動脈

art gallery *garō* 画廊

article 1 essay *rombun* 論文 2 (newspaper) article [*shimbun*] *ki′ji* [新聞]記事

artificial *jinkō* [*no*] 人工[の] artificial insemination *jinkō jusei* 人工受精 artificial respiration *jinkō ko′kyū* 人工呼吸

artificial flowers *zōka* 造花

artist 1 *geijutsuka* 芸術家 2 painter *gaka* 画家; *ekaki* 絵かき

artistic *geijutsuteki* [*na*] 芸術的[な]

art museum *bijutsukan* 美術館

art studio *atorie* アトリエ; *sutajio* スタジオ

as 1 as … as … *to onaji gu′rai* …と同じぐらい She's lived in Japan as long as I have *Ka′nojo wa watashi to onaji gu′rai no kikan, Niho′n ni su′nde iru.* 彼女は私と同じぐらいの期間, 日本に住んでいる.; [*na*] *dake* [な]だけ Take as much as you like. *Suki′ na dake to′tte kudasa′i.* 好きなだけ取って下さい. Do it as soon as possible. *Dekiru dake ha′yaku shite kudasa′i.* できるだけ早くして下さい. 2 like; in the manner of … *yō′* [*ni*] …よう[に] Do as he said. *Ka′re ga itta yō′ ni shinasa′i.* 彼が言ったようにしなさい. 3 for … *to shite* … として I use this table as my desk. *Kono te′buru o tsukue to shite tsukau.* このテーブルを机として使う.

asexual *musei no* 無性の

ash *hai* 灰

ashamed (adj) *hazukashi′·i* 恥ずかしい

ashore *riku-jō* 陸上 ——(irr) go ashore *jōriku-suru* 上陸する

ashtray *haizara* 灰皿

Asia *A′jia* アジア

Asian (person) *Ajia′jin* アジア人 ——(attr) *Ajia no* アジアの

as is *ari-no-mama′* ありのまま; *sono mama′* そのまま Leave it as is. *Sono mama′ ni shite kudasa′i.* そのままにして下さい.

ask ind-obj *ni*, obj *o* (v) 1 inquire *ki′k·u* 聞く Ask her. *Ka′nojo ni kiite kudasa′i.* 彼女に聞いて下さい. 2 request *tano′m·u* 頼む I asked him to get the tickets. *Ka′re ni kippu o kau yō′ni tano′nda.* 彼に切符を買うように頼んだ.

asleep (v) *nete i·ru* 寝ている She's asleep. *Ka′nojo wa nete iru.* 彼女は寝ている. ——(idiom) (lit., become numb) *shibire′·ru* しびれる My foot's asleep. *Ashi′ ga shibi′reta.* 足がしびれた.

aspirin *asupirin* アスピリン

assassinate obj *o* (irr) *ansatsu-suru* 暗殺する

assassination *ansatsu* 暗殺

assault *bōkō* 暴行 ——(idiom) assault (a person) *bōkō o ku-wae'·ru* 暴行を加える

assemblyman *gi'in* 議員 Diet assemblyman *kokkai-gi'in* 国会議員

assert obj *o* (irr) *shuchō-suru* 主張する assert one's opinion *i'ken o shuchō-suru* 意見を主張する

assign (v) *wariate'·ru* 割り当てる The group leader assigned (us) our) rooms. *Gurūpu rīdā wa heya' o waria'teta.* グループリーダーは部屋を割り当てた。

assignment 1 *wariate* 割り当て 2 (school) *shukudai* 宿題

assist obj *o* (v) *tetsuda'·u* 手伝う She is assisting me with my research. *Ka'nojo wa watashi no kenkyū o tetsuda'tte iru.* 彼女は私の研究を手伝っている。 ——(idiom) *sewa' o suru* 世話をする assist an old person *toshiyori no sewa'o suru* 年寄りの世話をする

assistance *e'njo* 援助 ask for assistance *e'njo o motome'ru* 援助を求める

assistant *jo'shu* 助手; assistant professor *jo-kyō'ju* 助教授

association (organization) *kyōkai* 協会

as soon as possible *dekiru dake ha'yaku* できるだけ早く

assume 1 obj *o* (irr) *katei-suru* 仮定する Assuming it is true, what should I do? *Sore o hontō da to katei-suru to, dō' sureba i'i deshō?* それを本当だと仮定すると、どうすればいいでしょう。 2 undertake *o·u* 負う assume responsibility *sekinin o ou* 責任を負う

aster *shi'on* 紫苑

asthma *zensoku* ぜん息

astigmatism *ranshi* 乱視

astonished compl *ni* (irr) *bikku'ri-suru* びっくりする I was astonished to hear that. *Sore o kiite bikku'ri-shita.* それを聞いてびっくりした。

astrology *sense'igaku* 占星学

astronomy *temmo'ngaku* 天文学

at *...de...* で I bought it at Isetan. *Isetan de katta.* 伊勢丹で買った。; *...ni...* I have my own word processor at home. *Ie' ni jibun no wā'puro ga a'ru.* 家に自分のワープロがある。 Tomorrow I have to get up at 6:00. *Ashita rokuji ni oki'nakereba nara'nai.* 明日、六時に起きなければならない。 The two nations are at war. *Nikokukan ga sensō jō'tai ni a'ru.* 二国間が戦争状態にある。 see also stare at

athlete *se'nshu* 選手

athlete's foot *mizumu'shi* 水虫

athletic *kyōsō* [na] 強壮[な] an athletic person *kyōsō na hito'* 強壮な人

athletic meet *undō'kai* 運動会; *kyōgi'kai* 競技会

athletics 1 physical exercise *undō* 運動 2 sports *supō'tsu* スポーツ 3 physical education *ta'iiku* 体育 4 calisthenics *taisō* 体操

Atlantic Ocean *Taise'iyō* 大西洋

atmosphere 1 *ta'iki* 大気 2 *fun'i'ki* 雰囲気 a homey atmosphere *kateiteki na fun'i'ki* 家庭的な雰囲気 This place has a good atmosphere. *Koko wa fun'i'ki ga i'i.* ここは雰囲気がいい.

atom *ge'nshi* 原子 atom bomb *genshi ba'kudan* 原子爆弾

atomic *genshi [no]* 原子[の] atomic/nuclear age *genshi ji'dai* 原子時代 atomic/nuclear power *genshi'ryoku* 原子力

at once *su'gu ni* すぐに When I called, he came at once. *Yonda'ra ka're wa su'gu ni kite' kureta.* 呼んだら彼はすぐに来てくれた.

attach obj *o* (v) *tsuke'・ru* 付ける; *soe'・ru* 添える Attach this document to the request. *Shinseisho ni kono sho'rui o soe-nasa'i.* 申請書にこの書類を添えなさい.

attached *shozoku no* 所属の; *fuzoku* 付属 a high school attached to a university *daigaku fuzoku kō'kō* 大学付属高校

attack *kōgeki* 攻撃 ——obj *o* (irr) *kōgeki-suru* 攻撃する

attempt *kokoromi* 試み ——obj *o* (v) *kokoromi'・ru* 試みる

attend (irr) *shusseki-suru* 出席する Did you attend the meeting? *Sono ka'i ni shusseki-shima'shita ka?* その会に出席しましたか.

attendance *shusseki* 出席 take attendance *shusseki o to'ru* 出席をとる

attention *chūmoku* 注目; *chū'i* 注意 attract attention *chū'i o hiku* 注意をひく

attitude *ta'ido* 態度 That student has a bad attitude. *Sono gakusei wa ta'ido ga waru'i.* その学生は態度が悪い.

attorney *bengo'shi* 弁護士

attract obj *o* (v) *hikitsuke'・ru* 引きつける There's something about him that attracts women. *Ka're wa dokoka onna' o hikitsuke'ru tokoro' ga a'ru.* 彼はどこか女を引きつけるところがある.

attractive *miryokuteki [na]* 魅力的[な] Don't you think she's attractive? *Ka'nojo wa miryokuteki da to omoimase'n ka?* 彼女は魅力的だと思いませんか.

aubergine *see* eggplant

auction *seriuri* せり売り

audit *kaikei ka'nsa* 会計監査 do an audit *kaikei ka'nsa o okonau* 会計監査を行なう ——obj *o* (irr) audit a course *chōkō-suru* 聴講する

auditorium *kōdō* 講堂

August *hachigatsu'* 八月 August 8 *hachigatsu yōka* 八月八日

aunt 1 (one's own) *oba* おば 2 (another's) *obasan* おばさん

aurora borealis *see* northern lights

Australia *Ō sutora'ria* オーストラリア

Australian (person) *Ō sutoraria'jin* オーストラリア人 ——(attr) *Ō sutora'ria no* オーストラリアの

Austria *Ōsutoria* オーストリア

Austrian (person) *Ōsutoria′jin* オーストリア人 ——(attr) *Ōsutoria no* オーストリアの

author 1 *sakka* 作家; *cho′sha* 著者 2 novelist *shōsetsuka* 小説家 3 playwright *gekisa′kka* 劇作家

authorities *tō′kyoku* 当局

authority *ke′nryoku* 権力; *ke′n'i* 権威

autobiography *jiden* 自伝

automatic *jidō[teki] [na]* 自動[的][な] automatic transmission *jidō hensoku-ki* 自動変速機 automatic vending machine *jidō hamba′i-ki* 自動販売機

automobile *jidō′sha* 自動車 automobile accident *jidōsha ji′ko* 自動車事故

autonomy *ji′chi* 自治 be deprived of (one's) autonomy *ji′chi o ubawareru* 自治を奪われる the people's autonomy *jūmin ji′chi* 住民自治

autumn *a′ki* 秋 ——(idiom) autumn leaves *kō′yō* 紅葉

average *heikin* 平均 average life span *heikin ju′myō* 平均寿命 determine the average *heikin o da′s·u* 平均をだす; *heibon [na]* 平凡[な]

avoid obj *o* (v) *sake′·ru* 避ける There was no way I could avoid the accident. *Ji′ko o dōshite′ mo sake′ru koto ga deki′nakatta.* 事故をどうしても避けることができなかった.

awake (v) *[me′ga] sa′mete i·ru* [目が]覚めている; *o′kite i·ru* 起きている Are you awake? *O′kite ima′su ka?* 起きていますか.

awaken see wake

away obj *o* (v) 1 take away *to′r·u* 取る Take this away, please. *Kore o to′tte kudasa′i.* これを取って下さい. 2 take (clear) away *sage′·ru* 下げる May I take away the dishes? *O-sara o sa′gete mo i′i desu ka?* お皿を下げてもいいですか. ——(idiom) 1 be away on business *shutchō-chū* 出張中 Mr. Tanaka's away on business. *Tanaka-san wa shutchō-chū′ desu.* 田中さんは出張中です. 2 not at home *ru′su ni suru* 留守にする The Tanakas are away for the weekend. *Tanaka-san-tachi wa shū′matsu de ru′su ni shite iru.* 田中さんたちは, 週末で留守にしている.

awful *taihen [na]* 大変[な] an awful person *taihen na hito′* 大変な人 Yesterday was awful. *Kinō′ wa taihen de′shita.* きのうは大変でした.

awkward *buki′yō [na]* 不器用[な] I'm awkward. *Watashi wa buki′yō desu.* 私は不器用です. ——(adj) *gigochina′·i* ぎごちない an awkward sentence *gigochinai bu′n[shō]* ぎごちない文[章]

awning *hiyoke* 日よけ

ax *o′no* 斧

azalea *tsutsu′ji* つつじ

B

B.A. (academic degree) *see* Bachelor of Arts

baboon *hi′hi* ひひ

baby 1 (human) *a′kachan* 赤ちゃん 2 (other than human) ... *no ko* ...の子 a baby lion *ra′ion no ko* ライオンの子

babysitter *komo′ri* 子守

baby-sitting *komo′ri* 子守 ——obj *o* (irr) *komo′ri-suru* 子守する

baccalaureate *ga′kushi* 学士

bachelor *dokushin* [*sha*] 独身[者]

Bachelor of Arts *bunga′kushi* 文学士

Bachelor of Science *riga′kushi* 理学士

back 1 (Anat) *senaka* 背中 2 the rear *ushiro′* 後ろ in the back *ushiro ni* 後ろに enter from the back *ushiro′ kara ha′iru* 後ろから入る 3 reverse side *ura* 裏 front and back *omote′ to ura* 表と裏 ——(v) 1 go back *modo′r·u* 戻る 2 go back home *ka′er·u* 帰る ——(irr) back up *ba′kku-suru* バックする back the car up *kuruma o ba′kku-suru* 車をバックする ——(idiom) I'm back! *Tadaima′!* ただいま.

back door 1 *uraguchi* 裏口 2 (kitchen door) *katte′guchi* 勝手口

background *haikei* 背景

backpack *ba′kkupakku* バックパック; *ryu′kku* リュック

backside *rimen* 裏面 *see also* buttocks

back street *ura-do′ri* 裏通り

backstroke *haiei* 背泳

backyard *ura niwa* 裏庭

bacon *be′kon* ベーコン bacon & eggs *bekon-e′ggu* ベーコンエッグ

bacteria *ba′ikin* 黴菌; *bakute′ria* バクテリア

bad (adj) *waru′·i* 悪い bad weather *waru′i te′nki* 悪い天気 My grades were bad. *Watashi wa seiseki ga wa′rukatta.* 私は成績が悪かった. ——(idiom) 1 I have a bad cold. *Waru′i kaze o hi′ite iru.* 悪い風邪をひいている. 2 I feel bad. *Ki′bun ga waru′i.* 気分が悪い. 3 That's too bad. *Sore wa ikemase′n ne.* それはいけませんね.

badger *anaguma* 穴熊

bad habit *waru′i kuse′* 悪い癖

bad luck *aku-un* 悪運 ——(idiom) I had bad luck. *U′n ga wa′rukatta.* 運が悪かった.

badminton *badomi′nton* バドミントン

bad-tempered (adj) *okorippo′·i* 怒りっぽい ——(idiom) *kigen ga waru′·i* 機嫌が悪い

baffled (v) be baffled *mai′r·u* まいる I was completely baffled by the student's question. *Gakusei no shitsumon ni wa matta′ku ma′itta.* 学生の質問には全くまいった.

baffling *fuka′kai* [*na*] 不可解[な] a baffling problem *fuka′kai na mondai* 不可解な問題 ——(attr) *wa′ke no wakara′nai* 訳のわからない a baffling explanation *wa′ke no wakara′nai setsumei* 訳のわからない説明

bag *fukuro* 袋 *see also* handbag; suitcase

baggage *ni′motsu* 荷物

bail (Leg) *hoshakukin* 保釈金 pay (someone's) bail *hoshakukin o tsumu* 保釈金をつむ ——(idiom) furnish bail for someone *hito no hoshaku hoshōnin ni na′ru* 人の保釈保証人になる

bait *esa′* 餌

bake obj *o* (v) *yak·u* 焼く I baked a cake. *Kē′ki o yaita.* ケーキを焼いた. ——(v) be baked *yake·ru* 焼ける Is the cake baked yet? *Kē′ki wa mō yakema′shita ka?* ケーキはもう焼けましたか.

baked (attr) *yaki-* 焼き baked sweet potato *yaki-imo* 焼き芋

baker *pa′n·ya-san* パン屋さん

bakery *pa′n·ya* パン屋

baking dish [*ōbun-yō*] *fuka′-zara* [オーブン用]深皿

baking powder *bēkingu pa′udā* ベーキングパウダー

baking soda *jūsō* 重曹

balance 1 scale *hakari′* はかり; *tembin* 天秤 2 remaining money *zandaka* 残高 What's my balance? *Zandaka wa i′kura ni narima′su ka?* 残高はいくらになりますか. ——(v) be equal in amount *tsuria′u* 釣り合う ——obj *o* (irr) balance the books *ke′ssan-suru* 決算する

baldheaded *hage-a′tama* [*no*] はげ頭[の]

ball (for playing games) *tama′* 球; *bōru* ボール

balloon *fūsen* 風船

ballot *tōhyō* 投票 ——(irr) cast a ballot *tōhyō-suru* 投票する

ballpoint pen *bōrupen* ボールペン

bamboo *take′* 竹 bamboo shoots *take′no ko* 竹の子

ban obj *o* (v) *kinji′·ru* 禁じる ——(pass) *kinjirare′·ru* 禁じられる Pornography is banned in Japan. *Niho′n de wa po′runo ga kinjira′-rete iru.* 日本ではポルノが禁じられている.

banana *ba′nana* バナナ

band 1 cord *himo′* 紐 2 sash *o′bi* 帯 3 rubber band *wagomu* 輪ゴム 4 musical group *bando* バンド; *gakudan* 楽団 *see also* belt; sash

bandage 1 surgical dressing *hōtai* 包帯 2 adhesive bandage *ban-sōkō* ばんそうこう ——(idiom) bandage (a wound) *hōtai o suru* 包帯をする

bandleader *shiki′sha* 指揮者

bang (sound) *do′n* どん; *bata′n* ばたん ——(adv) with a bang *do′n to* どんと hit with a bang *do′n to u′ts·u* どんと打つ; *bata′n* *to* ばたんと The door shut with a bang. *Do'a wa bata'n to shima't-ta.* ドアはばたんとしまった.

Bangladesh *Bangurade'shu* バングラデシュ ——(attr) *Bangurade'shu no* バングラデシュの

Bangladeshi *Banguradeshu'jin* バングラデシュ人

banish obj *o* (irr) *tsuihō-suru* 追放する

banishment *tsuihō* 追放

bank 1 (of a canal or river) *dote* 土手 2 financial institution *ginkō* 銀行 Bank of Japan *Nihon Gi'nkō* 日本銀行

bankbook *yokin tsū'chō* 預金通帳

banker *ginkōka* 銀行家

bankruptcy *hasan* 破産 declare bankruptcy *hasan o senkoku-suru* 破産を宣告する

banquet *enkai* 宴会

baptism (Chr) 1 *senrei* 洗礼 2 (ceremony) *senre'i-shiki* 洗礼式

baptize (Chr) (idiom) 1 *senrei o hodoko's·u* 洗礼を施す 2 be baptized *senrei o uke'·ru* 洗礼を受ける

bar 1 drinking establishment *bā'* バー; *suna'kku* スナック 2 bar of music *shōsetsu* 小節 3 rod *bō* 棒 ——obj *o* (v) 1 block *fusag·u* ふさぐ 2 prevent; exclude (irr) *bōshi-suru* 防止する

barber *tokoya[-san]* 床屋[さん]

barbershop *tokoya* 床屋

barbiturate *barubitsuru-sa'n'en* バルビツル酸塩

bare *hadaka [no]* 裸[の] completely bare *suppa'daka [no]* 素裸[の]

barefooted *hadashi [no]* 裸足[の] walk barefooted *hadashi de aru'·ku* 裸足で歩く

bargain 1 a good buy *horidashimono'* 掘り出し物 2 bargain sale *uridashi* 売り出し; *bāgen sē'ru* バーゲンセール ——obj *o* (v) *negi'r·u* 値切る

bark 1 (of a tree) [*ki' no] kawa'* [木の]皮 2 dog's bark *inu no nakigo'e* 犬の鳴き声 ——(v) *hoe'·ru* 吠える Does the dog bark? *Kono inu' wa hoema'su ka?* この犬は吠えますか.

barley *ōmugi* 大麦

barn *naya* 納屋

barometer *kiatsukei* 気圧計; *baromē'tā* バロメーター

baron *da'nshaku* 男爵

barracks *hei-ei* 兵営; *heisha* 兵舎

barrel *taru* 樽

barrier *shōheki* 障壁

bartender *bāte'ndā* バーテンダー

basal metabolic rate (BMR) *kiso taisha'ritsu* 基礎代謝率

base 1 *kitei* 基底 2 (military) *ki'chi* 基地 3 (baseball) -*rui* 塁 first base *ichi'-rui* 一塁 get to first base *ichi'-rui ni de'ru* 一塁に出る *see also* basis

baseball **1** (ball) *bōru* ボール **2** (game) *yakyū* 野球 baseball stadium *yakyūjō* 野球場 baseball player *yakyū no se'nshu* 野球の選手

basement *chi'ka* 地下; *chika'shitsu* 地下室

bashful (adj) *hazukashi'·i* 恥ずかしい ——(v) be bashful *hazukashiga'r·u* 恥ずかしがる Don't be bashful. *Hazukashigarana'ide [kudasa'i].* 恥ずかしがらないで[下さい]. ——(idiom) a bashful person *hazukashiga'riya* 恥ずかしがり屋

basic *kihonteki* [na] 基本的[な] a basic principle *kihonteki gensoku* 基本的の原則; *komponteki* [na] 根本的[な]; *honshitsuteki* [na] 本質的 [な]

basically *komponteki ni* 根本的に That idea was basically mistaken. *Sono kanga'e wa komponteki ni machiga'tte ita.* その考えは根本的にまちがっていた.; *kihonteki ni* 基本的に; *honshitsuteki ni* 本質的に

basin **1** (Geo) *bonchi* 盆地 the Kofu Basin *Kōfu Bo'nchi* 甲府盆地 **2** washbasin *semme'nki* 洗面器

basis **1** foundation *dodai* 土台; *kiso'* 基礎 **2** standard *kijun* 規準

basket **1** *kago* かご **2** bamboo basket *zaru* ざる

bass (fish) *suzuki* 鱸

bass (voice) *ba'su* バス; *bē'su* ベース

bassinet *yuri'kago* 揺りかご

bastard (illegitimate child) *shisei'ji* 私生児

bat (animal) *kō'mori* こうもり

bat (baseball) *ba'tto* バット

bath **1** *furo'* 風呂 take a bath *furo' ni ha'ir·u* 風呂に入る bathtub *furo o'ke* 風呂桶 **2** public bath *se'ntō* 銭湯

bathing suit *mizugi* 水着

bathrobe **1** (W) *basurō'bu* バスローブ **2** (J) *yukata* ゆかた

bathroom (for bathing) *furoba* 風呂場

batik *rōzome* ろう染め

batter **1** (baseball) *da'sha* 打者; *ba'ttā* バッター **2** (for cooking) *neriko* 練粉

battery **1** *de'nchi* 電池 **2** car battery *batterī* バッテリー

battle *tatakai* 戦い ——comp *ni* (v) battle with *tataka·u* 戦う

battlefield *senjō* 戦場

bay *wa'n* 湾 Tokyo Bay *Tōkyō'-wan* 東京湾

bay leaf *gekke'iju no ha* 月桂樹の葉

B.C. (before Christ) *kigenze'n* 紀元前

be (v) **1** (animate) *i·ru* いるI will be at home tomorrow. *Ashita uchi ni iru.* 明日家にいる. Where are you now? *I'ma do'ko ni ima'su ka?* 今どこにいますか.; (inanimate) *a'r·u* ある Your wallet is on the dresser. *Ana'ta no saifu wa tansu no ue' ni a'ru.* あなたの財布はたんすの上にある. **2** (copula) *desu* です This is a book. *Kore wa ho'n desu.* これは本です.

beach *hamabe* 浜辺; *ka'igan* 海岸

bead *tama'* 玉

beads (necklace) *kubika'zari* 首飾り; *ne'kkuresu* ネックレス

beak *kuchibashi* くちばし

beam 1 (piece of wood) *keta'* 桁; *hari'* 梁 2 (of light) *kōsen* 光線

bean 1 *mame'* 豆 2 string beans *saya-i'ngen* さやいんげん 3 soybeans *daizu* 大豆

bean curd *tō'fu* 豆腐

bean sprouts *moyashi* もやし

bear (animal) *kuma'* 熊

bear obj *o* (v) 1 endure *tae'·ru* 耐える It's more than I can bear. *Sore wa watashi ni'wa taerare'nai koto' desu.* それは私には耐えられないことです。; (irr) *ga'mun-suru* がまんする You'll just have to bear it. *Sore o ga'man-shina'kute wa nara'nai.* それをがまんしなくてはならない。 2 give birth *um·u* 産む bear a child *ko o umu* 子を産む *see also* born

beard *hige* 髭

beast *kedamono* 獣

beat obj *o* (v) 1 hit *tata'k·u* 叩く beat a drum *taiko o tata'ku* 太鼓を叩く; *nagu'·ru* 殴る beat a person *hito o nagu'ru* 人を殴る 2 defeat *makas·u* 負かす beat the B team *B chimu o makasu* B チームを負かす

beater 1 whisk *awadate'ki* あわだて器 2 electric mixer *mi'kisā* ミキサー

beautiful (adj) *utsukushi'·i* 美しい beautiful person *utsukushi'i hito'* 美しい人

beauty *utsuku'shisa* 美しさ

beauty parlor *biyō'shitsu* 美容室

because ... *kara* ... から I didn't go because I had no money. *Okane ga na'katta kara ikana'i.katta.* お金がなかったから行かなかった。; ... *node* ... ので I was late because the train was behind schedule. *Densha ga okureta' node chikoku-shima'·shita.* 電車が遅れたので遅刻しました。

beckon ind-obj *ni,* obj *o* (irr) *tema'neki-suru* 手招きする

become compl *ni* (v) *na'r·u* なる become sick *byōki ni na'ru* 病気になる When spring comes, it will become warm. *Ha'ru ni na'ru to atata'kaku naru.* 春になると暖かくなる。

becoming compl *ni* (v) *nia'·u* 似合う That color is becoming to you. *Sono iro' wa ana'ta ni nia'u.* その色はあなたに似合う。

bed 1 (W) *be'ddo* ベッド 2 (J) *toko* 床 ——(v) go to bed *ne·ru* 寝る ——(idiom) get/crawl into bed *toko ni ha'ir·u* 床に入る

bedding 1 (W) *shi'ngu* 寝具 2 (J) *futon* 布団

bedridden *netakiri* [*no*] 寝たきり[の] The old woman is bedridden. *Sono rōfu'jin wa netakiri de'su.* その老婦人は寝たきりです。

bedroom   *shinshitsu* 寝室

bee   *hachi* 蜂 honey bee *mitsu'bachi* 蜜蜂

beef   *gyūniku* 牛肉

beer   *bi'ru* ビール draft beer *nama bi'ru* 生ビール

beet   *bi'to* ビート

beetle   *kōchū* 甲虫; *kabuto'mushi* かぶと虫

before   **1** ahead of (in time, space, rank, etc.) ... [no] *ma'e* ...[の]
前 a week before *isshūkan ma'e* 一週間前 15 minutes before four
o'clock *yo'ji jūgofu'n ma'e* 4時15分前; *tema'e* 手前 That store is
just before (you get to) the bank. *Ano mise' wa ginkō no cho'tto
tema'e desu.* あの店は銀行のちょっと手前です.   **2** formerly *ma'e
wa* 前は We lived in Chicago before. *Ma'e wa wata'shi-tachi wa
Shika'go ni su'nde ita.* 前は私たちはシカゴに住んでいた.

beg   obj *o* (v) *ko'u* 乞う beg for something *mono' o ko'u* 物を
乞う

beggar   *kojiki'* こじき

begging   *monogo'i* 物ごい

begin   (v) *hajimar·u* 始まる What time does it begin? *Na'nji ni
hajimarima'su ka?* 何時に始まりすか. ——obj *o* (v) *hajime·ru* 始
める When do you begin it? *I'tsu sore o hajimema'su ka?* いつそ
れを始めますか. Have you begun ikebana classes? *Ike'bana no
ke'iko o hajimema'shita ka?* 生け花の稽古を始めましたか. *see
also* start

beginner   *shoshi'nsha* 初心者

begonia   *begonia* ベゴニア

behavior   *furuma'i* 振舞い

behind   *ushi'ro* [ni] 後ろ[に] There's a vacant lot behind our house.
Uchi no ushiro ni akichi ga a'ru. 家の後ろに空地がある. ——(v)
be behind/be late *okure·ru* 遅れる The plane is two hours behind
schedule. *Hikō'ki wa niji'kan mo okurete iru.* 飛行機は二時間も遅
れている. I'm behind in my work. *Shigoto ga okure'te iru.* 仕事が
遅れている.

being   (existence)   *sonzai* 存在 reason/justification for being *sonzai
ri'yū* 存在理由

belch   *geppu* げっぷ ——(idiom) to belch *geppu ga de'·ru* げっぷ
が出る I belched. *Geppu ga de'ta.* げっぷが出た.

Belgian   (person)   *Berugi'jin* ベルギー人 ——(attr) *Berugi no* ベ
ルギーの

Belgium   *Berugi'* ベルギー

belief   (Chr) *shinkō* 信仰; (Budd) *shinjin* 信心

believe   obj *o* (v) *shinji'·ru* 信じる believe in God *Ka'mi o shinji'ru*
神を信じる Believe me! *Watashi o shi'njite kudasa'i!* 私を信じて
下さい.

bell   1 *be'ru* ベル the bell rings *be'ru ga naru* ベルが鳴る   2 doorbell *yobirin* 呼び鈴   3 church/temple bell *kane* 鐘

bellboy   *bōi-san* ボーイさん

belong to   compl *ni* (irr) *zoku-suru* 属する I belong to the language department. *Gogaku-ka ni zoku'-shite iru.* 語学科に属している. ──(idiom) belong to ... *no mono'* ... の物 That belongs to me. *Sore wa watashi no mono' desu.* それは私の物です.

below   *shita* 下 He lives in the apartment below. *Ka're wa shita no heya' ni su'nde iru.* 彼は下の部屋に住んでいる.

belt   *bando* バンド; *beruto* ベルト

bench   *benchi* ベンチ

bend   (v) *magar·u* 曲がる The road bends to the right. *Michi ga migi ni magaru.* 道が右に曲がる.   ──obj *o* (v) *mager·u* 曲げる bend one's legs *ashi' o mageru* 足を曲げる

beneath   *shita* [*ni*] 下[に]

benefactor   *onjin* 恩人

beneficial   *yūeki* [*na*] 有益[な] a beneficial measure *yūeki na shu'dan* 有益な手段   ──(idiom) *tame' ni nar·u* ためになる That would be beneficial to you. *Sore wa ana'ta no tame' ni naru.* それはあなたのためになる.

benefit   1 *ri'eki* 利益 If you get permanent residence status, what benefits will you receive? *Eijū'ken ga to'retara, do'nna ri'eki ga shōjima'su ka?* 永住権がとれたらどんな利益が生じますか.; *onkei* 恩恵 Citizenship provides a number of benefits. *Shimi'nken ni wa samaza'ma na onkei ga a'ru.* 市民権にはさまざまな恩恵がある.   2 retirement benefits *taishoku'kin* 退職金

Bengal   *Bengaru* ベンガル

Bengalese   see Bengali

Bengali   1 (language) *Bengaru-go* ベンガル語   2 (person) *Benga'-rujin* ベンガル人   ──(attr) *Bengaru no* ベンガルの

bent   (v) be/become bent *magar·u* 曲がる This spoon is bent. *Kono su'pūn wa magatte iru.* このスプーンは曲がっている.   ──(attr) *magatta* 曲がった a bent rod *magatta bō* 曲がった棒

berry   *be'rī* ベリー

berth   *dan* 段 lower berth *gedan* 下段 upper berth *jōdan* 上段

beside   *so'ba* [*ni*] そば[に] I have an alarm clock beside my bed. *Watashi no be'ddo no so'ba ni mezamashi-do'kei ga oite a'ru.* 私のベッドのそばに目覚し時計が置いてある.

besides   1 above and beyond *sono ue'* [*ni*] その上[に] Besides that, I have nothing to say. *Sono ue' iu koto' wa nani mo na'i.* その上言うことは何もない.   2 in addition *hoka* [*ni*] ほか[に] Is there something else to see besides that? *Sono' hoka ni na'nika mi'ru tokoro ga arima'su ka?* そのほかに何か見る所がありますか.

3

other than ... *i'gai* 以外 I have no friend besides him. *Ka're i'gai ni wa tomodachi wa na'i.* 彼以外には友達はない.

best (adj) *ichiban i'·i* 一番いい the best way *ichiban i'i hōhō* 一番いい方法

bet *kake'* 賭け ——ind-ob *ni*, obj *o* (v) *kake'·ru* 賭ける place a bet of a thousand yen on a favorite horse *ninki' uma ni se'n-en o kake'ru* 人気馬に千円を賭ける

betray obj *o* (v) *uragi'·ru* 裏切る betray someone *hito o uragi'ru* 人を裏切る ——(pass) *uragirare'·ru* 裏切られる She betrayed me. *Watashi wa ka'nojo ni uragira'reta.* 私は彼女に裏切られた.

better (adj) *mo'tto i'·i* もっといい That's much better. *Sore wa mo'tto i'i.* それはもっといい. ——(idiom) ... *yori* ... [*no*] *hō'* より ... [*no*]方 A is better than B. *B yori A no hō' ga i'i.* BよりAの方がいい. It's better to go by plane. *Hikō'ki de itta hō' ga i'i.* 飛行機で行った方がいい.

between [... *no*] *aida* [*ni*] [...の]間[に] between two people *futari' no aida* 二人の間 That store is between the bank and the post office. *Ano mise' wa ginkō to yūbi'nkyoku no aida ni a'ru.* あの店は銀行と郵便局の間にある.

beverage *nomi'mono* 飲み物

beware ind-obj *ni* (irr) *yōjin-suru* 用心する ——(idiom) *ki o tsuke'·ru* 気をつける Beware of the dog! *Inu'ni ki o tsuke'te kudasa'i.* 犬に気をつけて下さい.

beyond *mukō'* 向こう Beyond the Alps lies Italy. *A'rupusu no mukō ga Itaria de'su.* アルプスの向こうがイタリアです. ——(attr) ... *o koeta* ... を越えた The village lies beyond the hills. *Sono mura' wa yama' o koeta tokoro ni a'ru.* その村は山を越えたところにある.

biased view *henken* 偏見

bias tape *baiasu tē'pu* バイアステープ

bib *yodare'kake* よだれ掛け

Bible *Se'isho* 聖書 Old Testament *Kyūyaku Se'isho* 旧約聖書 New Testament *Shin'yaku Se'isho* 新約聖書

bicarbonate of soda *jūsō* 重曹

bicycle *jite'nsha* 自転車

bid **1** (in bridge) *seri'ne* せり値 **2** (at an auction) *nyūsatsu* 入札 ——(v) **1** (bridge) [*serifuda o*] *senge'n-suru* [せり札を]宣言する; **2** (auction) *nyūsatsu-suru* 入札する

bifocal lenses *nishōten re'nzu* 二焦点レンズ

big *ō'ki na* 大きな ——(adj) *ōki'·i* 大きい a big town *ōki'i machi'* 大きい町 Our house in France was big. *Fura'nsu no wata'shi-tachi no ie' wa ō'kikatta.* フランスの私たちの家は大きかった. ——(v) be too big *ōki-sugi'·ru* 大きすぎる This (suit) coat is too big. *Kono uwagi wa ōki-sugi'ru.* この上着は大きすぎる.

bigamy *jūkon* 重婚

Big Dipper *Ōkuma-za* 大熊座

bigotry *henken* 偏見

bike *see* bicycle; motorbike

bilingual *bairi'ngaru* バイリンガル; *iko'kugo* [*no*] 二国語[の]; *nige'ngo heiyō* [*no*] 二言語併用[の]

bill 1 debit note *seikyūsho* 請求書 Send me the bill. *Seikyūsho o okutte kudasa'i.* 請求書を送って下さい. 2 tab *kanjō'* 勘定 How much is my bill? *Kanjō' wa i'kura desu ka?* 勘定はいくらですか. 3 paper money *-satsu* 札 ¥1,000 bill *sen-e'n-satsu* 千円札 ¥10,000 bill *ichiman-e'n-satsu* 一万円札 4 (Leg) *hōan* 法案 5 bird's beak *kuchibashi* くちばし

billboard *kamban* 看板

bill collector *shūkin-nin* 集金人

billfold *saifu* 財布; *satsu-ire* 札入れ

billiards *biriya'do* ビリヤード

billion *jū'oku* 十億

bind obj *o* (v) 1 *shiba'r·u* 縛る 2 bind books (irr) *seihon-suru* 製本する *see also* tie

binge *donchan sa'wagi* どんちゃん騒ぎ

binoculars *sōgankyō* 双眼鏡

biography *denki* 伝記

biology (science) *seibutsu'gaku* 生物学

bird *tori* 鳥 small bird *kotori* 小鳥

bird watching *bādo-uo'tchingu* バードウォッチング

birth *umare* 生まれ Where is your place of birth? *Umare wa do'ko desu ka?* 生まれはどこですか. *see also* childbirth

birth certificate *shusshō shōmeisho* 出生証明書

birth control *sanji se'igen* 産児制限; (contraception) *hinin* 避妊 birth control pill *keikō hini'n-yaku* 経口避妊薬

birthday *tanjō'bi* 誕生日 When is your birthday? *O-tanjō'bi wa i'tsu desu ka?* お誕生日はいつですか.

birthmark *aza'* あざ

biscuit (sweet) *bisuke'tto* ビスケット

bisexual *ryōsei* [*no*] 両性[の]

bisexuality *ryōse'iai* 両性愛

bishop 1 (Church of England) *kantoku* 監督 2 (Cath) *sō'jō* 僧正

bit 1 a little amount *suko'shi* 少し 2 a little while *cho'tto* ちょっと 3 (bridle) *kutsuwa* くつわ

bite 1 one mouthful *hito'kuchi* 一口 2 a snack *oya'tsu* おやつ ——obj *o* (v) 1 bite; chew *ka'm·u* かむ Bite down on this! *Kore o ka'nde kudasa'i.* これをかんで下さい. 2 grab onto with the teeth *kamitsuk·u* かみつく Be careful, the dog bites! *Inu'ga kamitsuku' kara, ki o tsuke'te kudasa'i!* 犬がかみつくから気をつけて下さい.

——(pass) be bitten *kamare′·ru* かまれる The child was bitten by
a dog. *Kodomo ga inu′ ni kama′reta* 子供が犬にかまれた. **3** bite
into *kaji′r·u* かじる take a bite out of an apple *ringo o hito′kuchi
kaji′ru* リンゴを一口かじる

bitter (adj) **1** (taste) *niga′·i* 苦い bitter medicine *niga′i kusuri* 苦い
薬 **2** (experience) *kurushi′·i* 苦しい bitter experience *kurushi′i
keiken* 苦しい経験

bizarre *he′n* [*na*] 変[な] That's bizarre! (masc) *He′n da nā!* 変だな
あ. (fem) *He′n ne!* 変ね.; *fūga′wari* [*na*] 風変わり[な]

black *kuro* 黒 ——(adj) *kuro′·i* 黒い black shoes *kuro′i kutsu′* 黒
い靴

black belt *kuro-o′bi* 黒帯

blackboard *kokuban* 黒板

blackhead (blemish) *kuro-ni′kibi* 黒にきび

blackmail obj *o* (v) *yusur·u* ゆする

blacksmith *kajiya* かじ屋

bladder *bōkō* 膀胱

blade (for cutting) *ha′* 刃 razor blade *kamisori no ha′* かみそりの
刃 double-edged blade *ryō-ba* 両刃

blame **1** responsibility for *sekinin* 責任 take the blame *sekinin o
to′ru* 責任をとる **2** fault *se′i* せい I was to blame. *Watashi no se′i
deshita.* 私のせいでした. ——obj *o* (v) *seme′·ru* 責める Blame
yourself, not others. *Jibun o se′mete, hito o seme′ru na.* 自分を責
めて人を責めるな.

blank *yohaku* 余白 Leave a blank space. *Yohaku o noko′shite oite
kudasa′i.* 余白を残しておいて下さい.

blanket *mō′fu* 毛布 electric blanket *denki mō′fu* 電気毛布

blazer *bure′zā* ブレザー

bleach *buri′chi* ブリーチ; *hyōha′ku-zai* 漂白剤

bleed (irr) *shukketsu-suru* 出血する ——(idiom) *chi ga de′·ru* 血
が出る I cut my hand and it's bleeding. *Te′ o kitte chi ga de′te
iru.* 手を切って血が出ている.

blind *mōmoku* [*no*] 盲目[の] blind person *mōjin* 盲人 color blind
shikimō 色盲 ——(idiom) That person is blind. *Ano′ hito wa
me′ga mie′nai.* あの人は目が見えない.

blink (irr) *maba′taki-suru* まばたきする

blister (on skin) *mizubu′kure* 水ぶくれ; *mame′* まめ

block **1** *buro′kku* ブロック **2** (toy) *tsumiki* 積木 **3** (city block)
kukaku 区画 one city block *ikku′kaku* 一区画 two city blocks
niku′kaku 二区画 **4** (pulley) *ka′ssha* 滑車 ——obj *o* (v) *samata-
ge′·ru* 妨げる

blockade *fūsa* 封鎖 ——obj *o* (irr) *fūsa-suru* 封鎖する

blockhead *dekuno′bō* でくのぼう

blond (hair) *kimpatsu* 金髪

blood   *chi* 血; (Tech) *ketsu'eki* 血液

blood pressure   *ketsuatsu* 血圧

bloodshot eyes   *jūketsu-shita me'* 充血した目

blood type   *ketsueki-gata* 血液型 blood type A *A-gata* A型

blood vessel   *kekkan* 血管

bloom   *hana'* 花; *hanaza'kari* 花ざかり   ——(v)*sak·u* 咲く This flower blooms in spring. *Kono hana' wa ha'ru ni saku.* この花は春に咲く.

blossom   *see* bloom

blot   stain *shimi* 染み   ——obj *o* (v) *suito'r·u* 吸い取る

blotter   *suitori'gami* 吸取紙

blouse   *bura'usu* ブラウス

blow   obj *o* (v) 1 *fu'k·u* 吹く   2 blow out *fukike's·u* 吹き消す blow out a candle *rōsoku o fukike'su* ろうそくを吹き消す   3 blow up *fukurama's·u* ふくらます blow up a balloon *fūsen o fukurama'su* 風船をふくらます   ——(v) *fu'k·u* 吹く A cool breeze is blowing. *Suzushi'i kaze ga fu'ite iru.* 涼しい風が吹いている.   ——(idiom) blow one's nose *hana o kam·u* 鼻をかむ

blowfish   *fu'gu* 河豚

blue   *a'o* 青 blue sky *aozo'ra* 青空; *burū'* ブルー Blue is becoming to you. *Ana'ta ni wa burū' ga nia'u.* あなたにはブルーが似合う.   ——(adj) *ao'·i* 青い The sky is blue. *So'ra ga ao'i desu.* 空が青いです.

blueprint   *aoja'shin* 青写真

blunt   (dull)   (adj) *nibu'·i* 鈍い   ——(attr) *kire'nai* 切れない a blunt knife *kire'nai na'ifu* 切れないナイフ

blush   (idiom) [*kao ga*] *akaku na'r·u* [顔が]赤くなる He blushed when he heard that. *Ka're wa sore o kiite, kao ga akaku na'tta.* 彼はそれを聞いて顔が赤くなった.

boar   *ino'shishi* 猪

board   (of wood)   *i'ta* 板 cutting board *mana'ita* まな板   ——(v) board a vehicle [*ni*] *nor·u* [に]乗る

boardinghouse   *geshuku* 下宿

boast   *jiman* 自慢   ——obj *o* (v) *hoko'r·u* 誇る   ——(idiom) *jiman o suru* 自慢をする She boasts about her son. *Ka'nojo wa musuko no jiman o suru.* 彼女は息子の自慢をする.

boat   *fu'ne* 船; rowboat *bō'to* ボート

bob   (bobbed hair)   *dampatsu* 断髪

bobby pin   *hea'pin* ヘアピン

Bodhisattva   *bo'satsu* 菩薩

body   1 (Anat) *karada* 体   2 car body *shatai* 車体; *bodi* ボディー

bodybuilding   *bodi-bi'ru* ボディービル

body language   *bodi-ra'ngeji* ボディランゲージ

boil (on skin) *o-de'ki* おでき; *dekimono* できもの

boil (cook) obj *o* (v) **1** (in a seasoned liquid) *ni·ru* 煮る boil vegetables *yasai o niru* 野菜を煮る **2** (in water) *yude'·ru* ゆでる boil potatoes *jagaimo o yude'·ru* じゃがいもをゆでる **3** (water) *wakas·u* 沸かす boil water *oyu o wakasu* お湯を沸かす

boiler *bo'irā* ボイラー

boisterous (noisy) (adj) *yakamashi'·i* やかましい ——(v) be boisterous *sawa'g·u* 騒ぐ ——(idiom) **1** boisterous boy *sōzōshi'i otoko'no ko* 騒々しい男の子 **2** boisterous girl *otemba na onna' no ko* おてんばな女の子

bold (fearless) *daita'n [na]* 大胆[な]

Bolivia *Boribia* ボリビア

Bolivian (person) *Boribia' jin* ボリビア人 ——(attr) *Boribia no* ボリビアの

bolt *oneji* 雄ねじ nuts and bolts *oneji to meneji* 雄ねじと雌ねじ; *boruto* ボルト

bomb *bakudan* 爆弾

bond (security) *shōken* 証券

bone *hone'* 骨 ——(idiom) to bone meat *niku no hone' o hazus·u* 肉の骨を外す

bonito *katsuo* 鰹

bonus *bō'nasu* ボーナス

book *ho'n* 本

bookcase *ho'mbako* 本箱

bookends *ho'ntate* 本立て

bookkeeper *chōbo-ga'kari* 帳簿係

bookkeeping *bo'ki* 簿記

bookmark *shiori* しおり

bookshelf *ho'ndana* 本棚

bookstore *ho'n'ya* 本屋

boom (economic) *keiki* 景気

boots **1** naga-gutsu 長靴 **2** rubber boots *gomu-gutsu* ゴム靴 **3** (fashion) *bū'tsu* ブーツ

border (boundary) *kyōkai* 境界 border with China *Chū'goku to no kyōkai* 中国との境界; *kyōka'i-sen* 境界線 draw a border line *kyōka'i-sen o hiku* 境界線を引く; *saka'i* 境 extend the border *saka'i o hirogeru* 境を拡げる the border between philosophy and religion *tetsu'gaku to shū'kyō to no saka'i* 哲学と宗教との境; national border *kokkyō* 国境

bore (a hole) (idiom) *ana' o ake·ru* 穴を開ける

bored be/become bored (irr) *taikutsu-suru* 退屈する The children seem to be bored. *Kodomo-tachi wa taikutsu-shite iru yō' desu.* 子供たちは退屈しているようです; (v) *aki·ru* 飽きる I'm bored. *A'kita.* 飽きた.

boredom *taikutsu* 退屈

boring (adj) *tsumara'na·i* つまらない The party was boring. *Pāti wa tsumarana'katta.* パーティーはつまらなかった.

born (v) *umare·ru* 生まれる Where were you born? *Do'ko de umarema'shita ka?* どこで生まれましたか.

borrow ind-obj *ni*, obj *o* (v) *kari·ru* 借りる May I borrow this? *Kore o karite' mo i'i desu ka?* これを借りてもいいですか.

boss 1 *shu'jin* 主人; (store) *tenchō* 店長 2 company head *shachō* 社長 3 division chief *buchō* 部長

botanical garden *shokubutsu'en* 植物園

botany *shokubutsu'gaku* 植物学

both *do'chira mo* どちらも; *do'tchi mo* どっちも Both are expensive. *Do'tchi mo taka'i.* どっちも高い. ... *tomo* ... とも both persons *futari tomo* 二人とも Both are my friends. *Futari tomo watashi no tomodachi de'su.* 二人とも私の友達です.; *ryōhō* 両方 I need both. *Ryōhō i'ru.* 両方いる.

bother obj *o* (v) *kama'u* かまう Don't bother. *Kamawa'naide kudasa'i.* かまわないで下さい. She doesn't bother about her appearance. *Ka'nojo wa minari o kamawa'nai.* 彼女は身形をかまわない. ——(idiom) a bother *tesū ga kaka'r·u* [koto] 手数がかかる [事] The children were no bother. *Kodomo'-tachi wa tesū ga kakara'nakatta.* 子供たちは手数がかからなかった. ——(idiom) I'm sorry to have bothered you. *O-jama shima'shita.* お邪魔しました.

bothersome *mendō' [na]* 面倒[な] It's bothersome, I'm sure, but would you please write this in Japanese? *Go-mendō' deshō ga, sore o Nihongo de ka'ite itadakemase'n ka?* ご面倒でしょうが、それを日本語で書いていただけませんか.; *ya'kkai [na]* やっかい[な] It's become really bothersome. *Taihen ya'kkai na koto' ni na'tta.* 大変やっかいなことになった.

bottle *bi'n* びん empty bottle *kara bin* 空びん baby bottle *honyū' bin* 哺乳瓶

bottle opener *sennu'ki* 栓抜き

bottom 1 *soko* 底 The water's so clear one can see the bottom. *Mizu ga su'nde ite, soko ga mie'ru.* 水が澄んでいて底が見える. 2 lower part *shita no hō'* 下の方; (Tech) *ka'bu* 下部

bouillon *bu'iyon* ブイヨン

boundary *see* border

bound for *-iki/-yuki* 行き Take the train bound for Tachikawa. *Tachikawa-yuki no densha ni notte kudasa'i.* 立川行きの電車に乗って下さい.

bouquet *hanataba* 花束

bourbon *bā'bon* バーボン

bow 1 knot *musubime* 結び目 2 (archery) *yumi'* 弓 bow and arrow *yumi'ya* 弓矢 3 (violin) *baiorin no yumi'* バイオリンの弓

bow   *o-jigi* お辞儀 ——(idiom) to bow *o-jigi o suru* お辞儀をする

bowl   **1** (for eating) *chawan* 茶わん   **2** sugar bowl *satō'-ire* 砂糖入れ   **3** serving bowl *fuka'-zara* 深皿   **4** large (eating) bowl *domburi* どんぶり

bowling alley   *bōringu-jō* ボーリング場

box (container)   *hako* 箱 cardboard box *dambōru'-bako* ダンボール箱

boxing (sport)   *bo'kushingu* ボクシング

box lunch   *bentō'* 弁当 box lunch sold at a railroad station *ekiben* 駅弁

box office   *kippu u'riba* 切符売り場

boy   **1** *otoko' no ko* 男の子   **2** (polite address) *bo'tchan* 坊ちゃん

boycott   *boiko'tto* ボイコット

boyfriend   *bōifure'ndo* ボーイフレンド

boy scout   *bōisuka'uto* ボーイスカウト

bracelet   *udewa* 腕輪; *bure'suretto* ブレスレット

brag   obj *o* (v) *jiman-suru* 自慢する

braid   *osa'ge* おさげ ——obj *o* (v) *amiko'm·u* 編み込む

brain   *nō* 脳 brain concussion *nō shintō* 脳震盪; (coll) *nōmi'so* 脳みそ He has no brains. *Ka're wa nōmi'so ga tarinai.* 彼は脳みそが足りない.

brake   *burē'ki* ブレーキ apply the brakes *burē'ki o kake'·ru* ブレーキをかける

branch (Bot)   *eda* 枝

branch office   *shutchōjo* 出張所

branch store   *shiten* 支店

brand name   *burando* ブランド; *shōhyō* 商標

brandy   *bura'ndē* ブランデー

brass   *shinchū* しんちゅう

brassiere   *bura'jā* ブラジャー

brat   *kozō'* 小僧; *gaki'* 餓鬼

brave   *yūkan* [na] 勇敢[な] a brave person *yūkan na hito'* 勇敢な人 ——(adj) *isamashi'·i* 勇ましい a brave man *isamashi'i otoko'* 勇ましい男

bravely   *isama'shiku* 勇ましく The opposition fought bravely. *Aite' wa isama'shiku tatakatta.* 相手は勇ましく戦った.

Brazil   *Burajiru* ブラジル

Brazilian (person)   *Burajiru'jin* ブラジル人 ——(attr) *Burajiru no* ブラジルの

bread   *pa'n* パン

breadcrumbs   *panko* パン粉

break (v)   **1** *koware'·ru* 壊れる It broke. *Sore wa kowa'rete shimatta.* それは壊れてしまった.   **2** fracture *ore'·ru* 折れる The bone broke. *Hone'ga o'reta.* 骨が折れた.   **3** shatter *ware·ru* 割れる

The dish broke. *O-sara ga wareta.* お皿が割れた. ——obj *o* (v) *kowa's·u* 壊す I broke it. *Watashi wa sore o kowa'shite shimatta.* 私はそれを壊してしまった. **2** *o'r·u* 折る break off a limb of a tree *ki' no eda o o'ru* 木の枝を折る **3** discontinue *uchiki'r·u* 打ち切る break off relations *kankei o uchiki'ru* 関係を打ち切る

breakables *waremono* 割れ物

breakdown *koshō* 故障; (Med) *suijaku* 衰弱 nervous breakdown *shinkei su'ijaku* 神経衰弱

break down (irr) *koshō-suru* 故障する The machine broke down. *Kika'i ga koshō-shita.* 機械が故障した.

breakfast *asago'han* 朝御飯; *chōshoku* 朝食

break through obj *o* (irr) *to'ppa-suru* 突破する break through the front line *zensen o to'ppa-suru* 前線を突破する

break up obj *o* (irr) *kaisan-suru* 解散する

breakup *kaisan* 解散

breast **1** *mune'* 胸 **2** a woman's breast *chi'busa* 乳房

breast-feeding *bonyū* 母乳

breath *i'ki* 息 hold one's breath *i'ki o korosu* 息を殺す

breathe (idiom) *i'ki o suru* 息をする

breathing exercise *kokyū u'ndō* 呼吸運動

breeze *soyo'kaze* そよ風

bribe *wa'iro* 賄賂; *baishū* 買収 ——ind-obj *ni*, obj *o* (irr) *baishū-suru* 買収する

brick *re'nga* れんが brick wall *renga-zu'kuri no hei* れんが造りの塀

bride *yome* 嫁; *hana'-yome* 花嫁

bridge **1** *hashi'* 橋 **2** (card game) *buri'dji* ブリッジ **3** (for the teeth) *buri'dji* ブリッジ

brief (span of time) (attr) *tanjikan no* 短時間の

briefcase *shorui ka'ban* 書類かばん

briefly **1** in a short time *tanjikan ni* 短時間に **2** in a cursory manner *hitoto'ri* ひととおり I looked it over briefly. *Hitotōri sore ni me' o tō'shita.* ひととおりそれに目を通した.

briefs *buri'fu* ブリーフ

bright *hana'yaka [na]* 華やか[な] a bright color *hana'yaka na iro'* 華やかな色 ——(adj) **1** *akaru'·i* 明るい This is a nice, bright room. *Kono heya' wa akaru'kute i'i desu.* この部屋は明るくていいです. **2** glaring *mabushi'·i* まぶしい The sunlight's too bright here. *Koko de'wa hizashi ga mabushi'i.* ここでは日ざしがまぶしい. **3** intelligent *kashiko'·i* 賢い He's very bright. *Ka're wa totemo kashiko'i.* 彼はとても賢い. ——(idiom) intelligent *atama' ga i'i* 頭がいい She's bright. *Ka'nojo wa atama' ga i'i.* 彼女は頭がいい.

bring obj *o* (irr) *mo'tte kuru* 持って来る Did you bring your lunch? *O-bentō o mo′tte kima′shita ka?* お弁当を持って来ましたか.

bring together   obj *o* (v) *awase′·ru* 合わせる

Britain   *Igirisu* イギリス *see also* England

British   (attr) *Igirisu no* イギリスの *see also* English

Britisher   *Igirisu′jin* イギリス人

broadcast   *hōsō* 放送 ——ind-obj *ni*, obj *o* (irr) *hōsō-suru* 放送する broadcast a program to the entire world *bangumi o ze′nsekai ni hōsō-suru* 番組を全世界に放送する

broadcasting station   *hōsō′kyoku* 放送局

broad-minded   *kandai* [na] 寛大[な] a broad-minded person *kandai na hito′* 寛大な人

brocade   *ni′shiki* 錦

broccoli   *buro′kkorī* ブロッコリー

broil   obj *o* (v) *yak·u* 焼く

broken   (v) *kowa′rete i·ru* 壊れている

bronchitis   *kikanshi′en* 気管支炎

bronze   *seidō* 青銅

brooch   *buro′chi* ブローチ

broom   *hōki* ほうき

brothel   *baishun ya′do* 売春宿

brother   1 *kyō′dai* 兄弟   2 (one's own, younger) *otōto′* 弟   3 (one's own, older) *a′ni* 兄   4 (another's, younger) *otōto-san* お弟さん   5 (another's older) *o-nī′-san* お兄さん

brother-in-law   1 (one's own, younger) *giri no otōto′* 義理の弟; *gitei* 義弟   2 (one's own, older) *giri no a′ni* 義理の兄; *gikei* 義兄   3 (another's, younger) *giri no otōto-san* 義理の弟さん   4 (another's, older) *giri no o-nī′-san* 義理のお兄さん

brow   *hitai* 額

brown   *chairo* 茶色 brown shoes *chairo no kutsu′* 茶色の靴

brown bread   *hōru hoito no pan* ホールホイートのパン; *kuro-pan* 黒パン

brown rice   *ge′mmai* 玄米

brown sugar   1 (refined) *aka-za′tō* 赤砂糖   2 (unrefined) *kuro-za′tō* 黒砂糖

bruise   *aza′* あざ ——obj *o* (v) *kizutsuke′·ru* 傷つける

brush   1 *bu′rashi* ブラシ   2 paintbrush *hake* はけ   3 writing/painting brush *fude* 筆   4 toothbrush *ha-bu′rashi* 歯ブラシ   5 hairbrush *hea-bu′rashi* ヘアブラシ ——obj *o* (v) 1 (teeth) *migak·u* みがく   2 (clothes) [*bu′rashi o*] *kake·ru* [ブラシを]かける   3 (hair) (irr) *bura′sshingu-suru* ブラッシングする

Brussels sprouts   *mekya′betsu* 芽キャベツ

brutal   *zangyaku* [na] 残虐[な]

B.S. (academic degree)   *see* Bachelor of Science

bubble   1 *shabon-dama* シャボン玉   2 foam *awa′* 泡

bucket   *baketsu* バケツ

buckwheat   *so'ba* そば

bud   *tsubomi'* つぼみ ——(idiom) to bud *hana no me' ga de'·ru* 花の芽が出る

Buddha   **1** (the historical Buddha) Sakyamuni *Sha'kuson* 釈尊; (coll) *O-Shaka-sama* お釈迦様   **2** buddha(s) *hotoke* 仏

Buddhism   *Bu'kkyō* 仏教

Buddhist (follower of Buddhism) *Bukkyō'-to* 仏教徒

Buddhist priest   *bō'zu* 坊主; (coll) *o-bō-san* お坊さん; (Tech) *sō'ryo* 僧侶

budget   *yosan* 予算

buffet (smorgasbord) *ba'ikingu* バイキング; (R.R.) *byu'ffe kā* ビュッフェカー

bug   *mu'shi* 虫

build   *obj o* (v) *tate'·ru* 建てる

building   **1** *tate'mono* 建物   **2** ferroconcrete building *bi'ru* ビル

bulb   **1** electric light bulb *denkyū* 電球   **2** plant bulb *kyūkon* 球根

Bulgaria   *Burugaria* ブルガリア

Bulgarian (person) *Burugaria' jin* ブルガリア人 ——(attr) *Burugaria no* ブルガリアの

bullet   *tama'* 弾; *dangan* 弾丸

bulletin board   *keijiban* 掲示板

bully (youth) *ijime'kko* いじめっ子; (adult) *ijime'ya* いじめ屋 ——*obj o* (v) *ijime'·ru* いじめる

bump   **1** (on the head) *kobu'* こぶ   **2** (in the road) *dekoboko* でこぼこ ——(v) **1** *butsukar·u* ぶつかる The ball bumped against the wall. *Bōru wa hei ni butsukatta.* ボールは塀にぶつかった.   **2** bump into (meet by chance) *meguria·u* 巡り合う ——ind-obj *ni, o* (v) *butsuke'·ru* ぶつける I bumped my head on the door. *Do'a ni atama'o butsuketa.* ドアに頭をぶつけた.

bundle   *ta'ba* 束

bunion   *mame'* まめ

burden   **1** *omoni* 重荷 bear a heavy burden *omoni o ou* 重荷を負う   **2** charge *futan* 負担 a student's financial burden *gakusei no gakuhi fu'tan* 学生の学資負担

bureau (department) *kyo'ku* 局 bureau director *kyokuchō* 局長

bureaucracy   *kanryōsei* 官僚制

bureaucrat   *kanryō* 官僚

bureaucratic   *kanryōteki* [na] 官僚的[な]

burglar   *dorobō* どろぼう

burglary   *oshikomi gō'tō* 押し込み強盗; (Leg) *yatō'zai* 夜盗罪

burial   *maisō* 埋葬 *see also* funeral service

burlesque (show) *sutori'ppu* ストリップ

Burma   *Bi'ruma* ビルマ

Burmese 1 (language) *Biruma-go* ビルマ語 **2** (person) *Biruma′ jin*
ビルマ人 ——(attr) *Bi′ruma no* ビルマの *see also* Myanmar
burn *yakedo* やけど ——(v) **1** receive a burn (irr) *yakedo-suru* や
けどする I burned myself. *Yakedo-shita.* やけどした. **2** *yake·ru*
焼ける The house burned down. *Ie′ ga yakete shima′tta.* 家が焼け
てしまった.; *moe·ru* 燃える The fire's burning well. *Hi′wa yo′ku
moete iru.* 火はよく燃えている. ——obj *o* (v) *mo·su* 燃す; *moyas·u*
燃やす I burned the leaves from the garden yesterday. *Kinō niwa
no ochiba o moya′shita.* きのう庭の落葉を燃やした.
burp *ge′ppu* げっぷ *see also* belch
burst (v) **1** (irr) *haretsu-suru* 破裂する The water main burst. *Sui-
dōkan ga haretsu-shita.* 水道管が破裂した. **2** explode (irr) *bakuhatsu-suru* 爆発する **3** rip; break (v) *ware·ru* 割れる The balloon
burst. *Fūsen ga wareta.* 風船が割れた.; *yabure′·ru* 破れる The bag
burst. *Fukuro′ ga yabu′reta.* 袋が破れた. ——obj *o* (v) *yabu′r·u*
破る burst a paper bag *kamibu′kuro o yabu′ru* 紙袋を破る ——
(idiom) **1** burst into flame *pa′tto moeaga′·ru* ぱっと燃え上がる
2 burst out laughing *dotto waraida′su* どっと笑い出す
bury obj *o* (v) **1** *ume·ru* 埋める **2** inter *hōmu′r·u* 葬る
bus *ba′su* バス
bush *ki′* 木 rosebush *bara no ki′* バラの木; (Tech) *kamboku* 灌木
see also plant
business 1 *eigyō* 営業 **2** clerical business *ji′mu* 事務 **3** commerce
shō′gyō 商業 **4** one's employment *shoku′gyō* 職業 **5** enterprise
jitsugyō 実業 **6** job *shigoto* 仕事 **7** trade *shō′bai* 商売 **8** an errand *yō′* 用; *yōji* 用事 ——(idiom) It's none of my business.
Watashi ni wa [nani mo] kankei na′i. 私には[何も]関係ない.
business card *meishi* 名刺
business deal *shō′bai no tori′hiki* 商売の取り引き
businessman 1 *shokugyō′ jin* 職業人 **2** entrepreneur *jitsugyō′ka* 実
業家 **3** salaried employee *sarari′man* サラリーマン **4** dealer;
trader *gyō′sha* 業者
business office 1 *jimusho* 事務所 **2** general affairs section *sōmu-ka*
総務課
business trip *shutchō* 出張 She's on a business trip. *Ka′nojo wa
shutchō-shite iru.* 彼女は出張している.
bus stop *teiryū jo* 停留所; (coll) *basu-tei* バス停
bustling *nigi′yaka* [na] にぎやか[な] Shinjuku is a bustling town.
Shinjuku wa nigi′yaka na machi′ desu. 新宿はにぎやかな街です.
busy (adj) *isogashi′·i* 忙しい Are you busy now? *I′ma isogashi′i
desu ka?* 今忙しいですか?
but 1 *ga* が I tried, but it was no use. *Yatte mima′shita ga, dame′
deshita.* やってみましたが, だめでした; *ke′redomo* けれども I'm
tired, but I'm going to the office. *Tsuka′rete iru ke′redomo, kaisha*

ni iku. 疲れているけれども、会社に行く.; *de'mo* でも I may not be able to do it, but I intend to do my best. *Deki'nai ka mo shire-mase'n. De'mo sei-i'ppai yatte mi'ru tsumori desu.* できないかも知れません. でも精いっぱいやってみるつもりです. **2** except [...*no*] *hoka* [*ni*] [...の]ほか[に] No one went but me. *Watashi no hoka ni wa dare mo' ika'nakatta.* 私のほかにはだれも行かなかった. **3** however *shika'shi* しかし Hiragana and katakana syllabaries have no meaning, but Chinese ideograms do. *Hiragana to katakana ni wa i'mi ga arimase'n. Shika'shi kanji ni wa i'mi ga arima'su.* ひらがなとかたかなには意味がありません. しかし漢字には意味があります.

butcher *niku'ya[-san]* 肉屋[-さん]

butcher shop *niku'ya* 肉屋

butt (cigarette) *suigara* 吸いがら

butter *ba'tā* バター

butterfly *chō'* 蝶; *chō'chō* 蝶蝶

butterfly stroke *ba'tafurai* バタフライ

buttocks *o-shiri* おしり fall on one's buttocks [*doshi'n to*] *shirimo'-chi o tsuku* [どしんと]しりもちをつく

button *bo'tan* ボタン button a button *bo'tan o tomeru* ボタンを留める

buy ind-obj *ni*, obj *o* (v) *ka·u* 買う Where did you buy that? *Do'ko de sore o kaima'shita ka?* どこでそれを買いましたか.

by **1** (near; beside) *so'ba* [*no/ni*] そば[の/に] Sit by me. *Watashi no so'ba ni suwatte kudasa'i.* 私のそばに坐って下さい. **2** (by means of) ...*de* ...で She went by plane. *Ka'nojo wa hikō'ki de itta.* 彼女は飛行機で行った.

by all means *ze'hi* 是非 Please come, by all means. *Ze'hi ki'te kudasa'i.* 是非来て下さい.

by no means *kesshite* (+neg) 決して By no means will I go. *Kesshite ikana'i.* 決して行かない.

by the way (incidentally) *tokoro' de* ... ところで...

C

cabaret *kya'barē* キャバレー

cabbage *kya'betsu* キャベツ

cabin *koya* 小屋 *see also* cottage

cabinet **1** cupboard *shokki'-dana* 食器棚 **2** file cabinet *fa'iringu kya'binetto* ファイリング・キャビネット **3** government *na'ikaku* 内閣

cabinet minister *da'ijin* 大臣

cable (wire rope) *kē'buru* ケーブル

cable (message) *dempō* 電報 send an international cable *kokusai de'mpō o u'tsu* 国際電報を打つ

cactus *saboten* サボテン

Caesarean section *teiō se'kkai* 帝王切開

cafe *keisho'kudō* 軽食堂; *kissa'ten* 喫茶店

cage 1 (large) *ori'* おり 2 (lightweight, for birds, insects, etc.) *kago* かご

cake *kē'ki* ケーキ

calamity *saigai* 災害

calcium *karushū'mu* カルシウム

calculate (compute) obj *o* (irr) *keisan-suru* 計算する

calculation *keisan* 計算

calculator *keisa'nki* 計算機; *dentaku*

calculus 1 *bibun-sekibu'ngaku* 微分積分学 2 differential calculus *bibu'ngaku* 微分学 3 integral calculus *sekibu'ngaku* 積分学

calendar *kare'ndā* カレンダー

calf 1 young cow *ko-ushi* 子牛 2 back part of lower leg *fukura'-hagi* ふくらはぎ

call obj *o* (v) *yob·u* 呼ぶ Someone's calling you! *Da'reka ga ana'ta o yonde iru.* だれかがあなたを呼んでいる. ——(irr) telephone *denwa-suru* 電話する I called the office. *Kaisha ni denwa-shita.* 会社に電話した.

calligraphy 1 (J) *shū'ji* 習字; *sho'dō* 書道 2 (English) *ei-shū'ji* 英習字

callus *ta'ko* たこ

calm *oda'yaka [na]* 穏やか[な] a calm sea *oda'yaka na u'mi* 穏やかな海 ——(attr) *ochitsuita* 落ち着いた a calm person *ochitsuita hito'* 落ち着いた人 ——(v) become calm *ochitsuk·u* 落ち着く Be calm! *Ochitsuki-nasa'i!* 落ち着きなさい. ——obj *o* (v) *shizume·ru* 静める

calorie *ka'rori* カロリー

cam *ka'mu* カム

Cambodia *Kambojia* カンボジア *see also* Kampuchea

Cambodian 1 (language) *Kambojia-go* カンボジア語 2 (person) *Kambojia'jin* カンボジア人 ——(attr) *Kambojia no* カンボジアの

camel *rakuda* らくだ

camellia *tsu'baki* 椿

cameo *ka'meo* カメオ

camera *ka'mera* カメラ

cameraman *kamera'man* カメラマン

camouflage *gisō* 擬装; *kamufurā'ju* カムフラージュ; *gomakashi* ごまかし

camp *kya'mpu* キャンプ ——(irr) *kya'mpu-suru* キャンプする

campaign **1** *undō* 運動 political campaign *seiji u'ndō* 政治運動 **2** (military) *gunji kō'dō* 軍事行動

camper (car) *kyampingu'-kā* キャンピングカー

camphor **1** *shō'nō* 樟脳 **2** camphor injection *kamfuru chū'sha* カンフル注射 **3** (tree) *kusu'noki* 楠

campus *kya'mpasu* キャンパス; university campus *daigaku kō'nai* 大学構内

can **1** (container) *ka'n* 缶 empty can *aki-kan* 空き缶 **2** canned goods *kanzume'* 缶詰

can (be able to) obj *ga* (v) *deki'·ru* できる Can you do it? *Dekima'su ka?* できますか. see also potential verb forms in tables 1–3 pp. xxi–xxxv.

Canada *Ka'nada* カナダ

Canadian (person) *Kanada'jin* カナダ人 ——(attr) *Ka'nada no* カナダの

canal *u'nga* 運河

canary *kanaria* カナリア

cancel obj *o* (v) **1** cross out *kes·u* 消す **2** revoke *torikes·u* 取り消す cancel an order *chūmon o torikesu* 注文を取り消す **3** do away with *nakus·u* なくす They canceled that regulation. *Sono kiso'ku o nakushita.* その規則をなくした.

cancer *ga'n* 癌

Cancer *Kani-za* 蟹座

candidacy *rikkō'ho* 立候補; declare candidacy *kō'ho ni ta'tsu* 候補に立つ

candidate *kōho'sha* 候補者

candle *rōsoku* ろうそく

candlestick *rōsoku'-tate* ろうそくたて

candy **1** *kya'ndi* キャンディー **2** sweets *o-ka'shi* お菓子 **3** hard candy *ame* 飴 **4** chocolate candy *chokorē'to* チョコレート

candy store *kashi'ya* 菓子屋

cane (staff) *tsu'e* 杖; *sute'kki* ステッキ

canker (sore) *kaiyō* 潰瘍

canned (food) *kanzume'* [no] 缶詰[の]

cannibal **1** *tomogui* 共食い、 **2** (of humans) *hitokui jinshu* 人食い人種

cannon *taihō* 大砲

canoe *ka'nū* カヌー

can opener *kanki'ri* 缶切り

cantalope see muskmelon

canteen (flask) *suitō* 水筒

canvas (cloth) *zu'kku* ズック

canyon *fuka'i tani* 深い谷; (Tech) *keikoku* 渓谷

cap (hat) *bōshi* 帽子

capability *see* ability

capable *yūnō* [*na*] 有能[な] a capable assistant *yūnō na jo'shu* 有能
な助手 ——obj *ga* (v) *deki'·ru* できる capable of understanding
ri'kai ga deki'ru 理解ができる

capacity *yōryō'* 容量

cape 1 (clothing) *kē'pu* ケープ 2 (geographic) *misaki* 岬

capital 1 (W) city *shu'fu* 首府 2 (J) *shuto* 首都; old capital (e.g.,
Kyoto) *miyako* 都 3 money resources *shiki'n* 資金; *shihon* 資本

capitalism *shihonshu'gi* 資本主義

capitalist 1 *shihonshugi'sha* 資本主義者 2 (financier) *shihonka* 資
本家

capital letter *ōmoji* 大文字

capital punishment *shike'i* 死刑

Capricorn *Yagi-za* 山羊座

capsize (v) *hikkuri-kae·ru* ひっくり返る The boat capsized. *Fu'ne
ga hikkuri-ka'etta.* 船がひっくり返った. ——obj *o* (v) *hikkuri-
ka'es·u* ひっくり返す capsize a boat *fu'ne o hikkuri-ka'esu* 船をひ
っくり返す

capsule *ka'puseru* カプセル

captain (army) *rikugun ta'i-i* 陸軍大尉; (aircraft) *ki'chō* 機長;
(boat) *se'nchō* 船長

captive *ho'ryo* 捕虜; *toriko'* とりこ *see also* hostage

capture obj *o* (v) *tora'e·ru* 捕らえる

car *kuruma* 車; (coll) personal car *ma'ikā* マイカー

caramel *kyarameru* キャラメル

carbohydrate *tansuika'butsu* 炭水化物

carbon *ta'nso* 炭素

carbon paper *kābo'nshi* カーボン紙

carcass *shitai* 死体

card 1 *ka'do* カード 2 playing card *tora'mpu* トランプ 3 calling
card; business card *meishi* 名刺 4 postcard *hagaki* 葉書; picture
postcard *e-ha'gaki* 絵葉書 5 Christmas card *Kurisumasu kā'do*
クリスマスカード

cardiac disease *shinzō-byō* 心臓病

cardiogram *shinde'nzu* 心電図

cardiograph *shindenzu'kei* 心電図計; *shindenkei* 心電計

care (attention) *chū'i* 注意 scrupulous care *saishin no chū'i* 細心の
注意 ——compl *ni* (irr) take care; pay attention *chū'i-suru* 注意
する Take care not to fall! *Ochi'nai yō ni chū'i-shite kudasa'i.* 落
ちないように注意して下さい. ——(idiom) 1 take care of ... [*no*]
sewa' o suru ... [の]世話をする Mother took good care of Dad.
Ha'ha wa yo'ku chichi' no sewa'o shita. 母はよく父の世話をした.
2 be taken care of *sewa' ni na'r·u* 世話になる The Tanakas took
care of me while I was in Tokyo. *Tōkyō de wa, Tanaka-san-tachi*

no o-sewa' ni na'tta. 東京では田中さんたちのお世話になった. **3** I don't care. *Kamaimase'n.* 構いません.

career *kya'ria* キャリア; *keireki* 経歴; academic career *gakureki* 学歴

carefree *no'nki* [na] のんき[な]

careful (adj) *chūi-buka'·i* 注意深い He/She's a careful person. *Ano' hito wa chūi-buka'i.* あの人は注意深い.

carefully 1 cautiously *chūi-bu'kaku* 注意深く The child crossed the street carefully. *Kodomo wa chūi-bu'kaku michi o watatta.* 子供は注意深く道を渡った. **2** conscientiously *te'inei ni* ていねいに I explained it carefully. *Watashi wa sore o te'inei ni setsumei-shita.* 私はそれをていねいに説明した. **3** gingerly *shinchō ni* 慎重に Treat that carefully! *Sore o shinchō ni atsukatte kudasa'i.* それを慎重に扱って下さい.

carelessness *fuchū'i* 不注意 It was because of my carelessness. *Watashi no fuchū'i no tame' deshita.* 私の不注意のためでした.

caress *a'ibu* 愛撫 ——obj *o* (irr) *a'ibu-suru* 愛撫する

caretaker 1 custodian *kanrinin* 管理人 **2** of a residence *rusuban* 留守番

carfare *ryo'hi* 旅費; *kōtsū'hi* 交通費

cargo *ka'motsu* 貨物

carnation *kānē'shon* カーネーション

carol *kya'roru* キャロル Christmas carol *Kurisumasu kya'roru* クリスマス・キャロル

carp *ko'i* 鯉 carp streamer *koino'bori* こいのぼり

carpenter *da'iku* 大工

carpet *jū'tan* じゅうたん; *kāpetto* カーペット

carrot *ninjin* 人参

carry obj *o* (v) **1** *motte ik·u* 持って行く **2** transport *hakob·u* 運ぶ **3** carry in the arms *dak·u* 抱く **4** carry on the back *o·u* 負う; *seo'·u* 背負う **5** carry (someone) on the back (irr) *o'mbu-suru* おんぶする **6** carry on the shoulders *katsu'g·u* かつぐ **7** carry something (e.g., a suitcase) that hangs from the hands *sa'gete ik·u* 下げて行く ——(idiom) be carried away with *muchū ni na'r·u* 夢中になる He's carried away with his work. *Ka're wa shigoto ni muchū ni' na'tte iru.* 彼は仕事に夢中になっている.

carry out (perform) obj *o* (v) *hata's·u* 果たす carry out one's mission *shi'mei o hata'su* 使命を果たす

carry-out food *mochikaeri ryo'ri* 持ち帰り料理

cart (vehicle) *nigu'ruma* 荷車

carton (cardboard) *dambōru'-bako* ダンボール箱

cartoon *manga* 漫画

cartridge 1 (for firearms) *dan'yakutō* 弾薬筒 **2** (for ink; recording tape; film) *kā'toridji* カートリッジ

carve obj *o* (v) *kizam·u* 刻む; *ho'r·u* 彫る

carving 1 hand carving *tebori* 手彫り 2 sculpture *chōkoku* 彫刻

case 1 box *hako* 箱 2 criminal case *keiji ji'ken* 刑事事件 3 legal suit; trial *soshō* 訴訟 4 medical case; patient *kanja* 患者 —— (idiom) in case ... [no] *baai* ... [の]場合 in case of rain *a'me no baai* 雨の場合 in case it rains *a'me ga futta baai* 雨が降った場合; *ma'nichi* 万一 in case something happens ... *man'ichi no koto' ga a'ttara* ... 万一のことがあったら

cash *genki'n* 現金 cash payment *genkin-ba'rai* 現金払い

cashier 1 *suitō-ga'kari* 出納係 2 restaurant cashier *re'ji* レジ

cash register *re'ji* レジ

casket *ka'n* 棺; *kan'oke* 棺桶

casserole (food) *gura'tan* グラタン; (dish) *ōbun-yō fuka'-zara* オーブン用深皿

cassette tape *kasetto tē'pu* カセットテープ cassette tape recorder *kasetto tēpu rekō'dā* カセットテープレコーダー

cast 1 rigid surgical dressing *gi'pusu* ギブス 2 (of a drama) *shutsue'nsha* 出演者

caste system *kāsuto-sei* カースト制

castle *shiro* 城; *-jō* 城 Osaka Castle *Ōsaka'-jō* 大阪城

castor oil *himashi'-yu* ひまし油

casual (adj) *nanigena'·i* 何気ない

casual dress *fuda'n-gi* 普段着; *kajuaru do'resu* カジュアルドレス

casualty *keganin* けが人 The accident resulted in no casualties. *Ji'ko wa keganin o dasa'nakatta.* 事故はけが人を出さなかった.

cat *ne'ko* 猫 stray cat *noraneko* 野良猫

catalogue 1 *katarogu* カタログ 2 (of a school or company) *yōran* 要覧

cataract (eye disease) *hakuna'ishō* 白内障

catastrophe *dai-sa'igai* 大災害

catch obj *o* (v) 1 *tsukamae·ru* つかまえる; *tsuka'm·u* つかむ catch hold of (someone's) hand *te' o tsuka'mu* 手をつかむ 2 catch (a ball) *uke'r·u* うける 3 catch (a cold) *hik·u* ひく I caught a cold. *Kaze o hiita.* 風邪をひいた. 4 catch (a disease) ... *ni kaka'r·u* ...にかかる catch pneumonia *hai-en ni kaka'ru* 肺炎にかかる 5 catch (fish) *tsur·u* 釣る ——(v) be caught; apprehended *tsukamar·u* つかまる He was caught by the police. *Ka're wa keisatsu ni tsukamatta.* 彼は警察につかまった. ——(idiom) catch one's breath *i'ki o no'm·u* 息をのむ

catcher (baseball) *ho'shu* 捕手; *kya'tchā* キャッチャー

catechism *kyōgi mo'ndō* 教義問答

category *kate'gorī* カテゴリー; *hanchū* 範疇; *han, i'* 範囲 We don't handle things in that category. *Sono han'i'-nai no koto' wa toriatsukawa'nai.* その範囲内のことは取り扱わない.

caterpillar   *kemushi* 毛虫

cathedral   *dai-se'idō* 大聖堂

Catholic   *Katori'kku* カトリック

catsup   *kecha'ppu* ケチャップ

Caucasian   *hakujin* 白人

cauliflower   *karifura'wā* カリフラワー

causative (Gram)   *shiekitai* 使役態

cause (producing)   *gen'in* 原因 They don't know the cause. *Gen'in ga wakara'nai.* 原因がわからない. ——obj *o* (v) bring about *oko's·u* 起こす cause a problem *mondai o oko'su* 問題を起こす ——(caus) *sase·ru* させる cause an injury *kega o saseru* けがをさせる *see also* causative verb forms in tables 1–3, pp. xxi–xxxv.

cause and effect   *i'nga* 因果

caution   *yōjin* 用心 Caution is important in such matters. *Kō iu mondai de' wa yōjin ga kanjin de'su.* こういう問題では用心が肝心です. ——(caus) *chū'i-sase·ru* 注意させる

cautious (adj) *yōjin-buka'·i* 用心深い; *chūi-buka'·i* 注意深い —— (irr) be cautious *chū'i-suru* 注意する Be cautious of pickpockets! *Su'ri ni chū'i-shite kudasa'i!* すりに注意して下さい.

cavalry   *kiheitai* 騎兵隊

cave   *hora-ana* 洞穴; *dōkutsu* 洞窟

caviar   *kya'bia* キャビア

cavity (tooth)   *mushiba* 虫歯

cease (v) *yam·u* 止む It seems that wars will never cease. *Sensō wa i'tsu made mo yamanai yō' desu.* 戦争はいつまでも止まないようです. ——obj *o* (v) *yame·ru* 止める The workers ceased their complaining and cooperated to complete the project. *Rōdō'sha wa fuhei o yamete, kyōryokuteki ni shigoto o o'eta.* 労働者は不平を止めて、協力的に仕事を終えた。

cedar   1 *sugi* 杉   2 red cedar *akasugi* 赤杉

ceiling   *tenjō* 天井

celebrate   obj *o* (v) *iwa'·u* 祝う celebrate a person's success *hito no seikō o iwa'u* 人の成功を祝う

celebration   *iwai* 祝い birthday celebration *tanjō'bi no o-iwai* 誕生日のお祝い, Let's have a drink in celebration. *O-iwai ni i'ppai yarimashō'.* お祝いに一杯やりましょう.

celebrity   *yūme'ijin* 有名人; *me'ishi* 名士

celery   *se'rori* セロリ

cell   1 (Biol) *saibō* 細胞   2 a communist cell *kyōsan-tō sa'ibō* 共産党細胞   3 (of a jail) *dokubō* 独房   4 (of a grid) *masu'* 桝   5 battery *de'nchi* 電池

cellar   *chika'shitsu* 地下室

cello   *che'ro* チェロ

Celsius   *see* centigrade

cement   *semento* セメント

cemetery   *bo'chi* 墓地

censorship   *ken'etsu* 検閲

censure   *hi'nan* 非難 ——obj *o* (v) *hi'nan-suru* 非難する

census   *kokusei chō'sa* 国勢調査

center   1 *mannaka* 真中 the center of the room *heya no mannaka* 部屋の真中   2 core; heart *chūshin* 中心 the center of a circle *en no chūshin* 円の中心; *-shin* 心 center of gravity *jūshin* 重心 center of Tokyo *toshin* 都心

centigrade   *se'sshi* 摂氏

centimeter   *se'nchi* センチ

centipede   *mukade* 百足

central   *chūō'* [*no*] 中央[の] central post office *chūō yūbi'nkyoku* 中央郵便局

century   *se'iki* 世紀 twentieth century *nijusse'iki* 二十世紀

ceramic   *tō'ki no* 陶器の

ceramics   *tō'ki* 陶器

cereal   1 (grain) *koku'rui* 穀類   2 (breakfast food) *shi'riaru* シリアル

ceremony   *shiki'* 式 wedding ceremony *kekko'n shiki* 結婚式

certain   1 a certain … *a'ru* … ある a certain person *a'ru hito* ある人 at certain stores *a'ru mise' de wa* ある店では   2 correct; reliable *ta'shika* [*na*] 確か[な] certain information *ta'shika na jōhō* 確かな情報 That's certain. *Sore wa ta'shika desu.* それは確かです.

certainly   1 *mochi'ron* もちろん Certainly I will go. *Mochi'ron iki-ma'su.* もちろん行きます.; *ta'shika ni* 確かに That was certainly a mistake. *Sore wa ta'shika ni machiga'tte ita.* それは確かに間違っていた.   2 really *hontō ni* 本当に He/She's certainly stupid! *Ano' hito wa hontō ni ba'ka da!* あの人は本当にばかだ.

certificate   *shōmeisho* 証明書

certification   *shōmei* 証明

certify   ind-obj *ni*, obj *o* (irr) *shōmei-suru* 証明する

chain   1 *kusari* 鎖   2 car chains *chē'n* チェーン

chair   1 *isu* 椅子   2 chair of a meeting *gi'chō* 議長; *gichō'dan* 議長団 ——obj *o* (irr) *shikai-suru* 司会する

chairperson   1 *shika'isha* 司会者   2 (of a business meeting) *gi'chō* 議長   3 (of a club or society) *kaichō* 会長   4 (of a committee) *ii'nchō* 委員長

chalk   *chō'ku* チョーク

challenge   *cha'renji* チャレンジ; *chōsen* 挑戦 ——ind-obj *ni*, obj *o* (irr) *cha'renji-suru* チャレンジする challenge the world record *sekai ki'roku ni cha'renji-suru* 世界記録にチャレンジする

chamber music   *shitsuna'igaku* 室内楽

chamber music orchestra   *shitsunai ga'kudan* 室内楽団

champagne *shampe'n* シャンペン

champignon *shampi'nion* シャンピニオン

champion **1** (sports) *cha'mpion* チャンピオン; *senshuken hoji'sha* 選手権保持者 **2** (animal) *yūshō-* 優勝 champion horse *yūshō-ba* 優勝馬

chance *cha'nsu* チャンス; *kika'i* 機会 ——(adv) by chance *gūzen [ni]* 偶然[に] I met him/her by chance. *Gūzen sono' hito ni atta.* 偶然その人に会った.

change **1** (natural) *he'nka* 変化 **2** (deliberate) *henkō* 変更 **3** (money) *o-tsuri* お釣り Here's your change. *O-tsuri de' su.* お釣りです.; *kozeni* 小銭; *komakai o-kane* 細かいお金 Do you have any change? *Komakai o-kane ga arima' su ka?* 細かいお金がありますか. ——compl *ni* (v) *kawar·u* 変わる My address has changed. *Watashi no jūsho ga kawarima' shita.* 私の住所が変わりました. The meeting place has been changed. *Kaigi no basho ga kawarima'-shita.* 会議の場所が変わりました. ——ind-obj *ni*, obj *o* (irr) **1** exchange; change money *ryōgae-suru* 両替えする Would you change this ¥10,000 bill for me, please? *Ichiman'e'n-satsu o ryō-gae-shite itadakemase'n ka?* 一万円札を両替えしていただけませんか. **2** replace *kae·ru* 替える Change the sheets, please. *Shītsu o kaete kudasa'i.* シーツを替えて下さい

changeable (adj) *kawari-yasu'·i* 変わりやすい The weather in the mountains is changeable. *Yama' no te'nki wa kawari-yasu'i.* 山の天気は変わりやすい. He is a man of changeable moods. *Ka're wa ki no kawari-yasu'i otoko' desu.* 彼は気の変わりやすい男です.

change of life (menopause) *kōne'nki* 更年期

channel **1** (radio; television) *channeru* チャンネル **2** (waterway) *kaikyō* 海峡 the English Channel *Igirisu Ka'ikyō* イギリス海峡

chant *eishō* 詠唱 ——obj *o* (irr) *eishō-suru* 詠唱する

chaos **1** *konton* 混沌 **2** utter confusion *dai-ko'nran* 大混乱 **3** bustle *ko'nzatsu* 混雑 **4** disorder *muchi'tsujo* 無秩序

chapel *reihaidō* 礼拝堂

chapter *-shō* 章 one chapter *i'ssho* 一章 Chapter One *da'i-i'sshō* 第一章

character **1** personal trait *jinkaku* 人格; *seikaku* 性格 a person of strong character *seikaku no tsuyo'i hito* 性格の強い人 **2** (in a play/novel) *ji'mbutsu* 人物 **3** Chinese ideogram *kanji* 漢字

characteristic *tokuchō* 特徴 What is its chief characteristic? *Sore ni wa do'nna tokuchō ga arima' su ka?* それにはどんな特徴がありますか. ——(attr) *tokuchō [no]* 特徴[の]

charcoal *sumi'* 炭

charge **1** (amount of money) *ryō'kin* 料金 **2** (of a battery) *jūden* 充電 ——obj *o* (v) **1** record as a debt on one's account *tsuke'·ru* 付ける Charge it, please. *Tsuke'te kudasa'i.* 付けて下さい. **2** in/

take charge of (irr) *tantō-suru* 担当する I'm in charge of that class. *Watashi wa sono ku'rasu o tantō-shite iru.* 私はそのクラスを担当している.

charge account   *see* account

charge card   *see* credit card

charity   *jizen* 慈善

charley horse   *keiren* けいれん

charm   **1** amulet; talisman *o-mamori* お守り   **2** attraction *miryoku* 魅力

chart   **1** *zu* 図   **2** (nautical) *kaizu* 海図   **3** (medical) *ka'rute* カルテ

chase   obj *o* (v) **1** chase away *o·u* 追う; *oihara'·u* 追い払う   **2** chase out *oida's·u* 追い出す   **3** chase after *oikake'·ru* 追いかける   **4** pursue *oimotome'·ru* 追い求める; (irr) *tsuikyū-suru* 追求する

chasm   *mizo* 溝

chassis   *shatai* 車体

chat   *o-sha'beri* おしゃべり   ——ind-obj *ni*, obj *o* (irr) *o-sha'beri-suru* おしゃべりする

chauffeur   *unte'nshu* 運転手

cheap   (adj) *yasu'·i* 安い, cheap clothes *yasu'i fuku'* 安い服 That's cheap! *Sore wa yasu'i desu!* それは安いです. This was very cheap. *Kore wa totemo ya'sukatta.* これはとても安かった.

cheating (on exams) *kanningu* カンニング

check   **1** draft *kogi'tte* 小切手 write a check *kogi'tte o ki'ru* 小切手を切る   **2** mark "√" *che'kku māku* チェックマーク   ——obj *o* (v) **1** (irr) *che'kku-suru* チェックする; *tenken-suru* 点検する Would you please check and see if it's O.K.? *I'i ka dō' ka tenken-shite kudasaimase'n ka?* いいかどうか点検して下さいませんか. **2** restrain *tome·ru* 止める   ——(idiom) make a check mark *che'kku o tsuke'·ru* チェックを付ける

checking account   *tōza yo'kin* 当座預金

checkup (medical) *shintai ke'nsa* 身体検査

cheek   *hō'* ほお; *ho'ho* ほほ;   (coll) *hoppe'ta* ほっぺた

cheerful   *yōki* [na] 陽気[な]   ——(adj) *akaru·i* 明るい, a cheerful person *akarui hito'* 明るい人

cheerfully   *ni'koniko* [to] にこにこ[と] He smiled cheerfully. *Ka're wa ni'koniko waraima'shita.* 彼はにこにこ笑いました.

cheering squad   *ōe'ndan* 応援団

cheese   *chi'zu* チーズ

chef   *see* cook

chemical   *ka'gaku ya'kuhin* 化学薬品   ——(attr) *kagaku no* 化学の

chemistry   *ka'gaku* 化学

chemotherapy   *ka'gaku ryō'hō* 化学療法

cherry   **1** (tree) *sakura* [*no ki'*] 桜[の木]   **2** (blossoms) *sakura* [*no hana'*] 桜[の花]   **3** (fruit) *sakurambo* さくらんぼ

chess   *che'su* チェス

chest   **1** (Anat) *mune'* 胸   **2** chest of drawers *tansu* たんす

chestnut   *kuri'* 栗

chew   obj *o* (v) *ka'm·u* かむ chew gum *ga'mu o ka'mu* ガムをかむ   Chew it well! *Yo'ku ka'nde kudasa'i.* よくかんで下さい.

chewing gum   *chūinga'mu* チューインガム

chic   *shi'kku* [*na*] シック[な]

chicken   **1** (bird) *niwatori* 鶏   **2** (meat) *toriniku* 鶏肉

chief   **1** division chief *buchō* 部長   **2** section chief *kachō* 課長   —— (attr) *o'mo* [*na*] 主[な] The chief cause is … *O'mo na gen'in wa* … 主な原因は…

child   **1** (one's own) *kodomo* 子供   **2** (another's) *o-kosan* お子さん

childbirth   **1** *o-san* お産   **2** natural childbirth *shizen bu'mben* 自然分娩

childish   (adj) *kodomoppo'·i* 子供っぽい

childlike   (adj) **1** *kodomo-rashi'·i* 子供らしい   **2** innocent *adokena'·i* あどけない

Chile   *Chi'ri* チリ

Chilean   (person) *Chiri'jin* チリ人   ——(attr) *Chi'ri no* チリの

chili (pepper)   *tōga'rashi* とうがらし

chill   *samuke'* 寒気 feel a chill *samuke' ga suru* 寒気がする   —— obj *o* (v) *hiya's·u* 冷やす Chill it for five minutes. *Gofu'nkan hiya-shi-nasa'i.* 5分間冷やしなさい.

chilly   (adj) *tsumeta'·i* 冷たい   ——(irr) be chilly *hiebi'e-suru* 冷え冷えする

chimney   *entotsu* 煙突

chin   *ago'* あご

China   *Chū'goku* 中国

chinaware   **1** *setomono* 瀬戸物   **2** porcelain *ji'ki* 磁器

Chinese   **1** (language) *Chūgoku-go* 中国語   **2** (person) *Chūgoku'jin* 中国人   ——(attr) *Chū'goku no* 中国の

Chinese ideogram   *kanji* 漢字

chiropractor   [*sekitsui*] *shiatsu chiryō'sha* [脊椎]指圧治療者

chirp   *tori no nakigo'e* 鳥の鳴き声   ——(v) *saezu'r·u* さえずる   ——(adv) *chu'nchun* [*to*] ちゅんちゅん[と] Sparrows chirp. *Suzume ga chu'nchun to naku.* 雀がちゅんちゅんと鳴く.

chisel   *no'mi* のみ

chlorine   *e'nso* 塩素; *ka'ruki* カルキ

chocolate   **1** (flavor) *chokore'to* チョコレート   **2** (candy) *chokore'to* チョコレート   **3** hot chocolate *ko'koa* ココア

choice   *sentaku* 選択

choir *seikatai* 聖歌隊

choke (v) [*no'do ga*] *tsuma'r·u* [のどが]詰まる I choked. *No'do ga tsuma'tta.* のどが詰まった; *muse·ru* むせる I choked on a grain of rice. *Gohan tsu'bu de museta.* 御飯粒でむせた.

choose obj o (v) *erab·u* 選ぶ; (irr) *sentaku-suru* 選択する

chop (cut of meat) **1** porkchop *pōku cho'ppu* ポークチョップ **2** lambchop *ramu cho'ppu* ラムチョップ

chop obj o (v) *war·u* 割る chop wood *maki o waru* 薪を割る

chopsticks *ha'shi* 箸

chord (Music) *wa'-on* 和音

chorus *gasshō'dan* 合唱団

Christ *Kirisuto* キリスト Jesus Christ *Iesu Ki'risuto* イエスキリスト

Christian *Kuri'suchan* クリスチャン; *Kirisutokyō'to* キリスト教徒 ——(attr) *Kirisutokyō no* キリスト教の

Christianity *Kirisutokyō* キリスト教

Christmas *Kuri'sumasu* クリスマス

chrome **1** *kurō'mu* クローム **2** chromium plating *kurōmu me'kki* クロームメッキ

chromosome *senshokutai* 染色体

chronic *mansei* [*no*] 慢性[の] chronic gastritis *mansei i'en* 慢性胃炎 My asthma is chronic. *Watashi no zensoku wa mansei de'su.* 私の喘息は慢性です.

chrysanthemum *kiku'* 菊

chuckle (v) *ku'sukusu wara·u* くすくす笑う

church *kyōkai* 教会

cicada *semi* 蟬

cigarette *tabako* たばこ (Give me) a pack of cigarettes, please. *Tabako o hito'-hako kudasa'i.* たばこを一箱下さい.

cigarette butt *suigara* 吸い殻

cigarette lighter *ra'itā* ライター

cinnamon *shina'mon* シナモン

circle *maru* 丸; *wa* 輪; *e'n* 円

circulation **1** *junkan* 循環 blood circulation *ketsu'eki no junkan* 血液の循環 **2** (of money) *kin'yū* 金融 **3** (of newspapers, books) *hakkō bu'sū* 発行部数

circumference *enshū* 円周

circumstances *jijō* 事情; actual circumstances *jitsujō* 実情; present circumstances *genjō* 現状

citizen **1** (of a city) *shi'min* 市民 **2** (of a country) *kokumin* 国民

citizenship *shimi'nken* 市民権; *kokuseki* 国籍

citric acid *kuensan* くえん酸

citrus fruit *kankitsu'-rui* 柑橘類

city *tokai* 都会; *to'shi* 都市 large city *dai-to'shi* 大都市; -*shi* 市 Kobe City *Kobe'-shi* 神戸市

city hall *shiya'kusho* 市役所

civilian *minka'njin* 民間人

civilization *bummei* 文明

civil rights *kōmi'nken* 公民権

civil servant *kōmu'in* 公務員

civil war *nairan* 内乱

claim 1 assertion; strong opinion *shuchō* 主張 2 demand *yōsei* 要請 ——obj *o* (irr) 1 assert *shuchō-suru* 主張する 2 lay claim to *yōkyū-suru* 要求する

clam 1 *hama'guri* 蛤 2 short-necked clam *asari* あさり

clan *u'ji* 氏; *shi'zoku* 氏族

clap (irr) *ha'kushu-suru* 拍手する Please do not clap. *Ha'kushu-shina'ide kudasa'i.* 拍手しないで下さい.

clarinet *kurarine'tto* クラリネット

class 1 school class *ku'rasu* クラス 2 class session *ju'gyō* 授業 Do you have a class today? *Kyō' wa ju'gyō ga arima'su ka?* 今日は授業がありますか. 3 social status *kaikyū* 階級 labor class *rōdōsha ka'ikyū* 労働者階級; -*ryū* 流 upper class *jōryū* 上流 middle class *chūryū* 中流 lower class *karyū* 下流 4 rank -*ryū* 流 first-class university *ichiryū da'igaku* 一流大学 second-class *niryū* 二流 third-class *sanryū* 三流; -*tō* 等 first-class car (on a train) *ittō'-sha* 一等車 second-class *nitō* 二等 third-class *santō* 三等

classic literature *koten* 古典

classification *bunrui* 分類

classify obj *o* (irr) *bunrui-suru* 分類する

classroom *kyōshitsu* 教室

classmate *dōkyū'sei* 同級生

clatter (irr) *ga'tagata-suru* がたがたする Last night the shutters clattered so, I couldn't sleep. *Yū'be amado ga ga'tagata-shite, nemurena'katta.* ゆうべ雨戸ががたがたして, 眠れなかった.

clay 1 *ne'ndo* 粘土 2 potter's clay *tō'do* 陶土

clean 1 *ki'rei* [*na*] きれい[な] a clean room *ki'rei na heya'* きれいな部屋 2 sanitary *seiketsu* [*na*] 清潔[な] a clean bathroom *seiketsu na o-tea'rai* 清潔なお手洗い ——obj *o* (irr) *sōji-suru* 掃除する ——(idiom) make clean *ki'rei ni'suru* きれいにする

Clean Government Party (Japanese political party) *Kōmei-tō* 公明党

cleaning 1 *sōji* 掃除 2 dry-cleaning *kuri'ningu* クリーニング

cleanser *kure'nzā* クレンザー

cleanup *katazuke* 片付け

clean up obj *o* (v) *katazuke'·ru* 片付ける Clean up this room, please. *Kono heya' o katazu'kete kudasa'i.* この部屋を片付けて下さい.

clear *aki'raka* [*na*] 明らか[な] a clear mistake *aki'raka na machiga'i* 明らかな間違い ——(v) be/become clear **1** (weather) *hare'ru* 晴れる The sky's clear. *So'ra ga ha'rete iru.* 空が晴れている. **2** be easily understandable (irr) *hakki'ri-suru* はっきりする That point's clear. *Sono ten wa hakki'ri-shite iru.* その点ははっきりしている. ——(idiom) **1** be declared innocent *mu'zai ni nar·u* 無罪になる He was cleared of the charge. *Ka're wa mu'zai ni na'tta.* 彼は無罪になった. **2** remove obj *o* (v) *sage'·ru* 下げる Clear the dishes, please. *O-sara o sa'gete kudasa'i.* お皿を下げてください. **3** clear up *aki'raka ni suru* 明らかにする The matter was cleared up. *Mondai wa aki'raka ni shita.* 問題は明らかにした. **4** clear the throat *sekiba'rai o suru* 咳払いをする

clearly *hakki'ri* [*to*] はっきり[と] I can't see clearly. *Hakki'ri mie' nai.* はっきり見えない. Please speak clearly. *Hakki'ri itte kudasa'i.* はっきり言って下さい.; *aki'raka ni* 明らかに He is clearly mistaken. *Ka're wa aki'raka ni machiga'tte iru.* 彼は明らかに間違っている.

clergy *seisho'kusha* 聖職者

clerk 1 (information-desk) *annai-ga'kari* 案内係 **2** (office) *jimu'in* 事務員 **3** (store) *ten'in* 店員

clever *ki'yō* [*na*] 器用[な] He's clever with his hands. *Ka're wa tesaki' ga ki'yō desu.* 彼は手先が器用です. ——(adj) **1** *kashiko'·i* 賢い **2** shrewd; cunning *zuru'·i* ずるい ——(idiom) intelligent *atama'ga i'·i* 頭がいい She's clever. *Ka'nojo wa atama ga i'i.* 彼女は頭がいい.

cleverly *takumi ni* 巧みに; *kashiko'ku* 賢く

clew *see* clue

client (Leg) *irainin* 依頼人; *kokyaku* 顧客

cliff *gake* 崖; *zeppeki* 絶壁

climate *kikō* 気候

climax *chō'ten* 頂点

climb (v) *nobor·u* 登る climb a mountain *yama' ni noboru* 山に登る

cling (v) *kuttsu'k·u* くっつく The little girl was clinging to her mother. *Onna' no ko wa haha-oya no so'ba ni kuttsu'ite ita.* 女の子は母親のそばにくっついていた.; *shigamitsu'k·u* しがみつく

clinic 1 private *i'in* 医院 **2** hospital *byōin* 病院

clipping (from newspapers, etc.) *kiri-nuki* 切り抜き

clitoris *kurito'risu* クリトリス; (Tech) *inkaku* 陰核

clock 1 *tokei* 時計 **2** alarm clock *mezamashi-do'kei* 目覚し時計 **3** (table/desk/mantel) *oki-do'kei* 置時計 **4** wall clock *hashira-do'kei* 柱時計 ——(idiom) measure time *jikan o hakar·u* 時間を計る

clog (v) *tsuma'r·u* 詰まる

clogs *geta* 下駄

cloisonné *shippōyaki* 七宝焼き

cloning *fukusei* 複製

close 1 nearby *chi'kaku* [no] 近く[の] My house is close to yours. *Watashi no ie' wa anata no ie' no chi'kaku desu.* 私の家はあなたの家の近くです. 2 intimate; familiar *missetsu* [na] 密接[な] a close relationship *missetsu na kankei* 密接な関係 ——(adj) 1 *chika'·i* 近い, The subway is close. *Chikatetsu wa chika'i.* 地下鉄は近い. 2 intimate; familiar *shitashi'·i* 親しい a close friend *shitashi'i tomodachi* 親しい友達 ——(idiom) *na'ka no i'·i* 仲のいい a close friend *na'ka no i'i tomodachi* 仲のいい友達

close *obj o* (v) *shime'·ru* 閉める Close the door! *Do'a o shi'mete kudasa'i.* ドアを閉めて下さい. ——(v) *shima'r·u* 閉まる This door doesn't close well. *Kono do'a wa yo'ku shimara'nai.* このドアはよく閉まらない. The store was closed. *Sono mise' wa shima'tte ita.* その店は閉まっていた.

closet *oshi-ire* 押し入れ

cloth 1 *kire'* きれ; *nuno* 布 2 (for clothing) *ki'ji* 生地 3 face cloth *tenugui* 手ぬぐい 4 cleaning cloth *zōkin* ぞうきん 5 dish-cloth *fukin* 布巾

clothesline *monohoshi-za'o* 物干し竿

clothespin *sentaku-ba'sami* 洗たくばさみ

clothing 1 (W) *fuku'* 服; *yōfuku* 洋服 2 (J) *wafuku* 和服; *kimono* 着物 3 apparel *kiru mono'* 着る物 4 garments *i'rui* 衣類

cloud *ku'mo* 雲

cloudy *kumori'* [no] 曇り[の] a cloudy sky *kumori-zo'ra* 曇り空 ——(v) be/become cloudy *kumo'r·u* 曇る It's cloudy. *Kumo'tte iru.* 曇っている. My glasses have become cloudy. *Me'gane ga kumo'tte kita.* メガネが曇ってきた.

clover *kurōbā* クローバー

clown *pi'ero* ピエロ; *dōke* 道化 ——(v) *fuzake'·ru* ふざける

club 1 golf club *ku'rabu* クラブ 2 clubhouse *kurabu ha'usu* クラブハウス 3 school club *ku'rabu* クラブ club activities *kurabu ka'tsudō* クラブ活動 4 member's club (bar) *kaiinsei ku'rabu* 会員制クラブ 5 stick *bō'* 棒 6 (suit of playing cards) *ku'rabu* クラブ ——(idiom) to club *bō de tata'k·u* 棒で叩く

clue *tega'kari* 手掛かり clue to a robbery *settō no tega'kari* 窃盗の手掛かり

clumsily *heta' ni* 下手に It's written clumsily. *Heta' ni ka'ite a'ru.* 下手に書いてある.

clumsy *heta'* [na] 下手[な] a clumsy waiter *heta' na ue'tā* 下手なウエーター; *buki'yō* [na] 不器用[な] I'm clumsy. *Watashi wa buki'yō desu.* 私は不器用です. see also awkward

clutter *garakuta* がらくた ——obj *o* (v) *chirakas·u* 散らかす
Don't clutter the floor with old newspapers and magazines. *Furushi'mbun ya zasshi de yuka o chirakasa'naide kudasa'i.* 古新聞や
雑誌で床を散らかさないで下さい。 ——(v) be full of clutter; be
cluttered *chirakar·u* 散らかる The room is cluttered. *Heya' ga
chirakatte iru.* 部屋が散らかっている。

coach *kō'chi* コーチ ——(idiom) to coach *kō'chi o suru* コーチ
をする

coal *sekita'n* 石炭

coarse (rough) *so'matsu* [na] 粗末[な] coarse fare *so'matsu na shokuji*
粗末な食事 ——(adj) *ara'·i* 粗い, coarse woodgrain *ara'i mokume* 粗い木目

coast (seaside) *kaigan* 海岸

coat 1 *kō'to* コート 2 overcoat *ō'ba* オーバー 3 suit coat; jacket
uwagi 上着

cobalt *kobaruto* コバルト cobalt treatment *kobaruto ryōhō* コバル
ト療法

cockroach *gokiburi* ごきぶり

cocktail *ka'kuteru* カクテル

cocoa *ko'koa* ココア see also chocolate

coconut *kokona'ttsu* ココナッツ

cocoon *ma'yu* 繭

cod *ta'ra* 鱈 cod roe *tarako* たらこ

code *angō* 暗号

coeducation *da'njo kyōgaku* 男女共学

coffee *kōhī* コーヒー instant coffee *insutanto kō'hi* インスタントコ
ーヒー coffee bean *kōhī'-mame* コーヒー豆

coffee cup *kōhī-ja'wan* コーヒー茶わん

coffee house/shop *kissa'ten* 喫茶店

coffin *ka'n* 棺; *ka'n-oke* 棺桶

cognac *konya'kku* コニャック

cohabitate (irr) *dōsei-suru* 同棲する

cohabitation *dōsei* [*se'ikatsu*] 同棲[生活]

coin (currency) *kō'ka* 硬貨; *-dama* 玉 a hundred-yen coin *hyaku-e'n-dama* 百円玉

coincidence *gūzen* 偶然

cold 1 (of the weather) *sa'musa* 寒さ the cold of winter *fuyu' no
sa'musa* 冬の寒さ 2 (illness) *kaze* 風邪 catch a cold *kaze o hiku*
風邪をひく I have a cold. *Kaze o hiite iru.* 風邪をひいている。
——(adj) 1 (of the weather) *samu'·i* 寒い It's very cold today, isn't
it? *Kyō' wa totemo samu'i desu ne.* 今日はとても寒いですね。 It's
cold! *Samu'i!* 寒い。 2 cold to the touch; indifferent *tsumeta'·i* 冷
たい The water's cold. *Mizu ga tsumeta'i.* 水が冷たい。 He's a cold
person. *Ka're wa tsumeta'i hito' desu.* 彼は冷たい人です。 ——(v)

become cold *hie′·ru* 冷える It gets cold at night. *Yo′ru wa hie′ru.* 夜は冷える.

cold sore *hōshin* 疱疹

cold war *reisen* 冷戦

collapse obj *o* (v) *taore′·ru* 倒れる She collapsed with a heart attack. *Ka′nojo wa shinzō-ma′hi de tao′reta.* 彼女は心臓麻痺で倒れた.

collar *e′ri* 襟

colleague *dōryō* 同僚

collect obj *o* (v) **1** *atsume′·ru* 集める I collect Japanese stamps. *Watashi wa Niho′n no kitte o atsu′mete iru.* 私は日本の切手を集めている. **2** collect payment (irr) *shūkin-suru* 集金する ——(v) be/become collected *atsuma′r·u* 集まる Many contributions were collected. *Kifu′kin ga takusa′n atsuma′tta.* 寄付金がたくさん集まった.

collected (attr) *atsuma′tta* 集まった collected money/contributions *atsuma′tta kane* 集まった金

collection 1 (of stamps, etc.) *kore′kushon* コレクション **2** contribution *ki′fu* 寄付 **3** church offering *kenkin* 献金

college 1 *daigaku* 大学 **2** junior college *tanki da′igaku* 短期大学; (abbr) *tandai* 短大 **3** faculty; department *gakubu* 学部

collision 1 *shōtotsu* 衝突 head-on collision *shōmen shō′totsu* 正面衝突 **2** (rear-end) *tsuitotsu* 追突

colloquial *kōgo no* 口語の; *kōgoteki [na]* 口語的[な]

colon (Gram) *ko′ron* コロン

Colombia *Koro′mbia* コロンビア

Colombian (person) *Korombia′jin* コロンビア人 ——(attr) *Koro′mbia no* コロンビアの

colonel *taisa* 大佐 army colonel *rikugun ta′isa* 陸軍大佐

color *iro′* 色 ——(idiom) to color (something) *iro′ o nur·u* 色をぬる

colorful *hana′yaka [na]* 華やか[な] The children's room is colorful, isn't it? *Kodomo-beya wa hana′yaka desu ne.* 子供部屋は華やかですね. He lives a colorful life. *Ka′re wa hana′yaka na seikatsu o okutte iru.* 彼は華やかな生活を送っている.

column 1 (newspaper) *ra′n* 欄 advertisement column *kōkoku′-ran* 広告欄 **2** pillar *hashira* 柱

comb *kushi′* 櫛 ——obj *o* (v) *toka′s·u* とかす comb hair *kami′ o toka′su* 髪をとかす

combination *gappei* 合併; *kumiawase* 組み合わせ

combine obj *o* (irr) *gappei-suru* 合併する; (v) *awase′·ru* 併せる

come obj *o* (irr) *ku′ru* 来る Please come tomorrow. *Ashita ki′te kudasa′i.* 明日来て下さい. She came yesterday. *Ka′nojo wa kinō ki′ta.* 彼女はきのう来た. He didn't come. *Ka′re wa ko′nakatta.* 彼は来なかった.

come back (v) **1** *modo'r·u* 戻る What time are you coming back to the office? *Na'nji ni kaisha ni modorima'su ka?* 何時に会社に戻りますか。 **2** return home *ka'er·u* 帰る My husband hasn't come back home yet. *Shu'jin wa ma'da ka'ette imase'n.* 主人はまだ帰っていません。

comedian *kome'dian* コメディアン

comedy *ki'geki* 喜劇

come off (v) *tore'·ru* とれる A button came off. *Bo'tan ga to'reta.* ボタンがとれた。

come out (irr) *de'te kuru* 出てくる He came out of the room. *Ka're wa heya' kara de'te kita.* 彼は部屋から出てきた。

comet *suisei* 彗星

comfort obj o (v) *nagusame'·ru* 慰める

comfortable *raku'* [na] 楽[な] a comfortable life *raku' na seikatsu* 楽な生活 This chair is more comfortable. *Kono isu no hō' ga raku' desu.* この椅子の方が楽です; *-yasusō'* [na] やすそう[な] Those shoes look comfortable. *Sono kutsu' wa haki-yasusō'desu.* その靴ははきやすそうです。

comic book *manga* 漫画

command *meirei* 命令 ——ind-obj *ni*, obj *o* (irr) *meirei-suru* 命令する

commander *chūsa* 中佐 navy commander *kaigun chū'sa* 海軍中佐

commentary **1** *kaisetsu* 解説 **2** (annotations) *kaisetsusho* 解説書

commentator *kaisetsu'sha* 解説者 radio news commentator *ra'jio no nyū'su kaisetsu'sha* ラジオのニュース解説者; *nyūsu-kya'sutā* ニュースキャスター

commerce *shō'gyō* 商業

commercial **1** *shōgyō no* 商業の **2** (on radio/TV) *komā'sharu* コマーシャル

committee *ii'nkai* 委員会 committee member *i'in* 委員

common *kyōtsū* [na] 共通[な] a common characteristic *kyōtsū na tokuchō* 共通な特徴

common sense *jōshiki* 常識

commotion *sa'wagi* 騒ぎ great commotion *ōsa'wagi* 大騒ぎ

communicate ind-obj *ni*, obj *o* (v) *tsutae·ru* 伝える I'll communicate that to her. *Ka'nojo ni sore o tsutaete oku.* 彼女にそれを伝えておく。

communication *komyunikē'shon* コミュニケーション; *dentatsu* 伝達

Communion service (Chr) *Seisa'n-shiki* 聖餐式

communism **1** (ideology) *kyōsanshu'gi* 共産主義 **2** (system) *kyō-sansei* 共産制

communist (person) *kyōsanshugi'sha* 共産主義者

Communist Party *Kyōsan-tō* 共産党

community 1 *kyōdōtai* 共同体 2 local community *chiiki sha'kai*
地域社会 3 village; settlement *mura'* 村 4 society *sha'kai* 社会
community center *kōmi'nkan* 公民館; *kōka'ido* 公会堂; *komyuniti
se'ntā* コミュニティーセンター
commute (v) *kayo·u* 通う I commute from Chiba. *Chi'ba kara
kayotte iru.* 千葉から通っている.
commuting 1 (to school) *tsūgaku* 通学 2 (to work) *tsūkin* 通勤
companion *tsure* 連れ; *nakama* 仲間
company 1 firm *kaisha* 会社 2 (joint) stock company *kabushiki-
ga'isha* 株式会社; limited *yūgen-ga'isha* 有限会社 3 guests *kyaku*
客; *o-kyaku-san* お客さん ——(idiom) Keep me company! *Tsuki-
a'tte kudasa'i!* 付き合って下さい.
comparative *hikaku-* 比較 comparative literature *hikaku-bu'ngaku*
比較文学
comparatively *wariai ni* 割り合いに; *wari ni* 割りに This persimmon is comparatively sweet. *Kono kaki' wa wari ni ama'i.* この柿
は割りに甘い.; *hikakuteki ni* 比較的に
compare comp *to*, ind-obj *ni*, obj *o* (v) *kurabe·ru* 比べる compare
A with B *A o B to kuraberu* AをBと比べる A is big compared to
B. *B ni kuraberu to, A ga ōki'i.* Bに比べるとAが大きい. ——
(irr) *hikaku-suru* 比較する Compare these two. *Kono futatsu' o
hikaku-shite mi'te kudasa'i.* この二つを比較してみて下さい.
comparison *hikaku* 比較
compass *rashimban* 羅針盤
compassionate (adj) *nasake-buka'·i* 情深い
compensate ind-obj *ni*, obj *o* (irr) *baishō-suru* 賠償する compensate
for damages *songai o baishō-suru* 損害を賠償する; *tsuguna'·u* 償う
I will compensate you for expenses incurred. *Kaka'tta hi'yō o
ana'ta ni tsugunaima'su.* かかった費用をあなたに償います.
compensation 1 allowance *te'ate* 手当 2 reparation *baishō* 賠償;
hoshō 補償
compete comp *to* (irr) *kyōsō-suru* 競争する The Whites are com-
peting with the Reds for the prize. *Shōkin o me'ate ni, shi'ro to
a'ka ga kyōsō-shite iru.* 賞金を目当に, 白と赤が競争している.
competent *see* capable
competition *kyōsō* 競争 free competition *jiyū kyō'sō* 自由競争
price-cutting competition *nesage kyō'sō* 値下げ競争
competitive *kyōsō* [*no*] 競争[の]
competitor 1 *aite'* 相手 2 (business) *ra'ibaru* ライバル
complain (idiom) *fuhei o i·u* 不平を言う; *mo'nku o i·u* 文句を言う
He's always complaining. *Ka're wa i'tsumo na'nika mo'nku o itte
iru.* 彼はいつも何か文句を言っている.
complaint *mo'nku* 文句; *kō'gi* 抗議 register a complaint *kō'gi o
mōshiko'mu* 抗議を申し込む

complement *ho'go* 補語 ——obj *o* (v) *ogina·u* 補う

complete *kanzen [na]* 完全[な] a complete success *kanzen na seikō* 完全な成功 ——(v) *dekiagar·u* 出来上がる When will the house be completed? *Ie'wa i'tsu dekiagarima'su ka?* 家はいつ出来上がりますか. ——obj *o* (v) **1** *oe·ru* 終える After completing a day's work, I like to watch television. *Ichinichi' no shigoto o oete, te'rebi o mi'ru no ga tanoshi'mi desu.* 一日の仕事を終えてテレビを見るのが楽しみです。 *shiage'·ru* 仕上げる I want you to complete it for me within a week. *Isshūkan i'nai ni shia'gete moraita'i.* 一週間以内に仕上げてもらいたい。 **2** perfect (caus) *kansei-sase'·ru* 完成させる Complete the chart, please. *Zu o kansei-sa'sete kudasa'i.* 図を完成させて下さい。

completely *kanzen ni* 完全に; *sukka'ri* すっかり I'm completely pooped! *Sukka'ri kutabi'reta.* すっかりくたびれた。

completion *kanryō* 完了; *shūryō* 終了

complex *fukuzatsu [na]* 複雑[な] a complex problem *fukuzatsu na mondai* 複雑な問題

complexion *kao-iro* 顔色

complicated *fukuzatsu [na]* 複雑[な]

compliment *obe'kka* おべっか; *oseji* お世辞 You're full of compliments, aren't you? *Oseji ga uma'i desu ne.* お世辞がうまいですね。 ——obj *o* (v) *home'·ru* 誉める She complimented me on my success. *Ka'nojo wa seikō o ho'mete kureta.* 彼女は成功を誉めてくれた。

comply comp *ni* (v) *ōji·ru* 応じる; *shitaga·u* 従う comply with an order *meirei ni shitagau* 命令に従う

composed (attr) *ochitsuita* 落ち着いた a composed person *ochitsuita hito'* 落ち着いた人 ——(v) be composed *ochitsuk·u* 落ち着く

composer *sakkyo'kuka* 作曲家

composition (literary) *sakubun* 作文

comprehend obj *o* (irr) *ri'kai-suru* 理解する It took time for me to comprehend it. *Sore o ri'kai-suru no ni, ji'kan ga kaka'tta.* それを理解するのに時間がかかった。 ——(pot) *ri'kai-deki'·ru* 理解できる I can't comprehend that. *Watashi ni' wa sore ga ri'kai-deki'nai.* 私にはそれが理解できない。

comprehension *ri'kai* 理解

compromise *dakyō* 妥協 a compromise plan *dakyō-an* 妥協案 ——comp *to* (irr) *dakyō-suru* 妥協する He compromises with no one. *Ka're wa da're to mo dakyō-shina'i.* 彼はだれとも妥協しない。

compulsory *kyōsei [no]* 強制[の]; *hisshū [no]* 必修[の] compulsory subject in school *hisshū ka'moku* 必修課目

compulsory education *gimukyō'iku* 義務教育

computer *kompyū'tā* コンピューター

comrade *dō'shi* 同志; *nakama* 仲間

concave *ō-* 凹 concave lens *ō-re'nzu* 凹レンズ

conceal ind-obj *ni*, obj *o* (v) *kaku's·u* 隠す She concealed her real intention. *Ka'nojo wa ho'n'i o kaku'shita.* 彼女は本意を隠した.
——(v) be concealed *kakure'·ru* 隠れる The letter was concealed beneath these documents. *Tegami wa kono shorui no shita'ni ka-ku'rete ita.* 手紙はこの書類の下に隠れていた.

conceited (attr) *kido'tta* 気取った ——(v) be conceited *kido'tte i·ru* 気取っている

conceive 1 become impregnated (irr) *ninshin-suru* 妊娠する 2 think of obj *o* (v) *omoitsuk·u* 思いつく

concentrate compl *ni* (v) *ko'r·u* 凝る concentrate on a plan *keika-ku ni ko'ru* 計画に凝る; (irr) *shūchū-suru* 集中する concentrate on the study of Japanese *Nihon-go no benkyō ni shūchū-suru* 日本語の勉強に集中する

concept *ga'inen* 概念

concern *shimpai* 心配 There's no call for concern. *Shimpai wa irana'i.* 心配はいらない. see also interest

concerning ... *ni tsu'ite* ...について What are your thoughts con-cerning this matter? *Kono mondai ni tsu'ite dō' kangaema'su ka?* この問題についてどう考えますか.

concert *ko'nsāto* コンサート; *onga'kukai* 音楽会

conclude (decide; agree upon) obj *o* (irr) *kettei-suru* 決定する

conclusion *kettei* 決定; *ketsuron* 結論 A conclusion was reached. *Ketsuron ga de'ta.* 結論が出た. No conclusion was reached. *Ke-tsuron wa de'nakatta.* 結論は出なかった.

conclusive *ketteiteki* [*na*] 決定的[な] ——(attr) *tettei-shita* 徹底した a conclusive argument *tettei-shita gi'ron* 徹底した議論

concrete 1 (building material) *konkuri'to* コンクリート 2 actual *gutaiteki* [*na*] 具体的[な] concrete plans *gutaiteki na keikaku* 具体的な計画

condemn ind-obj *ni*, obj *o* (irr) *senkoku-suru* 宣告する ——obj *o* (irr) *hinan-suru* 非難する

condition 1 provision *jōke'n* 条件 2 state *jōtai* 状態 3 circum-stances; physical condition *guai* 具合 My physical condition's not good. *Karada no guai ga yo'ku na'i.* 体の具合がよくない.

condolence *o-kuyami* お悔やみ

condom *suki'n* スキン; *kondo'mu* コンドーム

conductor 1 (orchestra) *shiki'sha* 指揮者 2 (train) *shashō* 車掌

confer ind-obj *ni*, obj *o* (irr) *sōdan-suru* 相談する confer with a lawyer *bengo'shi ni sōdan-suru* 弁護士に相談する

conference *kaigi* 会議

confess ind-obj *ni*, obj *o* (irr) 1 *ha'kujō-suru* 白状する The child confessed that he had stolen the money. *Kodomo wa sono o-kane o* *nusunda koto'o ha'kujō-shita.* 子供はそのお金を盗んだことを白状した. **2** (Leg) *jikyō-suru* 自供する The criminal confessed. *Ha'nnin wa jikyō-shita.* 犯人は自供した.

confession 1 *ha'kujō* 白状 **2** (Leg) *jikyō* 自供

confidence 1 *shin'yō* 信用; *shinrai* 信頼 **2** self-confidence *jishin* 自信 ——obj *o* (irr) have confidence in *shin'yō-suru* 信用する; *shinrai-suru* 信頼する I have confidence in that person. *Ano'hito o shinrai-suru.* あの人を信頼する.

confirm obj *o* (irr) *kakunin-suru* 確認する

confirmation 1 *kakunin* 確認 **2** confirmation ceremony (Cath) *kenshin no hiseki* 堅信の秘跡; (Prot) *kenshi'nrei* 堅信礼

conflict 1 clash *kuichigai* 食い違い, **2** strife *tōsō* 闘争 ——comp *to* (v) be contrary to *kuichiga·u* 食い違う My idea conflicts with his. *Watashi no kanga'e wa ka're no to kuichigatte iru.* 私の考えは彼のと食い違っている. **2** battle with (irr) *tōsō-suru* 闘争する

confront (v) *muka·u* 向かう confront face-to-face *men to mukau* 面と向かう

confrontation *tairitsu* 対立

Confucianism *Ju'kyō* 儒教

Confucius *Kōshi* 孔子

confuse comp *to*, obj *o* (irr) *kondō-suru* 混同する confuse rights with obligations *ke'nri to gi'mu o kondō-suru* 権利と義務を混同する ——(caus) *konran-sase·ru* 混乱させる confuse the situation *keisei o konran-saseru* 形勢を混乱させる

confused (v) be confused *awate·ru* あわてる She was confused as to what to do. *Ka'nojo wa dō shiyo' ka to awateta.* 彼女はどうしようかとあわてた.; *magotsuk·u* まごつく I was confused by all the questions. *Iroiro na shitsumon ni magotsu'ita.* 色々な質問にまごついた.

confusedly *awatete* あわてて

confusion 1 mix-up *kondō* 混同 **2** disorder *konran* 混乱

congratulate (idiom) *iwai o i·u* 祝いを言う I congratulate you. *O-iwai o mōshi-agema'su.* お祝いを申し上げます.

Congratulations! *Omedetō gozaima'su!* おめでとうございます.

Congress (W) *Kokkai* 国会

congressman *gi'in* 議員

connect obj *o* (v) *tsunag·u* つなぐ connect line A to line B *A-sen o B-sen ni tsunagu* A 線を B 線につなぐ

connection 1 *sesshoku* 接触 The electrical connection is bad. *De'nki no sesshoku ga waru'i.* 電気の接触が悪い. **2** contact *renraku* 連絡 **3** personal contact *ko'ne* コネ One needs connections. *Ko'ne ga hitsuyō de'su.* コネが必要です.

connotation *nyu'ansu* ニュアンス; (Tech) *naihōteki i'mi* 内包的意味

conquer obj *o* (irr) *seifuku-suru* 征服する

conscience *ryó'shin* 良心

conscientious *ryōshinteki* [na] 良心的[な] He is a conscientious person. *Ka're wa ryōshinteki na hito' desu.* 彼は良心的な人です。

conscientiously *ryōshinteki'ni* 良心的に work conscientiously *ryōshinteki ni hataraku* 良心的に働く

conscious obj *o* (irr) be conscious of *i'shiki-suru* 意識する ——compl *ni* (v) notice *kizu'k·u* 気づく I wasn't conscious of that. *Sore ni kizuka'nakatta.* それに気づかなかった。 ——(idiom) be conscious *i'shiki ga a'r·u* 意識がある Is he conscious? *Ka're wa ishiki ga arima'su ka?* 彼は意識がありますか。

consciousness *i'shiki* 意識 ——(idiom) lose consciousness *ki o ushina·u* 気を失う

consensus *dōi* 同意；*gōi* 合意

consent *shōchi* 承知 ——(irr) consent to *shōchi-suru* 承知する； ——compl *ni* (irr) *dōi-suru* 同意する

consequence *kekka* 結果

consequently *shitagatte* 従って *see also* therefore

conservation *hozon* 保存; energy conservation *shō-ene'* [*rugī*] 省エネ[ルギー]

conservatism *hoshushu'gi* 保守主義

conservative 1 not liberal *hoshuteki* [na] 保守的[な] That person is conservative. *Ano' hito wa hoshuteki de'su.* あの人は保守的です。 2 subdued *jimi'* [na] 地味[な] a conservative color *jimi'na iro'* 地味な色

Conservative Party *Hoshu-tō* 保守党

conserve obj *o* (irr) *hozon-suru* 保存する

consider obj *o* (v) *kangae'·ru* 考える 2 deliberate (irr) *kō'ryo-suru* 考慮する ——(caus) *kangaesase'·ru* 考えさせる Let me consider it a bit. *Suko'shi kangaesa'sete kudasa'i.* 少し考えさせて下さい。 3 consider to do/be . . . *to kangae'·ru* . . . と考える I consider him to be fair. *Watashi wa ka're ga kōhei da to kanga'ete iru.* 私は彼が公平だと考えている。

consideration *kō'ryo* 考慮 take into consideration *kō'ryo ni ireru* 考慮に入れる

consign ind-obj *ni*, obj *o* (irr) *itaku-suru* 委託する consign goods to an agent *shinamono o dairinin ni itaku-suru* 品物を代理人に委託する

consistent be consistent (irr) *i'tchi-suru* 一致する；*ikkan-suru* 一貫する His logic is consistent. *Ka're no ro'nri wa shu'bi ikkan-shite iru.* 彼の論理は首尾一貫している。 ——(idiom) without contradictions *mujun no na'i* 矛盾のない

consolation *nagusame* 慰め

console obj *o* (v) *nagusame'·ru* 慰める There's no way to console her. *Ka'nojo wa nagusameyō' ga na'i.* 彼女は慰めようがない.

consort 1 (mate) *haigū'sha* 配偶者 2 (empress) *kōgō'* 皇后

conspicuous (v) be conspicuous *medа'ts·u* 目立つ I put it where it wouldn't be conspicuous. *Sore o medata'nai toko'ro ni oita.* それを目立たない所に置いた.

constant *taema* [*no*] *na'i* 絶え間[の]ない; *tsu'ne* [*no*] 常[の]; *kawaranai* 変らない Racial discrimination is a constant problem, occurring in every period of history. *Do'no jidai de'mo, jinshu sa'betsu wa kawaranai mondai de'su.* どの時代でも人種差別は変わらない問題です.

constantly *tsu'ne ni* 常に As she's constantly saying ... *Ka'nojo ga tsu'ne ni itte iru yō'ni ...* 彼女が常に言ってるように ...

constipated (irr) be constipated *bempi-suru* 便秘する I'm constipated. *Bempi-shite iru.* 便秘している.

constipation *bempi* 便秘

constitution 1 (document) *ke'mpō* 憲法 2 (physical) *taishitsu* 体質 He was born with a delicate constitution. *Ka're wa umaretsuki kayowa'i taishitsu desu.* 彼は生まれつきか弱い体質です.

construction 1 building *kensetsu* 建設 2 structure; framework *kumitate* 組み立て 3 construction work *kō'ji* 工事 under construction *kōji-chū* 工事中 4 construction company *kenchiku-ga'-isha* 建築会社

consul *ryō'ji* 領事

consulate *ryōji'kan* 領事館

consult ind-obj *ni*, obj *o* (irr) *sōdan-suru* 相談する I'll consult with him about that. *Sono koto' ni tsu'ite, ka're ni sōdan-suru.* その事について彼に相談する.

consultant *ko'mon* 顧問; *komo'n-yaku* 顧問役; *sōdan-yaku* 相談役

consultation *sōdan* 相談

contact (irr) 1 come into contact with *sesshoku-suru* 接触する 2 contact a person *renraku-suru* 連絡する

contact lens *kontakuto re'nzu* コンタクトレンズ

contagious *densensei* [*no*] 伝染性[の] contagious disease *densembyō* 伝染病

container 1 *iremono* 入れ物; *yō'ki* 容器 2 (for freight) *konte'na* [*sha*] コンテナ[車]

contemporary (attr) *onaji se'dai* [*no*] 同じ世代[の]; *tōdai* [*no*] 当代 [の] *see also* modern

content (satisfied) compl *ni* (irr) *ma'nzoku-suru* 満足する Are you content with that? *Sore ni ma'nzoku-shite ima'su ka?* それに満足していますか.

contents 1 *naka'mi* 中身 2 *naiyō* 内容 the contents of a letter *tegami no naiyō* 手紙の内容 3 (table of contents) *mokuji* 目次

contest *ko'ntesuto* コンテスト; *konkū'ru* コンクール
continue (v) *tsuzuk·u* 続く How long will it continue? *I'tsu made tsuzukima'su ka?* いつまで続きますか. ——obj o (v) 1 *tsuzuke'ru* 続ける Please continue it. *Dō'zo sore o tsuzukete kudasa'i.* どうぞそれを続けて下さい. 2 continue (doing) *-tsuzuke'·ru* 続ける continue running *hashiri-tsuzuke'ru* 走り続ける Continue reading, please. *Dō'zo yomi-tsuzuke'te kudasa'i.* どうぞ読み続けて下さい.
contraceptive 1 contraceptive device *hiningu* 避妊具 2 birth control pill *keikō hini'nyaku* 経口避妊薬
contract *keiyaku* 契約 make a contract *keiyaku o musubu* 契約を結ぶ ——obj o (irr) *keiyaku-suru* 契約する
contradict (irr) *mujun-suru* 矛盾する That contradicts what the newspaper article said. *Sore wa shimbun-ki'ji to mujun-shite iru.* それは新聞記事と矛盾している.
contradiction *mujun* 矛盾 Her words were full of contradictions. *Ka'nojo no hanashi' wa mujun-da'rake deshita.* 彼女の話は矛盾だらけでした.
contrary compl *ni* (irr) be contrary to *hansu'ru* 反する contrary to one's expectations *kitai ni hansu'ru* 期待に反する ——(adv) on the contrary *sore do'koro ka* それどころか
contrast *taishō* 対照 ——comp *to*, ind-obj *ni*, obj o (irr) *taishō-suru* 対照する when one contrasts A with B … *A o B to taishō-shite mi'ru to …* AをBと対照してみると…; *taisu'ru* 対する literary style contrasted with colloquial style *kōgotai ni taisu'ru bungotai* 口語体に対する文語体
contrastive *taishōteki* [na] 対照的[な]
contrastively *taishōteki ni* 対照的に
contribution 1 *kōken* 貢献 2 (community) service *hō'shi* 奉仕 3 (money) *kifu'kin* 寄付金
control 1 rule *shi'hai* 支配 2 regulation *tōsei* 統制 ——obj o (irr) 1 rule *shi'hai-suru* 支配する 2 regulate *tōsei-suru* 統制する
controlled economy *tōsei kei'zai* 統制経済
controversy *ronsō* 論争
convenient 1 handy *be'nri* [na] 便利[な] a convenient kitchen *be'nri na daidokoro* 便利な台所 2 suitable *tsugō ga i'i* 都合がいい a convenient day *tsugō ga i'i hi* 都合がいい日 Is tomorrow convenient for you? *Ashita' wa go-tsugō ga i'i desu ka* 明日は御都合がいいですか.
convent *jo'shi shūdō'in* 女子修道院
convention 1 meeting *taikai* 大会 2 general convention *sōkai* 総会 3 custom *shūkan* 習慣
conversation 1 *kaiwa* 会話 English conversation *Ei-ka'iwa* 英会話 2 informal conversation *zatsudan* 雑談; *danwa* 談話

converse comp *to* (irr) *kaiwa-suru* 会話する; *zatsudan-suru* 雑談する

conversion 1 transformation *tenkan* 転換 2 (monetary) *ryōgae* 両替 3 (Budd) awakening *hosshin* 発心 4 change of denomination/religion *kaishū* 改宗 5 (political) *tenkō* 転向

convict 1 (offender) *zainin* 罪人 2 (one serving time) *chōekinin* 懲役人 ——(idiom) *yūzai ni sho'su* 有罪に処す

convince compl *ni* (irr) *nattoku-suru* 納得する I was convinced of it. *Watashi wa sore ni nattoku-shita.* 私はそれに納得した. ——(caus) *nattoku-sase·ru* 納得させる Do you think you can convince him? *Ka're o nattoku-saseru koto' ga deki'ru to omoima'su ka?* 彼を納得させることができると思いますか.

cook *ko'kku-san* コックさん; *ryōrinin* 料理人 ——ind-obj *ni*, obj *o* (irr) *ryō'ri-suru* 料理する; (v) *tsuku'r·u* 作る cook a meal *go'han o tsuku'ru* ご飯を作る 3 cook rice *go'han o tak·u* ご飯を炊く *see also* bake; boil; broil; fry; roast

cookie *ku'kkī* クッキー

cool (adj) *suzushi'·i* 涼しい This house is cool, even in summer. *Kono uchi' wa natsu de'mo suzushi'i.* この家は夏でも涼しい. ——obj *o* (irr) *sama's·u* 冷ます Give the milk to the baby after cooling it a bit. *Sono mi'ruku wa suko'shi sama'shite kara a'kachan ni nomase-nasa'i.* そのミルクは少し冷ましてから赤ちゃんに飲ませなさい.

cooperate compl *ni* (irr) *kyōryoku-suru* 協力する

cooperation *kyōryoku* 協力

copper *dō'* 銅

copperplate *dōban-zuri* 銅版刷り

copy *ko'pī* コピー; *utsushi* 写し; *fukusha* 複写 ——obj *o* (irr) *ko'pī-suru* コピーする; (v) *utsu's·u* 写す *see also* imitate

coral *sa'ngo* 珊瑚

cord 1 *tsuna* 綱 2 rope *nawa'* 縄 3 string *himo* 紐 4 telephone cord *kō'do* コード

corduroy *kōruten* コールテン; *kōju'roi* コージュロイ

core *shi'n* 芯 core of an apple *ringo no shi'n* りんごの芯 rotten to the core *shi'n made kusa'tte iru* 芯まで腐っている *see also* center; heart

cork *ko'ruku* コルク

corkscrew *koruku-nu'ki* コルク抜き

corn (plant; ear) *tōmo'rokoshi* とうもろこし

corner 1 (of a room) *su'mi* すみ 2 (at a street intersection) *ka'do* 角 3 (of a table) *hashi/haji* 端

cornet *korune'tto* コルネット

corn soup *kōn sū'pu* コーンスープ

cornstarch *kōnsutā'chi* コーンスターチ

corporal (military) *go′chō* 伍長

corporation 1 (Leg) *shadan hō′jin* 社団法人 2 (limited) *yūgen-ga′isha* 有限会社 3 (stock) *kabushiki-ga′isha* 株式会社

corpse *shitai* 死体

correct *seikaku* [na] 正確[な] Is this clock correct? *Kono tokei wa seikaku de′su ka?* この時計は正確ですか. ——(adj) *tadashi′·i* 正しい ——obj *o* (v) *nao′s·u* 直す correct a mistake *machiga′i o nao′su* 間違いを直す

correspond to compl *ni* (irr) *sōtō-suru* 相当する There is no English to correspond to that word. *Sono kotoba′ ni sōtō-suru Ei-go wa na′i.* その言葉に相当する英語はない.

correspondence (written) *tsūshin* 通信 ; *buntsū* 文通

corruption 1 (business; political) *baishū* 買収 2 (personal) *da′raku* 堕落

cosmetics *keshō* [-hin] 化粧[品]

cost 1 price *nedan* 値段 2 expense *hi′yō* 費用 ——(idiom) high costs *bukka′daka* 物価高

costly (adj) *taka′·i* 高い costly perfume *taka′i kōsui* 高い香水

costume *fukusō* 服装

cottage (for vacationing) *bessō′* 別荘

cotton 1 *momen* 木綿; cotton fabric *me′n* 綿 2 raw cotton *wata* 綿 cotton field *wata-ba′take* 綿畑 3 absorbent cotton *dasshi′men* 脱脂綿

couch *naga-isu* 長いす ; *so′fā* ソファー

cough *seki′* 咳 ——(idiom) to cough *seki′ ga de′·ru* 咳が出る I coughed all night. *Hitoban-jū seki′ ga de′ta.* 一晩中咳が出た.

council 1 *kyō′gi* 協議 2 city council *shigikai* 市議会

counselor *ka′unserā* カウンセラー

count (title) *hakushaku* 伯爵 ——obj *o* (v) *kazoe′·ru* 数える Count (them) and see! *Kazo′ete goran!* 数えてごらん.

counter (for the display and sale of goods) *uriba* 売り場

counterfeit *nisemono* にせもの

countermeasure *taisaku* 対策

country 1 nation *kuni* 国 2 rural area *inaka* 田舎

country bumpkin *inakamono* 田舎者

country music *ka′ntorī* カントリー

couple (husband and wife) *fū′fu* 夫婦

courage *do′kyō* 度胸 muster courage *do′kyō o sueru* 度胸をすえる

course (academic study) *kamoku* 課目 ; *kō′su* コース

court (Leg) *saibansho* 裁判所 Supreme Court *Saikō Saibansho* 最高裁判所

courtesy *reigi′* 礼儀

cousin 1 (one's own) *ito′ko* いとこ 2 (another's) *o-itoko-san* おいとこさん

cover 1 lid *futa* ふた 2 bedcover (comforter) *futon* 蒲団; *kakebu′ton* 掛け蒲団 ——obj *o* (v) *kabuse′·ru* かぶせる cover with dirt *tsuchi o kabuse′ru* 土をかぶせる ——(idiom) put a lid on *futa o suru* ふたをする

cow *ushi* 牛 dairy cow *nyūgyū* 乳牛

coward *yowa′mushi* 弱虫 You coward! *Yowa′mushi!* 弱虫.

cowardly *okubyō′* [*na*] 臆病[な] a cowardly person *okubyō′ na hito* 臆病な人

co-worker *dōryō* 同僚

crab *kani* 蟹

crabby *iji′waru* [*na*] いじわる[な] a crabby person *iji′waru na hito* いじわるな人 ——(idiom) be crabby *iji′waru o suru* いじわるをする Don't be crabby! *Iji′waru o shina′ide!* いじわるをしないで.

crabs (Pithirius pubis) *kejira′mi* 毛じらみ

crack *hibi* ひび ——obj *o* (v) *war·u* 割る crack an egg *tama′go o waru* 卵を割る

cracker *kura′kkā* クラッカー

cradle *yurikago* 揺りかご

cramp (muscular) *keiren* けいれん get a cramp *keiren o oko′su* けいれんを起す

cramped *kyū′kutsu* [*na*] 窮屈[な] Five people riding in a small car would be cramped. *Kogata-sha ni gonin noru to, kyū′kutsu de-shō′.* 小型車に5人乗ると窮屈でしょう.

crane 1 (bird) *tsu′ru* 鶴 2 (machine) *kurē′n* クレーン

craving *yokkyū* 欲求

crawl (v) *ha′·u* 這う Is your baby already crawling? *Ana′ta no a′kachan wa mō′ achi′kochi ha′tte ikima′su ka?* あなたの赤ちゃんはもうあちこち這って行きますか. ——(idiom) creep *yotsumbai ni na′r·u* 四つん這いになる

crawl (swimming stroke) *kurō′ru* クロール

crazy a crazy person *kichiga′i* 気違い ——(idiom) 1 be/become crazy *kichiga′i ni na′ru* 気違いになる; *ki ga kuru′·u* 気が狂う She's crazy! *Ka′nojo wa ki ga kuru′tte iru.* 彼女は気が狂っている. 2 fanatic about -*ki′chigai* 気違い, I'm crazy about Bach. *Watashi wa Bahha-ki′chigai desu.* 私はバッハ気違いです.

cream *kuri′mu* クリーム fresh cream *nama kuri′mu* 生クリーム sour cream *sawā kuri′mu* サワークリーム

creator *sōzō′sha* 創造者

credit 1 credit account *kashikata ka′njō* 貸方勘定 2 (installment payment plan) *kure′jitto* クレジット 3 unit of academic credit *ta′n·i* 単位

credit card *kurejitto kā′do* クレジットカード

creditor *kashikata* 貸方

creep *see* crawl

cremate (idiom) *kasō ni suru* 火葬にする
cremation *kasō* 火葬
crematory *kasōba* 火葬場
crepe 1 (J) *chirimen* ちりめん 2 (W) *kurḗpu* クレープ
crew *norikumi'in* 乗り組み員
crib (for a baby) *bebī-bé'ddo* ベビーベッド
cribbage *kuribḗji* クリベージ
crime 1 *tsu'mi* 罪 2 criminal offense *hanzai* 犯罪 3 violation of
a law or regulation *ihan* 違反
criminal (person) *ha'nnin* 犯人
crimson *kurenai* [-iro] 紅[色]
crippled *bi'kko* [no] びっこ[の] ——(idiom) 1 be crippled *bi'kko
o hik·u* びっこをひく 2 a crippled person *ashi no fu'jiyū na hito*
足の不自由な人
crisis *ki'ki* 危機
crisp (attr) *ka'rikari-shita* かりかりした; *pa'ripari-shita* ぱりぱり
した
critic 1 *hihyōka* 批評家   2 *hyōronka* 評論家 art critic *geijutsu
hyōronka* 芸術評論家; drama critic *engeki hyōronka* 演劇評論家;
music critic *ongaku hyōronka* 音楽評論家; literary critic *bungei
hyōronka* 文芸評論家
critical 1 censorious *hihanteki* [na] 批判的[な] a critical attitude
hihanteki na ta'ido 批判的な態度 2 crucial *da'iji* [na] 大事[な] a
critical decision *da'iji na ke'tsugi* 大事な決議
criticism 1 objective criticism *hihyō* 批評; subjective criticism
shukanteki na hihyō 主観的な批評; positive criticism *kōteiteki na
hihyō* 肯定的な批評; art criticism *geijutsu hi'hyō* 芸術批評; drama
criticism *engeki hi'hyō* 演劇批評; literary criticism *bungei hi'hyō*
文芸批評; music criticism *ongaku hi'hyō* 音楽批評 2 negative
criticism *hihan* 批判
criticize obj *o* (irr) 1 (objectively) *hihyō-suru* 批評する 2 (nega-
tively) *hihan-suru* 批判する
critique *hyōron* 評論 *see also* criticism
crooked bogus *i'nchiki* [na] いんちき[な] a crooked company *i'n-
chiki na kaisha* いんちきな会社 ——(attr) bent *magatta* 曲がっ
た a crooked stick *magatta bō* 曲がった棒
crop (harvest) *shūkaku* 収穫
cross *jūji* 十字 Red Cross *Seki-jū'ji* 赤十字; (Chr) *jūjika* 十字架
——loc *o* (v) cross over *watar·u* 渡る cross a bridge *hashi'o wataru*
橋を渡る 2 cut across *yokogi'r·u* 横切る cross the playing field
gurraundo o yokogi'ru グラウンドを横切る *see also* crucifix
crossing 1 railroad crossing *fumikiri* 踏み切り 2 street intersection *kōsa'ten* 交差点 3 pedestrian crossing *ōdan ho'dō* 横断歩道
crossroads *jūji'ro* 十字路

crotch *mata'* また

crow (bird) *ka'rasu* 烏 ——(v) *nak·u* 鳴く A rooster crows cock-a-doodle-doo. *O'ndori wa koke'kokkō to naku.* 雄鶏はコケコッコーと鳴く.

crowd (of people) *hitogomi* 人ごみ ——(v) be crowded *ko'm·u* 込む The train's crowded. *Densha ga ko'nde iru.* 電車が込んでいる.

crown (headdress) *kammuri* 冠

crown prince *kōta'ishi* 皇太子 *see also* prince

crown princess *kōtaishi'hi* 皇太子妃 *see also* princess

crucial *jūdai* 重大[な]; *ketteiteki* [na] 決定的[な]

crucifix (cross of Christ) *Kirisuto no jūjika* キリストの十字架

crude *zonza'i* [na] ぞんざい[な]

cruel *zankoku* [na] 残酷[な]

cruelty *zankoku* 残酷

crumb 1 *panku'zu* パンくず; 2 bread crumbs *panko* パン粉

crush obj *o* (v) *tsubus·u* つぶす crush grapes *budō o tsubusu* ぶどうをつぶす ——(v) be crushed *tsubure·ru* つぶれる The house was crushed in the earthquake. *Ie' wa jishin de tsubureta.* 家は地震でつぶれた.

crust (of baked goods) *kawa'* 皮 piecrust *pai-gawa* パイ皮

crutch *matsuba-zu'e* 松葉杖

cry 1 *naki-go'e* 泣き声 2 shout *sakebi-go'e* 叫び声 ——(v) 1 shed tears *nak·u* 泣く The baby's crying. *A'kachan ga naite iru.* 赤ちゃんが泣いている. Don't cry! *Nakana'ide!* 泣かないで. 2 cry out; shout *sake'b·u* 叫ぶ Someone's crying out! *Da'reka ga sake'nde iru.* だれかが叫んでいる. ——(idiom) shed tears *na'mida o naga's·u* 涙を流す

crystal 1 *su'ishō* 水晶 a crystal formation *su'ishō no kesshō* [tai] 水晶の結晶[体] 2 (tableware) *kurisutaru ga'rasu* クリスタルガラス

Cuba *Kyū'ba* キューバ

Cuban (person) *Kyūba'jin* キューバ人 ——(attr) *Kyū'ba no* キューバの

cube 1 (Geom) *rippōtai* 立方体 2 (Math) *sanjō* 三乗

cuckoo *ka'kkō* かっこう

cucumber *kyū'ri* きゅうり

cue 1 *hi'nto* ヒント; *anji* 暗示 2 signal in a play *a'izu* 合図 3 billiard cue *kyū* キュー

cuff (clothing) *sode-guchi* 袖口; *ka'fusu* カフス

cuisine 1 *ryō'ri* 料理 2 (W) *seiyō ryō'ri* 西洋料理 3 (J) *washoku* 和食

cultivate (a field) obj *o* (v) *tagaya's·u* 耕す

culturally *bunkateki ni* 文化的に

culture (of a given people) *bu'nka* 文化

cultured (educated) (attr) *kyōyō no a′ru* 教養のある

cultured pearls *yōshoku shi′nju* 養殖真珠

cup **1** *chawan* 茶碗; coffee cup *kōhī-ja′wan* コーヒー茶碗; teacup (W) *kōcha-ja′wan* 紅茶茶碗; (J) *yunomi* 湯飲み   **2** measuring cup *keiryō ka′ppu* 計量カップ   **3** one cup of *i′ppai* 一杯 *see also* Appendix 1: glassfuls

cure (treatment) *chiryō* 治療   ——(v) be cured *nao′r·u* 治る I'm cured! *Byōki ga nao′tta!* 病気が治った.   ——obj *o* (v) remedy *nao′s·u* 治す cure a disease *byōki o nao′su* 病気を治す

curfew *monge′n* 門限

curiosity *kōki′shin* 好奇心 have curiosity *kōki′shin o mo′tsu* 好奇心を持つ

curious (idiom) *kōki′shin ga a′ru* 好奇心がある I'm curious. *Watashi wa kōki′shin ga a′ru.* 私は好奇心がある.

curl *makige* 巻き毛   ——obj *o* (v) *chijira′s·u* 縮らす   ——(v) *chijire′r·u* 縮れる

curly (attr) *chijire′ta* 縮れた

currency *tsū′ka* 通貨; *ka′hei* 貨幣

current **1** (of a stream, etc.) *nagare* 流れ   **2** contemporary *ge′nzai no* 現在の

curriculum vitae *rirekisho* 履歴書

curry (stew) *karē* カレー curry with rice *karē-ra′isu* カレーライス

curse (hex) *noroi* 呪い   ——obj *o* (v) **1** blaspheme *nonoshi′r·u* ののしる **2** put a curse on *noro′·u* 呪う   ——(idiom) swear *akuta′i o tsuk·u* 悪態をつく

curse word *akuta′i* 悪態

curtain **1** drapes *kā′ten* カーテン   **2** (theater) *maku* 幕   ——(idiom) curtain time *kaimaku* 開幕

curve *kā′bu* カーブ

cushion **1** (J) *zabu′ton* 座ぶとん   **2** (W) *ku′sshon* クッション

custom (social convention) **1** *shūkan* 習慣 Japanese customs *Niho′n no shūkan* 日本の習慣   **2** usual practice *kanrei* 慣例 according to custom *kanrei ni shitagatte* 慣例に従って

customer *kyaku* 客; *o-kyaku-san* お客さん

customhouse *zeikan* 税関

customs *zeikan* 税関; (tax) *kanzei* 関税 How much (in) customs did you have to pay? *Kanzei wa i′kura harawana′kute wa narimase′n deshita ka?* 関税はいくら払わなくてはなりませんでしたか

cut haircut *sampatsu* 散髪; *ka′tto* カット   ——obj *o* (v) **1** *ki′r·u* 切る cut with a knife *na′ifu de ki′ru* ナイフで切る   **2** cut grass [*kusa o*] *kar·u* [草を]刈る   **3** cut hair (irr) *sampatsu-suru* 散髪する   **4** cut (school) [*gakkō o*] *sabo′r·u* [学校を]さぼる   **5** delete (irr) *shōryaku-suru* 省略する   **6** cut across *yokogi′r·u* 横切る   ——(v) able to cut *kire'·ru* 切れる This knife cuts well. *Kono na'ifu wa yo'ku kire'ru.* このナイフはよく切れる.

cute (adj) *kawai'·i* 可愛い

cylinder *shi'rindā* シリンダー

cynical *hiniku* [*na*] 皮肉[な]

cynicism *hiniku* 皮肉

cypress *ito'sugi* 糸杉; (J) *hinoki* 檜

cyst *hōnō* 包嚢

Czech *see* Czechoslovakian

Czechoslovakia *Che'kosurobakia* チェコスロバキア; *Che'ko* チェコ

Czechoslovakian 1 (language) *Che'kosurobakia-go* チェコスロバキア語 2 (person) *Chekosurobakia'jin* チェコスロバキア人; *Cheko'-jin* チェコ人 ——(attr) *Che'kosurobakia no* チェコスロバキアの

D

dad *pa'pa* パパ *see also* father; father-in-law

daffodil *rappa-zu'isen* ラッパ水仙

dahlia *da'riya* ダリヤ

daily *ma'inichi* [*no*] 毎日[の] daily schedule *ma'inichi no suke'jūru* 毎日のスケジュール; *nichijō* [*no*] 日常[の] daily life *nichijō se'ikatsu* 日常生活

dainty *koma'yaka* [*na*] こまやか[な]

dairy farm *rakunōjō* 酪農場

dairyman *rakunōka* 酪農家

dairy products *nyūse'ihin* 乳製品

daisy *hina'-giku* 雛菊; *furansu'-giku* フランス菊

dam *da'mu* ダム ——obj *o* (v) *sekitome'·ru* せきとめる

damage *hi'gai* 被害 ——ind-obj *ni*, obj *o* (v) *kizutsuke'·ru* 傷つける damage one's reputation *me'iyo o kizutsuke'ru* 名誉を傷つける ——(idiom) be/become damaged *kizu ga tsu'k·u* 傷がつく These goods are damaged. *Kono shinamono wa kizu ga tsu'ite iru.* この品物は傷がついている.

damascene (inlay) *zōgan* 象眼

damask *damasuku-ori* ダマスク織り; *aya-ori* 綾織り

damn *chikushō* 畜生 ——obj *o* (v) *noro'·u* 呪う

damp (v) be/become damp *shimer·u* 湿る The plants in the garden are damp from the dew. *Niwa no kusa'ki wa tsu'yu de shimette iru.* 庭の草木は露で湿っている. ——(attr) *shimetta* 湿った a damp towel *shimetta tenugui* 湿った手拭い

dance 1 *odori* 踊り 2 (J) *Nihon-bu'yō* 日本舞踊 3 Japanese clas-

sical dance *mai* 舞　**4** (W) *da'nsu* ダンス　——obj *o* (v) *odor·u*
踊る; (irr) *da'nsu-suru* ダンスする

dandelion *ta'mpopo* たんぽぽ

dandruff *fuke* ふけ

Dane *Demmāku'jin* デンマーク人

danger *kiken* 危険

dangerous *kiken* [*na*] 危険[な] a dangerous place *kiken na tokoro'*
危険な所　——(adj) *abuna·i* 危ない It's dangerous. *Abunai'.* 危な
い.

Danish (language) *Demmāku-go* デンマーク語　——(attr) *Dem-*
mā'ku no デンマークの

dare *see* challenge

daring *daita'n* [*na*] 大胆[な]

dark (adj) *kura·i* 暗い　——(v) be/become dark *kure·ru* 暮れる
It's become dark. *Hi ga kureta.* 日が暮れた.

darn obj *o* (v) *tsukuro'·u* 繕う

dash **1** short race *tankyori kyō'sō* 短距離競走　**2** the mark "—"
da'sshu ダッシュ

data *shi'ryō* 資料

date **1** engagement *dē'to* デート　**2** the day on which something
occurs *hizuke* 日付け What is the date of the meeting? *Ka'igi no*
hizuke wa i'tsu desu ka? 会議の日付けはいつですか.; *ni'chiji* 日時
Let me know the date. *Ni'chiji o oshiete kudasa'i.* 日時を教えて
下さい.　**3** day of the month [*hi-*]*nichi* [日]にち What is the date
today? *Kyō' wa na'nnichi desu ka?* 今日は何日ですか.　**4** (fruit)
natsume' [*yashi*] 棗[椰子]　——comp *to* (irr) have a date with
(someone) *dē'to-suru* デートする

daughter **1** (one's own) *musume'* 娘　**2** (another's) *o-jō'-san* お嬢
さん

daughter-in-law **1** (one's own) *yome* 嫁　**2** (another's) *o-yome-san*
お嫁さん

dawn *yoake* 夜明け It's dawn. *Yoake de'su.* 夜明けです.

day **1** *hi* 日　**2** all day *ichinichi-jū'* 一日中　**3** every day *ma'inichi*
毎日　**4** once a day *ichinichi ikka'i* 一日一回　**5** day before yesterday *ototo'i* おととい　**6** day after tomorrow *asa'tte* あさって　**7**
one day *ichinichi* 一日

daydream *hakujitsu-mu* 白日夢　——(irr) *bon'ya'ri-suru* ぼんやり
する

daylight **1** *chūkō* 昼光　**2** sunlight *ni'kkō* 日光

daytime *hiruma* 昼間

daze (irr) be in a daze *bōtto-suru* ぼうっとする I was in a daze.
Watashi wa bōtto-shite ita. 私はぼうっとしていた.

dazzling (adj) *mabushi'·i* 眩しい

DC, D.C., d.c. *see* direct current

deacon (Prot) *shitsu'ji* 執事

dead (attr) *shinda* 死んだ a dead cat *shinda ne'ko* 死んだ猫

deadline *shimekiri* 締め切り

deadlock *yukizumari* 行き詰まり a break in the deadlock *yukizumari no dakai* 行き詰まりの打開

deaf (attr) *mimi no kikoenai* [*hito'*] 耳の聞こえない[人] ——(idiom) hard of hearing *mimi ga tō·i* 耳が遠い

deaf-mute *rō'a* ろうあ; *rōa'sha* ろうあ者

deal (cards) ind-obj *ni*, obj *o* (v) *kuba'r·u* 配る

dealer 1 (retail) *ko-uri'shō* 小売商 2 (wholesale) *oroshi'shō* 卸商

dean (of a university) *gakubu'chō* 学部長

dear *shin'ai na* 親愛な ——(adj) *itoshi'·i* 愛しい

death *shi'* 死 death penalty *shike'i* 死刑 natural death *rōsu'ishi* 老衰死

deathbed *rinjū no toko* 臨終の床 He gave his last wish on his deathbed. *Ka're wa rinjū no toko de yuigon o tsuta'eta.* 彼は臨終の床で遺言を伝えた.

debate *tō'ron* 討論 ——obj *o* (irr) *tō'ron-suru* 討論する

debit *karikata* 借方

debris *ku'zu* 屑

debt *shakki'n* 借金

debtor *karikata* 借方; *karinushi* 借り主

decade *jūne'nkan* 十年間

decadence *taihai* 退廃

decadent *taihaiteki* [*na*] 退廃的[な] ——(irr) be/become decadent *taihai-suru* 退廃する

decay (v) 1 rot *kusa'r·u* 腐る 2 deteriorate *otoroe'·ru* 衰える

deceased (the) *shi'sha* 死者; *shibō'sha* 死亡者

deceit *gomakashi* ごまかし

deceitful (adj) *zuru'·i* ずるい

deceive obj *o* (v) 1 *azamu'k·u* 欺く 2 cheat *dama's·u* だます ——(pass) *damasare'·ru* だまされる I was deceived by him. *Watashi wa ka're ni damasa'reta.* 私は彼にだまされた.

December *jūnigatsu* 十二月 December 12 *jūnigatsu juni'nichi* 十二月十二日

decent (adj) *migurushiku na'·i* 見苦しくない I haven't a single decent dress to wear. *Migurushiku na'i fuku o itchaku mo mo'tte ina'i.* 見苦しくない服を一着も持っていない.

deception 1 deceit *gomakashi* ごまかし 2 cheating *manchaku* まん着 3 fraud *sa'gi* 詐欺

decide obj *o* (v) 1 *kime'·ru* 決める decide on the date *hidori o kimeru* 日取りを決める; (irr) *kettei-suru* 決定する We have not yet decided the matter. *Sono ke'n ni ka'nshite wa mada kettei-shite ina'i.* その件に関してはまだ決定していない. ——(v) be decided *kimar·u* 決まる When was it decided? *I′tsu kimarima′shita ka?* いつ決まりましたか. ——(idiom) decide to do (something) ... *koto′ ni suru* ...ことにする I decided to buy that dress. *Sono do′resu o kau koto′ ni shita.* そのドレスを買うことにした.

deciduous   *datsurakusei [no]* 脱落性[の]

decimal   *jusshin* 十進; *jusshi′nhō* 十進法

decimal point   *shōsū′ ten* 小数点

decision   1 *kettei* 決定   2 result; vote *ke′tsugi* 決議   3 contest *kesshō* 決勝

decisive   *ketteiteki na* 決定的な

deck   1 (on ship) *kampan* 甲板   2 (of cards) *hito′kumi [no tora′mpu]* 一組[のトランプ]

declaration   1 *senge′n* 宣言 declaration of independence *dokuritsu se′ngen* 独立宣言   2 public declaration *seimei* 声明

declare   ind-obj *ni*, obj *o* (irr) *seimei-suru* 声明する; *senge′n-suru* 宣言する

decline (refuse)   obj *o* (v) *kotowa′r·u* 断る decline an invitation *shō′tai o kotowa′ru* 招待を断る

decompose   (irr) *fuhai-suru* 腐敗する

decomposition   *fuhai* 腐敗

decompress   obj *o* (irr) *gen′atsu-suru* 減圧する   ——(idiom) *atsu′-ryoku o heras·u* 圧力を減らす

decorate   obj *o* (v) *kazar·u* 飾る

decoration   *kazari* 飾り

decrease   1 decline *genshō* 減少 a ¥100,000 decrease *jūman′en no genshō* 十万円の減少   2 reduction (in size) *shukushō* 縮小 ——obj *o* (v) 1 cut down *heras·u* 減らす decrease the budget to one-third *yosan o sambun-no-ichi′ ni herasu* 予算を三分の一に減らす   2 reduce (the size) (irr) *shukushō-suru* 縮小する reduce the size of a photograph *shashin o shukushō-suru* 写真を縮小する ——(v) *her·u* 減る The budget has decreased. *Yosan ga hette iru.* 予算が減っている.

dedicate   obj *o* (irr) *kentei-suru* 献呈する; (v) *sasage′·ru* 捧げる

deduction   1 *suitei* 推定   2 (subtraction) *sashihiki* 差引

deed   1 act *kō′i* 行為   2 title deed *kenri shō′sho* 権利証書   3 deed of transfer *jōto shō′sho* 譲渡証書

deep   (adj) *fuka′·i* 深い a deep river *fuka′i kawa* 深い川

deepfreeze   obj *o* (irr) *reitō-suru* 冷凍する

deer   *shika′* 鹿

deerskin   *shika-gawa* 鹿皮

defeat   *haiboku* 敗北 ——obj *o* (v) *makas·u* 負かす defeat an opponent in an argument *gi′ron de aite o makasu* 議論で相手を負かす ——(v) be/become defeated *make·ru* 負ける I was defeated in the contest. *Kyōsō ni maketa.* 競争に負けた.

defect   *kette'n* 欠点; *kekkan* 欠陥

defection   1 *haishin* 背信   2 apostasy *hensetsu* 変節   3 (from a political party) *dattō* 脱党

defective   *fuka'nzen [na]* 不完全[な]

defend   obj *o* (v) 1 *fuse'g·u* 防ぐ defend against invasion by the enemy *teki no shinryaku o fuse'gu* 敵の侵略を防ぐ I'm just managing to defend myself against the cold. *Yatto samuke'o fuse'ide iru.* やっと寒気を防いでいる. 2 vindicate (irr) *benkai-suru* 弁解する

defendant   *hikokunin* 被告人

defense   *bōei* 防衛 defense budget *bōe'i-hi* 防衛費

Defense Agency   *Bōe'i-chō* 防衛庁

defensive   *shusei[no]* 守勢[の]

deference   *sonkei* 尊敬; *ke'ii* 敬意

defer to   obj *o* (irr) *sonkei-suru* 尊敬する

deficiency   *fusoku* 不足

deficit   *fusoku* 不足

define   obj *o* (irr) 1 *te'igi-suru* 定義する   2 delimit *gentei-suru* 限定する

definite   (attr) *meikaku na* 明確な; *hakki'ri-shita* はっきりした

definition   *te'igi* 定義

deflate   (idiom) *kū'ki o nuk·u* 空気を抜く

deformed   *katawa [no]* 片端[の] a deformed bird without wings *hane no na'i katawa no tori* 羽根のない片端の鳥

deformity   *katawa* 片端

defrost   obj *o* (irr) *kaitō-suru* 解凍する

defy   obj *o* (v) 1 (irr) *mu'shi-suru* 無視する defy public opinion *yo'ron o mu'shi-suru* 世論を無視する   2 *anado'r·u* 侮る No child should defy his parents. *Kodomo wa oya' o anado'tte wa nara'nai.* 子供は親を侮ってはならない.

degeneracy   *daraku* 堕落

degenerate   (irr) *daraku-suru* 堕落する

degrading   (adj) *iyashi·i* 卑しい

degree   1 extent *te'ido* 程度   2 (measurement) *-do* 度 a 45-degree angle *yonjūgo'-do no ka'kudo* 45度の角度 The temperature is 60 degrees. *O'ndo wa rokujū'-do desu.* 温度は60度です.   3 academic degree *ga'ku-i* 学位

dehumanization   *ningen shikkaku* 人間失格; *hi'ningenka* 非人間化

dehumidifier   *joshitsu'ki* 除湿器

dehydrate   (irr) *dassui-suru* 脱水する

dejection   *rakutan* 落胆

delay   (caus) *okurase·ru* 遅らせる ——(adv) without delay *sassoku* 早速

delegate *dairi* 代理; *dairinin* 代理人 ——compl *ni* (irr) *inin-suru* 委任する

delegation *daihyō'dan* 代表団; *dairi ha'ken* 代理派遣

delete obj *o* (irr) *sa'kujo-suru* 削除する

deliberately *ko'i ni* 故意に; *wa'zato* わざと I didn't do it deliberately. *Wa'zato shita wa'ke ja na'i.* わざとした訳じゃない.

delicate *derikē'to* [na] デリケート[な] a delicate matter *derikē'to na kotogara* デリケートな事柄 ——(adj) *kayowa'·i* か弱い, delicate skin *kayowa'i ha'da* か弱い肌

delicately *binkan ni* 敏感に; *yasashiku* 優しく; *te'inei ni* 丁寧に Handle delicately! *Te'inei ni toriatsukatte kudasa'i!* 丁寧に取り扱って下さい.

delicious (adj) *oishi·i* おいしい delicious steak *oishii sutē'ki* おいしいステーキ It was delicious. *Oishi'katta.* おいしかった.

delightful *yu'kai* [na] 愉快[な] a delightful person *yu'kai na hito'* 愉快な人 I had a delightful time. *Totemo yu'kai deshita.* とても愉快でした.

delinquent (juvenile) **1** (masc) *furyō shō'nen* 不良少年 **2** (fem) *furyō shō'jo* 不良少女

delirium *seishin sa'kuran* 精神錯乱

deliver ind-obj *ni*, obj*o* **1** *todoke'·ru* 届ける Would you deliver (it), please? *Todo'kete itakema'su ka?* 届けていただけますか. **2** (irr) *haitatsu-suru* 配達する Do you deliver? *Haitatsu-shima'su ka?* 配達しますか.

delivery *haitatsu* 配達 newspaper delivery *shimbun ha'itatsu* 新聞配達

delivery room *bumbe'n-shitsu* 分娩室

deluge *dai-kō'zui* 大洪水

delusion *mō'sō* 妄想

deluxe *dera'kkusu* [na] デラックス[な]

demand **1** requirement *yōkyū* 要求 **2** request *yōbō* 要望 **3** consumer demand [*shōhisha no*] *juyō* [消費者の] 需要 supply and demand *juyō to kyōkyū* 需要と供給

democracy **1** *minshushu'gi* 民主主義 **2** system *minshusei* 民主制

democratic *minshuteki* [na] 民主的[な]

Democratic Socialist Party (Japanese political party) *Mi'nshu Shakai-tō* 民主社会党; (abbr) *Minsha-tō* 民社党

demolish obj *o* (v) **1** tear down *torikowas'·u* 取り壊す demolish a house *ie'o torikowasu* 家を取り壊す **2** ruin (irr) *hakai-suru* 破壊する **3** destroy (irr) *funsai-suru* 粉砕する demolish enemy installations *teki no ki'chi o funsai-suru* 敵の基地を粉砕する ——(pass) *hakai-sareru* 破壊される Everything was demolished. *Ze'mbu ga hakai-sareta.* 全部が破壊された.

demon *a'kuma* 悪魔

demonic *a'kumateki* [na] 悪魔的[な]

demonstrate obj *o* (v) *shimes'u* 示す

demonstration   **1** *jitsuen* 実演   **2** teaching demonstration *jitchi kyō'ju* 実地教授   **3** strike *de'mo* デモ

demoralize (idiom) *shi'ki o kuji'k·u* 士気をくじく

den   **1** lair *dōkutsu* 洞窟   **2** study *shosai* 書斎

denial *hitei* 否定

Denmark *Demmā'ku* デンマーク

denomination   **1** religious sect *shū'ha* 宗派   **2** sect (Chr) *kyō'ha* 教派

denotation   **1** *hyōji* 表示; (Tech) *gaien* 外延   **2** (explicit meaning) *shijiteki i'mi* 指示的意味

denote obj *o* (irr) *hyōji-suru* 表示する; obj *o* (v) *shimes·u* 示す

denounce obj *o* (v) *hi'nan-suru* 非難する   denounce a person as a traitor *hito o uragirimono da' to hi'nan-suru* 人を裏切り者だと非難する

dense (v) be dense *shige'r·u* 茂る   The trees are dense on that mountain. *Sono yama' wa ki' ga shige'tte iru.* その山は木が茂っている。 ——(attr) *misshū-shita* 密集した

density *nō'do* 濃度

dent *kubomi* 窪み

dentist *ha'isha* 歯医者; *ha'isha-san* 歯医者さん

dentistry *shika-i'gaku* 歯科医学

denture *ireba* 入れ歯

deny obj *o* (v) **1** contradict (irr) *hitei-suru* 否定する   The defendant denied the testimony of the witness for the prosecution. *Hikokunin wa kensatsu'-gawa no shō'gen o hitei-shita.* 被告人は検察側の証言を否定した。   **2** disavow *uchikes·u* 打ち消す   His actions denied the false rumor. *Ka're wa kōdō ni yotte, waru'i uwasa o uchike-shita.* 彼は行動によって悪いうわさを打ち消した。

deodorant *bōshū'-zai* 防臭剤

depart (v) *ta'ts·u* たつ; (irr) *shuppatsu-suru* 出発する   He departed for Europe. *Ka're wa Yōro'ppa ni shuppatsu-shita.* 彼はヨーロッパに出発した。

department   **1** *-ka* 科   Japanese-language department (e.g., of a school) *Nihongo-ka* 日本語科   orthopedic department *seikei ge'ka* 整形外科   **2** (government)*-shō* 省 (U.S.) Department of Agriculture *Nōmu'-shō* 農務省

department store *depā'to* デパート

departure *shuppatsu* 出発

dependence   **1** reliance *izon* 依存   **2** trust *shinrai* 信頼

dependent (supported family member) *fuyō ka'zoku* 扶養家族 ——compl *ni* (v) be dependent on *tayo'r·u* 頼る   He's too depen-

dent on his friend. *Ka're wa tomodachi ni tayori-su'gite iru.* 彼は
友達に頼りすぎている。

depending on ... *ni yotte* ...によって Opinions differ depending
on the person. *Hito ni yotte i'ken ga chigau.* 人によって意見が違
う。

depend on (irr) *izon-suru* 依存する; (v) *tayo'r·u* 頼る ——(pot)
tayore'·ru 頼れる I have no other friend I can depend on. *Hoka
ni tayore'ru tomodachi ga inai.* 外に頼れる友達がいない。

depict obj *o* (v) **1** draw *ega'k·u* 描く **2** describe (irr) *byōsha-suru*
描写する

deplorable *a'ware* [na] 哀れ[な]

deplore obj *o* (v) *kuya'm·u* 悔やむ As a fellow human being, I deplore the tragedy of Bangladesh. *Onaji ningen to shite, Bangurade'shu no hi'geki o kuya'mu.* 同じ人間として、バングラデシュの
悲劇を悔やむ。; *nage'k·u* 嘆く deplore the corruption in politics
seiji no fuhai o nage'ku 政治の腐敗を嘆く

deport obj *o* (irr) *tsuihō-suru* 追放する

deposit 1 (bank) *yokin* 預金 **2** guaranty money *hoshō-kin* 保証金
——obj *o* (v) *azuke'·ru* 預ける deposit money in the bank *ginkō
ni kane o azuke'ru* 銀行に金を預ける deposit valuables at the
front desk of a hotel *furonto ni kichōhin o azuke'ru* フロントに貴
重品を預ける

depot (railroad) *e'ki* 駅

depressing *inki na* 陰気な

depression 1 (economic) *fuke'iki* 不景気 **2** (psychological) *utsubyō*
鬱病 **3** (atmospheric) *teiki'atsu* 低気圧

deprive obj *o* (v) *uba'·u* 奪う deprive (someone) of pleasure *tanoshimi' o uba'u* 楽しみを奪う

depth *fuka'sa* 深さ

deride obj *o* (v) *azake'r·u* あざける deride a person for his cow-
ardice *okubyō da to itte azake'ru* 臆病だと言ってあざける

derive compl *ni* (v) *hikida's·u* 引き出す

derogatory *keibetsuteki* [na] 軽蔑的[な]

dermatology *hifu-ka* 皮膚科

descend loc *o* (v) *kudar·u* 下る descend a mountain *yama' o
kudaru* 山を下る descend from heaven *te'n kara kudaru* 天から
下る

descendant *shi'son* 子孫

describe obj *o* (irr) **1** *byōsha-suru* 描写する **2** record *kijutsu-suru*
記述する

description *byōsha* 描写; *kijutsu* 記述

desert *sabaku* 砂漠

desert obj *o* (v) *misute·ru* 見捨てる ——(pass) *misuterare'·ru* 見

捨てられる The child was deserted by its parents. *Sono kodomo wa oya′ ni misutera′reta.* その子供は親に見捨てられた.

deserted (adj) *sabishi′·i* 寂しい a deserted beach *sabishii hamabe′* 寂しい浜辺

deserve (idiom) *ka′chi ga a′r·u* 値がある His services deserve to be recognized. *Ka′re no kōseki wa mitomerareru ka′chi ga a′ru.* 彼の功績は認められる価値がある.

design 1 (clothing) *deza′in* デザイン 2 (architectural) *sekkei* 設計

designate ind-obj *ni*, obj *o* (irr) *shimei-suru* 指名する designate a person for an office *hito′ o ni′mmu ni shimei-suru* 人を任務に指名する ——(pass) *shimei-sare′·ru* 指名される be designated chairperson *gi′chō ni shimei-sareru* 議長に指名される

desirable (adj) *nozomashi′·i* 望ましい A house facing the south is desirable. *Minami-muki no ie′ ga nozomashi′i.* 南向きの家が望ましい.

desire *yoku′* 欲; *yokubō* 欲望 ——(adj)...*[ga] hoshi′·i* ...[が]欲しい She has everything she desires. *Ka′nojo wa hoshi′i mono wa ze′mbu mo′tte iru.* 彼女は欲しいものは全部持っている. ——obj *o* (v) *hoshiga′r·u* 欲しがる Money is something that all people desire. *O-kane wa su′bete no hito′ ga hoshiga′ru mono′ desu.* お金は全ての人が欲しがるものです. see also **want**

desk *tsukue* 机

desolation *kōhai* 荒廃

despair *zetsubō* 絶望

desperate 1 *inochi-gake [no]* 命懸け[の] make a desperate effort *inochi-gake no do′ryoku o suru* 命懸けの努力をする 2 hopeless *zetsubōteki [na]* 絶望的[な] It was a desperate situation. *Zetsubōteki na jōtai de′shita.* 絶望的な状態でした.

despise obj *o* (irr) *keibetsu-suru* 軽蔑する

despot *dokusai ku′nshu* 独裁君主

dessert *dezā′to* デザート

destination *mokute′kichi* 目的地

destiny *u′mmei* 運命

destitute (irr) be destitute *ketsubō-suru* 欠乏する The refugees are destitute. *Nammin wa ketsubō-shite iru.* 難民は欠乏している.

destroy obj *o* (irr) *hakai-suru* 破壊する

destroyer (ship) *kuchikukan* 駆逐艦

destruction *hakai* 破壊

detach obj *o* (v) *hazu′s·u* 外す Detach the stereo headphones, please. *Sutereo no heddohō′n o hazu′shite kudasa′i.* ステレオのヘッドホーンを外して下さい.

details *shōsai* 詳細 I'll let you know the details later. *Sono shōsai wa a′to de shirasema′su.* その詳細は後で知らせます.

detain obj *o* (v) *hikitome′·ru* 引き止める ——(pass) *hikitomera-*

re'·ru 引き止められる I'm sorry to be late. I was detained by the teacher. *Okurete sumimase'n. Sense'i ni hikitomera'rete shimaima'-shita.* 遅れてすみません。先生に引き止められてしまいました。

detective **1** private detective *tantei* 探偵 detective story *tantei shō'-setsu* 探偵小説 **2** police detective *ke'iji* 刑事

detention *kōryū* 拘留 He was put under detention by the police. *Ka're wa keisatsu ni kōryū-sa'reta.* 彼は警察に拘留された。

detergent *senzai* 洗剤

deteriorate (v) *kowarekaka'r·u* 壊れかかる The house is beginning to deteriorate. *Ie' wa kowarekaka'tte iru.* 家は壊れかかっている。

determination *ke'sshin* 決心

determine (decide) obj *o* (irr) *ke'sshin-suru* 決心する

determined *da'nko to shite* 断固として I am determined to go to China. *Da'nko to shite Chū'goku ni iku.* 断固として中国に行く。

detest obj *o* (v) *kira·u* 嫌う He detests spinach. *Ka're wa hōre'nsō o kiratte iru.* 彼はほうれん草を嫌っている。

detestable (adj) *nikurashi'·i* 憎らしい a detestable person *nikura-shi'i hito'* 憎らしい人

detour *mawari'michi* 回り道; (Tech) *ukai* 迂回

devastation *kōhai* 荒廃

develop (irr) *seichō-suru* 成長する; *hatten-suru* 発展する —— (caus) *hatten-sase'·ru* 発展させる Large companies developed that village into a factory town. *Daiga'isha ga sono mura' o kōjō-chi'tai ni hatten-saseta.* 大会社がその村を工場地帯に発展させた。 —— obj *o* (irr) develop (film) [*fui'rumu o*] *genzō-suru* [フィルムを]現像する

developing (film) *genzō* 現像 ——(attr) *hatten to'jō* [*no*] 発展途上 [の] developing nation *hatten tojō'-koku* 発展途上国

development **1** growth *seichō* 成長 A child's development is rapid. *Kodomo wa seichō ga haya'i.* 子供は成長が早い。 **2** exploitation; utilization *kaihatsu* 開発 development of an undeveloped area *mikai chi'iki no kaihatsu* 未開地域の開発 **3** expansion *hatten* 発展 foster the development of industry *sangyō no hatten o haka'ru* 産業の発展をはかる **4** progress *hattatsu* 発達 scientific and technological development *kagaku gi'jutsu no hattatsu* 科学技術の発達

device **1** invention *kōan* 考案 **2** means *shu'dan* 手段 **3** contrivance *kufū* 工夫

devil *a'kuma* 悪魔

devise obj *o* (irr) *kufū-suru* 工夫する

devote compl *ni*, obj *o* (v) **1** dedicate *sasage'·ru* ささげる He devoted his life to the study of history. *Ka're wa rekishi no kenkyū ni isshō o sasa'geta.* 彼は歴史の研究に一生をささげた。 **2** be absorbed in (irr) *netchū-suru* 熱中する be devoted to one's work *shigoto ni netchū-shite iru* 仕事に熱中している

devoted (self-sacrificing) *kenshinteki* [*na*] 献身的[な] a devoted teacher *kenshinteki na sense'i* 献身的な先生

devotion 1 dedication *kenshin* 献身 2 love *aijō* 愛情

devour obj *o* (v) *musabo'r·u* むさぼる ——(attr) *musabori-* むさぼり devour food *shokuji o musabori-ku'u* 食事をむさぼり食う devour books *ho'n o musabori-yo'mu* 本をむさぼり読む

dew *tsu'yu* 露

dexterous *ki'yō* [*na*] 器用[な] She's dexterous. *Ka'nojo wa ki'yō desu.* 彼女は器用です.

dextrose *budōtō* ぶどう糖

diabetes *tōnyō-byō* 糖尿病

diagnose obj *o* (irr) *shindan-suru* 診断する

diagnosis *shindan* 診断

diagonal *nana'me* [*no*] 斜め[の] a diagonal pattern *nana'me no moyō'* 斜めの模様

diagonally *nana'me ni* 斜めに draw a line diagonally *nana'me ni se'n o hiku* 斜めに線を引く

diagram *zu* 図; *zuhyō* 図表

dial *daiyaru* ダイヤル ——obj *o* (v) *mawas·u* 回す Please dial 110. *Hyaku-tōban o mawashite kudasa'i.* 110番を回して下さい.

dialect *hōge'n* 方言 Okinawan dialect *Okinawa hō'gen* 沖縄方言

dialogue *taiwa* 対話

dial tone *hasshi'n-on* 発信音

diameter *chokkei* 直径

diamond 1 *daiyamo'ndo* ダイヤモンド 2 (suit of playing cards) *daiya* ダイヤ

diaper *omu'tsu* おむつ

diaper rash *jimma'shin* じんましん

diaphragm 1 (Anat) *ōkaku'maku* 横隔膜 2 (contraceptive device) *pe'ssarī* ペッサリー

diarrhea *geri* 下痢

diary *nikki* 日記 keep a diary *nikki o tsuke'ru* 日記をつける

dice *saiko'ro* さいころ throw/roll dice *saiko'ro o furu* さいころをふる ——(idiom) chop *sainome'ni ki'r·u* さいの目に切る

dictation 1 *kakitori* 書き取り 2 (secretarial) *kōjutsu* [*hi'kki*] 口述 [筆記]

dictator *dokusai ku'nshu* 独裁君主

dictionary *ji'sho* 辞書; *jiten* 辞典

die (stamp) *kata* 型

die (v) 1 *shin·u* 死ぬ 2 pass away *nakunar·u* 亡くなる 3 die instantly (irr) *sokushi-suru* 即死する 4 die in war (irr) *senshi-suru* 戦死する

diesel *ji'zeru* ジーゼル

diet 1 *shoku se'ikatsu* 食生活 2 dieting *genshoku* 減食; *biyō'shoku* 美容食 ——(irr) *da'ietto-suru* ダイエットする; *genshoku-suru* 減食する

diet (national assembly) *kokkai* 国会

diet member *kokkai gi'in* 国会議員

differ comp *ni* (irr) *sōi'-suru* 相違する differ from one's expectations *a'n ni sōi'-suru* 案に相違する ——comp *to* (v) *kotonar·u* 異なる

difference 1 *chigai* 違い 2 conflict *sōi'* 相違

different *betsu [no]* 別[の] I'm driving a different car now. *I'ma wa betsu no kuruma o unten-shite iru.* 今は別の車を運転している. ——comp *to* (v) be different *chiga·u* 違う It's different from mine. *Watashi no' to chigau.* 私のと違う. No, that's different. *Ie', chigaima'su.* いいえ, 違います.

difficult (adj) *muzukashi'·i* 難しい Japanese is difficult, isn't it? *Nihon-go wa muzukashi'i desu ne'.* 日本語は難しいですね.

difficult to (do) *-niku'·i* にくい It's so dark it's difficult to see. *Kura'kute, mie-niku'i.* 暗くて見えにくい. *see also* hard; hard to (do)

difficulty *ko'nnan* 困難

dig obj *o* (v) *ho'r·u* 掘る dig potatoes *imo' o ho'ru* 芋を掘る

digest obj *o* (irr) *shōka-suru* 消化する

digestion *shōka* 消化

dignified *songen [na]* 尊厳[な] ——(adj) stately *ikameshi'·i* いかめしい ——(attr) *hin no a'ru* 品のある a dignified person *hin no a'ru hito* 品のある人

dignity *igen* 威厳

digress (irr) *dassen-suru* 脱線する

digression *dassen* 脱線

dike *dote* 土手

dilate (v) *hirogar·u* 広がる The pupils of the eyes dilate in the dark. *Hitomi wa kurayami de hirogaru.* 瞳は暗闇で広がる.

dilemma *jire'mma* ジレンマ

diligent *kimben [na]* 勤勉[な]

dilute obj *o* (v) *usume·ru* 薄める dilute with water *mizu de usumeru* 水で薄める

dim (adj) *usu-gura'·i* 薄暗い

dimension *jigen* 次元

diminish obj *o* (v) *heras·u* 減らす ——(caus) *genshō-sase·ru* 減少させる

dimple *e'kubo* えくぼ

dine (irr) *shokuji-suru* 食事する

diner (on train) *shokudō'sha* 食堂車; *byu'ffe* ビュッフェ

dining room *shokudō* 食堂

dinner *yūshoku* 夕食

dip obj *o* (v) *hita's·u* 浸す

diphtheria *jifuteria* ジフテリア

diploma *sotsugyō shō'sho* 卒業証書

diplomacy *gaikō* 外交

diplomat *gaikō'kan* 外交官

diplomatic relations *kokkō* 国交; *gaikō ka'nkei* 外交関係

dipper *hishaku* ひしゃく

direct *chokusetsu [no]* 直接[の]; *chok[u]-* 直 direct flight *chokkōbin* 直航便

direct current (DC, D.C., d.c.) *chokuryū* 直流

direction *hōkō* 方向

directly 1 straight *chokusetsu [ni]* 直接[に] 2 immediately *su'gu [ni]* すぐ[に] I'll go directly. *Su'gu iku.* すぐ行く.

director 1 (company) *jūyaku* 重役 2 a member of a board of directors *ri'ji* 理事 3 (stage) *enshutsuka* 演出家; (screen) *kantoku* 監督 4 (university program) *shunin* 主任

dirt 1 *gomi'* ごみ 2 filth; grime *aka'* あか 3 soil *tsuchi'* 土 4 mire *doro* 泥

dirty 1 (adj) *kitana'·i* 汚い 2 unsanitary *fuketsu [na]* 不潔[な] ——obj *o* (v) *yogos·u* 汚す I dirtied my white dress. *Shiro'i do'resu o yogoshite shima'tta.* 白いドレスを汚してしまった. ——(v) be/ become dirty *yogore·ru* 汚れる It's not dirty. *Yogorete inai.* 汚れていない.

disabled *fu'gu [na]* 不具[な]

disadvantage *fu'ri* 不利

disagree (irr, neg) *itchi-shina·i* 一致しない All their verbal accounts disagree. *Minna' no hanashi' ga itchi-shinai.* みんなの話が一致しない.

disagreeable *iya' [na]* いや[な] I smell something disagreeable. *Iya' na nio'i ga suru.* いやな臭いがする.

disagreement *fu'itchi* 不一致 ——(idiom) have a difference of opinions *i'ken ga awa'nai* 意見が合わない The two of them had a disagreement. *Futari' wa i'ken ga awa'nakatta.* 二人は意見が合わなかった.

disappear 1 (v) *kie·ru* 消える The snow disappeared. *Yuki' wa kiete shima'tta.* 雪は消えてしまった. 2 vanish from sight *mie'na-ku-na'r·u* 見えなくなる He disappeared into the crowd. *Ka're wa gunshū no na'ka ni mie'naku natta.* 彼は群衆の中に見えなくなった.

disappointed compl *ni* (irr) 1. be disappointed *gakka'ri-suru* がっかりする I was disappointed with her singing. *Ka'nojo no uta' ni* *gakka'ri-shita.* 彼女の歌にがっかりした. **2** dejected *shitsubō-suru* 失望する

disapprove of compl *ni* (irr, neg) *sansei-shina·i* 賛成しない He disapproved of the plan. *Ka're wa sono keikaku ni sansei-shina'katta.* 彼はその計画に賛成しなかった.

disarmament *gu'mbi shukushō* 軍備縮小

disaster *saigai* 災害 disaster area *saiga'ichi* 災害地

disbursements *shishutsu* 支出

discard obj *o* (v) *sute·ru* 捨てる

discharge **1** (of a gun) *happō* 発砲 **2** (Biol) *haisetsu'butsu* 排泄物 **3** (mucous) *hana-mizu* 鼻水 **4** (from the ears) *mimi-dare* 耳だれ **5** (from the eyes) *meyani'* 目やに **6** (from an abscess) *umi'* うみ ——obj *o* (caus) discharge from a hospital *taiin-sase·ru* 退院させる ——(irr) be discharged from a hospital *taiin-suru* 退院する ——(idiom) **1** fire *kubi ni suru* 首にする I discharged her. *Watashi wa ka'nojo o kubi ni shita.* 私は彼女を首にした. **2** be fired *kubi ni na'r·u* 首になる He was discharged. *Ka're wa kubi ni na'tta.* 彼は首になった.

disciple *deshi* 弟子

discipline **1** *ku'nren* 訓練 **2** upbringing *shitsuke* 躾

disclose (idiom) *a'rawa ni suru* あらわにする

disconnect obj *o* (v) *hazus·u* 外す

discontinue obj *o* (irr) *chūshi-suru* 中止する ——(pass) *chūshi-sare·ru* 中止される That class has been discontinued. *Sono ku'rasu wa chūshi-sarete iru.* そのクラスは中止されている.

discount *waribiki* 割り引き ——obj *o* (irr) *benkyō-suru* 勉強する; (v) *waribi'k·u* 割り引く Will you give me a discount? *Mō cho'tto waribi'ite kudasaimase'n ka?* もうちょっと割り引いて下さいませんか.

discount house *oroshido'n-ya* 卸問屋

discourage obj *o* (caus) *rakutan-sase·ru* 落胆させる I don't want to discourage her. *Ka'nojo o rakutan-saseta'ku na'i.* 彼女を落胆させたくない. ——(irr) be discouraged *gakka'ri-suru* がっかりする Don't be discouraged. *Gakka'ri-shina'ide.* がっかりしないで.

discourse *danwa* 談話

discourteous *shitsu'rei* [na] 失礼[な]; *bu'rei* [na] 無礼[な] a discourteous person *bu'rei na hito'* 無礼な人

discourtesy *shitsu'rei* 失礼; *bu'rei* 無礼

discover obj *o* (v) *mitsuke·ru* 見つける I discovered a nice, inexpensive shop. *Ya'sukute, i'i mise' o mitsuketa.* 安くていい店を見つけた.; (irr) *hakken-suru* 発見する The police discovered the corpse. *Keisatsu wa shitai o hakken-shita.* 警察は死体を発見した.

discovery *hakken* 発見

discreet *shinchō* [*na*] 慎重[な]

discrimination *sa'betsu* 差別 sex discrimination *sei sa'betsu* 性差別 race discrimination *jinshu sa'betsu* 人種差別

discuss obj *o* (irr) *tō'gi-suru* 討議する

discussion *tō'gi* 討議

disease *byōki* 病気

disgrace *fume'iyo* 不名誉 ——(idiom) **1** disgrace oneself *haji'o ka'k·u* 恥をかく **2** be disgraced (lit., lose face) *memboku o ushina·u* 面目を失う

disgusted (irr) be disgusted *unza'ri-suru* うんざりする

disgusting *iya'* [*na*] いや[な]

dish *sara* 皿

dishcloth *fuki'n* 布巾

dishonest *fushō'jiki* [*na*] 不正直[な]

dishonor *fume'iyo* 不名誉

dishpan *arai-o'ke* 洗い桶

dishwasher [*jidō*] *shokki ara'iki* [自動]食器洗い機

disinfect obj *o* (irr) *shōdoku-suru* 消毒する

disinfectant *shōdoku'-zai* 消毒剤

disinherit (Leg) obj *o* (irr) *haichaku-suru* 廃嫡する

dislike [... *ga*] *kirai* [*na*] [...が]きらい[な] food that one dislikes *kirai na tabemono'* きらいな食べ物 I dislike that. *Watashi wa sore ga kirai de'su.* 私はそれが嫌いです。 ——obj *o* (v) *kira·u* 嫌う ——(pass) *kiraware·ru* 嫌われる She is disliked by everyone. *Ka'nojo wa minna' ni kirawarete iru.* 彼女はみんなに嫌われている。

dislocation (Med) *dakkyū* 脱臼

disloyal *fuchū' jitsu* 不忠実[な]

dismiss obj *o* (v) **1** cause to leave (caus) *ikase·ru* 行かせる **2** fire (irr) *menshoku-suru* 免職する

disobedience *fujū' jun* 不従順

disobedient *fujū' jun* [*na*] 不従順[な]

disobey (idiom) *iu koto' o kikana·i* 言う事を聞かない My son disobeys me. *Musuko wa watashi no iu koto' o kikanai.* 息子は私の言う事を聞かない。

disorder **1** *midare* 乱れ **2** confusion *konran* 混乱

disorderly **1** *detarame* [*na*] でたらめ[な]; *mechakucha* [*na*] めちゃくちゃ[な] This room is disorderly. *Kono heya' wa mechakucha de'su.* この部屋はめちゃくちゃです。 **2** (of behavior) *rambō'* [*na*] 乱暴[な] The students are disorderly. *Sono se'ito-tachi wa rambō' desu.* その生徒たちは乱暴です。

display obj *o* (v) *kazar·u* 飾る

disposable (attr) *tsukai-sute* [*no*] 使い捨て[の] disposable diapers *tsukai-sute no omu'tsu* 使い捨てのおむつ

disposition *kishitsu* 気質 She has a sunny disposition. *Ka'nojo wa akaru'i kishitsu no hito' desu.* 彼女は明るい気質の人です.

dispute 1 argument *ronsō* 論争 2 strife; strike *sō'gi* 争議

disqualification *mushi'kaku* 無資格; *shikkaku* 失格

disregard obj *o* (irr) *mu'shi-suru* 無視する You may disregard that. *Sore o mu'shi-shite mo i'i desu.* それを無視してもいいです.

disrespect *bu'rei* 無礼

disrupt obj *o* (caus) *bunretsu-sase-ru* 分裂させる

dissatisfaction *fuma'nzoku* 不満足

dissatisfied *fuman* [*na/no*] 不満[な/の] I am dissatisfied with my present job. *Watashi wa jibun no ge'nzai no shigoto ni fuman de'su.* 私は自分の現在の仕事に不満です.

dissect obj *o* (irr) *kaibō-suru* 解剖する

dissection *kaibō* 解剖 dissection of a cadaver *jintai ka'ibō* 人体解剖

dissent *i'gi* 異議

dissertation *rombun* 論文 Ph.D. dissertation *hakase ro'mbun* 博士論文

dissolve (v) *toke'·ru* 溶ける ——obj *o* (v) *toka's·u* 溶かす

distance *kyo'ri* 距離 long distance *chō-kyo'ri* 長距離 short distance *tan-kyo'ri* 短距離 measure a distance *kyo'ri o haka'ru* 距離を計る

distant *tōku* [*no*] 遠く[の] ——(adj) *tō·i* 遠い

distasteful *iya'* [*na*] いや[な]

distemper (disease) *jisute'mpā* ジステンパー

distill obj *o* (irr) *jōryū-suru* 蒸留する

distinction *ku'betsu* 区別

distinguish comp *to*, obj *o* (irr) *ku'betsu-suru* 区別する

distinguished *yūmei* [*na*] 有名[な] a distinguished scientist *yūmei na kaga'kusha* 有名な科学者 ——(adj) *nadaka'·i* 名高い She is distinguished as a woodblock artist. *Ka'nojo wa hanga'ka to shite nadaka'i.* 彼女は版画家として名高い.

distort (v) *yugam·u* ゆがむ Her face distorted with rage. *Ka'nojo no kao wa ikari' de yuganda.* 彼女の顔は怒りでゆがんだ. ——(pass) *yugamerare·ru* ゆがめられる The meaning was distorted. *I'mi ga yugamera'reta.* 意味がゆがめられた. ——(attr) *yuganda* ゆがんだ a distorted facial expression *yuganda kao* ゆがんだ顔

distract obj *o* (v) *magira's·u* 紛らす

distress 1 suffering *kutsū* 苦痛; *ku'nō* 苦悩 2 peril *saigai* 災害 a distress area *saiga'i-chi* 災害地

distribute ind-obj *ni*, obj *o* (v) *kuba'r·u* 配る distribute leaflets *bira o kuba'ru* ビラを配る; (irr) *bumpai-suru* 分配する distribute food *shoku'ryō o bumpai-suru* 食糧を分配する

distributor (Elec) *haidemban* 配電盤

district 1 *chiku'* 地区 2 (electoral) *senkyo'ku* 選挙区 3 (residential) *jūta'kuchi* 住宅地

district attorney *ke'nji* 検事

disturb obj *o* (irr) *jama-suru* 邪魔する I'm sorry to have disturbed you. *O-jama-shima'shita.* お邪魔しました.

ditch *dobu* どぶ in a ditch *dobu no na'ka* どぶの中

dive (v) *mogu'r·u* もぐる dive for pearls *shinju o to'ri ni mogu'ru* 真珠を取りにもぐる; *tobiko'm·u* 飛び込む dive into the water *mizu no na'ka e tobiko'mu* 水の中へ飛び込む

divide ind-obj *ni*, obj *o* (v) 1 *wake'·ru* 分ける The landlord divided the land and sold it. *Ō'ya-san wa ji'sho o wa'kete, bunjō-shita.* 大家さんは地所を分けて分譲した. 2 partition *kugi'r·u* 区切る divide a room into two *heya' o futatsu' ni kugi'ru* 部屋を二つに区切る 3 (Math) *war·u* 割る Six divided by two equals three. *Roku o ni' de waru to san ni na'ru.* 6を2で割ると3になる; *Roku waru ni' wa san.* 6割る2は3. ——(caus) *bunretsu-sase·ru* 分裂させる

divine *shinsei na* 神聖な

diving board *tobikomi-dai* 飛び込み台

division 1 (Math) *wari'zan* 割り算 2 a split *bunretsu* 分裂 3 department -*bu* 部 language division *gogaku'-bu* 語学部

divorce *rikon* 離婚

dizzy (irr) feel dizzy *fu'rafura-suru* ふらふらする I feel dizzy. *Fu'rafura-suru'n desu.* ふらふらするんです.; *memai ga suru* めまいがする

do obj *o* (irr) *suru* する do work *shigoto o suru* 仕事をする do the wash *sentaku o suru* 洗濯をする Do it! *Shi-nasa'i.* しなさい.

dock *sambashi* 桟橋

doctor 1 (medical) *isha* 医者; (pol) *o-isha-san* お医者さん 2 (Ph. D.) *ha'kase/ha'kushi* 博士

Doctor of Philosophy *ha'kase/ha'kushi* 博士; (degree of) *hakase'-gō* 博士号

doctrine *shu'gi* 主義; (Chr) *kyō'ri* 教理

document *kiroku* 記録; *shorui* 書類 ——(idiom)to document *bu'n-sho de shōmei-suru* 文書で証明する

dodge (v) 1 move aside *dok·u* どく 2 evade *nige'·ru* 逃げる Every time I bring the matter up he dodges it. *Sono hanashi' o mochi-dasu to, i'tsu mo ka're wa ni'gete shimau.* その話を持ち出すといつも彼は逃げてしまう. ——obj *o* (v) avoid *sake'·ru* 避ける dodge a blow *u'tte kuru no o sake'ru* 打ってくるのを避ける

dog *inu'* 犬 stray dog *nora-inu* のら犬

dogcatcher *inu' no hokakunin* 犬の捕獲人; *inutori* 犬捕り

doggie bag (idiom) *nokorimono o irete mochika'eru fukuro* 残りものを入れて持ち帰る袋

doghouse *inu-goya* 犬小屋
dogmatic *dokudanteki* [na] 独断的[な]; *kyōjōshugi* [no] 教条主義 [の]
dogwood *hanami'zuki* はなみずき
doll *ningyō* 人形 paper doll *kami ni'ngyō* 紙人形
dollar *do'ru* ドル $100 *hyaku'-doru* 百ドル
dolphin *iruka* いるか
domain *ryō'chi* 領地
domestic (national) *koku'nai* [no] 国内[の]; *kokunai-* 国内 domestic airline *kokuna'i-sen* 国内線
domestic animal *kachiku* 家畜
domesticated (attr) 1 *kainarasa'reta* 飼い馴らされた 2 *hitonare-shita* 人馴れした
dominant 1 prominent *meda'tta* 目立った dominant color *meda'tta iro'* 目立った色 2 leading *yūsei* [na] 優勢[な]
Dominican (of the Dominican Republic) (person) *Dominika'jin* ドミニカ人 ──(attr) *Domi'nika no* ドミニカの
Dominican Republic *Domi'nika* ドミニカ
donation 1 *ki'fu* 寄付 2 (at a Christian church) *kenkin* 献金 3 (at a Shinto shrine) *hōnō'-butsu* 奉納物 4 (at a Buddhist temple) *o-saisen* お賽銭
done (v, past) *de'kita* できた The work is done. *Shigoto ga de'kita.* 仕事ができた.
donkey *ro'ba* ろば
donor *kizō'sha* 寄贈者
don't *-na'ide* ないで Don't do it! *Shina'ide kudasa'i.* しないで下さい. *see also* imperative verb form in tables 1–4, pp. xxi–xl.
donut *see* doughnut
doom *metsubō* 滅亡
door 1 *do'a* ドア 2 front door *ge'nkan* 玄関 3 back door *katte-guchi* 勝手口 4 (J) *to* 戸; *tobira* 扉
doorknob *nigiri* にぎり; *totte* 把手
dormitory *ryō'* 寮 men's dormitory *danshi ryō'* 男子寮 women's dormitory *joshi ryō'* 女子寮
dose *ikka'i-bun* 一回分
dot *te'n* 点
double *nijū* [no] 二重[の] double (storm) windows *nijū ma'do* 二重窓 ──(idiom) to double *ba'i ni suru* 倍にする
double-cross obj *o* (v) *uragi'r·u* 裏切る
doubt *utagai* 疑い ──obj *o* (v) *utaga·u* 疑う
doubtful (adj) *ayashi·i* 怪しい
dough *neriko* 練り粉; *ki'ji* 生地
doughnut *dō'natsu* ドーナツ
dove *ha'to* 鳩

down 1 *shita* 下 put down *shita ni oku* 下に置く 2 (feathers) *umō* 羽毛 down comforter *umō-bu'ton* 羽毛布団

downstairs *ka'ika* 階下

downstream *karyū ni* 下流に

downtown *hanka'gai* 繁華街; *chūshi'ngai* 中心街

doze (irr) *inemu'ri-suru* 居眠りする

dozen *dā'su* ダース one dozen *ichi-dā'su* 1ダース

Dr. (M.D.; Ph.D.) *sense'i* 先生 Dr. Smith *Su'misu sensei* スミス先生

draft 1 (manuscript) *shitagaki* 下書き 2 (bank) *tegata* 手形 3 (military) *chōhei* 徴兵 4 (air) *sukimaka'ze* すき間風 5 draft beer *nama bi'ru* 生ビール

draftsman *seizukō* 製図工

drag obj *o* (v) *hik·u* 引く The suitcase is heavy; I'll have to drag it behind me. *Sū'tsukēsu wa omo'i no de, hiite mo'tte ikana'kereba nara'nai.* スーツケースは重いので, 引いて持って行かなければならない.

dragon *ryū'*; *tatsu* 竜

dragonfly *tombo* とんぼ

drain *haisui* 排水 drain pipe *haisuikan* 排水管 ——obj *o* (v) 1 *nagas'·u* 流す Is it OK to drain the tub? *O-fu'ro no mizu o naga'-shite mo i'i desu ka?* お風呂の水を流してもいいですか? 2 drain (liquid) off *sute'·ru* 捨てる Drain off the liquid from the boiled noodles. *Me'n no yudeji'ru o sutete kudasa'i.* めんのゆで汁を捨てて下さい.

drama *ge'ki* 劇; (Tech) *engeki* 演劇; (coll) *shi'bai* 芝居

dramatist *gikyoku sa'kka* 戯曲作家; *geki sa'kka* 劇作家

drapes *kā'ten* カーテン

drastic *mōretsu na* 猛烈な

draw obj *o* (v) 1 sketch; paint *ka'k·u* かく The child drew a picture. *Kodomo wa e' o ka'ita.* 子供は絵をかいた. 2 depict *ega'k·u* 描く 3 draw a line *se'n o hik·u* 線を引く 4 draw water *mizu o kum·u* 水をくむ 5 draw a card *tora'mpu o to'r·u* トランプをとる

drawer *hikidashi* 引き出し

drawing 1 *e'* 絵 2 sketch *zu* 図; *suke'tchi* スケッチ 3 illustration *irasuto* イラスト; *sashie* 挿し絵

draw near (v) *chikayor'·u* 近寄る

dread *osore'* 恐れ ——obj *o* (v) *osore'·ru* 恐れる

dream *yume'* 夢 ——(idiom) to dream *yume' o mi'·ru* 夢を見る Last night I dreamed of you. *Saku'ban, ana'ta no yume' o mi'ta.* 昨晩, あなたの夢を見た.

dress 1 clothing *fuku* 服 2 (ladies) *fuji'n fuku* 婦人服; *wampi'su* ワンピース; *do'resu* ドレス ——obj *o* (v) 1 *ki·ru* 着る dress oneself *fuku' o kiru* 服を着る 2 ind-obj *ni*, obj *o* (v) *kise·ru* 着せる

Dress your sister, please. *Imōto ni fuku' o kisete kudasa'i.* 妹に服を着せて下さい.

dressmaking *yōsai* 洋裁

dried (attr) *kansō-shita* 乾燥した dried lumber *kansō-shita zaimoku* 乾燥した材木; *ho'shita* 干した dried fruit *ho'shita kuda'mono* 干した果物; *hoshi-* 干し dried persimmon *hoshi-ga'ki* 干し柿

drier *see* dryer

drift (v) *nagare'·ru* 流れる

drill **1** tool *ki'ri* 錐 **2** practice *renshū* 練習 ——(caus) to drill *renshū-sase·ru* 練習させる ——(idiom) to drill a hole *ana' o ake·ru* 穴を開ける

drink obj *o* (v) *no'm·u* 飲む drink milk *mi'ruku o no'mu* ミルクを飲む Did you drink your juice? *Jū'su o nomima'shita ka?* ジュースを飲みましたか.

drinking fountain *mizuno'miki* 水飲み器

drinks *nomi'mono* 飲み物

drip (v) *shitata'r·u* したたる

drive (for recreation) *dora'ibu* ドライブ ——obj *o* (irr) *unten-suru* 運転する

driver (person) *unte'nshu* 運転手

driving *unten* 運転 driving without a license *mumenkyo u'nten* 無免許運転 drunken driving *yopparai u'nten* 酔っ払い運転

drizzle *kirisame* 霧雨

drool (idiom) *yodare o naga's·u* よだれを流す

drop (of liquid) *shizuku* しずく; *-teki* 滴 a few drops *nisanteki* 二, 三滴

drop obj *o* (v) *oto's·u* 落とす I dropped my handbag. *Handoba'ggu o oto'shite shimatta.* ハンドバッグを落としてしまった.

drought *hideri* 日照り

drown (v) *obore-shi'n·u* おぼれ死ぬ

drugs **1** medicine *kusuri'* 薬 **2** narcotics *mayaku* 麻薬

drugstore *kusuriya* 薬屋

drum *taiko* 太鼓

drunk a drunk *yopparai* 酔っ払い ——(v) be/become drunk *yo'·u* 酔う He's drunk. *Ka're wa yo'tte iru.* 彼は酔っている.

dry (v) be dry *kawa'k·u* 乾く Is the washing dry? *Sentakumono wa kawa'ite imasu ka?* 洗濯物は乾いていますか.; (irr) *kansō-suru* 乾燥する It's very dry this year. *Kotoshi wa sugo'ku kansō-shite iru.* 今年はすごく乾燥している. ——obj *o*(v) **1** make dry *kawaka's·u* 乾かす **2** hang out to dry *ho's·u* 干す

dry cleaner's *dorai-kuri'ningu* ドライクリーニング

dryer (apparatus) **1** *kansō'ki* 乾燥器 **2** hair dryer [*hea*] *dora'iyā* [ヘア]ドライヤー

duck (bird) **1** (domestic) *ahiru* あひる **2** (wild) *ka'mo* 鴨

dues   *kaihi* 会費

duet   **1** (instrumental) *nijū'sō* 二重奏   **2** (vocal) *nijū'shō* 二重唱

duke   *kō'shaku* 公爵

dull   (adj) **1** uninteresting *tsumara'na·i* つまらない It was a dull book. *Tsumara'nai ho'n deshita.* つまらない本でした。 **2** sluggish *nibu'·i* 鈍い   ——(attr) not sharp *kire'nai* 切れない a dull knife *kire'nai na'ifu* 切れないナイフ

dumb   (mute) *oshi* おし   ——(attr) *kuchi no kike'nai* 口の利けない This child has been dumb since birth. *Kono' ko wa umaretsuki kuchi no kike'nai ko desu.* この子は生まれつき口の利けない子です。

dumbfounded   (v) be/become dumbfounded *akire·ru* あきれる I was dumbfounded! *Akireta!* あきれた。

dump truck   *da'mpukā* ダンプカー

dune   (coll) *suna-yama* 砂山; (Tech) *sakyū* 砂丘

duplicate   (photocopy) obj *o* (irr) *ko'pi-suru* コピーする; *fukusha-suru* 複写する

duplicator   *fukusha'ki* 複写機; Xerox *ze'rokkusu* ゼロックス

durable   (attr) *nagamochi' [no]* 長持ち[の]; *mochi' ga/no i'i* 持ちが/のいい durable fabric *mochi no i'i ki'ji* 持ちのいい生地 Those goods are durable. *Kono shinamono wa mochi' ga i'i.* この品物は持ちがいい。

during   *-chū/-jū* 中 during the morning *gozen-chū* 午前中 I was busy during the whole day. *Ichinichi-jū isoga'shikatta.* 一日中忙しかった。

dusk   *higure* 日暮れ; *tasogare* たそがれ

dust   *hokori* 埃; *chiri* ちり

duster   *hataki'* はたき

dusty   (adj) *hokorippo'·i* ほこりっぽい

Dutch   **1** (language) *Oranda-go* オランダ語   **2** (people) *Oranda'jin* オランダ人   ——(attr) *Oranda no* オランダの

duty   **1** work *ki'mmu* 勤務; *kimmu ji'kan* 勤務時間 off duty *kimmu'gai* 勤務外 **2** task *ni'mmu* 任務 **3** obligation *gi'mu* 義務 It is not my duty to do that. *Sore o suru gi'mu wa na'i.* それをする義務はない。 **4** tax *zeikin* 税金 Is this subject to duty? *Kore wa zeikin ga kakarima'su ka?* これは税金がかかりますか。

duty-free   *menzei [no]* 免税[の]

dwarf   *kobito* 小人

dye   *senryo'* 染料   ——obj *o* (v) *some·ru* 染める

dynamic   *dainami'kku [na]* ダイナミック[な]   ——(adj) *chikara-zuyo'·i* 力強い

dynamite   *dainama'ito* ダイナマイト

dynamo   *hatsude'nki* 発電機

dynasty   *ō'chō* 王朝

E

each　*ka′ku* 各 each area *ka′ku hōme′n* 各方面; *-zu′tsu* ずつ Give me one each of those. *Sore o hitotsu-zu′tsu kudasa′i.* それを一つずつ下さい.

eager　*ne′sshin* [*na*] 熱心[な] an eager student *ne′sshin na gakusei* 熱心な学生 The pupils are all eager to study. *Se′ito wa minna′ benkyō ni ne′sshin desu.* 生徒はみんな勉強に熱心です.

eagerly　*ne′sshin ni* 熱心に She listened eagerly to the lecture. *Ka′nojo wa ne′sshin ni kōgi o kiita.* 彼女は熱心に講義を聞いた.

eagle　*washi* 鷲

ear　**1** *mimi′* 耳　**2** (of grain) [*koku′motsu no*] *ho′* [穀物の]穂

earache　(Tech) *jitsū* 耳痛　——(idiom) have an earache *mimi′ ga ita′·i* 耳が痛い

eardrum　*komaku* 鼓膜

early　(adj) *haya′·i* 早い It's early. *Haya′i desu.* 早いです.　——(adv) *ha′yaku* 早く The plane arrived early. *Hikō′ki wa ha′yaku tsu′ita.* 飛行機は早く着いた.

earn　obj *o* (v) **1** profit *mōke′·ru* 儲ける We earned ¥100,000. *Jū-man-en mō′keta.* 十万円儲けた.　**2** work for wages *kase′g·u* 稼ぐ earn pocket money *ko′zukai o kase′gu* 小遣いを稼ぐ　**3** receive salary, wage, etc. *mora·u* 貰う How much salary do you earn? *Kyū′ryō wa i′kura moratte ima′su ka?* 給料はいくら貰っていますか.

earnest　*majime* [*na*] 真面目[な] an earnest person *majime na hito′* 真面目な人 Is she in earnest? *Ka′nojo wa majime de′su ka?* 彼女は真面目ですか.

earnestly　*majime ni* 真面目に work earnestly *majime ni hataraku* 真面目に働く

ear, nose, and throat specialist　(Tech) *ji·bi inkōka′·i* 耳鼻咽喉科医; (coll., lit., ear and nose department) *jibika* 耳鼻科

earring　*mimi-ka′zari* 耳飾り; *iyari′ngu* イヤリング

earth　**1** soil *tsuchi′* 土　**2** (planet) *chikyū* 地球

earthquake　*jishin* 地震

earthworm　*mimizu* みみず

ease　(v) be at ease *ochitsuk·u* 落ち着く I'm never at ease with him around. *Ka′re ga so′ba ni iru to ochitsukana′i.* 彼がそばにいると落ち着かない.　——(adv) with ease *rakuraku* [*to*] 楽々[と]

easel　*da′i* 台; (Tech) *gaka* 画架

easily　*raku′ ni* 楽に He ran 200 meters easily. *Ka′re wa nihyaku mē′toru o raku′ ni hashi′tta.* 彼は200メートルを楽に走った.

east　**1** *higashi* 東 east entrance/exit *higashi-guchi* 東口　**2** the East; the Orient *Tō′yō* 東洋; East Asia *Higashi A′jia* 東アジア

Easter　*Fukkatsu′sai* 復活祭; *I′sutā* イースター

easy *raku'* [*na*] 楽[な] easy work *raku' na shigoto* 楽な仕事; *kantan* [*na*] 簡単[な] an easy problem *kantan na mondai* 簡単な問題 ── (adj) *yasashi·i* やさしい I only understand easy Japanese. *Yasashii Nihon-go' shika wakara'nai.* やさしい日本語しか分からない。; *ta-yasu'·i* たやすい an easy task *tayasu'·i koto'* たやすい事 ── (idiom) **1** It is easy (it is nothing, you don't have to thank me)! *O-yasu'i go-yō' desu!* お易いご用です。 **2** Take it easy! *Ochitsuki-nasa'i!* 落ち着きなさい。

easygoing *no'nki* [*na*] のんき[な]

easy-payment plan *bunkatsu-ba'rai* 分割払い

easy to (do) (adj) *-yasu'·i* やすい This is easy to read. *Kore wa yomi-yasu'i.* これは読みやすい。

eat (irr) *shokuji-suru* 食事する eat alone *hito'ri de shokuji-suru* 一人で食事する What time are we going to eat? *Na'nji ni shokuji-shima'su ka?* 何時に食事しますか。 ──obj *o* (v) *tabe'·ru* 食べる Do you eat raw fish? *Sashimi o tabema'su ka?* さしみを食べますか。 Let's eat! *Tabemashō'!* 食べましょう。

eave *noki* 軒

ebb tide *hikishio* 引き潮; *kanchō* 干潮

ebony *kokuta'n* 黒檀

eccentric (attr) *kawatta* 変わった eccentric person *kawatta hito'* 変わった人

echo *kodama* こだま

eclipse **1** (lunar) *gesshoku* 月食 **2** (solar) *nisshoku* 日食

ecology (science) *seita'igaku* 生態学

economical *keizaiteki* [*na*] 経済的[な] This way is (more) economical. *Kono hō' ga keizaiteki de'su.* この方が経済的です。

economic depression *fuke'iki* 不景気

economics **1** *ke'izai* 経済 **2** (study of) *keiza'igaku* 経済学

economize obj *o* (irr) *ken'yaku-suru* 倹約する economize on food *tabemono' o ken'yaku-suru* 食べ物を倹約する *see also* conserve

economy *ke'izai* 経済 national economy *kokumin ke'izai* 国民経済

Ecuador *Ekua'doru* エクアドル

Ecuadorian (person) *Ekuadoru' jin* エクアドル人 ──(attr) *Ekua'doru no* エクアドルの

eczema *shisshin* 湿疹

edge **1** end *hashi'*/*haji'* 端 edge of a table *tēburu no hashi'* テーブルの端 **2** border; brink *fuchi'* 淵 edge of a cliff *gake no fuchi'* 崖の淵 **3** outskirts *-ha'zure* はずれ the edge of town *machi-ha'zure* 町はずれ

edible (pot) *taberare'·ru* 食べられる Is this edible? *Kore wa tabe-rarema'su ka?* これは食べられますか。

edit obj *o* (irr) *henshū-suru* 編集する

edition **1** (of a book) *-han*/*-ban* 版 first edition of a book *shohan*

初版 limited edition *gentei-ban* 限定版　**2** (of a newspaper) *-kan* 刊 morning edition *chōkan* 朝刊 evening edition *yūkan* 夕刊

editor *henshūsha* 編集者

editorial *shasetsu* 社説

educate obj o (irr) *kyōiku-suru* 教育する

educated (attr) *kyōyō no a′ru* 教養のある an educated person *kyōyō no a′ru hito′* 教養のある人

education *kyōiku* 教育 She received her education in America. *Ka′nojo wa kyōiku o Amerika de u′keta.* 彼女は教育をアメリカ で受けた.

eel *unagi* 鰻 Do you eat eel? *Unagi o tabema′su ka?* 鰻を食べま すか.

eerie *buki′mi* [*na*] 不気味[な]

effect **1** result *kekka* 結果 cause and effect *gen′in to kekka* 原因と 結果　**2** efficacy *kō′ka* 効果 It had no effect. *Kō′ka ga na′katta.* 効果がなかった.　**3** in effect *yūkō* [*na*] 有効[な] That law is still in effect. *Sono hōritsu wa ma′da yūkō de′su.* その法律はまだ有効で す.

effective *kōkateki* [*na*] 効果的[な] an effective method *kōkateki na hōhō* 効果的な方法 ——(idiom) *kikime ga i′·i* ききめがいい This medicine is effective. *Kono kusuri wa kikime ga i′i.* この薬はきき めがいい.

effeminate (adj) *onnappo′·i* 女っぽい

effete (attr) *suitai-shita* 衰退した effete civilizations *suitai-shita shobu′mmei* 衰退した諸文明

efficiency *nōritsu* 能率 improve efficiency *nōritsu o ageru* 能率を上 げる

efficiently *nōritsuteki ni* 能率的に; *nōritsu yo′ku* 能率よく work efficiently *nōritsu yo′ku hatara′ku* 能率よく働く

effort *do′ryoku* 努力 We expended every effort. *Wata′shi-tachi wa arayu′ru do′ryoku o tsuku′shita.* 私たちはあらゆる努力を尽くした.

egg **1** *tama′go* 卵 raw egg *nama ta′mago* 生卵　**2** fried egg (sunny-side up) *medama-yaki* 目玉焼き　**3** hard-boiled egg *yude ta′mago* ゆで卵　**4** poached egg *otoshi ta′mago* 落とし卵　**5** scrambled egg *sukura′mburu* スクランブル; *iri ta′mago* 炒り卵　**6** soft-boiled egg *hanjuku ta′mago* 半熟卵

eggbeater *awadate′ki* 泡立て器

eggplant *na′su* 茄子

egg white *shi′romi* 白身

egg yolk *kimi* 黄身

ego *ji′ga* 自我 a person with a strong ego *ji′ga no tsuyo′i hito′* 自 我の強い人

egocentric *ji′ko chūshinshu′gi* [*no*] 自己中心主義[の]

egoism *rikoshu′gi* 利己主義

egoist *rikoshugi'sha* 利己主義者

egotism 1 self-centeredness *ji'ko chūshin* 自己中心 2 conceit *hitori-yo'gari* ひとりよがり

egotist *ji'ko chūshinshugi'sha* 自己中心主義者

egret *shirasagi* 白鷺

Egypt *Ejiputo* エジプト

Egyptian (person) *Ejiputo'jin* エジプト人 ——(attr) *Ejiputo no* エジプトの

eight *hachi* 八; *yattsu'* 八つ *see also* Appendix 1

eighteen *jūhachi* 十八; 18 years old *jūha'ssai* 十八歳

eighth 1 (ordinal) *hachiban-me* 八番目 2 (fraction) *hachi'bun no ichi* 八分の一

eighth day of the month *yōka* 八日

eighty *hachijū'* 八十 *see also* Appendix 1

either *do'tchi [de] mo* どっち[で]も Either will do. *Do'tchi demo i'i.* どっちでもいい.; *do'chira [de] mo* どちら[で]も

ejaculation *shasei* 射精

elapse (v) *ta'ts·u* 経つ Several days elapsed. *I'kunichika [ga] ta'tta.* 幾日か[が]経った.

elastic band *gomu'himo* ゴムひも; *wagomu* 輪ゴム

elasticity 1 resilience *danryoku* 弾力 2 flexibility *shinshuku* 伸縮

elbow (Anat) *hiji'* 肘

elderly (attr) *toshito'tta* 年とった an elderly person *toshito'tta hito* 年とった人 ——(idiom) elderly person *rōjin* 老人

elder statesman *genrō* 元老

elect obj *o* (v) select *era'b·u* 選ぶ 2 vote into office (irr) *se'nkyo-suru* 選挙する *see also* choose

election *se'nkyo* 選挙 local election *chihō se'nkyo* 地方選挙

elective course (in school) *sentaku ka'moku* 選択課目

electric (attr) *de'nki [no]* 電気[の] electric blanket *denki mō'fu* 電気毛布

electricity *de'nki* 電気

electricity meter *de'nki no mētā* 電気のメーター

electric power company *denryoku-ga'isha* 電力会社

electrocardiogram *see* cardiogram

electrocardiograph *see* cardiograph

electroencephalogram *see* encephalogram

electroencephalograph *see* encephalograph

elegant *yū'ga [na]* 優雅[な]

element 1 essential factor *yō'so* 要素 2 (chemical) *genso* 元素

elementary school *shōga'kkō* 小学校

elephant *zō'* 象

elevator *erebē'tā* エレベーター

eleven *jūichi* 十一; 11 years old *jūissai* 十一歳

eligibility *shikaku* 資格 eligibility for membership *kaiin to na'ru shikaku* 会員となる資格

eliminate obj *o* (v) *torinozok·u* 取り除く eliminate impurities *fujumbutsu o torinozoku* 不純物を取り除く

El Salvador *Eru Saruba'doru* エルサルバドル

else (in addition) *hoka ni* 外に Is there something else? *Hoka ni na'nika arima'su ka?* 外に何かありますか.

embark (irr) *shuppan-suru* 出帆する

embarrass obj *o* (v) *komarase'·ru* 困らせる I don't want to embarrass anyone. *Hito' o komarase'ru yō na koto wa shita'ku nai.* 人を困らせるような事はしたくない.

embarrassed (adj) *hazukashi'·i* 恥ずかしい I was embarrassed. *Hazuka'shikatta.* 恥ずかしかった.　——(irr) *tōwaku-suru* 当惑する I was embarrassed for an answer. *Dō o-kotae shite i'i ka, tōwaku-shita.* どうお答えしていいか当惑した.　——(attr) *koma'tta* 困った an embarrassed look *koma'tta kao* 困った顔

embarrassing *ya'kkai* [na] やっかい[な] an embarrassing situation *ya'kkai na jijō* やっかいな事情　——(adj) *hazukashi'·i* 恥ずかしい It's embarrassing! *Hazukashi'i!* 恥ずかしい.　——(attr) *koma'tta* 困った It's an embarrassing matter! *Koma'tta koto' desu!* 困った事です.

embassy *taishi'kan* 大使館 British embassy *Igirisu taishi'kan* イギリス大使館

embezzlement *ōryō* 横領

embrace obj *o* (v) *dakishime'·ru* 抱き締める

embroidery *shishū* 刺しゅう

embryo **1** (human, animal) *ta'iji* 胎児 **2** (plant) *haiga* 胚芽

emerald *emera'rudo* エメラルド

emergency **1** urgency *kyū* [na] 急[な] an emergency *kyū na baai* 急な場合 In an emergency, what does one do? *Kyū na baai, na'ni o shima'su ka?* 急な場合何をしますか.　**2** contingency *kinkyū* [no] 緊急[の]; *hijō* [na/no] 非常[な/の] Emergency circumstances require emergency measures. *Kinkyū no baai ni wa hijō no shu'dan o yōsuru.* 緊急の場合には非常の手段を要する.

emergency exit *hijō'guchi* 非常口

emigrant *imin* 移民

emigrate (irr) *ijū-suru* 移住する

emotion *kanjō* 感情

emotional *kanjōteki* [na] 感情的[な]

emperor **1** *kōtei* 皇帝 **2** the Japanese emperor *tennō'* 天皇 His Imperial Majesty, the (Japanese) Emperor *Tennō-he'ika* 天皇陛下

emphasize obj *o* (irr) *kyō'chō-suru* 強調する

employ obj *o* (v) *yato'·u* 雇う employ a person *hito o yato'u* 人を雇う　——(v) **1** be employed *tsutome'·ru* 勤める Is he employed?

Ka're wa tsuto'mete imasu ka? 彼は勤めていますか. **2** (irr) secure employment *shūshoku-suru* 就職する

employee 1 *jūgyō'in* 従業員 **2** company employee *sha'in* 社員

employer 1 *koyō'sha* 雇用者 **2** company boss *shachō* 社長

employment *koyō* 雇用 *see also* job; occupation

employment agency *shokugyō anteijo'* 職業安定所; (abbr) *shokuan* 職安

empress *kōgō'* 皇后 Her Imperial Majesty, the (Japanese) Empress *Kōgō-he'ika* 皇后陛下

empty *kara'* [no] 空[の] an empty bottle *karabin* 空瓶 This bottle's empty. *Kono bi'n wa kara' desu.* この瓶は空です. ——(v) be/become empty *suk·u* 空く The train's empty. *Densha wa suite iru.* 電車は空いている. ——(idiom) empty out *kara' ni suru* 空にする Empty this. *Kore o kara' ni shite kudasa'i.* これを空にして下さい.

enamel *enameru* エナメル

encephalogram *nō'ha kiroku'zu* 脳波記録図

encephalograph *nō'ha sokutei sō'chi* 脳波測定装置

enclose (with a letter) obj *o* (irr) *dōfū-suru* 同封する I'm enclosing a check. *Kogi'tte o dōfū-shite oku.* 小切手を同封しておく.

encore *ankō'ru* アンコール

encounter 1 meeting *deai* 出会い, **2** conflict *sōgū* 遭遇 ——compl *ni* (v) *dea·u* 出会う I encountered an old friend. *Furu'i tomodachi ni deatta.* 古い友達に出会った.

encourage obj *o* (v) **1** *susume·ru* 勧める **2** urge *hage'm·u* 励む ——(caus) *hagemase'·ru* 励ませる ——(caus-pass) *hagemasare'·ru* 励まされる I was encouraged by my father. *Chichi ni hagemasa'reta.* 父に励まされた.

encouragement *shōrei* 奨励

encyclopedia *hyakkaji'ten* 百科事典

end 1 *owari* 終わり **2** end of the bus/train line *shūten* 終点 **3** last part of a calendar division of time *-matsu* 末 end of the week *shūmatsu* 週末 end of the month *getsumatsu* 月末 end of the year *nemmatsu* 年末 **4** limit *hate'* 果て to the ends of the earth *se'kai no hate' made* 世界の果てまで **5** the (tail) end *mattan* 末端 **6** conclusion; settlement *ketsumatsu* 結末 end of a war *sensō no ketsumatsu* 戦争の結末 *see also* complete; finish

endless *mugen* [no] 無限[の] endless desires *mugen no yokubō* 無限の欲望 ——(adj) **1** interminable *kagirina'·i* 限りない, endless love *kagirina'·i aijō* 限りない愛情 **2** boundless *hateshina'·i* 果てしない the endless sea *hateshina'·i u'mi* 果てしない海

endorse obj *o* (irr) *uragaki-suru* 裏書きする

endowment (financial) *kiki'n* 基金

endurance 1 perseverance *ni'ntai* 忍耐 **2** doggedness *gambari* 頑張り

endure (v) *ta'e·ru* 耐える ——(pot) *taerare'·ru* 耐えられる That's more than I can endure. *Sore wa watashi ni wa taerarena'i koto' desu.* それは私には耐えられないことです. ——obj *o* (irr) *ga'-man-suru* 我慢する You'll just have to endure it. *Sore o ga'man-shina'kute wa nara'nai.* それを我慢しなくてはならない.; (coll) *Ga'man-shina'kucha!* 我慢しなくちゃ.

enema *kanchō* かんちょう

enemy *teki* 敵

energetic *ge'nki [ippai]* 元気[いっぱい]; *ge'nki ga i'i* 元気がいい She's energetic, isn't she? *Ka'nojo wa ge'nki ga i'i desu ne'.* 彼女は元気がいいですね.

energetically *ikioi-yo'ku* 勢いよく

energy 1 spirit *ge'nki* 元気 I have no energy these days. *Dō'mo, konogoro ge'nki ga na'i.* どうもこのごろ元気がない. 2 vitality *se'iryoku* 精力 That sapped his energy. *Ka're wa sono tame'ni se'iryoku ga otoro'eta.* 彼はそのために精力が衰えた. 3 (Physics) *ene'rugī* エネルギー kinetic energy *undō ene'rugī* 運動エネルギー

enforce obj *o* (irr) *jisshi-suru* 実施する enforce regulations *kitei o jisshi-suru* 規定を実施する

enforcement *jisshi* 実施; *shikkō* 執行

engaged (to be married) comp *to* (irr) be/become engaged *kon'ya-ku-suru* 婚約する They are engaged. *Ka'rera wa kon'yaku-shite iru.* 彼らは婚約している.

engagement 1 (for marriage) *kon'yaku* 婚約 2 appointment *ya-kusoku* 約束 I have an engagement. *Yakusoku ga a'ru.* 約束がある. 3 previous engagement *sen'yaku* 先約

engine 1 (of a car/ship) *e'njin* エンジン 2 (of a train) *kika'nsha* 機関車

engineer *enjini'a* エンジニア; *gishi* 技師 electrical engineer *denki gi'shi* 電気技師 mechanical engineer *kikai gi'shi* 機械技師 mining engineer *kōzan gi'shi* 鉱山技師

engineering *kōgaku* 工学

England *Ingura'ndo* イングランド; *Igi'risu* イギリス

English 1 (language) *Ei-go* 英語 2 (person) *Igirisu' jin* イギリス人 ——(attr) *Igirisu no* イギリスの

engrave obj *o* (v) *ho'r·u* 彫る; *kizam·u* 刻む

engraving (copperplate) *dōban* 銅板

enigma *nazo* 謎

enjoy obj *o* (v) *tanoshi'm·u* 楽しむ enjoy reading a book *ho'n o tanoshi'nde yo'mu* 本を楽しんで読む Enjoy yourself! *Tanoshi'nde itte irassha'i!* 楽しんで行っていらっしゃい.

enjoyable *yu'kai [na]* 愉快[な] ——(adj) *tanoshi'·i* 楽しい

enlarge obj *o* (v) 1 stretch *hikinoba's·u* 引き伸ばす I'd like to have this photograph enlarged. *Kono shashin o hikinoba'shite itadaki-ta'i.* この写真を引き伸ばしていただきたい。 **2** make more spacious (irr) *ō'kiku-suru* 大きくする We enlarged the bedroom. *Shinshitsu o ō'kiku-shita.* 寝室を大きくした。

enlargement *kakuchō* 拡張

enlightenment **1** *keihatsu* 啓発 **2** (Budd) *satori* 悟り

enlist (in the armed forces) *chōhei ni ōji'·ru* 徴兵に応じる

enormous **1** (size) *kyodai [na]* 巨大[な] **2** (space) *kōdai [na]* 広大[な] **3** (amount) *bakudai [na]* 莫大[な]

enough *jūbu'n [na]* 十分[な] That's enough! *Sore de jūbu'n desu.* それで十分です。 ——(v) be enough *tari·ru* 足りる Do you think it will be enough? *Sore de tariru to omoima'su ka?* それで足りると思いますか。 That's not enough. *Sore de' wa tarina'i.* それでは足りない。

enroll in school (irr) *nyūgaku-suru* 入学する

en route *tochū [de]* 途中[で]

ensign (U.S. Navy) *kaigun shō'i* 海軍少尉

enter (v) **1** *ha'ir·u* 入る enter a room *heya' ni ha'iru* 部屋に入る enter (join) a firm *kaisha ni ha'iru* 会社に入る **2** enter school (irr) *nyūgaku-suru* 入学する

enterprise *ji'gyō* 事業 government enterprise *se'ifu no ji'gyō* 政府の事業 public enterprise *kōkyō ji'gyō* 公共事業; *ki'gyō* 企業 start up an enterprise *ki'gyō o oko'su* 企業を興す

entertain obj o (v) **1** *motenas·u* もてなす entertain guests *o-kya-ku-sa'ma o motenasu* お客様をもてなす **2** (for business reasons) (irr) *se'ttai-suru* 接待する entertain a guest of the company *kaisha no kyaku o se'ttai-suru* 会社の客を接待する

entertainment **1** hospitality *motenashi* もてなし; *se'ttai* 接待 **2** performance *moyōshi-mono* 催し物; *shō'* ショー **3** amusement *goraku* 娯楽

enthusiasm *netchū* 熱中

enthusiastic *netsuretsu [na]* 熱烈[な] enthusiastic welcome *netsure-tsu na kangei* 熱烈な歓迎; *nekkyōteki [na]* 熱狂的[な] enthusiastic support *nekkyōteki shi'ji* 熱狂的支持 ——compl *ni* (irr) be enthusiastic *netchū-suru* 熱中する He's enthusiastic about everything he does. *Ka're wa monogo'to ni netchū-shigachi de'su.* 彼は物事に熱中しがちです。

entire *ze'mbu [no]* 全部[の] She wrote the entire novel in six weeks. *Ka'nojo wa rokushū'kan de sono shōsetsu o ze'mbu ka'ita.* 彼女は六週間でその小説を全部書いた。

entirely *kanzen ni* 完全に entirely mistaken *kanzen ni machiga'tte iru* 完全に間違っている

entomology *konchū'gaku* 昆虫学

entrance 1 *iriguchi* 入口 **2** back (kitchen) entrance *katte-guchi* 勝手口 **3** vestibule *ge'nkan* 玄関 **4** gate *mo'n* 門

entrust ind-obj *ni*, obj *o* (irr) *itaku-suru* 委託する entrust to a committee *ii'nkai ni itaku-suru* 委員会に委託する

entry (in a ledger) *kinyū* [*ji'kō*] 記入[事項]; *kisai* [*ji'kō*] 記載[事項]

envelope *fūtō* 封筒

envious (adj) *urayamashi'.i* うらやましい, I'm envious! *Urayamashi'i!* うらやましい. see also jealous

environment *kankyō* 環境

envy *urayami* うらやみ ——obj *o* (v) *uraya'm.u* うらやむ envy (someone's) success *seikō o uraya'mu* 成功をうらやむ

epic (poem) *joji'shi* 叙事詩

epidemic *densembyō* 伝染病 ——(attr) *ryūkōsei* [*no*] 流行性[の] epidemic parotitis (mumps) *ryūkōsei jikase'n-en* 流行性耳下腺炎

Epiphany (Chr festival) **1** (Prot) *Epefa'ni no shukujitsu* エペファニーの祝日 **2** (Cath) *Shuke'n-sai* 主顕祭

epoch *shinkigen* 新紀元; *shinji'dai* 新時代

equal *byōdō* [*no*] 平等[の] All people are equal. *Su'bete no ningen wa byōdō de'su.* すべての人間は平等です. see also equivalent to

equality *byōdō* 平等

equalize (make uniform) obj *o* (v) *soroe'.ru* そろえる

equals (in number) *ikō'ru* イコール Two plus two equals four. *Ni' tasu ni' ikō'ru yo'n.* 2足す2イコール4

equator *sekidō* 赤道

equilibrium *heikō* 平衡

equinox *higan* 彼岸; vernal *shumbun* 春分; autumnal *shū'bun* 秋分

equipment 1 furnishings *bihin* 備品 **2** conveniences *se'tsubi* 設備

equivalent to (adj) *hitoshi'.i* 等しい This is equivalent in length to that. *Sore to kore wa na'gasa ga hitoshi'i.* それとこれは長さが等しい. ——(attr) ...*ni junzuru* ...に準ずる treatment equivalent to that of a regular member *seika'iin ni junzuru toriatsukai* 正会員に準ずる取り扱い

era *jidai* 時代 Meiji era *Meiji ji'dai* 明治時代

erase obj *o* (v) *kes.u* 消す Don't erase this. *Kore o kesana'ide kudasa'i.* これを消さないで下さい.

eraser 1 rubber eraser *keshigomu* 消しゴム **2** blackboard eraser *kokuba'n-fuki* 黒板ふき

erect *massu'gu* [*ni*] まっすぐ[に] stand erect *massu'gu ni ta'tsu* まっすぐに立つ ——obj *o* (v) *tate'.ru* 建てる

erection (erect penis) *bokki* 勃起

ermine *shiroten* しろてん ermine fur *shiroten no kegawa* しろてんの毛皮

erosion *shinshoku* 浸蝕; *fushoku* 腐蝕

erotic *erochi'kku* [*na*] エロチック[な] ——(adj) *iroppo'.i* 色っぽい

errand *o-tsukai* お使い、send someone on an errand *da'reka o o-tsukai ni yaru* だれかをお使いにやる; *yōji* 用事 I have a little errand to do. *Cho'tto yōji ga a'ru.* ちょっと用事がある.

error *machiga'i* 間違い

eruption (of a volcano) *funka* 噴火

escalator *esukarē'tā* エスカレーター

escape *tōsō* 逃走 ——(v) *nige'・ru* 逃げる see also leak

Eskimo *Esuki'mō* エスキモー

especially *to'ku ni* 特に; especially cold *to'ku ni samu'i* 特に寒い; *wa'zawaza* わざわざ I bought this especially for you. *Kore wa wa'zawaza ana'ta no tame' ni katte kita.* これはわざわざあなたのために買ってきた. ——(idiom) not especially *betsu ni* 別に I'm not especially busy tomorrow. *Ashita' wa betsu ni isoga'shiku na'i.* 明日は別に忙しくない.

essential *hissu [no]* 必須[の]; *hitsuyō [na]* 必要[な] an essential point *hitsuyō na ten* 必要な点

establish obj *o* (irr) **1** found *setsuritsu-suru* 設立する; *sōritsu-suru* 創立する **2** fix *kakuritsu-suru* 確立する establish a reputation *meisei o kakuritsu-suru* 名声を確立する

estate **1** residence and land *yashiki'* 屋敷 **2** property *za'isan* 財産

esthetic see aesthetic

esthetics see aesthetics

estimate *mitsumori* 見積もり Would you give me an estimate? *Mitsumori o shite kudasaimase'n ka?* 見積もりをして下さいませんか. ——obj *o* (v) *mitsumor・u* 見積もる make a rough estimate *ōyoso no tokoro' o mitsumoru* おおよそのところを見積もる

etching *etchingu* エッチング

eternally *eikyū ni* 永久に

eternity *eien* 永遠

ether *ēteru* エーテル

ethics *ri'nri* 倫理; (the study of) *rinri'gaku* 倫理学

Ethiopia *Echio'pia* エチオピア

Ethiopian **1** (language) *Echiopia'-go* エチオピア語 **2** (person) *Echiopia'jin* エチオピア人 ——(attr) *Echio'pia no* エチオピアの

ethnic *jinshuteki [na]* 人種的[な]; *minzokuteki [na]* 民族的[な]

ethnology *minzoku'gaku* 民族学

etiquette *reigi* 礼儀; *reigi sa'hō* 礼儀作法

etymology *gogen* 語源; (the study of) *goge'ngaku* 語源学

Eucharist **1** (Prot) *Seisa'n-shiki* 聖餐式 **2** (Cath) *Mi'sa* ミサ

Eurasian *[Ō'a] konketsu* [欧亜]混血

Europe *Yōro'ppa* ヨーロッパ

European (person) *Yoroppa'jin* ヨーロッパ人 (attr) *Yōro'ppa no* ヨーロッパの

euthanasia *anra'kushi* 安楽死

evacuate obj *o* (v) *utsu′s·u* 移す ——(pass) be evacuated *utsusare′·ru* 移される 1,200 people were evacuated. *Se′n-nihyaku′nin no hito′ ga utsusa′reta.* 千二百人の人が移された.

evacuation *sokai* 疎開 evacuation from a danger zone *kiken ku′iki kara no sokai* 危険区域からの疎開

evade (v) *nige′·ru* 逃げる ——obj *o* (v) 1 evade taxes (irr) *datsuzei-suru* 脱税する 2 equivocate *haguraka′s·u* はぐらかす He cleverly evaded the question. *Ka′re wa shitsumon o u′maku haguraka′shita.* 彼は質問をうまくはぐらかした.

evaluate obj *o* (irr) *hyō′ka-suru* 評価する evaluate highly *ta′kaku hyō′ka-suru* 高く評価する ——(pass) *hyō′ka-sare·ru* 評価される Her work is not evaluated very highly. *Ka′nojo no shigoto wa amari ta′kaku hyō′ka-sarete ina′i.* 彼女の仕事はあまり高く評価されていない.

evaluation *hyō′ka* 評価

evangelical *fukuin* [no] 福音[の] evangelical preaching *fukuin dendō se′kkyō* 福音伝道説教

evangelism *dendō* 伝道

evangelist (Chr) *dendō′sha* 伝道者

evaporate obj *o* (irr) *jōhatsu-suru* 蒸発する

evaporated milk *eba-mi′ruku* エバミルク

evasion *ka′ihi* 回避

even 1 smooth *name′raka* [na] なめらか[な] 2 equal; uniform *kintō* [no] 均等[の] 3 indeed ... [de]mo ... [で]も Even a child can do it. *Kodomo de′mo deki′ru.* 子供でもできる.

even if -te[de]mo て[で]も Even if I read it, I probably won't understand. *Yo′nde mc, wakara′nai deshō.* 読んでも分からないでしょう.

evening 1 *yūgata* 夕方 towards evening *yūgata chika′ku ni* 夕方近くに; *ban* 晩 this evening *ko′mban* 今晩 In the evening I watch TV. *Ban wa te′rebi o mi′ru.* 晩はテレビを見る. 2 last evening *yūbe* ゆうべ ——(idiom) Good evening! *Komban wa!* 今晩は.

evening dress *i′buningu* イブニング

evening newspaper *yūkan* 夕刊

evening star (e.g., Venus) *yoi no myō′jō* 宵の明星

even number *gūsū* 偶数

event 1 occurrence *deki′goto* 出来事 2 incident *ji′ken* 事件 political event *seijiteki ji′ken* 政治的事件 3 sports event *shiai* 試合

even-tempered *oda′yaka* [na] 穏やか[な]

eventually 1 *yagate* やがて 2 in the end *saishūteki ni* 最終的に 3 finally *kekkyoku* 結局

ever (at any time) ... *koto′ ga ar·u* ...ことがある. Have you ever been to Paris? *Pa′ri ni itta koto′ ga arima′su ka?* パリに行ったことがありますか.

evergreen *jōryo'kuju* 常緑樹

every 1 all *su'bete* [*no*] すべて[の] in every respect *su'bete no ten de* すべての点で 2 each interval of *mai-* 毎 every day *ma'inichi* 毎日 every month *maitsuki* 毎月 every morning *ma'iasa* 毎朝 every night *ma'iban* 毎晩 every week *maishū* 毎週 every week (lit., every week on Thursday) *maishū mokuyo'bi ni* 毎週木曜日に every year *maitoshi* 毎年; -*go'to* ごと every Thursday *mokuyōbi-go'to ni* 木曜日ごとに

everybody *minna'* みんな Everybody come! *Minna ki'te kudasa'i!* みんな来て下さい.

everyday *fudan*[-] 普段 everyday clothes *fuda'ngi* 普段着; *fu'dan* [*no*] 普段[の]; *nichijō* 日常 everyday experience *nichijō saha'nji* 日常茶飯事

everyone 1 *minna'* みんな; *mina* 皆 2 (anyone) *da're* [*de*] *mo* だれ[で]も

every other -*oki* [*ni*] おき[に] every other week *isshūkan-oki* 一週間おき

everything *su'bete* すべて *see also* anything

every time ... *tabi ni* ... たびに every time the telephone rings *denwa ga naru tabi' ni* 電話が鳴るたびに

everywhere *do'ko* [*de*] *mo* どこ[で]も

evidence *shōko* 証拠

evident *aki'raka* [*na*] 明らか[な] His intentions are evident. *Ka're no i'to wa aki'raka desu.* 彼の意図は明らかです.

evidently 1 clearly *aki'raka ni* 明らかに She's evidently mistaken. *Ka'nojo wa aki'raka ni machiga'tte iru.* 彼女は明らかに間違っている. 2 no doubt *oso'raku ... deshō* おそらく...でしょう Evidently he was busy. *Ka're wa oso'raku isoga'shikatta deshō.* 彼はおそらく忙しかったでしょう.

evil *a'ku* 悪 ——(adj) *waru'·i* 悪い、

evolution *shi'nka* 進化 human evolution *ningen no shi'nka* 人間の進化 the theory of evolution *shinka'ron* 進化論

exact 1 precise *sokku'ri* [*na*] そっくり[な] an exact duplicate *sokku'ri na mo'sha* そっくりな模写 2 accurate *seikaku* [*na*] 正確[な] an exact record *seikaku na kiroku* 正確な記録

exactly *chōdo* 丁度 It's exactly one o'clock. *Chōdo ichi' ji desu.* 丁度一時です.; *pitta'ri* ぴったり It fits exactly. *Pitta'ri desu.* ぴったりです.

exaggerated *ōgesa* [*na*] 大げさ[な] an exaggerated tale *ōgesa na hanashi'* 大げさな話

exaggeration *kochō* 誇張 a slight exaggeration *shō'shō no kochō* 少々の誇張

examination 1 test *shike'n* 試験 2 medical examination *shinsatsu*

診察　**3** physical examination *shintai ke'nsa* 身体検査　　**4** audit *ka'nsa* 監査

examine obj *o* (v) *shirabe'·ru* 調べる Did you examine the data? *Shi'ryō o shirabema'shita ka?* 資料を調べましたか。　　——(v) have oneself examined *mi'te mora·u* 診てもらう You should have the doctor examine you. *O-isha-san ni mi'te moratta hō' ga i'i desu.* お医者さんに診てもらった方がいいです。

example **1** *re'i* 例 To give an example ... *Re'i o ageru to ...* 例をあげると ... ; for example *tato'eba* 例えば　　**2** model (for copying) *teho'n* 手本　　——(idiom) set an example *mohan o shimes·u* 模範を示す

exceed obj *o* (v) *koe·ru* 越える exceed 80 km/hr *hachi-ju'kkiro o koeru* 八十キロを越える

excellence *yūshūsa* 優秀さ

excellent **1** *suteki* [na] すてき[な] an excellent dinner *suteki na gochisō* すてきな御馳走　　**2** superior; top class *yūshū* [na] 優秀[な] an excellent school *yūshū na gakkō* 優秀な学校　　——(attr) *sugu'reta* すぐれた an excellent musical performance *sugu'reta ensō* すぐれた演奏

except ... *o nozoite* ...を除いて Except Sunday, we have school every day. *Nichiyō'bi o nozoite, ma'inichi gakkō ga a'ru.* 日曜日を除いて毎日学校がある。

exception *reigai* 例外 without exception *reigai na'shi* [ni] 例外なし[に]

exceptionally *see* very

excess *yobun* [na] 余分[な] excess baggage *yobun na ni'motsu* 余分な荷物

excessively *-sugi'·ru* 過ぎる It's excessively hot. *Atsusugi'ru.* あつ過ぎる。 Last night I drank excessively. *Yūbe nomi-su'gita.* ゆうべ飲み過ぎた。

exchange **1** comp *to* (irr) *kōkan-suru* 交換する They exchanged views on the subject. *Ka'rera wa sono mondai ni tsuite tagai ni i'ken o kōkan-shita.* 彼らはその問題について互いに意見を交換した。　　**2** (money) obj *o* (irr) *ryōgae-suru* 両替する I want to exchange $200 for yen. *Nihyaku do'ru o e'n ni ryōgae-shite itadakita'i.* 200ドルを円に両替していただきたい。　　——obj *o* (v) *torika·e·ru* 取り替える May I exchange these shoes? *Kono kutsu' o torikaete' mo i'i desu ka?* この靴を取り替えてもいいですか。

exchange rate *kawase sō'ba* 為替相場

excited (irr) be/become excited *kōfun-suru* 興奮する Don't get excited! *Kōfun-shina'ide kudasa'i!* 興奮しないで下さい。

exclamation **1** *kantan* 感嘆　　**2** outcry *sakebi'* 叫び　　**3** (Gram) *kantō'shi* 間投詞

exclamation point *kanta'nfu* 感嘆符
exclusive (cliquish) *haitateki* [*na*] 排他的[な]
excursion *ensoku* 遠足
excuse *iiwake* 言い訳 She made an excuse for being late. *Ka'nojo wa chikoku no iiwake o shita.* 彼女は遅刻の言い訳をした. ── ind-obj *ni*, obj *o* (v) **1** forgive *yuru's·u* 許す ──(pot) *yuruse'·ru* 許せる I absolutely cannot excuse that. *Sore wa kesshite yuruse'na'i.* それは決して許せない. **2** exempt (irr) *me'njo-suru* 免除する ──(pass) *me'njo-sare·ru* 免除される He was excused from the exam. *Ka're wa shike'n o me'njo-sareta.* 彼は試験を免除された. **3** excuse oneself from (doing something) (irr) *ji'tai-suru* 辞退する
Excuse me. **1** Forgive me. *Gomen-nasa'i.* ごめんなさい. **2** Excuse me, but … *Sumimase'n ga* … すみませんが… **3** Excuse me, (I must leave). *Shitsu'rei-shimasu.* 失礼します. **4** Excuse me for intruding. *O-jama-shima'su.* お邪魔します. **5** Excuse me for having bothered you. *O-jama-shima'shita.* お邪魔しました. **6** Excuse me, I'd like to ask … *Cho'tto ukagaima'su ga* … ちょっと伺いますが…
executive **1** department *ka'mbu* 幹部 **2** (of a company) *jūyaku* 重役
exercise **1** physical exercise *taisō* 体操; *ta'iiku* 体育 **2** practice *renshū* 練習 practice exercises *renshū mo'ndai* 練習問題 ──(irr) *undō-suru* 運動する Do you exercise every day? *Ma'inichi undō-shima'su ka?* 毎日運動しますか.
exhausted (v) be/become exhausted *tsukare'·ru* 疲れる; *kutabire'·ru* くたびれる I'm exhausted! *Kutabi'reta!* くたびれた.
exhaust gas *haiki-ga'su* 排気ガス
exhaustion *tsukare* 疲れ; *karō* 過労
exhibit *-ten* 展 art exhibit *biju'tsuten* 美術展 ──obj *o* (v) **1** *mise'·ru* 見せる **2** (irr) *tenji-suru* 展示する
exhibition *tenra'nkai* 展覧会
exist (irr) *sonzai-suru* 存在する
existence *sonzai* 存在 the existence of God *Ka'mi no sonzai* 神の存在
existentialism *jitsuzonshu'gi* 実存主義
existentialist *jitsuzonshugi'sha* 実存主義者
exit *de'guchi* 出口 emergency exit *hijō'-guchi* 非常口
exotic **1** *ekizochi'kku* [*na*] エキゾチック[な] **2** (lit., feeling of a foreign country) *ikoku jō'cho no* 異国情緒の
expand obj *o* (irr) *kakuchō-suru* 拡張する
expect obj *o* (v) **1** await *ma'ts·u* 待つ I'm expecting her. *Ka'nojo o ma'tte iru.* 彼女を待っている. **2** hope (irr) *kitai-suru* 期待する ──(pot) *kitai-deki'·ru* 期待できる One can't expect much to

come of that. *Sore ni ō'ku wa kitai-deki'nai.* それに多くは期待で
きない.

expected *atarimae* [*no*] 当たり前[の] something which is expected
atarimae no koto' 当たり前のこと; ... *hazu* [*no*] ...はず[の] He is
expected to arrive tomorrow. *Ka're wa ashita tsu'ku hazu desu.* 彼
はあした着くはずです. ——(ad) as expected *yaha'ri* やはり Just
as I expected, it was expensive. *Yaha'ri, sore wa ta'kakatta.* やは
りそれは高かった.

expedite obj *o* (v) *hayame'·ru* 早める expedite a negotiation *kōshō
o hayame'ru* 交渉を早める

expedition *ensei* 遠征; *tanken* 探検

expenditure *shi'shutsu* 支出 fiscal expenditure *zaisei shi'shutsu* 財
政支出

expense 1 cost *hi'yō* 費用 The expenses will come to about ¥50,
000. *Hi'yō wa goman-en gu'rai ni na'ru.* 費用は五万円ぐらいにな
る. 2 (business) *ke'ihi* 経費 3 (household) *kakei* 家計 4 (traveling) *ryohi* 旅費

expensive (adj) *taka'·i* 高い Meat is expensive. *Niku'wa taka'i.* 肉
は高い.

experience *keiken* 経験 have experience *keiken ga a'ru* 経験がある
have no experience *keiken ga na'i* 経験がない ——obj *o* (irr) *kei-
ken-suru* 経験する ——(idiom) to have experienced (something)
... *koto' ga a'r·u* ... ことがある Have you ever had the experience
of climbing Mt. Fuji? *Fu'ji-san ni nobotta koto' ga arima'su ka?*
富士山に登ったことがありますか.

experiment (scientific) *jikken* 実験

expert *ku'rōto* 玄人; *pu'ro* プロ ——(attr) *jōzu'* [*na*] 上手[な]
She's expert at painting. *Ka'nojo wa e' ga jōzu' desu.* 彼女は絵が
上手で.

explain ind-obj *ni*, obj *o* (irr) *setsumei-suru* 説明する

explanation *setsumei* 説明

explicit (attr) *hakki'ri-shita* はっきりした He was not explicit
about it. *Ka're wa hakki'ri-shita koto' wa iwana'katta.* 彼ははっ
きりしたことは言わなかった.

explode (irr) *bakuhatsu-suru* 爆発する

exploit obj *o* (irr) *sa'kushu-suru* 搾取する exploit workers *rōdō'sha
o sa'kushu-suru* 労働者を搾取する

exploration *tanken* 探検

explosion *bakuhatsu* 爆発

export *yushutsu* 輸出 export business *yushutsu bō'eki* 輸出貿易
export goods *yushutsu-hin* 輸出品 ——obj *o* (irr) *yushutsu-suru* 輸
出する

exposure (camera setting) *roshutsu* 露出 exposure meter *roshutsu-
kei* 露出計

express **1** (train) *kyūkō* 急行 **2** limited express *tokubetsu kyū'kō* 特別急行; *tokkyū* 特急 **3** (mail) *sokutatsu* 速達 Send this by express mail, please. *Sokutatsu ni shite kudasa'i.* 速達にして下さい。 ——obj *o* (irr) express in words *hyōge'n-suru* 表現する

expression **1** (facial) *hyōjō'* 表情 **2** (verbal) *hyōge'n* 表現

expressway *kōsoku dō'ro* 高速道路

extend obj *o* (v) *noba'su* 伸ばす extend life *jumyō o noba'su* 寿命を伸ばす ——(v) be extended *nobi'·ru* 伸びる It will extend to a height of 30 cm. *Sore wa sanjusse'nchi ni nobi'ru.* それは30センチに伸びる。

extension **1** enlargement *kakuchō* 拡張 **2** postponment *enki* 延期

exterior *ga'ibu* 外部

extinct *zetsumetsu [no]* 絶滅[の] an extinct species *zetsumetsu'shu* 絶滅種 ——(irr) be/become extinct *zetsumetsu-suru* 絶滅する

extinguish obj *o* (v) *kes·u* 消す extinguish a fire *hi' o kesu* 火を消す

extinguisher *see* fire extinguisher

extra *yobun [no]* 余分[の] Do you have any extra paper? *Yobun no kami' ga arima'su ka?* 余分の紙がありますか。

extract obj *o* (v) *nuk·u* 抜く extract a tooth *ha' o nuku* 歯を抜く

extraordinary *ijō [na]* 異常[な]; *hibon [na]* 非凡[な]

extravagance *zeita'ku* ぜいたく

extravagant *zeita'ku [na]* ぜいたく[な] extravagant living *zeita'ku na seikatsu* ぜいたくな生活

extreme *kyokutan [no]* 極端[の]

extremely *hijō ni* 非常に It's extremely cold this winter. *Kotoshi no fu'yu wa hijō ni samu'i.* 今年の冬は非常に寒い。

extrovert *gaikōteki [na]* 外向的[な] He's an extrovert. *Ka're wa gaikōteki de'su.* 彼は外向的です。

eye *me'* 目

eyebrow *ma'yuge* 眉毛

eyelash *ma'tsuge* まつ毛

eyelid *ma'buta* まぶた

eyesight *shiryoku* 視力 ——(idiom) **1** poor eyesight [*me' ga*] *yo'ku mie'nai* [目が]よく見えない She has poor eyesight. *Ka'nojo wa me' ga yo'ku mie'nai.* 彼女は目がよく見えない。 **2** good eyesight [*me' ga*] *yo'ku mie'·ru* [目が]よく見える

F

fabric **1** cloth *ki'ji* 生地 **2** textile *orimono* 織物

face **1** *kao* 顔 wash one's face *kao o arau* 顔を洗う **2** honor *memboku* 面目 lose face *memboku o ushinau* 面目を失う; *kao* 顔 cause (someone) to lose face *kao o tsubusu* 顔をつぶす ——*dir ni* (v) *muka·u* 向かう It's on the right as you face the front. *Shō-me'n ni mukatte migi-gawa de'su.* 正面に向かって右側です. —— *dir ni obj o* (v) *muke·ru* 向ける Face the blackboard (lit., turn your eyes to the blackboard)! *Kokuban ni me' o muke-nasa'i!* 黒板に目を向けなさい.

face card *e'fuda* 絵札

face powder *oshiroi* おしろい

facetious (attr) *fuza'keta* ふざけた Don't be facetious! *Fuza'keta mane o suru' na!* ふざけたまねをするな.

face value *gakumen ka'kaku* 額面価格

facilities *be'ngi* 便宜 facilities for doing research *kenkyū no be'ngi* 研究の便宜

fact *ji'jitsu* 事実 investigate the facts *ji'jitsu o shirabe'ru* 事実を調べる ——(idiom) in fact *jitsu' wa* 実は; *hontō wa* 本当は In fact, I didn't have time. *Hontō wa, jikan ga na'katta.* 本当は時間がなかった.

faction 1 *habatsu* 派閥 2 sect; coterie *ha* 派

factionalism *habatsu a'rasoi* 派閥争い

factor (cause; component) *yōin* 要因

factory *kōjō'* 工場

faculty (teachers) *kyōju'kai* 教授会; (member of) *kyōshoku'in* 教職員

fad *ryūkō [no]* 流行[の] a dance fad *ryūkō no da'nsu* 流行のダンス take up the latest fad *ryūkō o ou* 流行を追う

fade (v) *same'·ru* さめる a color that won't fade *same'nai iro* さめない色 ——(idiom) *iro' ga ochi'·ru* 色が落ちる Will these jeans fade when I wash them? *Kono jīpan o arau to, iro' ga ochima'su ka?* このジーパンを洗うと色が落ちますか.

faded (attr) *shioreta* しおれた a faded flower *shioreta hana'* しおれた花

Fahrenheit *ka'shi* 華氏

fail compl *ni* (irr) 1 fall short of a goal *shippai-suru* 失敗する fail in a new venture *atarashi'i kokoromi' ni shippai-suru* 新しい試みに失敗する 2 make a failing grade *rakudai-suru* 落第する He failed algebra. *Ka're wa daisū' de rakudai-shita.* 彼は代数で落第した.

faint (adj) *usu·i* 薄い ——(irr) *kizetsu-suru* 気絶する ——(idiom) 1 *ki o ushina·u* 気を失う She was so shocked, she fainted. *Ka'nojo wa sho'kku no amari, ki o ushina'tta.* 彼女はショックのあまり、気を失った. 2 feel faint *ki ga tōku na'r·u* 気が遠くなる I feel faint. *Ki ga tōku narisō' desu.* 気が遠くなりそうです.

fair 1 exhibition *hakura'nkai* 博覧会 2 market *i'chi* 市 3 impartial *kōhei* [*na*] 公平[な] a fair opinion *kōhei na i'ken* 公平な意見

fairly 1 rather *ka'nari* かなり It's fairly far. *Ka'nari tōi.* かなり遠い.; *ke'kkō* けっこう It's fairly difficult. *Ke'kkō muzukashi'i.* けっこう難しい. 2 with impartiality *kōhei ni* 公平に She treats people fairly. *Ka'nojo wa hito' o kōhei ni toriatsukau.* 彼女は人を公平に取り扱う.

fairway (golf) *feau'ē* フェアウェー

fairy *yōsei* 妖精

fairy tale *otogiba'nashi* おとぎ話

faith (Chr) *shinkō* 信仰; (Budd) *shinji'n* 信心

faithful *chūjitsu* [*na*] 忠実[な] He's a faithful employee. *Ka're wa sho'kumu ni chūjitsu na hito' desu.* 彼は職務に忠実な人です.

fake *nisemono* にせもの This woodblock print is a fake. *Kono hanga wa nisemono de'su.* この版画はにせものです.

falcon *hayabusa* 隼; *taka* 鷹

fall autumn *a'ki* 秋 ——(v) 1 *ochi'·ru* 落ちる It fell! *O'chite shimatta!* 落ちてしまった. Don't fall! *Ochi'naide!* 落ちないで. 2 stumble *korob'u* ころぶ She fell off her bike. *Ka'nojo wa jite'nsha ni notte koronda.* 彼女は自転車に乗ってころんだ. 3 (of blossoms) *chir·u* 散る The (cherry) blossoms fell early this year. *Kotoshi wa hana' ga ha'yaku chitte shima'tta.* 今年は花が早く散ってしまった.

false *u'so* [*no*] うそ[の] a false report *u'so no hōkoku* うその報告

falsehood *u'so* うそ

false teeth *ireba* 入れ歯

falsetto *ura-goe* 裏声

fame *meisei* 名声 His fame spread throughout the world. *Ka're no meisei wa sekai-jū'ni hiromatta.* 彼の名声は世界中に広まった.

familiar *najimi* [*no*] なじみ[の] a familiar product *najimi no shinamono* なじみの品物 ——compl *ni* (v) be familiar with *naji'm·u* なじむ He's familiar with Japanese customs. *Ka're wa Nihon no shūkan ni naji'nde iru.* 彼は日本の習慣になじんでいる.

family 1 (one's own) *ka'zoku* 家族; *uchi* 家 My family spends summer vacations in Karuizawa. *Uchi de wa Karu'izawa e hisho' ni ikima'su.* 家では軽井沢へ避暑に行きます. 2 (another's) *go-ka'zoku* 御家族 Do you live with your family? *Go-ka'zoku to issho ni su'nde imasu ka?* 御家族と一緒に住んでいますか.

famine *kiki'n* 飢きん

famous *yūmei* [*na*] 有名[な] a famous sculptor *yūmei na chōkoku'-ka* 有名な彫刻家 She is famous. *Ka'nojo wa yūmei de'su.* 彼女は有名です.

fan 1 (folding) *sensu* 扇子 2 (flat) *uchi'wa* うちわ 3 (electric) *sempū'ki* 扇風機 ——obj *o* (v) *ao'g·u* あおぐ

fanatic (person) *kyōshi'nsha* 狂信者 ——(attr) *kichigai-me'ita* 気違いめいた

fanatical *kyōshinteki* [*na*] 狂信的[な]

fancy daydream *kūsō* 空想 ——(attr) elaborate *ko'tta* 凝った fancy pattern *ko'tta gara* 凝った柄

fang 1 (snake's) *do'kuga* 毒牙 2 (animal's) *ki'ba* きば

fantastic 1 *fūga'wari* [*na*] 風変わり[な] 2 splendid *suteki* [*na*] すてき[な]

fantasy *fa'ntaji* ファンタジー; *musō* 夢想; *gensō* 幻想

far *mukō* [*no*] 向こう[の] very far *zutto mukō* ずっと向こう —— (adj) *tō·i* 遠い far place *tōi tokoro'* 遠い所 Is it far? *Tō'i desu ka?* 遠いですか.

fare *ryō'kin* 料金

Far East *Kyokutō* 極東

far-fetched *kojitsuke* [*no*] こじつけ[の]

farm *nōjō'* 農場 ——obj *o* (v) *tagaya's·u* 耕す

farm equipment *nō'gu* 農具

farmer *hyakushō'* 百姓; *nōmin* 農民

farming *nō'gyō* 農業

farsighted (eyesight) *enshi* [*no*] 遠視[の]

fart *onara* おなら ——(idiom) to fart *onara o suru* おならをする

farther *see* further

fascinated by compl *ni* (irr) *utto'ri-suru* うっとりする fascinated by a musical selection *o'ngaku no shirabe ni utto'ri-suru* 音楽の調べにうっとりする; *miryō-suru* 魅了する ——(pass) *miryō-sare·ru* 魅了される be fascinated by a woman *onna' ni miryō-sare'ru* 女に魅了される

fascination *miryoku* 魅力

fascism *fashi'zumu* ファシズム

fashion *fa'sshon* ファッション

fashionable *hayari* [*no*] はやり[の] a fashionable restaurant *hayari no re'sutoran* はやりのレストラン; *ryūkō* [*no*] 流行[の] fashionable style *ryūkō no suta'iru* 流行のスタイル

fast *danjiki* 断食 ——(irr) *danjiki-suru* 断食する

fast (adj) *haya'·i* 速い That runner is fast. *Sono se'nshu wa haya'i.* その選手は速い. ——(v) be fast (e.g., a timepiece) *susum·u* 進む My watch is fast. *Watashi no tokei wa susunde iru.* 私の時計は進んでいる. ——(adv) *ha'yaku* 速く run fast *ha'yaku hashi'ru* 速く走る

fasten obj *o* (v) *tome·ru* 留める fasten down with nails *kugi de tomeru* 釘で留める fasten a button *bo'tan o tomeru* ボタンを留める

fat *abura* 脂 cut off the fat *abura o kiritoru* 脂を切りとる fry in fat *abura de itame'ru* 脂で炒める; (Tech) *shibō* 脂肪 fatty meat *shibō no ō'i niku'* 脂肪の多い肉 ——(adj) *futo'·i* 太い fat legs *futo'i ashi'* 太い足 ——(v) be/become fat *futo'r·u* 太る I've gotten a little fat. *Suko'shi futo'tta.* 少し太った. He's fat. *Ka're wa futo'tte iru.* 彼は太っている・ ——(attr) *futo'tta* 太った a fat person *futo'tta hito'* 太った人

fatal 1 *shukumeiteki* [*na*] 宿命的[な] 2 crucial *chimeiteki* [*na*] 致命的[な]

fatalism *shukume'iron* 宿命論

fatalist *shukumeiro'nsha* 宿命論者

fatalities *shibō'sha* 死亡者 There were no fatalities in the automobile accident. *Jidōsha ji'ko de shibōsha wa dena'katta.* 自動車事故で死亡者は出なかった.

fatally 1 *shukumeiteki* [*ni*] 宿命的[に] 2 critically *chimeiteki* [*ni*] 致命的[に]

fate *u'mmei* 運命 a whim of fate *u'mmei no itazura* 運命のいたずら; *shukumei* 宿命 That's fate! *Sore wa shukumei de'su!* それは宿命です.

father 1 (one's own) *chichi'* 父; (address) *o-tō'san* お父さん 2 (another's) *o-tō'san* お父さん 3 (Chr) priest *shi'mpu* [*-san*] 神父[さん]

father-in-law 1 (one's own) *giri no chichi'* 義理の父 2 (another's) *giri no o-tō'san* 義理のお父さん

fatigue *karō* 過労

faucet 1 *jaguchi* 蛇口 2 (handle) *ko'kku* コック

fault 1 defect *kette'n* 欠点 That's one of his faults. *Sore wa ano'hito no kette'n desu.* それはあの人の欠点です. 2 responsibility *sekinin* 責任 That's his fault. *Sore wa ka're no sekinin de'su.* それは彼の責任です. 3 blame *se'i* せい It was my fault. *Watashi no se'i deshita.* 私のせいでした.

favor compl *ni* (irr) *sansei-suru* 賛成する The majority was in favor of the motion. *Kaha'nsū ga dō'gi ni sansei-shita.* 過半数が動議に賛成した. ——(idiom) *o-negai* お願い I have a favor to ask. *O-negai ga a'ru.* お願いがある.

favorite *hi'iki* [*no*] ひいき[の] a favorite Kabuki actor *hi'iki no kabuki ya'kusha* ひいきの歌舞伎役者

favoritism *ekohi'iki* えこひいき

fawn *kojika* 子鹿

fear *kyō'fu* 恐怖 sense of fear *kyōfu'kan* 恐怖感 see also worry

fearful (adj) *osoroshi'·i* 恐ろしい; *kowa'·i* 怖い have a fearful experience *kowa'i me ni a'u* 怖い目に会う

feasible *jikkō-kanō* [*na*] 実行可能[な] Do you think it's feasible? *Sore wa jikkō-kanō da' to omoima'su ka?* それは実行可能だと思いますか.

feast 1 *gochisō* ごちそう 2 banquet *enkai* 宴会 ——ind-obj *ni,* obj *o* (irr) give a feast *gochisō-suru* ごちそうする   ——(idiom) be treated to a feast *gochisō ni na'ru* ごちそうになる

feather   *hane* 羽 feather bed *hane-bu'ton* 羽ぶとん

feature   **1** characteristic *tokuchō* 特徴   **2** facial features *kao-katachi* 顔形   **3** merit *torie'* 取柄 Her honesty is her only redeeming feature. *Shō ji'ki dake' ga ka'nojo no torie' desu.* 正直だけが彼女の取柄です.

February   *nigatsu'* 二月 February **2** *ni'gatsu futsuka* 二月二日

federation   *remmei* 連盟

fee   **1** *ryō'kin* 料金   **2** *-ryō* 料 doctor's fee *shinsatsu'-ryō* 診察料   **3** honorarium *sharei* 謝礼   **4** tutorial fee *gessha* 月謝

feed   *esa'* 餌   ——obj *o* (caus) *tabesase'·ru* 食べさせる

feel   compl *ni* (v) *fure·ru* 触れる I realized this material was silk when I felt it. *Kono ki'ji wa ki'nu da to, furete waka'tta.* この生地は絹だと, 触れてわかった.   ——obj *o* (v) **1** *sawar·u* 触る Feel this! *Kore o sawatte goran!* これを触ってごらん.   **2** (emotion) *kanji·ru* 感じる I feel (sorrow at) the loss of my father. *Chichi o ushinatte, kanashimi o kanji'ru.* 父を失って, 悲しみを感じる.   ——(idiom) feel sick *ki'bun ga waru·i* 気分が悪い I feel sick. *Ki'bun ga waru'i.* 気分が悪い.

feeling   **1** sensation *kanji* 感じ a good feeling *kanji ga i'i* 感じがいい; a disgusting feeling *iya'na kanji* いやな感じ   **2** mood *kimochi* 気持ち She understands other people's feelings. *Ka'nojo wa hito no kimochi ga yo'ku waka'ru.* 彼女は人の気持ちがよくわかる.   **3** emotion *kanjō* 感情 a person of strong feelings *kanjō no hageshi'i hito* 感情の激しい人   ——(idiom) have a feeling (about/toward) ... *kanji ga suru* ...感じがする I don't have a very good feeling toward him/her. *Ano' hito ni wa amari i'i kanji ga shina'i.* あの人にはあまりいい感じがしない.

fellow   **1** companion *dō'shi* 同志   **2** guy *aitsu* あいつ; *ya'tsu* 奴

fellowship   (companionship) *shimboku* 親睦 see also scholarship

felony   *jūzai* 重罪

female   **1** (human) *josei* 女性; (woman) *onna' no hito* 女の人; (young girl) *onna' no ko* 女の子   **2** (bird) *mendori* 雌鳥   **3** (animal) *mesu'* 雌

feminine   *shito'yaka* [*na*] しとやか[な]   ——(adj) *onna-rashi'·i* 女らしい

femininity   *onna-ra'shisa* 女らしさ

feminism   **1** *da'njo dōkenshu'gi* 男女同権主義   **2** women's liberation *ūman-ri'bu* ウーマンリブ

fence   *hei* 塀

fencing   *fe'nshingu* フェンシング

fermentation   *hakkō* 発酵

fern   *shi'da* 羊歯

ferryboat 1 (for passengers and vehicles) *feribō'to* フェリーボート 2 (for passengers only) *renrakusen* 連絡船

fertile *hiyoku* [na] 肥沃[な]

fertilizer *hi'ryō* 肥料

fervor *netsujō* 熱情

festival *matsuri* 祭り; *o-ma'tsuri* お祭り

fetish *ju'butsu* 呪物

fetus *ta'iji* 胎児

feudalism *hōken* 封建

feudal system *hōken se'ido* 封建制度

fever *netsu'* 熱 Do you have a fever? *Netsu' ga arima'su ka?* 熱がありますか.

few 1 *suko'shi* 少し Give me a few. *Suko'shi kudasa'i.* 少し下さい. 2 mere *wa'zuka na* わずかな Only a few people came to the party. *Sono pā'ti ni wa wa'zuka na hito' shika ko'nakatta.* そのパーティーにはわずかな人しか来なかった. ——(adj) *sukuna'·i* 少ない There were only a few people. *Hito' ga sukuna'katta.* 人が少なかった.

fiancé; fiancée *kon'yaku'sha* 婚約者 (see heir; heiress)

fiber *se'n'i* 繊維

fiction (literature) 1 novel *shōsetsu* 小説 2 story *monoga'tari* 物語

fidelity 1 *chūjitsu'do* 忠実度 2 sound *hakushi'ndo* 迫真度

field 1 open field *no'hara* 野原 2 cultivated field *hatake* 畑 3 grass field *kusahara* 草原 4 one's specialty *semmon* 専門 That's not in my field. *Sore wa watashi no semmon-ga'i desu.* それは私の専門外です.

fierce (adj) 1 *hageshi'·i* 激しい a fierce wind *hageshi'i kaze* 激しい風 2 frightful *kowa'·i* 怖い a fierce dog *kowa'i inu'* 怖い犬

fifteen *jū'go* 十五; 15 years old *jūgo'sai* 十五歳

fifth 1 (ordinal) *gobam-me* 五番目 2 (fraction) *gobun no ichi* 五分の一

fifth day of the month *itsuka* 五日

fifty *gojū'* 五十 see also Appendix 1

fig *ichi'jiku* いちじく

fight 1 *tatakai* 戦い 2 quarrel *kenka* けんか ——comp to (v) 1 *tataka·u* 戦う 2 quarrel (irr) *kenka-suru* けんかする

figure 1 numeral *sūji* 数字 the figure 4 *sūji no yo'n* 数字の4 2 human body *ji'ntai* 人体 3 appearance *su'gata* 姿 a slim figure *hosso'ri-shita su'gata* ほっそりした姿 ——obj *o* (irr) *keisan-suru* 計算する ——(idiom) *sūji ga a'·u* 数字が合う That doesn't figure. *Sūji ga awa'nai.* 数字が合わない.

file 1 (tool) *yasuri* やすり 2 nail file *tsume ya'suri* 爪やすり 3

(folder) *fa'iru* ファイル file cabinet *fairu kya'binetto* ファイルキャビネット

filial piety *oya kō'kō* 親孝行

Filipina; Filipino *Firipi'njin* フィリピン人

fill (idiom) **1** make full *ippai ni suru* いっぱいにする Fill the glass, please. *Koppu ippai ni shite kudasa'i.* コップいっぱいにして下さい. **2** fill a car gas tank *mantan ni suru* 満タンにする Fill the tank, please. *Mantan ni shite kudasa'i.* 満タンにして下さい.

filling (in a tooth) *jūten* 充てん

filling station *gasorin suta'ndo* ガソリンスタンド

film **1** (for a camera) *fi'rumu* フィルム color film *karā fi'rumu* カラーフィルム black-and-white film *shiro-kuro fi'rumu* 白黒フィルム **2** a movie *eiga* 映画

filter *fi'rutā* フィルター ——obj *o* (v) *kos·u* こす; (irr) *ro'kasuru* ろ過する

fin *hire* ひれ

finally **1** at last *yatto* やっと I finally did it! *Yatto de'kita!* やっとできた. **2** in the end *tō'tō* とうとう It finally stopped raining. *Tō'tō a'me ga yanda.* とうとう雨がやんだ. **3** ultimately *kekkyoku* 結局 He finally made a mess of everything. *Kekkyoku ka're wa na'ni mo ka'mo mecha'kucha ni shite shima'tta.* 結局彼は何もかもめちゃくちゃにしてしまった.

finance **1** *za'isei* 財政 national finance *kokka za'isei* 国家財政 **2** private finances *kojin sho'toku* 個人所得

finance company *yūshi-ga'isha* 融資会社

finance department *zaimu'-bu* 財務部; finance section *zaimu-ka* 財務課

financial affairs (of a company) *zaisei* 財政

financing (loan) *yūshi* 融資

find obj *o* (v) *mitsuke·ru* 見つける Did you find a good one? *I'i no o mitsukema'shita ka?* いいのを見つけましたか.

fine (penalty) *bakkin* 罰金 ——obj *o* (irr) *bassu'ru* 罰する

fine (exceptional) *rippa [na]* 立派[な] a fine boy *rippa na otoko' no ko* 立派な男の子 a fine attitude *rippa na ta'ido* 立派な態度

Fine, thank you! *Ge'nki desu!* 元気です.

finger *yubi'* 指 index finger *hitosashi'-yubi* 人差し指 middle finger *naka'-yubi* 中指 ring finger *kusuri'-yubi* 薬指 little finger *ko-yubi* 小指 thumb *oya-yubi* 親指

fingernail *tsume* 爪

fingerprint *shimon* 指紋

finish *shiage* 仕上げ rough finish *ara-shi'age* 荒仕上げ ——(v) *su'm·u* 済む Are you finished? *Sumima'shita ka?* 済みましたか.; *owar·u* 終わる The work is finished. *Shigoto ga owa'tta.* 仕事が終

わった. ——obj *o* (v) finish (something) *owar·u* 終わる finish high school *kōtōga'kkō no katei o owaru* 高等学校の課程を終わる; *oe·ru* 終える finish school and get a job *gakkō o oete, shūshoku-suru* 学校を終えて就職する; *sumase'·ru* 済ませる Finish this work! *Kono shigoto o sumase-nasa'i!* この仕事を済ませなさい.; (finalize) *shiage'·ru* 仕上げる

finish (doing something) *-owar·u* 終わる Have you finished reading that novel? *Sono shōsetsu o yomi-owarima'shita ka?* その小説を読み終わりましたか.

Finland *Fi'nrando* フィンランド

Finn *Finrando'jin* フィンランド人

Finnish (language) *Finrando-go* フィンランド語 ——(attr) *Fi'nrando no* フィンランドの

fir *mo'mi-no-ki* もみの木

fire 1 *hi'* 火 2 bonfire *takibi* たき火 3 conflagration *ka'ji* 火事 Fire! *Ka'ji da!* 火事だ. 4 flame *ho'nō* 炎 ——obj *o* (v) fire (a gun) [*jū' o*] *u'ts·u* [銃を]撃つ ——(idiom) 1 discharge *kubi ni suru* 首にする 2 be discharged *kubi ni na'r·u* 首になる

fire alarm *kasai hōchi'ki* 火災報知器

firecracker *kanshakudama* かんしゃく玉

fire department *shōbō'sho* 消防署

fire engine *shōbō'sha* 消防車

fire extinguisher *shōka'ki* 消火器

fire fighter *shōbōshi* 消防士

firefly *ho'taru* 蛍

fire hydrant *shōkasen* 消火栓

fire insurance *kasai ho'ken* 火災保険

fireman *see* fire fighter

fireplace 1 (W) *da'nro* 暖炉 2 (J) *irori* 囲炉裏

fireplug *see* fire hydrant

fire station *shōbō'sho* 消防署

firewood *maki* 薪

fireworks *ha'nabi* 花火

firm (company) *kaisha* 会社

firm (hard; resolved) (adj) *kata·i* 堅い firm resolution *katai ke'-sshin* 堅い決心 ——(v) become firm *kataku-na'r·u* 堅くなる Leave it in the refrigerator until it gets firm. *Kataku-na'ru made, reizō'ko ni irete o'ite kudasai.* 堅くなるまで冷蔵庫に入れておいて下さい.

first 1 (in rank) *ichi'ban* 一番 I was first. *Watashi wa ichi'ban de-shita.* 私は一番でした. 2 primary *da'i-ichi* [*no*] 第一[の] The first goal is this. *Da'i-ichi' no mokuhyō wa kore de'su.* 第一の目標はこれです. 3 earliest *saisho* [*no*] 最初[の] first experience *saisho no keiken* 最初の経験 4 (ordinal) *ichiban-me'* 一番目 5 first gear of a car *dai-ichi gi'ya* 第一ギヤ ——(adv) 1 first time *haji'mete*

初めて Is this your first time in Japan? *Niho'n wa haji'mete desu ka?* 日本は初めてですか.　　**2** at first *hajime [ni]* 初め[に] At first it's difficult. *Hajime wa muzukashi'i.* 初めは難しい.

first aid　*ōkyū te'ate* 応急手当

first day of the month　*tsuitachi* 一日

first day of the year　*ganjitsu* 元日

first generation　*i'ssei* 一世

first name　*namae* 名前

fiscal　**1** fiscal expenditure *zaisei shi'shutsu* 財政支出　**2** fiscal year *kaikei ne'ndo* 会計年度

fish　*sakana* 魚　——(idiom) to fish *sakana o tsur'u* 魚を釣る

fisherman　*ryō'shi* 漁師

fishery　*gyogyō* 漁業

fishhook　*tsuri-bari* 釣り針

fishing　*uo-tsuri* 魚釣り

fishing rod　*tsuri-zao* 釣り竿

fish market　*uo i'chiba* 魚市場

fishmonger　*sakanaya* 魚屋

fist　*kobushi* 拳

fit　compl *ni* (v) *a'・u* 合う Those shoes don't fit me (lit., my feet). *Sono kutsu' wa watashi'no ashi'ni awa'nai.* その靴は私の足に合わない.　——ind-obj *ni*, obj *o* (v) *awase'・ru* 合わせる I had this dress altered to fit me. *Kono fuku no sa'izu o awa'sete moratta.* この服のサイズを合わせてもらった.

fitting　*karinui* 仮縫い

five　*itsu'tsu* 五つ; *go'* 五 see also Appendix 1

fix　obj *o* (v) *nao's・u* 直す Can you fix it? *Nao'su koto' ga dekima'su ka?* 直すことができますか.　——(v) be/become fixed *nao'r・u* 直る The radio is fixed. *Ra'jio wa na'otta.* ラジオは直った. It can't be fixed. *Naora'nai.* 直らない.　——(idiom) be in a fix *koma'r・u* 困る I'm in a fix. *Koma'tta.* 困った.

fixed　**1** established *kisei [no]* 既成[の] fixed moral principles *kisei no dōtoku* 既成の道徳　**2** prescribed *kitei [no]* 規定[の] a fixed time *kitei no jikan* 規定の時間　——(v) be fixed *kimar'・u* 決まる The date's fixed. *Hinichi wa kimatte iru.* 日にちは決まっている.　——(attr) *kimatta* 決まった a fixed way of doing *kimatta hōhō* 決まった方法

fixture　*bihin* 備品

flag　**1** *hata'* 旗　**2** national flag *kokki* 国旗

flame　*ho'nō* 炎

flamingo　*furami'ngo* フラミンゴ

flannel　*fura'nneru* フランネル; *ne'ru* ネル

flap　obj *o* (v) *habata'k・u* 羽ばたく; (irr) *haba'taki-suru* 羽ばたきする

flash 1 *hirameki'* ひらめき 2 flash bulb *fura'sshu* フラッシュ
——(v) *hirame'k·u* ひらめく

flashlight *kaichū de'ntō* 懐中電灯

flat 1 *taira* [na] 平ら[な] a flat surface *taira na hyōme'n* 平らな表
面 2 flat tire *panku* パンク 3 (Music) *hen-* 変 A flat *hen'-i* 変イ
——(adj) *hirata'·i* 平たい The bottom of the bathtub is flat. *Furo-
o'ke no soko ga hirata'i.* 風呂桶の底が平たい。

flatter (idiom) *oseji o i·u* お世辞を言う You're flattering me! *Oseji
ga uma'i desu ne'!* お世辞がうまいですね。

flattery *oseji* お世辞 That's flattery! *Sore wa oseji deshō'!* それは
お世辞でしょう。

flavor *aji* 味 ——(idiom) 1 add flavor *aji o tsuke'·ru* 味を付ける
2 have flavor *aji ga a'r·u* 味がある

flavorful (attr) *aji no a'ru* 味のある

flavorless (attr) *aji no na'i* 味のない

flaw 1 scratch *kizu* 傷 2 defect *kette'n* 欠点

flax *asa'* 麻

flea *nomi'* のみ flea powder *nomitoriko* のみ取り粉

flesh (human) *nikutai* 肉体 2 meat *niku'* 肉

flexible (idiom) *yūzū ga kik·u* 融通がきく

flight (airline) 1 (domestic) *kokunaibin* 国内便 2 (international)
kokusaibin 国際便

flight attendant *kyakushitsu jōmu'in* 客室乗務員

flight number *hikō ba'ngō* 飛行番号; Flight 104 *hyakuyombin* 104
便

flint (for lighter) *ishi'* 石

flippers (for skin diving) *ashihire* 足ひれ

flirt compl *to* (v) *fuzake'·ru* ふざける

float *uki* 浮き ——(v) *ukab·u* 浮かぶ float on water *mizu ni uka-
bu* 水に浮かぶ; *uk·u* 浮く float (up) to the surface of the water
suimen ni uku 水面に浮く

flock *mure'* 群れ ——(v) *muraga'r·u* 群がる

flood *kōzui* 洪水

flood tide *manchō* 満潮

floor 1 *yuka* 床 2 *-kai* 階 1st floor *ikkai* 一階 2nd floor *nikai* 二
階 3rd floor *sangai* 三階 4th floor *yonkai* 四階 what floor *nangai*
何階

floor lamp [*furoa*] *suta'ndo* [フロア]スタンド

floppy disk *furoppī-di'suku* フロッピーディスク

florist *hana'ya* 花屋

flounder *hirame* 平目 ——(v) *magotsuk·u* まごつく

flour 1 wheat flour *komugiko* 小麦粉 2 soy flour *ki'nako* きな
粉

flow *nagare'* 流れ ——(v) *nagare'·ru* 流れる The river flows to the sea. *Kawa' wa u'mi ni nagare'ru.* 川は海に流れる.

flower *hana'* 花

flower garden *hanazono* 花園

flowerpot *ueki'-bachi* 植木鉢

flu *infurue'nza* インフルエンザ

fluctuate (v) *furatsuk·u* ふらつく; (irr) *hendō-suru* 変動する

fluently *pe'rapera* ぺらぺら; *ryūchō ni* 流ちょうに; *su'rasura [to]* すらすら[と] That person speaks Japanese fluently. *Sono' hito wa su'rasura to Nihon-go o hana'su.* その人はすらすらと日本語を話す.

fluffy (attr) *fu'wafuwa-shita* ふわふわした fluffy pillow *fu'wafuwa-shita makura* ふわふわした枕

fluid *ryūtai* 流体; (liquid) *ekitai* 液体 ——(attr) *ryūdōsei no* 流動性の

flunk compl *ni* (irr) *rakudai-suru* 落第する

fluorescent light *keikōtō* 蛍光灯

fluoride treatment (for teeth) *[ha' no] fusso chi'ryō* [歯の]ふっ素治療

fluorine *fu'sso* ふっ素

flush (the toilet) *mizu o naga's·u* 水を流す

flush toilet *suisen be'njo* 水洗便所

flustered (v) be/become flustered *awate·ru* あわてる Don't be flustered! *Awatena'ide!* あわてないで. ——(adv) in a dither *awatete* あわてて He left the house flustered. *Ka're wa awatete ie' o de'ta.* 彼はあわてて家を出た.

flute *fue* 笛 play a flute *fue o fuku* 笛を吹く; (W) *furū'to* フルート

fly (insect) *hae* 蝿

fly loc *o* (v) *to'b·u* 飛ぶ This species of bird doesn't fly. *Kono shu'rui no tori wa tobana'i.* この種類の鳥は飛ばない. ——(idiom) **1** fly in an airplane *hikō'ki ni no'r·u* 飛行機に乗る **2** go by plane *hikō'ki de ik·u* 飛行機で行く Are you going to fly to Osaka? *Ōsaka ni hikō'ki de ikima'su ka?* 大阪に飛行機で行きますか.

fly swatter *haeta'taki* 蝿たたき

foam *awa'* 泡 foam on water *mizu no awa'* 水の泡 make foam *awa' o tate'ru* 泡をたてる

foam rubber *suponji* スポンジ

focus *shō'ten* 焦点 the focus of a problem *mondai no shō'ten* 問題の焦点 ——(v) be in focus *a'·u* 合う Is the camera in focus? *Pinto ga a'tte ima'su ka?* ピントが合っていますか. ——obj *o* (v) **1** *awase'r·u* 合わせる focus a camera *pinto o awase'ru* ピントを合わせる **2** focus on *shibo'r·u* 絞る Let's focus on this prob-

lem. *Kono mondai ni shō'ten o shiborimashō'.* この問題に焦点を
絞りましょう.

fog *kiri* 霧 dense fog *fuka'i kiri* 深い霧 The fog is thick. *Kiri ga
fuka'i.* 霧が深い.

foggy (idiom) become foggy *kiri ga ta'ts·u* 霧がたつ

fold obj *o* (v) *tatam·u* たたむ Fold the shirts, please. *Sha'tsu o
tatande o'ite kudasa'i.* シャツをたたんでおいて下さい.

folder (file holder) *fa'iru* ファイル

folding chair *oritatami'-isu* 折りたたみ椅子

foliage *happa* 葉っぱ

folk etymology *minkan go'gen* 民間語源; *tsūzoku go'gen* 通俗語源

folk music *fō'ku* フォーク

folk song (J) *min'yō* 民謡

folk tale *minwa* 民話

follow compl *ni* (v) comply with *shitaga·u* 従う Follow the leader!
Ri'dā ni shitagai-nasa'i! リーダーに従いなさい. ——(idiom) **1**
a'to ni tsu'k·u 後につく Follow me! *Watashi no a'to ni tsu'ite kite
kudasa'i!* 私の後について来て下さい. **2** tail *a'to o tsuke'·ru* 後を
つける Follow that cab! *Sono ta'kushī no a'to o tsuke'te kudasa'i!*
そのタクシーの後をつけて下さい.

following *tsugi' no* 次の the following quotation *tsugi' no in'yō* 次
の引用

follow-up *afutā-ke'ā* アフターケアー

fondle obj *o* (v) *nade'·ru* 撫でる fondle a cat *ne'ko o nade'·ru* 猫を
撫でる

food *tabemono'* 食べ物; *ryō'ri* 料理 Chinese food *Chūka ryō'ri* 中
華料理 Korean food *Chōsen ryō'ri* 朝鮮料理 Western food *Seiyō
ryō'ri* 西洋料理; *-shoku* 食 Japanese food *Washoku* 和食

food poisoning *shoku chū'doku* 食中毒

foodstuff 1 *shokuryōhin* 食料品 **2** canned goods *kanzu'me* 缶詰

fool *ba'ka* ばか You fool! *Ba'ka!* ばか! ——obj *o* (v) **1** trick;
cheat *gomaka's·u* ごまかす **2** deceive *dama's·u* だます ——
(pass) *damasare'·ru* だまされる I was fooled by his sweet talk.
Ano' hito no ama'i kotoba ni damasa'reta. あの人の甘い言葉にだ
まされた. ——(idiom) be made a fool of *baka ni sare'·ru* ばかに
される He made a fool of me. *Ano' hito ni baka ni sa'reta.* あの
人にばかにされた.

foolish (adj) *bakarashi'·i* ばからしい That was a foolish thing to
do. *Sore wa bakarashi'i koto' deshita.* それはばからしいことでし
た.

foot 1 *ashi'* 足 **2** (measurement) *fi'to* フィート

footprint *ashi-a'to* 足跡

footstep *ashi-oto'* 足音 I can hear footsteps. *Ashi-oto' ga kikoeru.*
足音が聞こえる.

footstool *ashi-dai* 足台; *da'i* 台
footwear *hakimono* 履物
for 1 ... *de* ... で for ¥1,000 *se'n-en de* 千円で I bought this for ¥1,000. *Se'n-en de kore o katta.* 千円でこれを買った。 2 during ... *[no] aida* ... [の]間 I haven't seen him for a long time. *Naga'i aida ka're ni awa'nakatta.* 長い間彼に会わなかった。 Would you mind watching the baby for an hour? *Ichiji'kan no aida, kono' ko o mi'te ite kudasaimase'n ka?* 一時間の間この子を見ていて下さいませんか。 3 for the purpose of ... *[no] tame [ni]* ... [の]ため[に] I walk for exercise. *Undō no tame' ni aruku.* 運動のために歩く。 This is for you. *Kore wa ana'ta no tame' desu.* これはあなたのためです。
forbidden (pass) *kinjirare·ru* 禁じられる Alcohol is forbidden. *O-sake wa kinjirarete iru.* お酒は禁じられている。
force 1 physical force *chikara'* 力 2 violence *bō'ryoku* 暴力 3 power; influence *se'iryoku* 勢力 ——obj *o* (irr) *mu'ri-suru* 無理する Don't force it! *Mu'ri-shina'ide!* 無理しないで。 Don't force the issue! *Mu'ri-shite mondai o kaiketsu-suru' na!* 無理して問題を解決するな。 ——(adv) with force *shi'ite* 強いて I'm not going to force my son to study. *Shi'ite musuko' ni benkyō o sase'nai.* 強いて息子に勉強をさせない。
forecast *yohō* 予報 weather forecast *tenki yo'hō* 天気予報
foreclose obj *o* (caus) *ha'ijo-saseru* 排除させる
forehead *hitai* 額; (coll) *ode'ko* おでこ
foreign *gaikoku no* 外国の
foreign correspondent *kaigai tokuha'in* 海外特派員; *tokuha'in* 特派員
foreign country *gaikoku* 外国
foreign diplomacy *gaikō* 外交
foreign diplomat *gaikō'kan* 外交官
foreigner *gaikoku'jin* 外国人; *gaijin* 外人
foreign exchange *gaikoku ka'wase* 外国為替
foreign language *gaikokugo* 外国語
foreign minister *gaimu da'ijin* 外務大臣
foreign policy *gaikō se'isaku* 外交政策
foreign relations *gaikō* 外交
foresee obj *o* (irr) *yo'chi-suru* 予知する foresee a calamity *saigai o yo'chi-suru* 災害を予知する
foresight (idiom) have foresight *mesaki' ga kik·u* 目先がきく
foreskin (Anat) *hō'hi* 包皮
forest 1 *mori* 森 2 grove; wood *hayashi* 林 3 dense forest *mi-tsurin* 密林
foretell obj *o* (irr) *yogen-suru* 予言する
forever 1 always *i'tsu made mo* いつまでも I'll love you forever.

I'tsu made mo a'ishite iru. いつまでも愛している。 **2** eternally *eikyū ni* 永久に It will last forever. *Eikyū ni mo'tsu.* 永久に持つ.

foreword *maegaki* 前書き

forfeit obj *o* (irr) *sōshitsu-suru* 喪失する

forget obj *o* (v) **1** *wasure•ru* 忘れる I forgot the appointment. *Ya-kusoku o wasureta.* 約束を忘れた。 **2** let slip one's mind (irr) *uk-ka'ri-suru* うっかりする Oh, I forgot! *A, ukka'ri-shite ita!* あ、うっかりしていた.

forgive obj *o* (v) *yuru's•u* 許す Forgive me for (doing) that. *Sore o yuru'shite kudasa'i.* それを許して下さい.; (irr) *ka'nnin-suru* 堪忍する ——(pot) *ka'nnin-deki•ru* 堪忍できる I can't forgive that. *Sore wa ka'nnin-deki-nai.* それは堪忍できない.

Forgive me! (idiom) **1** It was rude of me! *Shitsu'rei-shima'shita!* 失礼しました. **2** I was wrong! *Ka'mben-shite [kudasa'i]* 堪弁して下さい].

forgiveness *yurushi* 許し

forgiving *kan'yō [na]* 寛容[な] a forgiving person *kan'yō na hito'* 寛容な人

fork *fō'ku* フォーク

form **1** shape *katachi* 形 **2** figure *su'gata* 姿 a graceful/beautiful form *yū'bi na su'gata* 優美な姿 **3** established procedure *keishiki* 形式 dramatic form *gikyoku no keishiki* 戯曲の形式 **4** (for a document) *yōshi* 用紙

formal *seishiki [no]* 正式[の] a formal dinner *seishiki no bansa'nkai* 正式の晩餐会

formal dress *reifuku* 礼服

formally *seishiki ni* 正式に They're not formally married yet. *Sono futari' wa ma'da seishiki ni kekkon-shite ina'i.* その二人はまだ正式に結婚していない.

former **1** *mo'to no* もとの her former house *ka'nojo no mo'to no ie'* 彼女のもとの家 **2** the former (aforementioned) *ze'nsha* 前者

formerly *mo'to [wa]* もと[は]; *ma'e [wa]* 前[は] Formerly, Japan's capital was Kyoto. *Ma'e wa, Nihon no shu'to wa Kyō'to deshita.* 前は日本の首都は京都でした.

forsake obj *o* (v) *misute•ru* 見捨てる forsake a friend *tomodachi o misuteru* 友達を見捨てる

for sale *urimono* 売り物 Is this for sale? *Kore wa urimono de'su ka?* これは売り物ですか。 ——(idiom) "House For Sale" *Uriya* 売り家

fort *toride* 砦

fortunate *saiwai [na]* 幸い[な] a fortunate occurrence *saiwai na deki'goto* 幸いな出来事 We're fortunate to have money. *Wata'-*

shi-tachi wa o-kane ga a'ru kara saiwai de'su. 私たちはお金がある から幸いです.

fortunately *saiwai ni* 幸いに Fortunately, the person wasn't hurt. *Sono' hito wa saiwai ni kega' o shina'ide su'nda.* その人は幸いに けがをしないで済んだ.

fortune *za'isan* 財産 She lost all her fortune. *Ka'nojo wa za'isan o ze'mbu ushinatte shima'tta.* 彼女は財産を全部失ってしまった. ——(idiom) **1** good fortune *kōun* 幸運 **2** bad fortune *fukō'* 不幸 **3** Read my fortune (lit., palm), please. *Teso'o mi'te kudasa'i.* 手 相を見て下さい.

fortune teller *urana'ishi* 占い師; *ekisha* 易者

fortunetelling *uranai* 占い

forty *yo'njū* 四十 *see also* Appendix 1

forward *ma'e e* 前へ go forward *ma'e e susumu* 前へ進む

fossil *kaseki* 化石

foster child **1** (female) *yō'jo* 養女 **2** (male) *yōshi* 養子

foul (smelling) (adj) *kusa'·i* 臭い

found (v) be found *mitsukar·u* 見付かる Was your wallet found? *Saifu wa mitsukarima'shita ka?* 財布は見付かりましたか. *see also* establish

foundation **1** base *ki'so* 基礎 the foundation of a building *bi'ru no ki'so* ビルの基礎 **2** fund (or endowment or organization that administers such) *kiki'n* 基金 relief fund *kyūsai ki'kin* 救済基金 The Asia Foundation *Ajia Ki'kin* アジア基金 The Japan Founda- tion *Kokusai Kōryū Ki'kin* 国際交流基金

founder *sōritsu'sha* 創立者; *sōshi'sha* 創始者

fountain *funsui* 噴水

fountain pen *manne'nhitsu* 万年筆; *pe'n* ペン

four *shi'*; *yo'n* 四; *yottsu'* 四つ *see also* Appendix 1

fourteenth day of the month *jū' yokka* 十四日

fourth **1** (ordinal) *yombam-me'* [*no*] 四番目[の] **2** (fraction) *yom- bun no ichi* 四分の一 **3** fourth gear of a car *da'i-yo'n gi'ya* 第四 ギヤ

fourth day of the month *yokka* 四日

fox *kitsune* 狐

fraction **1** small number *shōsū'* 少数 **2** one part *ichi'bu* 一部

fracture **1** *hibi'* ひび **2** bone fracture *kossetsu* 骨折 ——(idiom) to fracture *hone'o o'r·u* 骨を折る He fractured his leg. *Ka're wa ashi no hone' o o'tta.* 彼は足の骨を折った.

fragile (adj) *koware-yasu'·i* こわれやすい ——(idiom) "Fragile" *waremono* われもの

fragment *kakera* 欠けら a fragment of rock *iwa no kakera* 岩の欠 けら

fragrance *kaori* 香り

fragrant (attr) *kaori no i'·i* 香りのいい

frail (adj) *kayowa'·i* か弱い

frame *fuchi* 縁 picture frame *gaku-buchi* 額縁 ——(idiom) to frame *gaku-buchi ni ire·ru* 額縁に入れる I'd like to have this picture framed. *Kono e' o gaku-buchi ni irete itadakita'i.* この絵を額縁に入れていただきたい.

framework *waku-gumi* 枠組

France *Furansu* フランス

franchise *tokken* 特権; *tokkyo* 特許

frank *sotchoku* [na] 率直[な] She's a frank person. *Ka'nojo wa sotchoku na hito' desu.* 彼女は率直な人です.

frankly *sotchoku ni* 率直に Frankly speaking ... *Sotchoku ni ie'ba* ... 率直に言えば...

frantic *kyo'ki* [no] 狂気[の]

frantically *kyo'ki ni* 狂気に

fraud *sa'gi* 詐欺

freckles *sobaka'su* そばかす

free 1 unrestricted *jiyū'* 自由 free trade *jiyū bo'eki* 自由貿易 free will *jiyū i'shi* 自由意志 2 gratis *ta'da* [no] ただ[の] Was it free? *Ta'da deshita ka?* ただでしたか. 3 not engaged *hima* [na] 暇[な] free time *hima na jikan* 暇な時間 Call me when you're free. *Hima na toki denwa-shite kudasa'i.* 暇な時電話して下さい. Are you free on Saturday? *Doyo'bi wa hima de'su ka?* 土曜日は暇ですか. ——obj *o* (v) let go; separate from *hana'su* 離す You mustn't let the dog free. *Inu' o hana'shite wa ikenai.* 犬を離してはいけない. ——(idiom) free (something/someone); give freedom to *jiyū' ni suru* 自由にする

freedom *jiyū'* 自由

freelance *jiyū ke'iyaku* [no] 自由契約[の]; *furī* [no] フリー[の] —— (idiom) work freelance *jiyū ke'iyaku de hataraku* 自由契約で働く

freely *jiyū' ni* 自由に

free of charge *sa'bisu* サービス

free time *hima* 暇

freeway *kōsoku do'ro* 高速道路

freeze (v) *kōr·u* 凍る Water freezes at 0° C. *Re'ido de mizu ga kōru.* 零度で水が凍る. The faucet won't budge; it's frozen. *Jaguchi ga kōtte ugoka'nai.* 蛇口が凍って動かない. ——obj *o* (v) *kōra·se·ru* 凍らせる; (irr) *reitō-suru* 冷凍する Freeze the meat. *Niku' o reitō-shite kudasa'i.* 肉を冷凍して下さい.

freezer *reitō'ko* 冷凍庫

freight 1 (light) *ni'motsu* 荷物 2 (heavy) *ka'motsu* 貨物 freight train *kamotsu re'ssha* 貨物列車 3 freight expenses *u'nchin* 運賃; *yuso'ryō* 輸送料

freighter *kamotsusen* 貨物船
French 1 (language) *Furansu-go* フランス語 2 (person) *Furansu'jin* フランス人 (attr) *Furansu no* フランスの
french fries *poteto fura'i* ポテトフライ
frequency *hi'ndo* 頻度
frequently *tabitabi* たびたび; *yo'ku* よく Do you come here frequently? *Yo'ku koko e kima'su ka?* よくここへ来ますか.
fresh *shinsen* [na] 新鮮[な] fresh air *shinsen na kū'ki* 新鮮な空気 ——(adj) *atarashi'·i* 新しい Is this bread fresh? *Kono pa'n wa atarashi'i desu ka?* このパンは新しいですか.
freshly *-tate* [no] 立て[の] freshly made *dekitate* 出来立て freshly painted *nuritate* 塗り立て
freshman *ichine'nsei* 一年生
friction 1 chafing *masatsu* 摩擦 trade friction *bōeki ma'satsu* 貿易摩擦 2 clash; disagreement *fu'wa* 不和 friction between two persons *hito to hito no aida no fu'wa* 人と人の間の不和
friction tape *zetsuen tē'pu* 絶縁テープ
Friday *kin'yō'bi* 金曜日
fried 1 ...*fu'rai*... フライ fried oysters *kaki fu'rai* かきフライ; *-yaki* 焼き fried egg *medama-yaki* 目玉焼き 2 deep-fried (attr) *ageta* 揚げた
friend 1 *tomodachi* 友達; *yūjin* 友人 2 close friend *shin'yū* 親友 3 buddy *nakama* 仲間 ——comp *to* (irr) make friends *na'kayoku-suru* 仲良くする Be friends! *Na'kayoku-shite!* 仲良くして! Won't you be this child's friend? *Kono' ko to na'kayoku-shimase'n ka?* この子と仲良くしませんか.
friendly *yūkō* 友好; *yūkōteki na* 友好的な friendly relations *yūkō ka'nkei* 友好関係 ——(irr) to be friendly; make oneself agreeable *aisōyo'ku-suru* 愛想よくする
friendship *yūjō* 友情; *yūkō* 友好
frightened (irr) be/become frightened *bi'kubiku-suru* びくびくする I'm frightened by thunder and lightning. *Kaminari ga ochina'i ka to bi'kubiku-suru.* 雷が落ちないかとびくびくする.; *doki'tto-suru* どきっとする I'm frightened every time the telephone rings. *Denwa ga naru tabi' ni, doki'tto-suru.* 電話が鳴るたびにどきっとする.
frightening (adj) *kowa'·i* 怖い That movie was frightening. *Sono e'iga wa ko'wakatta.* その映画は怖かった. That person looks frightening. *Sono' hito wa kowa'i kao o shite iru.* その人は怖い顔をしている.
fringe benefits *te'ate* 手当
frog 1 *kaeru* 蛙 2 bullfrog *ga'ma* がま
from 1 ...*kara*... から Where are you leaving from? *Do'ko kara ikima'su ka?* どこから行きますか.; from (place/time) to (place/

time) ... *kara* ... *made* ...から...まで from July to September *shichigatsu' kara ku'gatsu made* 七月から九月まで; from (person/place) to (person/place) ... *kara* ... *ni* ...から...に This letter came to me from my uncle in America. *Kono tegami wa Amerika no oji-san kara watashi ni okura'rete kita.* この手紙はアメリカのおじさんから私に送られてきた. **2** born in *shusshin* 出身 I'm from Hokkaido. *Hokka'idō shusshin de'su.* 北海道出身です. ——(adv) from now/here on *kore kara* これから I'm going to study harder from now on. *Kore kara mo'tto benkyō-shita'i to omou.* これからもっと勉強したいと思う. Where are you going from here? *Kore kara do'ko e ikima'su ka?* これからどこへ行きますか.

front 1 before ... *[no] ma'e [ni]* ...[の]前[に] It's in front of the post office. *Yūbi'nkyoku no ma'e ni a'ru.* 郵便局の前にある. **2** the front *omote'* 表 She went out front. *Ka'nojo wa omote' ni de'ta.* 彼女は表に出た.

front desk *furonto* フロント

frost *shimo'* 霜 ——(idiom) to frost *shimo' ga ori'·ru* 霜がおりる When I got up this morning there was frost. *Ke'sa o'kitara shimo' ga o'rite ita.* 今朝起きたら霜がおりていた.

frostbite *shimoyake* 霜焼け

frosting (on sweets) *a'ishingu* アイシング; *satō-go'romo* 砂糖衣

frown *shikamettsura* しかめっつら ——(idiom) to frown *shika-mettsura o suru* しかめっつらをする; *ma'yu o hisome'·ru* 眉をひそめる

frozen (attr) *reitō [-shita]* 冷凍[した] frozen goods *reitō sho'kuhin* 冷凍食品 frozen fish *reitō'-gyo* 冷凍魚

fruit 1 *kuda'mono* 果物 **2** dried fruit *dorai furu'tsu* ドライフルーツ ——(idiom) produce fruit *mi ga na'r·u* 実がなる Last year this tangerine tree didn't bear fruit. *Kyo'nen, kono mi'kan no ki wa mi ga nara'nakatta.* 去年このみかんの木は実がならなかった.

fruit store *kudamonoya* 果物屋

frustrating (adj) *jiretta'·i* じれったい This bumper-to-bumper driving is frustrating. *Kono noronoro u'nten wa mattaku jiretta'i.* このののろ運転はまったくじれったい.

fry obj *o* (v) *itame'·ru* 炒める; *yak·u* 焼く fry eggs *tamago o yaku* 卵を焼く ——(idiom) *fura'i ni suru* フライにする

frying pan *furai pan* フライパン

fuel *nenryō'* 燃料

fuel oil (for kerosene stove) *tōyu* 灯油

fulfill obj *o* (v) *mita's·u* 満たす fulfill a condition *jōken o mita's·u* 条件を満たす ——(irr) *suikō-suru* 遂行する fulfill an obligation *gi'mu o suikō-suru* 義務を遂行する

full 1 *ippai [no]* いっぱい[の] Is it full? *Ippai de'su ka?* いっぱいで

すか. I'm full. *Onaka ga ippai de'su.* おなかがいっぱいです. **2** at its peak *man-* 満 full moon *ma'ngetsu* 満月 full tank *mantan* 満タン full tide *manchō* 満潮 full bloom *mankai [no]* 満開[の]

full of *-da'rake [no]* だらけ[の] full of faults *ketten-da'rake* 欠点だらけ

full-time *jōkin [no]* 常勤[の] full-time instructor *jōkin kō'shi* 常勤講師 How many full-time workers are there in this company? *Kono kaisha ni wa jōkin sha'in ga na'nnin ima'su ka?* この会社には常勤社員が何人いますか.

fumes *ga'su* ガス; *kemuri* 煙

fun *yu'kai [na]* 愉快[な] It was fun. *Yu'kai deshita.* 愉快でした. ——(adj) *tanoshi'i* 楽しい a fun game *tanoshii gē'mu* 楽しいゲーム It was a lot of fun. *Totemo tano'shikatta.* とても楽しかった.

function *yakume'* 役目 My room functions both as a sitting room and a bedroom. *Watashi no heya' wa ima to shinshitsu no futa'tsu no yakume' o suru.* 私の部屋は居間と寝室の二つの役目をする.; *yakushoku* 役職 What is his function in the company? *Ka're wa kaisha de do'nna yakushoku ni tsuite ima'su ka?* 彼は会社でどんな役職についていますか.

fundamental *kisoteki [na]* 基礎的[な] fundamental problem *kisoteki na mondai* 基礎的な問題

funds **1** (endowment) *kiki'n* 基金 the International Monetary Fund (IMF) *Kokusai Tsūka Ki'kin* 国際通貨基金 **2** (scholarship) *shiki'n* 資金 *shōgaku shi'kin* 奨学資金

funeral service *sōshiki* 葬式; *o-sōshiki* お葬式

fungus *shinki'n-rui* 真菌類

funnel *jō'go* じょうご

funny (adj) *okashi'-i* おかしい

fur *kegawa* 毛皮

furnace *ro* 炉 see also boiler

furnished *kagutsuki* 家具付き furnished apartment *kagutsuki apā'to* 家具付きアパート

furniture *ka'gu* 家具

further (ahead) *mo'tto saki* もっと先 My house is further ahead. *Uchi wa mo'tto saki de'su.* 家はもっと先です.

fuse (electrical) *hyū'zu* ヒューズ

fuss *izakoza* いざこざ; *go'tagota* ごたごた ——(irr) *go'tagota-suru* ごたごたする They're fussing about that at home. *Sore de ie' ga go'tagota-shite iru.* それで家がごたごたしている.

futile *muda [na]* 無駄[な] futile plans *muda na keikaku* 無駄な計画

futility *muda* 無駄

future *shō'rai* 将来 in the near future *chikai shō'rai [ni]* 近い将来[に]; *mi'rai* 未来

future tense (Gram) *mirai-kei* 未来形
fuzzy (attr) *kebada'tta* 毛羽立った

G

gabfest (coll) *mudaba'nashi* むだ話
gag (idiom) *no'do ga tsuma'r·u* のどが詰まる I gagged on a piece of toast. *Tōsuto o hito'kuchi ta'bete, no'do ga tsuma'tta.* トースト を一口食べてのどが詰まった.
gaily *kaikatsu ni* 快活に
gain 1 profit; earning *ri'eki* 利益 ——(v) increase *fue'·ru* 増える gain a pound in weight *taijū ga ichi-po'ndo fue'ru* 体重が一ポンド 増える ——(idiom) gain a profit *ri'eki o u'·ru* 利益を得る
galaxy *gi'nga* 銀河 galactic system *ginga-kei* 銀河系
gale *kyōfū* 強風
gall bladder *tannō* 胆のう
gallery (picture) *garō* 画廊
gallop [*uma no*] *haya-ashi* [馬の]早足 ——(idiom) The horse galloped off. *Uma' ga ka'kete itta.* 馬が駆けて行った.
gamble ind-obj *ni*, obj *o* (v) *kake'·ru* 賭ける ——(idiom) *gya'mburu o suru* ギャンブルをする My husband never gambles. *Uchi no shu'jin wa kesshite gya'mburu o shimase'n.* うちの主人は決っ してギャンブルをしません. see also bet
gambling *bakuchi* ばくち She lost ¥100,000 gambling. *Ka'nojo wa bakuchi de jūman-en tora'reta.* 彼女はばくちで十万円取られた.
game 1 *asobi* 遊び 2 sport *supo'tsu* スポーツ 3 contest *shiai* 試 合 4 parlor game *gē'mu* ゲーム 5 prey *emono* 獲物
gander *gachō no osu'* 鵞鳥の雄
gang *gya'ngu* ギャング
gangrene *e'sso* 壊そ; *da'sso* 脱そ
gangster *gyangu'-dan no ichi'in* ギャング団の一員; (abbr) *gya'ngu* ギャング ——(attr) *gya'ngu no* ギャングの
gap *sukima* 透き間
garage *sha'ko* 車庫; *garēji* ガレージ
garbage *gomi'* ごみ dispose of garbage *gomi' o sute'ru* ごみを捨て る
garbage can *gomi-bako* ごみ箱
garbage collector *gomi'ya* [*-san*] ごみ屋[さん]
garden 1 *niwa* 庭 2 Japanese traditional garden *Nihon te'ien* 日 本庭園 3 (flower) *hanazono* 花園 4 (rock) *sekitei* 石庭 5 (vegetable) *yasai-ba'take* 野菜畑 6 (botanical) *shokubutsu kō'en* 植物 公園; *shokubutsu'en* 植物園

gardener *uekiya* [-*san*] 植木屋[さん]

gargle (irr) *ugai-suru* うがいする

garlic *ninniku* にんにく garlic press *ninniku tsubu′shiki* にんにくつぶし器

garment *i′fuku* 衣服; *i′rui* 衣類

garter *kutsushita-dome* 靴下留め

gas (for gas appliances) *ga′su* ガス

gas company *gasu-ga′isha* ガス会社

gash *wareme* 割れ目

gas meter *gasu me′tā* ガスメーター

gasoline *gasorin* ガソリン put in gasoline *gasorin o ireru* ガソリンを入れる; (coll) *sekiyu* 石油 Gasoline's expensive. *Sekiyu ga taka′i.* 石油が高い.

gasp (idiom) to gasp *i′ki o kira′s·u* 息を切らす After I ran up the flight of stairs, I was gasping for breath. *Kaidan o i′kki ni kakenobori, i′ki o kira′shite ita.* 階段を一気に駆けのぼり、息を切らしていた.

gas station *gasorin suta′ndo* ガソリンスタンド

gate *mo′n* 門 front gate *omotemon* 表門 main gate *seimon* 正門 back gate *uramon* 裏門

gatekeeper *mo′mban* 門番

gather obj *o* (v) *atsume′·ru* 集める gather teaching materials *kyōzai o atsume′ru* 教材を集める ——(v) be gathered *atsuma′r·u* 集まる Many people were gathered there. *Soko ni hito′ ga takusan atsuma′tte ita.* そこに人がたくさん集まっていた.

gathering *atsumari* 集まり

gaudy *hade′* [na] 派手[な] a gaudy color *hade′ na iro′* 派手な色

gauze *gā′ze* ガーゼ gauze mask *gā′ze no ma′suku* ガーゼのマスク

gay *dōsei-a′isha* 同性愛者; (male) *ho′mo* ホモ; *ge′i* ゲイ; (female) *rezubi′an* レズビアン; (abbr) *re′zu* レズ see also cheerful; happy

gaze obj *o* (v) *mitsume·ru* 見つめる gaze at the sky *so′ra o mitsumeru* 空を見つめる gaze into a person's face *hito no kao o mitsumeru* 人の顔を見つめる

gear 1 equipment *dōgu* 道具 fishing gear *tsuri dō′gu* 釣り道具 2 car gears *gi′ya* ギヤ first gear *da′i-ichi gi′ya* 第一ギヤ second gear *da′i-ni gi′ya* 第二ギヤ third gear *da′i-san gi′ya* 第三ギヤ fourth gear *da′i-yon gi′ya* 第四ギヤ reverse gear *bakku gi′ya* バックギヤ put into gear *gi′ya o ireru* ギヤを入れる

gearshift *gi′ya* ギヤ

gelatin *zerachin* ゼラチン

gem *hōseki* 宝石

Gemini *Futago-za* 双子座

gene *ide′nshi* 遺伝子

genealogy 1 *kakei* 家系 2 (the study of) *keizu'gaku* 系図学

general (army) *ta'ishō* 大将 ——(adv) in general *ippanteki ni* 一般的に

general anesthetic *zenshin ma'sui* 全身麻酔

general assembly *sōkai* 総会

general delivery *kyoku-dome* 局止め

general headquarters (military) *sōshire'ibu* 総司令部

generalize *gaikatsu suru* 概括する ——(neg) *ichigai ni [wa]* 一概に[は] One cannot generalize. *Ichigai ni' wa iena'i.* 一概には言えない.

generation *-dai* 代 for many generations *na'ndai ni mo watatte* 何代にもわたって; *sedai* 世代 the younger generation *waka'i sedai* 若い世代

generation gap *sedai no gya'ppu* 世代のギャップ

generator 1 *hatsude'nki* 発電機 2 (car) *jenerēta* ジェネレーター

generous *kandai [na]* 寛大[な] a generous person *kandai na hito'* 寛大な人

genetics *ide'ngaku* 遺伝学

genitals *seisho'kuki* 生殖器

genius *tensai* 天才 He is a genius in chemistry. *Ka're wa ka'gaku no tensai de'su.* 彼は化学の天才です.

gentile *ihō'jin* 異邦人

gentle (adj) *yasashi·i* 優しい She is very gentle. *Ka'nojo wa totemo yasashi'i.* 彼女はとても優しい.

gentleman *shi'nshi* 紳士

gentlewoman *kifu'jin* 貴婦人; *shuku'jo* 淑女

gently 1 *yasashiku* 優しく; *yawara'kaku* 柔らかく 2 quietly *shi'-zuka ni* 静かに; *sotto* そっと

genuine *hommono* 本物 Is this genuine? *Kore wa hommono de'su ka?* これは本物ですか.

geography 1 *chi'ri* 地理 2 (the study of) *chiri'gaku* 地理学

geology 1 *chishitsu* 地質 2 (the study of) *chishitsu'gaku* 地質学

geometry *kika'gaku* 幾何学

geranium *zeranyū'mu* ゼラニューム

germ 1 bacillus *baikin* ばい菌 2 embryo, bud (e.g., wheat germ) *ha'iga* 胚芽

German 1 (language) *Doitsu-go* ドイツ語 2 (person) *Doitsu'jin* ドイツ人 ——(attr) *Do'itsu no* ドイツの

Germany *Do'itsu* ドイツ East Germany *Higashi Do'itsu* 東ドイツ West Germany *Nishi Do'itsu* 西ドイツ

germinate *me' o da'su* 芽を出す

gestation *kaitai* 懐胎 gestation period *kaitai ki'kan* 懐胎期間

gesture *je'suchā* ジェスチャー; *mi'buri* 身振り

get obj *o* (v) 1 receive *mora·u* 貰う From whom did you get that?

Da're ni sore o moraima'shita ka? だれにそれを貰いましたか. **2** acquire (irr) *kakutoku-suru* 獲得する get the right to ... *no ke'nri o kakutoku-suru* ...の権利を獲得する **3** go and bring (irr) *to'tte kuru* 取ってくる Would you get the paper for me, please. *Shimbun o to'tte kite kudasaimase'n ka?* 新聞を取ってきて下さいませんか. **4** get to (arrive) *tsu'k·u* 着く What time does the plane get to Narita? *Hiko'ki wa na'nji ni Na'rita ni tsukima'suka?* 飛行機は何時に成田に着きますか.

get off loc *o* (v) *ori'·ru* 降りる get off the train *de'nsha o ori'ru* 電車を降りる

get on loc *ni* (v) *nor·u* 乗る get on the train *de'nsha ni noru* 電車に乗る

Get out! *De'te ikinasa'i!* 出て行きなさい.; (masc) *De'te ike!* 出て行け.; (fem) *De'te itte!* 出て行って.

get up (v) *oki'·ru* 起きる What time do you get up in the morning? *A'sa na'nji ni okima'su ka?* 朝何時に起きますか. Get up! *Okinasa'i!* 起きなさい.

Ghana *Gā'na* ガーナ

Ghanaian (person) *Gāna'jin* ガーナ人 ——(attr) *Gā'na no* ガーナの

ghost *yū'rei* 幽霊

giant *kyojin* 巨人

gift **1** *okurimono* 贈り物 **2** thank-you gift *o-rei* お礼 **3** souvenir *o-miyage* おみやげ

gifted *tensaiteki* [na] 天才的[な]

giggle (v) *ko'rokoro-wara·u* ころころ笑う

gill *era* えら

gin *ji'n* ジン

ginger *shōga* 生姜

giraffe *kirin* きりん

girdle *ko'rusetto* コルセット

girl **1** *onna' no ko* 女の子 **2** (polite address) *o-jō'san* お嬢さん

girlfriend *gārufure'ndo* ガールフレンド; *onna to'modachi* 女友達

girl scout *gāru suka'uto* ガールスカウト

gist *yōryō'* 要領; *yōte'n* 要点

give ind-obj *ni*, obj *o* (v) **1** give to another *age·ru* 上げる Give this to Ms. Tanaka, please. *Kore o Tanaka-san ni agete kudasa'i.* これを田中さんに上げて下さい. **2** (someone) gives me *kure·ru* くれる He gave this to me. *Ka're wa kore o kureta.* 彼はこれをくれた.; (polite) *kudasa'r·u* 下さる Mr. Tanaka gave this to me. *Tanaka-san ga kore o kudasaima'shita.* 田中さんがこれを下さいました. **3** give to an inferior (or animal or plant) *yar·u* やる Did you give the plants water? *Ueki ni mizu o yarima'shita ka?* 植木に水をやりましたか.

give up obj *o* (v) quit *yame·ru* やめる I gave up cigarettes. *Tabako o yameta.* たばこをやめた. **2** resign oneself to *akirame'·ru* あきらめる I gave up going to Europe this year. *Kotoshi Yōro'ppa e iku koto' wa akira'meta.* 今年ヨーロッパへ行くことはあきらめた.

glacier *hyō'ga* 氷河

glad (adj) *ureshi'·i* うれしい I'm glad! *Ureshi'i!* うれしい.

gladly (willingly) *yoroko'nde* 喜んで I'll gladly keep the children. *Yoroko'nde kodomo o azukarima'su.* 喜んで子供を預かります.

glamorous *miwakuteki* [na] 魅惑的[な]

glance (v) *futo mi'·ru* ふと見る I just happened to glance in that direction. *Futo sotchi no hō' o mi'ta.* ふとそっちの方を見た. —— (idiom) *me' o tō'su* 目を通す I only had time to glance at the headlines this morning. *Ke'sa wa shimbun no midashi ni me' o tō'su gurai shika jikan ga na'katta.* 今朝は新聞の見出しに目を通すぐらいしか時間がなかった.

gland *se'n* 腺 lymph glands *rimpasen* リンパ腺

glare *mabu'shisa* まぶしさ ——obj *o* (v) *nira'm·u* にらむ He glared at me with anger in his eyes. *Ka're wa oko'tta me' de watashi o nira'nda.* 彼は怒った目で私をにらんだ.

glaring (adj) *mabushi'·i* まぶしい

glaringly *gi'ragira to* ぎらぎらと

glass 1 tumbler *koppu* コップ **2** plate glass *garasu* ガラス **3** wine glass *wain gu'rasu* ワイングラス **4** magnifying glass *kakudaikyō* 拡大鏡 **5** one glass/cup of *i'ppai* 一杯 *see also* Appendix 1: glassfuls

glassware *garasu'ki* ガラス器

glaucoma *ryokuna'ishō* 緑内障

glaze (for pottery) *uwagu'suri* 釉薬

gleam (irr) *pika'pika-suru* ぴかぴかする

glide loc *o* (v) *sube'r·u* 滑る

glimmer (idiom) *ho'noka ni kagaya'k·u* ほのかに輝く

glimpse (idiom) catch a glimpse of *chira'ri to mie'·ru* ちらりと見える I just caught a glimpse of her from the back. *Ka'nojo no ushiro-su'gata ga chira'ri to mi'eta.* 彼女の後ろ姿がちらりと見えた.

glitter (idiom) *pika'pika* [*to*] *kagaya'k·u* ぴかぴか[と]輝く

globe *kyū'* 球

globefish *fu'gu* 河豚

gloomy *inki* [na] 陰気[な] ——(adj) *uttōshi'·i* うっとうしい

glorify obj *o* (v) *hometatae'·ru* ほめたたえる

glory *eikō* 栄光

glossary *yōgo ka'isetsu* 用語解説

glossy (irr) be glossy *tsu'yatsuya-suru* つやつやする ——(attr) *tsu'yatsuya-shita* つやつやした

glove *tebu'kuro* 手袋 a pair of gloves *tebu'kuro hito'kumi* 手袋一組

glow (v) *hika'r·u* 光る; (irr) *hakunetsu-suru* 白熱する

glucose *budōtō* ぶどう糖

glue **1** (rice) *nori* 糊 **2** (fish, animal, vegetable) *nikawa* 膠 **3** (fast-setting) *setchaku'-zai* 接着剤 ——obj *o* (v) *tsuke'·ru* 付ける; (coll) *kuttsuke'·ru* くっ付ける

gnat *bu'yo* ぶよ

gnaw obj *o* (v) *kaji'·ru* かじる

go (v) *ik·u* 行く Let's go! *Ikimashō'!* 行きましょう. When are you going to Kyoto? *I'tsu Kyō'to ni ikima'su ka?* いつ京都に行きますか. I went to see a movie with a friend yesterday. *Kinō tomodachi to e'iga o mi'ni itta.* きのう友達と映画を見に行った.

goal **1** *gō'ru* ゴール **2** purpose *mokuhyō* 目標 **3** aim *me'ate* 目当て

go around (circulate) (v) *haya'r·u* はやる A bad cold's been going around. *Waru'i kaze ga haya'tte iru.* 悪い風邪がはやっている.

goat *ya'gi* 山羊

go back (v) *modo'r·u* 戻る go back the way one came *ki'ta michi o modo'ru* 来た道を戻る Go back to your seat. *Se'ki ni modori-nasa'i.* 席に戻りなさい.

go (back) home (v) *ka'er·u* 帰る What time do you go home? *Na'nji ni kaerima'su ka?* 何時に帰りますか.

gobble (food) obj *o* (v) *musaboriku'·u* むさぼり食う

go-between **1** *chūka'isha* 仲介者 **2** (marriage) *baishaku'nin* 媒酌人

god **1** *ka'mi* 神 **2** (Chr) *Ka'mi-sama* 神様

goddess *me'gami* 女神

go down loc *o* (v) *ori'·ru* 降りる go down the stairs *kaidan o ori'ru* 階段を降りる

goggles *fūbō me'gane* 風防めがね; *gō'guru* ゴーグル

gold **1** (metal) *ki'n* 金 18-kt. gold *jūhachi kin* 18金 **2** white gold *howaito gō'rudo* ホワイトゴールド **3** (color) *kin-iro* 金色

golden (made of gold) *kinsei no* 金製の

gold-filled *kimbari [no]* 金張り[の]

goldfish *ki'ngyo* 金魚

gold plating *kimme'kki* 金メッキ

golf *go'rufu* ゴルフ ——(idiom) play golf *go'rufu o suru* ゴルフをする

golf bag *gorufu ba'ggu* ゴルフバッグ

golf ball *gorufu bō'ru* ゴルフボール

golf club **1** wood; iron *gorufu ku'rabu* ゴルフクラブ **2** organization *gorufu ku'rabu* ゴルフクラブ

golf course *gorufu-jō* ゴルフ場

gonorrhea   *rimbyō* 淋病

good   (adj) *i′·i* いい a good idea *i′i kanga′e* いい考え

Good!   *Yo′katta!* よかった.

Good afternoon.   *Konnichi wa.* こんにちは.

Goodbye   **1** *Sayōnara.* さようなら.   **2** (when leaving home) *Itte′ kima′su.* 行って来ます.   **3** (to one leaving) *Itte irassha′i.* 行っていらっしゃい.

Good evening.   *Komban wa.* 今晩は.

good-for-nothing   (person) *namakemono* 怠け者 *see also* lazy person

Good Friday   (Prot) *Juna′mbi* 受難日; (Cath) *Se′i-kin′yō′bi* 聖金曜日

good-looking   **1** (man) *bina′nshi* 美男子   **2** (woman) *bi′jo* 美女; *bi′jin* 美人

good luck   *kō-un* 幸運   ——(idiom) Good luck! *U′maku iku yō′ni!* うまく行くように.

Good morning.   *O-hayō [gozaima′su].* おはよう[ございます].

good-natured   *o-hitoyoshi [no]* お人よし[の]   ——(idiom) *hito′ ga i′i* 人がいい She's good-natured. *Ka′nojo wa hito′ ga i′i.* 彼女は人がいい.

Good night   *O-yasumi [-nasa′i].* おやすみ[なさい].

goods   **1** *shinamono* 品物   **2** manufactured goods *seihin* 製品

good sport   (attr) *kishō no i′i* 気性のいい

good-tempered   *oda′yaka [na]* 穏やか[な]   ——(adj) *yasashi·i* 優しい

goodwill   *yūkō* 友好

goose   *gachō* 鵞鳥

gooseflesh; goose pimples   *toriha′da* 鳥肌

go out   loc *o* (v) *de′·ru* 出る He went out of the room. *Ka′re wa heya′ o de′ta.* 彼は部屋を出た.; (irr) *gaishutsu-suru* 外出する We hardly ever go out anymore. *Wata′shitachi wa konogoro mō′ hoto′ndo gaishutsu-shina′i.* 私たちはこのごろもうほとんど外出しない. *see also* leave

gorgeous   **1** beautiful *karei [na]* 華麗[な]   **2** elegant *gōka [na]* 豪華[な]   ——(adj) *utsukushi′·i* 美しい

gorilla   *go′rira* ゴリラ

gospel   (Chr) **1** *fukuin* 福音   **2** (one of the four gospels in the New Testament) *fukuinsho* 福音書 The Gospel of Mark *Ma′ruko ni yoru fukuinsho* マルコによる福音書

gossip   *uwasa [-ba′nashi]* うわさ[話]   ——(idiom) to gossip *uwasa-ba′nashi o suru* うわさ話をする

gothic   *goshi′kku* ゴシック

go through   loc *o* (v) *tō′r·u* 通る Does the Bullet Train go through Kyoto on the way to Osaka? *Shinkansen wa Kyō′to o tō′tte Ō′saka ni ikima′su ka?* 新幹線は京都を通って大阪に行きますか. This bus goes through Yotsuya. *Kono ba´su wa Yotsuya o tō´ru.* このバスは四ツ谷を通る.; *kugurinuke´·ru* 潜り抜ける When you go through the tunnel, turn right. *To´nneru o kugurinuke´tara, migi ni magarinasa´i.* トンネルを潜り抜けたら，右に曲がりなさい.

go up loc *o* (v) *agar·u* 上がる go up the stairs *kaidan o agaru* 階段を上がる

gourd *hyōta´n* ひょうたん

gourmet *shokutsū* 食通

govern obj *o* (v) *osame´·ru* 治める

government 1 *seiji* 政治 2 national government *se´ifu* 政府 3 cabinet; administration *na´ikaku* 内閣

governor 1 *chi´ji* 知事 2 prefectural governor *ken-chi´ji* 県知事 3 governor of Tokyo *to-chi´ji* 都知事 4 governor of a U.S. state *shū-chi´ji* 州知事

gown 1 bathrobe *ga´un* ガウン 2 (sleeping) *nemaki* 寝間着 3 evening dress *yaka´i-fuku* 夜会服

grab obj *o* (v) 1 *tsuka´m·u* つかむ 2 grab onto (coll) *hittsuka´m·u* ひっつかむ 3 take hold of *torae´·ru* 捕らえる

grace 1 charm *yū´bi* 優美 2 (Chr) [God's] grace *[Ka´mi no] megumi* [神の]恵み 3 (Budd) *oboshimeshi* おぼしめし

graceful *yū´bi [na]* 優美[な]

gracefully *yū´bi ni* 優美に; *shito´yaka ni* しとやかに

gracious *yū´bi [na]* 優美[な] ——(adj) *yasashi´·i* 優しい ——(attr) *kō´i ni mi´chita* 好意に満ちた

grade 1 score *seiseki* 成績 2 rank (in school) *-sei* 生 first grade *ichine´n-sei* 一年生 3 quality *-tō* 等 first grade *ittō* 一等 ——obj *o* (irr) grade (school) papers *saiten-suru* 採点する

gradually *danda´n [to/ni]* だんだん[と/に] You'll gradually come to understand. *Dandan waka´tte ku´ru deshō´.* だんだん分かってくるでしょう.

graduate *sotsugyō´-sei* 卒業生 ——obj *o* (irr) *sotsugyō´-suru* 卒業する ——(idiom) graduate (from college) *[daigaku o] de´·ru* 大学を出る He graduated from college. *Ka´re wa daigaku o de´te iru.* 彼は大学を出ている.

graduate school *daigaku´in* 大学院 graduate-school student *daigakui´n-sei* 大学院生

graduation ceremony *sotsugyō´-shiki* 卒業式

graft 1 corruption *shūwai* 収賄; *oshoku* 汚職 2 (Bot) *tsugiki* つぎ木 ——obj *o* (v) *tsug·u* つぐ

grain 1 cereal *koku´motsu* 穀物 2 (of wood) *mokume* 木目 3 a grain of (cereal) *hito´-tsubu no* 一粒の

gram *gu´ramu* グラム 400 grams *yonhyaku gu´ramu* 400グラム

grammar *bumpō* 文法

grammar school *shōga´kkō* 小学校

grammatical *bumpō-jō no* 文法上の

granary *kokusō* 穀倉

grand *sōdai* [na] 壮大[な]

grandchild 1 (one's own) *mago* 孫 2 (another's) *o-mago-san* お孫さん

granddaughter 1 (one's own) *mago-mu'sume* 孫娘 2 (another's) *o-mago-san* お孫さん

grandfather 1 (one's own) *so'fu* 祖父; (address) *o-ji'-san* おじいさん 2 (another's) *o-ji'-san* おじいさん

grandfather clock *hashira-do'kei* 柱時計

grandmother 1 (one's own) *so'bo* 祖母; (address) *o-bā'-san* おばあさん 2 (another's) *o-bā-san* おばあさん

grandson 1 (one's own) *mago* 孫 2 (another's) *o-mago-san* お孫さん

grandstand *shōmen kanra'nseki* 正面観覧席

granite *kakō'gan* 花崗岩

grant *hojokin* 補助金 a grant from a foundation *kiki'n hojo'kin* 基金補助金 ——ind-obj *ni*, obj *o* (v) 1 consent to *yuru's·u* 許す 2 concede; admit *mitome·ru* 認める I grant that. *Sore o mitomeru.* それを認める. ——(pass) consented to *yurusare'·ru* 許される The request was granted. *Yōkyū wa yurusa'·reta.* 要求は許された.

grape *budō* ぶどう a bunch of grapes *budō hito'-fusa* ぶどう一房

grape arbor *budō-dana* ぶどう棚

grapefruit *gurēpu-furū'tsu* グレープフルーツ

graph *zu* 図; *gu'rafu* グラフ

graphic arts *gurafikku ā'to* グラフィックアート

grapple comp to (v) *tokkumia'·u* 取っ組み合う

grasp obj *o* (v) *tsuka'm·u* つかむ grasp the meaning *i'mi o tsuka'mu* 意味をつかむ; *tsukamae'·ru* 捕まえる She grasped my arm. *Ka'nojo wa watashi no ude'o tsukama'eta.* 彼女は私の腕を捕まえた.

grass 1 *kusa'* 草 2 lawn *shibafu* 芝生

grasshopper *inago* いなご; *batta* ばった

gratefully *ariga'taku* ありがたく

grater *oroshi'gane* おろし金

gratitude *ka'nsha* 感謝 a feeling of gratitude *ka'nsha no kimochi* 感謝の気持ち express gratitude *ka'nsha no i'' o arawa'su* 感謝の意を表わす

gratuity *sharei* 謝礼

grave (tomb) *haka'* 墓

gravel *jari* 砂利

gravestone *haka-ishi* 墓石

graveyard *bo'chi* 墓地; *hakaba* 墓場

gravity *i'nryoku* 引力 the gravity of the earth *chikyū no i'nryoku* 地球の引力

gray 1 *hai-iro* 灰色; *nezumi-iro* 鼠色 **2** gray hair *shiraga'* 白髪

grease 1 *abura* 油 a grease stain *abura'-jimi* 油じみ **2** lard *rā'do* ラード **3** machine lubricant *junkatsu'-yu* 潤滑油

greasy (adj) *abura'kko·i* 油っこい greasy food *abura'kkoi shoku'ji* 油っこい食事

great 1 wonderful *suteki* [*na*] すてき[な] **2** mighty *idai* [*na*] 偉大 [な] ——(adj) *sugo'·i* すごい

great- *hi-* ひ great-grandchild *hi'-mago* ひ孫; *hi* ひい great-grandfather *hi-oji'-san* ひいおじいさん great-grandmother *hi-obā'-san* ひいおばあさん

Great Britain *Igirisu* イギリス; *Eikoku* 英国

Greece *Gi'risha* ギリシャ

greed *don'yoku* 貪欲

greedy *yokuba'ri* [*na*] 欲ばり[な] ——(idiom) greedy about food *kuishi'mbō* 食いしん坊

Greek 1 (language) *Girisha'-go* ギリシャ語 **2** (person) *Girisha'jin* ギリシャ人 ——(attr) *Gi'risha no* ギリシャの

green *mi'dori* 緑; *gurin* グリーン ——(attr) *mi'dori-iro no* 緑色 の

greengrocer *yaoya* [*-san*] 八百屋[さん]

greenhouse *onshitsu* 温室

green light *ao shi'ngō* 青信号

greenroom *gakuya* 楽屋

greens *ao'mono* 青物

greet compl *ni* (v) **1** (irr) *a'isatsu-suru* あいさつする **2** welcome *mukae·ru* 迎える

greeting *a'isatsu* あいさつ

grief 1 *urei* 憂い **2** sadness *kanashimi* 悲しみ

grieve obj *o* (v) **1** *kanashi'm·u* 悲しむ **2** pine *nage'k·u* 嘆く

grill *gu'riru* グリル

grin (v) *ni'yaniya-wara·u* にやにや笑う

grind obj *o* (v) *hik·u* ひく grind coffee beans *kōhī'-mame o hiku* コーヒー豆をひく

gripe (idiom) *fuhei o i·u* 不平を言う She's always griping about something. *Ka'nojo wa i'tsumo na'nika fuhei o itte iru.* 彼女はいつ も何か不平を言っている.

groan obj *o* (v) *ume'k·u* うめく

groceries *shokuryōhin* 食料品 *see also* foodstuff

grocery *yaoya* 八百屋

groom *hanamu'ko* 花婿 bride and groom *hanamu'ko to hana'yome* 花婿と花嫁

grouchy *fuki'gen* [*na*] 不きげん[な]

ground 1 *ji'men* 地面 2 earth *tsuchi'* 土 3 land *tochi* 土地

ground beef *hiki-niku* ひき肉

group 1 *kumi* [-*gumi*] 組 2 (for an excursion/activity) *dantai* 団体 3 meeting; assembly *atsumari'* 集まり 4 coterie; faction *ha* 派 the Akamon Group *Akamon-ha* 赤門派 ——obj *o* (v) *atsume'·ru* 集める

grove *ko'dachi* 木立ち; *hayashi* 林

grow (v) 1 mature (irr) *seichō-suru* 成長する as one grows older *seichō-suru' ni shitagatte* 成長するに従って 2 grow up (be reared) *soda'ts·u* 育つ I grew up in Texas. *Te'kisasu de soda'tta.* テキサスで育った. 3 sprout *hae'·ru* 生える Weeds have grown up in the lawn. *Shibafu ni zassō ga ha'ete kita.* 芝生に雑草が生えてきた. ——obj *o* (v) raise *sodate'·ru* 育てる grow plants *shoku'butsu o sodate'ru* 植物を育てる

grown-up (mature) (attr) *seichō-shita* 成長した; (person) *seijin* 成人 *see also* adult

growth *seichō* 成長

grudge *urami'* 恨み He has a grudge against me. *Ka're wa watashi ni urami'o mo'tte iru.* 彼は私に恨みをもっている. ——obj *o* (v) begrudge *ura'm·u* 恨む

gruel (rice) *o-kayu* おかゆ

grumble (idiom) *bu'tsubutsu o i·u* ぶつぶつを言う

guarantee *hoshō* 保証 ——obj *o* (irr) *hoshō-suru* 保証する

guarantor *hoshōnin* 保証人

guard 1 *shuei* 守衛 2 security officer *hoa'nkan* 保安官 3 gate guard *mo'mban* 門番 ——obj *o* (v) *mamo'r·u* 守る

guardian *hogo'sha* 保護者; (Leg) *kōkennin* 後見人

guardianship *ho'go* 保護

Guatemala *Guatemara* グアテマラ

Guatemalan (person) *Guatemara'jin* グアテマラ人 ——(attr) *Guatemara no* グアテマラの

guess *suisoku* 推測 It's only a guess. *Ta'nnaru suisoku de'su.* 単なる推測です. ——obj *o* (irr) *suisoku-suru* 推測する ——(idiom) … *to omo'·u* … と思う I guess I can do it. *Sore ga deki'ru to omo'u.* それができると思う.

guest *o-kyaku-san* お客さん

guide *ga'ido* ガイド; *annai-ga'kari* 案内係 ——obj *o* (irr) *anna'i-suru* 案内する

guidebook *ryokō a'nnai* 旅行案内

guideline *shishin* 指針

guilt 1 *tsu'mi* 罪 2 (Leg) *yūzai* 有罪

guilty (attr) *yūzai* [*no*] 有罪(の) He was judged guilty. *Ka're wa yūzai to hanketsu-sa'reta.* 彼は有罪と判決された.

guitar *gi'tā* ギター

gulf   *wa'n* 湾 Gulf of Mexico *Mekishiko'-wan* メキシコ湾

gull   *kamome* 鷗

gum (chewing gum)   *ga'mu* ガム

gums   *ha'guki* 歯ぐき

gun   *teppo'* 鉄砲; *jū'* 銃 see also pistol; rifle

gut   *harawata'* はらわた

gutter   1 ditch *mizo* みぞ; *dobu* どぶ fall in the gutter *dobu no na'ka e ochi'ru* どぶの中へ落ちる   2 drain *to'i* とい

gymnasium   *taiku'kan* 体育館

gymnastics   1 *taisō* 体操   2 (school) *ta'iiku* 体育

gynecologist   *fujinka'-i* 婦人科医

gynecology   *fujinka* 婦人科

H

habit   1 practice *shūkan* 習慣 I'm in the habit of getting up early. *Watashi wa haya'oki no shūkan de'su.* 私は早起きの習慣です.   2 peculiarity *kuse'* 癖 get into a habit *kuse' ga tsu'ku* 癖がつく bad habit *waru'i kuse'* 悪い癖 break a habit *kuse' o nao'su* 癖を直す

habitual   *jōshū-* 常習 habitual criminal *jōshū'-han* 常習犯; *jōshūteki [na]* 常習的[な] habitual liar *jōshūteki uso'tsuki* 常習的うそつき

haddock   see cod

haggle   obj *o* (v) *negi'r·u* 値切る

hail   *arare* あられ ——(idiom) to hail *arare ga fu'r·u* あられが降る

hair (human)   1 (head) *kami'* 髪; *kami-no'-ke* 髪の毛   2 (body) *ke* 毛   3 (chest) *munage* 胸毛   4 curly hair *makige* 巻毛   5 straight hair *chokumō* 直毛

hairbrush   *hea-bu'rashi* ヘアブラシ

haircut   *sampatsu* 散髪 ——(irr) get a haircut *sampatsu-suru* 散髪する

hairdo   *kami-gata* 髪型

hairdresser   *biyō'shi* 美容師

hair dryer   *hea-dora'iyā* ヘアドライヤー

hair oil   [*kami-yō*] *a'bura* [髪用]油

hairpin   *hea-pin* ヘアピン

hair rinse   *ri'nsu* リンス

hair spray   *hea-supu'rē* ヘアスプレー

hairstyle   *hea-suta'iru* ヘアスタイル

hairy (animal, human)   (adj) *kebuka'·i* 毛深い

half   1 *hambu'n* 半分 Give me half of it. *Hambun kudasa'i.* 半分下

さい. **2** half a day *hannichi'* 半日 **3** half fare *hangaku* 半額 **4** half price *hanne* 半値 **5** half a year *hantoshi* 半年 **6** one-half *nibun no ichi'* 二分の一

half-blooded *konketsu* 混血

halfhearted *fune'sshin [na]* 不熱心な ——(idiom) *chūto-ha'mpa [na]* 中途半端[な]

half-moon *ha'ngetsu* 半月

half-open *hambiraki [no]* 半開き[の]

half past *-ha'n* 半 half past six *rokuji-ha'n* 六時半

halfway *chūto* 中途

hall **1** *rōka* 廊下 **2** public *kaikan* 会館 **3** municipal *kōkaidō* 公会堂 **4** entry *genkan* 玄関

Halloween *Ha'rouin* ハロウィーン

halo **1** aureole *go'kō* 後光 **2** (sun/moon) *ka'sa* かさ

halt obj *o* (irr) *teishi-suru* 停止する

ham *ha' mu* ハム

hamburger *hambā'gā* ハンバーガー *see also* ground beef

hammer *ha'mmā* ハンマー; *kanazu'chi* 金づち

hand **1** (Anat) *te'* 手 both hands *ryōte* 両手 by hand *te' de* 手で one hand *katate* 片手 with one hand *katate de* 片手で **2** worker *hitode* 人手 We're short of hands. *Hitode ga tarina'i.* 人手が足りない. **3** (of a clock) *ha'ri* 針 the long hand *chōshin* 長針 the short hand *tanshin* 短針

handbag *handoba'ggu* ハンドバッグ

handbook *te'biki* 手引き

hand carving *tebori* 手彫り

handful *hito'tsukami [no]* 一つかみ[の]; *te-i'ppai [no]* 手いっぱい[の]

handicap *handikya'ppu* ハンディキャップ

handicapped person **1** (physical) *shintai shōga'isha* 身体障害者 **2** (mental) *seishin shōga'isha* 精神障害者

handicraft *te-za'iku* 手細工; *shugei* 手芸

handkerchief *hanka'chi* ハンカチ

handle *totte* 取っ手 ——obj *o* (v) *toriatsuka'·u* 取り扱う Handle with care! *Toriatsukai chū'i!* 取り扱い注意.

handlebar *handoru* ハンドル

hand luggage *te-ni'motsu* 手荷物

handmade *tesei [no]* 手製[の] handmade wallet *tesei no saifu* 手製の財布

hand over ind-obj *ni*, obj *o* (v) **1** pass *watas·u* 渡す **2** yield; cede *yuzur·u* 譲る hand over one's business to one's son *musuko ni shō'bai o yuzuru* 息子に商売を譲る

handrail *tesuri'* 手すり

handsome *ha'nsamu [na]* ハンサム[な] *see also* good-looking

hand towel   *tenugui* 手ぬぐい

handwriting   (idiom) *ji'[no kakika'ta]* 字[の書き方] My handwriting is bad. *Watashi wa ji' ga heta' desu.* 私は字が下手です。

handy   **1** convenient *be'nri* [na] 便利[な]   **2** skillful *ki'yō* [na] 器用 [な]

handyman   *zatsu-eki'fu* 雑役夫

hang   (v) **1** *kaka'r·u* 掛かる Your suit's hanging in the closet. *Sebiro wa yō'fuku-da'nsu ni kaka'tte iru.* 背広は洋服ダンスに掛かっている。   **2** hang down *burasaga'r·u* ぶら下がる   ——obj *o* (v) *kake'·ru* 掛ける Hang your coats here. *Kō'to wa koko ni ka'kete kudasa'i.* コートはここに掛けて下さい。   ——(idiom) execute *kō-shu'kei ni suru* 絞首刑にする

hanger (for clothes)   *ha'ngā* ハンガー

hangover   *futsuka-yoi* 二日酔い

haphazardly   *detarame ni* でたらめに; *ii kagen ni* いい加減に

happen   (v) *oki'·ru* 起きる That often happens. *Sore wa yo'ku okima'su.* それはよく起きます。   *oko'r·u* 起こる One thing happened after another. *A'to kara a'to kara iroiro na koto' ga oko'tta.* あとからあとからいろいろなことが起こった。

happening   *deki'goto* 出来事

happily (fortunately)   *saiwai ni* 幸いに Happily, she wasn't hurt. *Saiwai ni ka'nojo wa kega' o shina'katta.* 幸いに彼女はけがをしなかった。

happiness   *kōfuku* 幸福

happy   **1** fortunate *shiawase* [na] 幸せ[な]   **2** full of happiness *kōfuku* [na] 幸福[な] a happy life *kōfuku na kurashi* 幸福な暮らし   ——(adj) **1** joyful *yorokobashi'·i* 喜ばしい   **2** glad *ureshi'·i* うれしい

happy-go-lucky   *nonki* [na] のんき[な]

Happy New Year!   *Shi'nnen omedetō gozaima'su!* 新年おめでとうございます。

harass   obj *o* (v) *kurushime'·ru* 苦しめる; *nayamas·u* 悩ます

harbor   *minato* 港

hard   (adj) **1** difficult *muzukashi·i* 難しい   **2** firm *kata·i* 堅い

hard-boiled egg   *yude ta'mago* ゆで卵

hard candy   *ame* 飴

harden   (v) *kataku-na'r·u* 堅くなる

hardheaded   *ga'nko* [na] がんこ[な] hardheaded person *ga'nko na hito'* がんこな人

hard of hearing   *mimi' ga tōi* 耳が遠い

hardship   *ko'nnan* 困難

hard to (do)   **1** (physically) difficult *-niku'·i* にくい hard to read *yomi-niku'i* 読みにくい   **2** (emotionally) difficult *-gata'·i* がたい hard to excuse *yurushi-gata'i* 許しがたい

hardware 1 *kanamono* 金物 hardware store *kanamonoya* 金物屋 2 (computer) *hādo-ueā* ハードウェアー

harlot *baishu'nfu* 売春婦

harm *ga'i* 害 ——obj *o* (irr) *gai-su'ru* 害する I meant you no harm. *Ana'ta o gai-su'ru tsumori wa na'katta.* あなたを害するつもりはなかった.

harmful (idiom) be harmful (to) *ga'i ni na'r·u* 害になる

harmony *chōwa* 調和

harp *hā'pu* ハープ; *tate'goto* 堅琴

harpoon *mo'ri* 銛

harpsichord *hāpushikō'do* ハープシコード

harsh (adj) *kibishi·i* 厳しい harsh punishment *kibishi'i ke'ibatsu* 厳しい刑罰

harvest *shūkaku* 収穫 ——obj *o* (v) *kari-ire'·ru* 刈り入れる

has *see* have

haste *isogi* 急ぎ in great haste *ō-i'sogi de* 大急ぎで

hat *bōshi* 帽子

hatchet *te-ono* 手斧

hate *nikushimi* 憎しみ ——obj *o* (v) *kira·u* 嫌う; *niku'm·u* 憎む ——(adj) [...*ga*] *kira·i* [...が] 嫌い I hate spinach! *Hō're'nsō ga kirai desu!* ほうれん草が嫌いです.

hateful *iya* [*na*] 嫌[な] ——(adj) *nikurashi'·i* 憎らしい

hatred *nikushimi* 憎しみ

haughty *gōman* [*na*] 傲慢[な] a haughty attitude *gōman na ta'ido* 傲慢な態度; *erasō'* [*na*] えらそう[な] ——(v) be haughty *iba'r·u* いばる She's haughty. *Ka'nojo wa iba'tte iru.* 彼女はいばっている.

haul obj *o* (v) *hakob·u* 運ぶ

haunted house *yū'rei no de'ru ie'* 幽霊の出る家

have obj *ga* (v) *a'r·u* ある Do you have any small change? *Koma-ka'i o-kane ga arima'su ka?* こまかいお金がありますか. ——obj *o* (v) own *mo'ts·u* 持つ Do you have a camera? *Ka'mera o mo'tte imasu ka?* カメラを持っていますか.

hawk *taka* 鷹

hay *magusa* まぐさ; *hoshikusa* 干し草

hay fever *kafunshō* 花粉症

hazard 1 danger *kiken* 危険 2 risk *bōken* 冒険

haze *mo'ya* もや

hazy (irr) be hazy *mo'yamoya-suru* もやもやする

he *ka're* 彼

head (Anat) *atama'* 頭; *kubi* 首

head (of an organization) *-chō* 長; (of a company) *shachō* 社長; (of a division) *buchō* 部長; (of a school) *kōchō* 校長; (of a university) *gakuchō* 学長

headache (Tech) *zutsū* 頭痛 ——(idiom) have a headache *atama′ ga ita′·i* 頭が痛い

headlight *heddora′ito* ヘッドライト

headline *midashi* 見出し

head (main) office *ho′nsha* 本社

head of lettuce *re′tasu i′kko* レタス一個

head of the line *sentō* 先頭

head-on collision *shōmen shō′totsu* 正面衝突

headquarters 1 *ho′mbu* 本部 2 (military) *shire′ibu* 司令部

headset *heddose′tto* ヘッドセット; *iya′hōn* イヤホーン

heal (v) *nao′r·u* 治る be healed of a sickness *byōki ga nao′ru* 病気が治る ——obj *o* (v) *nao′s·u* 治す heal a wound *kizu o nao′su* 傷を治す

health *kenkō* 健康 health insurance *kenkō ho′ken* 健康保険

health foods *shizen sho′kuhin* 自然食品; *kenkō sho′kuhin* 健康食品

healthful *kenkōteki [na]* 健康的[な] healthful activity *kenkōteki na katsudō* 健康的な活動

healthy *ge′nki [na]* 元気[な]; *kenkō [na]* 健康[な] a healthy person *kenkō na hito′* 健康な人 He's not very healthy. *Ka′re wa amari kenkō ja na′i.* 彼はあまり健康じゃない.

hear obj *o* (v) *kik·u* 聞く hear a sound *oto′ o kiku* 音を聞く I heard it on the radio. *Sore o ra′jio de kiita.* それをラジオで聞いた. ——obj *ga* (pot) *kikoe·ru* 聞こえる Can you hear? *Kikoema′su ka?* 聞こえますか. I heard a bird singing. *Kotori no ko′e ga kikoeta.* 小鳥の声が聞こえた. ——(idiom) hear a sound *oto′ ga suru* 音がする

hearing 1 (ability) *chō′ryoku* 聴力 2 (sense of) *chōkaku* 聴覚

hearing aid *hochō′ki* 補聴器

hearse *reikyū′sha* 霊柩車

heart 1 (Tech) *shinzō* 心臓 heart disease *shinzōbyō* 心臓病 2 *koko′ro* 心 a warm heart *a tataka′i koko′ro* 暖かい心 with all one's heart *koko′ro o ko′mete* 心をこめて from the bottom of one's heart *koko′ro [no soko] kara* 心[の底]から take to heart *koko′ro ni kake′ru* 心にかける 3 (suit of playing cards) *hāto* ハート

heart attack *shinzō ma′hi* 心臓麻痺

heartbeat *shinzō no kodō* 心臓の鼓動; *dōki* 動悸

heartburn *muneyake* 胸やけ

heart trouble *shinzōbyō* 心臓病

heat 1 *a′tsusa* 暑さ; *netsu* 熱 ——obj *o* (v) *atatame′·ru* 暖める heat the soup *sū′pu o atatame′ru* スープを暖める

heater 1 *hi′tā* ヒーター; *sutō′bu* ストーブ; gas stove *gasu sutō′bu* ガスストーブ 2 (electric) *denne′tsuki* 電熱器

heathen *ikyō′to* 異教徒

heating *dambō* 暖房

heating pad *denki a′nka* 電気あんか; *denki ma′tto* 電気マット
heat resistant *tai-netsusei* [no] 耐熱性[の]
heat wave *nekki* 熱気
heaven (Chr) *te′ngoku* 天国; (Budd) *gokuraku* 極楽
heavy (adj) *omo·i* 重い
Hebrew **1** (language) *Heburai-go* ヘブライ語 **2** (person) *Hebura′i-jin* ヘブライ人 ——(attr) *Heburai no* ヘブライの
hedge *kaki′ne* 垣根; *ikegaki* 生け垣
hedge clippers *ueki-ba′sami* 植木ばさみ
heel **1** (foot) *kakato* かかと **2** (shoe) *hi′ru* ヒール
height **1** *se′* 背 What is your height? *Se′ wa nan-se′nchi desu ka?* 背は何センチですか. **2** (measurement) *ta′kasa* 高さ
heir; heiress *sōzokunin* 相続人
helicopter *heriko′putā* ヘリコプター
helium *heriu′mu* ヘリウム
hell *jigoku* 地獄
Hello. **1** (daytime) *Konnichi wa.* 今日は. **2** (nighttime) *Komban wa.* 今晩は. **3** (on the telephone) *Mo′shi-moshi.* もしもし.
helm *ka′ji* 舵
helmet **1** (W) *herume′tto* ヘルメット **2** (J) *ka′buto* かぶと
help **1** assistance *tetsuda′i* 手伝い; *e′njo* 援助 **2** rescuing *tasuke′* 助け ——obj *o* (v) **1** assist *tetsuda′u* 手伝う Would you help me, please? *Tetsuda′tte kudasaimase′n ka?* 手伝って下さいませんか. **2** rescue *tasuke′·ru* 助ける Help! *Tasukete!* 助けて.
helpful (idiom) **1** be helpful *yaku′ ni ta′ts·u* 役に立つ This dictionary is helpful. *Kono ji′sho wa yaku′ ni ta′tsu.* この辞書は役に立つ. The map wasn't very helpful. *Sono chi′zu wa amari yaku′ ni tata′nakatta.* その地図はあまり役に立たなかった. **2** be of help (to someone) *sewa′ ni na′r·u* 世話になる You were very helpful. *Taihen o-se′wa ni narima′shita.* 大変お世話になりました.
helping **1** a helping *ichininmae* 一人前 **2** second helping *o-ka′wari* おかわり Would you like a second helping? *O-ka′wari wa ika′ga desu ka?* おかわりはいかがですか.
helpless (adj) *tayorina′·i* 頼りない
helplessly *tayorina′ku* 頼りなく; *shikata-na′ku* 仕方なく
helplessness *tayorina′sa* 頼りなさ
Help yourself! *Dō′zo go-jiyū ni!* どうぞご自由に.
hem *fuchi* 縁; *suso* 裾 ——(idiom) to hem *suso o kagar·u* 裾をかがる Hem this for me, please. *Suso o kagatte kudasa′i.* 裾をかがって下さい.
hemisphere *hankyū* 半球
hemorrhage *shukketsu* 出血 ——(irr) *shukketsu-suru* 出血する
hemorrhoid(s) *ji* 痔
hemp *asa* 麻

hen   *mendori* 雌鳥

her   1 *ka'nojo* 彼女 Please help her. *Ka'nojo o tetsuda'tte kudasa'i.* 彼女を手伝って下さい． 2 (possessive) *ka'nojo no* 彼女の her coat *ka'nojo no kō'to* 彼女のコート 3 to her *ka'nojo ni* 彼女に

herb   *yakusō* 薬草

herd   *mure'* 群

here   1 *koko* ここ There's a telephone here. *Koko ni denwa ga aru.* ここに電話がある． Turn here. *Koko o magatte kudasa'i.* ここを曲がって下さい． 2 this direction *kotchi'* こっち; *kochira* こちら The toilet is here. *To'ire wa kochira de'su.* トイレはこちらです．

here and there   *achira ko'chira* あちらこちら; *atchi ko'tchi* あっちこっち

hereditary   1 *idensei [no]* 遺伝性[の] 2 heredity *iden* 遺伝

heretic   *ita'nsha* 異端者

heritage   1 (wealth) *isan* 遺産 2 tradition *dentō* 伝統

hermit   *into'nsha* 隠遁者

hernia   *herunia* ヘルニア

hero   1 protagonist (novel) *shuji'nkō* 主人公; (film; play) *shuyaku* 主役 2 great man *eiyū* 英雄 3 brave man *yū'shi* 勇士

heroine   (novel) *hiro'in* ヒロイン; (film; play) *shuyaku* 主役

heron   *sagi* 鷺

herpes   *he'rupesu* ヘルペス

herring   *ni'shin* 鰊; herring roe *kazu-no-ko* 数の子

hers   *ka'nojo no* 彼女の This is hers. *Kore wa ka'nojo no desu.* これは彼女のです．

herself   *ka'nojo jishi'n* 彼女自身

hesitate   (v) 1 *tamera'·u* ためらう 2 pause (irr) *chū'cho-suru* ちゅうちょする 3 be at a loss (irr) *u'rouro-suru* うろうろする

heterosexual   *ise'iai [no]* 異性愛[の]

heterosexuality   *ise'iai* 異性愛

hexagonal   *rokka'ku-kei [no]* 六角形[の]

Hey!   *Cho'tto!* ちょっと．

Hi!   *Yā'!* やあ．

hiccups   *sha'kkuri* しゃっくり

hidden   (attr) *kaku'shita* 隠した

hide   (v) *kakure'·ru* 隠れる The child hid in the closet. *Kodomo wa oshiire no na'ka ni kaku'reta.* 子供は押し入れの中に隠れた． ——obj *o* (v) *kaku's·u* 隠す hide one's face *kao o kaku'su* 顔を隠す

hide-and-seek   *kakure'mbo* かくれんぼ

hierachy   *kaisō se'ido* 階層制度; *kaikyū so'shiki* 階級組織

high   (adj) *taka'·i* 高い high mountain *taka'i yama'* 高い山 The price is high. *Nedan ga taka'i.* 値段が高い． ——(idiom) high (living) costs *bukka'daka* 物価高 ——(adv) *ta'kaku* 高く jump high *ta'kaku tobu* 高く飛ぶ

highball *haibō'ru* ハイボール

high beam (headlight) *uwamuki ra'ito* 上向きライト

high blood pressure *kōketsu'atsu* 高血圧

highchair *kodomo'-isu* 子供椅子

highest *saikō* [no] 最高[の]; *saikō'do* [no] 最高度[の]

high jump *hai-ja'mpu* ハイジャンプ

highland *kōgen* 高原

high-rise *kōsō ke'nchiku* 高層建築

high school *kōkō* 高校

high-strung (attr) *ki no hatta* 気の張った He is high-strung. *Ka're wa ki no hatta hito desu.* 彼は気の張った人です.

high tide *manchō* 満潮

highway *haiuē'* ハイウェー; *kōsoku dō'ro* 高速道路

hijack *haija'kku* ハイジャック

hiking *ha'ikingu* ハイキング

hill 1 *oka* 丘 2 slope *saka* 坂; *sha'men* 斜面

hilly (idiom) *kyūryō no ō'i* 丘陵の多い, hilly terrain *kyūryō no ō'i chita'i* 丘陵の多い地帯

him 1 *ka're* 彼 Please invite him. *Ka're o shō'tai-shite kudasa'i.* 彼を招待して下さい. 2 to him *ka're ni* 彼に Give this to him, please. *Kore o ka're ni agete kudasa'i.* これを彼に上げて下さい.

himself *ka're ji'shin* 彼自身

Hindi *Hindī-go* ヒンディー語

hindrance *jama* 邪魔; *bōgai* 妨害

Hinduism *Hinzūkyō* ヒンズー教

hinge *chōtsu'gai* ちょうつがい

hint *hi'nto* ヒント

hip 1 *koshi* 腰; (coll) *o-shiri* お尻 2 (for measurement) *hi'ppu* ヒップ

hippopotamus *ka'ba* かば

hire obj *o* (v) *yato'·u* 雇う hire a housekeeper *kase'ifu o yato'u* 家政婦を雇う

his *ka're no* 彼の This is his. *Kore wa ka're no desu.* これは彼のです.

historian *rekishika* 歴史家

historic *rekishiteki* [na] 歴史的[な]

history *rekishi* 歴史; *-shi* 史 Japanese history *Niho'n-shi* 日本史

hit 1 (baseball) *a'nda* 安打; *hi'tto* ヒット 2 (song) *hi'tto* ヒット ——obj *o* (v) 1 *bu'ts·u* ぶつ hit one's opponent *aite' o bu'tsu* 相手をぶつ 2 (with the fist) *nagu'r·u* なぐる 3 (against) *butsuke· ru* ぶつける I hit my head against the door. *Atama' o do'a ni butsuketa.* 頭をドアにぶつけた. 4 knock down (with a car) *hane′·ru* はねる   **5** strike (with an instrument) *u′ts·u* 打つ hit with a hammer *ha′mmā de u′tsu* ハンマーで打つ ——(v) **1** [*ni*] *atar·u* に当たる Something hit the window. *Na′nika ga ma′do ni atatta.* 何かが窓に当たった.   **2** bump into *butsukar·u* ぶつかる I hit the door. *Do′a ni butsukatta.* ドアにぶつかった.

hive   *mitsu′bachi no su* 蜜蜂の巣

hives   *jimma′shin* じんましん

hoard   obj *o* (v) *takuwae′·ru* 蓄える; (irr) *chozō-suru* 貯蔵する

hoarse voice   *shagare-goe* しゃがれ声

hobby   *shu′mi* What are your hobbies? *Shu′mi wa na′n desu ka?* 趣味は何ですか.

hockey   *ho′kkē* ホッケー

hodgepodge   *mecha′kucha* めちゃくちゃ; *gottama′ze* [*no*] ごった混ぜ[の]

hoe   *kuwa* 鍬

hog   *buta* 豚

hold   obj *o* (v) **1** *mo′ttei·ru* 持っている Hold this, please. *Kore o mo′tte ite kudasai.* これを持っていて下さい.   **2** hold onto *tsu-kamar·u* つかまる Hold onto the hand strap, please. *Tsurikawa ni tsukamatte kudasa′i.* つり皮につかまって下さい.

hole   *ana′* 穴

holiday   **1** *yasumi′* 休み   **2** fixed holiday *kyūjitsu* 休日   **3** festival day *saijitsu* 祭日   **4** (national) [*kokumin no*] *shuku′jitsu* [国民の] 祝日

Holland   *Oranda* オランダ

hollow   **1** depression *kubomi* 窪み   **2** cave *hora-ana* 洞穴   **3** cavity *kūdō* 空洞   **4** valley *tanima* 谷間 ——(idiom) It's hollow. *Na′ka ga aite iru.* 中が空いている.

holly   *hi′iragi* 柊

holy   *shinsei* [*na*] 神聖[な]

home   **1** (one's own) *uchi* 家   **2** (another's) *o-taku* お宅   **3** family *katei* 家庭   **4** residence *jitaku* 自宅   **5** native place *ko′kyo* 故郷; *furu′sato* ふるさと   **6** native land *kuni* 国

home economics   *kase′igaku* 家政学; *katei-ka* 家庭科

homely   **1** *shi′sso* [*na*] 質素な   **2** homely woman (coll) *bu′su* 醜子   **3** homely man (coll) *buo′toko* 醜男

homemade   *hōmu-mē′do* [*no*] ホームメード[の]; *jikasei* [*no*] 自家製 [の]

home run   *hōmu′ran* ホームラン

homesick   (idiom) be/become homesick *hōmushi′kku ni na′r·u* ホームシックになる; *hōmushi′kku ni kaka′r·u* ホームシックにかかる

homework   (for school) *shukudai* 宿題

homicide   *hito-goroshi* 人殺し; (Tech) *satsuji′n-han* 殺人犯

homonym *dōon-igi'-go* 同音異議語

homosexual *homose'kusharu* ホモセクシャル ——(attr) *dōse'i-ai no* 同性愛の

homosexuality *dōse'i-ai* 同性愛

Honduran (person) *Honjurasu'-jin* ホンジュラス人 ——(attr) *Ho'njurasu no* ホンジュラスの

Honduras *Ho'njurasu* ホンジュラス

honest *shōji'ki* [na] 正直[な] an honest person *shōji'ki na hito'* 正直な人 She's honest. *Ka'nojo wa shoji'ki desu.* 彼女は正直です.

honestly *shōji'ki ni* 正直に

honey *hachimitsu* 蜂密

honeydew melon *me'ron* メロン

honeymoon (trip) *shinkon ryo'kō* 新婚旅行

honor 1 *me'iyo* 名誉 a matter of honor *me'iyo ni kakawa'ru mondai* 名誉にかかわる問題 2 reputation *membuku* 面目 preserve one's honor *membuku o tamo'tsu* 面目を保つ

honorable (attr) *sonkei-subeki* 尊敬すべき an honorable person *sonkei-sube'ki hito* 尊敬すべき人

honorarium *sharei* 謝礼

honorary *me'iyo* [no] 名誉[の] honorary citizen *meiyo shi'min* 名誉市民

honorific speech *keigo* 敬語

hood 1 (of a car) *fū'do* フード; *bonne'tto* ボンネット 2 (on a garment) *zu'kin* 頭巾

hoof *hizume* ひづめ

hook 1 *kagi* 鉤 2 crochet hook *kagiba'ri* 鉤針 3 fish hook *tsuribari* 釣り針

hop (v) *tob·u* 跳ぶ ——(idiom) *pyo'n-pyon-tob·u* ぴょんぴょん跳ぶ

hope 1 *kibō* 希望 2 expectation *kitai* 期待 ——obj *o* (irr) *kibō-suru* 希望する She hopes to work for one more year. *Ka'nojo wa mō ichi'nen hatarakita'i to kibō-shite iru.* 彼女はもう一年働きたいと希望している.; *nozom·u* 望む ——(idiom) ...*da to i'·i*...だといい I hope it will be a good day tomorrow. *Ashita' o-ten'ki da to i'i desu ne'.* 明日お天気だといいですね.

hopeful (attr) *nozomi a'ru* 望みある a hopeful future *nozomi a'ru mi'rai* 望みある未来 ——(idiom) be hopeful *nozomi ga a'r·u* 望みがある

hopeless (attr) *nozomi no na'i* 望みのない; *dō shiyō mo na'i* どうしようもない a hopeless situation *dō shiyō mo na'i jōtai* どうしようもない状態

horizon *chiheisen* 地平線

horizontal *suihei* [no] 水平[の]

hormone *ho'rumon* ホルモン

horn 1 (animal) *tsuno'* 角 2 (music) *ho'run* ホルン 3 (automobile) *keiteki* 警笛; *kura'kushon* クラクション

hornet *suzume'bachi* 雀蜂

horrible (adj) 1 *sugo'・i* すごい 2 frightening *osoroshi'・i* 恐ろしい

horror *kyo'fu* 恐怖; horror movie *hora e'iga* ホラー映画

hors d'oeuvre *o'doburu* オードブル

horse *uma'* 馬

horseback riding *jōba* 乗馬

horsepower *bariki* 馬力

horse race *keiba* 競馬

horseradish [*seiyō*] *wa'sabi* [西洋] わさび

horseshoe *teitetsu* 蹄鉄

horticulture *engei* 園芸

hose 1 *ho'su* ホース fire hose *shōbō hō'su* 消防ホース watering hose *mizu-maki hō'su* 水まきホース 2 stockings *suto'kkingu* ストッキング

hospital *byōin* 病院 emergency hospital *kyūkyū byō'in* 救急病院

hospitality *motenashi* もてなし

hospitalize obj *o* (caus) *nyūin-sase-ru* 入院させる ——(v) be hospitalized *nyūin-suru* 入院する

host *shujin* 主人; *shujin-yaku* 主人役

hostage *hitojichi* 人質 take as hostage *hitojichi ni suru* 人質にする

hostess 1 *onna shu'jin* 女主人 2 bar hostess *ho'sutesu* ホステス 3 air hostess *see* stewardess; flight attendant

hostile (attr) *te'ki-ni mi'chita* 敵意に満ちた

hot (adj) 1 (temperature) *atsu'・i* 熱い 2 (spicy) *kara'・i* 辛い

hot chocolate *ko'koa* ココア

hotel *ho'teru* ホテル

hothouse *onshitsu* 温室

hot pepper *tōga'rashi* とうがらし

hot plate 1 *hotto pure'to* ホットプレート 2 (electric) *denki ko'nro* 電気コンロ 3 (gas) *gasu ko'nro* ガスコンロ

hot spring *onsen* 温泉

hot water *oyu* お湯

hot-water bottle [*go'mu*] *yuta'mpo* [ゴム]湯たんぽ

hot-water heater (gas) *yuwakashi'ki* 湯沸かし器

hour an hour *ichiji'kan* 一時間 an hour from now *ichiji'kan saki* 一時間先 I'm leaving in an hour. *Ichiji'kan de dekakeru.* 一時間で出かける.

house *uchi* うち; *ie'* 家

house call *ōshin* 往診

housecoat *heyagi'* 部屋着

household *katei* [*no*] 家庭[の]

housekeeper *kase'ifu* 家政婦

House of Councillors   (J) *Sangi'in* 参議院
House of Representatives   (J) *Shūgi'in* 衆議院; (US) *Ka'in* 下院
housewife   *shu'fu* 主婦
housework   *ka'ji* 家事
housing   *jūtaku* 住宅   housing problem *jūtaku mo'ndai* 住宅問題
How?   *dō' [yatte]* どう[やって]   How does one get there? *Soko e' wa dō' yatte ikima'su ka?* そこへはどうやって行きますか.   How do you make miso soup? *Dō' yatte misoshiru o tsukurima'su ka?* どうやってみそ汁を作りますか.
How about...   *...wa ika'ga desu ka?* ...はいかがですか.   How about some coffee? *Kōhi' wa ika'ga desu ka?* コーヒーはいかがですか.
How are things with you? *Dō' desu ka?* どうですか.
How are you?   **1** *O-ge'nki desu ka?* お元気ですか.   **2** (very polite) *Go-kigen ika'ga desu ka?* ごきげんいかがですか.
How do you do? [*Hajimema'shite*] *dō'zo yoroshiku.* [初めまして]どうぞよろしく.
How do you say "X" in Japanese?   *"X" wa Nihon-go de dō' iima'su ka?*「X」は日本語でどう言いますか.
however   *keredomo* けれども
How far is it from here? *Koko kara dono ku'rai desu ka?* ここからどのくらいですか.
How many?   **1** *i'kutsu* いくつ   **2** how many people *na'nnin* 何人
How much?   **1** *i'kura* いくら   How much is it? *I'kura desu ka?* いくらですか.   **2** *dono ku'rai* どのくらい   How much do you want? *Dono ku'rai irima'su ka?* どのくらいいりますか.   How much time will it take? *Jikan wa dono kurai kaka'ru deshō ka?* 時間はどのくらいかかるでしょうか.
How old?   *i'kutsu* いくつ   How old are you? *O-iku'tsu desu ka?* おいくつですか.; *na'nsai* 何才   How old is your son? *Musuko-san wa na'nsai desu ka?* 息子さんは何才ですか.
hue   *iro-ai* 色合い
hug   obj *o* (v) *dakishime'·ru* 抱きしめる
huge   (adj) *deka'·i* でかい
Huh?   *E'?* えっ.
hull (of a seed; nut)   *kara'* 殻
human being   *ningen* 人間
humanitarian   *hakuaishugi'sha* 博愛主義者
humanity   **1** human nature *ningensei* 人間性   **2** human race *ji'nrui* 人類
humanize   obj *o* (irr) *ningenka-suru* 人間化する
human relations   *ningen ka'nkei* 人間関係
humble   *kenson [no]* 謙遜[の] ——(irr) be humble *kenson-suru* 謙遜する

humid (adj) hot and humid *mushi-atsu'·i* 蒸し暑い ——(attr)
shikke no ō'i 湿気の多い

humidifier *kashitsu'ki* 加湿器

humidity *shikke/shikki* 湿気

humiliate (idiom) *haji' o kakase'·ru* 恥をかかせる

humility *kenson* 謙遜

humor *yū'moa* ユーモア

humorous *kokkei* [na] 滑稽[な]

hump *kobu'* こぶ a camel's hump *rakuda no kobu'* らくだのこぶ

humpback *nekoze* 猫背

hunchback *semushi'* せむし

hundred *hyaku'* 百 one hundred *hyaku'* 百 three hundred *sam-byaku'* 三百 *see also* Appendix 1

Hungarian 1 (language) *Hangari-go* ハンガリー語 2 (person)
Hangari'jin ハンガリー人 ——(attr) *Hanga'ri no* ハンガリーの

Hungary *Hanga'ri* ハンガリー

hunger *kūfuku* 空腹; *ki'ga* 飢餓

hungry (idiom) I'm hungry! *Onaka ga suita!* おなかがすいた.

hunt obj *o* (v) *kar·u* 狩る

hunter *karyū'do* 狩人

hunting *shuryō* 狩猟 hunting license *shuryō kyoka'shō* 狩猟許可証

hurricane *bōfū'·u* 暴風雨

hurriedly *iso'ide* 急いで

hurry (v) *iso'g·u* 急ぐ Are you in a hurry? *Iso'ide imasu ka?* 急い
でいますか. Don't hurry! *Isoga'naide!* 急がないで. We'll have to
hurry! *Isoga'nakereba [nara'nai]!* 急がなければ[ならない]. Hurry
up! *Iso'ide!* 急いで!

hurt (adj) *ita'·i* 痛い, It hurts! *Ita'i!* 痛い. ——(v) 1 *ita'm·u* 痛
む Does it hurt? *Itamima'su ka?* 痛みますか. 2 be injured *kizu-
tsu'k·u* 傷つく ——obj *o* (v) *kizutsuke'·ru* 傷つける I'm sorry. I
didn't mean to hurt your feelings. *Gomennasa'i. Kanjō o kizutsuke'-
ru tsumori wa zenzen na'katta.* ごめんなさい. 感情を傷つけるつも
りは全然なかった.

husband 1 (one's own) *shu'jin* 主人 2 (another's) *go-shu'jin* 御主
人

Hush! *Shi!* しっ.

hut *koya* 小屋

hyacinth *hiyashi'nsu* ヒヤシンス

hydrangea *ajisai* あじさい

hydrant 1 *kyūsuisen* 給水栓 2 fireplug *shōkasen* 消火栓

hydrofoil boat *suichūyo'kusen* 水中翼船

hydrogen *su'iso* 水素

hygiene *eisei* 衛生

hymn *sambika* 賛美歌

hyperactive (v) be hyperactive *kappatsu-sugi′·ru* 活発すぎる
hypertension (high blood pressure) *kōketsu′atsu* 高血圧 ——
(idiom) *ka′do no kinchō* 過度の緊張
hyphen *ha′ifun* ハイフン
hypnotize (idiom) *saimi′njutsu o kake′·ru* 催眠術をかける
hypochondriac *yū-utsushō* [*ka′nja*] 憂うつ症[患者]
hypocrite *gize′nsha* 偽善者
hypodermic [*hika-*]*chū′sha* [皮下]注射
hypothesis *kasetsu* 仮説
hypothetical *kasetsu no* 仮説の; *kateiteki* [*na*] 仮定的[な]
hysteria *hisute′rī* ヒステリー
hysterical *hisuteri′kku na* ヒステリックな

I

I *watashi* わたし; (polite) *watakushi* 私; (plain, masc) *bo′ku* ぼく
ice *kōri* 氷
ice bag *hyōnō* 氷のう
iceberg *hyō′zan* 氷山
ice cream **1** *aisukurī′mu* アイスクリーム **2** nondairy ice cream
so′futo ソフト; *sofuto kuri′mu* ソフトクリーム
iced coffee *aisu kō′hī* アイスコーヒー
iced tea *aisu tī′* アイスティー
Iceland *Aisura′ndo* アイスランド
Icelandic **1** (language) *Aisurando-go* アイスランド語 **2** (person)
Aisurando′ jin アイスランド人 ——(attr) *Aisura′ndo no* アイスラ
ンドの
ice skate; ice skating *sukē′to* スケート ——(v) *sukē′to-suru* スケ
ートする *sukē′to* スケート
ice water *kōri′ mizu* 氷水
icicle *tsurara* つらら
icon *shōzō* 肖像
idea *kanga′e* 考え That's a good idea. *Sore wa i′i kanga′e desu.*
それはいい考えです。 I have an idea. *Kanga′e ga a′ru.* 考えがあ
る。
ideal *risō* 理想 ——(attr) *risōteki* [*na*] 理想的[な]
idealist *risōshugi′ sha* 理想主義者
ideally *risōteki ni* 理想的に
identical *sokku′ri* [*na*] そっくり[な] That's identical to mine. *Sore
wa watashi no′ to sokku′ri desu.* それは私のとそっくりです。; identical twins *ichira′nsei sōse′iji* 一卵性双生児
identification card *mibun shōmeisho′* 身分証明書

identify 155 **illiterate**

identify obj *o* (irr) **1** *shiteki-suru* 指摘する Identify the authors of the following novels. *Ka'ki no shōsetsu no cho'sha o shiteki-shite kudasa'i.* 下記の小説の著者を指摘して下さい. **2** *kakunin-suru* 確認する He identified the man as the criminal. *Ka're wa sono otoko' o ha'nnin de a'ru to kakunin-shita.* 彼はその男を犯人であると確認した. ——compl *ni* (irr) be identified with *kankei-suru* 関係する She is identified with that movement. *Ka'nojo wa sono undō ni kankei-shite iru.* 彼女はその運動に関係している.

ideograph (Chinese/Japanese character) *kanji* 漢字

ideology *ideo'rogī* イデオロギー

idiom *kan'yō'ku* 慣用句

idiosyncracy *tokuisei* 特異性; *kuse'* 癖

idiot *hakuchi* 白痴

idle (irr) **1** be idle *u'rouro-suru* うろうろする Saturday I was idle all day. *Doyō'bi ichinichi-jū u'rouro-shite ita.* 土曜日一日中うろうろしていた. **2** (of a motor) *karama'wari-suru* 空回りする ——(attr) *tsukawarete inai* 使われていない an idle machine *tsukawarete inai kika'i* 使われていない機械 ——(idiom) **1** lie unused *asobasete a'r·u* 遊ばせてある This land is lying idle. *Kono tochi wa asobasete a'ru.* この土地は遊ばせてある. **2** be unemployed *shitsugyō-shite iru* 失業している

if *mo'shi . . . -tara [-dara]* もし . . . たら[だら] If you come to Tokyo, stop by our place. *Mo'shi Tōkyō ni kita'ra, kochira ni' mo yotte kudasa'i.* もし東京に来たらこちらにも寄って下さい.; *-tara [-dara]* たら[だら] If you're cold, light the stove. *Sa'mukattara, sutō'bu o tsuke'te kudasa'i.* 寒かったらストーブをつけて下さい.; *. . . to* と If I don't go now, I won't be on time. *I'ma ikanai to, ma ni awa'nai.* 今行かないと間に合わない.; *-ba* ば If you read it, you'll understand. *Yo'meba, waka'ru deshō.* 読めばわかるでしょう. *see also* conditional and provisional verb forms in tables 1–4, pp. xxi–xl.

ignition (car) *iguni'shon* イグニッション

ignorance *mu'chi* 無知

ignorant *mu'chi* [na] 無知[な]

ignore obj *o* (irr) *mu'shi-suru* 無視する He ignored the traffic signal. *Ka're wa shingō o mu'shi-shita.* 彼は信号を無視した.

ill *byōki* [no] 病気[の] a sick person *byōki no hito'* 病気の人 He is ill. *Ka're wa byōki de'su.* 彼は病気です.

illegal *fuhō* [na] 不法[な] illegal entry into a country *fuhō nyu'-koku* 不法入国; *higō'hō* [na] 非合法[な] an illegal business *higō'hō na shō'bai* 非合法な商売

illegitimate child *shise'iji* 私生児

illiterate (attr) *yomi'kaki ga deki'nai* 読み書きができない

ill-mannered *reigi-shi'razu* [*na*] 礼儀知らず[な] an ill-mannered person *reigi-shi'razu na hito'* 礼儀知らずな人

illness *byōki* 病気 He's suffering from a serious illness. *Ka're wa omoi byōki ni kaka'tte iru.* 彼は重い病気にかかっている.

illogical *hironriteki* [*na*] 非論理的[な]

ill-tempered (adj) *ki-muzukashi'·i* 気難しい She is ill-tempered. *Ka'nojo wa ki-muzukashi'i.* 彼女は気難しい.

illusion *gensō* 幻想

illustration 1 artwork; diagram *irasuto* イラスト 2 example *re'i* 例 *see also* drawing

image 1 impression *imē'ji* イメージ 2 likeness *shōzo* 肖像

imaginary *kasō* [*no*] 仮想[の]

imagination *sōzō* 想像 power of imagination *sōzō'ryoku* 想像力 I'll leave that to your imagination. *Go-sōzō ni o-makase shima'su.* 御想像におまかせします.

imagine obj *o* (irr) *sōzō-suru* 想像する ——(idiom) I can't imagine it! *Sōzō mo tsuka'nai!* 想像もつかない. *see also* think

imitate obj *o* (v) *mane·ru* 真似る ——(idiom) *mane o suru* 真似をする

imitation *nise* [*no*] 偽[の]; *nisemono* 偽物; *jinzō* [*no*] 人造[の]; imitation ivory *jinzō zo'ge* 人造象牙; *jinkō* [*no*] 人工[の] imitation pearl *jinkō shi'nju* 人工真珠

immature *mijuku* [*na*] 未熟[な] an immature writing style *mijuku na bu'nshō* 未熟な文章 ——(idiom) *aoni'sai* 青二才 He's still immature. *Ka're wa ma'da aoni'sai desu.* 彼はまだ青二才です.

immediate 1 direct *chokusetsu* [*no*] 直接[の] the immediate cause *chokusetsu no gen'in* 直接の原因 2 close *mijika*[*na*] 身近[な] people in one's immediate circle *mijika na hito'bito* 身近な人々

immediately *ta'dachi ni* 直ちに; *su'gu ni* すぐに I'll have to take care of that immediately. *Su'gu ni sore o shina'kereba* [*nara'nai*]. すぐにそれをしなければ[ならない].; *sassoku* さっそく I'll let you know immediately. *Sassoku o-shirase shima'su.* さっそくお知らせします.

immigration *nyūkoku* 入国 immigration office *nyūkoku kanri ji-mu'sho* 入国管理事務所

immoral *fudō'toku* [*na*] 不道徳[な] That's immoral. *Sore wa fudō'-toku desu.* それは不道徳です.

immortal *fumetsu* [*no*] 不滅[の]

impatient 1 short-tempered *ta'nki* [*na*] 短気[な] an impatient person *ta'nki na hito'* 短気な人 2 hasty *se'kkachi* [*na*] せっかち[な] ——(adj) *machidōshi'·i* 待ち遠しい The children are impatient. *Kodomo'-tachi wa machidōshi'i.* 子供たちは待ち遠しい. ——(idiom) *ki ga mijika·i* 気が短い She is impatient. *Ka'nojo wa ki ga mijika'i.* 彼女は気が短い.

imperative 1 *meireiteki* [*na*] 命令的[な] 2 (Gram) *meireikei* 命令形 ——(attr) urgent *sashisema'tta* 差し迫った

imperfect *fuka'nzen* [*na*] 不完全[な]

imperfection 1 incompleteness *fukanze'nsa* 不完全さ 2 flaw *kekkan* 欠陥

imperial *teikoku* [*no*] 帝国[の] The Imperial Hotel *Teikoku Hoteru* 帝国ホテル

imply obj *o* (v) *fuku'm·u* 含む; (irr) *i'mi-suru* 意味する

impolite *shitsu'rei* [*na*] 失礼[な]; *bure'i* [*na*] 無礼[な] impolite manner of speaking *bure'i na iikata* 無礼な言い方; *reigi-shi'razu* [*na*] 礼儀知らず[な] an impolite person *reigi-shi'razu na hito'* 礼儀知らずな人

import *yunyū* 輸入 import goods *yunyūhin* 輸入品 ——obj *o* (irr) *yunyū-suru* 輸入する

importance *jūyōsei* 重要性 have importance *jūyōsei ga a'ru* 重要性がある

important *daiji* [*na*] 大事[な] Caution is important. *Chū'i ga da'iji desu.* 注意が大事です.; *taisetsu* [*na*] 大切[な] Time is very important to me. *Watashi ni wa jikan ga totemo taisetsu de'su.* 私には時間がとても大切です.; *jūyō* [*na*] 重要[な] This is the important point. *Koko ga jūyō na ten de'su.* ここが重要な点です. ——(idiom) an important person *era'i hito* 偉い人

impossible *fuka'nō* [*na*] 不可能[な]

impostor *sagi'shi* 詐欺師

impressed compl *ni* (irr) be impressed (by) *kangeki-suru* 感激する I was impressed by the scenery of the Inland Sea. *Seto-na'ikai no ke'shiki ni kangeki-shita.* 瀬戸内海の景色に感激した.

impression 1 feeling *kanji* 感じ give a good impression *i'i kanji o ataeru* いい感じを与える What is your impression of him? *Ka're ni wa do'nna kanji o ukema'shita ka?* 彼にはどんな感じを受けましたか. 2 thoughts *kansō* 感想 What is your impression of Japan? *Niho'n ni taisuru go-kansō wa ika'ga desu ka?* 日本に対する御感想はいかがですか. 3 image *inshō* 印象 first impression *dai-ichi i'nshō* 第一印象 receive an impression *inshō o uke'ru* 印象を受ける 4 deep impression *kammei* 感銘 That book left a deep impression on me. *Sono ho'n ni wa fuka'i kammei o u'keta.* その本には深い感銘を受けた.

imprisonment *kankin* 監禁

improve (v) *yo'ku-nar·u* よくなる Things will gradually improve, I'm sure. *Monogoto wa dandan yo'ku na'ru deshō.* 物事はだんだんよくなるでしょう. ——obj *o* (irr) *kaizen-suru* 改善する improve the living conditions of the poor *himmin no seikatsu o kaizen-suru* 貧民の生活を改善する

improvement *kaizen* 改善

improvise (idiom) *ma ni awase'·ru* 間に合せる I'll improvise with this material. *Kono ki'ji de ma ni awase'ru.* この生地で間に合せる。

impulse *shōdō* 衝動

impure *fuketsu* [na] 不潔[な]

in ...*ni* に I live in Tokyo. *Tōkyō ni su'nde iru.* 東京に住んでいる。;...*de* で The plane will arrive in an hour. *Ichiji'kan de hikō'ki ga tsuku.* 一時間で飛行機が着く。 The children are playing in the park. *Kodomo'-tachi wa kōen de asonde iru.* 子供たちは公園で遊んでいる。

inaccurate *fuse'ikaku* [na] 不正確[な] inaccurate records *fuseikaku na kiroku* 不正確な記録 ——(v) be inaccurate *machiga'tte i·ru* 間違っている The newspaper account is inaccurate. *Sono shimbun kiji wa machigatte iru.* その新聞記事は間違っている。

inactive *fuka'ppatsu* [na] 不活発[な] ——;(attr) not in use *tsuka-warete inai* 使われていない an inactive machine *tsukawarete inai kika'i* 使われていない機械

inattention *fuchū'i* 不注意

incapable (v) (neg) *deki'na·i* できない; -*deki'na·i* できない incapable of understanding *ri'kai-deki'nai* 理解できない;...*koto ga/wa deki'na·i* ことが/はできない This motorbike is incapable of going 100 km/h. *Kono ōtobai wa hya'kkiro o da'su koto' ga de-ki'nai.* このオートバイは100キロを出すことができない。

incense *kō* 香; an incense stick *se'nkō* 線香

incense burner *kōro* 香炉

inch *i'nchi* インチ

incident *ji'ken* 事件

inclination *keikō* 傾向 ——(idiom) have an inclination *ki ga suru* 気がする I have no inclination to study these days. *Kono-goro benkyō-suru ki ga shina'i.* このごろ勉強する気がしない。

include obj *o* (v) *fuku'm·u* 含む Does the price include tax? *Kono nedan wa zeikin o fuku'nde imasu ka?* この値段は税金を含んでいますか?

including -*tsuki* 付き including bath and toilet *basu-toire-tsuki* バストイレ付き including two meals *nishoku-tsuki* 二食付き

income *shūnyū* 収入

income tax *shotoku'zei* 所得税 income tax form *shotoku'zei shinkokusho* 所得税申告書

incompetence *munō'ryoku* 無能力

incomplete *fuka'nzen* [na] 不完全[な]

inconsistency *futō'itsu* 不統一; *mujun* 矛盾 That idea is full of inconsistencies. *Sono kanga'e wa mujun-da'rake desu.* その考えは矛盾だらけです。

inconvenient *fu'ben* [na] 不便[な] an inconvenient kitchen *fu'ben* *na daidokoro* 不便な台所 ——(idiom) not suitable *tsugō ga waru´·i* 都合が悪い Tomorrow is inconvenient for me. *Ashita´ wa watashi wa tsugō ga waru´i.* 明日は私は都合が悪い.

incorporate obj *o* (v) **1** take in *toriire´·ru* 取り入れる **2** combine (irr) *gappei-suru* 合併する ——(idiom) form a limited corporation *yūgen-gaisha ni suru* 有限会社にする

incorrect (v) be incorrect *machiga´tte i·ru* 間違っている This English is incorrect. *Kono Ei-go wa machiga´tte iru.* この英語は間違っている. ——(attr) *machiga´tta* 間違った an incorrect announcement *machiga´tta hōkoku* 間違った報告

increase **1** *zōka* 増加 **2** sudden increase *gekizō* 激増 ——(v) *mas·u* 増す Exports increased 20% over last year. *Yushutsu ga kyo´nen yo´ri ni´-wari mashita.* 輸出が去年より二割増した.; *fue´·ru* 増える Because of the depression, the number of unemployed has increased. *Fuke´iki de shitsugyō´sha ga fu´ete kite iru.* 不景気で失業者が増えてきている. ——obj *o* (v) *fuya´s·u* 増やす increase the staff *hitode o fuya´su* 人手を増やす

incredible (adj) *shinjirarena´·i* 信じられない That's incredible! *Shinjirarena´i koto´ desu!* 信じられないことです.

indebted (idiom) be indebted to *o´n o uke´·ru* 恩を受ける

indebtedness (financial) **1** *fusai* 負債 **2** debt *shakki´n* 借金

indecent *waisetsu* [*na*] わいせつ[な]

indefinite *aimai* [*na*] あいまい[な] She gave an indefinite answer. *Ka´nojo wa aimai na henji´ o shita.* 彼女はあいまいな返事をした. ——(attr) *bakuzen to shita* 漠然とした I have only an indefinite recollection. *Bakuzen to shita kioku shika na´i.* 漠然とした記憶しかない.

indefinitely *muse´igen ni* 無制限に

independence **1** *dokuritsu* 独立 spirit of independence *dokuritsu se´ishin* 独立精神 Declaration of Independence *Dokuritsu Se´ngen* 独立宣言 **2** self-reliance *dokuritsu do´ppo* 独立独歩

independent **1** self-supporting *jikyū* 自給 **2** self-governing *dokuritsu-* 独立 an independent state *dokuritsu´-koku* 独立国 **3** free from influence *do´kuji* [*no*] 独自[の] That person has independent ideas. *Ano´ hito wa do´kuji no kanga´e o mo´tte iru.* あの人は独自の考えを持っている. ——(attr) *dokuritsu-shita* 独立した My children all have independent personalities. *Watashi no kodomo wa minna dokuritsu-shita ko´sei o mo´tte iru.* 私の子供はみんな独立した個性を持っている.

index *sakuin* 索引

index finger *hitosashi´-yubi* 人差し指

India *I´ndo* インド

Indian (American) [*Amerika*] *I´ndian* [アメリカ]インディアン

Indian (person) *Indo´jin* インド人 ——(attr) *I´ndo no* インドの

indicate obj *o* (irr) *shitei-suru* 指定する

indictment 1 *ki'so* 起訴 2 prosecution *kokuhatsu* 告発

indifference *muka'nshin* 無関心

indifferent *muka'nshin* [na] 無関心[な] an indifferent attitude *muka'nshin na ta'ido* 無関心な態度

indigestion *shōka fu'ryō* 消化不良

indigo 1 (color) *ai-iro* あい色 2 (dye) *a'i* あい

indirect *kansetsu* [no] 間接[の]

indirectly *kansetsu ni* 間接に

individual *ko'jin* 個人 ——(attr) 1 *ko'jin no* 個人の rights of the individual *ko'jin no ke'nri* 個人の権利 2 of a unique character *dokutoku no* 独特の his own individual way *ka're dokutoku no yarikata* 彼独特のやり方

individuality *ko'sei* 個性

individually 1 person by person *hitori-hito'ri de* 一人一人で 2 item by item *betsu-betsu ni* 別々に Wrap them individually, please. *Betsu-betsu ni tsutsu'nde kudasa'i.* 別々に包んで下さい。

Indonesia *Indone'shia* インドネシア

Indonesian 1 (language) *Indoneshia-go* インドネシア語 2 (person) *Indoneshia'jin* インドネシア人 ——(attr) *Indone'shia no* インドネシアの

indoors *shitsu'nai* 室内

industrious *kimben* [na] 勤勉[な] an industrious worker *kimben na jūgyō'in* 勤勉な従業員

industriously *kimben ni* 勤勉に work industriously *kimben ni hataraku* 勤勉に働く

industry *sangyō* 産業;*-gyō* 業 manufacturing industry *seizō kō'gyō* 製造工業 iron and steel industry *tekkō'-gyō* 鉄鋼業

ineffective *mukō* [no] 無効[の]; *muda* [na] 無駄[な] ineffective effort *muda na do'ryoku* 無駄な努力 ——(idiom) be/become ineffective *mukō ni na'r·u* 無効になる Our efforts were ineffective. *Wata'shitachi no do'ryoku wa mukō ni na'tta.* 私たちの努力は無効になった。

inequality *fubyō'dō* 不平等 social inequality *shakaiteki fubyō'dō* 社会的不平等

inexpensive (adj) *yasu'·i* 安い an inexpensive restaurant *yasu'i re'sutoran* 安いレストラン

inexperienced *mijuku* [na] 未熟[な] ——(attr) *keiken no na'i* 経験のない We can't hire an inexperienced person. *Keiken no na'i hito o yato'u koto wa deki'nai.* 経験のない人を雇うことはできない。

infant *yō'ji* 幼児

infect (v) be/become infected *u'm·u* うむ The wound is infected. *Kizu wa u'nde iru.* 傷はうんでいる。

infection *kansen* 感染

inferior *soaku* [na] 粗悪[な] This product is inferior. *Kono seihin wa soaku de'su.* この製品は粗悪です。 ——(v) be inferior *oto'r·u* 劣る This one is inferior to that one. *Kore wa sore yo'ri mo oto'tte iru.* これはそれよりも劣っている。 ——(attr) *oto'tta* 劣った inferior goods *oto'tta shinamono* 劣った品物

inferiority complex *rettō'kan* 劣等感

infidelity *uwaki* 浮気

infinite *mugen* [no] 無限[の]

infinitive (Gram) *fute'ishi* 不定詞

inflation *infure* インフレ

influence 1 *eikyō* 影響 2 power *se'iryoku* 勢力 ——(idiom) exert influence *eikyō o oyobo's·u* 影響を及ぼす

influential *yūryoku* [na] 有力[な] an influential businessman *yūryoku na jitsugyō'ka* 有力な実業家

influenza *ryūkan* 流感; *infurue'nza* インフルエンザ

inform ind-obj *ni*, obj *o* (v) *shirase'ru* 知らせる Inform me of the result as soon as possible. *Kekka o dekiru dake ha'yaku shirasete kudasa'i.* 結果をできるだけ早く知らせて下さい。

informal (attr) *kuda'keta* くだけた informal talk *kuda'keta hanashi'* くだけた話

information 1 *tsūchi* 通知 2 report *hōdō* 報道 3 knowledge *jōhō* 情報 4 *annai* 案内 information desk *anna'ijo* 案内所

infrequently *tama ni* たまに That happens only infrequently. *Sore wa tama ni' shika okora'nai.* それはたまにしか起こらない。

ingredient(s) 1 *seibun* 成分; *yōin* 要因 2 (cooking) *genza'iryō* 原材料

inhabitant *jūmin* 住民

inhale obj *o* (v) *suiko'm·u* 吸い込む inhale a chestful of fresh air *shinsen na kū'ki o mune ippai suiko'mu* 新鮮な空気を胸一杯吸い込む

inherit obj *o* (irr) *sōzoku-suru* 相続する

inheritance *sōzoku* 相続

inhuman *hi'ningenteki* [na] 非人間的[な]

initial 1 initial letter *kashira mo'ji* 頭文字 2 beginning *saisho no* 最初の

injection *chūsha* 注射 ——obj *o* (irr) give/receive an injection *chūsha-suru* 注射する

injure (idiom) cause an injury *kega' o sase·ru* 怪我をさせる

injured (attr) *kega'-shita* 怪我した ——(idiom) be injured *kega' o suru* 怪我をする

injury *kega'* 怪我

injustice *futō* 不当

ink 1 *inku* インク; *inki* インキ 2 India ink *sumi'* 墨

Inland Sea *Seto-na'ikai* 瀬戸内海

in-laws *giri no na′ka* 義理の仲

inlay *zōgan-za′iku* 象眼細工

inn 1 (J) *ryokan* 旅館; (tourist guest-house with limited service) *minshuku* 民宿

innocence 1 *mujaki′sa* 無邪気さ 2 (Leg) *mu′zai* 無罪

innocent 1 *mu′jaki* [na] 無邪気[な] an innocent child *mu′iaki na kodomo* 無邪気な子供 2 pure *seijō* [na] 清浄[な] ——(attr) *tsu′mi no na′i* 罪のない an innocent victim *tsu′mi no na′i higa′isha* 罪のない被害者

inquire obj *o* (v) *tazune′·ru* 尋ねる

inquiry 1 *toiawase* 問い合せ a telephone inquiry *denwa no toiawase* 電話の問い合せ 2 survey *chō′sa* 調査

insane *kichiga′i* [no] 気違い[の]

insanity *seishimbyō* 精神病

inscribe (idiom) *me′i o ire·ru* 銘を入れる

inscription *me′i* 銘

insect *mushi* 虫

insect repellent *mushi-yoke* 虫よけ

insert obj *o* (v) *ire·ru* 入れる insert a bookmark in a book *ho′n no aida ni shiori o ireru* 本の間にしおりを入れる

inside [no] *na′ka* [ni] [の]中[に] She's inside the house. *Ka′nojo wa ie no na′ka ni iru.* 彼女は家の中にいる。 It's inside the box. *Sore wa hako no na′ka ni a′ru.* それは箱の中にある。

inside out *ura-ga′eshi* 裏返し

insincere (attr) *se′i-i no na′i* 誠意のない

insist on obj *o* (irr) *shuchō-suru* 主張する insist on one's innocence *mu′jitsu o shuchō-suru* 無実を主張する I must insist on this point. *Kono ten o do′ko made mo shuchō-suru.* この点をどこまでも主張する。

inspect obj *o* (v) *shirabe′·ru* 調べる; (irr) *tenken-suru* 点検する

inspection *ke′nsa* 検査; *shi′nsa* 審査; *tenken* 点検

inspire obj *o* (v) *hagema′s·u* 励ます ——(pass) *hagemasare′·ru* 励まされる Everyone was inspired by his words. *Minna′ga ka′re no kotoba′ ni hagemasa′reta.* みんなが彼の言葉に励まされた。

in spite of *…no ni* …のに He didn't come, in spite of the fact that he said he would. *Ka′re wa ku′ru to itta′ no ni, ko′nakatta.* 彼は来ると言ったのに来なかった。

installment plan *bunkatsu-ba′rai* 分割払い

instant *see* moment

instantaneous *so′kuji* 即時; *soku-* 即 instantaneous death *sokushi* 即死

instant (foods) (attr) *i′nsutanto* インスタント instant coffee *insutanto kō′hi* インスタントコーヒー; *sokuseki* 即席 instant ramen *sokuseki rā′men* 即席ラーメン

instantly *see* immediately

instead of ... *[no] kawari ni* ...[の]かわりに instead of going *iku kawari ni* 行くかわりに She went instead of Mr. Smith. *Ka'nojo wa Su'misu-san no kawari ni itta.* 彼女はスミスさんのかわりに行った.

instep *ashi-no-kō'* 足の甲

instinct *ho'nnō* 本能

institute (for research) *kenkyūjo* 研究所

instruct ind-obj *ni*, obj *o* (v) *oshie·ru* 教える

instruction *oshie* 教え; *kyōju* 教授

instructions *shi'ji* 指示

instructor *kō'shi* 講師

instrument 1 (musical) *gakki* 楽器   2 means *shu'dan* 手段 an instrument for gaining control *shiha'iken o kakutoku-suru shu'dan* 支配権を獲得する手段

insufficient *fusoku* [*-busoku*] [*no*] 不足[の] insufficient funds *shikinbu'soku* 資金不足 insufficient sleep *suimin-bu'soku* 睡眠不足

insulation 1 (Elec) *zetsuentai* 絶縁体   2 house insulation *dannetsu'-zai* 断熱材

insult *bujoku* 侮辱 ——obj *o* (irr) *bujoku-suru* 侮辱する

insurance 1 *hoken* 保険   2 car insurance *jidōsha ho'ken* 自動車保険   3 fire insurance *kasai ho'ken* 火災保険   4 hospital/health insurance *kenkō ho'ken* 健康保険   5 insurance policy *hoken shō'sho* 保険証書   6 life insurance *seimei ho'ken* 生命保険   7 theft insurance *tōnan ho'ken* 盗難保険   8 unemployment insurance *shitsugyō ho'ken* 失業保険

intellect *chiteki nō'ryoku* 知的能力; *chisei* 知性

intellectual *interi* インテリ ——(attr) *richiteki* [*na*] 理知的[な]

intelligence 1 *chi'nō* 知能   2 information *jōhō* 情報 intelligence division *jōhō'bu* 情報部

intelligent 1 rational *chiteki* [*na*] 知的[な] Man is an intelligent being. *Ningen wa chiteki na dōbutsu de'su.* 人間は知的な動物です. 2 smart *rikō* [*na*] りこう[な] ——(adj) *kashiko'·i* 賢い, an intelligent child *kashiko'i kodomo* 賢い子供 ——(idiom) *atama'ga i'·i* 頭がいい, She's intelligent. *Ka'nojo wa atama' ga i'i.* 彼女は頭がいい.

intend ...*tsumori* つもり I intend to go tomorrow. *Ashita' iku tsumori de'su.* 明日行くつもりです. I don't intend to go. *Ikanai tsumori de'su.* 行かないつもりです.

intention *i'shi* 意志 make clear one's intention *jibun no i'shi o aki'raka ni suru* 自分の意志を明らかにする That wasn't my intention at all. *Sō iu i'shi wa watashi ni' wa mōtō nak'atta.* そういう意志は私には毛頭なかった.

intentionally *wa'zato* わざと I can't think he did that intentionally.

Ka're ga wa'zato sō shita' to wa omoe'nai. 彼がわざとそうしたとは思えない.

intently   *jitto* じっと stare at intently *jitto mi'ru* じっと見る

intercourse (sexual)   *se'kkusu* セックス; *seikō* 性交

interest (on money)   *ri'shi* 利子; *risoku* 利息

interest   **1** *kyō'mi* 興味 Do you have any interest in antiques? *Kottōhin ni kyō'mi ga arima'su ka?* 骨董品に興味がありますか.; *kanshin* 関心 I have an interest in modern art. *Watashi wa modan ā'to ni kanshin o mo'tte iru.* 私はモダンアートに関心を持っている.   **2** hobby *shu'mi* 趣味 We have many common interests. *Wata'shitachi wa iroiro na ten de shu'mi ga kyōtsū-shite iru.* 私たちはいろいろな点で趣味が共通している.

interesting (adj) *omoshiro'·i* 面白い She's a very interesting writer. *Ka'nojo wa totemo omoshiro'i sakka de'su.* 彼女はとても面白い作家です. ——(attr) *kyō'mi no a'ru* 興味のある It was an interesting talk. *Kyō'mi no a'ru hanashi' deshita.* 興味のある話でした.

interfere with   obj *o* (irr) *jama-suru* 邪魔する Don't interfere with your father's work. *Otō'-san no shigoto no jama o shina'ide.* お父さんの仕事の邪魔をしないで.

interior   **1** inside *na'ibu* 内部   **2** an inner area *o'ku* [*no*] 奥[の] the interior of a mountainous area *yama no o'ku* 山の奥

interior decoration   *interia* インテリア

intermission   *kyūkei* 休憩

intern   *intā'n* インターン

international   *kokusaiteki* [*na*] 国際的[な]; *kokusai-* 国際 international relations *kokusai ka'nkei* 国際関係 international telephone call *kokusai de'nwa* 国際電話

interpret   obj *o* (irr)   **1** orally translate *tsū'yaku-suru* 通訳する   **2** construe *ka'ishaku-suru* 解釈する

interpretation   **1** oral translation *tsū'yaku* 通訳   **2** construction *ka'ishaku* 解釈

interpreter   *tsū'yaku* 通訳 simultaneous interpreter *dōji tsū'yaku* 同時通訳

interrogation   *torishirabe* 取り調べ; *jimmon* 尋問

interrogative (Gram)   **1** (word) *gimo'nshi* 疑問詞   **2** (sentence) *gimo'n-bun* 疑問文

interrupt   obj *o* (v)   **1** interfere with *saegi'r·u* さえぎる; (irr) *jama-suru* 邪魔する   **2** suspend (irr) *chūshi-suru* 中止する

interruption   **1** interference *jama* 邪魔   **2** suspension *chūshi* 中止

intersection (of streets)   *kōsaten* 交差点

interval   *aida* 間 for a short interval of time *shiba'raku no aida* しばらくの間 *see also* space

interview   **1** *kaiken* 会見 press interview *kisha ka'iken* 記者会見   **2**

(for a job) *mensetsu* 面接 ——compl *ni* (irr) *mensetsu-suru* 面接する

intestine (Tech) *chō'* 腸; (coll) *harawata* はらわた

intimacy *shitashimi'* 親しみ

intimate *missetsu* [*na*] 密接[な] an intimate relationship *missetsu na kankei* 密接な関係 ——(adj) *shitashi'·i* 親しい, an intimate friend *shitashi'i tomodachi* 親しい友達

intonation (Tech) *yokuyō* 抑揚; (coll) *intonē'shon* イントネーション

intoxicated (v) be/become intoxicated *yo'·u* 酔う He's intoxicated. *Ka're wa yo'tte iru.* 彼は酔っている。; (coll) *yoppara'·u* 酔っ払う

intoxication *yoi'* 酔い

intrauterine device *shikyū'nai hini'ngu* 子宮内避妊具; *pe'ssarī* ペッサリー

introduce ind-obj *ni*, obj *o* (irr) *shōkai-suru* 紹介する Let me introduce Mr. Tanaka. *Tanaka-san o go-shōkai shima'su.* 田中さんを御紹介します。; *dōnyū-suru* 導入する Today I'm going to introduce the *kanji* of Lesson Twelve. *Kyō wa jūni'-ka no kanji o dōnyū-shima'su.* 今日は十二課の漢字を導入します。

introduction 1 presentation *shōkai* 紹介 Professor Tanaka needs no introduction. *Tanaka-sense'i wa go-shōkai-suru ma'de mo arimase'n.* 田中先生は御紹介するまでもありません。; *dōnyū* 導入 2 (of a book) *maegaki* 前書き; *jobun* 序文

introvert *naikōteki* [*na*] 内向的[な] She's an introvert. *Ka'nojo wa naikōteki de'su.* 彼女は内向的です。

intuition *chokkan* 直感; *kan* 勘 know by intuition *kan de waka'ru* 勘で分かる

invade obj *o* (irr) *shinnyū-suru* 侵入する

invalid (person) *byōnin* 病人

invasion *shinryaku* 侵略

invent obj *o* (irr) *hatsumei-suru* 発明する

inventor *hatsumeika* 発明家

invest obj *o*, compl *ni* (irr) *tōshi-suru* 投資する

investigate obj *o* (v) *shirabe'·ru* 調べる; (irr) *chō'sa-suru* 調査する

investigation *torishirabe* 取り調べ; *chō'sa* 調査

investment *tōshi* 投資

invitation *shō'tai* 招待 receive an invitation *shō'tai o uke'ru* 招待を受ける accept an invitation *shō'tai ni ōji'ru* 招待に応じる

invite obj *o* (v) 1 *mane'k·u* 招く Who shall we invite to the party? *Pā'tī ni da're o manekimashō' ka?* パーティーにだれを招きましょうか。 2 (informally) *saso·u* 誘う 3 (formally) *shō'tai-suru* 招待する 4 call *yob·u* 呼ぶ invite Mr. Tanaka to dinner *Tanaka-san o yūshoku ni yobu* 田中さんを夕食に呼ぶ How about inviting Mr. Tanaka over? *Tanaka-san o uchi ni yonda'ra ika' ga desu ka?*

田中さんを家に呼んだらいかがですか. ——(pass) **1** (informally) *sasoware-ru* 誘われる I'm late because I was invited out for a beer by a friend. *Tomodachi ni sasowarete, bi'ru o no'mi ni itta' kara okureta.* 友達に誘われてビールを飲みに行ったから遅れた. **2** (formally) *shō'tai-sare-ru* 招待される be invited to a formal dinner *bansan ni shō'tai-sareru* 晩さんに招待される

involve obj o (v) *makiko'm·u* 巻き込む ——(pass) *makikomare'·ru* 巻き込まれる be involved in a war *sensō ni makikomare'ru* 戦争に巻き込まれる ——(attr) involved *fukuzatsu* [na] 複雑[な] an involved matter *fukuzatsu na mondai* 複雑な問題

iodine *yōdochi'nki* ヨードチンキ; (abbr) *yōchin* ヨーチン

Iran *I'ran* イラン

Iranian (person) *Ira'njin* イラン人 ——(attr) *I'ran no* イランの

Iraq *I'raku* イラク

Iraqi (person) *Iraku'jin* イラク人 ——(attr) *I'raku no* イラクの

Ireland *Airura'ndo* アイルランド

iris **1** (flower) *ayame* あやめ; *hana shō'bu* 花しょうぶ **2** (of eye) (Tech) *kōsai* 虹彩

Irish (person) *Airurando'jin* アイルランド人 ——(attr) *Airura'n-do no* アイルランドの

iron **1** (metal) *tetsu* 鉄 **2** golf iron *a'ian* アイアン **3** (for clothes) *airon* アイロン ——(idiom) to iron [...ni] *airon o kake'r·u*[...に] アイロンをかける

irrational *fugō'ri* [na] 不合理[な]

irregular *fuki'soku* [na] 不規則[な]

irresponsible *muse'kinin* [na] 無責任[な]

irrigation *kangai* かんがい

irritable (adj) *okorippo'·i* おこりっぽい ——(irr) be/become irritable *i'raira-suru* いらいらする

is **1** ...*wa* ...*desu* ...は...です This is a book. *Kore wa ho'n desu.* これは本です. **2** (v) *i·ru* いる My husband is in his study. *Shu'jin wa shosai ni ima'su.* 主人は書斎にいます. *see also* be

Islam *Isuramu-kyō* イスラム教

island *shima* [-*jima*] 島 Awaji Island *Awaji'-shima* 淡路島; -*tō* 島 Guam Island *Guamu-tō* グアム島

isolate obj o (caus) *koritsu-sase·ru* 孤立させる

Israel *Isura'eru* イスラエル

Israeli (person) *Isuraeru'jin* イスラエル人 ——(attr) *Isura'eru no* イスラエルの

it *sore* それ Give it to me. *Sore o kudasa'i.* それを下さい. *see also* this; that

Italian **1** (language) *Itaria-go* イタリア語 **2** (person) *Itaria'jin* イタリア人 ——(attr) *Itaria no* イタリアの

Italy *Itaria* イタリア

itchy (adj) *kayu'·i* かゆい, It's itchy! *Kayu'i!* かゆい.
item 1 thing *shinamono* 品物 2 newspaper item *ki'ji* 記事 3 part of a document *kajō* 箇条; *kōmoku* 項目
itinerary *ryotei* 旅程
IUD, IUCD *see* intrauterine device
ivory *zōge* 象牙
ivy *tsuta* 蔦

J

jack 1 (car) *ja'kki* ジャッキ 2 (face card) *ja'kku* ジャック
jacket 1 *ja'ketto* ジャケット 2 suit coat *uwagi* 上着
jade *hisui* ひすい
jail *rōya'* 牢屋 ——(idiom) imprison *keimu'sho ni ire·ru* 刑務所に入れる
jam 1 fruit jam *ja'mu* ジャム 2 traffic jam *kōtsū jū'tai* 交通渋滞 3 deadlock *ikizumari* 行き詰まり Negotiations are in a jam. *Kōshō wa ikizumari jō'tai ni na'tta.* 交渉は行き詰まり状態になった.
janitor *yōmu'in* 用務員
January *ichigatsu* 一月 January 1 *ichigatsu tsuitachi* 一月一日
Japan *Niho'n* 日本
Japanese 1 (language) *Nihon-go* 日本語 2 (person) *Nihonji'n* 日本人 ——(attr) *Nihon no* 日本の
Japan Sea *Niho'nkai* 日本海
Japan Travel Bureau *Niho'n Kōtsū Kō'sha* 日本交通公社
jar 1 *tsubo* つぼ 2 (large) jar *kame* かめ 3 water jar *mizu-game* 水がめ
jaundice *ōdan* 黄疸
jaw *ago'* あご
jazz *ja'zu* ジャズ
jealous (adj) *shitto-buka'·i* しっと深い a jealous person *shittobuka'i hito* しっと深い人 ——(idiom) be/become jealous *yaki'mochi o yak·u* やきもちをやく He was jealous. *Ka're wa yaki'mochi o yaita.* 彼はやきもちをやいた.
jealousy *yaki'mochi* やきもち; *shitto* しっと
jeans *ji'pan* ジーパン
jeep *ji'pu* ジープ
jello *ze'rī* ゼリー
jelly *ze'rī* ゼリー
jellyfish *kurage* くらげ
jerk 1 sudden movement *kyū'na ugoki'* 急な動き 2 stupid person *orokamono* おろか者 ——(idiom) to jerk *kyū' ni hik·u* 急に引く

jest *fuzake'* ふざけ ——(v) *fuzake'·ru* ふざける; *chaka's·u* 茶化す

Jesus (Prot) *Ie'su* イエス; (Cath) *Ie'zusu* イエズス

jet lag *ji'sa-boke* 時差ぼけ

jetliner *jetto'ki* ジェット機; *jetto ryoka'kki* ジェット旅客機

Jew *Yudaya'jin* ユダヤ人

jewel 1 *hōseki* 宝石 2 precious stone *ishi'* 石

jewelry *hōseki* 宝石 jewelry box *hōseki'-bako* 宝石箱

Jewish (person) *Yudaya'jin* ユダヤ人 ——(attr) *Yudayakyō no* ユダヤ教の

jigsaw puzzle *hame-e* はめ絵; *jigusō pa'zuru* ジグソーパズル

job *shigoto* 仕事 have a job *shigoto ga a'ru* 仕事がある

jobless *mu'shoku* 無職

jockstrap *sapō'tā* サポーター

jogging *jogingu* ジョギング; *ranningu* ランニング

join comp *to*, ind-obj *ni*, obj *o* (v) 1 tie together *musub·u* 結ぶ join two pieces of string *i'to to i'to to o musubu* 糸と糸とを結ぶ 2 put together; fix together *tsunagi-awase'r·u* つなぎ合せる join hands *te' to te' o tsunagi-awase'ru* 手と手をつなぎ合せる ——obj *o* (irr) *gappei-suru* 合併する ——(idiom) 1 join in ... [to] *tsukia·u* ...[と]付き合う Join me! *Tsukia'tte kudasa'i!* 付き合って下さい。 2 join an association *kaiin ni na'r·u* 会員になる

joint 1 (Anat) *kansetsu* 関節 2 *kyōdō* 共同 joint research project *kyōdō ke'nkyū* 共同研究

joke *jōda'n* 冗談 That's no joke! *Jōda'n ja na'i!* 冗談じゃない。; poor joke *dajare* だじゃれ ——(v) *fuzake'·ru* ふざける

joker 1 (face card) *jō'kā* ジョーカー 2 one who jests *fuzakeya* ふざけや

jolly *yōki* [*na*] 陽気[な]

Jordan *Yo'rudan* ヨルダン

Jordanian (person) *Yoruda'njin* ヨルダン人 ——(attr) *Yo'rudan no* ヨルダンの

journalist *jānari'suto* ジャーナリスト; *shimbun* [*zasshi*] *ki'sha* 新聞[雑誌]記者

journey *tabi'* 旅 see also trip

joy *yorokobi* 喜び

joyfully *ureshisō' ni* うれしそうに

Judaic *Yudayakyō no* ユダヤ教の

Judaism *Yudayakyō* ユダヤ教

judge 1 (court) *saiba'nkan* 裁判官 2 (contest) *shinsa'in* 審査員 ——obj *o* (irr) *sa'iban-suru* 裁判する; *shi'nsa-suru* 審査する

judgment (Leg) *hanketsu* 判決

jug *mizusa'shi* 水差し

juice 1 *shi'ru* 汁 2 juice or fruit-flavored soft drink *jū'su* ジュース 3 fruit juice *furūtsu jū'su* フルーツジュース

July *shichigatsu'* 七月 July 7 *shichigatsu nanoka* 七月七日

jump loc *o* (v) *tob·u* 跳ぶ Jump! *Tonde goran!* 跳んでごらん.

jump rope *nawa-to'bi* なわ飛び

June *rokugatsu'* 六月 June 6 *rokugatsu muika* 六月六日

June beetle *kofukiko'gane* こふきこがね; (coll) *ka'nabun* かなぶん

jungle *ja'nguru* ジャングル

junior 1 college junior *daigaku sanne'n-sei* 大学三年生 2 one's junior (in rank) *kōhai* 後輩

junk shop *kuzu'ya* くず屋

Jupiter *Mokusei* 木星

juror *baishi'n-in* 陪審員

jury *baishin* 陪審

just 1 exactly *chōdo* ちょうど It's just 2:00. *Chōdo ni'ji desu.* ちょうど二時です.; *pitta'ri* ぴったり This blouse just fits. *Kono bura'-usu wa pitta'ri desu.* このブラウスはぴったりです. 2 fair *kōhei* [*na*] 公平[な]

justice *se'igi* 正義

justify (idiom) *tadashi'i to suru* 正しいとする

just like *marude*...[*no*] *yō'* [*na*] まるで...[の]よう[な] The scenery there was just like a picture postcard. *Asoko no ke'shiki wa maru-de eha'gaki no yō' deshita.* あそこの景色はまるで絵葉書のようでした.

just now (a moment ago) *sa'kki* さっき Who is that person who was here just now? *Sa'kki ki'te ita hito wa da're desu ka?* さっき来ていた人はだれですか.

juvenile delinquency *shōnen hikō* 少年非行

juvenile delinquent 1 (masc) *furyō shō'nen* 不良少年 2 (fem) *furyō shō'jo* 不良少女

K

Kampuchea *Kampuchea* カンプチェア see also Cambodia

kangaroo *kanga'rū* カンガルー

karma (Budd) *gō'* 業

Kashmir *Kashimī'ru* カシミール

Kashmiri 1 (language) *Kashimīru-go* カシミール語 2 (person) *Kashimiru' jin* カシミール人 ——(attr) *Kashimī'ru no* カシミールの

keel *se'mbi* 船尾

keep obj *o* (v) **1** store (irr) *hozon-suru* 保存する **2** hold *mo′ts·u* 持つ; *to′tte ok·u* 取っておく Let's keep this. *Kore o to′tte okimashō′.* これを取っておきましょう。 **3** obey; guard *mamo′r·u* 守る keep the commandments *okite o mamo′ru* おきてを守る **4** keep (raise) a pet *ka′·u* 飼う Do you keep a dog? *Inu′ o ka′tte imasu ka?* 犬を飼っていますか。 **5** hold in trust *azuka′r·u* 預かる Would you keep this money for me? *Kono o-kane o azuka′tte kudasaimase′n ka?* このお金を預かって下さいませんか。

keeper (of animals) *kainushi* 飼い主

keep on (doing) *-tsuzuke·ru* 続ける He knows the danger of getting lung cancer, but he keeps on smoking. *Ka′re wa haigan no ko′wasa o shirina′gara, tabako o sui-tsuzuke′te iru.* 彼は肺癌のこわさを知りながら、たばこを吸い続けている。

keepsake *katami* 形見

keep up with compl *ni* (v) *oitsu′·ku* 追い付く ——(pot) *oitsuke′·ru* 追い付ける I can't keep up with my work. *Shigoto ni oitsuke′nai.* 仕事に追い付けない。

kelp *ko′mbu* 昆布

kennel *inu-goya* 犬小屋

kernel **1** *kaku* 核 **2** core *shi′n* 芯

kerosene **1** *sekiyu* 石油 **2** fuel for kerosene stove *tōyu* 灯油

ketchup *kecha′ppu* ケチャップ

kettle **1** (for cooking) *kama* かま **2** teakettle *yuwa′kashi* 湯沸かし; *yakan* やかん

key **1** *kagi′* 鍵 key to a problem *mondai no kagi* 問題の鍵 Do you have the house key? *Ie no kagi′ o mo′tte imasu ka?* 家の鍵を持っていますか。 **2** car key *ki′-* キー **3** (music) key of... *-chō′* 調 the key of A *i′-chō* イ調

keyboard *kemban* 鍵盤

keynote speaker *kichō enzetsu′sha* 基調演説者

key ring *ki-ri′ngu* キーリング

kick obj *o* (v) **1** *ke′r·u* 蹴る **2** kick violently *kettoba′s·u* 蹴っとばす

kid **1** young goat *koyagi* 子やぎ **2** (leather) *ki′ddo* キッド

kidnap obj *o* (irr) *yūkai-suru* 誘拐する

kidnapper *yūka′ihan* 誘拐犯

kidney **1** (Anat) *jinzō* 腎臓 **2** (food) *mame* まめ

kill obj *o* (v) *koros·u* 殺す *see also* assassinate; murder

kill time (idiom) *jikan o tsubus·u* 時間をつぶす

kiln *kama* かま

kilogram *ki′ro* キロ one kilogram *ichiki′ro* 1キロ two kilograms *ni′kiro* 2キロ three kilograms *san′kiro* 3キロ

kilometer *ki′ro* キロ thirty kilometers *sanju′kkiro* 30キロ eighty kilometers *hachiju′kkiro* 80キロ

kin 1 (same family line) *dōzoku* 同族 2 relative *shinseki* 親戚

kind 1 *shi'nsetsu* [*na*] 親切[な] a kind person *shi'nsetsu na hito'* 親切な人 2 variety *shu'rui* 種類 3 kind of: this kind of *konna* こんな that kind of *sonna* そんな that (distant) kind of *anna* あんな what kind of (?) *do'nna* どんな What kind of clothes are you looking for? *Do'nna fuku o sagashite ima'su ka?* どんな服を探していますか. ——(idiom) be kind to *shi'nsetsu ni suru* 親切にする She was kind to me. *Ka'nojo wa watashi ni shi'nsetsu ni shite kureta.* 彼女は私に親切にしてくれた.

kindergarten *yōchi'en* 幼稚園

kindhearted *shi'nsetsu* [*na*] 親切[な] ——(adj) *yasashi·i* 優しい

kindling *takigi* たき木

kindness *shi'nsetsu* 親切

king 1 *ōsama* 王様; *koku-ō'* 国王 2 (face card) *ki'ngu* キング

kingdom *ōkoku* 王国

kinky hair *chijireta kami'* 縮れた髪

kiss *kuchizuke* ロづけ; *ki'su* キス ——comp *ni* (irr) *kuchizuke-suru* ロづけする

kit *yō'gu* 用具 carpenter's kit *mokkō yō'gu* 木工用具

kitchen *daidokoro* 台所

kite 1 (toy) *ta'ko* 凧 flying a kite *tako'-age* 凧あげ 2 (bird) *to'bi* [*to'mbi*] 鳶

kitten *kone'ko* 子猫

Kleenex *ti'sshu* ティッシュ

knapsack *nappusa'kku* ナップサック; *ryu'kku* リュック

knead obj *o* (v) *ne'r·u* 練る

knee *hiza* ひざ

kneel (v) *hizamazu'k·u* ひざまずく

knife 1 *na'ifu* ナイフ; *ha'mono* 刃物 2 kitchen knife *hōchō* 包丁

knit obj *o* (v) *a'm·u* 編む Did you knit that sweater yourself? *Jibun de sono sē'tā o amima'shita ka?* 自分でそのセーターを編みましたか.

knitting *ami'monō* 編み物

knitting needle *ami'bō* 編み棒

knob *totte* 把手

knock obj *o* (v) 1 *tata'k·u* 叩く 2 (on a door) (irr) *no'kku-suru* ノックする

knockout *nokku-a'uto* ノックアウト

knot *musubime* 結び目

know obj *o* (v) *shir·u* 知る Do you know Mr. Tanaka? *Tanaka-san o shitte ima'su ka?* 田中さんを知っていますか. I don't know him. *Shirimase'n.* 知りません.

knowledge *chi'shiki* 知識 a person of knowledge *chi'shiki no a'ru hito* 知識のある人

knuckles *genkotsu* げんこつ

Korea 1 (North) *Kita Chōse'n* 北朝鮮　2 (South) *Ka'nkoku* 韓国

Korean 1 (language): (North) *Chōsen-go* 朝鮮語; (South) *Kankoku-go* 韓国語　2 (person); (North) *Chōsenji'n* 朝鮮人; (South) *Kankoku'jin* 韓国人　——(attr) (North) *Chōse'n no* 朝鮮の; (South) *Ka'nkoku no* 韓国の

kung-fu *kanfū'* 功夫; カンフー

Kuwait *Kuē'to* クウェート

Kuwaiti (person) *Kuēto'jin* クウェート人　——(attr) *Kuē'to no* クウェートの

L

lab *see* laboratory

label 1 (product) *ra'beru* ラベル　2 (for packages, etc.) *fuda* 札

labor 1 work *rōdō* 労働 labor union *rōdō ku'miai* 労働組合 manual labor *jūrō'dō* 重労働　2 (workers) *rōdō'sha* 労働者 management and labor *keie'isha to rōdō'sha* 経営者と労働者　3 childbirth *bumben* 分娩　——(irr) *rōdō-suru* 労働する

laboratory 1 (language) *ra'bo* ラボ　2 (research) *jikke'n-shitsu* 実験室

labor pains *jintsū* 陣痛

lace *rē'su* レース

lack *ketsubō* 欠乏; *fusoku* 不足 lack of money *kane no fusoku* 金の不足

lacquer 1 *urushi* 漆　2 lacquer ware *urushi* 漆; *nurimono* 塗り物; *shikki* 漆器　——(idiom) apply lacquer *urushi o nur·u* 漆を塗る

ladder *hashigo* はしご

ladle *shakushi* 杓子; (coll) *ota'ma* おたま

lady 1 *fujin* 婦人　2 (titled) *kifu'jin* 貴婦人

laity *hira-shi'nto* 平信徒

lake *mizuu'mi* 湖

lamb 1 (animal) *kohitsu'ji* 子羊　2 (meat) *kohitsu'ji no niku'* 子羊の肉; *ra'mu* ラム

lame *bi'kko* びっこ[の]　——(idiom) be lame *bi'kko o hik·u* びっこをひく; *ashi'ga fu'jiyū [na]* 足が不自由[な] He's lame. *Ka're wa ashi' ga fu'jiyū desu.* 彼は足が不自由です。

lamp 1 *ra'mpu* ランプ　2 floor lamp *[de'nki no] suta'ndo* [電気の]スタンド

lampshade *de'nki no ka'sa* 電気のかさ

land 1 property *tochi* 土地　2 the land; the shore *riku* 陸　——(irr) to land *chakuriku-suru* 着陸する

landing (plane) *chakuriku* 着陸

landlady; landlord *ō′ya* 大家; *ō′ya-san* 大家さん; *ya′nushi* 家主

landowner *jinushi* 地主

landscape *ke′shiki* 景色; *fū′kei* 風景 landscape painting *fūkei-ga* 風景画

language 1 *kotoba* 言葉; (Tech) *ge′ngo* 言語 2 *-go* 語 English *Ei-go* 英語 French *Furansu-go* フランス語 Japanese *Nihon-go* 日本語 Spanish *Supein-go* スペイン語 3 (the study of) *go′gaku* 語学

lantern 1 (paper) *chōchi′n* 提灯 2 (metal) *tō′rō* 灯籠 3 (stone) *ishi-dō′rō* 灯籠

Laos *Ra′osu* ラオス

Laotian 1 (language) *Raosu-go* ラオス語 2 (person) *Raosu′jin* ラオス人 ——(attr) *Ra′osu no* ラオスの

lap (Anat) *hiza* ひざ

lapel (idiom) *eri no orikaeshi* えりの折り返し

lard *rā′do* ラード

large (adj) 1 (size) *ōki′·i* 大きい 2 (space) *hiro′·i* 広い 3 (amount) *ō′·i* 多い

large-size 1 *ōgata* [*no*] 大型[の] large-size car *ōgata′sha* 大型車 2 L-size *Eru-sa′izu* Lサイズ

lark *hibari* ひばり

larva *yōchū* 幼虫

laryngitis *kōtō′en* 喉頭炎

last 1 final *sa′igo* [*no*] 最後[の] the last item *sa′igo no mono* 最後のもの 2 end *owari* [*no*] 終わり[の] the last sentence *owari no bu′nshō* 終わりの文章 3 previous *saku-* 昨 last evening *saku′ban* 昨晩 last night *saku′ya* 晩夜; *sen-* 先 last month *se′ngetsu* 先月 last week *senshū* 先週

last name *myō′ji* 名字

late (adj) *oso′·i* 遅い It's late! *Oso′i desu!* 遅いです. She's always late getting home. *Ka′nojo wa kaeri ga i′tsumo oso′i desu.* 彼女は帰りがいつも遅いです. ——(v) 1 be late *okure·ru* 遅れる He is always late handing in his homework. *Ka′re wa i′tsumo shukudai o okurete da′su.* 彼はいつも宿題を遅れて出す. 2 be tardy (irr) *chikoku-suru* 遅刻する 3 become late *osoku-na′r·u* 遅くなる I'll be late tonight. *Ko′mban osoku-na′ru.* 今晩遅くなる. ——(idiom) until late *osoku ma′de* 遅くまで from early in the morning till late at night *a′sa ha′yaku kara yo′ru osoku′ made* 朝早くから夜遅くまで

later *a′to de* 後で I'll do it later. *A′to de suru.* 後でする.

latest *motto′mo saikin no* もっとも最近の the latest news *motto′mo saikin no nyū′su* もっとも最近のニュース

Latin (language) *Raten-go* ラテン語

latitude *i′do* 緯度

latter *kō′sha* 後者

laugh *warai* 笑い ——(v) *wara·u* 笑う ——(idiom) **1** laugh loudly *ge′ragera-wara·u* げらげら笑う **2** laugh heartily *wa′haha to wara·u* わはははと笑う **3** laugh contemptuously *sesera-wara′·u* せせら笑う She laughed contemptuously. *Ka′nojo wa sesera-wara′tte ita.* 彼女はせせら笑っていた.

laughter *warai* 笑い; *warai-go′e* 笑い声

launch obj *o* (caus) **1** (ship) *shinsui-sase·ru* 進水させる **2** (rocket) *noridasase′·ru* 乗り出させる

launder obj *o* (irr) *sentaku-suru* 洗濯する

laundry *sentaku* 洗濯

laurel *gekke′iju* 月桂樹

lavatory [*o-*]*tearai* [お]手洗い; (term used by men) *benjo′* 便所; (polite) *o-be′njo* お便所

lavender *rabe′ndā* ラベンダー

law *hōritsu* 法律

lawlessness *muhō* 無法

lawn *shibafu* 芝生

lawn mower *shibakari′ki* 芝刈り機

lawsuit *soshō* 訴訟

lawyer *bengo′shi* 弁護士

laxative *gezai* 下剤

lay (place) obj *o* (v) *ok·u* 置く Lay it here. *Koko ni oite kudasa′i.* ここに置いて下さい.

layer *sō′* 層 be in layers *sō′o na′s·u* 層をなす

layman *hira-shi′nto* 平信徒

lazy (v) be lazy *namake′·ru* 怠ける Don't be lazy. *Nama′kete wa ikena′i.* 怠けてはいけない.

lazy person *namakemono* 怠け者

lead *sentō* 先頭 take the lead *sentō ni ta′tsu* 先頭に立つ ——obj *o* (irr) **1** give leadership *shidō-suru* 指導する lead students *se′ito o shidō-suru* 生徒を指導する **2** guide *anna′i-suru* 案内する He led the way. *Ka′re wa saki ni ta′tte anna′i-shita.* 彼は先にたって案内した. **3** conduct *shiki′-suru* 指揮する lead an orchestra *gakudan o shiki′-suru* 楽団を指揮する

lead (metal) *namari* 鉛

leader *shidō′sha* 指導者

leadership *shidō* 指導

leaf *ha* 葉

leaflet *bira* ビラ

league (alliance) *remmei* 連盟

leak (v) *more′·ru* 漏れる Gas is leaking! *Ga′su ga mo′rete iru!* ガスが漏れている.; *mo′r·u* 漏る There's rain leaking through the roof. *Tenjō kara a′me ga mo′tte iru.* 天井から雨が漏っている.

lean (v) *katamu'k·u* 傾く The tower is leaning. *Tō' wa katamu'ite iru.* 塔は傾いている.

lean meat *akami* 赤身; *shibō no sukuna'i niku'* 脂肪の少ない肉

lean on compl *ni* (v) **1** depend on *tayo'r·u* 頼る lean on one's son *musuko ni tayo'ru* 息子に頼る **2** prop oneself against *motare'·ru* もたれる lean on a desk *tsukue ni motare'ru* 机にもたれる

leap loc *o* (v) *tob·u* 跳ぶ *see* jump

leap year *urū'doshi* うるう年

learn ind-obj *ni*, obj *o* (v) **1** *nara'·u* 習う I learned French from a Frenchman. *Furansu' jin ni tsuite Furansu-go o nara'tta.* フランス人についてフランス語を習った. **2** memorize *oboe'·ru* 覚える How many *kanji* have you learned? *Kanji o dore kurai oboema'shita ka?* 漢字をどれくらい覚えましたか.

learning *gaku'mon* 学問

lease *keiyaku* 契約 lease of a house *shakuya ke'iyaku* 借家契約 ——obj *o* (v) rent (from someone) *kari·ru* 借りる lease a room *heya' o kariru* 部屋を借りる

leash *kawa himo* 皮ひも

least (adj) **1** amount *ichiban sukuna'·i* 一番少ない **2** size *ichiban chisa'·i* 一番小さい ——(adv) at least *se'mete* せめて I'd like to have stayed at least one more day. *Se'mete mō ichinichi tomarita'katta.* せめてもう一日泊まりたかった.

leather *kawa'* 皮 leather jacket *kawa ja'ketto* 皮ジャケット

leave loc *o* (v) **1** go out of *de'·ru* 出る leave the room *heya' o de'ru* 部屋を出る **2** go out *dekake'·ru* 出かける She's already left. *Ka'nojo wa mō' dekaketa.* 彼女はもう出かけた. **3** depart on a trip (irr) *shuppatsu-suru* 出発する He left for America. *Ka're wa Amerika e shuppatsu-shita.* 彼はアメリカへ出発した. **4** depart via boat (irr) *shuppan-suru* 出帆する The ship leaves tomorrow. *Fu'ne wa ashita shuppan-suru.* 船は明日出帆する. ——(v) be left over *noko'r·u* 残る There is nothing left! *Nani mo noko'tte inai!* 何も残っていない. ——obj *o* (v) leave behind *noko's·u* 残す ——(pass) be left behind *nokosare'·ru* 残される Everyone went on ahead and I was left alone. *Minna' ga saki ni itte, watashi hito'ri nokosa'rete shimatta.* みんなが先に行って私一人残されてしまった.

leaves *happa* 葉っぱ

Lebanese (person) *Rebano'njin* レバノン人 ——(attr) *Reba'non no* レバノンの

Lebanon *Reba'non* レバノン

lecture *kō'gi* 講義 ——obj *o* (irr) *kō'gi-suru* 講義する

ledger *motochō* 元帳

leek *ri'ki* リーキ; *seiyō ne'gi* 西洋ネギ

left (side; direction) *hidari* 左 left side *hidari-gawa* 左側

left hand *hidarite* 左手

left-handed (person) *hidari-kiki* 左利き

leftovers *nokorimono* 残り物

left turn *sasetsu* 左折

left-wing; the Left *sa'ha* 左派; *sa'yoku* 左翼

leg *ashi'* 足

legal *hōritsu-jō* [*no*] 法律上[の]; *hōritsu* [*no*] 法律[の] It's legal. *Hōritsu de yurusa'rete iru.* 法律で許されている.

legend *densetsu* 伝説

legislature 1 state *shūgi'kai* 州議会 2 national *kokkai* 国会

legitimate *seitō* [*na*] 正当[な]

leisure 1 *rejā* レジャー 2 free time *hima* 暇 ——(irr) be at lei-sure *nombi'ri-suru* のんびりする

lemon *re'mon* レモン

lend ind-obj *ni*, obj *o* (v) *kas·u* 貸す Would you lend me that book? *Sono ho'n o watashi ni kashite kudasaimase'n ka?* その本を私に貸して下さいませんか.

length *na'gasa* 長さ

lengthen obj *o* (v) *noba's·u* 延ばす I had the skirt lengthened. *Su-kā'to no suso o noba'shite moratta.* スカートのすそを延ばしてもらった.

lens *re'nzu* レンズ concave lens *ō-re'nzu* 凹レンズ convex lens *totsu-re'nzu* 凸レンズ bifocal lens *nishōten re'nzu* 二焦点レンズ

Leo (constellation) *Shishi-za* 獅子座

leopard *hyō'* 豹

leotard *re'otādo* レオタード

leper *raibyō ka'nja* らい病患者; *Hansen-shi-byō ka'nja* ハンセン氏病患者

leprosy *raibyō* らい病; *Hansen-shi-byō* ハンセン氏病

lesbian *onna no dōsei a'isha* 女の同性愛者 ——(attr) *re'zu no* レズの

less (Math) minus *mainasu* マイナス ——(adj) *yori sukuna'·i* より少ない This year's profit was less than last year's. *Kotoshi no ri'eki wa kyo'nen yori sukuna'katta.* 今年の利益は去年より少なかった.

lesson 1 *gakka* 学課 2 class *ju'gyō* 授業 3 private lesson *re'ssun* レッスン 4 (music, ikebana, etc.) *ke'iko* 稽古

let obj *o* (v) 1 allow *yuru's·u* 許す I don't let the children watch television at night. *Kodomo ga yo'ru te'rebi o mi'ru no o yurusanai.* 子供が夜テレビを見るのを許さない. 2 rent *kas·u* 貸す let a room *heya' o kasu* 部屋を貸す

letter 1 epistle *tegami* 手紙 2 (symbol) *ji'* 字; *mo'ji* 文字 3 (ir typesetting) *katsuji* 活字

lettuce *re'tasu* レタス

leukemia *hakketsubyō* 白血病

level *heime'n* 平面; *taira* [*na*] 平ら[な]

lever *te'ko* てこ

lewd *suke'be* [*na*] すけべ[な]

liability *sekinin* 責任

liar *uso'tsuki* うそつき

liberal *kandai* [*na*] 寛大[な]

liberal arts *kyōyō ka'moku* 教養課目 liberal arts division(of a college or university) *kyōyō ga'kubu* 教養学部

Liberal Democratic Party (J) *Jiyū'-minshu-tō* 自由民主党; (abbr) *Jimin-tō* 自民党

liberalism *jiyūshu'gi* 自由主義

liberation *kaihō* 解放

Liberia *Riberia* リベリア

Liberian (person) *Riberia'jin* リベリア人 ——(attr) *Riberia no* リベリアの

liberty 1 freedom *jiyū'* 自由 2 release *kaihō* 解放

Libra *Tembin-za* 天秤座

librarian *toshoka'n-in* 図書館員; *shi'sho* 司書

library *toshokan* 図書館

Libya *Ri'bia* リビア

Libyan (person) *Ribia'jin* リビア人 ——(attr) *Ri'bia no* リビアの

lice *shirami* しらみ

license 1 *me'nkyo* 免許 2 license plate *nambā purē'to* ナンバープレート license plate number [*kuruma no*] *nambā* [車の]ナンバー

lick obj *o* (v) *name'·ru* なめる lick ice cream *aisukurī'mu o name'ru* アイスクリームをなめる

lid *futa* ふた take off the lid *futa o akeru* ふたをあける

lie (falsehood) *u'so* うそ It's no lie! *U'so ja na'i!* うそじゃない. ——(idiom) tell a lie *u'so o tsuk·u* うそをつく I never lie. *Watashi wa kesshite u'so o tsuka'nai.* 私はけっしてうそをつかない.

lie (recline) (idiom) *yoko ni na'r·u* 横になる Why don't you lie down for a while? *Suko'shi yoko ni na'ttara?* すこし横になったら?

lieutenant 1 2d Lt. *shō'-i* 少尉 2 1st Lt./Lt. (J.G.) *chū-i* 中尉 3 full Lt. *ta'i-i* 大尉

life 1 *se'imei* 生命 save a person's life *se'imei o sukuu* 生命を救う the origin of life *se'imei no ki'gen* 生命の起源 2 life (vs. death) *i'nochi* 命 3 living *seikatsu* 生活 comfortable life *jūjitsu-shita seikatsu* 充実した生活 an ordinary life *heibon na seikatsu* 平凡な生活 Life is miserable! *Seikatsu wa kurushi'i!* 生活は苦しい. 4 human life *ji'nsei* 人生 the problems of life *ji'nsei no mondai* 人生の問題

life (activity span) *se'imei* 生命 the life span of an athlete *supō'tsu no senshu se'imei* スポーツの選手生命

lifeboat *hinan-yō bō'to* 避難用ボート

lifeguard *kanshi'-in* 監視員; *kyūjo'in* 救助員

life insurance *seimei ho'ken* 生命保険

life preserver *kyūmei yō'gu* 救命用具

life style *seikatsu yō'shiki* 生活様式

lifetime (life span) **1** *jumyō* 寿命 The lifetime of a washing machine is about 5 years. *Senta'kuki no jumyō wa gonen-gu'rai desu.* 洗濯機の寿命は五年ぐらいです。 **2** (one's) *isshō* 一生

life vest *kyūmei-dō'i* 救命胴衣

lift obj *o* (v) *mochiage·ru* 持ち上げる Can you lift this bundle? *Kono ni'motsu o mochiageru koto' ga dekima'su ka?* この荷物を持ち上げることができますか。 see also **elevator**

light **1** electric light *de'nki* 電気 Turn on the light, please. *De'nki o tsuke'te kudasa'i.* 電気をつけて下さい。 Leave the light on, please. *De'nki o tsuke'te oite kudasa'i.* 電気をつけておいて下さい。 Turn off the light. *De'nki o keshite kudasa'i.* 電気を消して下さい。 **2** illumination *shōmei* 照明 **3** sunlight *hikari* 光 **4** traffic light *shingō* 信号

light (adj) **1** (not heavy) *karu·i* 軽い a light load *karui ni'motsu* 軽い荷物 **2** minor *karu·i* 軽い a light injury *karui kega'* 軽い怪我 **3** (not dark) *akaru·i* 明るい It's still light outside. *Soto wa ma'da akaru'i.* 外はまだ明るい。

light (ignite) (idiom) **1** *hi' o tsuke'·ru* 火をつける light a cigarette *tabako ni hi' o tsuke'ru* たばこに火をつける **2** light the stove *sutō'bu o tsuke'·ru* ストーブをつける

light bulb *denkyū* 電球

lighthouse *tōdai* 灯台

lighter *ra'itā* ライター

lightly *sotto* そっと touch lightly *sotto fureru* そっと触れる walk lightly *sotto aru'ku* そっと歩く

lightning *inazuma* 稲妻

likable (adj) *konomashi'·i* 好ましい ——(attr) *kōkan no mote'ru* 好感の持てる

like **1** [...*ga*] *suki'* [*na*] [...が]好き[な] Is there someone you like? *Suki' na hito ga ima'su ka?* 好きな人がいますか。 I like Japan. *Watashi wa Niho'n ga suki' desu.* 私は日本が好きです。 **2** as ... *no yō'* [*na*] ...のよう[な] I'd like something like this. *Kono yō' na mono' ga hoshi'i desu.* このような物がほしいです。 see also **look alike**; **look like**.

lilac *raira'kku* ライラック

lily *yuri* 百合

lily of the valley *suzu'ran* 鈴蘭

limb **1** (of a tree) *eda* 枝 **2** (Anat) *te'-ashi* 手足

lime **1** (mineral) *se'kkai* 石灰 **2** (fruit) *ra'imu* ライム

limit **1** prescribed limit *seige'n* 制限 age limit *nenrei se'igen* 年齢
制限 speed limit *seigen so'kudo* 制限速度 time limit *seigen ji'kan*
制限時間 **2** recognized limit *ka'giri* 限り to the limit of one's
ability *dekiru ka'giri* できる限り There is a limit to human power.
Ningen no chikara' ni wa kagi'ri ga a'ru. 人間の力には限りがある.
——obj *o* (irr) *seige'n-suru* 制限する limit one's movements *kōdō
o seige'n-suru* 行動を制限する

limited **1** *gentei-* 限定 limited edition *gentei-ban* 限定版 **2** *yūgen*
有限 a limited company/corporation *yūgen-ga'isha* 有限会社

limitless *mugen* [*no*] 無限[の] limitless desires *mugen no yokubō* 無
限の欲望 ——(idiom) *kiri' ga na'i* きりがない Academic research
is limitless. *Gakujutsu ke'nkyū to iu mono' wa kiri' ga na'i.* 学術研
究というものはきりがない.

limp *shina'yaka* [*na*] しなやか[な] ——(idiom) walk with a limp
bi'kko o hik·u びっこをひく He's limping. *Ka're wa bi'kko o hiite
iru.* 彼はびっこをひいている.

line **1** *se'n* 線 draw a line *se'n o hiku* 線を引く **2** railroad line
-sen 線 Yamanote line *Yamanote-sen* 山の手線 **3** clothesline
tsuna' 綱 **4** queue *re'tsu* 列 in one line *ichi'-retsu ni* 一列に

lineage *kettō* 血統

linen *asa'* 麻; *ri'nneru* リンネル

lines (to a play) *serifu* せりふ

line up (v) *narab·u* 並ぶ Line up, please. *Narande kudasa'i.* 並ん
で下さい. ——obj *o* (v) *narabe·ru* 並べる Line up these chairs
in one row, please. *Kono isu o ichi'-retsu ni narabete kudasa'i.*
この椅子を一列に並べて下さい.

lingerie *ra'njeri* ランジェリー

linguistics *gengo'gaku* 言語学

lining *ura'* 裏

linoleum *rinoryū'mu* リノリウム

lint *rinto'-fu* リント布; *ri'nto* リント

lion *raion* ライオン

lip *kuchibiru* くちびる

lipstick *kuchibeni* 口紅 put on lipstick *kuchibeni o tsuke'ru* 口紅を
つける

liquid **1** *ekitai* 液体 **2** liquid content *su'ibun* 水分

liquor **1** *sake* 酒 **2** (J) *nihonshu* 日本酒 **3** (W) *yōshu* 洋酒

liquor store *sakaya* 酒屋

list **1** *hyō* 表; *ri'suto* リスト **2** roll of names *meibo* 名簿 ——
obj *o* (irr) record *kinyū-suru* 記入する List these items in the cata-

logue. *Kono kōmoku o mokuroku ni kinyū-shite kudasa'i.* この項目を目録に記入して下さい. ——(v) tilt *katamu'k·u* 傾く The boat is listing. *Fu'ne ga katamu'ite iru.* 船が傾いている.

listen obj *o* (v) *kik·u* 聞く listen to music *o'ngaku o kiku* 音楽を聞く Listen to me! *Watashi no iu koto o kiki-nasa'i!* 私の言う事を聞きなさい.

liter *rittoru* リットル one liter *ichi-ri'ttoru* 1 リットル ten liters *jū ri'ttoru* 10 リットル

literally *moji-dō'ri* 文字通り

literature *bu'ngaku* 文学 comparative literature *hikaku bu'ngaku* 比較文学 English literature *Ei bu'ngaku* 英文学 Japanese literature *Nihon bu'ngaku* 日本文学 modern literature *gendai bu'ngaku* 現代文学

litter 1 *ku'zu* くず 2 (of puppies, etc.) *hito'hara no ko* 一腹の子 ——obj *o* (v) *chiraka's·u* 散らかす

little (adj) *chisa'·i* 小さい a little child *chīsa'i kodomo* 小さい子供 ——(adv) 1 (quantity) *suko'shi* 少し I have a little money. *O-kane wa suko'shi arima'su.* お金は少しあります. 2 (time; distance) *cho'tto* ちょっと Wait a little bit! *Cho'tto ma'tte kudasa'i!* ちょっと待って下さい. It's a little far. *Cho'tto tōi.* ちょっと遠い.

Little Dipper *Koguma-za* 小熊座

live (attr) *i'kite iru* 生きている live fish *i'kite iru sakana* 生きている魚

live 1 (v) (irr) *seikatsu-suru* 生活する live on one's salary *gekkyū de seikatsu-suru* 月給で生活する Can one live on ¥100,000 a month? *Tsuki' ni jūman-en de seikatsu-dekima'su ka?* 月に十万円で生活できますか.; *kuras·u* 暮らす just manage to live *dō' ni ka kurashite iku* どうにか暮らしていく live happily *kōfuku ni kurasu* 幸福に暮らす 2 be alive *iki'·ru* 生きる as long as I live *i'kite iru ka'giri* 生きている限り I can't go on living any more. *Mō' i'kite irarena'i.* もう生きていられない. ——loc *ni* (v) dwell *su'm·u* 住む Where do you live? *Do'ko ni su'nde ima'su ka?* どこに住んでいますか.

livelihood *seikei* 生計

lively 1 *ge'nki* [*na*] 元気[な] a lively child *ge'nki na kodomo* 元気な子供 2 active *kappatsu* [*na*] 活発[な] a lively person *kappatsu na hito'* 活発な人 3 bustling *nigi'yaka* [*na*] にぎやか[な] a lively town *nigi'yaka na machi'* にぎやかな町 ——(irr) be lively; spry *pi'npin-suru* ぴんぴんする For eighty, my grandfather is still very lively. *O-ji'-san wa hachijū' ni shite wa pi'npin-shite iru.* おじいさんは八十にしてはぴんぴんしている.

liver 1 (Anat) *kanzō* 肝臓 2 (food) *re'bā* レバー

living (alive and well) *kenzai* 健在 Are your parents living? *Go-ryō'shin wa go-kenza'i desu ka?* 御両親は御健在ですか.

living expenses   *seikatsu'-hi* 生活費
living room   *ima* 居間; *kyakuma* 客間
lizard   *tokage* とかげ
load   *ni'motsu* 荷物   ——obj *o* (v) *tsum·u* 積む load baggage onto a truck *tora'kku ni ni'motsu o tsumu* トラックに荷物を積む
loan   *yūshi* 融資; *rō'n* ローン car loan *kuruma rō'n* 車ローン ——obj *o* (v) *kas·u* 貸す Loan me your pencil, please. *Empitsu o kashite kudasa'i.* 鉛筆を貸して下さい. *see also* **lend**
lobby (of a building)   *ro'bī* ロビー
lobster   (J) *ise'-ebi* 伊勢えび; (W) *umiza'rigani* 海ざりがに
local   **1** *ki'njo no* 近所の a local store *ki'njo no mise'* 近所の店   **2** local train *kaku-eki te'isha* 各駅停車
location   *basho* 場所 The location is not good. *Basho wa yo'ku na'i.* 場所は良くない.
lock   *kagi'* 鍵; padlock *jōmae* 錠前   ——obj *o* (v) [*kagi' o*] *kake'·ru* [鍵を]かける Did you lock the front door? *Omote no kagi'o kakema'shita ka?* 表の鍵をかけましたか.   ——(v) be locked [*kagi' ga*] *kaka'r·u* [鍵が]かかる It's locked. *Kagi' ga kaka'tte iru.* 鍵がかかっている.
lodge   *ro'dji* ロッジ
lodging   *ya'do* 宿
log   *maruta* 丸太
logic   **1** *ro'nri* 論理   **2** (the study of) *ronri'gaku* 論理学
logical   **1** reasonable *gōriteki* [*na*] 合理的[な]   **2** following logic *ronriteki* [*na*] 論理的[な]
loincloth   *fundoshi* ふんどし
lonely   (adj) *sabishi'·i* 寂しい Are you lonely? *Sabishi'i desu ka?* 寂しいですか.
long   (adj) *naga'·i* 長い a long rope *naga'i tsuna'* 長い綱 a long time *naga'i aida* 長い間 That was a long movie! *Ano e'iga wa naga'katta.* あの映画は長かった.   ——(idiom) a long time (since) *hisashiburi* ひさしぶり It's been a long time! *O-hisashiburi de'su!* おひさしぶりです.
long ago   *mukashi* 昔
long-distance   *chō-kyo'ri* 長距離 make a long-distance (phone) call *chō-kyori de'nwa o kake'ru* 長距離電話をかける
longitude   *ke'ido* 経度
long-playing record   *erupi'* LP; *erupiban* LP盤
long-waisted   *dōnaga no* 胴長の
look   obj *o* (v) *mi'·ru* 見る Would you look at this, please. *Kore o mi'te kudasaimase'n ka?* これを見て下さいませんか. Don't look! *Mi'naide!* 見ないで. You mustn't look! *Mi'te wa ikena'i!* 見てはいけない.
Look!   *Hora!* [*Mi'te goran-nasa'i!*] ほら[見てごらんなさい].

look after **1** ... [*no*] *sewa'o suru* ...[の]世話をする **2** (children) [*no*] *mendō' o mi'ru* [の]面倒を見る

look alike compl *ni* (v) *ni·ru* 似る They (two persons) look alike. *Futa'ri wa nite iru.* 二人は似ている.

look back obj *o* (v) *furimu'k·u* 振り向く Don't look back! *Furimuka'naide!* 振り向かないで.

look like ...[*no*] *yō'* [*na*] ...[の]よう[な] It looks like it's going to be a hot day tomorrow. *Ashita' wa atsuku na'ru yō' desu.* 明日は暑くなるようです.; ...*mi'tai* [*na*] ...みたい[な] That looks like Mrs. Tanaka. *Ano kata' wa Tanaka-san mi'tai desu.* あの方は田中さんみたいです. ——(adj) ...*rashi'·i* ...らしい It looks like Mrs. Tanaka's hard up for money. *Tanaka-san wa o-kane ni koma'tte iru rashi'i.* 田中さんはお金に困っているらしい.

Look out! *Abuna'i!* 危い.

loop *wa'* 輪

loose (adj) *yuru'·i* 緩い The strap is loose. *Bando ga yuru'i.* バンドが緩い. ——obj *o* (v) let loose *hana's·u* 離す

loosen obj *o* (v) *yurume'·ru* 緩める loosen a rope *tsuna' o yurume'ru* 綱を緩める ——(v) be/become loose *yuru'm·u* 緩む The screw was loose. *Ne'ji wa yuru'nde ita.* ねじは緩んでいた.

lopsided (attr) *katamu'ita* 傾いた

lose (v) **1** lose weight *yase·ru* やせる You've lost weight! *Yasema'shita ne!* やせましたね. **2** be defeated compl *ni* (v) *make·ru* 負ける We lost to the A team. *Ē chi'mu ni maketa.* A チームに負けた. ——obj *o* (v) *nakus·u* なくす I lost my commuter pass. *Te'iki-ken o nakushita.* 定期券をなくした.; *ushina·u* 失う lose color (pale) *iro' o ushinau* 色を失う ——(irr) *so'n-suru* 損する I lost a lot (of money) by not buying that. *Sore o kawana'katta no de, zu'ibun so'n-shita.* それを買わなかったので随分損した.

loss *sonshitsu* 損失

lost (v) **1** be lost *nakunar·u* なくなる It's lost! *Nakunatta!* なくなった. **2** lose one's way *mayo'·u* 迷う I've lost my way! *Watashi wa michi ni mayo'tte shimatta!* 私は道に迷ってしまった. ——(idiom) *ma'igo ni na'r·u* 迷子になる The child got lost. *Kodomo wa ma'igo ni na'tta.* 子供は迷子になった.

lost-and-found office *ishitsu'butsu toriatsukaijo* 遺失物取り扱い所

lost article *wasuremono* 忘れ物

lot **1** land *tochi* 土地; *kukaku* 区画 one lot of land *tochi no ikku'-kaku* 土地の一区画 **2** vacant lot *akichi* 空地

lot (large quantity) *takusan* たくさん He has a lot of books. *Ka're wa ho'n o takusan mo'tte iru.* 彼は本をたくさん持っている.; *ōze'i* 大勢 A lot of people came. *Hito' ga ōze'i kita.* 人が大勢来た.

lotion *rō'shon* ローション

lottery *kujibiki* くじ引き

lotus **1** (flower) *hasu no hana'* 蓮の花 **2** (root) *renkon* 蓮根

loud garish *hade'* [*na*] 派手な[な] a loud color *hade' na iro'* 派手な色
——(adj) **1** noisy *yakamashi'·i* やかましい You're being too loud!
Yakamashi'i! やかましい. **2** *ōki'·i* 大きい loud voice *ōki'i ko'e*
大きい声

loudspeaker *supi'kā* スピーカー; *kakuse'iki* 拡声器

love **1** *a'i* 愛; *ko'i* 恋; *ren'ai* 恋愛 **2** affection *aijō* 愛情 **3** heterosexual love *ise'i-ai* 異性愛 **4** homosexual love *dōse'i-ai* 同性愛

love affair *jō'ji* 情事

love at first sight *hitome-bore* 一目ぼれ

love letter *rabu-re'tā* ラブレター

lover *koibito* 恋人

love song *ko'i no uta'* 恋の歌

low (adj) *hiku'·i* 低い My grades were low. *Tensū wa hiku'katta.*
点数は低かった. This chair is too low. *Kono isu wa hiku-sugiru.* こ
の椅子は低すぎる.

low beam (headlight) *shitamuki ra'ito* 下向きライト

lower (adj) *mo'tto hiku'·i* もっと低い This chair is lower (than
that one). *Kono isu' wa* [*ano isu' yori*] *mo'tto hiku'i.* この椅子は
[あの椅子より]もっと低い. ——obj *o* (v) *oro's·u* 降ろす Lower
the shades, please. *Buraindo o oro'shite kudasai.* ブラインドを降
ろして下さい.

lower berth *gedan* 下段

Lower House *kain* 下院; (J) House of Representatives *Shūgi'in* 衆
議院

low-priced (adj) *yasu'·i* 安い

low tide *kanchō* 干潮

loyal *chūjitsu na* 忠実な

lubrication **1** *junkatsu* 潤滑; *kyūyu* 給油 **2** (car) lube job *gurisu-
a'ppu* グリースアップ

luck *u'n* 運 good luck *kō-un* 幸運 bad luck *aku-un* 悪運

lucky (idiom) be lucky *u'n ga i'·i* 運がいい I was lucky. *U'n ga
yo'katta.* 運がよかった.

luggage *ni'motsu* 荷物 hand luggage *te ni'motsu* 手荷物

lukewarm (adj) *nuru'·i* ぬるい

lullaby *komori'uta* 子守歌

lumbago *yōtsū* 腰痛 ——(idiom) have lumbago *koshi ga ita'i* 腰
が痛い

lumber *zaimoku* 材木

lump **1** a clot; mass *katamari* 塊り **2** swelling *kobu'* こぶ

lunar eclipse *gesshoku* 月食

lunch *hirugo'han* 昼御飯

lung *hai* 肺 lung disease *haibyō* 肺病

lust *yoku'* 欲; *nikuyoku'* 肉欲

luster *hikari* 光
luxurious *zeitaku'* [*na*] ぜいたく[な] a luxurious apartment *zeita-ku' na apāto* ぜいたくなアパート
luxury *zeitaku'* ぜいたく
lymph gland *rimpa-sen* リンパ腺
lyrics *ka'shi* 歌詞

M

M.A. *see* Master of Arts
macaroni *makaroni* マカロニ
machine *kika'i* 機械
machine gun *kikanjū* 機関銃
machinist *kikaikō* 機械工
mackerel *saba* さば
mad 1 insane *kichiga'i* 気違い、 2 rabid dog *kyōken* 狂犬 ——obj *o* (v) be angry *oko'r·u* 怒る He's mad! *Ka're wa oko'tte iru!* 彼は怒っている。 ——(idiom) 1 be/become angry *hara'ga tats·u* 腹が立つ; *hara'o tate'·ru* 腹を立てる She's mad! *Ka'nojo wa hara'o ta'tete iru.* 彼女は腹を立てている。 2 be/go insane *ki ga kuru'·u* 気が狂う He's gone mad. *Ka're wa ki ga kuru'tte iru.* 彼は気が狂っている。
made in -*sei* 製 made in Japan *Nihon-sei* 日本製
made-to-order *atsurae* [*no*] あつらえ[の]
madness *kyō'ki* 狂気
magazine 1 *zasshi* 雑誌 2 weekly *shūka'n-shi* 週刊誌 3 monthly *gekkan-shi* 月刊誌 4 quarterly *kika'n-shi* 季刊誌
maggot *uji* うじ
magic *ma'jutsu* 魔術; *mahō* 魔法; *te'jina* 手品
magician *tejina'shi* 手品師
magnet *ji'shaku* 磁石
magnetic force *ji'ryoku* 磁力
magnetic pole *jikyoku* 磁極
magnetism *ji'ryoku* 磁力; *ji'ki* 磁気
magnificent *sōdai* [*na*] 壮大[な]
magnify obj *o* (irr) *kakudai-suru* 拡大する
magnifying glass *kakudaikyō* 拡大鏡; *mushi-me'gane* 虫眼鏡
mahjong *mā'jan* 麻雀
mahogany *maho'gani* マホガニー
maid *o-te'tsudai* お手伝い; *o-te'tsudai-san* お手伝いさん
mail *yūbin* 郵便 ——obj *o* (v) *da's·u* 出す mail a letter *tegami o da'su* 手紙を出す

mailbox 1 (for collection) *po'suto* ポスト; (for delivery) *yūbi'n-uke* 郵便受 2 P.O. box *shishoba'ko* 私書箱

mail carrier *yūbin'ya* 郵便屋; *yūbin'ya-san* 郵便屋さん

mail order *tsūshin ha'mbai* 通信販売

main *o'mo [na]* 主[な] the main product *o'mo na sambutsu* 主な産物 the main point *o'mo na ten* 主な点

mainland *ho'ndo* 本土

mainly *o'mo ni* 主に The students are mainly Americans. *Gakusei wa o'mo ni Amerika'jin desu* 学生は主にアメリカ人です.

maintain (support) obj *o* (irr) *i'ji-suru* 維持する ——(pass) *i'ji-sare·ru* 維持される Private schools are largely maintained by donations. *Shi'ritsu no gakkō wa hoto'ndo kifu-kin de i'ji-sarete iru.* 私立の学校はほとんど寄付金で維持されている.

maintenance 1 support *i'ji* 維持 2 servicing *se'ibi* 整備

major 1 (army rank) *shōsa* 少佐 2 (academic specialization) *senkō* 専攻 3 (Music) *-chō'chō* 長調 C-major *ha-chō'chō* ハ長調 A flat major *hen i-chō'chō* 変イ長調 *see also* key; major scale

majority 1 *daita'sū* 大多数 2 (vote) *kaha'nsū* 過半数

major scale *chō-o'nkai* 長音階

make obj *o* (v) 1 *tsuku'r·u* 作る make dinner *go'han o tsuku'ru* 御飯を作る; *tsuku'r·u* 造る make by hand *te' de tsuku'ru* 手で造る 2 create (irr) *sōzō-suru* 創造する 3 put together *koshirae·ru* こしらえる

make-believe *manegoto* 真似事 *see also* pretend

maker 1 *tsuku'tta hito* 作った人 2 manufacturer *mē'kā* メーカー 3 The Maker (God) *Sōzō'shu* 創造主; *Tsukuri'nushi* 造り主

make (someone) **do** (something) (caus) *-sase'ru* させる The mother made the child clean up his room. *Okā'-san wa kodomo ni heya' o katazuke-sa'seta.* お母さんは子供に部屋を片付けさせた. *see also* causative verb forms tables 1–3 pp. xxi–xxxv.

make-up (cosmetics) *keshō* 化粧; *keshōhin* 化粧品 ——obj *o* (irr) apply make-up *keshō-suru* 化粧する

malaria *mararia* マラリア

Malaysia *Marē'shia* マレーシア

Malaysia 1 (language) *Marēshia-go* マレーシア語 2 (person) *Marēshia'jin* マレーシア人 ——(attr) *Marē'shia no* マレーシアの

male *otoko'* 男; *dansei* 男性

mallard *magamo* 真鴨

man 1 *otoko' no hito* 男の人 2 young (unmarried) man *seinen* 青年 3 human being *ningen* 人間

manage obj *o* (v) 1 control (irr) *ka'nri-suru* 管理する 2 deal with *atsuka·u* 扱う I don't manage children well. *Watashi wa kodomo o atsuka'u no ga nigate de'su.* 私は子供を扱うのが苦手で

す. ——(idiom) contrive to do *dō' ni ka* [*suru*] どうにか[する] Somehow I manage to live. *Dō' ni ka kurashite iru.* どうにか暮らしている.

management 1 supervision *ka'nri* 管理 2 operation *un'ei* 運営 3 administration *keiei* 経営 4 the management *keie'isha* 経営者 5 control *torishimari* 取締り

manager *manē'ja* マネージャー; *shiha'inin* 支配人

Manchurian *Manshū'jin* 満州人 ——(attr) *Ma'nshū no* 満州の

mandarin duck *oshi'dori* おし鳥

mane *tategami* たてがみ

maneuver obj *o* (v) [*a'kuji o*] *takura'm·u* [悪事を]企む He maneuvered to topple his rival. *Ka're wa ra'ibaru o keotosu tame' ni a'kuji o takura'nda.* 彼はライバルを蹴落とすために悪事を企んだ.

maneuvers (military) *enshū* 演習; *sakusen kō'dō* 作戦行動

manger *kaibao'ke* 飼い葉桶

mania *ma'nia* マニア; -*kyō* 狂 suicidal mania *jisatsu-kyō* 自殺狂; -*kichiga'i* 気違い baseball mania *yakyū-ki'chigai* 野球気違い

maniac *kichiga'i* 気違い ——(idiom) a maniac *ki no kuru'tta hito* 気の狂った人

manicure *manikyua* マニキュア

manifestation *araware* 現われ

manipulate obj *o* (v) *ayatsu·ru* 操る manipulate public opinion *se'ron*[*yo'ron*] *o ayatsuru* 世論を操る ——(idiom) 1 manipulate people *hito o atsuka·u* 人を扱う 2 manipulate people to one's own advantage *hito o riyō-suru* 人を利用する

mankind *ningen* 人間; *ji'nrui* 人類

manly (adj) *otoko-rashi'·i* 男らしい

man-made *jinkō* [*no*] 人工[の] man-made satellite *jinkō e'isei* 人工衛星; *jinzō* [*no*] 人造[の] man-made lake *jinzō'ko* 人造湖

mannequin *manekin* マネキン

manner 1 method *hōhō* 方法 the best manner *ichiban i'i hōhō* 一番いい方法 2 way of (doing something) -*kata* 方 manner of doing *shikata* 仕方; *yarikata* やり方 manner of eating *tabekata* 食べ方 manner of making *tsukurikata* 作り方

manners *reigi* 礼儀 a person with good manners *reigi tadashi'i hito* 礼儀正しい人; *gyōgi* 行儀 a child with good manners *gyōgi no i'i kodomo* 行儀のいい子供

mansion *teitaku* 邸宅

manual (guide) *te'biki* 手引き

manufacture obj *o* (irr) *seizō-suru* 製造する

manufacturer *mē'kā* メーカー

manufacturing industry *seizō kōgyō* 製造工業

manure *koyashi'* 肥やし

manuscript *genkō* 原稿 manuscript paper *genkō yō'shi* 原稿用紙

many 1 (objects) *ōˊku no* 多くの There are not so many books. *Sonna ni ōˊku no hoˊn wa naˊi.* そんなに多くの本はない.; *takusaˊn [no]* たくさん[の]; There are many nice things in that store. *Ano miseˊ ni wa iˊi mono ga takusan aˊru.* あの店にはいい物がたくさんある. 2 (people) *ōzeˊi [no]* 大勢[の] Many people gathered. *Ōzeˊi no hito ga atsumaˊtta.* 大勢の人が集まった.

map *chiˊzu* 地図 a map of Kyoto *Kyōˊto no chiˊzu* 京都の地図 road map *dōro chiˊzu* 道路地図

maple 1 (tree) *moˊmiji* もみじ 2 (flavor) *mēˊpuru* メープル maple syrup *mēpuru shiˊroppu* メープルシロップ

marathon *marason* マラソン

marble *dairiˊseki* 大理石

March *saˊngatsu* 三月 March 3 *saˊngatsu mikka* 三月三日

march 1 *kōshin* 行進 2 (music) *kōshiˊnkyoku* 行進曲 ——(irr) *kōshin-suru* 行進する

mare *mesu umaˊ* 雌馬

margarine *māˊgarin* マーガリン

margin 1 (of written or printed page) *yohaku* 余白 2 border *fuchiˊ* 縁

marijuana *marifana* マリファナ

marine products *kaisaˊmbutsu* 海産物

marines *kaiheitai* 海兵隊

marionette *ayatsuri niˊngyō* 操り人形

mark 1 sign *shirushi* 印 2 maker's mark *māˊku* マーク 3 technical symbol *kigō* 記号 4 goal *meˊate* 目当 5 target *mato* 的 ——(idiom) mark (something) *shirushi o tsukeˊ·ru* 印を付ける

mark down obj *o* (irr) *nesage-suru* 値下げする

marker 1 felt-tip pen *majikku iˊnki* マジックインキ; *majiˊkku* マジック 2 sign *hyōshiki* 標識

market 1 *shijō* 市場 The company is seeking a new market in foreign countries. *Sono kaisha wa gaikoku ni atarashiˊi shijō o motoˊmete iru.* その会社は外国に新しい市場を求めている. 2 local marketplace *iˊchiba* 市場; *iˊchi* 市 fish market *uo iˊchiba* 魚市場

mark up obj *o* (irr) *neage-suru* 値上げする

marmalade *māmarēˊdo* マーマレード

marriage 1 *kekkon* 結婚 2 (love) *renˊai keˊkkon* 恋愛結婚 3 (arranged) *miai keˊkkon* 見合い結婚 4 (ceremony) *kekkoˊn-shiki* 結婚式

married comp *to* (irr) get married *kekkon-suru* 結婚する Are you married? *Kekkon-shite imaˊsu ka?* 結婚していますか. ——(attr) *kekkon-shita* 結婚した my married (younger) brother *kekkon-shita otóto* 結婚した弟

marry comp *to* (irr) *kekkon-suru* 結婚する Whom did Mr. Tana-

ka marry? *Tanaka-san wa daʹre to kekkon-shimaʹshita ka? 田中
さんはだれと結婚しましたか.

Mars *Kasei* 火星

marsh *numaʹ* 沼

marshmallow *mashumaro* マシュマロ

martial arts *buʹdō* 武道

martyr *junkyōʹsha* 殉教者

marvelous (adj) *sugoʹ·i* すごい

Marxism *Marukusushuʹgi* マルクス主義

mascara *masukara* マスカラ

masculine *danseiteki* [na] 男性的[な] ——(adj) *otoko-rashiʹ·i* 男
らしい

mask 1 *men* 面 2 (gauze mask for mouth and nose) *gaʹze no
maʹsuku* ガーゼのマスク 3 (surgical) *maʹsuku* マスク 4 (theatrical) *o-men* お面 ——(idiom) put on a mask *men o kabuʹr·u*
面をかぶる

masking tape *tēʹpu* テープ

masochism *mazohiʹzumu* マゾヒズム; (abbr) *maʹzo* マゾ

masochistic *mazohisutoteki* [na] マゾヒスト的[な]; *mazoteki* [na]
マゾ的[な]

mason *sekkō* 石工

Mass (Cath) *misa* ミサ

mass media *masu-meʹdia* マスメディア

mass production *masupuʹro* マスプロ

massage *massāʹji* マッサージ ——(obj *o*) (v) *mom·u* もむ Shall I
massage your shoulders? *Kaʹta o monde agemashoʹ ka?* 肩をもん
で上げましょうか.

masseur; masseuse *amma* あんま

mast *maʹsuto* マスト

master 1 (of a house, employer, etc.) *shuʹjin* 主人 ——obj *o* (irr)
maʹsutā-suru マスターする

Master of Arts *bungaku shūʹshi* 文学修士

Master of Science *rigaku shūʹshi* 理学修士

masterpiece 1 *kessaku* 傑作 2 famous masterpiece *meisaku* 名作

masturbate (irr) *jiʹi-suru* 自慰する; *shuin-suru* 手淫する ——
(idiom) *masutābēʹshon o suru* マスターベーションをする

masturbation *masutābēʹshon* マスターベーション; *jiʹi* 自慰; *shuin*
手淫; (coll) *oʹnani* オナニー

match 1 (for lighting a fire) *maʹtchi* マッチ 2 a game *shiai* 試合
3 things that go well together *soroi* そろい a matched ensemble
soroi no fuku そろいの服 ——compl *ni* (irr) suit *sōtō-suru* 相当
する a penalty that matches the offense *ihan ni sōtō-suru bakkin*
違反に相当する罰金

mate (spouse) *haigūʹsha* 配偶者

material 1 cloth *ki´ji* 生地 2 constituents *zairyo´* 材料 3 data *shi´ryō* 資料

materialism *busshitsushu´gi* 物質主義; (Tech) *yuibutsu´ron* 唯物論

materialize (irr) *jitsugen-suru* 実現する; *seiritsu-suru* 成立する

mathematics *sūgaku* 数学

matter 1 (physics) *busshitsu* 物資 2 thing; affair *koto´* 事 a serious matter *shinkoku na koto´* 深刻な事 ——(idiom) 1 It doesn't matter. *Kamaimase´n.* 構いません. 2 What's the matter? *Dō´ shima´shita ka?* どうしましたか. 3 It's no matter. *Nan demo na´i.* 何でもない.

mattress 1 (W) *ma´ttoresu* マットレス; *ma´tto* マット 2 (J) *futon* ふとん; *shiki-bu´ton* 敷きぶとん

mature (adj) *seijin-rashi´·i* 成人らしい ——(irr) *seijuku-suru* 成熟する become sexually mature *seiteki ni seijuku-suru* 性的に成熟する This fruit matures in three months. *Kono kudamono wa san-ka´getsu de seijuku-suru.* このくだ物は三か月で成熟する. ——(attr) *seijuku-shita* 成熟した

maxim *kakugen* 格言; *kotowaza* ことわざ

maximum *saikō* [*no*] 最高[の]; *saida´igen* [*no*] 最大限[の]

May *go´gatsu* 五月 May 5 *go´gatsu itsuka* 五月五日

may (permission) *-te* [*-de*] *mo i·i* て[で]もいい You may go. *Itte´ mo i´i.* 行ってもいい. You may swim here. *Koko de oyo´ide mo i´i.* ここで泳いでもいい. May I borrow this? *Kore o karite´ mo i´i desu ka?* これを借りてもいいですか.

maybe *ka´ mo shirena´i* かもしれない Maybe she won't come. *Ka´nojo wa ko´nai ka mo shirena´i.* 彼女は来ないかもしれない.

mayonnaise *mayone´´zu* マヨネーズ

mayor *shichō´* 市長

me *watashi* 私 Help me, please. *Watashi o tetsuda´tte kudasa´i.* 私を手伝って下さい. Are you giving this to me? *Watashi ni kore o kudasa´ru no desu ka?* 私にこれを下さるのですか.

meadow *kusahara* 草原

meal *go´han* 御飯; *shokuji* 食事 Is the meal ready? *Shokuji ga dekima´shita ka?* 食事ができましたか.

mealtime *shokuji ji´kan* 食事時間

mean 1 ill-tempered *iji´waru* [*na*] 意地悪[な] a person who looks mean *ijiwaru-sō´ na kaotsuki no hito´* 意地悪そうな顔付きの人 2 dirty; base *hiretsu* [*na*] 卑劣[な] a mean trick *hiretsu na shu´dan* 卑劣な手段 ——obj *o* (irr) denote *i´mi-suru* 意味する What does that action mean? *Sono kō´i wa na´ni o i´mi-shima´su ka?* その行為は何を意味しますか. ——(idiom) (intend) *tsumori* つもり I didn't mean to say that. *Sore o iu tsumori wa na´katta.* それを言うつもりはなかった.

meaning *i´mi* 意味 What is the meaning of this word? *Kono* *kotoba' wa dō' iu i'mi desu ka?* この言葉はどういう意味ですか.

meaningless *mui'mi* 無意味 What she said was meaningless. *Ka'-nojo no itta koto' wa mu'imi deshita.* 彼女の言った事は無意味でした.

meantime in the meantime *sono uchi ni* その内に

measles *hashika'* はしか

measure 1 measurements *sumpō* 寸法 2 tape measure *me'jā* メジャー; *makijaku* 巻き尺 ——obj *o* (v) *haka'r·u* 計る Measure it, please. *Sumpō o haka'tte mite kudasa'i.* 寸法を計ってみて下さい.

measures (steps) *shu'dan* 手段 The government will no doubt take measures to check inflation. *Se'ifu wa infure bōshi no shu'dan o to'ru deshō.* 政府はインフレ防止の手段を取るでしょう.

meat *niku'* 肉 eat meat *niku'o tabe'ru* 肉を食べる; *mi* 身 separate the meat from the bone *mi o mushiru* 身をむしる

meat market *niku'ya* 肉屋

mechanic *shūrikō* 修理工

mechanical *kikaiteki [na]* 機械的[な]

medal *medaru* メダル gold medal *kin me'daru* 金メダル

mediate comp *to*, obj *o* (irr) *chūkai-suru* 仲介する

mediation *chūkai* 仲介

medical science *i'gaku* 医学

medicine *kusuri* 薬

medieval *chū'sei [no]* 中世[の]

mediocre *nami no* 並の mediocre goods *nami no seihin* 並の製品

meditate (irr) *mokusō-suru* 黙想する

Mediterranean Sea *Chichū'kai* 地中海

medium-sized *chūgata [no]* 中型[の]

meek *nyūwa [na]* 柔和[な] ——(adj) *otonashi'·i* おとなしい

meet sports meet *shiai* 試合 ——compl *ni* (v) 1 *a'·u* 会う Did you meet Mr. Tanaka? *Tanaka-san ni aima'shita ka?* 田中さんに会いましたか. ——obj *o* (v) *demukae·ru* 出迎える I have to go to Narita Airport to meet a client tomorrow. *Ashita Narita kū'kō ni o-kyaku-san o demukae ni ikana'kereba nara'nai.* 明日成田空港にお客さんを出迎えに行かなければならない. 2 encounter *dea'·u* 出会う meet with difficulty *ko'nnan ni dea'u* 困難に出会う; *meguria'·u* めぐり会う

meeting 1 gathering *atsuma'ri* 集まり; *shūkai* 集会 2 conference *ka'igi* 会議; (informal) *hanashiai* 話し合い 3 preliminary planning session *uchiawase'-kai* 打ち合せ会 4 general meeting; plenary session *sōkai* 総会 5 encounter *deai* 出会い

melancholy *yūtsu'kan* 憂うつ感 ——(attr) *yūutsu [na]* 憂うつ[な]

melody *me'rodi* メロディー

melon *me'ron* メロン

melt (v) *toke'r·u* 溶ける The ice melted. *Kōri ga to'keta.* 氷が溶

けた. ——obj *o* (v) *toka'su* 溶かす The sun melted the snow. *Ta'iyō ga yuki'o toka'shita.* 太陽が雪を溶かした.

member   **1** (of an association/club) *kai-in* 会員   **2** (of a church) *kyōka'i-in* 教会員   **3** (of a committee) *i'-in* 委員

membrane   *maku'* 膜 mucous membrane *ne'mmaku* 粘膜

memento   *katami* 形見

memo   *me'mo* メモ

memoir   *kaiko'roku* 回顧録

memorial   *kinen* [*no*] 記念[の]

memorize   obj *o* (irr) *anki-suru* 暗記する

memory   *kioku* 記憶 power of memory *kioku'ryoku* 記憶力

mend   obj *o* (v)   **1** *nao'su* 直す   **2** darn *tsukuro'u* 繕う

menopause   *gekkei heishiki* 月経閉止期

menstrual period   *gekkei* [*ki'kan*] 月経[期間]

menstruation   *se'iri* 生理

mental   *se'ishin* [*no*] 精神[の] mental hospital *seishin byō'in* 精神病院

mentality   **1** quality of mind *seishi'nryoku* 精神力   **2** way of thinking *kangaeka'ta* 考え方

mention   **1** obj *o* (irr) *genkyū-suru* 言及する   **2** touch on [*ni*] *fure·ru* [に]触れる He mentioned that in his speech. *Ka're wa supi'chi no naka de sono koto' ni furema'shita.* 彼はスピーチの中でそのことに触れました. ——(idiom) Don't mention it! *Dō' itashima'shite!* どういたしまして.

menu   *menyū* メニュー

meow   *nyā'nyā* にゃあにゃあ

merchandise   **1** goods *shō'hin* 商品; *shinamono* 品物   **2** trade goods *bōekihin* 貿易品

merchant   *shō'nin* 商人

merciful   (adj) *nasake-buka'·i* 情深い; *jihi-buka'·i* 慈悲深い

mercury   *suigin* 水銀

Mercury   *Suisei* 水星

mercy   *awaremi* 哀れみ God's mercy *Ka'mi no awaremi* 神の哀れみ; *nasake* 情; *jihi* 慈悲 beg for mercy *jihi o ko'u* 慈悲を請う ——obj *o* (v) have mercy on *aware'm·u* 哀れむ Please have mercy on me! *Dō'ka aware'nde kudasai'!* どうか哀れんで下さい.

mere   *hon no* ほんの a mere baby *hon no akambō* ほんの赤ん坊

merely   *ta'n ni* 単に I merely suggested it. *Ta'n ni sō itta da'ke desu.* 単にそう言っただけです.

merger   *gappei* 合併

meridian   *shigo'sen* 子午線 the magnetic meridian *jiki shigo'sen* 磁気子午線

merit   **1** value *ka'chi* 価値 have merit *ka'chi ga a'ru* 価値がある   **2** redeeming feature *torie'* 取り柄 His (one) merit is that he tries hard. *Majime na tokoro' ga ka're no torie' desu.* 真面目な所が彼の取り柄です.

merrily *tanoshige ni* 楽しげに

merry 1 lively *nigi'yaka* [na] にぎやか[な] 2 fun *yu'kai* [na] 愉快[な] It was quite a merry party. *Taihen yu'kai na pā'tī deshita.* 大変愉快なパーティーでした.

Merry Christmas! *Kuri'sumasu omedetō!* クリスマスおめでとう.

merry-go-round *merigō'raundo* メリーゴーラウンド

mess (idiom) 1 in disorder *chirakatte i·ru* 散らかっている My room is a mess. *Heya' wa chirakatte iru.* 部屋は散らかっている. 2 disheveled *kushakusha* くしゃくしゃ My hair is a mess. *Kamino'-ke ga kushakusha de'su.* 髪の毛がくしゃくしゃです.

message 1 speech *o-hanashi* お話 2 communication *me'ssēji* メッセージ; *kotozuke* 言付け I have a message for Ms. Tanaka. *Tanaka-san ni kotozuke ga a'ru.* 田中さんに言付けがある.; *dengon* 伝言 message board *dengon-ban* 伝言板

messenger *shi'sha* 使者

messy (adj) *kitana'·i* きたない ──(attr) *darashi no na'i* だらしのない ──(v) *chirakatte i·ru* 散らかっている

metabolism *shinchin ta'isha* 新陳代謝

metal *ki'nzoku* 金属 metal goods *kinzoku se'ihin* 金属製品

metamorphosis (Bot) *hentai* 変態; (Geol) *hensei* 変成

metaphor *i'n'yu* 隠喩 see also simile

metaphysical *keijijō no* 形而上の

meteorite *inseki* 隕石

meter *mētoru* メートル one meter *ichi-mē'toru* 1メートル ten meters *jū-mē'toru* 10メートル

method 1 *hōhō* 方法 2 *-kata* 方 method of doing *shikata* 仕方 method of making *tsukurikata* 作り方 method of teaching *oshie-kata* 教え方

metric (system) *mētoru* [*hō*] メートル[法]

metropolitan *tokai no* 都会の

mew see meow

Mexican (person) *Mekishiko'jin* メキシコ人 ──(attr) *Mekishiko no* メキシコの

Mexico *Mekishiko* メキシコ

microphone *maikuro'fon* マイクロフォン; (abbr) *ma'iku* マイク

microscope *kembikyō* 顕微鏡

microwave oven *denshi re'nji* 電子レンジ

middle *mannaka* 真中 see also center

middle-aged *chūnen no* 中年の

middle class *chūryū ka'ikyū* 中流階級

Middle East *Chūtō* 中東

middle school *chūga'kkō* 中学校

midnight *mayo'naka* 真夜中
midwife *josa'mpu* 助産婦
might (adv) with all one's might *isshōke'mmei [ni]* 一生懸命[に]
see also may; maybe
migraine *henzu'tsū* 偏頭痛
migrate (irr) *ijū-suru* 移住する
mild 1 (temperature) *ondan [na]* 温暖[な] 2 (disposition) *onwa [na]* 温和[な]
mildew *kabi'* かび ——(idiom) to mildew *kabi' ga hae'·ru* かびが生える These clothes are mildewed. *Kono fuku' wa kabi' ga ha'ete iru.* この服はかびが生えている.
mile *ma'iru* マイル
military *gu'ntai [no]* 軍隊[の]
military person *gunjin* 軍人
milk 1 *gyūnyū* 牛乳; *mi'ruku* ミルク 2 (condensed) *kondensu mi'ruku* コンデンスミルク 3 (powdered) *kona mi'ruku* 粉ミルク 4 (evaporated) *eba-mi'ruku* エバミルク 5 (skimmed) *dasshi fu'nnyū* 脂脱粉乳; *sukimu mi'ruku* スキムミルク
milkshake 1 (with ice cream) *shē'ku* シェーク 2 (without ice cream) *miruku sē'ki* ミルクセーキ
Milky Way *Ama-no'-gawa* 天の川
millet *ki'bi* きび
millimeter *mirimē'toru* ミリメートル; (abbr) *mi'ri* ミリ one millimeter *ichi'-miri* 1ミリ ten millimeters *jū'-miri* 10ミリ
million *hyakuma'n* 百万 *see also* Appendix 1
millionaire *hyakumanchō'ja* 百万長者
mimic *monomane'shi* 物まね師 ——obj o (v) *mane·ru* 真似る ——(idiom) to mimic *mane o suru* 真似をする
mimicry *monomane* 物まね
mind 1 *se'ishin* 精神 He's not in his right mind. *Ka're wa se'ishin ni ijō ga a'ru.* 彼は精神に異状がある. 2 heart *koko'ro* 心 I didn't have that in mind. *Sore wa kokoro ni mo na'katta.* それは心にもなかった. ——(idiom) 1 care about (v) *kama'·u* 構う I don't mind. *Kamaimase'n.* 構いません.; ...*-te [-de] mo i·i* ...て[で]もいい Do you mind if I smoke? *Tabako o sutte' mo i'i desu ka?* たばこを吸ってもいいですか. 2 care for *mendō' o mi'·ru* 面倒をみる Would you mind the children for me while I'm out? *Ru'su no aida, kodomo no mendō' o mi'te kudasaimase'n ka?* 留守の間, 子供の面倒をみて下さいませんか.
mine (excavation) *kō'zan* 鉱山 mining industry *kō'gyō* 鉱業
mine (possessive pronoun) *watashi no* 私の It's mine. *Watashi no' desu.* 私のです.
mineral *kō'butsu* 鉱物 ——(attr) *kō'butsu no* 鉱物の
mineralogy *kōbutsu'gaku* 鉱物学

mineral spring *kōsen* 鉱泉 *see also* hot spring; spa
mineral water *kōsui* 鉱水; *mineraru uō'tā* ミネラルウォーター
mini (ature) *kogata* [*no*] 小型[の] minibus *kogata ba'su* 小型バス; *mini-* ミニ minicomputer *minikompyū'tā* ミニコンピューター
minimum *saitei* [*no*] 最低[の]; *saite'igen* [*no*] 最低限[の]
minister **1** clergyman *bo'kushi* 牧師 **2** governmental minister *da'ijin* 大臣 prime minister *sōri da'ijin* 総理大臣
Minister of Education *Mombu Da'ijin* 文部大臣
Minister of Finance *Ōkura Da'ijin* 大蔵大臣
Minister of Foreign Affairs *Gaimu Da'ijin* 外務大臣
Minister of Justice *Hōmu Da'ijin* 法務大臣
ministry *-shō* 省; (agency) *-chō* 庁
Ministry of Education *Mombu'shō* 文部省
Ministry of Finance *Ōkura'shō* 大蔵省
Ministry of Foreign Affairs *Gaimu'shō* 外務省
Ministry of Justice *Hōmu'shō* 法務省
mink *mi'nku* ミンク
minor **1** (in age) *mise'inen* 未成年 **2** (subject in school) *fuku-se'nkō* 副専攻 ——(adj) *karu·i* 軽い a minor injury *karui kega'* 軽い怪我 ——(attr) of minor importance *jūyō de na'i* 重要でない
minor scale *tan-o'nkai* 短音階; *-ta'nchō* 短調 A-flat minor *hen i-ta'nchō* 変イ短調 *see also* key
minority **1** *shōsū'* 少数 **2** (J) minority (opposition) party *ya'tō* 野党
minus (Math) *mainasu* マイナス
minute (time) *-fun* [*-pun*] 分 one minute *i'ppun* 一分 two minutes *ni'fun* 二分 ten minutes past twelve *jūniji juppu'n-sugi* 十二時十分すぎ
minute (diminutive) **1** (size) *koma'ka* [*na*] 細か[な] **2** (space) *bisai* [*na*] 微細[な] ——(adj) *komaka'·i* 細かい
minute hand *chōshin* 長針
minutes (record) *kiroku* 記録
miracle *kiseki* 奇跡
mirror **1** *kaga'mi* 鏡 **2** dressing table with mirror *kyōdai* 鏡台 **3** three-way mirror *sammen-kyō* 三面鏡 **4** rear view mirror *bakku mi'rā* バックミラー
misappropriation *ōryō* 横領
miscarriage *ryū'zan* 流産
mischief *itazura* いたずら make mischief *itazura o suru* いたずらをする
miser *ke'chimbo* けちんぼ
miserable *hisan* [*na*] 悲惨[な] a miserable life *hisan na seikatsu* 悲惨な生活 a miserable existence *hisan na sonzai* 悲惨な存在

misery *hisan* 悲惨

misfortune *fukō'* 不幸 meet misfortune *fukō' ni dea'u* 不幸に出会う

mishap *ji'ko* 事故; *saina'n* 災難

mislead obj *o* (v) *mayowa's·u* 迷わす ——(caus) *gokai-sase·ru* 誤解させる

miss (adj) long for *natsukashi'·i* なつかしい Do you miss America? *Amerika ga natsukashi'i desu ka?* アメリカがなつかしいですか. ——compl *ni* (v) fail to hit a mark *hazure·ru* 外れる

miss (unmarried woman) **1** *-san* さん Miss Smith *Su'misu-san* スミスさん **2** (younger woman) *ojō'-san* お嬢さん **3** (older woman) *oba-san* おばさん

missile *misa'iru* ミサイル

missionary *senkyō'shi* 宣教師

mist *kasumi* 霞

mistake *machiga'i* 間違い ——obj *o* (v) make a mistake *machiga'e·ru* 間違える I made a mistake. *Machiga'eta.* 間違えた.

mistaken (v) be mistaken *machiga'tte i·ru* 間違っている Aren't you mistaken? *Machiga'tte imase'n ka?* 間違っていませんか.; (irr) *kanchi'gai-suru* 勘違いする He's mistaken. *Ka're wa kanchi'gai-shite iru.* 彼は勘違いしている. ——(attr) *machiga'tta* 間違った a mistaken estimate *machiga'tta mitsumori* 間違った見積もり

mistaken identity *hito-chi'gai* 人違い

mistletoe *yadori'gi* 宿り木

mistress *mekake'* 妾

misty (v) be misty *kasum·u* 霞む It's misty. *Kasunde iru.* 霞んでいる.

misunderstand obj *o* (irr) *gokai-suru* 誤解する Please don't misunderstand. *Gokai-shina'ide kudasa'i.* 誤解しないで下さい.

misunderstanding *gokai* 誤解

mite (bug) *dani'* だに

mittens *tebu'kuro* 手袋; *mi'ton* ミトン

mix obj *o* (v) *maze'·ru* 混ぜる Mix well. *Yo'ku ma'zete kudasa'i.* よく混ぜて下さい. ——(v) be/become mixed *maji'·ru* 混じる Oil and water don't mix. *Mizu to abura wa majira'nai.* 水と油は混じらない.

mixer (appliance) *mi'kisā* ミキサー

mixing bowl *bōru* ボール

mix-up **1** confusion *kondō* 混同 **2** misunderstanding *ikichigai* 行き違い

mob *gunshū* 群集

model **1** *mokei* 模型 **2** example *teho'n* 手本 **3** fashion model *mo'deru* モデル **4** ideal *mohanteki* [*na*] 模範的[な] a model son *mohanteki na musuko'* 模範的な息子

moderate 1 *te′kido* [no] 適度[の] a moderate amount of sleep *te′kido no suimin* 適度の睡眠 2 calm *oda′yaka* [na] 穏やか[な] a moderate person *oda′yaka na hito* 穏やかな人 ——obj *o* (irr) moderate (a meeting) *shikai-suru* 司会する

modern 1 *kindaiteki* [na] 近代的[な] 2 modern-day *ge′ndai* [no] 現代[の] modern literature *gendai bu′ngaku* 現代文学; *ki′ndai* [no] 近代[の] modern theater *kinda′igeki* 近代劇

modest (attr) *kenson-shita* 謙遜した

moist (adj) *shimeppo′-i* 湿めっぽい moist air *shimeppo′i kū′ki* 湿めっぽい空気 ——(attr) *shimetta* 湿めった Wrap (it) in a moist cloth! *Shimetta nuno′ de tsutsumi-nasa′i!* 湿めった布で包みなさい。

moisture *shikke/shikki* 湿気

molar *kyū′shi* 臼歯

molasses *mora′shisu* モラーシス

mold (form) *kata* 型 ——(idiom) to mold [*kata ni irete*] *tsuku′r·u* [型に入れて]作る

mold (fungus) *kabi* かび ——(idiom) to mold *kabi ga hae′·ru* かびが生える

mole 1 (animal) *mogura* もぐら 2 (blemish) *hokuro* ほくろ

molest (idiom) ...*ni itazura o suru* ...にいたずらをする molest a person *hito ni itazura o suru* 人にいたずらをする

mom *ma′ma* ママ *see also* mother; mother-in-law

moment *shunkan* 瞬間 a moment's time *isshun no aida* 一瞬の間

monastery *shūdō′in* 修道院

Monday *getsuyō′bi* 月曜日 on Monday *getsuyō′bi ni* 月曜日に

money *o-kane* お金

money order *kawase* 為替

Mongolian 1 (language) *Mongoru-go* モンゴル語 2 (person) *Mongoru′jin* モンゴル人 ——(attr) *Mo′ngoru no* モンゴルの

monitor (for television, video, etc.) *mo′nitā* モニター

monk *shūdō′sō* 修道僧

monkey *sa′ru* 猿

monkey wrench *supa′na* スパナ

mononucleosis (Tech) *densensei tankaku-shō* 伝染性単核症; (coll) *kissu-byō* キッス病

monopoly *dokusen* 独占; *dokuse′nken* 独占権

monorail *monorē′ru* モノレール

monotonous *tanchō* [na] 単調[な]

monster *kaibutsu* 怪物

month 1 *tsuki′* 月 2 all month *ikkagetsu-jū* 一か月中 3 every month *maitsuki* 毎月 4 once a month *ikka′getsu ni ichido* 一か月に一度 5 month before last *sen-se′ngetsu* 先々月 6 last month *se′ngetsu* 先月 7 this month *kongetsu* 今月 8 next month *ra′ige-*

tsu 来月　**9** month after next *sara'igetsu* 再来月　**10** one month *ikka'getsu* 一か月

monthly *maitsuki* [*no*] 毎月[の]

monthly payment *tsuki-ba'rai* 月払い

monument *kine'n-hi* 記念碑

moo *mō'* もう

mood **1** atmosphere *fun'i'ki* 雰囲気 a quiet mood *oda'yaka na fun'i'ki* 穏やかな雰囲気　**2** temperament *kigen* 機嫌 Today the boss is in a good mood. *Kyō', shachō wa kigen ga i'i.* 今日, 社長は機嫌がいい.

moody *fuki'gen* [*na*] 不機嫌[な]

moon **1** *tsuki'* 月　**2** half-moon *ha'ngetsu* 半月　**3** full moon *ma'ngetsu* 満月　**4** new moon *shi'ngetsu* 新月　**5** crescent moon *mika-zuki* 三日月

moonlight *gekkō* 月光

mop *moppu* モップ　——obj *o* (v) *fuk·u* 拭く Please mop it up. *Fuite kudasa'i.* 拭いて下さい.

morals *dōtoku* 道徳 a question of morals *dōtoku-jō no mondai* 道徳上の問題

more **1** *mo'tto* もっと Give me more. *Mo'tto kudasa'i.* もっと下さい.　**2** *mō'* もう I don't need/want any more. *Mō' irimase'n.* もういりません.

more and more *masu'masu* ますます Fares are becoming more and more expensive. *U'nchin wa masu'masu ta'kaku natte kite iru.* 運賃はますます高くなってきている.

more or less *tashō* 多少 The opinions of those two more or less agree on this point. *Kono ten de' wa futa'ri no i'ken wa tashō a'tte iru.* この点では二人の意見は多少合っている.

moreover *sa'rani* さらに

more than ...*yo'ri* ...より This costs more than that. *Kore wa sore yo'ri taka'i.* これはそれより高い. My son likes to play more than to study. *Musuko wa benkyō-suru yo'ri asobitaga'ru.* 息子は勉強するより遊びたがる.

morgue *shitai anchijo* 死体安置所

morning **1** *a'sa* 朝　**2** before noon *go'zen* 午前 during the morning *gozen-chū* 午前中　**3** this morning *ke'sa* 今朝

morning newspaper *chōkan* 朝刊

morning star *ake no myōjō* 明けの明星

Moroccan (person) *Morokko'jin* モロッコ人　——(attr) *Mo'rokko no* モロッコの

Morocco *Mo'rokko* モロッコ

mortal (fatal) *chimeiteki* [*na*] 致命的[な]; *chimei-* 致命 a mortal wound *chime'ishō* 致命傷

mortar *u'su* 臼; *suri'bachi* すり鉢

mortgage *teitō* 抵当 deed of mortgage *teitō shō'sho* 抵当証書 (idiom) **1** to mortgage *teitō ni ire·ru* 抵当に入れる **2** be mortgaged *teitō ni ha'itte i·ru* 抵当に入っている

mosquito *ka* 蚊 be bitten by a mosquito *ka ni sasare'ru* 蚊に刺される

mosquito net *kaya* 蚊帳

mosquito repellent (incense) *katorise'nkō* 蚊取り線香

moss *koke'* 苔

most 1 greatest (lit., number one) *ichiban* 一番 I like this the most. *Kore ga ichiban suki' desu.* これが一番好きです. **2** the greater part *daibu'bun* 大部分 Most people have TV sets. *Daibu'bun no hito' ga te'rebi o mo'tte iru.* 大部分の人がテレビを持っている.

moth *ga* 蛾

mothballs (naphthalene) *nafutarin* ナフタリン

mother 1 (one's own) *ha'ha* 母; (address) *okā'-san* お母さん **2** (another's) *okā'-san* お母さん

mother-in-law 1 (one's own) *shūtome* 姑; *giri no ha'ha* 義理の母 **2** (another's) *o-shūtome-san* お姑さん

motherland *bo'koku* 母国

Mother's Day *Ha'ha no hi* 母の日

mother tongue *bokoku-go* 母国語

motion 1 (in parliamentary procedure) *dō'gi* 動議 I wish to make a motion. *Dō'gi o teishutsu-shima'su.* 動議を提出します. **2** action; movement *dō'sa* 動作

motionlessly *jitto* じっと He sat motionlessly. *Ka're wa jitto suwatte ita.* 彼はじっとすわっていた.

motive *dō'ki* 動機 Her motives are not good. *Ka'nojo no dō'ki wa waru'i.* 彼女の動機は悪い. What was your motive for writing this? *Kore o ka'ita dō'ki wa na'n desu ka?* これを書いた動機は何ですか.

motor 1 (of a car) *e'njin* エンジン gasoline engine *gasorin e'njin* ガソリンエンジン **2** electric motor *mō'tā* モーター

motorbike *mōtābaiku* モーターバイク; *ba'iku* バイク

motorboat *mōtābō'to* モーターボート

motorcycle *ōto'bai* オートバイ

motor scooter *sukū'tā* スクーター

motto *mo'ttō* モットー

mound *tsuka'* 塚

mountain *yama'* 山

mountain climbing *to'zan* 登山

mountain range *sammyaku* 山脈

mourn (for) obj *o* (v) *nagek·u* 嘆く; *kanashi'm·u* 悲しむ

mourning *mo* 喪 mourning clothes *mofuku* 喪服

mouse 1 *nezumi* 鼠 **2** pet mouse *hatsuka ne'zumi* 二十日鼠 **3**

house mouse *ie ne´zumi* 家鼠   **4** field mouse *no ne´zumi* 野鼠

mousetrap   *nezumi´tori* 鼠取り

mouth   **1** *kuchi* 口   **2** (of a river) *kakō* 河口

mouthful   *kuchi ippai* 口いっぱい

mouthwash   *ugai* うがい; *uga´i-yaku* うがい薬

move   (v) **1** *ugo´k·u* 動く Don't move! *Ugoka´naide!* 動かないで. **2** change residence *utsu´·ru* 移る I moved here two years ago. *Ninen ma´e koko ni utsu´tta.* 二年前ここに移った. ——obj *o* (v) **1** *utsu´s·u* 移す; *ugoka´s·u* 動かす Move your chair a little, please. *Isu o cho´tto ugoka´shite kudasai.* 椅子をちょっと動かして下さい. **2** change residence *hikko´s·u* 引っ越す They recently moved into the house next door. *Sono hito´-tachi wa saikin tonari no ie´ ni hikko´shite kita.* その人たちは最近隣の家に引っ越してきた. —— compl *ni* (irr) be moved; stirred by *kandō-suru* 感動する I was moved by what he/she said. *Ano´ hito no itta´ koto´ ni kandō-shita.* あの人の言ったことに感動した.

movement (campaign)   *undō* 運動 start a movement *undō o oko´su* 運動を起こす

movers   *unsōya* 運送屋

movie   *e´iga* 映画

movie actor;actress   *eiga´ ha´iyū* 映画俳優

movie camera   *mūbi ka´mera* ムービーカメラ

movie projector   *eisha´ki* 映写機

movie theater   *eiga´kan* 映画館

moving company   *unsō-ga´isha* 運送会社

mow   obj *o* (v) *kar·u* 刈る

mower   *see* lawn mower

M.P.   **1** military police *ke´mpei* 憲兵   **2** member of parliament [*kokkai*] *gi´in* [国会]議員

Mr.   *-san* さん Mr. Smith *Su´misu-san* スミスさん

Mr. and Mrs.   *-san fusa´i* さん夫妻 Mr. and Mrs. Smith *Su´misu-san fusa´i* スミスさん夫妻; (polite) *-san go-fusa´i* さん御夫妻 Mr. and Mrs. Smith *Su´misu-san go-fusa´i* スミスさん御夫妻

Mrs.   *-san* さん Mrs. Smith *Su´misu-san* スミスさん

Ms.   *-san* さん Ms. Smith *Su´misu-san* スミスさん

M.S. (academic degree)   *see* Master of Science

much   *takusan* たくさん I don't need very much. *Takusa´n wa irimase´n.* たくさんはいりません. I have much work to do tomorrow. *Ashita shigoto ga takusan a´ru.* 明日仕事がたくさんある. *see also* how much

mud   *doro´* 泥

muddy   *dorodoro* [*no*] どろどろ[の]; *doro-da´rake* [*no*] 泥だらけ[の]

muffin   *ma´fin* マフィン

muffler   *ma´furā* マフラー

mug *jo'kki* ジョッキ beer mug *biru jo'kki* ビールジョッキ

muggy (adj) *mushiatsu'·i* 蒸し暑い Japan is muggy in the summer. *Niho'n no na'tsu wa mushiatsu'i desu.* 日本の夏は蒸し暑いです.

mulberry *ku'wa* 桑 mulberry tree *ku'wa no ki* 桑の木 mulberry fruit *ku'wa no mi* 桑の実

mule *ra'ba* らば

multiplication (Math) *kake'zan* 掛け算; (Tech) *jō'hō* 乗法

mummy *mi'ira* ミイラ

mumps *otafuku'kaze* おたふく風邪; (Tech) *jikase'n-en* 耳下腺炎

murder *hito-goroshi* 人殺し; *satsujin* 殺人 ——obj *o* (v) *koros·u* 殺す

murderer *satsuga'isha* 殺害者; (Tech) *satsuji'nhan* 殺人犯

murmur (v) *bu'tsubutsu-i·u* ぶつぶつ言う

muscle *ki'nniku* 筋肉

museum 1 *hakubu'tsukan* 博物館 2 art museum *biju'tsukan* 美術館

mushroom 1 (imported varieties) *masshurū'mu* マッシュルーム; *shampi'nion* シャンピニオン 2 (domestic varieties) *ki'-no-ko* 茸 3 (poisonous varieties) *doku ki'-no-ko* 毒茸 4 (an edible fungus from red-pine roots) *matsutake* 松茸

music *o'ngaku* 音楽

musical play *myū'jikaru* ミュージカル

musician *ongakuka* 音楽家

muskmelon *masuku-me'ron* マスクメロン

muslin *mo'surin* モスリン; (cotton) *kya'rako* キャラコ

must *-na'kereba nara'nai* なければならない I must go home. *Kaera'nakereba nara'nai.* 帰らなければならない. The vegetables must be fresh. *Yasai wa atara'shiku na'kereba nara'nai.* 野菜は新しくなければならない.

mustache *hige* 髭; *kuchi hige* 口髭

mustard 1 (W) *masutā'do* マスタード 2 (J) *karashi* 辛子

must not *-te [-de] wa ikena'i* て[で]はいけない You must not do that. *Sore o shite' wa ikena'i.* それをしてはいけない.

mutter (v) *bu'tsubutsu-i·u* ぶつぶつ言う

mutton *ma'ton* マトン; *hitsuji no niku* 羊の肉 *see also* lamb

mutually *o-tagai ni* お互いに Next Monday would be mutually convenient for the meeting. *Ko'ndo no mi'tingu wa getsuyō'bi ga o-tagai ni be'nri desu.* 今度のミーティングは月曜日がお互いに便利です.

my *watashi no* 私の my pen *watashi no pe'n* 私のペン

Myanmar *Miyanma* ミャンマー *see also* Burma

myself *jibun* 自分 by myself *jibun de* 自分で I did it by myself. *Jibun de shima'shita.* 自分でしました.

mysterious *shi'mp*i [*no*] 神秘[の]; *shimpiteki* [*na*] 神秘的[な]

mystery   *shi'mpi* 神秘; *o'kugi* 奥義
mystery story   *suiri shō'setsu* 推理小説
myth   *shin'wa* 神話

N

nail   1 finger/toe nail *tsume* 爪   2 fastener *kugi* 釘   ——(idiom) to nail *kugi o u'tsu* 釘を打つ
nail clippers   *tsumeki'ri* 爪切り
nail file   *yasuri* やすり; *tsume ya'suri* 爪やすり
nail polish   *manikyua'-eki* マニキュア液; (remover) *jokō'-eki* 除光液
naive   1 innocent *mu'jaki* [*na*] 無邪気[な]   2 unsophisticated *soboku* [*na*] 素朴[な] a naive nature *soboku na hitogara* 素朴な人柄
naked   1 *hadaka* [*no*] 裸[の]   2 stark naked *suppa'daka* [*no*] 素っ裸[の]
name   1 *namae* 名前 What's your name? *O-namae wa na'n to iima'su ka?* お名前は何と言いますか.   2 given name *namae* 名前   3 family name *myō'ji* 名字   4 maiden name *kyūsei* 旧姓   ——(idiom) to name *namae o tsuke'·ru* 名前を付ける
name card   *meishi* 名刺
name tag   *nafuda* 名札; *hyōsatsu* 表札
nap   *hirune* 昼寝   ——(irr) *inemu'ri-suru* 居眠りする
naphthalene   *nafutarin* ナフタリン
napkin   *na'pukin* ナプキン
narcissus   *suisen* 水仙
narcotic   *mayaku* 麻薬
narrate   ind-obj *ni*, obj *o* (v) *nobe'·ru* 述べる
narrative   1 *jojutsu* 叙述   2 story *monoga'tari* 物語
narrow   (adj) *sema'·i* 狭い. The streets in town are narrow. *Machi no dō'ro wa sema'i.* 町の道路は狭い.
narrow-minded   (attr) *kokoro no sema'i* 心の狭い, a narrow-minded person *kokoro no sema'i hito* 心の狭い人
nation   *kuni* 国
national   *koku-* 国; *kokuritsu* [*no*] 国立[の] national park *kokuritsu kō'en* 国立公園; *kokumin* 国民 national income *kokumin sho'toku* 国民所得
nationalism   *kokusuishu'gi* 国粋主義; *nashonari'zumu* ナショナリズム
nationality   *kokuseki* 国籍
native   1 local resident *tochi no hito'* 土地の人   2 aborigine *genjū'min* 原住民   ——(attr) indigenous *dochaku* [*no*] 土着[の]

native language *bokoku-go* 母国語

natural   **1** *shizen [no]* 自然[の] Japan's natural beauty *Nihon no shizen no utsuku'shisa* 日本の自然の美しさ   **2** as expected *atarimae [no]* 当たり前[の] It is natural to exchange greetings with people you know. *Shitte iru hito' ni a'ttara a'isatsu-suru' no ga atarimae de'su.* 知っている人に会ったら挨拶するのが当たり前です.; *tōzen [no]* 当然[の] Her punishment is a natural result. *Ka'nojo ga basserareru no wa tōzen de'su.* 彼女が罰せられるのは当然です.

natural science *shizen ka'gaku* 自然科学

nature   **1** disposition *seishitsu* 性質 a person's nature *hito no seishitsu* 人の性質; *ko'njō* 根性 a person of perverse nature *ko'njō no maga'tta hito* 根性の曲がった人   **2** Nature *Daishi'zen* 大自然; *shizen* 自然

nature worship *shizen sū'hai* 自然崇拝

nausea *hakike'* 吐き気 ——(idiom) feel nauseated *hakike' ga suru* 吐き気がする

navel *o-heso* おへそ

navigation *kō'kai* 航海

navy *kaigun* 海軍

near *chika'ku [no]* 近く[の] Is your house near? *O-uchi wa chika'ku desu ka?* お家は近くですか. ——(adj) *chika'·i* 近い The supermarket is near my house. *Sū'pā wa uchi kara chika'i desu.* スーパーは家から近いです.

nearly *hoto'ndo* ほとんど It's nearly done. *Hoto'ndo de'kite iru.* ほとんどできている. The sugar's nearly gone. *O-satō wa hoto'ndo na'i.* お砂糖はほとんどない.

nearsighted *kinshi [no]* 近視[の]; *kingan [no]* 近眼[の] I'm nearsighted. *Watashi wa kingan de'su.* 私は近眼です.

neat   (attr) *kichi'nto-shita* きちんとした a neat room *kichi'nto-shita heya'* きちんとした部屋 ——(v) be neat *kichi'nto-shite i·ru* きちんとしている My daughter's room is always neat. *Musume no heya' wa i'tsumo kichi'nto-shite iru.* 娘の部屋はいつもきちんとしている.

neatly *ki'rei ni* きれいに She writes neatly. *Ka'nojo wa [ji'o] ki'rei ni ka'ku.* 彼女は[字を]きれいに書く.

necessary *hitsuyō [na]* 必要[な] necessary documents *hitsuyō na sho'rui* 必要な書類 Caution is necessary. *Chū'i ga hitsuyō de'su.* 注意が必要です.

necessities *hitsujuhin* 必需品

neck   **1** *kubi* 首 I have a stiff neck. *Watashi wa kubi o nechiga'eta.* 私は首を寝違えた.   **2** (on clothing) *eri'* えり

necklace *ne'kkuresu* ネックレス; *kubika'zari* 首飾り

necktie *ne'kutai* ネクタイ

necromancy *uranai* 占い

need *hitsuyō* 必要 ——obj *ga* (v) *ir·u* 要る I need that. *Sore ga iru.* それが要る. I don't need that. *Sore wa iranai.* それは要らない.

needle *ha'ri* 針

needlework *hari shi'goto* 針仕事

needy *hinkon* [*na*] 貧困[な] a needy person *hinko'nsha* 貧困者

negation *hitei* 否定

negative 1 *hitei* [*teki na*] 否定[的な] a negative reply *hiteiteki na kota'e* 否定的な答 a negative attitude *hiteiteki na ta'ido* 否定的な態度   2 (Photog) *ne'ga* ネガ   3 (Gram) *uchikeshi* [*no*] 打ち消し[の]

neglect obj *o* (v) *okota'r·u* 怠る neglect to answer a letter *tegami no henji o okota'r·u* 手紙の返事を怠る ——(idiom) *naozari ni suru* なおざりにする neglect one's work *shigoto o naozari ni suru* 仕事をなおざりにする

negligee *negurije* ネグリジェ

negligence 1 *taiman* 怠慢   2 carelessness *fuchū'i* 不注意

negotiate comp *to*, obj *o* (irr) *kōshō-suru* 交渉する The employees negotiated with the company concerning bonuses. *Sha'in wa bō'nasu ni tsuite kaisha to kōshō-shita.* 社員はボーナスについて会社と交渉した.

negotiation *kōshō* 交渉 The negotiation ended in failure. *Kōshō wa shippai ni owa'tta.* 交渉は失敗に終わった.

Negro 黒人

neighbor *tonari no hito* 隣の人

neighborhood *ki'njo* 近所

neither 1 *do'chira mo* (+neg) どちらも; *dotchi mo* (+neg) どっちも Neither will do. *Dotchi mo ikena'i.* どっちもいけない.   2 neither... nor ... *mo*... *mo* (+neg). ...も... も I have neither time nor money. *Jikan mo o-kane mo na'i.* 時間もお金もない.

Nepal *Nepa'ru* ネパール

Nepalese 1 (language) *Nepa'ru-go* ネパール語   2 (person) *Nepa'ru'jin* ネパール人 ——(attr) *Nepa'ru no* ネパールの

nephew 1 (one's own) *oi* 甥   2 (another's) *oigo-san* 甥ごさん

Neptune *Kaiōsei* 海王星

nerve (Anat) *shinkei* 神経

nerve-racking (idiom) *kibone ga ore'·ru* 気骨が折れる

nervous *shinkeishitsu* [*na*] 神経質[な] ——(irr) be nervous *do'ki-doki-suru* どきどきする; (v) *agar·u* 上がる I was so nervous, I didn't do well on my speech. *Agatte, supi'chi ga u'maku deki'nakatta.* 上がって、スピーチがうまくできなかった.

nervous breakdown *shinkei su'ijaku* 神経衰弱

nervous system *shinkei ke'itō* 神経系統

nest *su* 巣

net *ami'* 網

Netherlands, The *see* Holland

network (radio/TV) *hōsō'mō* 放送網

neurology *shinke'igaku* 神経学

neuropsychiatry *shinkei seishimbyōgaku* 神経精神病学

neurotic *noirō'ze [no]* ノイローゼ[の]

neutral **1** *chūritsu [no]* 中立[の] a neutral country *chūritsu'-koku* 中立国 **2** (gear of a car) *nyū'toraru* ニュートラル **3** a neutral color (gray) *hai-iro* 灰色

neutrality *chūritsu* 中立

never **1** by no means *kesshite* 決して I never wake up before 7:00. *Shichiji' made wa kesshite me' ga same'nai.* 七時までは決して目がさめない. **2** in no case *zenzen* 全然 He never calls. *Ka're wa zenzen denwa-shina'i.* 彼は全然電話しない. **3** not once ...*koto' ga na'i* ...ことがない I've never been to Paris. *Pa'ri ni itta koto' ga na'i.* パリに行ったことがない.

Never mind. *Dō'zo, go-shimpai na'ku.* どうぞ御心配なく.; *Dō' itashima'shite.* どういたしまして.

nevertheless *sore ni' mo kakawara'zu* それにもかかわらず; *sore de' mo* それでも

new (adj) *atarashi'·i* 新しい a new car *atarashi'i kuruma* 新しい車 Is that dress new? *Sono fuku' wa atarashi'i desu ka?* その服は新しいですか.

newlyweds *shinkon fū'fu* 新婚夫婦

news *nyū'su* ニュース

newscast *nyū'su* ニュース

newspaper **1** *shimbun* 新聞 newspaper delivery *shimbun ha'itatsu* 新聞配達 **2** morning edition *chōkan* 朝刊 **3** evening edition *yūkan* 夕刊

New Testament *Shin'yaku Se'isho* 新約聖書

New Year's *o-shōgatsu'* お正月; *shi'nnen* 新年

New Year's Day *ganjitsu* 元日

New Year's Eve *ōmi'soka* 大みそか

New Zealand *Nyūjira'ndo* ニュージーランド

New Zealander *Nyūjirando' jin* ニュージーランド人

next **1** *tsugi' [no]* 次の] **2** (time) *rai-* 来 next month *ra'igetsu* 来月 next week *raishū* 来週 next year *rainen* 来年

next door *o-tonari* お隣

next time *ko'ndo* 今度; *kono tsugi'* この次

Nicaragua *Nikara'gua* ニカラグア

Nicaraguan (person) *Nikaragua' jin* ニカラグア人 ——(attr) *Nikara'gua no* ニカラグア の

nice (adj) *i'·i* いい She's a nice person. *Ka'nojo wa i'i hito' desu.* 彼女はいい人です.

nickname *nikkunē'mu* ニックネーム; *adana* あだ名
nicotine *nikochin* ニコチン
niece **1** (one's own) *mei* 姪 **2** (another's) *meigo-san* 姪ごさん
Nigeria *Naijeria* ナイジェリア
Nigerian (person) *Naijeria'jin* ナイジェリア人 ——(attr) *Naijeria no* ナイジェリアの
night **1** *yo'ru* 夜; *ban* 晩 **2** all night *yodōshi* 夜通し **3** every night *ma'iban* 毎晩 **4** once a night *hito'ban ni ichido* 一晩に一度 **5** middle of the night *yonaka* 夜中 **6** night before last *ototoi no ban* おとといの晩 **7** last night *saku'ban* 昨晩 **8** tomorrow night *ashita no ban* 明日の晩; *myō'ban* 明晩 **9** one night *hito'ban* 一晩
nightclub *naito ku'rabu* ナイトクラブ
nightgown *nemaki* 寝間着
nightingale *naichingē'ru* ナイチンゲール
nightmare *a'kumu* 悪夢
nihilism *kyomushu'gi* 虚無主義
nine *koko'notsu* 九つ; *kyū'* 九 *see also* Appendix 1
nineteen **1** *jū-ku'* 十九 **2** nineteen years old *jūkyū'-sai* 十九歳
nineteenth *jūku'-nichi* 十九日
ninety *kyū'-jū* 九十 *see also* Appendix 1
ninth **1** (ordinal) *kyūbam-me* 九番目 **2** (fraction) *kyūbun no ichi* 九分の一
ninth day of the month *kokonoka* 九日
nipple **1** (Anat) *chi'kubi* 乳首 **2** (for baby bottle) *honyū'bin no kuchi* 哺乳びんの口
nirvana (Budd) *nehan* 涅槃
nitrogen *chi'sso* 窒素
No! *Iie'!* いいえ.; *Chigaima'su!* 違います.
noble **1** lofty *kō'ki* [na] 高貴[な] **2** member of nobility *ki'zoku* 貴族 ——(adj) *tōto'·i* 尊い
nobody *dare mo* (+neg) だれも Nobody came. *Dare mo ko'nakatta.* だれも来なかった.
nod obj *o* (v) *unazuk·u* うなずく He nodded in agreement. *Ka're wa unazuite shōchi-shita.* 彼はうなずいて承知した.
no doubt *oso'raku* おそらく No doubt she won't agree. *Oso'raku ka'nojo wa shōchi-shina'i deshō.* おそらく彼女は承知しないでしょう.
noise **1** *zatsuon* 雑音 **2** din *sōon* 騒音 **3** uproar *sa'wagi* 騒ぎ
noisy (adj) *yakamashi'·i* やかましい; *urusa'·i* うるさい
nominate obj *o* (irr) *shimei-suru* 指名する
nonchalant *muto'nchaku* [na] 無頓着[な]
noncommissioned officer *kashi'kan* 下士官
none (idiom) ...*mo* (+neg) ...も none *dore mo* どれも None of them suit me. *Dore mo watashi ni awa'nai.* どれも私に合わない.;

not one *hitotsu mo* 一つも I have none (at all). *Watashi wa hitotsu mo mota'nai.* 私は一つも持たない.

nonprofit *hi'eiri [teki na]* 非営利[的な] nonprofit organization *hieiri da'ntai* 非営利団体

nonresident *hizaijū'sha* 非在住者

nonsense *na'nsensu* ナンセンス; *mui'mi* 無意味

nonstop *chokkō [no]* 直行[の] a nonstop flight *chokkōbin* 直行便

noodles 1 *me'nrui* 麺類 **2** (bleached-flour) *udon* うどん **3** (buckwheat) *so'ba* そば **4** (Chinese-style) *rā'men* ラーメン

noon 1 *hiru'* 昼 **2** midday *shō'go* 正午

no one *dare mo* (+neg) だれも There was no one there. *Dare mo ina'katta.* だれもいなかった.

No parking. *Chūsha kinshi.* 駐車禁止.

normal 1 standard *seijō [na]* 正常[な] normal pulse *seijō na myaku'haku* 正常な脈搏 **2** average *heikin [no]* 平均[の] My baby is heavier than normal. *Uchi no akambō no taijū wa heikin i'jō desu.* 家の赤ん坊の体重は平均以上です.

north *kita* 北 north exit *kita-guchi* 北口; *hoku-* 北 North America *Hokubei* 北米

northeast *hokutō* 北東

northern lights *hokkō* 北光; *ōrora* オーロラ

North Pole *Hokkyoku* 北極

northwest *hokusei* 北西

Norway *Noruuē'* ノルウェー

Norwegian 1 (language) *Noruuē-go* ノルウェー語 **2** (person) *Noruuē'jin* ノルウェー人 ——(attr) *Noruuē no* ノルウェーの

nose *hana* 鼻

nosebleed *hanaji* 鼻血

nose drops *hana-gu'suri* 鼻薬

nostalgia *kyōshū* 郷愁

nostalgic *kyōshū no* 郷愁の ——(attr) *ka'iko ni fuketa* 懐古にふけた

nostril (Tech) *bikō* 鼻孔; (coll) *hana no ana'* 鼻の穴

not is not *na'·i* ない That's not so! *Sō' ja na'i!* そうじゃない.; (polite) *arimase'n* ありません That's not so! *Sō' de wa arimase'n!* そうではありません. *see also* tables 1–4, pp. xxi–xl.

not at all *mattaku* まったく I don't understand his Japanese at all. *Ka're no Nihon-go wa mattaku wakara'nai.* 彼の日本語はまったく分からない.

note 1 *me'mo* メモ; *oboegaki* 覚え書き **2** (music) *ompu* 音符 ——compl *ni*, (irr) *chū'i-suru* 注意する

notebook *nō'to* ノート

notes 1 *me'mo* メモ **2** footnotes *kyakuchū* 脚注 **3** commentary *chū* 注; *chūshaku* 注釈

No, thank you! *Ke′kkō desu!* 結構です.

nothing *nani mo* (+neg) 何も She said nothing. *Ka′nojo wa nanimo iwana′katta.* 彼女は何も言わなかった. I want (need) nothing. *Nani mo iranai.* 何もいらない.

nothingness *mu′* 無; *kyo′mu* 虚無

notice information *shirase* 知らせ ——(idiom) to notice [*ni*] *ki ga′ tsuk·u* [に]気が付く I didn't notice it. *Sore ni ki ga′ tsuka′-nakatta.* それに気が付かなかった.

notify ind-obj *ni,* obj *o* (v) *shirase·ru* 知らせる When you arrive, notify me. *Tsu′itara shirasete kudasa′i.* 着いたら知らせて下さい.

not only ... but *...ba′kari de naku* ばかりでなく Not only can she speak French, but she can speak Chinese as well. *Ka′nojo wa Furansu-go ba′kari de naku, Chūgoku-go mo deki′ru.* 彼女はフランス語ばかりでなく中国語もできる.

not yet *ma′da* まだ Isn't it time for dinner yet? *Go′han wa ma′da desu ka?* 御飯はまだですか. Not yet. *Ma′da desu.* まだです.

noun *meishi* 名詞

novel *shōsetsu* 小説

novelist *shōsetsuka* 小説家

November *jūichigatsu′* 十一月 November 11 *jūichigatasu jūichini-chi* 十一月十一日

now *i′ma* 今 What time is it now? *I′ma na′nji desu ka?* 今何時ですか.

nowadays *i′ma de wa* 今では; *konogoro* このごろ

now and then *tokidoki* 時々 He comes to visit now and then. *Ka′re wa tokidoki asobi ni ku′ru.* 彼は時々遊びに来る.

nowhere *doko*[*ni*] *mo* (+neg) どこ[に]も She was nowhere to be found. *Ka′nojo wa doko ni mo ina′katta.* 彼女はどこにもいなかった.

nuclear *ka′ku* [*no*] 核[の] nuclear age *kaku ji′dai* 核時代

nuclear arms *kaku bu′sō* 核武装; *kaku he′iki* 核兵器

nude 1 *hadaka* [*no*] 裸[の] sleep in the nude *hadaka de neru* 裸で寝る They were nude. *Ka′rera wa hadaka de′shita.* 彼らは裸でした. 2 representation of a nude *nū′do* ヌード 3 nude model *nūdo mo′deru* ヌードモデル

nuisance *me′iwaku* 迷惑 I'm sorry to have been such a nuisance. *Taihen go-me′iwaku o o-kake shima′shita.* たいへん御迷惑をおかけしました.

numb (v) be/become numb *shibire′·ru* しびれる My hands were numb with the cold. *Sa′musa de te′ga shibi′reta.* 寒さで手がしびれた.

number 1 quantity *ka′zu* 数 Let us know the number you need. *Hitsuyō na ka′zu o shirasete kudasa′i.* 必要な数を知らせて下さい. 2 (in a listing) *bangō′* 番号 telephone number *denwa ba′ngō* 電話番

号; -*ban* 番 number one *ichi'-ban* 一番 number two *ni'-ban* 二番 number three *samban* 三番 **3** track number -*bansen* 番線 What is the track number for the train that goes to Shibuya? *Shibuya-yuki wa nambansen de'su ka?* 渋谷行きは何番線ですか.

number one (the best) *ichi'-ban* 一番 He was number one. *Ka're wa ichi'-ban deshita.* 彼は一番でした.

numeral *sūji* 数字 the numeral 2 *ni'no sūji* 2の数字

numerous *tasū'* [*no*] 多数[の]

nun *ama* 尼

nunnery *joshi shūdō'in* 女子修道院

nurse *kango'fu* 看護婦; (polite) *kango'fu-san* 看護婦さん ——obj *o* (irr) tend a sick person *ka'mbyō-suru* 看病する

nursemaid *u'ba* うば

nursery **1** children's room *kodomo-beya* 子供部屋 **2** day-care center *takujisho* 託児所 **3** (for plants) *uekiya* 植木屋

nursery school *hoiku'en* 保育園

nursing (breast-feeding) *bonyū* 母乳 Are you nursing your baby? *A'kachan wa bonyū desu ka?* 赤ちゃんは母乳ですか.

nursing bottle *honyū'bin* 哺乳瓶

nut *ki'nomi* 木の実

nut (for screwing onto a bolt) *meneji* 雌ねじ

nutrition *eiyō* 栄養

nutritious (attr) *eiyō no a'ru* 栄養のある It's nutritious food. *Eiyō no a'ru tabemono'desu.* 栄養のある食べ物です.

nylon *na'iron* ナイロン nylon stockings *nairon suto'kkingu* ナイロンストッキング

O

oak *ka'shi* 樫; *kashiwa* 柏; *na'ra* 楢

oar *ōru* オール; *ka'i* かい

oasis *o'ashisu* オアシス

oath *chikai* 誓い

oatmeal *ōtomi'ru* オートミール

oats *karasu'mugi* からす麦

obedience *fukujū* 服従

obedient *jūjun* [*na*] 従順[な] an obedient disposition *jūjun na sei-shitsu* 従順な性質; *su'nao* [*na*] 素直[な] an obedient child *su'nao na kodomo* 素直な子供

obediently *jūjun ni* 従順に

obey ind-obj *ni* (irr) *fukujū-suru* 服従する ——(idiom) listen to what (someone) says *iu koto' o kik•u* 言う事を聞く My son doesn't obey me. *Musuko wa watashi no iu koto' o kikana'i.* 息子は私の言う事を聞かない.

obituary *shibō ko'kuji* 死亡告示

object 1 *mono'* 物 2 purpose; subject *taishō* 対象 object of worship *shinkō no taishō* 信仰の対象 object of research *kenkyū no taishō* 研究の対象 3 aim *mokuteki* 目的 My object in coming to Japan is to collect material for my dissertation. *Niho'n ni kita mokuteki wa rombun no zairyō' o atsume'ru koto' desu.* 日本に来た目的は論文の材料を集める事です. ——comp *ni* (irr) oppose *hantai-suru* 反対する I am going to object to that. *Sore ni hantai-shima'su.* それに反対します.

objection *hantai* 反対; *hantai i'ken* 反対意見; *i'gi* 異議 If there are no objections, we will proceed to the next item. *I'gi ga na'kereba, tsugi no gidai ni ha'iru.* 異議がなければ次の議題に入る.

objective *mokuhyō* 目標 long-range objective *chōki mo'kuhyō* 長期目標 We will set an objective of a 10% increase in production. *Ichiwari zō'san o mokuhyō to suru.* 一割増産を目標とする. ——(attr) unbiased *kyakkanteki* [*na*] 客観的[な] an objective view *kyakkanteki na kenkai* 客観的な見解

obligation *gi'mu* 義務 fulfill an obligation *gi'mu o hata'su* 義務を果たす I have an obligation. *Gi'mu ga a'ru.* 義務がある.

obligatory *gimuteki* [*na*] 義務的[な]; *gimu-* 義務 obligatory term of service *gimu-ne'ngen* 義務年限

oblong *chōhōkei* [*no*] 長方形[の]

obnoxious *iya'* [*na*] いや[な]

obscene *waisetsu* [*na*] わいせつ[な] obscene book *waisetsu-bon* わいせつ本

obscenity *waisetsu* わいせつ

obscure *aimai* [*na*] あいまい[な] ——(adj) *usugura'·i* 薄暗い

observation *kansatsu* 観察

observatory *temmondai* 天文台

observe *obj o* (v) 1 keep *mamo'r·u* 守る observe the law *hōritsu o mamo'ru* 法律を守る 2 watch (irr) *kansatsu-suru* 観察する 3 observe classroom instruction (irr) *sankan-suru* 参観する

obsolete (attr) *sutareta* すたれた obsolete custom *sutareta shūkan* すたれた習慣

obstacle *jama* [*mono*] 邪魔[物] There wasn't a single obstacle in my path. *Watashi no ma'e ni wa jama ni na'ru mono wa issai na'katta.* 私の前には邪魔になる物はいっさいなかった.; *shōgai* 障害 The problem has become an obstacle. *Kono mondai ga shōgai ni na'tte iru.* この問題が障害になっている.

obstetrician *sanka'-i* 産科医

obstetrics *sanka* 産科; *sanka'gaku* 産科学

obstetrics and gynecology (department of) *sanfujinka* 産婦人科

obstinate *ga′nko* [*na*] 頑固[な]; *gōjō* [*na*] 強情[な]; *gōjoppari* [*na*] 強情っぱり[な] He's obstinate! *Ka′re wa gōjoppari′ desu!* 彼は強情っぱりです.

obstruct obj *o* (v) **1** bar; cut off *saegi′r·u* さえぎる ——(pass) be obstructed *saegirare′·ru* さえぎられる Our view of the ocean was obstructed by trees. *Ki′ ni saegira′rete, u′mi ga mie′nakatta.* 木にさえぎられて海が見えなかった. **2** (irr) interfere *bōgai-suru* 妨害する They obstructed business with a strike. *Ka′rera wa suto′ de eigyō o bōgai-shita.* 彼らはストで営業を妨害した.

obstruction *bōgai* 妨害

obtain *see* get

obvious *aki′raka* [*na*] 明らか[な] Her purpose is obvious. *Ka′nojo no mokuteki wa aki′raka desu.* 彼女の目的は明らかです. That's an obvious mistake. *Sore wa aki′raka na machiga′i desu.* それは明らかな間違いです.

obviously *aki′raka ni* 明らかに That's obviously a mistake. *Sore wa aki′raka ni machiga′i desu.* それは明らかに間違いです.

occasion *...baai* ...場合 on occasions when the store is not open *...mise′ ga aite inai baai...* 店が開いてない場合...; *...[no] sai ni* ...[の]際に My husband gave me this on the occasion of our silver-wedding anniversary. *Wata′shi-tachi no ginko′n-shiki no sai ni, shu′jin wa kore o kurema′shita.* 私たちの銀婚式の際に, 主人はこれをくれました.

occasionally *tama ni* たまに I go to the movies only occasionally. *Tama ni′ shika eiga o mi′nai.* たまにしか映画を見ない.

Occident *Se′iyō* 西洋

Occidental (person) *seiyō′jin* 西洋人 ——(attr) *Se′iyō no* 西洋の

occupant *sen′yū′sha* 占有者

occupation *shoku′gyō* 職業 What is your occupation? *Shoku′gyō wa na′n desu ka?* 職業は何ですか.

occupy (a country) obj *o* (irr) *senryō-suru* 占領する

occur (v) *oko′r·u* 起こる When did the accident occur? *Ji′ko wa i′tsu okorima′shita ka?* 事故はいつ起こりましたか.

occurrence *deki′goto* 出来事

ocean *u′mi* 海; *-yo* 洋 Atlantic Ocean *Taise′iyō* 大西洋 Pacific Ocean *Taihe′iyō* 太平洋

o'clock *-ji* 時 1:00 o'clock *ichi′ji* 一時 2:00 o'clock *ni′ji* 二時 3:00 o'clock *sa′nji* 三時 at 3:00 *sa′nji ni* 三時に

octave *okutā′bu* オクターブ

October *jūgatsu* 十月 October 10 *jūgatsu tōka* 十月十日

octopus *ta′ko* 蛸

odd *he′n* [*na*] 変[な] She's an odd person. *Ka′nojo wa he′n na hito′ desu.* 彼女は変な人です. ——(adj) *okashi′·i* おかしい That's odd! *Okashi′i na!* おかしいな.

odd number *kisū'* 奇数

odor *nio'i* 臭い

of *...no ...*の teacher of English *Ei-go no sense'i* 英語の先生 one of my students *se'ito no hito'ri* 生徒の一人

Of course! *Mochi'ron!* もちろん.

off (v) be separated from *hazure·ru* 外れる The phone's off the hook. *Juwa'ki ga hazurete iru.* 受話器が外れている. **2** be out of operation *keshite a'r·u* 消してある Are the lights off? *De'nki wa keshite arima'su ka?* 電気は消してありますか. **3** be mistaken *machiga'·u* 間違う This figure's off. *Kono sūji ga machiga'tte iru.* この数字が間違っている.

off and on *...-tari...-tari suru ...*たり...たりする The cleaning lady comes off and on. I can't depend on her. *Kase'ifu ga kita'ri ko'nakattari suru. Tayo'ru koto' wa deki'nai.* 家政婦が来たり来なかったりする. 頼ることはできない.

offense **1** *warugi* 悪気 I meant no offense (by saying what I did). *Warugi de itta wa'ke ja na'i.* 悪気で言った訳じゃない. **2** (Leg) *hanzai* 犯罪

offensive **1** *iya' [na]* いや[な] an offensive odor *iya' na nio'i* いやな臭い **2** battle *tatakai* 戦い

offer obj *o* (v) **1** volunteer *mōshide'·ru* 申し出る She offered to chair the committee. *Ka'nojo wa ka'igi de no shinkō'-yaku o mōshide'ta.* 彼女は会議での進行役を申し出た. **2** present (irr) *teikyō-suru* 提供する

offering **1** contribution *ki'fu* 寄付 **2** oblation (Chr) *kenkin* 献金; (Budd) *saisen* 賽銭; (Shinto) *hōnō* 奉納

offhand *yō'i nashi ni* 用意なしに

office **1** *jimu'sho* 事務所 **2** university office *o'fisu* オフィス **3** teacher's private office *kenkyū'shitsu* 研究室 **4** head office *ho'nsha* 本社; *honten* 本店 **5** branch office *shutchō jo* 出張所; *shiten* 支店 **6** government office *yakusho* 役所

office building *ofisu bi'rudingu* オフィスビルディング; (abbr) *ofisu bi'ru* オフィスビル

office hours *shitsumu ji'kan* 執務時間

officer **1** (military) *shō'kō* 将校 **2** (police) *keikan* 警官 **3** (governmental) *yakunin* 役人; *kōmu'in* 公務員 **4** (church) *yaku'in* 役員

office work *ji'mu* 事務 office worker *jimu'in* 事務員

official *kō-* 公- official document *kōbunsho* 公文書

officially *kōshiki ni* 公式に

offshore *oki [ni]* 沖[に]

often *yo'ku* よく Do you eat Japanese food often? *Yo'ku Nihon ryō'ri o tabema'su ka?* よく日本料理を食べますか.; *tabitabi* 度々 Pardon me for calling so often. *Tabitabi denwa-shite, shitsu'rei-shima'shita.* 度々電話して失礼しました.

ogre *oni'* 鬼

oh *a'a* ああ; *o'o* おお; (fem) *ara'* あら

oil 1 *abura* 油 2 fuel oil (light) *keiyu* 軽油 3 heavy oil *jūyu* 重油 4 lubricating oil *junkatsu'yu* 潤滑油 5 petroleum *sekiyu* 石油 *see also* salad oil

oil field *yuden* 油田

oil filter *oirufi'rutā* オイルフィルター

oil painting *abura'-e* 油絵

oil paints *abura-e'nogu* 油絵の具

oily 1 (adj) *aburakko'·i* 油っこい 2 (covered with oil) *abura-da'rake no* 油だらけの

ointment *nurigu'suri* 塗り薬

OK *ōkē.* オーケー. 1 I'm OK (No need to worry). *Daijō'bu desu.* 大丈夫です。 2 Good. *I'i.* いい. Tomorow's OK. *Ashita wa i'i.* 明日はいい. 3 OK (I'll do it). *Shōchi-shima'shita.* 承知しました.

old (adj) *furu'·i* 古い an old car *furu'i kuruma* 古い車 ——(attr) elderly *toshito'tta* 年とった; *toshiyori* [no] 年寄り[の]; an old person *toshiyori'* [no kata'] 年寄り[の方] ——(idiom) 1 How old are you? *O-toshi wa o-ikutsu de'su ka?* お年はおいくつですか. 2 be/become old *toshi' o to'r·u* 年をとる He's old. *Ka're wa toshi' o to'tte iru.* 彼は年をとっている. 3 from old *mukashi kara* 昔から an old friend *mukashi kara' no tomodachi* 昔からの友達

older 1 (animate) *toshiue* [no] 年上[の] She's older than I. *Ka'nojo wa watashi yo'ri toshiue de'su.* 彼女は私より年上です. 2 (animate) *ue* [no] 上[の] the older child *ue no kodomo* 上の子供 3 (inanimate) *mo'tto furu'·i* もっと古い This is older. *Kore no hō' ga mo'tto furu'i.* これの方がもっと古い.

old-fashioned *jidai o'kure* [no] 時代遅れ[の]

old person *toshiyori'* 年寄り; (polite) *nempai no kata'* 年輩の方

Old Testament *Kyū'yaku Se'isho* 旧約聖書

olive *ori'bu* オリーブ

olive oil *oribu o'iru* オリーブオイル

omelet *omuretsu* オムレツ

omen *kizashi* 兆し; *zenchō* 前兆

omission 1 (not deliberate) *teochi* 手落ち 2 (deliberate) *shōryaku* 省略

omit *obj o* (v) 1 *nukas·u* 抜かす 2 neglect *okota'r·u* 怠る

omnipotent *zennō* [no] 全能[の]

omniscient *ze'nchi* [no] 全知[の]

on ...*ni* ...に; ...*no ue' ni* ...の上に Put it on the table. *Tēburu no ue' no oite kudasa'i.* テーブルの上に置いて下さい.

once 1 some indefinite time in the past *i'tsuka* いつか; *i'tsu datta ka* いつだったか I think I met him once. *I'tsu datta ka, ka're* *ni a'tta koto ga a'ru to omou.* いつだったか、彼に会ったことがあると思う. **2** one time *ichido* 一度 once a week *isshū'kan ni ichido* 一週間に一度 I'd like to go there once. *Ichido soko ni itte mita'i to omou.* 一度そこに行ってみたいと思う.

once more *mō ikka'i* もう一回; *mō ichido* もう一度 Please say it once more. *Mō ichido itte kudasa'i.* もう一度言って下さい.

once upon a time *mukashi mukashi* 昔々

one *hito'tsu* 一つ; *ichi'* 一 — see also Appendix 1

one by one *hitotsu hito'tsu* 一つ一つ Please carry them one by one. *Hitotsu hito'tsu hakonde kudasa'i.* 一つ一つ運んで下さい.

one of each *hitotsu-zu'tsu* 一つずつ Give me one of each. *Hitotsu-zu'tsu kudasa'i.* 一つずつ下さい.

oneself *jibun* 自分

one-storied house *hiraya* 平屋

one-way **1** (street; traffic) *ippō tsū'kō* 一方通行 **2** (ticket) *kata-michi* [*ki'ppu*] 片道[切符]

onion *tamane'gi* 玉ねぎ

onlooker *bōka'nsha* 傍観者

only *ta'da* ただ She only looked at me with a blank stare. *Ka'nojo wa watashi o ta'da bon'ya'ri mi'te ita.* 彼女は私をただぼんやり見ていた.; ... *dake* ...だけ Only Sunday is free. *Nichiyō'bi dake'ga aite iru.* 日曜日だけがあいている.; ... *shika* (+neg)...しか There's only ¥5,000 left. *Gosen-en shika noko'tte ina'i.* 五千円しか残っていない.

onomatopoeia **1** *giseigo* 擬声語 **2** mimesis *gitaigo* 擬態語

opaque *futō'mei* [*na*] 不透明[な]

open obj *o* (v) *ake·ru* 開ける Open the window, please. *Ma'do o akete kudasa'i.* 窓を開けて下さい. ——(v) *ak·u* 開く What time does the store open? *Sono mise wa nanji ni akima'su ka?* その店は何時に開きますか.

opening **1** opportunity *kika'i* 機会; *suki* 隙 watch for an opening *suki o ukagau* 隙をうかがう **2** (of a meeting) *kaikai* 開会 **3** job opening *shūshoku'-guchi* 就職口; (abbr) *kuchi* 口 There are no job openings. *Kuchi ga na'i.* 口がない. **4** beginning *hajimari* 始まり

open-minded (idiom) *kokoro no hiro'·i* 心の広い

opera *o'pera* オペラ

operate obj *o* (irr) **1** *sō'sa-suru* 操作する **2** perform surgery *shu'jutsu-suru* 手術する

operation **1** (Med) *shu'jutsu* 手術 **2** (Mech) *sō'sa* 操作

operator (telephone) *kōka'nshu* 交換手

operetta *opere'tta* オペレッタ; *kika'geki* 喜歌劇

ophthalmologist *ganka'-i* 眼科医

ophthalmology *ganka* 眼科

opinion **1** *i'ken* 意見 **2** evaluation *hyō'ka* 評価

opium *ahen* あへん

opponent *taikō'sha* 対抗者; *aite* 相手

opportunity *kika'i* 機会 grasp an opportunity *kika'i o tsuka'mu* 機会をつかむ; *cha'nsu* チャンス

oppose compl *ni* (irr) **1** *hantai-suru* 反対する oppose a proposal/ motion *teian ni hantai-suru* 提案に反対する **2** resist *teikō-suru* 抵抗する oppose an attack *kōgeki ni teikō-suru* 攻撃に抵抗する **3** defy *hankō-suru* 反抗する Youth oppose the advice of their elders. *Wakamono wa sempai no chūkoku ni hankō-suru.* 若者は先輩の忠告に反抗する.

opposite *hantai* [no] 反対[の] opposite direction *hantai no hōkō* 反対の方向 opposite side *hantai-gawa* 反対側

opposition **1** *hantai* 反対; *taikō* 対抗 **2** opponent *aite* 相手

opposition party *ya'tō* 野党

oppress obj *o* (irr) *appaku-suru* 圧迫する

optimism *rakkanshu'gi* 楽観主義; *rakka'nron* 楽観論

optimist *rakkanshugi'sha* 楽観主義者; *rakkanro'nsha* 楽観論者

optimistic *rakkanteki* [na] 楽観的[な]

option *sentaku'ken* 選択権 business option *sentaku baiba'iken* 選択売買権

optometrist *kenga'nshi* 検眼師

optometry *kengan* 検眼

or **1** *ka* か this or that *are ka kore* あれかこれ What will you have, coffee or tea? *Kōhī ka kōcha, do'chira ni shima'su ka?* コーヒーか紅茶, どちらにしますか. **2** *soreto'mo* それとも Will you have coffee or would you prefer tea? *Kōhī ni shima'su ka? Soreto'mo, kōcha ni shima'su ka?* コーヒーにしますか. それとも紅茶にしますか. **3** or else *mata' wa* または I'll have to either write or (else) wire. *Tegami o da'su ka, mata' wa dempō o u'tsu ka shina'kereba nara'nai.* 手紙を出すかまたは電報を打つかしなければならない.

orally *kōtō de* 口頭で I informed them orally. *Kōtō de ka'rera ni shiraseta.* 口頭で彼らに知らせた.

orange **1** (color) *orenji iro* オレンジ色 **2** (fruit) *ore'nji* オレンジ **3** navel orange *nē'buru* ネーブル **4** mandarin orange *mi'kan* みかん

orangutan *oran'ū'tan* オランウータン

orbit *kidō* 軌道 the earth's orbit *chikyū no kidō* 地球の軌道

orchard *kaju'en* 果樹園

orchestra *ōke'sutora* オーケストラ; *gakudan* 楽団 chamber music orchestra *shitsunai ga'kudan* 室内楽団 symphony orchestra *kangen ga'kudan* 管弦楽団

orchid *ra'n* 蘭

order 1 sequence *ju′njo* 順序 2 system *tejun* 手順 3 method *chitsu′jo* 秩序 4 command *meirei* 命令; *iitsuke* 言い付け 5 (for merchandise) *chūmon* 注文 6 request *chūmon* 注文 ——(adv) in order *ju′nyo yoku* 順序よく; *jumban ni* 順番に Arrange those in order, please. *Sore o jumban ni narabete kudasa′i.* それを順番に並べて下さい。; *-jun* 順 in order according to age *nenrei-jun ni* 年齢順に ——obj *o* (v) 1 *meiji′ru* 命じる; *iitsuke′·ru* 言い付ける 2 place an order (irr) *chūmon-suru* 注文する

ordinary 1 usual *futsū* [*no*] 普通[の] ordinary rate *futsū ryo′kin* 普通料金 2 general *ippan* [*no*] 一般[の] ordinary people *ippan no hito′bito* 一般の人々 3 regular *tsūjō* [*no*] 通常[の] ordinary session of the Diet *tsūjō ko′kkai* 通常国会 4 average *heibon* [*na*] 平凡[な] an ordinary life *heibon na seikatsu* 平凡な生活

organ 1 musical instrument *orugan* オルガン 2 internal organ *naizō* 内臓

organic 1 *yūki* 有機 organic chemistry *yūki ka′gaku* 有機化学 organic farming *yūki nō′gyō* 有機農業 2 (physiological) *kika′n* [*no*] 器官[の] organic disease *kikan shi′kkan* 器官疾患

organic food *shizen sho′kuhin* 自然食品

organization 1 *so′shiki* 組織 2 association *dantai* 団体

organize obj *o* (irr) 1 form an organization *so′shiki-suru* 組織する 2 put in order *se′iri-suru* 整理する Organize these papers, please. *Kono shorui o se′iri-shite kudasa′i.* この書類を整理して下さい。

orgasm *oruga′sumusu* オルガスムス

Orient *Tō′yō* 東洋

Oriental (person) *Tōyō′jin* 東洋人 ——(attr) *Tō′yō no* 東洋の

origin *ki′gen* 起源 the origin of the Japanese language *Nihon-go no ki′gen* 日本語の起源

original 1 former *mo′to no* 元の 2 primary form *ge′nshi no* 原始の 3 (text) *gembun* 原文 4 (writing) *gensaku* 原作 5 (design) *ori′jinaru* オリジナル

originally *mo′to wa* 元は Originally this was a Kyushu company. *Kono kaisha wa mo′to wa Kyū′shū no kaisha de′shita.* この会社は元は九州の会社でした。

ornament *kazari* 飾り

ornithologist *chōrui ga′kusha* 鳥類学者

ornithology *chōru′igaku* 鳥類学

orphan *ko′ji* 孤児

orphanage *koji′-in* 孤児院

orthodontist *kyōsei shika′-i* 矯正歯科医

orthopedics *seikeige′ka* 整形外科

osmosis *shintō* 浸透

ostrich *dachō* 駝鳥

other 1 *hoka no* ほかの 2 different in nature *betsu no* 別の

otherwise *mo'shi sō' de na'kereba* もしそうでなければ

otter *kawauso* かわうそ

Ouch! *Ita'i!* 痛い.

ought *...hō' ga i'·i* ...方がいい We ought to buy the tickets right away. *Kippu o ha'yaku katta hō' ga i'i.* 切符を早く買った方がいい.

our *wata'shi-tachi no* 私たちの

ourselves *watashi-tachi ji'shin* 私たち自身

out 1 (baseball) *a'uto* アウト to be out *a'uto ni na'r·u* アウトになる 2 the outside *so'to* 外 ——(v) be depleted *kire'·ru* 切れる I'm out of gasoline. *Gasorin ga ki'reta.* ガソリンが切れた. That item is sold out. *Sono shinamono wa uri-ki'rete imasu.* その品物は売り切れています. ——(idiom) 1 He's out just now. *Ka're wa i'ma gaishutsu-shite iru.* 彼は今外出している. 2 Put the garbage out! *Gomi' o sute-nasa'i!* ごみを捨てなさい.

outcome *kekka* 結果

outer space [*ta'iki kengai no*] *u'chū* [大気圏外の]宇宙

outdoors *oku'gai* [*de*|*ni*] 屋外[で|に]

outfit *yōhin* 用品 ——obj *o* (irr) *ju'mbi-suru* 準備する

outing *ensoku* 遠足

outlet (Elec) *ko'nsento* コンセント

outline 1 *aramashi* あらまし 2 (of a story) *arasuji* あらすじ 3 general remarks *gairon* 概論

outlook *mitōshi* 見通し business outlook *ji'gyō no mitōshi* 事業の見通し The outlook isn't clear. *Hakki'ri mitōshi ga tsukana'i.* はっきり見通しがつかない.

out-of-order *koshō* [*-chū*] 故障[中]

out-of-the-way *he'mpi* [*na*] へんぴ[な]

outside 1 *so'to* 外 go outside *so'to e iku* 外へ行く 2 exterior *ga'ibu* 外部

outstanding (attr) *meda'tta* 目立った an outstanding (theatrical) performance *meda'tta e'ngi* 目立った演技

oval *tamago-gata* [*no*] 卵形[の]

ovary *ransō* 卵巣

oven *ō'bun* オーブン

over 1 above *...no ue'* [*ni*] ...の上[に] over the sink *nagashi no ue'* [*ni*] 流しの上[に] 2 beyond *...o koete* ...を越えて over the hill *yama'o koete iku* 山を越えて ——(v) be over *owar·u* 終わる That's over! *Sore wa owatta!* それは終わった. ——obj *o* (v) 1 exceed *koe·ru* 越える over the budget *yosan o koete iru* 予算を越えている 2 break through (irr) *toppa-suru* 突破する He received over

30,000 votes. *Kare no tokuhyō wa samman o toppa-shita.* 彼の得票は三万を突破した.

over and over   *na'ndo mo* 何度も I read the letter over and over. *Sono tegami o na'ndo mo yonda.* その手紙を何度も読んだ.

overcast   (attr) *kumo'tta* 曇った

overcoat   *ō'bā* オーバー

overcome   compl *ni* (v) *uchikats·u* 打ち勝つ   ——obj *o* (irr) *koku-fuku-suru* 克服する

overcooked   **1** overbaked/broiled/roasted *yaki-sugi* 焼きすぎ   **2** (in liquid) *ni-sugi* 煮すぎ

overcrowded   *tsumekomi-sugi* [*no*] 詰め込みすぎ[の]

over (do)   (v) *-sugi'·ru* すぎる

overdose   [*kusuri no*] *karyō* [薬の]過量

overdue   (idiom) *ki'gen ga su'gita* 期限が過ぎた

overeat   obj *o* (v) *tabe-sugi'·ru* 食べすぎる

overexposed (film)   *roshutsu ō'bā* 露出オーバー

overflow   (v) *afure'·ru* あふれる

overhead (expenses)   *ke'ihi* 経費

overhead projector   *ō-eichi-pī*; OHP

overnight   *ippaku* 一泊

overpass   **1** *rikkyō* 陸橋   **2** pedestrian overpass *hodōkyō* 歩道橋   **3** girder bridge *gā'do* ガード

overseas   *ka'igai* 海外 overseas travel *kaigai ryo'kō* 海外旅行

overshoes   *ōbāshū'zu* オーバーシューズ

oversight   *miotoshi* 見落とし

overtake   obj *o* (v) *oitsu'k·u* 追いつく

over there   *atchi* [*de*|*ni*] あっち[で/に]; *achira* [*de*|*ni*] あちら[で/に]

overtime (work)   *zangyō* 残業

overturn   obj *o* (v) *hikkurika'es·u* ひっくり返す   ——(v) be overturned *hikkurika'e·ru* ひっくり返る

overweight   *futori-sugi* 太りすぎ

overwork   *hataraki-sugi* 働きすぎ   ——(v) *hataraki-sugi'·ru* 働きすぎる

owe   (idiom) *shakki'n ga a'r·u* 借金がある I owe ¥100,000. *Watashi wa jūman-en no shakki'n ga a'ru.* 私は¥100,000の借金がある.

owl   *fuku'rō* ふくろう

own   one's own *jibun* [*ji'shin*] *no* 自分[自身]の   ——obj *o* (v) *mo'ts·u* 持つ Do you own a car? *Kuruma o mo'tte imasu ka?* 車を持っていますか.

owner   *mochi'nushi* 持主

ox   *oushi* 雄牛

oxygen   *sa'nso* 酸素

oyster   *ka'ki* かき

P

Pachinko *pachinko* パチンコ

Pacific Ocean *Taihe'iyō* 太平洋

pacifier *o-sha'buri* おしゃぶり

pacifist *heiwashugi'sha* 平和主義者

pack 1 bundle *tsutsumi'* 包み 2 backpack *senimotsu* 背荷物 ——obj *o* (v) 1 (irr) *nizu'kuri-suru* 荷造りする 2 pack a suitcase *ni'motsu o ire·ru* 荷物を入れる

package *kozu'tsumi* 小包み

packing *nizu'kuri* 荷造り

pact *jōyaku* 条約

pad 1 memo pad *memo-chō'* メモ帳 2 launching pad *hassha-dai* 発射台

page *pēji* ページ

pagoda *tō'* 塔 5-storied pagoda *go-jū no tō'* 五重の塔

pail *baketsu* バケツ

pain *itami'* 痛み

painful (adj) 1 (physically) *ita'·i* 痛い Is it painful? *Ita'i desu ka?* 痛いですか. 2 (mentally) *kurushi'·i* 苦しい It's psychologically painful to him. *Ka're no kokoro no na'ka wa kurushi'i.* 彼の心の中は苦しい.

paint *penki* ペンキ; *peinto* ペイント ——obj *o* (v) *nur·u* 塗る It's painted red. *Akaku nutte a'ru.* 赤く塗ってある.

paintbrush *hake'* はけ

painter 1 artist *gaka* 画家; *ekaki'* 絵かき 2 house painter *penkiya* [*-san*] ペンキ屋[さん]

painting *e'* 絵 oil painting *abura'-e* 油絵

paint thinner *shi'nnā* シンナー

pair 1 *-tsui* 対 one pair *ittsui* 一対 two pairs *ni'tsui* 二対 2 (of footwear) *-soku* 足 one pair of stockings *kutsu'shita issoku* 靴下一足 How many pairs of shoes do you have? *Kutsu' wa na'nzoku motte imasu ka?* 靴は何足持っていますか. 3 one pair of gloves *tebu'kuro hito'kumi* 手袋一組 4 one pair of trousers *zu'bon i'ppon* ズボン一本 5 one pair of undershorts *pa'ntsu ichi'mai* パンツ一枚

pajamas *pa'jama* パジャマ

Pakistan *Paki'sutan* パキスタン

Pakistani (person) *Pakisuta'njin* パキスタン人 ——(attr) *Paki'-sutan no* パキスタンの

pal *nakama'* 仲間

palace 1 *kyūden* 宮殿 2 imperial palace *go'sho* 御所; the Imperial Palace *kō'kyo* 皇居 3 detached palace *ri'kyū* 離宮

palate (Anat) *uwa-ago* 上あご; (Tech) *kōgai* 口蓋

pale (adj) *aojiro'·i* 青白い ——(v) become pale *aozame'·ru* 青ざめる; *ao'ku-nar·u* 青くなる ——(idiom) appear pale *ao'i kao o suru* 青い顔をする

palette *pa'retto* パレット

palm 1 (of the hand) *teno'hira* 手のひら 2 (tree) *shuro* しゅろ

Palm Sunday *Shuro no Nichiyō'bi* しゅろの日曜日

palpitate (irr) *do'kidoki-suru* どきどきする My heart's palpitating. *Mune' ga do'kidoki-suru.* 胸がどきどきする.

palsy *chūbū* 中風

pamper obj *o* (v) *amayaka's·u* 甘やかす ——(pass) *amayaka-sare·ru* 甘やかされる She was pampered when she was a child. *Ka'nojo wa kodomo no to'ki ni amayakasa'reta.* 彼女は子供の時に甘やかされた.

pamphlet *pa'mfuretto* パンフレット

pan (for cooking) 1 *na'be* 鍋 2 frying pan *furaipan* フライパン

Panama *Pa'nama* パナマ

Panamanian (person) *Panama'jin* パナマ人——(attr) *Pa'nama no* パナマの

pancake *hottokē'ki* ホットケーキ

panic *kyōfu* 恐怖

pansy *sanshoku su'mire* 三色すみれ

panties *pa'ntī* パンティー

pants 1 trousers *zu'bon* ズボン 2 underpants *pa'ntsu* パンツ

panty girdle *panti gādoru* ガードル

paper 1 *kami'* 紙 a sheet of paper *kami' ichimai* 紙一枚 2 newspaper *shimbun* 新聞 3 research paper *rombun* 論文 4 sandpaper *kamiya'suri* 紙やすり; *sandopē'pā* サンドペーパー 5 stationery *binsen* 便せん 6 tissue paper *chiri-gami* ちり紙; *ti'sshu* ティッシュ 7 tracing paper *torēshingu pē'pā* トレーシングペーパー 8 typing paper *taipu yō'shi* タイプ用紙 9 wallpaper *kabe-gami* 壁紙 10 wax paper *rō'gami* ろう紙

paperback (J) *bunko-bon* 文庫本; (W) *pēpāba'kku* ペーパーバック

paper bag *kami-bu'kuro* 紙袋

paperboy *shimbun ha'itatsu* [*shōnen*] 新聞配達[少年]

paper clip *kuri'ppu* クリップ

paper doll *kami ni'ngyō* 紙人形

paperweight *bunchin* 文鎮

paprika *papu'rika* パプリカ

parable *tatoeba'nashi* たとえ話

parachute *parashū'to* パラシュート

parade *parē'do* パレード

paradise 1 *rakuen* 楽園; *parada'isu* パラダイス 2 (Chr) *te'ngoku* 天国 3 (Budd) *gokuraku* 極楽

paraffin *para'fin* パラフィン

paragraph *danraku* 段落

Paraguay *Para'guai* パラグアイ

Paraguayan (person) *Paragua'ijin* パラグアイ人 ——(attr) *Para'guai no* パラグアイの

parakeet *i'nko* いんこ

parallel *heikō* [na] 平行[な] parallel lines *heikō'-sen* 平行線

paralysis *ma'hi* 麻痺

paralyzed *ma'hi-shite iru* 麻痺している He's paralyzed in both legs. *Ka're wa ryō-ashi ga ma'hi-shite iru.* 彼は両足が麻痺している。

parasite *kiseichū* 寄生虫

parasol *higa'sa* 日傘

parcel *kozu'tsumi* 小包

pardon 1 *yurushi'* 許し **2** (Leg) *ta'isha* 大赦 ——obj *o* (v) *yuru's·u* 許す pardon a convict *zainin o yuru'su* 罪人を許す

Pardon me. 1 *Sumimase'n.* すみません。; *Gomen nasa'i.* ごめんなさい。 **2** Pardon me, but... *Cho'tto o-ukagai-shima'su ga...* ちょっとおうかがいしますが... Pardon me, but where is the bank? *Cho'tto o-ukagai-shima'su ga, ginkō wa do'ko desu ka?* ちょっとおうかがいしますが、銀行はどこですか。 **3** Pardon me for going ahead. *O-saki ni shitsu'rei-shima'su.* お先に失礼します。

paregoric *geridome* 下痢止め

parent 1 *oya* 親 both parents (one's own) *ryō'shin* 両親; (another's) *go-ryō'shin* 御両親

parenthesis *ka'kko* かっこ

parish *kyō'ku* 教区

park 1 playground *yūe'nchi* 遊園地 **2** public park *kōen* 公園 national park *kokuritsu kō'en* 国立公園 ——obj *o* (irr) *chūsha-suru* 駐車する

parking *pā'kingu* パーキング

parking lot *chūshajō* 駐車場

parking meter *pākingume'tā* パーキングメーター

parliament *gi'kai* 議会

parliamentary procedure *gi'ji un'eihō* 議事運営法

parole *kari sha'kuhō* 仮釈放

parrot *ōmu* おうむ

parsley *pa'seri* パセリ

part 1 portion *bu'bun* 部分 **2** one part *ichi'bu* 一部 **3** (of a car, TV, etc.) *buhin* 部品; *pā'tsu* パーツ **4** role *yaku'* 役 leading part *shuyaku* 主役 ——comp *o* (v) *wakare'·ru* 別れる They (two persons) parted two years ago. *Futari wa ninen ma'e ni waka'reta.* 二人は二年前に別れた。

partially *bubunteki ni* 部分的に

participate compl *ni* (irr) *sanka-suru* 参加する Are you going to

participate in the conference? *Ka'igi ni sanka-shima'su ka?* 会議
に参加しますか.

participation *sanka* 参加

particle 1 (Gram) *joshi* 助詞 2 tiny fragment *mijin* 微塵; *ryū'shi*
粒子 elementary particle (in physics) *soryū'shi* 素粒子

particular *tokubetsu [na]* 特別[な] a particular reason *tokubetsu na
riyū* 特別な理由

particularly *to'ku ni* 特に This custom is observed particularly in
rural districts. *Kono shūkan wa to'ku ni inaka ni mirare'ru.* この
習慣は特に田舎に見られる.

particulars *shōsai* 詳細 We'll let you know the particulars later.
Shōsai wa a'to de shirasema'su. 詳細は後で知らせます.

partition *kugiri* 区切り ——obj *o* (v) *kugi'r·u* 区切る

partner 1 (in a game) *aite* 相手 2 friend *nakama'* 仲間 3 (business) *kyōdō keie'isha* 共同経営者

partnership *kyōdō* 共同 business partnership *kyōdō ke'iei* 共同経
営

part-time work *aruba'ito* アルバイト; *baito* バイト; *pāto* パート

party 1 (social gathering) *pā'tī* パーティー 2 organized group
dantai 団体 3 political party *seitō* 政党

pass 1 (commuter) *teiki'ken* 定期券; *te'iki* 定期 2 mountain
pass *tōge* 峠 ——compl *ni* (v) pass an exam (irr) *gōkaku-suru*
合格する; *uka'r·u* 受かる I passed. *Uka'tta.* 受かった. ——obj
o (v) 1 *watas·u* 渡す Please pass this memo to Ms. Tanaka.
Kono me'mo o Tanaka-san ni watashite kudasa'i. このメモを田中
さんに渡して下さい. 2 circulate *mawas·u* 回す After you've
read it, pass it on to the next person, please. *Yo'nde kara, tsugi'
no hito ni mawashite kudasa'i.* 読んでから次の人に回して下さい.
3 spend (time) *sugo's·u* 過ごす How did you pass the winter
holidays? *Fuyu-ya'sumi wa dō' yatte sugoshima'shita ka?* 冬休み
はどうやって過ごしましたか. 4 overtake *oiko's·u* 追い越す pass
a car *kuruma o oiko'su* 車を追い越す 5 pass beyond loc *o* (v)
tōri-sugi'·ru 通り過ぎる We passed the turnoff to your house.
Ana'ta no uchi' o tōri-su'gite shimatta. あなたの家を通り過ぎて
しまった.

passbook *tsūchō* 通帳

pass by loc *o* (v) 1 *tōrikaka'r·u* 通りかかる I happened to be
passing by, so I thought I'd stop in. *Tōrikaka'tta no de, yotte
mi'ta.* 通りかかったので寄ってみた. 2 pass by/through *tō'r·u* 通
る Does this bus pass by Shinjuku Station? *Kono ba'su wa Shinjuku'-eki o tōrima'su ka?* このバスは新宿駅を通りますか.

passenger 1 *kyaku* 客 passenger seat *kyakuseki* 客席 2 (on a
train or bus) *jōkyaku* 乗客 3 (on a ship) *senkyaku* 船客

passer-by *tsūkōnin* 通行人

passion *netsujō* 熱情; *jōnetsu* 情熱

passionate *netsuretsu* [na] 熱烈[な]

passive 1 passive role *ukemi'* [no] 受身[の] 2 with a passive bearing *shōkyokuteki* [na] 消極的[な] 3 (Gram) *ukemi'* 受身 4 (Gram) passive voice *judōtai* 受動態

passivity *shōkyokusei* 消極性

pass out 1 faint (irr) *kizetsu-suru* 気絶する; *shisshin-suru* 失神する 2 distribute obj *o* (v) *kuba'r·u* 配る

passport *pasupō'to* パスポート; *ryoken* 旅券

pass through loc *o* (v) *tōrinuke·ru* 通り抜ける pass through a gate *mo'n o tōrinuke'ru* 門を通り抜ける

past 1 *ka'ko* 過去 2 (Gram) past tense *kakokei* 過去形

paste *nori'* のり ——obj *o* (v) *har·u* 貼る

pasteurization *pasutsū'ru sakkinhō* パスツール殺菌法; *teion sa'-kkin* 低温殺菌

pastime *asobi* 遊び; *goraku* 娯楽

pastor *bo'kushi* 牧師

pastry *o-ka'shi* お菓子 see also cake; pie; sweets

pasture *bokujō* 牧場

patch 1 (on a garment) *tsugi* 継ぎ 2 a field *hatake* 畑 ——obj *o* (v) *hag·u* 接ぐ ——(idiom) to patch *tsugi o ate·ru* 継ぎを当てる

patent [*sembai*] *to'kkyo* [専売]特許

path 1 walkway *hodō* 歩道 2 mountain path *yama'michi* 山道

patience *ni'ntai* 忍耐

patient *kanja* 患者 outpatient *gairai ka'nja* 外来患者 ——(adj) *shimbō-zuyo'·i* 辛抱強い; *nintai-zuyo'·i* 忍耐強い a patient person *nintai-zuyo'·i hito* 忍耐強い人 ——(irr) be patient *ga'man-suru* 我慢する Be patient! *Ga'man-shinasa'i!* 我慢しなさい.

patriot *aiko'kusha* 愛国者

patriotism *aiko'kushin* 愛国心

patrol car *patokā* パトカー

patron *kōe'nsha* 後援者

pattern 1 model; guide *kata* 型 2 design *moyō* 模様

pause *kyūshi* 休止 ——(irr) *kyūshi-suru* 休止する

pave obj *o* (irr) *hosō-suru* 舗装する The street is not paved. *Michi' wa hosō-shite na'i.* 道は舗装してない. ——(attr) *hosō-shita* 舗装した a paved road *hosō-shita michi'* 舗装した道

pawnshop *shichi'ya* 質屋

pay obj *o* (v) 1 *hara'·u* 払う Did you pay the money? *O-kane o haraima'shita ka?* お金を払いましたか. ; *shihara'·u* 支払う pay a bill *kanjō o shihara'u* 勘定を支払う; *da's·u* 出す I paid ¥10,000. *Ichiman-en dashima'shita.* 一万円出しました. 2 pay (taxes) [*zei-kin o*] *osame'·ru* [税金を]納める

pay attention (irr)*chūmoku-suru* 注目する Pay attention, please. *Chūmoku-shite kudasa'i.* 注目して下さい.

payday *kyūryō'bi* 給料日

payment 1 *shiharai* 支払い 2 monthly payment *geppu* 月賦 3 payment of taxes *nōzei* 納税 4 advance payment *maekin* 前金

pea 1 *gurin pi'su* グリーンピース 2 (in pod) *sayae'ndō* さやえんどう

peace *heiwa* 平和 peace treaty *heiwa jō'yaku* 平和条約

peaceful *heiwa [na]* 平和[な]; *oda'yaka [na]* 穏やか[な]

peach *momo* 桃 peach blossoms *momo no hana'* 桃の花

peacock *kujaku* 孔雀

peak 1 (of a mountain) *chōjō'* 頂上 2 (high point) *chō'ten* 頂点

peanut *pi'natsu* ピーナツ peanut butter *pīnatsu ba'tā* ピーナツバター

pear 1 (W) *seiyō'nashi* 西洋梨 2 (J) *nashi* 梨

pearl *shinju* 真珠 cultured pearl *yōshoku shi'nju* 養殖真珠

pebble *koishi* 小石

peculiar 1 strange *he'n [na]* 変[な] a peculiar happening *he'n na koto'* 変な事 2 unique *dokutoku [no]* 独特[の] That's his own peculiar idea. *Sore wa ano' hito dokutoku no kanga'e desu.* それはあの人独特の考えです.

peculiarity 1 distinctive characteristic *tokushoku* 特色 a peculiarity of Japanese poetry *Nihon no shi'ika no tokushoku* 日本の詩歌の特色 2 idiosyncrasy *kuse'* 癖 a speech peculiarity *kotoba no kuse'* 言葉の癖

pedal *pedaru* ペダル

pedestrian *hokō'sha* 歩行者

pedestrian bridge *hodōkyō* 歩道橋

pediatrician *shōnika'-i* 小児科医

pediatrics *shōnika* 小児科

peel obj *o* (v) *muk·u* むく peel an apple *ringo [no kawa'] o muku* りんご[の皮]をむく

peep obj *o* (v) *nozok·u* 覗く peep through the keyhole *kagi-ana kara nozoku* 鍵穴から覗く

peer obj *o* (v) *jitto mi'·ru* じっと見る peer into a person's face *hito no kao o jitto mi'ru* 人の顔をじっと見る

peer (an equal) *dōhai* 同輩

pelican *perikan* ペリカン

pelvis *kotsuban* 骨盤

pen 1 *pe'n* ペン 2 ballpoint *bōrupen* ボールペン

penalty 1 *ba'tsu* 罰 2 fine *bakkin* 罰金

pencil *empitsu* 鉛筆 pencil sharpner *empitsu ke'zuri* 鉛筆削り

penetrate (v) 1 pierce *tsukitō'r·u* 突き通る The nail penetrated to the bone. *Kugi' wa hone' made tsukitō'tta.* 釘は骨まで突き通

った. **2** permeate *shimiko'm·u* 染み込む Lotion penetrates the skin. *Rō'shon wa ha'da ni shimiko'mu.* ローションは肌に染み込む.

penguin *pengin* ペンギン

penicillin *penishirin* ペニシリン

peninsula *hantō* 半島

penis (Anat) *pe'nisu* ペニス; (coll) *o-chi'nchin* おちんちん; (Tech) *inkei* 陰茎

penitentiary *keimu'sho* 刑務所

penmanship **1** (with a brush) *shūji* 習字 **2** (with a pen) *pen shū'ji* ペン習字

pen pal *pen-paru* ペンパル

pension *nenkin* 年金; *onkyū* 恩給

peony **1** (tree) *bo'tan* ボタン **2** (herbaceous) *shakuyaku* 芍薬

people **1** *hito'bito* 人々 **2** the people/public *jimmi'n* 人民

pepper **1** (ground black) *koshō'* 胡椒 **2** (green) *pi'man* ピーマン **3** (cayenne) *tōga'rashi* 唐辛子

percent *pā'sento* パーセント

perfect *kanzen* [na] 完全[な] ——obj o (caus) *kansei-sase'·ru* 完成させる

perfection **1** completion *kansei* 完成 **2** the acme of perfection *kampeki* 完璧

perfectionist *kanzenro'nsha* 完全論者; *kanzenshugi'sha* 完全主義者

perform obj o (irr) **1** execute *jikkō-suru* 実行する **2** give a performance *e'ngi-suru* 演技する

performance **1** action; execution *jikkō* 実行 **2** (theatrical) *kōen* 公演 **3** dramatic technique *engi-hō* 演技法; *e'ngi* 演技 **4** (musical) *ensō'kai* 演奏会

perfume *kōsui* 香水

perhaps *...ka mo shirenai* ...かもしれない Perhaps she'll come. *Ka'nojo wa ku'ru ka mo shirenai.* 彼女は来るかもしれない.

peril *kiken* 危険

period **1** (Gram) *shūshi'fu* 終止符; *ten* 点 put a period (in a sentence) *ten o u'tsu* 点を打つ **2** period of time *kikan* 期間 **3** age; era *jidai* 時代 the Kamakura period *Kamakura ji'dai* 鎌倉時代

periscope *sembōkyō* 潜望鏡

perishable (adj) *fuhai-shiyasu'·i* 腐敗しやすい

permanent wave *pā'ma* パーマ

permission *kyo'ka* 許可

permit obj o (v) *yuru's·u* 許す Do you permit your children to watch TV in the evening? *Kodomo ni yo'ru te'rebi o mi'ru no o yurushima'su ka?* 子供に夜テレビを見るのを許しますか.

perpendicular *suichoku* [no] 垂直[の] ——(adv) *ta'te* [no] 縦[の] a perpendicular line *ta'te no sen* 縦の線

perpendicularly *ta'te ni* 縦に Japanese is written both perpendicularly and horizontally. *Nihon-go wa ta'te ni mo ka'ku shi, yoko ni mo ka'ku.* 日本語は縦にも書くし、横にも書く.

perplexed (v) be perplexed *koma'r·u* 困る I was perplexed. *Koma'tchatta.* 困っちゃった.; (irr) *tōwaku-suru* 当惑する; *tomado'·u* 戸惑う

perseverance *shi'mbō* 辛抱

persevere obj *o* (v) *gamba'r·u* 頑張る; (irr) *shi'mbō-suru* 辛抱する

Persia *Pe'rusha* ペルシャ see also Iran

Persian (language) *Perusha-go* ペルシャ語 ——(attr) *Pe'rusha no* ペルシャの see also Iranian

persimmon 1 *kaki* 柿 2 astringent persimmon *shibu'-gaki* 渋柿 3 dried persimmon *hoshi'-gaki* 干し柿

persist obj *o* (v) *gamba'r·u* 頑張る ——compl *ni* (v) *koshitsu-suru* 固執する She persisted in her own plan. *Ka'nojo wa jibun no keikaku ni koshitsu-shita.* 彼女は自分の計画に固執した.

person 1 *hito'* 人; (polite) *kata'* 方 2 that person (referring to someone known to the speaker and the listener) *ano' hito* あの人; (polite) *ano kata'* あの方 3 that person (referring to someone either unknown or known only to either the speaker or the listener) *sono' hito* その人; (polite) *sono kata'* その方

personal *kojinteki [na]* 個人的[な]

personality *ko'sei* 個性 strong personality *tsuyo'i ko'sei* 強い個性; *seikaku* 性格 a clash of personalities *seikaku no fui'tchi* 性格の不一致; *jinkaku* 人格 personality development *jinkaku ke'isei* 人格形成

personnel 1 employee *shoku'in* 職員 2 *ji'nji* 人事 personnel matter *jinji mo'ndai* 人事問題 personnel department *jinjika* 人事課

perspective 1 viewpoint *shiten* 視点 2 prospect *mitō'shi* 見通し 3 distant view *enkei* 遠景 4 (artistic) *enkinhō* 遠近法

perspiration *a'se* 汗

perspire (idiom) *a'se o ka'k·u* 汗をかく

persuade obj *o* (caus) *nattoku-sase'·ru* 納得させる

Peru *Pe'rū* ペルー

peruse obj *o* (irr) *tsūdoku-suru* 通読する

Peruvian (person) *Perū' jin* ペルー人 ——(attr) *Pe'rū no* ペルーの

perversion 1 *akka* 悪化 2 (sexual) *seiteki tō'saku* 性的倒錯

pervert (person) *henshitsu'sha* 変質者

pessimism *hikanshu'gi* 悲観主義; *hika'nron* 悲観論

pessimist *hikanshugi'sha* 悲観主義者; *hikanro'nsha* 悲観論者

pessimistic *hikanteki [na]* 悲観的[な]

pet *pe'tto* ペット; *aigan dō'butsu* 愛玩動物 ——obj *o* (v) *nade'·ru* なでる

petal *hanabi'ra* 花びら

petroleum *sekiyu* 石油 *see also* gasoline

petunia *pechunia* ペチュニア

pew *kyōkai no seki* 教会の席

phantom *gen'ei* 幻影

pharmacist *kusuriya* [-san] 薬屋[さん]

pharmacology *yakugaku* 薬学

pharmacy *yakkyoku* 薬局; (coll) *kusuriya* [-san] 薬屋[さん]

Ph.D. *ha'kase/ha'kushi* 博士; *hakase'-go* 博士号

pheasant *kiji* 雉子

phenomenon *genshō* 現象

philatelist *kitte shūshūka* 切手収集家

philately *kitte shūshū* 切手収集

Philippine (attr) *Fi'ripin no* フィリピンの *see also* Filipina; Filipino

Philippines *Fi'ripin* フィリピン

philosopher *tetsuga'kusha* 哲学者

philosophy *tetsu'gaku* 哲学

phlegm *tan* 痰

phone *denwa* 電話 phone number *denwa ba'ngō* 電話番号 phone book *denwachō* 電話帳 ——(irr) *denwa-suru* 電話する

phonetics *onse'igaku* 音声学

phony *nisemono* 偽物

phosphorus *ri'n* 燐

photocopy *shashin fuku'sha* 写真複写 ——obj *o* (irr) *shashin de fukusha-suru* 写真で複写する; *fotosuta'tto de fukusha-suru* フォトスタットで複写する *see also* xerox

photograph *shashin* 写真 ——(idiom) take a photograph *shashin o to'r·u* 写真を撮る

photographer *kamera'man* カメラマン; (Tech) *shashinka* 写真家

photography *shashin sa'tsuei* 写真撮影

phrase *ku'* 句

physical *nikutaiteki* [na] 肉体的[な]

physical education *ta'iiku* 体育

physical therapy *butsuri ryō'hō* 物理療法

physician *isha* 医者; (polite) *o-isha-san* お医者さん

physics *bu'tsuri* 物理; (study of) *butsuri'gaku* 物理学 nuclear physics *kaku butsuri'gaku* 核物理学

physique *taikaku* 体格

piano *piano* ピアノ play the piano *piano o hiku* ピアノを弾く

pick *tsuru'hashi* つるはし ——obj *o* (v) **1** select *era'b·u* 選ぶ **2** (with fingers) *tsumam·u* つまむ ——(idiom) pick one's nose *hana o hoji'r·u* 鼻をほじる

picket (idiom) to picket *pike' o har·u* ピケを張る

pickles **1** (W) *pi'kurusu* ピクルス **2** (J) *tsukemono* 漬物; *o-shinkō* お新香

pickpocket *su'ri* すり ——obj *o* (v) *su'r·u* する ——(pass) *surare·ru* すられる I saw someone get his wallet pickpocketed on the train. *De'nsha no na'ka de hito' ga saifu o surare'ru no o mi'ta.* 電車の中で人が財布をすられるのを見た。

pick up obj *o* (v) *hiro·u* 拾う

picnic *pi'kunikku* ピクニック

picture *ka'iga* 絵画; *e'* 絵 ——obj *o* (v) *ega'k·u* 描く

picture frame *gakubuchi* 額縁

pie *pa'i* パイ apple pie *appuru pa'i* アップルパイ lemon pie *remo'n pai* レモンパイ pie shell *paigawa* パイ皮

piece **1** fragment *-hen* 片; *dampen* 断片 **2** (of something broken) *kakera* 欠けら a piece of broken glass *garasu no kakera* ガラスの欠けら **3** one part (of a whole) *bu'bun* 部分 **4** a/one piece (of) see Appendix 1

piecrust *paigawa* パイ皮

pier *sambashi* 桟橋

pierce obj *o* (v) *sa's·u* 刺す; *tsukisa's·u* 突き刺す I pierced my finger with a needle. *Watashi wa ha'ri de yubi' o tsukisa'shita.* 私は針で指を突き刺した。

pig *buta* 豚

pigeon *ha'to* 鳩

pigtail (braid) *o-sa'ge* お下げ

pilgrim *junre'isha* 巡礼者; (coll) *he'nro* 遍路; (polite) *o-henro-san* お遍路さん

pilgrimage *junrei* 巡礼

pill **1** *gan'yaku* 丸薬 **2** tablet *jōzai* 錠剤 **3** "the pill" (birth control) *keikō hini'nzai* 経口避妊剤

pillar *hashira* 柱

pillow *ma'kura* 枕

pillowcase *makura ka'bā* 枕カバー

pilot **1** (plane) *pairo'tto* パイロット; (Tech) *sōjū'shi* 操縦士 **2** (ship) *kōka'ishi* 航海士

pilot light *tanebi* 種火

pimp *pombiki* ぽん引き

pimple *ni'kibi* にきび

pin **1** brooch *buro'chi* ブローチ **2** safety pin *anze'n pin* 安全ピン **3** straight pin *machi'-bari* 待ち針 ——(idiom) to pin *pi'n de tome·ru* ピンで留める

pinch obj *o* (v) *tsune'·ru* つねる pinch someone's hand *te' o tsuneru* 手をつねる; *tsumam·u* つまむ pinch one's nose *hana o tsumamu* 鼻をつまむ

pine (tree) *ma'tsu* 松

pineapple *paina'ppuru* パイナップル pineapple juice *pain jū'su* パインジュース

ping-pong *pi'mpon* ピンポン; *takkyū* 卓球

pink *pi'nku* ピンク; *momo-iro* 桃色

pioneer *kaita'kusha*; 開拓者 *se'nkusha* 先駆者

pipe 1 (W) smoking pipe *paipu* パイプ 2 (J) smoking pipe *kiseru* キセル 3 tube *ka'n/ku'da* 管 4 duct *da'kuto* ダクト 5 metal pipe *tekkan* 鉄管

pipe wrench *kan-ba'sami* 管ばさみ

pirate *kaizoku* 海賊

Pisces *Uo-za* 魚座

pistol *pisutoru* ピストル

pitch dark *makku'ra* [na] 真暗[な]

pitcher 1 *mizusa'shi* 水差し 2 creamer *kurimu'-ire* クリーム入れ 3 baseball pitcher *pi'tchā* ピッチャー; *tō'shu* 投手

pitiable *kawaisō'* [na] かわいそう[な] That stray cat is pitiable. *Sono nora-neko wa kawaisō' desu.* そののら猫はかわいそうです.

pitiful *mi'jime* [na] みじめ[な] Those people lead pitiful lives. *Sono hito-tachi wa mi'jime na seikatsu o okutte i'ru.* その人たちはみじめな生活を送っている.; *a'ware* [na] 哀れ[な] a pitiful child who has lost both parents *ryō'shin o nakushita a'ware na kodomo* 両親をなくした哀れな子供; *kinodo'ku* [na] 気の毒[な] The refugee's condition was pitiful. *Nammin no yōsu wa kino'doku deshita.* 難民の様子は気の毒でした.

pity *awaremi* 哀れみ ——obj *o* (v) *aware'm·u* 哀れむ Lord, have pity on us. *Shu'yo, dō'ka aware'nde kudasa'i.* 主よ, どうか哀れんで下さい.

pizza *pi'za* ピザ; *piza'pai* ピザパイ

place 1 location *basho* 場所 a quiet place *shi'zuka na basho* 静かな場所 Where is the place for the picnic? *Pi'kunikku no basho wa do'ko desu ka?* ピクニックの場所はどこですか.; *tokoro'* 所 How about coming over to my place? *Watashi no tokoro'ni kimase'n ka?* 私の所に来ませんか. 2 rank *-i* 位 first place *ichi'-i* 一位 second place *ni'-i* 二位 ——obj *o* (v) *ok·u* 置く Place it here. *Koko ni oite kudasa'i.* ここに置いて下さい.

place mat *tēburu ma'tto* テーブルマット

(in) place of ...*no kawari ni* ...の代わりに In place of a ladder, use this chair. *Hashigo no kawari ni, kono isu o tsukatte kudasa'i.* はしごの代わりにこの椅子を使って下さい.

place on top of loc *ni*, obj *o* (v) *nose·ru* 載せる Place some cheese on top of the bread. *Pa'n ni chi'zu o nosete kudasa'i.* パンにチーズを載せて下さい.

plague *ekibyō* 疫病

plaid *kōshijima* [*no*] こうしじま[の]

plain 1 not fancy *jimi'* [*na*] じみ[な] a plain dress *jimi' na fuku'* じみな服 2 without design *mu'ji* [*no*] 無地[の] 3 wide expanse of land *heiya* 平野 4 evident *aki'raka* [*na*] 明らか[な] a plain fact *aki'raka na ji'jitsu* 明らかな事実

plan *keikaku* 計画 ——obj *o* (irr) *keikaku-suru* 計画する They're planning to put up some kind of large building there. *Asoko de na'ni ka ōki'i biru ke'nchiku o keikaku-shite iru.* あそこで何か大きいビル建築を計画している. ——(idiom) intend ...*tsumori* ... つもり I plan to buy a new car next year. *Rainen atarashi'i kuruma o kau tsumori de'su.* 来年新しい車を買うつもりです.

plane *hikō'ki* 飛行機 go by plane *hikō'ki de iku* 飛行機で行く

plane (tool) *kanna'* 鉋

planet *wakusei* 惑星; *-sei* 星 the planet Mars *Kasei* 火星

plank *i'ta* 板

plant 1 vegetation *shoku'butsu* 植物 2 garden plant *ueki* 植木 3 potted plant *hachiue* 鉢植 ——obj *o* (v) *ue·ru* 植える plant/set bulbs *kyūkon o ueru* 球根を植える Last year we planted roses in the back garden. *Kyo'nen, ura-niwa ni bara o ueta.* 去年裏庭にばらを植えた.

plaster *shikkui* しっくい

plaster cast *gi'pusu* ギプス

plaster of Paris *sekkō* 石膏

plastic *pura'suchikku* プラスチック

plate *o-sara* お皿

platform (train) [*puratto*]*hō'mu* [プラット] ホーム

platform ticket *nyūjō'ken* 入場券

platter *ōzara* 大皿

play 1 *asobi* 遊び 2 dramatic performance *shibai* 芝居; *ge'ki* 劇 3 drama *gikyoku* 戯曲 ——(v) *asob·u* 遊ぶ The children are playing together well. *Kodomo'-tachi wa na'kayoku asonde iru.* 子供たちは仲良く遊んでいる. ——(idiom) 1 play a game *gē'mu o suru* ゲームをする 2 play a flute *fue o fu'k·u* 笛を吹く 3 play the piano *piano o hik·u* ピアノを弾く

play area *undō'jō* 運動場

playground 1 *yūe'nchi* 遊園地 2 exercise field *undō'jō* 運動場

playmate *asobi-to'modachi* 遊び友達

playwright *geki sa'kka* 劇作家; (Tech) *gikyokuka* 戯曲家

plead ind-obj *ni*, obj *o* (v) 1 (irr) *be'ngo-suru* 弁護する 2 request; beg *nega'·u* 願う

pleasant (attr) 1 *kanji no i'i* 感じのいい; *kimochi no i'i* 気持ちのいい This is a pleasant, sunny room. *Kore wa hiatari ga yo'ku,* *kimochi no i'i heya' desu.* これは日当たりがよく気持ちのいい部屋です.　**2** amiable *aisō' no i'i* 愛想のいい She is a pleasant person. *Ka'nojo wa aisō' no i'i hito' desu.* 彼女は愛想のいい人です.

pleasantly *kokoroyo'ku* 快く He accepted the work pleasantly. *Ka're wa shigoto o kokoroyo'ku hikiu'kete kureta.* 彼は仕事を快く引き受けてくれた.

please obj *o* (caus) *yorokobase'・ru* 喜ばせる To please our son we let him go to Guam on his birthday. *Tanjo'bi ni yorokobaseyō' to omotte, musuko o Guamu-tō ni ika'seta.* 誕生日に喜ばせようと思って, 息子をグアム島に行かせた.

Please　**1** *dō'zo* どうぞ Please go ahead of me. *Dō'zo, o-saki ni.* どうぞお先に. Please take one. *O-hitotsu, dō'zo.* おーつどうぞ.　**2** be kind enough (to do/give something) *...kudasa'i* ...下さい A glass of water, please. *Mizu o i'ppai kudasa'i.* 水を一杯下さい.　**3** desire; petition *...negaima'su* ...願います; *o-negai-shima'su* お願いします To Shinjuku Station, please. *Shinjuku'-eki e o-negai-shima'su.* 新宿駅へお願いします.

pleased obj *o* (v) be pleased *yoroko'b・u* 喜ぶ She was pleased with it. *Ka'nojo wa sore o yoroko'nde ita.* 彼女はそれを喜んでいた.

——(idiom) be pleased *ki ni ir・u* 気にいる Are/Were you pleased with it? *Sore wa ki ni irima'shita ka?* それは気にいりましたか.

pleasure *tanoshi'mi* 楽しみ

pleat *hi'da* ひだ

plenty *jūbu'n* 十分; *takusan* たくさん That's plenty! *Mō' takusa'n desu!* もうたくさんです.

pleurisy *rokumakuen* 肋膜炎

pliers *pe'nchi* ペンチ; *yattoko* やっとこ

plot　**1** (story) *su'ji* 筋　**2** (scheme) *kuwadate* 企て　——obj *o* (v) *kuwadate'・ru* 企てる

plough *see* plow

plow *suki* すき　——obj *o* (v) *tagaya's・u* 耕す

plug　**1** electric socket *sashikomi* 差し込み; *ko'nsento* コンセント　**2** stopper *se'n* 栓

plum　**1** (W) *pu'ramu* プラム　**2** (J) *ume* 梅

plumber *suidō kōjiya* [-san] 水道工事屋[さん]; *haikan-kō* 配管工

plural *fukusū'* 複数

Pluto (planet) *Meiōsei* 冥王星

plywood *beniya'-ita* ベニヤ板

P.M. (afternoon, evening) *go'go* 午後　5 P.M. *go'go go'ji* 午後五時

pneumonia *haien* 肺炎

poached egg *otoshi ta'mago* 落とし卵

pocket *poke'tto* ポケット

pocketbook *saifu* 財布; *satsu'-ire* 札入れ

poem *shi* 詩

poet *shijin* 詩人

poetry *shi'ika* 詩歌

point 1 tip *saki* 先 pencil point *empitsu no saki* 鉛筆の先 2 cape; headland *misaki* 岬 3 aspect *ten* 点 important point *jūte'n* 重点 We don't agree on that point. *Sono ten de i'ken ga awana'i.* その点で意見が合わない. ——obj *o* (v) 1 point to *sa's·u* さす 2 point with the finger *yubisa's·u* 指さす

pointed (attr) *toga'tta* 尖った a pointed knife *toga'tta na'ifu* 尖ったナイフ

point of view *ke'nchi* 見地; *mikata* 見方 from another point of view *betsu no mika'ta de wa* 別の見方では

point out obj *o* (irr) *shiteki-suru* 指摘する point out an error *ayamari'o shiteki-suru* 誤りを指摘する

poised (dignified) *jōhi'n* [na] 上品[な] She's very poised. *Ka'nojo wa jōhi'n na kata' desu.* 彼女は上品な方です.

poison *doku'* 毒

poker (card game) *pō'kā* ポーカー

Poland *Pō'rando* ポーランド

Pole *Pōrando'jin* ポーランド人

pole *sao'* 竿; *bō* 棒

police 1 *keisatsu* 警察 police station *keisatsusho* 警察署 Call the police! *Keisatsu o yonde kudasa'i!* 警察を呼んで下さい. 2 riot police *kidōtai* 機動隊

police box *kōban* 交番

police officer *keisa'tsukan* 警察官; (abbr) *keikan* 警官; (coll) *oma'wari-san* お巡りさん

policy 1 stance; platform *seisaku* 政策 diplomatic policy *gaikō se'isaku* 外交政策 Japan's policy toward America *Nihon no tai-Bei se'isaku* 日本の対米政策 2 insurance policy *hoken shō'sho* 保険証書

Polish 1 (language) *Pōrando-go* ポーランド語 2 (person) *Pōrando'jin* ポーランド人 ——(attr) *Pō'rando no* ポーランドの

polish 1 *migaki* 磨 brass polish *shinchū mi'gaki* しんちゅうみがき silver polish *gin mi'gaki* 銀みがき 2 (furniture) *ka'gu no tsuyadashi'* 家具のつや出し 3 (nail) *manikyua* マニキュア 4 (shoe) *kutsu'zumi* 靴墨 ——obj *o* (v) *migak·u* 磨く I polished the shoes. *Kutsu' o migaita.* 靴を磨いた.

polish remover *jokō'eki* 除光液

polite *te'inei* [na] 丁寧[な] polite language *teinei-go* 丁寧語 polite speech *te'inei na kotoba-zu'kai* 丁寧な言葉遣い Japanese are very polite. *Nihonji'n wa totemo te'inei desu.* 日本人はとても丁寧です. ——(adj) *reigi tadashi'·i* 礼儀正しい Mrs. Tanaka is a polite person. *Tanaka-san wa reigi tadashi'i hito' desu.* 田中さんは礼儀正しい人です.

politely   *te′inei ni* 丁寧に He bowed politely. *Ka′re wa te′inei ni o-jigi-shita.* 彼は丁寧におじぎした.

politeness   *teine′isa* 丁寧さ; *reigi tada′shisa* 礼儀正しさ

political   (attr) *seijiteki* [*na*] 政治的[な]; *seiji-* 政治 political power/ influence *seiji′ryoku* 政治力

politician   *seijika* 政治家

politics   *seiji* 政治

pollen   *kafun* 花粉

pollution   *kōgai* 公害; *osen* 汚染 air pollution *kūki o′sen* 空気汚染 water pollution *suishitsu o′sen* 水質汚染

Polynesia   *Porine′shia* ポリネシア

Polynesian   1 (language) *Porineshia-go* ポリネシア語   2 (person) *Porineshia′jin* ポリネシア人   ——(attr) *Porine′shia no* ポリネシアの

pompous   (attr) *mottai-bu′tta* もったいぶった

pond   *ike′* 池 lotus pond *hasu no ike′* 蓮の池

pony   *kouma* 小馬

ponytail   *ponitē′ru* ポニーテール

pool   1 (of stagnant water) *mizutamari* 水たまり   2 swimming pool *pū′ru* プール   3 game *pū′ru* プール; a pool bar *pū′ru bā′* プールバー

poor   *bi′mbō* [*na*] 貧乏[な]   ——(adj) *mazushi′·i* 貧しい

poor sport   *kujikeyasu′i hito′* くじけやすい人

popcorn   *poppukō′n* ポップコーン

Pope   *Rōma Hō-ō′* ローマ法王

poppy   *keshi* けし

popsicle   *aisu kya′ndē* アイスキャンデー

popular   *ninki* [*no a′ru*] 人気[のある] a popular singer *ninki ka′shu* 人気歌手   ——(v) be popular *haya′r·u* はやる This color is popular this year. *Kotoshi kono iro′ga haya′tte iru.* 今年この色がはやっている.

popularity   *ninki* 人気 have popularity *ninki ga a′ru* 人気がある

population   *jinkō* 人口 the population of Tokyo *Tōkyō no jinkō* 東京の人口

porcelain   *ji′ki* 磁器

pore (in skin)   *ke-ana* 毛穴

pork   *butaniku* 豚肉

pornography   1 *po′runo* ポルノ   2 illustration *shunga* 春画

port   *minato* 港; *-kō* 港 Kobe Port *Kōbe′-kō* 神戸港

portable   *mochihakobi-deki′ru* 持ち運びできる; *keitai-* 携帯 portable TV *keitai-te′rebi* 携帯テレビ

porter   1 (hotel) *bōi-san* ボーイさん   2 redcap *akabō* 赤帽

portion   *bu′bun* 部分; *wakema′e* 分け前

portrait   *shōzō* 肖像

Portugal *Porutogaru* ポルトガル

Portuguese **1** (language) *Porutogaru-go* ポルトガル語   **2** (person) *Porutogaru´jin* ポルトガル人   ——(attr) *Porutogaru no* ポルトガルの

port wine *pōto wa´in* ポートワイン

position *i´chi* 位置 The position of the couch is not good. *So´fa no i´chi ga yo´yku na´i.* ソファーの位置がよくない. You hold an advantageous position. *Ana´ta wa yū´ri na i´chi o shi´mete iru.* あなたは有利な位置をしめている.

possess obj *o* (irr) *shoyū-suru* 所有する

possessions **1** property *shoyū´butsu* 所有物   **2** valuables *kichōhin* 貴重品

possessive **1** (attr) *shoyū´yoku no tsuyo´i* 所有欲の強い   **2** (Gram) *shoyū´kaku* 所有格

possibility *kanōsei* 可能性 There is a strong possibility that the project will be completed before the end of the year. *Puro´jekuto ga nemmatsu ma´de ni dekiagaru kanōsei wa jūbu´n aru.* プロジェクトが年末までにできあがる可能性は十分ある.

possible obj *ga* (v) *deki´·ru* できる Is it possible? *Sore ga dekima´su ka?* それができますか; …*koto´ ga deki´·ru* …ことができる Is it possible to get a visa to China? *Chū´goku no bi´za o te´ni ireru koto ga dekima´su ka?* 中国のビザを手に入れることができますか. ——(adv) as…as possible *dekiru da´ke* …できるだけ as soon/early as possible *dekiru dake ha´yaku* できるだけ早く as much/many as possible *dekiru dake takusa´n* できるだけたくさん I'll help you as much as possible. *Dekiru dake tetsuda´tte ageru.* できるだけ手伝ってあげる.; *narubeku* なるべく see also **able** (to); **can** (be able to)

post **1** stake *ku´i* 杭   **2** military base *kichi* 基地   **3** mailbox *po´suto* ポスト ——obj *o* (v) *har·u* 貼る;(irr) *keiji-suru* 掲示する

postage **1** *kitte-dai* 切手代   **2** mailing/shipping charge *sō´ryō* 送料 postage for a parcel *kozutsumi no sō´ryō* 小包の送料

postal code *yūbin ba´ngō* 郵便番号

postcard *hagaki* 葉書 picture postcard *eha´gaki* 絵葉書

poster *po´sutā* ポスター

posterity *shi´son* 子孫

postman *yūbin-ya* 郵便屋; *yūbin´ya-san* 郵便屋さん

post office *yūbi´nkyoku* 郵便局

post office box *shisho´-bako* 私書籍

positive **1** *kōteiteki [na]* 肯定的[な]   **2** constructive *sekkyokuteki [na]* 積極的[な]

postpone obj *o* (irr) *enki-suru* 延期する ——(pass) *enki-sare´ru* 延期される It was postponed. *Enki-sareta.* 延期された.

postponement *enki* 延期

postscript *soegaki* 添え書き; *tsuishin* 追伸

posture *shisei* 姿勢 She has good posture. *Ka'nojo wa shisei ga i'i.* 彼女は姿勢がいい.

pot 1 cooking vessel *na'be* 鍋 **2** flower pot *hachi* 鉢; *ueki'-bachi* 植木鉢 **3** (W) teapot *tipo'tto* ティーポット **4** (J) *kyūsu* 急須

potato 1 Irish potato; white potato *jagaimo* じゃが芋 **2** sweet potato *imo'* 芋; *satsumaimo* さつま芋 *see also* french fries

potato chips *poteto-chi'ppu* ポテトチップ

potential 1 *kanōsei* 可能性 **2** capability *hattensei* 発展性

potter *yakimono'shi* 焼物師; *tōgeika* 陶芸家

pottery 1 earthenware *yakimono* 焼物 **2** china *setomono* 瀬戸物; *tō'ki* 陶器

poultry 1 *tori* 鳥 **2** (meat) *toriniku* 鳥肉 *see also* chicken

pound *po'ndo* ポンド one pound *ichi-po'ndo* 一ポンド ——obj *o* (v) **1** pulverize *kuda'k·u* 砕く **2** strike *[tsu'yoku]* *u'ts·u* [強く] 打つ

pour obj *o* (v) *tsug·u* 注ぐ Pour me some beer, please. *Bi'ru o tsuide kuremase'n ka?* ビールを注いでくれませんか.

poverty *bi'mbō* 貧乏; *hinkon* 貧困

powder 1 *kona'* 粉 make into a powder *kona' ni suru* 粉にする **2** face powder *oshiroi* 白粉

powder room *keshō'-shitsu* 化粧室

power 1 strength *chikara'* 力 **2** ability *nō'ryoku* 能力 **3** influence *se'iryoku* 勢力 **4** (physical) *ta'iryoku* 体力 **5** (electrical) *de'nryoku* 電力 **6** (political) *seiken* 政権 **7** authority *ke'n'i* 権威

power failure *teiden* 停電

powerful influential *yūryoku* [*na*] 有力[な] ——(adj) stong *tsuyo'·i* 強い

practical *jitsuyōteki* [*na*] 実用的[な]

practice 1 *renshū* 練習 **2** rehearsal *o-sarai* おさらい **3** carrying out exercises *enshū* 演習 **4** practical application *ōyō* 応用 —— obj *o* (irr) *renshū-suru* 練習する

prairie *daisō'gen* 大草原

praise *sa'mbi* 賛美 ——obj *o* (v) **1** home'r·u 誉める People praised her for her sense of responsibility. *Minna' wa ka'nojo no sekini'nkan o ho'meta.* みんなは彼女の責任感を誉めた. **2** (Chr) praise (God) (irr) *[Kami-sama o] sa'mbi-suru* [神様を] 賛美する

prank *itazura* いたずら

prawn *kuruma'-ebi* くるまえび

pray obj *o* (v) *ino'r·u* 祈る pray to a god *ka'mi ni ino'ru* 神に祈る I pray that you'll get well soon. *Ichinichi mo ha'yaku kenkō ni na'ru yō inorima'su.* 一日も早く健康になるよう祈ります.

prayer 1 *inori* 祈り; *kitō* 祈禱 **2** silent prayer *mokutō* 黙禱

prayer beads (Budd) *juzu* じゅず; (Cath) *roza'rio* ロザリオ

prayer meeting *kitō'kai* 祈禱会

preach obj *o* (irr) (Chr) *sekkyō'-suru* 説教する; (Budd) *seppō-suru* 説法する

preacher *sekkyō'sha* 説教者

precede (v) [*ni*] *sakida'ts·u* [に]先立つ

precedent *senrei* 先例

precept *kyōkun* 教訓

precincts 1 shrine/temple grounds *ke'idai* 境内 2 electoral district *senkyo'ku* 選挙区 3 environs *shū'i* 周囲

precipice *zeppeki* 絶壁

precisely *kichi'nto* きちんと do precisely *kichi'nto-suru* きちんとする

predicate (Gram) *jutsugo* 述語

predict obj *o* (irr) *yogen-suru* 予言する

preface *jobun* 序文; *maegaki* 前書き

prefectural office 1 (Hokkaido) *dō'chō* 道庁 2 (Kyoto & Osaka) *fuchō* 府庁 3 (Tokyo) *to'chō* 都庁 4 (other prefectures) *ke'nchō* 県庁

prefecture *ke'n* 県 Iwate Prefecture *Iwate'-ken* 岩手県

prefer (idiom) ...*yo'ri*...[*no*] *hō' ga suki' desu* ...より...[の]方が好きです I prefer the mountains to the seashore. *U'mi yori yama' no hō' ga suki' desu.* 海より山の方が好きです.

preference *suki-ki'rai* 好き嫌い Children have definite preferences when it comes to food. *Kodomo wa tabemo'no no suki-ki'rai ga hageshi'i.* 子供は食べ物の好き嫌いが激しい.

preferred stock *yūse'n kabu* 優先株

prefix (Gram) *settō'ji* 接頭辞

pregnancy *ninshin* 妊娠

pegnant (irr) *ninshin-suru* 妊娠する She's pregnant. *Ninshin-shite iru.* 妊娠している. ——(idiom) She's pregnant. (lit., Her stomach's big.) *Ka'nojo wa onaka ga oki'i.* 彼女はお腹が大きい.

prejudice *henken* 偏見

premature (attr) *sō-* 早- premature birth *sō'zan* 早産 premature conclusion *sōkei na ha'ndan* 早計な判断

premise *zentei* 前提

premonition *yokan* 予感

preparation *shitaku'* 支度 preparation for dinner *yū'shoku no shitaku'* 夕食の支度; *ju'mbi* 準備 I have to make preparations for the party. *Pa'ti no ju'mbi o shina'kereba nara'nai.* パーティーの準備をしなければならない.; *yō'i* 用意 preparation for a trip *ryokō no yō'i* 旅行の用意

preparatory school 1 (in the school system) *shinga'ku-kō* 進学校; *juke'n-kō* 受験校 2 (outside the school system) *yobi-kō* 予備校

prepare obj *o* (irr) *shitaku-suru* 支度する; *ju'mbi-suru* 準備する; *yō'i-suru* 用意する

preposition (Gram) *zenchi'shi* 前置詞

prescription (for medicine) *shohōsen* 処方箋

present 1 *okurimono* 贈り物; *pure'zento* プレゼント 2 (of money) *o-rei* お礼 3 the present time *ge'nzai* 現在 up till the present *ge'nzai made* 現在まで 4 (Gram) present tense *genzai-kei* 現在形 ──(irr) be present; attend *shusseki-suru* 出席する ──ind-obj *ni*, obj *o* (v) 1 make a presentation (to a meeting) (irr) *teishutsu-suru* 提出する 2 make a report (irr) *happyō-suru* 発表する 3 give (a present) *age'ru* 上げる; *okur'u* 贈る

preserve obj *o* (irr) *i'ji-suru* 維持する; *hozon-suru* 保存する

preside obj *o* (irr) *shikai-suru* 司会する

president 1 (bank) *tōdori* 頭取 2 (club, society, association) *kaichō* 会長 3 (company) *shachō* 社長 4 (nation) *daitō'ryō* 大統領 5 (school) *kōchō* 校長 6 (university) *gakuchō* 学長 see also chairperson

press (news media) *hōdō ki'kan* 報道機関

press obj *o* (v) 1 press down *osae'ru* 押える 2 iron [*airon o*] *kake'ru* [アイロンを]かける Press this, please. *Airon o ka'kete kudasa'i.* アイロンをかけて下さい。 3 urge *seme'ru* 責める Don't press me. *Seme'naide kudasa'i.* 責めないで下さい。

pressure 1 *atsu'ryoku* 圧力 2 strain; tension *kinchō* 緊張

presume obj *o* (v) *mina's·u* 見なす; (irr) *suitei-suru* 推定する presume a person's innocence *hito o mu'zai to suitei-suru* 人を無罪と推定する; *katei-suru* 仮定する

presumption *katei* 仮定

presupposition *zentei* 前提

pretend (idiom) ...*furi' o suru* ...ふりをする pretend not to hear *kikanai furi' o suru* 聞かないふりをする

pretty *ki'rei* [*na*] きれい[な] a pretty girl *ki'rei na onna' no ko* きれいな女の子 ──(adj) *kawai'·i* 可愛い

prevent obj *o* (v) *fuse'g·u* 防ぐ There was no way I could prevent it. *Dō ni mo fusegi-yō'ga na'katta.* どうにも防ぎようがなかった。; (irr) *yobō-suru* 予防する prevent infection *kansen o yobō-suru* 感染を予防する

prevention *bōshi* 防止 crime prevention *hanzai bō'shi* 犯罪防止; *yobō* 予防 Fire Prevention Week *Kasai Yobō Shū'kan* 火災予防週間

preview *yokokuhen* 予告編 ──obj *o* (caus) *nairan-sase'·ru* 内覧させる

previous *ma'e no* 前の; *-sen* 先 previous engagement *sen'yaku* 先約

price 1 *nedan* 値段 The price is high. *Nedan ga taka'i.* 値段が

高い. **2** list price *teika* 定価 20% off the list price *teika yo'ri nijuppāse'nto no waribiki* 定価より20パーセントの割り引き **3** commodity prices *bukka* 物価 high prices *bukka'-daka* 物価高 Prices are high in Japan! *Niho'n de wa bukka ga taka'i!* 日本では物価が高い.

prickly *chi'kuchiku* ちくちく ——(irr) be/become prickly *chi'-kuchiku-suru* ちくちくする This sweater is prickly. *Kono sē'tā wa chi'kuchiku-suru* このセーターはちくちくする.

prickly heat (heat rash) *kabure* かぶれ; *asemo* 汗疹

pride 1 *hokori'* 誇り He is the pride of his school. *Ka're wa gakkō no hokori' desu.* 彼は学校の誇りです. **2** (in oneself) *jiman* 自慢 pride in one's ability *ude-ji'man* 腕自慢 national pride *o-kuni ji'man* お国自慢 **3** haughtiness *gōman* 傲慢 ——(idiom) have pride (in) ...[*ni*] *hokori'o mots·u* ...[に]誇りをもつ She has pride in her academic ability. *Ka'nojo wa jibun no gakuryoku ni hokori' o mo'tte iru.* 彼女は自分の学力に誇りをもっている.

priest 1 (Chr) *shi'mpu* 神父 **2** (Budd) *sō'* 僧; *sō'ryo* 僧呂; (coll) *obōsan* お坊さん **3** (Shinto) *ka'nnushi* 神主

primary school *shōga'kkō* 小学校

prime minister *shushō* 首相 Prime Minister Kaifu *Kai'fu shushō* 海部首相; *sōri da'ijin* 総理大臣

primitive *ge'nshi* [*no*] 原始[の]; *genshiteki* [*na*] 原始的[な]

prince 1 *ō'ji* 王子 **2** crown prince *kōta'ishi* 皇太子

princess 1 *hi'me* 姫 **2** (title) *-hide'nka* 妃殿下

principal 1 (head of a school) *kōchō* 校長 **2** main; chief *o'mo* [*na*] 主[な] principal product *o'mo na sambutsu* 主な産物

principle 1 general rule *gensoku* 原則 in principle *gensoku to shite* 原則として **2** theory *ge'nri* 原理 economic principle *keizai ge'nri* 経済原理

print 1 woodblock print *hanga* 版画; (Tech) *mokuhan* 木版 **2** photo *shashin* 写真 *insatsu-suru* 印刷する ——obj *o* (irr) **3** printed matter *insatsu'butsu* 印刷物

printing (presswork) *insatsu* 印刷

prison *keimu'sho* 刑務所

prisoner *shū'jin* 囚人

prisoner of war *ho'ryo* 捕虜

private 1 personal; individual *ko'jin* [*no*] 個人[の] private taxi *kojin ta'kushi* 個人タクシー It's a private matter. *Ko'jin no mondai de'su.* 個人の問題です. **2** one's private life *shi-se'ikatsu* 私生活 **3** (not public) *shi'ritsu* 私立 private school *shiritsu ga'kkō* 私立学校

privilege *tokken* 特権

prize *hōbi* 褒美; *shō'* 賞; *shōhin* 賞品 ——(idiom) hold dear *daiji' ni suru* 大事にする

probably *ta'bun...deshō'* 多分...でしょう He probably won't come. *Ka're wa ta'bun ko'nai deshō.* 彼は多分来ないでしょう.; *oso'raku...deshō'* 恐らく...でしょう She'll probably return in a few days. *Ka'nojo wa oso'raku ni-sannichi-chū ni wa ka'eru deshō.* 彼女は恐らく二三日中には帰るでしょう.; *...deshō'* ...でしょう You'll probably go by train, won't you? *Densha de iku'n deshō?* 電車で行くんでしょう. It'll probably be a nice day tomorrow. *Ashita' wa te'nki ni na'ru deshō.* 明日は天気になるでしょう. *see also* tables 1–4, pp. xxi–xl.

problem *mondai* 問題 a big problem *daimo'ndai* 大問題

procedure *tetsu'zuki* 手続き complicated procedure *fukuzatsu na tetsu'zuki* 複雑な手続き

proceeds *uriage* 売上げ

process 1 *sa'yō* 作用 process of growth *seichō sa'yō* 成長作用 2 proceedings *shinkō* 進行 in the process (of) *shinkō-chū* 進行中 3 *katei* 過程 Please explain the process by which this product is made. *Kono seihin ga tsukurare'ru made no katei o setsumei-shite kudasa'i.* この製品が作られるまでの過程を説明して下さい.

proclaim ind-obj *ni*, obj *o* (irr) *senge'n-suru* 宣言する

proclamation *senge'n* 宣言

produce 1 *seisa'mbutsu* 生産物 2 (agricultural) *nō-sa'mbutsu* 農産物 ——obj *o* (irr) 1 *sanshutsu-suru* 産出する produce oil *se-kiyu o sanshutsu-suru* 石油を産出する 2 manufacture *seisaku-suru* 製作する 3 (movies, art, etc.) *seisaku-suru* 制作する

producing (attr) *sanshutsu-* 産出 oil-producing country *sekiyu sanshutsu'-koku* 石油産出国

product *sambutsu* 産物 staple products *shuyō sa'mbutsu* 主要産物; *seisan* 生産 gross national product (GNP) *kokumin sō-se'isan* 国民総生産

production *seisan* 生産 cost of production *seisan-hi* 生産費 production control *seisan se'igen* 生産制限

profanity 1 irreverence *fukei* 不敬 2 profane act *bōtoku* 冒瀆 3 profane word *bōtokuteki na kotoba* 冒瀆的な言葉

profession 1 occupation *shoku'gyō* 職業 2 (Chr) public profession of faith *shinkō ko'kuhaku* 信仰告白

professional (person) *pu'ro* プロ; *kurō'to* 玄人

professor 1 *kyō'ju* 教授 2 assistant (associate) professor *jokyō'ju* 助教授 3 instructor *kō'shi* 講師; *kyō'shi* 教師

profile *yoko-gao* 横顔

profit *ri'eki* 利益 ——(idiom) make a profit *ri'eki o u'r·u* 利益を得る

program *purogu'ramu* プログラム; (TV; radio) *bangumi* 番組; (theater) *dashi'mono* 出し物

progress 1 advance *shinkō* 進行 The progress of the work has been delayed. *Shigoto no shinkō ga okurete iru.* 仕事の進行が遅れている. **2** improvement *shi'mpo* 進歩 scientific progress *ka'gaku no shi'mpo* 科学の進歩 **3** development; growth *hattatsu* 発達

progressive *shimpoteki* [na] 進歩的[な] progressive teaching methods *shimpoteki na kyōju-hō* 進歩的な教授法

progressive (person) *shimposhugi'sha* 進歩主義者

progressive party *shimpo-tō* 進歩党

prohibit obj *o* (irr) *kinshi-suru* 禁止する ——(pass) *kinshi-sare·ru* 禁止される Smoking is prohibited here. *Koko de wa tabako wa kinshi-sarete i'ru.* ここではたばこは禁止されている.

prohibited *kinshi* 禁止 Trespassing prohibited! *Tachi-iri kinshi!* 立ち入り禁止.

project *kikaku* 企画 ——obj *o* (v) **1** (on a screen) *utsu's·u* 写す **2** (plan) (irr) *kikaku-suru* 企画する; *keikaku-suru* 計画する

projector 1 (movie) *eishaki* 映写機 **2** (slide) *proje'kutā* プロジェクター

promise *yakusoku* 約束 make a promise *yakusoku o musubu* 約束を結ぶ keep a promise *yakusoku o mamo'ru* 約束を守る break a promise *yakusoku o yabu'ru* 約束を破る ——obj *o* (irr) *yakusoku-suru* 約束する

promissory note *yakusoku te'gata* 約束手形

promotion 1 *sokushin* 促進 **2** (in rank) *shōshin* 昇進

promptly *sassoku* 早速 He did it promptly. *Ka're wa sassoku shite kureta.* 彼は早速してくれた.

pronoun (Gram) *daime'ishi* 代名詞

pronounce obj *o* (irr) *hatsuon-suru* 発音する How do you pronounce your name? *O-namae wa dō' hatsuon-shima'su ka?* お名前はどう発音しますか.

pronunciation *hatsuon* 発音

proof (evidence) *shōko* 証拠 There is no proof. *Shōko ga na'i.* 証拠がない.

propaganda *senden* 宣伝

proper *tekitō* [na] 適当[な] I couldn't find the proper word. *Tekitō na kotoba' ga mitsukarana'katta.* 適当な言葉が見つからなかった. ——(attr) *kichi'nto-shita* きちんとした the proper way *kichi'nto-shita yari'kata* きちんとしたやり方

properly *kichi'nto* きちんと Do it properly! *Kichi'nto shinasa'i!* きちんとしなさい.

property 1 *za'isan* 財産 **2** possessions *shoyū'butsu* 所有物

prophecy *yogen* 予言

prophesy obj *o* (irr) *yogen-suru* 予言する

prophet *yoge'nsha* 予言者

proposal 1 (marriage) *puropō'zu* プロポーズ **2** plan; suggestion *teian* 提案

propose ind-obj *ni*, obj *o* (v) **1** (marriage) (irr) *puropōˈzu-suru* プロポーズする **2** suggest *mōshideˈ·ru* 申し出る; (irr) *teian-suru* 提案する

prose *sambun* 散文

prosecution 1 *kisoˈ* 起訴; *kokuhatsu* 告発 **2** the prosecution *kensatsu* 検察

prosecutor (Leg) *keˈnji* 検事

prospects *mikomi* 見込み Prospects are poor. *Mikomi wa amari naˈi.* 見込みはあまりない.

prosper (irr) *haˈnjō-suru* 繁盛する

prosperity *han'ei* 繁栄

prosperous *sakan* [*na*] 盛ん[な] a prosperous enterprise *sakan na jiˈgyō* 盛んな事業

prostate gland *zenritsusen* 前立腺

prostitute *baishuˈnfu* 売春婦; *shōˈfu* 娼婦

protect obj *o* (v) *mamoˈr·u* 守る protect from danger *kiken kara mamoˈr·u* 危険から守る; (irr) *hoˈgo-suru* 保護する protect domestic industry *kokunai saˈngyō o hoˈgo-suru* 国内産業を保護する

protection *hoˈgo* 保護 police protection *keisatsu no hoˈgo* 警察の保護

protein *taˈmpaku* 蛋白; *tampakuˈshitsu* 蛋白質

protest *kōˈgi* 抗議 register a protest *kōˈgi o mōshideˈr·u* 抗議を申し出る ——obj *o* (irr) *kōˈgi-suru* 抗議する

Protestant (person) *Puroteˈsutanto* プロテスタント; *Shinkyōˈto* 新教徒

proud 1 (attr) *hokoriˈ o moˈtta* 誇りを持った; *o-tokuˈi no* お得意の **2** haughty *kōman* [*na*] 高慢[な] a proud person *kōman na hito* 高慢な人 ——obj *o* (v) be proud *tokuigaˈr·u* 得意がる; (irr) *jiman-suru* 自慢する

prove ind-obj *ni*, obj *o* (irr) *shōmei-suru* 証明する prove a person's innocence *muˈzai o shōmei-suru* 無罪を証明する prove a theory *gakusetsu o shōmei-suru* 学説を証明する

proverb *kotowaza* ことわざ

prune obj *o* (v) *kiritor·u* 切り取る

prune (dried plum) **1** *kansō puˈramu* 乾燥プラム **2** (stewed) *nikomi puˈramu* 煮こみプラム

pruning shears *sentei-baˈsami* せん定ばさみ

psalm (Bible) *shiˈhen* 詩編

psoriasis *kansen* かんせん

psychiatrist *seishinkaˈ·i* 精神科医

psychiatry *seishin byōriˈgaku* 精神病理学

psychologist *shinrigaˈkusha* 心理学者

psychology *shinriˈgaku* 心理学

puberty   1 *toshigoro* 年頃   2 adolescence *shishu′nki* 思春期; *sei-shu′nki* 青春期

pubic region   *i′mbu* 陰部

public   1 *ōyake [no]* 公[の]; *kōritsu [no]* 公立[の] public school *kōritsu ga′kkō* 公立学校   2 public opinion *se′ron* 世論 public opinion poll *seron chō′sa* 世論調査

publication   1 *shuppan* 出版   2 published matter *shunppa′mbutsu* 出版物

publicity   *senden* 宣伝; *kōkoku* 広告

publicize   obj *o* (irr) *senden-suru* 宣伝する

public office   *yakusho* 役所

public relations   *kō′hō* 広報; *pī-ā′ru* ピーアール; PR

publish   obj *o* (irr) *shuppan-suru* 出版する; *hakkō-suru* 発行する

publisher   *shuppa′nsha* 出版社; *hakkōsho′* 発行所

pudding   *pu′rin* プリン

puddle   *mizutamari* 水たまり

pull   obj *o* (v)   1 *hik·u* 引く   2 (with a rope, etc.) *hippa′r·u* 引っぱる   3 pull out *nuk·u* 抜く

pulpit   *sekkyōdan* 説教壇

pulse   *myaku′* 脈 take one's pulse *myaku′o to′ru* 脈をとる Your pulse is rapid. *Myaku′ga haya′i.* 脈が速い。

pulverize   (idiom) *kona′ ni suru* 粉にする

pump   1 (for air) *kūki-i′re* 空気入れ   2 (for liquid) *po′mpu* ポンプ ——obj *o* (v) *kumiage′·ru* 汲み上げる pump water *mizu o kumiage′ru* 水を汲み上げる ——(idiom) pump air *kū′ki o ireru* 空気を入れる

pumpkin   *kabocha* かぼちゃ

pun   *share* しゃれ make a pun *share o iu* しゃれを言う

punch   obj *o* (v) *nagu′r·u* なぐる

punctual   [*jikan ni ka′nshite*] *kichōmen [na]* [時間に関して]きちょうめん[な] She is punctual. *Ka′nojo wa jikan ni ka′nshite kichō′men desu.* 彼女は時間に関してきちょうめんです。

puncture   *panku* パンク ——(irr) be/become punctured *panku-suru* パンクする

punish   obj *o* (irr) *bassuru* 罰する

punishment   *ba′tsu* 罰

pupil   1 student *se′ito* 生徒   2 (eye) *hitomi* 瞳

puppet   1 hand puppet *yubi ni′ngyō* 指人形   2 marionette *ayatsuri ni′ngyō* あやつり人形

puppy   *koinu* 子犬

purchase   *kaimono* 買い物; *kōnyū* 購入 ——obj *o* (v) *ka·u* 買う Where did you purchase that? *Sore o do′ko de kaima′shita ka?* それをどこで買いましたか。

pure 1 *junsui* [*no*] 純粋[の] 2 naive *junshin* [*na*] 純真[な] a pure heart *junshin na kokoro* 純真な心

purebred *junketsu* [*no*] 純血[の]

purity *seijunsa* 清純さ

purple *mura'saki* 紫; *murasaki-iro* 紫色 ——(attr) *murasaki-iro no* 紫色の

purpose *mokuteki* 目的 have a purpose *mokuteki ga a'ru* 目的がある

purposely *waza'waza* わざわざ I went there purposely to buy it, but the store was closed. *Waza'waza kai ni itta no ni, mise' ga shima'tte ita.* わざわざ買いに行ったのに、店がしまっていた.

purse 1 *saifu* 財布 2 (handbag) *handoba'ggu* ハンドバッグ

pursue compl *ni* (v) 1 *o·u* 追う 2 chase *oikake'·ru* 追いかける

pursuit *tsuikyū* 追求

pus *umi'* 膿

push obj *o* (v) *os·u* 押す Don't push! *Osana'ide!* 押さないで.

put obj *o* (v) *ok·u* 置く Put it here. *Koko ni oite kudasa'i.* ここに置いて下さい.

put away (store) obj *o* (v) *shima·u* しまう Put it away in the closet. *Oshiire ni shimatte kudasa'i.* 押し入れにしまって下さい.

put back obj *o* (v) *modo's·u* 戻す

put down obj *o* (v) *oro's·u* 降ろす

put in obj *o* (v) *ire·ru* 入れる I put in ¥200, but the ticket didn't come out. *Nihyaku-en ireta'n desu ga, kippu wa de'te kimase'n deshita.* 二百円入れたんですが、切符は出てきませんでした.

put off postpone obj *o* (irr) *enki-suru* 延期する ——(idiom) *atoma'washi ni suru* 後回しにする

put on (clothing) obj *o* (v) *ki·ru* 着る Wait a minute. I'm going to put on my coat. *Cho'tto ma'tte kudasai, kō'to o kima'su kara.* ちょっと待って下さい、コートを着ますから.; (shoes, pants, etc.) *hak·u* 履く

put out obj *o* (v) *da's·u* 出す Put the garbage out! *Gomi' o da'- shite kudasa'i!* ゴミを出して下さい. 2 extinguish *kes·u* 消す Did you put out the fire? *Hi'o keshima'shita ka?* 火を消しましたか. ——compl *ni* (irr) be disturbed; annoyed *dōyō-suru* 動揺する He was put out about my promotion. *Ka're wa watashi no shōshin ni dōyō-shita.* 彼は私の昇進に動揺した. ——(idiom) inconvenience *me'iwaku o kake'·ru* 迷惑をかける I hate to put you out, but will you take me to the station? *Go-me'iwaku deshō ga, e'ki made tsurete itte itadakemase'n ka?* ご迷惑でしょうが、駅まで連れて行っていただけませんか.

puzzle 1 game *pa'zuru* パズル 2 jigsaw puzzle *hame-e* はめ絵; *jigusō pa'zuru* ジグソーパズル 3 riddle *nazo* 謎

pyramid *pirami'ddo* ピラミッド

Q

quack (duck's cry) *gā′gā* ガーガー

quack *yabu-* 藪 quack (doctor) *yabu-isha* 藪医者

quadrant *shibu′n-en* 四分円

quail *uzura* うずら

quaint (adj) *omoshiro′·i* 面白い, What a quaint carving! *Na′nte omoshiro′i chōkoku na′n deshō!* なんて面白い彫刻なんでしょう. ——(attr) *ki′myō* [na] 奇妙[な] quaint customs *ki′myō na shūkan* 奇妙な習慣

qualification *shikaku* 資格 have no qualifications *shikaku ga na′i* 資格がない

qualitative analysis *teisei bu′nseki* 定性分析

quality **1** *shitsu* 質 a thing of good quality *shitsu no i′i mono* 質のいい物 **2** value *ka′chi* 価値 a thing of quality *ka′chi no a′ru mono* 価値のある物

quantitative analysis *teiryō bu′nseki* 定量分析

quantity *ryō′* 量 measure in terms of quantity *ryō′ de haka′ru* 量で計る We ought to have a large quantity. *Ryō′ ga ō′i hō ga i′i.* 量が多い方がいい.

quantum theory *ryōshi′ron* 量子論

quarantine **1** *ken′eki* 検疫 a ship under quarantine *ken′eki te′isen* 検疫停船 **2** hospital isolation ward *kakuri byō′tō* 隔離病棟

quarrel *kenka* けんか heated quarrel *kuchi-ge′nka* 口げんか ——comp *to* (irr) *kenka-suru* けんかする I quarreled with Mr. Tanaka. *Tanaka-san to kenka-shita′.* 田中さんとけんかした.

quarter 1 one-quarter *yombun no ichi* 四分の一 three-quarters *yombun no san* 四分の三 **2** a quarter of an hour *jū′gofun* 十五分; *jūgo-fu′nkan* 十五分間

quartet 1 (vocal) *shijū′shō* 四重唱 **2** (instrumental) *shijū′sō* 四重奏

quartz *su′ishō* 水晶

queen 1 *joō′* 女王 Queen Elizabeth *Erizabesu Joō′* エリザベス女王 **2** (face card) *kui′n* クイーン

queer *he′n* [na] 変[な] That's queer! *He′n da na′!* 変だな. He had a queer expression on his face. *Ka′re wa he′n na kao o shite ita.* 彼は変な顔をしていた. ——(adj) *okashi′·i* おかしい How queer! *Na′nte okashi′i!* なんておかしい.

question *shitsumon* 質問 Are there any questions? *Shitsumon ga arima′su ka?* 質問がありますか. ——obj *o* (irr) *shitsumon-suru* 質問する My students questioned me for an hour about my impression of Chinese students. *Gakusei wa ichiji′kan mo Chū′goku no gakusei ni taisuru watashi no inshō ni tsu′ite shitsumon-shita.* 学生は一時間も中国の学生に対する私の印象について質問した.

——(idiom) raise a question about *gimon ni suru* 疑問にする

questionable (adj) *utagawashi'·i* 疑わしい questionable behavior *utagawashi'i kōdō* 疑わしい行動 ——(attr) *gimon no a'ru* 疑問のある questionable policy *gimon no a'ru seisaku* 疑問のある政策

question mark *gimo'n-fu* 疑問符

quick (adj) *haya'·i* 速い

quick-freeze obj *o* (irr) *kyūsoku re'itō-suru* 急速冷凍する

quickly *iso'ide* 急いで Come quickly! *Iso'ide kite kudasa'i!* 急いで来て下さい.

quick-tempered *ta'nki* [na] 短気[な] ——(adj) *okorippo'·i* 怒りっぽい

quiet *shizuke'sa* 静けさ ——(attr) *shi'zuka* [na] 静か[な] a quiet place *shi'zuka na tokoro'* 静かな所

Quiet! *Shi'zuka ni [shite kudasa'i]!* 静かに[して下さい].

quietly *shi'zuka ni* 静かに Walk quietly, please. *Shi'zuka ni aru'ite kudasa'i.* 静かに歩いて下さい.

quilt *futon* 蒲団

quit (v) *yam·u* やむ It's quit raining. *A'me ga yanda.* 雨がやんだ. ——obj *o* (v) *yame·ru* やめる She quit the company. *Ka'nojo wa kaisha o yameta.* 彼女は会社をやめた. I quit smoking. *Tabako o yameta.* たばこをやめた.

quite *sōtō* 相当 It'll probably take quite a bit of time. *Sōtō jikan ga kaka'ru deshō.* 相当時間がかかるでしょう.; *daibu* 大分 He was quite late. *Ka're wa daibu oso'katta.* 彼は大分遅かった.

quota *buntan* 分担 this year's quota *kotoshi no buntan* 今年の分担

quotation *in'yō* 引用 a quotation from Shakespeare *Shēkusu'pia kara no in'yō* シェークスピアからの引用

quote obj *o* (irr) *in'yō-suru* 引用する To quote Shakespeare... *Shēkusu'pia kara in'yō-suru to...* シェークスピアから引用すると...

R

rabbi *ra'bi* ラビ

rabbit *usagi* 兎

rabid *kyōkembyō no* 狂犬病の

rabies *kyōkembyō* 狂犬病

race 1 (human) *jinshu* 人種 2 contest *kyōsō* 競争; *kyō'gi* 競技 3 (horse) *keiba* 競馬 4 (bicycle) *keirin* 競輪 5 (automobile) *kā rēsu* カーレース; *jidōsha rē'su* 自動車レース 6 (foot) *toho kyōsō* 徒歩競走

race track 1 (horseracing) *keiba-jō* 競馬場 **2** (bike racing) *keirin-jō* 競輪場 **3** (car racing) *rēsu-jō* レース場

rack 1 (pipe) *pa'ipu-tate* パイプ立て **2** (towel) *taoru'-kake* タオル掛け

racket (tennis) *rake'tto* ラケット

radar *rē'dā* レーダー

radial 1 *hōshajō* [*no*] 放射状[の] **2** radial tire *rajiaru ta'iya* ラジアルタイヤ

radiation 1 *hōsha* 放射 **2** (heat) *fukusha' netsu* 輻射熱 **3** (solar) *taiyō fukusha' netsu* 太陽輻射熱

radical 1 extreme *kyūshin*[*teki*] [*na*] 急進[的][な] radical ideas *kyūshin shi'sō* 急進思想 **2** revolutionary *kakumeiteki* [*na*] 革命的[な]

Radical *kyūshin-shugi'sha* 急進主義者

radio 1 *ra'jio* ラジオ **2** (transistorized) *toranjisutā ra'jio* トランジスターラジオ **3** (shortwave) *tampa hō'sō* 短波放送

radioactive *hōshasei* [*no*] 放射性[の]

radioactive fallout *hōshasei kōka'butsu* 放射性降下物 ——(idiom) (lit., ashes of death) *shi' no hai* 死の灰

radio announcer *rajio ana'unsā* ラジオアナウンサー

radio station *rajio hōsō'kyoku* ラジオ放送局

radio wave *de'mpa* 電波

radish *hatsuka da'ikon* 二十日大根

radium *raju'mu* ラジウム radium therapy *rajūmu ryō'hō* ラジウム療法

raft *ikada* いかだ

rag 1 *bo'ro* ぼろ **2** cleaning rag *zōkin* 雑巾

rail 1 guardrail *tesuri* 手すり **2** railroad track *se'nro* 線路

railroad 1 *tetsudō* 鉄道 **2** (private) *shitetsu* 私鉄 **3** (government) *kokuyū te'tsudō* 国有鉄道

railroad car 1 *[sha]ryō* [車]両 railroad car no. 5 *goryō-me* 五両目 **2** passenger car *kyakusha* 客車

railroad crossing *fumikiri* 踏切

railroad station *e'ki* 駅 Where is the railroad station? *E'ki wa do'chira desu ka?* 駅はどちらですか。

railroad track [*tetsudō*] *se'nro* [鉄道]線路

railroad underpass *ga'do* ガード

rain *a'me* 雨 ——(idiom) to rain *a'me ga fu'r·u* 雨が降る It rained last night. *Yūbe a'me ga fu'tta.* ゆうべ雨が降った。

rainbow *niji* 虹

raincoat *rēnkō'to* レーンコート; *kappa* かっぱ

rainfall *u'ryō* 雨量

rainstorm 1 *bōfū'-u* 暴風雨 **2** heavy rain *ōa'me* 大雨

rainwater *ama'mizu* 雨水

rainy season *tsuyu* 梅雨 The rainy season is over. *Tsuyu ga aketa.* 梅雨が明けた.

raise salary increase *bēsu-a'ppu* ベースアップ ——obj *o* (v) **1** *age·ru* 上げる raise one's voice *ko'e o ageru* 声を上げる Shall I raise the shades? *Buraindo o agemashō' ka?* ブラインドを上げましょうか. **2** (irr) *ta'kaku-suru* 高くする Could you raise (the height of) this mirror a little? *Kono kagami'o sukoshi ta'kaku-shite kudaisaimase'n ka?* この鏡を少し高くして下さいませんか. **3** rear *sodate'·ru* 育てる ——(pass) be raised *sodaterare'·ru* 育てられる I was raised by my grandmother. *Obā'-san ni sodatera'reta.* おばあさんに育てられた. **4** keep (animals) *ka'·u* 飼う They raise chickens. *Niwatori o ka'tte iru.* 鶏を飼っている. **5** raise a problem *oko's·u* 起こす We tried not to raise any unnecessary problems. *Fuhitsu'yō na mondai o okosana'i yō ni do'ryoku-shita.* 不必要な問題を起こさないように努力した.

raisin *hoshi-bu'dō* 干しぶどう; *rē'zun* レーズン

rake 1 (bamboo) *kumade* くまで **2** (metal) *rē'ki* レーキ ——obj *o* (v) *kakiatsume'·ru* かき集める

ramp *ra'mpu* ランプ

ranch *bokujō* 牧場

random *detarame* [*no*] でたらめ[の] ——(adv) at random *detarame ni* でたらめに

range 1 *re'nji* レンジ gas range *gasu re'nji* ガスレンジ **2** extent *ha'n'i* 範囲

rank (status) *chi'i* 地位

rape 1 (plant) *na'-no-hana* 菜の花 **2** sexual assault *bōkō* 暴行 ——obj *o* (irr) (Leg) *gōkan-suru* 強姦する

rapeseed *natane* 菜種 rapeseed oil *natane a'bura* 菜種油

rapidly *ha'yaku* 速く The work is progressing rapidly. *Shigoto ga ha'yaku susunde iru.* 仕事が速く進んでいる.

rapport *itchi* 一致 ——(irr) have rapport *itchi-suru* 一致する We have good rapport. *I'ken ga itchi-shite i'ru.* 意見が一致している.

rapprochement *shinzen* 親善; *shinkō kaifuku* 親交回復 *see also* reconciliation

rare *mare* [*na*] 稀[な] A movie that's worth seeing is rare. *Mi'ru ka'chi no aru eiga wa mare de'su.* 見る価値のある映画は稀です. ——(adj) *mezurashi'·i* 珍しい This is a rare gem. *Kore wa mezurashi'i ishi' desu.* これは珍しい石です.

rare (underdone) *nama-yake* [*no*] 生焼け[の]

rarely *me'tta ni* [+neg] めったに I rarely see him. *Ka're ni wa me'tta ni awa'nai.* 彼にはめったに会わない.

rash (on the skin) *hosshin*; *hasshin* 発疹

rasp *ishime ya'suri* 石目やすり

rasping 1 *mimiza'wari* [*na*] 耳障り[な] a rasping voice *mimiza'wari* *na ko'e* 耳障りな声 **2** (sound) *gi'gi* [to] ギーギー[と] a rasping sound *gi'gi to iu oto'* ギーギーという音

rat *nezumi* 鼠; *dobune'zumi* どぶ鼠

rate 1 exchange rate *kawase so'ba* 為替相場 **2** percentage *hiritsu* 比率 **3** frequency *hi'ndo* 頻度 ——obj *o* (irr) *hyō'ka-suru* 評価する How do you rate this? *Kore o dō' hyō'ka-shimasu ka?* これをどう評価しますか. ——(adv) at any rate *to'nikaku* とにかく ——(idiom) rate of speed *ha'yasa* 速さ at a rate of 80 km/hr *hachi-ju'kkiro no ha'yasa de* 80 キロの速さで

rather (somewhat) *ka'nari* かなり rather cold *ka'nari samu'i* かなり寒い

rather than *mu'shiro...[no] hō* むしろ...[の]方 I'd rather die than do that. *Sonna koto o suru kura'i nara, mu'shiro shinda hō' ga i'i.* そんな事をするくらいならむしろ死んだ方がいい.

rating 1 *i'chi* 位置 **2** evaluation *hyō'ka* 評価

ratio 1 proportion *wariai* 割合 **2** percentage *hiritsu* 比率

ration *haikyū* 配給 ——obj *o* (irr) *haikyū-suru* 配給する

rational 1 logical *gōriteki* [na] 合理的[な] a rational conclusion *gōriteki na ketsuron* 合理的な結論 **2** (having or showing reason) *riseiteki* [na] 理性的[な]

rat poison *neko-i'razu* 猫入らず

rattan *tō'* 籐

rattle 1 (child's toy) *garagara'* がらがら **2** (noise) *ga'tagata* がたがた ——(irr) *ga'tagata-suru* がたがたする

rattlesnake *garagara he'bi* がらがら蛇

rattrap *nezumi'tori* 鼠取り

raven *ōga'rasu* 大烏

raw *na'ma* [no] 生[の] raw egg *nama ta'mago* 生卵

rayon *rē'yon* レーヨン; *jinken* 人絹

razor *kamiso'ri* かみそり electric razor *denki ka'misori* 電気かみそり

razor blade *kamiso'ri no ha'* かみそりの刃

reach (v) arrive at *tsuk·u'* 着く When will you reach San Francisco? *I'tsu San Furanshi'suko ni tsukima'su ka?* いつサンフランシスコに着きますか. **2** extend to *todo'k·u* 届く Can you reach the top shelf? *Ue no tana ni te' ga todokima'su ka?* 上の棚に手が届きますか. ——ind-obj *ni* (irr) make contact with (a person) *renraku-suru* 連絡する I couldn't reach Mr. Tanaka. *Tanaka-san ni renraku-suru koto' ga deki'nakatta.* 田中さんに連絡することができなかった.

reaction *hannō* 反応 nuclear reaction *kaku ha'nnō* 核反応 What was the university president's reaction to the proposal? *Sono teian ni tsu'ite gakuchō no hannō wa dō' deshita ka?* その提案について学長の反応はどうでしたか.

read   ind-obj *ni*, obj *o* (v) *yo'm·u* 読む read a book *ho'n o yo'mu* 本を読む ——(pot) be able to read *yome'·ru* 読める Can you read Japanese? *Nihon-go ga yomema'su ka?* 日本語が読めますか.

reader (schoolbook)   *tokuhon* 読本; *ri'da* リーダー

reading   *do'kusho* 読書

ready   (idiom) **1** be ready [*shitaku ga*] *dekima'shita/de'kite i·ru* [支度が]できました/できている Are you ready to go? *Iku shitaku ga dekima'shita ka?* 行く支度ができましたか. Is supper ready? *Yū-shoku ga de'kite imasu ka?* 夕食ができていますか. **2** make ready *ju'mbi o suru* 準備をする I have to get ready to entertain guests. *Raikyaku o motenasu ju'mbi o shina'kereba nara'nai.* 来客をもてなす準備をしなければならない.

ready-made   *kisei [no]* 既製[の] ready-made clothing *kise'i fuku* 既製服

ready-to-wear   *dekiai [no]* できあい[の]

real   *hommono [no]* 本物[の] a real diamond *hommono no daiya-mo'ndo* 本物のダイヤモンド

real estate   *fudō'san* 不動産

realist   *genjitsushugi'sha* 現実主義者

realistic   *genjitsuteki [na]* 現実的[な]   ——(attr) feasible *jikkō-shiuru* 実行しうる

reality   *genjitsu* 現実

realization   *jitsugen* 実現

realize   (irr) *jitsugen-suru* 実現する   ——(idiom) *ki ga' tsuk·u* 気が付く I didn't realize it. *Ki ga tsuka'nakatta.* 気が付かなかった. *see also* know; understand

really   *hontō ni* 本当に Do you really think so? *Hontō ni sō omoi-ma'su ka?* 本当にそう思いますか.

Really?   *Hontō?* 本当.

realtor   *fudōsan'ya* 不動産屋

realty   *fudō'san* 不動産

reap   obj *o* (v) *kari-ire'·ru* 刈り入れる

rear   *ushiro* 後ろ

rearview mirror   *bakku mi'rā* バックミラー

reason   **1** rationality *ri'sei* 理性 **2** factor *gen'in* 原因 **3** purpose *riyū* 理由 without reason *riyū na'shi* 理由なし I don't understand the reason. *Riyū ga wakara'nai.* 理由がわからない. **4** explanation *wa'ke* 訳 for some reason or other *dō' iu wa'ke ka...* どういう訳か... ——(caus) reason with (cause someone to comply) *nattoku-sase'·ru* 納得させる ——(idiom) **1** The reason is that... *Na'ze nara...* なぜなら...; *Na'ze ka to iu to...* なぜかというと... **2** For some reason or other... *Dō' shita koto' ka...* どうしたことか...

reasonable   *gōriteki [na]* 合理的[な]

rebellion 1 resistance; opposition *hampatsu* 反発; *hankō* 反抗 2 uprising *hanran* 反乱

rebound (v) *haneka´e·ru* はね返る

recall obj *o* (v) *omoida´s·u* 思い出す ——(pot) *omoidase´·ru* 思い出せる I can't recall. *Sore ga omoidase´nai.* それが思い出せない.

receipt *ryōshūsho* 領収書; *uketori* [*-sho*] 受取[書]; *reshi´to* レシート...

receive ind-obj *ni*, obj *o* (v) 1 *mora·u* もらう Whom did you receive that from? *Da´re ni sore o moraima´shita ka?* だれにそれをもらいましたか. 2 *uke´·ru* 受ける receive a telephone call *denwa o uke´ru* 電話を受ける He received his elementary education in America. *Ka´re wa Amerika de shotō kyō´iku o u´keta.* 彼はアメリカで初等教育を受けた. 3 (from a superior) *itadak·u* いただく I received this pen from the teacher. *Kono pe´n o sense´i ni itadaita.* このペンを先生にいただいた. 4 obtain *e´·ru* 得る receive permission *kyo´ka o e´ru* 許可を得る

receiver 1 telephone receiver *juwa´ki* 受話器 2 addressee *uketorinin* 受取人 3 person who receives *uketoru hito´* 受け取る人 receiver of a gift *pure´zento o uketoru hito´* プレゼントを受け取る人 4 (in sports) *reshi´bā* レシーバー

recent *saikin* [*no*] 最近[の] Do you have any recent news from America? *Saikin no Amerika no nyū´su ga arima´su ka?* 最近のアメリカのニュースがありますか.

recently *saikin* 最近; *chika´goro* 近頃; *konogoro* このごろ I have not seen her recently. *Konogoro ka´nojo ni awa´nai.* このごろ彼女に会わない.

recipe *chōrihō* 調理法

recite (irr) *anshō-suru* 暗誦する

reckless 1 *mu´cha na* [*na*] むちゃな do a reckless thing *mu´cha na koto´ o suru* むちゃな事をする 2 *mukō´mizu* [*na*] 向こう見ず[な] a reckless adventure *mukō´mizu na bōken* 向こう見ずな冒険

reckless driving *bōsō* 暴走

reclamation 1 (filling in of coastland) *umetate* 埋め立て 2 (clearing of forest land) *kaitaku* 開拓

recognize obj *o* (v) *mitome·ru* 認める He doesn't recognize me as a colleague. *Ka´re wa watashi o dōryō to shite mitomete kurena´i.* 彼は私を同僚として認めてくれない. ——(idiom) *ki ga´ tsuk·u* 気が付く I didn't recognize you. *Ana´ta da to ki ga tsuka´nakatta.* あなただと気が付かなかった.

recollection *kioku* 記憶 I have no recollection of it. *Sō iu kioku wa na´i.* そういう記憶はない.

recommend obj *o* (v) *susume·ru* 勧める; (irr) *suisen-suru* 推薦する Would you recommend a good hotel? *I´i hoteru o suisen-shite* *kuremase′n ka?* いいホテルを推薦してくれませんか. ——(pass) be recommended *suisen-sare′·ru* 推薦される He was recommended for this position. *Ka′re wa kono sho′kumu ni suisen-sa′reta.* 彼はこの職務に推薦された.

recommendation *suisen* 推薦 a letter of recommendation *suisenjō* 推薦状; *assen* 斡旋 a job recommendation *shūshoku no assen* 就職の斡旋

reconcile obj *o* (caus) *wakai-sase·ru* 和解させる

reconciliation *wakai* 和解

record 1 an account *kiroku* 記録 an accurate record *seikaku na kiroku* 正確な記録 **2** the best performance, etc., officially recorded *kiroku* 記録 a new record *shin-ki′roku* 新記録 **3** phonograph record *rekō′do* レコード 45-RPM record *yo′njūgo ka′iten rekō′do* 45回転レコード long-playing record *erupi′* LP ——obj *o* (irr) make a sound recording *rokuon-suru* 録音する ——(idiom) **1** put on record *kiroku ni todo′mete ok·u* 記録にとどめておく **2** on record *kiroku ni notte i·ru* 記録にのっている

recording (disc, tape) *rokuon* 録音

record player [*rekōdo*] *purē′yā* [レコード] プレーヤー

recover (from an illness) (v) [*byōki ga*] *nao′r·u* [病気が]治る Have you recovered from your cold? *Kaze ga naorima′shita ka?* 風邪が治りましたか.; (irr) *kaifuku-suru* 回復する You'll soon recover. *Su′gu kaifuku-suru deshō.* すぐ回復するでしょう.

recreation *rekurie′shon* レクリエーション

rectangle *chōhōkei* 長方形

rectum (Anat) *chokuchō* 直腸; *kōmon* 肛門

recuperate (irr) *hoyō-suru* 保養する; *kaifuku-suru* 回復する

recuperation *hoyō* 保養; *kaifuku* 回復

recycle obj *o* (irr) *saisei-suru* 再生する

red 1 *a′ka* 赤 **2** bright red *makka′* 真赤 ——(adj) *aka·i* 赤い a red dress *akai do′resu* 赤いドレス The cover of the book is red. *Ho′n no hyōshi′ ga aka′i.* 本の表紙が赤い. ——(idiom) in the red *akaji* 赤字

Red (communist) *A′ka* 赤

redcap *akabō* 赤帽

Red Cross *Sekijūji* 赤十字 Red Cross Hospital *Sekijūji Byō′in* 赤十字病院

redhead *akage* 赤毛

red ink *akaji* 赤字

red light *aka shi′ngō* 赤信号

red pepper *tōga′rashi* 唐辛子

red tape *oyakusho shi′goto* お役所仕事

reduce obj *o* (v) **1** (in quantity) *heras·u* 減らす Reduce the amount of meat and increase the amount of vegetables you eat. *Niku′ o* *herashite, yasai o mo'tto tabenasa'i.* 肉を減らして，野菜をもっと食べなさい． **2** (in size) (irr) *shukushō-suru* 縮小する reduce the size of a photograph *shashin o shukushō-suru* 写真を縮小する **3** (in price) *waribi'k·u* 割り引く They reduced the price for me. *Nedan o waribi'ite kureta.* 値段を割り引いてくれた．

reduction 1 (in quantity) *genshō* 減少 **2** (in size) *shukushō* 縮小 **3** (in price) *waribiki* 割引

reed *a'shi* 葦

reel (fishing; tape) *riru* リール

reentry (into a country) *sainyū'koku* 再入国 reentry permit *sainyū'koku kyoka'sho* 再入国許可書

reference book *sankōsho* 参考書

refer to 1 obj *o* (irr) *sanshō-suru* 参照する refer to a written source *bunken o sanshō-suru* 文献を参照する **2** direct to loc *ni* (irr) *shōkai-suru* 照会する Let me refer that to a specialist in the field. *Sono bu'n'ya no semmonka ni shōkai-shimashō.* その分野の専門家に照会しましょう．

refine obj *o* (irr) *senren-suru* 洗練する ——(pass) be/become refined *senren-sare·ru* 洗練される a refined person *senren-sareta hito'* 洗練された人

reflect obj *o* (irr) **1** (light; sound; heat) *hansha-suru* 反射する The moon reflects the light of the sun. *Tsuki' wa ta'iyō no hikari' o hansha-suru.* 月は太陽の光を反射する． **2** contemplate *hansei-suru* 反省する reflect on one's conduct *ji'ko no kō'i o hansei-suru* 自己の行為を反省する ——(v) look back *kaerimi'·ru* 顧みる; *furika'ette mi'·ru* 振り返って見る When I reflect, I realize we had many misunderstandings. *Furika'ette miru to, wata'shitachi no aida ni gokai ga o'katta.* 振り返って見ると，私たちの間に誤解が多かった． **2** be reflected *utsu'r·u* 映る be reflected in a mirror *kagami' ni utsu'ru* 鏡に映る **3** be expressed (irr) *han'ei-suru* 反映する Public opinion is reflected in the National Diet. *Kokumin no se'ron wa gi'kai ni han'ei-suru.* 国民の世論は議会に反映する．

reflection 1 reflected image *ka'ge* 影 **2** (light; sound; heat) *hansha* 反射 **3** introspection *hansei* 反省 **4** expression *han'ei* 反映

reform obj *o* (irr) *kaikaku-suru* 改革する

reformation *kaikaku* 改革

refreshing *sawa'yaka* [*na*] さわやか[な]

refreshments *seiryō i'nryō* 清涼飲料

refrigerator *reizo'ko* 冷蔵庫

refugee *nammin* 難民; (political) *bōme'isha* 亡命者

refund *haraimodoshi* 払い戻し ——obj *o* (v) *haraimodo's·u* 払い戻す

refusal *kyo'hi* 拒否

refuse obj *o* (v) **1** decline *kotowa'r·u* 断る He refused the appointment. *Ka're wa ninmei o kotowa'tta.* 彼は任命を断った. **2** deny (irr) *kyo'hi-suru* 拒否する refuse a request *yōkyū o kyo'hi-suru* 要求を拒否する **3** refuse to listen to *kikiirena'·i* 聞き入れない

region *chi'hō* 地方 the Kansai region *Kansai chi'hō* 関西地方

register cash register *re'ji* レジ ——obj *o* (v) **1** (irr) *tōroku-suru* 登録する register as a student in the university *gakusei to shite daigaku ni tōroku-suru* 学生として大学に登録する **2** record *todoke'·ru* 届ける ——(idiom) register the birth of a child *shusshō to'doke o dasu* 出生届をだす

registration *tōroku* 登録 alien registration *gaikokujin tō'roku* 外国人登録 alien registration certificate *gaikokujin tōroku shōme'isho* 外国人登録証明書; *todoke'* 届 birth registration *shusshō to'doke* 出生届

regret *kō'kai* 後悔 ——obj *o* (v) *kanashi'm·u* 悲しむ; (irr) *kō'kai-suru* 後悔する I don't regret it. *Sore o kō'kai-shite ina'i.* それを後悔していない.

regrettable *zanne'n [na]* 残念[な] It is regrettable that he cannot come. *Zanne'n na koto' ni ka're wa korare'nai.* 残念なことに彼は来られない. ——(adj) *oshi'·i* 惜しい I did a very regrettable thing. *Taihen oshi'i koto' o shita.* 大変惜しい事をした.

regrettably *zannen na'gara* 残念ながら Regrettably I must decline the invitation. *Zannen na'gara go-shō'tai o kotowara'nakereba nara'nai.* 残念ながら御招待を断らなければならない.

regular **1** ordinary *futsū [no]* 普通[の] the regular way of doing (something) *futsū no yarikata* 普通のやりかた **2** scheduled *teirei [no]* 定例[の] a regular meeting *teirei ka'igi* 定例会議

regulate obj *o* (irr) **1** adjust *chōsei-suru* 調整する regulate the temperature *o'ndo o chōsei-suru* 温度を調整する **2** control *tōsei-suru* 統制する regulate industry *sangyō o tōsei-suru* 産業を統制する **3** restrict *seige'n-suru* 制限する regulate the flow of traffic *kōtsū o seige'n-suru* 交通を制限する ——(idiom) *kagen o mi'·ru* かげんを見る regulate the temperature of the bathwater *o-yu no kagen o mi'ru* お湯のかげんを見る

regulation **1** adjustment *chōsei* 調整 **2** control *tōsei* 統制 **3** limitation *seige'n* 制限 **4** rule *ki'soku* 規則

rehearsal *rihā'saru* リハーサル

reheat obj *o* (v) *atatame'·ru* 暖める

reign *tō'chi* 統治 ——obj *o* (v) *osame'·ru* 治める

reincarnation *umarekawari* 生まれ変わり

reindeer *tona'kai* となかい

reins *tazuna* 手綱

reject obj *o* (irr) *kyo'hi-suru* 拒否する reject a proposal *teian o kyo'hi-suru* 提案を拒否する

rejection 1 exclusion *ha'ijo* 排除 2 refusal *kyo'hi* 拒否 3 rejection of a motion in parliamentary procedure *hiketsu* 否決

relapse *saihatsu* 再発

related (attr) 1 *kankei no a'ru* 関係のある a related problem *kankei no a'ru mondai* 関係のある問題 2 connected with... ...[*ni*] *kansu'ru* ...[に]関する Please investigate everything related to this problem. *Kono mondai ni kansuru arayu'ru koto' o shira'bete kudasa'i.* この問題に関するあらゆる事を調べて下さい.

relation 1 relatedness *kankei* 関係 interpersonal relations *ningen ka'nkei* 人間関係 That has no relation to this. *Sore wa kore ni kankei ga na'i.* それはこれに関係がない. 2 interaction *kōsai* 交際 relations with people *hito to' no kōsai* 人との交際 3 family relation *shinseki* 親戚; *shinrui* 親類

relax (v) 1 (irr) *nombi'ri-suru* のんびりする a relaxed mood *nombi'ri-shita ki'bun* のんびりした気分 2 make oneself at home *kutsuro'g·u* くつろぐ Sunday's the only day I can relax. *Nichiyō'bi dake' wa kutsuro'gu koto' ga deki'ru.* 日曜日だけはくつろぐことができる. ——obj *o* (v) *yawarage'·ru* 和らげる relax tension *kinchō o yawarage'ru* 緊張を和らげる

release *kaihō* 解放 ——obj *o* (irr) *kaihō-suru* 解放する

reliable (adj) *tanomoshi'·i* 頼もしい ——(idiom) be reliable *ate ni na'r·u* 当てになる She's not reliable. *Ka'nojo wa ate ni narana'i.* 彼女は当てにならない.

relic *ibutsu* 遺物

relieved (irr) be relieved *hotto-suru* ほっとする I was relieved. *Hotto-shita.* ほっとした.

religion *shū'kyō* 宗教 the religions of the world *se'kai no shū'kyō* 世界の宗教 new religion *shinkō shū'kyō* 新興宗教

religious (attr) *shūkyōteki* [*na*] 宗教的[な] ——(idiom) be religious *shūkyō'shin ga a'r·u* 宗教心がある He is religious. *Ka're wa shūkyō'shin ga a'ru.* 彼は宗教心がある.

relish (pickles) 1 (W) *pi'kurusu* ピクルス 2 (J) *tsukemono* 漬物

reluctant (idiom) *ki ga susumana·i* 気が進まない I'm reluctant to give an answer to that. *Sore ni kotae'ru no wa ki ga susumana'i.* それに答えるのは気が進まない.

rely on compl *ni*, obj *o* (v) *tayo'r·u* 頼る He relies on his son. *Ka're wa musuko o tayo'tte iru.* 彼は息子を頼っている.

remain (v) *noko'r·u* 残る There's no meat remaining. *Niku' wa noko'tte inai.* 肉は残っていない. Would you please remain after the others have gone? *Minna' ga ka'etta ato, noko'tte kudasaimase'n ka?* みんなが帰った後、残って下さいませんか.

remainder *nokori* 残り

remedy (for illness) 1 *i'yaku* 医薬 2 medicine *kusuri* 薬 see also treatment

remember obj *o* (v) **1** call to mind *omoida's·u* 思い出す Don't you remember? *Omoidashimase'n ka?* 思い出しませんか. **2** keep in mind *oboe'·ru* 覚える I remember clearly my first day in Japan. *Watashi wa Niho'n de no saisho no hi' o hakki'ri oboe'ete iru.* 私は日本での最初の日をはっきり覚えている. **3** remember nostalgically *natsukashi'm·u* 懐かしむ

remind obj *o* (v) **1** (irr) *sa'isoku-suru* 催促する Remind me of that tomorrow. *Ashita sore o sa'isoku-shite kudasa'i.* 明日それを催促して下さい. **2** put (one) in mind of something *omowase'·ru* 思わせる Florence reminds me of Kyoto. *Furo'rensu wa Kyō'to o omowase'ru.* フローレンスは京都を思わせる. ——(caus) remind (one) of *omoidasase'·ru* 思い出させる She reminds me of my mother. *Sono' hito wa ha'ha o omoidasase'ru.* その人は母を思い出させる.

remove obj *o* (v) **1** (irr) *jo'kyo-suru* 除去する remove an obstacle *jamamono o jo'kyo-suru* 邪魔物を除去する **2** eliminate *to'r·u* 取る Can I remove the stains with this? *Kore de shimi o to'ru koto ga dekima'su ka?* これで染みを取ることができますか.; *torisar·u* 取り去る All impurities have been removed. *Fuju'mbutsu wa su'bete torisatte aru.* 不純物はすべて取り去ってある. **3** erase; cross out (irr) *massho-suru* 抹消する I want these lines removed from the manuscript. *Genkō kara kono gyō' o massho-shite hoshi'i.* 原稿からこの行を抹消してほしい.

remover (solvent) *hakuri'zai* 剥離剤

rendezvous (idiom) *a'u yakusoku* 会う約束

renew obj *o* (irr) *kōshin-suru* 更新する

renewal *kōshin* 更新 When is the time for renewal of a driver's license? *Unten menkyo'shō no kōshin wa i'tsu desu ka?* 運転免許証の更新はいつですか.

rent **1** *ya'chin* 家賃 **2** (for a room) *heya-dai* 部屋代 ——obj *o* (v) *kari·ru* 借りる rent a room *heya' o kariru* 部屋を借りる

rental agent's fee *asse'nryō* 斡旋料; *tesu̅'ryō* 手数料

repaint obj *o* (v) *nurinao's·u* 塗りなおす

repair obj *o* (v) *nao's·u* 直す Would you repair this, please? *Kore o nao'shite itadakema'su ka?* これを直していただけますか.

reparations *baishō* 賠償

repeat obj *o* (v) *kurika'es·u* 繰り返す In the language lab we repeat words over and over again. *Ra'bo de wa kotoba' o na'nkai mo kurika'esu.* ラボでは言葉を何回も繰り返す.

repellent *bō-* 防- insect repellent *bōchūzai* 防虫剤 water-repellent cloth *bōsu'i-fu* 防水布

repent obj *o* (v) **1** (irr) *kō'kai-suru* 後悔する **2** (Chr) *kuiaratame'·ru* 悔い改める repent of one's sins *tsu'mi o kuiaratame'ru* 罪を悔い改める

replace *torikae·ru* 取り替える

reply *kota'e* 答え; *henji* 返事 By when do you need a reply? *I'tsu made ni henji'o sureba i'i desu ka?* いつまでに返事をすればいいですか. ——obj *o* (v) *kota'e·ru* 答える He didn't reply. *Ka're wa kota'e·nakatta.* 彼は答えなかった. ——(idiom) *henji'o suru* 返事をする I must reply to this letter right away. *Kono tegami wa su'gu henji' o shina'kereba nara'nai.* この手紙はすぐ返事をしなければならない.

report *repo'to* レポート; *hōkoku* 報告 interim report *chūkan hō'-koku* 中間報告

report card *seisekihyō* 成績表

reporter *ki'sha* 記者 newspaper reporter *shimbun ki'sha* 新聞記者

represent obj *o* (v) **1** (irr) *daihyō-suru* 代表する He represented Japan at the international conference. *Ka're wa Niho'n o daihyō-shite, kokusai ka'igi ni shusseki-shita.* 彼は日本を代表して国際会議に出席した. **2** symbolize *arawa's·u* 表す White represents purity. *Shi'ro wa junketsu o arawa'su.* 白は純潔を表す.

representative **1** (official) *daihyō* 代表 **2** (personal) *dairi* 代理 I'm Ms. Tanaka's representative. *Watashi wa Tanaka-san no dairi de'su.* 私は田中さんの代理です.

reproduce **1** bear offspring obj *o* (irr) *seishoku-suru* 生殖する **2** copy obj *o* (irr) *fukusei-suru* 複製する

reptile *hachū'rui* は虫類

republic *kyōwa'koku* 共和国

reputation *me'iyo* 名誉; *hyōban* 評判

request **1** desire *o-negai* お願い, grant one's request *o-negai o kiku* お願いを聞く refuse one's request *o-negai o kikiire'nai* お願いを聞き入れない **2** demand *yōkyū* 要求 a request for damages *songai ba'ishō no yōkyū* 損害賠償の要求 comply with a request *yōkyū ni ōjiru* 要求に応じる ——ind-obj *ni*, obj *o* (v) **1** *nega'·u* 願う I requested a six-month research leave. *Watashi wa rokka'-getsu no kenkyū kyū'ka o negaima'shita.* 私は六か月の研究休暇を願いました. **2** ask *tano'm·u* 頼む Shall we request Ms. Tanaka to do it? *Sore o Tanaka-san ni tanomimashō' ka?* それを田中さんに頼みましょうか. **3** demand (irr) *yōkyū-suru* 要求する The employees are requesting a ¥20,000 increase. *Shokui'n wa niman-en no bēsu a'ppu o yōkyū-shite iru.* 職員は二万円のベースアップを要求している. **4** beg *ko'·u* 請う request permission *kyo'ka o ko'u* 許可を請う

require *ir·u* 要る This document requires the section chief's signature. *Kono shorui wa kachō no shomei ga irima'su.* この書類は課長の署名が要ります. ——(idiom) *hitsuyō to suru* 必要とする

required *hisshū* [*no*] 必修[の] required course of study *hisshū ka'moku* 必修課目

rescue obj *o* (v) *tasuke′·ru* 助けるrescue a person from drowning *oboreru hito′o tasuke′r·u* 溺れる人を助ける ——(v) be rescued *tasuka′r·u* 助かる A hundred people were rescued. *Hito ga hyaku′nin tasuka′tta.* 人が百人助かった.

research *kenkyū* 研究 research topic *kenkyū te′ma* 研究テーマ joint research *kyōdō ke′nkyū* 共同研究 ——obj *o* (irr) *kenkyū-suru* 研究する

resemble compl *ni* (v) *ni·ru* 似る That person resembles Mr. Tanaka. *Sono′ hito wa Tanaka-san ni nite iru.* その人は田中さんに似ている.

resent obj *o* (v) *ura′m·u* 恨む She resents you. *Ka′nojo wa ana′ta o ura′nde iru.* 彼女はあなたを恨んでいる.

resentment *urami′* 恨み

reservation *yoyaku* 予約 hotel reservation *ho′teru no yoyaku* ホテルの予約

reserve obj *o* (irr) *yoyaku-suru* 予約する

reserved (adj) *uchitoke′na·i* 打ち解けない a reserved person *uchitoke′nai hito* 打ち解けない人 ——(attr) kept in reserve *shitei-* 指定 reserved seat *shite′i-seki* 指定席; *yoyaku-* 予約 reserved table *yoya′ku-seki* 予約席

residence *jūtaku* 住宅

residential area *jūta′kuchi* 住宅地

resign obj *o* (v) **1** (irr) (from a job) *jishoku-suru* 辞職する; (from a position) *jinin-suru* 辞任する **2** acquiesce *akirame′·ru* 諦める

resignation **1** *jishoku* 辞職 **2** letter of resignation *jihyō* 辞表 **3** acquiescence *akirame* 諦め

resist obj *o* (irr) *teikō-suru* 抵抗する

resolution (decision) *ke′tsugi* 決議

resort **1** health resort *hoyō′chi* 保養地 **2** ski resort *suki-jō* スキー場 **3** summer resort *hisho′chi* 避暑地 **4** recourse *te′* 手 They had no other resort but to use force. *Bō′ryoku no hoka′ ni te′ ga na′katta.* 暴力の外に手がなかった.

resources **1** *shi′gen* 資源 natural resources *tennen shi′gen* 天然資源 **2** (financial) *zaigen* 財源

respect *ke′ii* 敬意 pay respect *ke′ii o hara′u* 敬意を払う ——obj *o* (irr) *sonkei-suru* 尊敬する I respect my teacher. *Sense′i o sonkei-shite iru.* 先生を尊敬している.; *sonchō-suru* 尊重する I respect your opinion. *Ana′ta no i′ken o sonchō-suru.* あなたの意見を尊重する.

respected (pass) be respected *sonkei-sare′·ru* 尊敬される At least I want to be respected by my children. *Sukuna′kutomo jibun no kodomo ni′ wa sonkei-sareta′i to omo′u.* 少なくとも自分の子供には尊敬されたいと思う. ——(attr) *sonkei-sareta* 尊敬された a respected person *sonkei-sa′reta hito′* 尊敬された人

respectively *sore′zore* それぞれ Mr. Tanaka and Ms. Yamada took positions in a bank and a publishing firm, respectively. *Tanaka-san wa ginkō ni, Yamada-san wa shuppa′nsha ni sore′zore shūshoku-shita.* 田中さんは銀行に山田さんは出版社にそれぞれ就職した.

respond compl *ni* (v) *kota′e·ru* 答える; (irr) *hannō-suru* 反応する

responsibility 1 *sekinin* 責任 sense of responsibility *sekini′nkan* 責任感 take responsibility *sekinin o to′ru* 責任を取る 2 duties *yakume′* 役目 What are the responsibilities of this job? *Kono shigoto no yakume′ wa na′n desu ka?* この仕事の役目は何ですか. 3 fault *se′i* せい That was my responsibility. *Sore wa watashi no se′i deshita.* それは私のせいでした.

rest 1 *yasumi′* 休み 2 a breather *kyūsoku* 休息 3 intermission *kyūkei* 休憩 4 remainder *nokori′* 残り I'll take care of the rest tomorrow. *Nokori′ wa ashita′ ni suru.* 残りは明日にする. ——loc *o* (v) *yasu′m·u* 休む Let's rest a bit. *Cho′tto yasumimashō′.* ちょっと休みましょう.

restaurant *re′sutoran* レストラン; *shokudō* 食堂 restaurant for students *gakkō no shokudō* 学校の食堂

restless (adj) *jiretta′·i* じれったい This bumper-to-bumper traffic makes me restless. *Noronoro u′nten de watashi wa jiretta′ku naru.* のろのろ運転で私はじれったくなる. ——(irr) *u′rouro-suru* うろうろする I feel restless, having been shut up in the house all day. *Ichinichi-jū uchi ni tojikomotte, u′rouro-suru.* 一日中家にとじこもってうろうろする. ——(attr) *ochitsukanai* 落ち着かない restless person *ochitsukanai hito′* 落ち着かない人

restore obj *o* (caus) *fukkō-sase·ru* 復興させる ——(idiom) *motodō′ri ni sase·ru* もとどおりにさせる

result *kekka* 結果 Inform me of the result. *Kekka o shirasete kudasa′i.* 結果を知らせて下さい.

resumé *rirekisho* 履歴書

resurrection *fukkatsu* 復活

retail *kouri* 小売り

retire (v) go to bed *yasu′m·u* 休む ——obj *o* (irr) go into retirement *taishoku-suru* 退職する; *intai-suru* 引退する

retirement *taishoku* 退職; *intai* 引退

retreat (v) *shirizo′k·u* 退く

return (v) 1 go back *modo′r·u* 戻る 2 return home *ka′er·u* 帰る What time will you return? *Na′nji ni kaerima′su ka?* 何時に帰りますか. 3 return to one's country (irr) *kikoku-suru* 帰国する ——obj *o* (v) *ka′es·u* 返す return a book *ho′n o ka′esu* 本を返す

return address *sashidashinin no jū′sho* 差出人の住所

return trip *ōfuku* 往復

reveal obj *o* (v) *arawa′s·u* 現す She finally revealed her true colors. *Ka'nojo wa tsu'i ni shō'tai o arawa'shita.* 彼女はついに正体を現した.

revealed (v) be revealed *araware'·ru* 現れる During the research a number of interesting facts were revealed. *Kenkyū-chū, i'kutsu ka no kyō'mi aru ji'jitsu ga arawa'reta.* 研究中いくつかの興味ある事実が現れた.

revelation **1** (Chr) *keiji* 啓示 **2** (Budd) *satori* 悟り **3** disclosure *ba'kuro* 暴露

revenge *fukushū* 復讐 ——(idiom) take revenge (on a person) [*hito ni*] *fukushū-suru* [人に]復讐する

revenue *shūnyū* 収入 revenue stamp *shūnyū i'nshi* 収入印紙; (Tech) *shotoku* 所得

reverse **1** opposite *gyaku* [*no*] 逆[の] in reverse order *gyaku no ju'njo de* 逆の順序で; *hantai* 反対 The car suddenly started to move in reverse. *Kuruma wa kyū ni hantai hō'kō ni hashirida'shita.* 車は急に反対方向に走りだした. **2** reverse gear *bakku gi'ya* バックギヤ

review *fukushū* 復習——*obj o* (irr) *fukushū-suru* 復習する

revise *obj o* (irr) *kaitei-suru* 改訂する

revision *kaitei* 改訂

revival **1** *fukkō* 復興 **2** (Chr) revival meeting *ribaibaru shū'kai* リバイバル集会

revolution *kakumei* 革命

revolutionary *kakumeiteki* [*na*] 革命的[な]

revue *re'byū* レビュー

reward *hōshū* 報酬; *hōbi* ほうび He received ¥100,000 as a reward. *Ka're wa hōbi ni jūman-en o mora'tta.* 彼はほうびに十万円をもらった.

rewrite *obj o* (v) *kakika'e·ru* 書きかえる

rhapsody (music) *kyōsō'kyoku* 狂想曲

rheumatism *ryūmachi* リューマチ

rhinoceros *sa'i* さい

rhododendron *shakunage* 石南花

rhubarb *rū'bābu* ルーバーブ

rhythm *ri'zumu* リズム; *hyōshi'* 拍子

rib (Anat) *rokkotsu* 肋骨

ribbon *ri'bon* リボン typewriter ribbon *ta'ipu no ri'bon* タイプのリボン

rice **1** (uncooked) *kome'* 米 **2** (cooked) *go'han* 御飯 **3** brown (unpolished) rice *ge'mmai* 玄米 **4** whole rice (with embryo buds) *haigaimai* 胚芽米 **5** glutinous rice *mochi-gome* 餅米

rice ball *o-ni'giri* おにぎり

rice bowl *chawan* 茶碗; *gohan-ja'wan* 御飯茶碗

rice paddy *ta'* 田; (coll) *tambo* 田んぼ

rice plant *i'ne* 稲
rice planting *ta-ue'* 田植え
rich 1 (flavor) *yu'taka na aji* 豊かな味 2 (person) *kanemo'chi* 金持ち
riddle *nazo* 謎
ride (v) [*ni*] *nor·u* [に]乗る I ride the train often. *Watashi wa yo'ku densha ni noru.* 私はよく電車に乗る.
ridiculous (adj) *bakarashi'·i* ばからしい ——(attr) *baka'geta* ばかげた
riding *jōba* 乗馬
rifle *raifuru'-jū* ライフル銃
right 1 privilege; power *jinken* 人権 infringement of another's rights *jinken shi'ngai* 人権侵害 2 claim *ke'nri* 権利 a legal right *hōritsujō no ke'nri* 法律上の権利 have no right *ke'nri ga na'i* 権利がない 3 copyright *chosa'kuken* 著作権 ——(adj) correct *tadashi'·i* 正しい
Right. *Sō'.* そう.; *Ha'i.* はい.
right (direction) *migi* 右 on the right *migi ni* 右に to the right *migi no hō'* 右の方 Go right. *Migi no hō' ni itte kudasa'i.* 右の方に行って下さい. Turn right at the next intersection. *Tsugi' no kōsaten de migi ni magatte kudasa'i.* 次の交差点で右に曲がって下さい.
right away *su'gu* [*ni*] すぐ[に]
right hand *migite* 右手 on the right-hand side *migite ni* 右手に
right-handed *migi-kiki* 右利き
right turn *usetsu* 右折 No right turn. *Usetsu kinshi.* 右折禁止.
right wing *u'yoku* 右翼
ring 1 *yubiwa* 指輪 2 circle *wa'* 輪 ——(v) *nar·u* 鳴る The telephone rang. *Denwa ga natta.* 電話が鳴った. ——obj *o* (v) *naras·u* 鳴らす ring a bell *be'ru o naras·u* ベルを鳴らす
ring finger *kusuri'-yubi* 薬指
rinse *ri'nsu* リンス ——obj *o* (v) *yusug·u* ゆすぐ; *susug·u* すすぐ rinse clothes *sentakumono o susugu* 洗濯物をすすぐ
riot *bōdō* 暴動
rip obj *o* (v) *sa'k·u* 裂く rip into two *futatsu' ni sa'ku* 二つに裂く
ripe (attr) *juku'shita* 熟した ripe fruit *juku'shita kuda'mono* 熟した果物
ripen (v) *juku's·u* 熟す
rise 1 mound *tsuka* 塚 2 a rise in prices *neagari* 値上り ——(v) 1 get up *oki'·ru* 起きる 2 stand *tachiaga'r·u* 立ち上がる 3 ascend *agar·u* 上がる smoke rises *kemuri ga agaru* 煙が上がる
risky *kiken* [*na*] 危険[な]
rival *ra'ibaru* ライバル
river *kawa'* 川

road 1 *dō′ro* 道路 road map *dōro chi′zu* 道路地図 2 *michi* 道 country road *inaka′michi* 田舎道 mountain road *yama′michi* 山道

roam loc *o* (v) *samayo′·u* さまよう; *arukimawa′r·u* 歩きまわる

roar (v) *hoe′·ru* 吠える

roast (cut of meat) *niku no katamari* 肉の塊 ——obj *o* (v) *yak·u* 焼く

rob obj *o* (v) 1 steal *nusu′m·u* 盗む 2 deprive of *uba·u* 奪う

robber 1 *dorobō* 泥棒 2 armed robber *gōtō* 強盗

robbery *tōnan* 盗難

robot *robo′tto* ロボット

rock *ishi′* 石 ——(v) *yure·ru* 揺れる

rock-and-roll *rokkun-rō′ru* ロックンロール; *ro′kku* ロック

rocket *roke′tto* ロケット

rock garden *sekitei* 石庭

rod *bō* 棒 iron rod *tetsubō* 鉄棒

roe 1 *gyoran* 魚卵 2 (cod) *tarako* 鱈子 3 (herring) *kazu-no-ko* 数の子 4 (salmon) *ikura* イクラ; *sujiko* 筋子

roll (v) *korogar·u* ころがる ——obj *o* (v) *korogas·u* ころがす

roll (dinner roll) *rōru′ pan* ロールパン

roller pin *me′mbō* めん棒

roller skates/skating *rōrā suke′to* ローラースケート

romance *ro′mansu* ロマンス; *ren'ai* 恋愛

Romania *Rūmania* ルーマニア

Romanian 1 (language) *Rūmania-go* ルーマニア語 2 (person) *Rūmania′ jin* ルーマニア人 ——(attr) *Rūmania no* ルーマニアの

romantic *roma′nchikku* [na] ロマンチック[な]

roof *ya′ne* 屋根 thatch roof *kayabuki ya′ne* かやぶき屋根 tile roof *kawara ya′ne* かわら屋根

room 1 *heya′* 部屋 room rent *heya-dai* 部屋代 2 leeway *yoyū* 余裕 There's no room in my schedule for that. *Suke′jūru ni wa sore o suru yoyū ga na′i.* スケジュールにはそれをする余裕がない。 3 space *yo′chi* 余地 There wasn't enough room to make a U-turn. *Yū-tan-suru yo′chi ga na′katta.* Uターンする余地がなかった。

room and board *geshuku* 下宿

root *ne′* 根 The roots are rotten. *Ne′ ga kusa′tte iru.* 根が腐っている。

rope 1 *rō′pu* ロープ; *tsuna* 綱 2 straw rope *nawa′* 縄

rosary *roza′rio* ロザリオ see also prayer beads

rose *bara* ばら rosebush *bara no ki′* ばらの木

rot (v) *kusa′r·u* 腐る The log rotted because of dampness. *Shikki de maruta ga kusa′tta.* 湿気で丸太が腐った。

rotary *rō′tari* ロータリー

rotate (irr) 1 turn *kaiten-suru* 回転する 2 take turns (caus) *kōtai-sase·ru* 交代させる

rouge *be'ni* 紅 lip rouge *kuchibeni* 口紅

rough *zarazara* [*na*] ざらざら[な] ——(adj) *ara·i* 荒い The waves are rough. *Nami' ga arai*. 波が荒い.; *arappo'·i* 荒っぽい a rough person *arappo'i hito* 荒っぽい人 ——(attr) rough (in texture) *za'razara-shita* ざらざらした a rough floor *za'razara-shita yuka* ざらざらした床

roughly 1 generally *daitai* [*ni*] 大体[に] The budget is roughly ¥100 million. *Yosan wa daitai ichi-oku-en de'su*. 予算は大体一億円です. **2** approximately *ōza'ppa* [*ni*] 大ざっぱ[に] estimate roughly *ōza'ppa ni mitsumo'ru* 大ざっぱに見積もる

round (adj) *maru'·i* 丸い

roundabout (adj) *mawarikudo'·i* 回りくどい a roundabout way of speaking *mawarikudo'i hanashi-kata* 回りくどい話し方

round-shouldered *nadegata* [*no*] なで肩[の]

round-trip ticket *ōfuku ki'ppu* 往復切符

route *rū'to* ルート; *michi* 道

routine *nichijō no* 日常の; *o-kimari no* お決まりの

row 1 *re'tsu* 列 in one row *ichi'retsu ni* 一列に in two rows *ni'retsu ni* 二列に **2** (opposed to column) *gyō'* 行 ——obj *o* (v) *ko'g·u* 漕ぐ We rowed a boat on the lake. *Mizuu'mi de bō'to o ko'ida*. 湖でボートを漕いだ.

royal *ō'ke no* 王家の

rub obj *o* (v) *kosu'r·u* こする Rub this with sandpaper. *Sandopē'-pā de kore o kosu'tte kudasa'i*. サンドペーパーでこれをこすって下さい.

rubber *go'mu* ゴム

rubber band *wagomu* 輪ゴム

rubbing alcohol *massāji-yō arukōru* マッサージ用アルコール

rubbish *gomi* ごみ; *garakuta* がらくた

ruby *ru'bi* ルビー

rudder *ka'ji* 舵 take the rudder *ka'ji o toru* 舵をとる

rude *bure'i* [*na*] 無礼[な] a rude person *bure'i na hito* 無礼な人 ——compl *ni* (irr) be rude *shitsu'rei-suru* 失礼する (I'm sorry) I was rude. *Shitsu'rei-shima'shita*. 失礼しました.

rug *jū'tan* じゅうたん

ruin *hōkai* 崩壊 ——(v) **1** *horobo's·u* 滅ぼす **2** (caus) *hōkai-sase'ru* 崩壊させる

ruins *ha'ikyo* 廃墟 the ruins of Rome *Rō'ma no ha'ikyo* ローマの廃墟

rule 1 regulation *ki'soku* 規則 **2** standard *kijun* 基準 **3** reign *shi'hai* 支配 ——obj *o* (v) *osame'·ru* 治める

ruler 1 (for measurement) *monosa'shi* 物差 **2** one who rules *shiha'isha* 支配者

rum *ramu'-shu* ラム酒

Rumania *see* Romania
Rumanian *see* Romanian
rumor *uwasa* うわさ
run loc *o* (v) *hashi'r·u* 走る I run one kilometer every morning. *Mai'asa ichi-kiro hashi'ru.* 毎朝1キロ走る.; *kake'·ru* 駆ける go at a run *ka'kete iku* 駆けていく
run away (v) *nige'·ru* 逃げる The thief ran away. *Dorobō wa ni'geta.* 泥棒は逃げた.
run out (exhaust) (v) *nakunar·u* なくなる I ran out of paper. *Kami' ga nakunatta.* 紙がなくなった.; *kire'·ru* きれる I ran out of gasoline. *Gasorin ga ki'reta.* ガソリンがきれた.
run over obj *o* (v) *hik·u* ひく ——(pass) be run over *hikare·ru* ひかれる Our cat was run over by a car. *Ne'ko wa kuruma ni hikareta.* 猫は車にひかれた.
rural *inaka no* 田舎の
rush hour *ra'sshu* ラッシュ; *rasshu a'wā* ラッシュアワー
Russia *Sobie'to* ソビエト; *So'ren* ソ連
Russian 1 (language) *Roshia-go* ロシア語 2 (person) *Roshia' jin* ロシア人 ——(attr) *So'bieto no* ソビエトの
rust *sabi'* さび ——(v) *sabi'·ru* さびる
rusty (attr) *sa'bita* さびた a rusty kitchen knife *sa'bita hōchō* さびた包丁
rye 1 (grain) *raimugi* ライ麦 2 (bread) *raimugi pa'n* ライ麦パン 3 (whiskey) *rai-ui'sukī* ライウイスキー

S

Sabbath *Ansoku'bi/Ansoku'jitsu* 安息日
sabotage *sabotā'ju* サボタージュ ——obj *o* (v) *sabo'r·u* サボる
saccharin *sakkarin* サッカリン
sack *fukuro'* 袋 paper sack *kami-bu'kuro* 紙袋
sacrament (Cath) *hiseki* 秘跡; (Prot) *seire'iten* 聖礼典
sacred *shinsei* [na] 神聖[な]
sacrifice *gisei* 犠牲 make a sacrifice *gisei o hara'u* 犠牲を払う They made a great sacrifice to accomplish the work. *Ka'rera wa sono ji'gyō ni ō'ki na gisei o hara'tta.* 彼らはその事業に大きな犠牲を払った. ——(idiom) *gisei ni suru* 犠牲にする He sacrificed his education to support his mother. *Ka're wa okā'-san no tame' ni jibun no kyō'iku o gisei ni shita.* 彼はお母さんのために自分の教育を犠牲にした.
sad (adj) *kanashi·i* 悲しい a sad event *kanashii koto'* 悲しい事 I

was sad to hear that. *Sore o kiite, kanashi'katta.* それを聞いて悲しかった.

saddle *kura'* くら

sadism *sadi'zumu* サディズム; (abbr) *sa'do* サド

sadist *sadi'suto* サディスト

sadistic *sadisuchi'kku [na]* サディスチック[な]; *sadoteki [na]* サド的[な]

sadness *kanashimi* 悲しみ

safe (for money) *ki'nko* 金庫

safe (secure) *anzen [na]* 安全[な] safe driving *anzen u'nten* 安全運転 Store it in a safe place. *Anzen na tokoro' ni hokan-shite kudasa'i.* 安全な所に保管して下さい.; *buji [na]* 無事[な] I heard you had a terrible typhoon; is your family safe? *Kono aida no taifu' wa hido'katta sō' desu ga, minasan wa buji de'shita ka?* この間の台風はひどかったそうですが, みなさんは無事でしたか.

safe-deposit box **1** *kichōhi'n-bako* 貴重品箱 **2** (in a bank) *kashi ki'nko* 借し金庫

safely *buji ni* 無事に We arrived safely. *Wata'shitachi wa buji ni tsukima'shita.* 私たちは無事に着きました.

safety **1** welfare *a'mpi* 安否 I'm concerned about his/her safety. *Ano' hito no a'mpi ga ki ni kaka'ru.* あの人の安否が気にかかる. **2** freedom from danger *anzen* 安全 Safety First. *Anzen Da'i-ichi.* 安全第一. safety belt *anzen be'ruto* 安全ベルト

safety pin *anze'n pin* 安全ピン

safflower *beni'bana* 紅花 safflower oil *benibana'yu* 紅花油

sag (v) *tarum·u* たるむ This skirt sags a bit in back. *Kono sukā'to wa ushirogawa ga suko'shi tarunde iru.* このスカートは後ろ側が少したるんでいる.; *tawa'm·u* たわむ A beam in the ceiling is sagging. *Tenjō no hari' ga tawa'nde iru.* 天井の梁がたわんでいる.

Sagittarius *Ite-za* 射手座

sail *ho'* 帆 ——(irr) set sail *shuppan-suru* 出帆する When does the ship sail? *Fu'ne wa i'tsu shuppan-shima'su ka?* 船はいつ出帆しますか. ——loc *o* (irr) navigate *kō'kai-suru* 航海する sail the Pacific *Taihe'iyō o kō'kai-suru* 太平洋を航海する ——(idiom) **1** go for a sail *funa-a'sobi ni iku* 船遊びに行く **2** sail a sailboat *yo'tto ni nor·u* ヨットに乗る Do you sail (in a sailboat)? *Yo'tto ni norima'su ka?* ヨットに乗りますか.

sailboat *yo'tto* ヨット

sailor *funa'nori* 船乗り; *sen'in* 船員; (navy) *su'ihei* 水兵

saint (W) *seijin* 聖人; (J) *hijiri* 聖

sake (adv) for the sake of... ...*[no] tame [ni]* ...[の]ため[に] I began jogging for the sake of my health. *Kenkō no tame'ni jogingu o hajime'ta.* 健康のためにジョギングを始めた.

salad *sa'rada* サラダ

salad dressing *dore'sshingu* ドレッシング

salad oil *sarada o'iru* サラダオイル

salaried worker *sarari'man* サラリーマン

salary 1 *sa'rari* サラリー; *kyū'ryō* 給料 2 monthly wage *gekkyū* 月給 3 base salary *kiho'nkyū* 基本給

sale *bāgen sē'ru* バーゲンセール; *ōu'ridashi* 大売出し

sales (proceeds) *uriage* 売上

salesperson *ten'in* 店員

saliva *tsubaki'* つばき

salmon 1 *sa'ke/sha'ke* 鮭 2 salted salmon *shio-za'ke* 塩鮭 3 salmon steak *sāmon sutē'ki* サーモンステーキ 4 salmon roe *ikura* イクラ; *sujiko'* 筋子 5 smoked salmon *sumōku sā'mon* スモークサーモン

salt 1 *shio'* 塩 salt shaker *shio-ire* 塩入れ 2 table salt *shoku'en* 食塩

salty (adj) *shio-kara'·i* 塩辛い; (coll) *shoppa'·i* しょっぱい

Salvadoran (person) *Eru Sarubadoru'jin* エルサルバドル人 —— (attr) *Eru Saruba'doru no* エルサルバドルの

salve *nuri-gu'suri* 塗り薬

same *onaji* 同じ Is it the same? *Onaji de'su ka?* 同じですか。 It's the same name. *Onaji namae de'su.* 同じ名前です。

sample *mihon* 見本 —— obj *o* (v) *tame'shite mi·ru* 試してみる May I sample this? *Kore o tame'shite mite mo i'i desu ka?* これを試してみてもいいですか。

sanatorium *ryōyōjo* 療養所; *sanatoryu'mu* サナトリウム

sanction 1 *ninka* 認可 2 *shobatsu* 処罰 This school should have stricter sanctions for misbehavior. *Kono gakkō wa kōsoku i'han ni taishite shobatsu o mo'tto kibi'shiku suru hō ga i'i.* この学校は校則違反に対して処罰をもっと厳しくする方がいい。 —— obj *o* (irr) *ninka-suru* 認可する。

sand *suna* 砂 sandbox *sunaba* 砂場 —— (idiom) to sand *kamiya'suri de migak·u* 紙やすりでみがく

sandal *sandaru* サンダル

sand dune *sakyū* 砂丘

sandpaper *kamiya'suri* 紙やすり; *sandopē'pā* サンドペーパー

sandstone *sagan* 砂岩

sandwich *sandoi'tchi* サンドイッチ

sandy (adj) *sunappo'·i* 砂っぽい —— (idiom) covered with sand *suna-da'rake [no]* 砂だらけ[の]

sandy beach *suna'hama* 砂浜

sane 1 *shōki [no]* 正気[の] Do you think that person is sane? *Ano' hito wa shō'ki da to omoima'su ka?* あの人は正気だと思いますか。 2 moderate *onken na* 穏健な a sane policy *onken na seisaku* 穏健

な政策 3 reasonable *gōriteki na* 合理的な sane measures *gōriteki na shu'dan* 合理的な手段

sanitary 1 *eiseiteki* [*na*] 衛生的[な] sanitary conditions *eiseiteki na jōtai* 衛生的な状態 sanitary engineering *eisei kō'gaku* 衛生工学 2 clean *seiketsu* [*na*] 清潔[な]

sanitary belt *gekke'i-tai* 月経帯

sanitary napkin *seiri-yō na' pukin* 生理用ナプキン

sanitation *eisei* 衛生 public sanitation *kōshū e' isei* 公衆衛生

Santa Claus *Santa Kurō'su* サンタクロース

sap *ju'eki* 樹液

sarcasm *hiniku* 皮肉

sarcastic *hiniku* [*na*] 皮肉[な]   ——(idiom) be sarcastic *hiniku o iu* 皮肉を言う

sardine 1 *iwashi* 鰯 2 dried sardine *niboshi* 煮干

sash 1 *o'bi* 帯 2 aluminum sash for windows and doors *arumi sa'sshi* アルミサッシ

Satan *Sa'tan* サタン; *a'kuma* 悪魔

satellite *eisei* 衛星

satin *shu'su* しゅす; *saten* サテン

satire *fūshi* 風刺

satisfaction *ma'nzoku* 満足

satisfy ——(irr) be satisfied *ma'nzoku-suru* 満足する Were you satisfied with it? *Sore ni ma'nzoku-shima'shita ka?* それに満足しましたか. ——(pot) *ma'nzoku-deki'·ru* 満足できる He couldn't be satisfied. *Ka're wa ma'nzoku-deki'nakatta.* 彼は満足できなかった. ——(caus) *ma'nzoku-sase·ru* 満足させる No matter how hard I try, I can't satisfy the teacher. *Iku'ra do'ryoku-shite mo, sense'i o ma'nzoku-saseru koto' ga deki'nai.* いくら努力しても先生を満足させることができない.

saturate obj *o* (caus) *shimikomase'·ru* しみ込ませる saturate a sponge with water *suponji ni mizu o shimikomase'ru* スポンジに水をしみ込ませる

Saturday *doyō'bi* 土曜日

Saturn *Dosei* 土星

sauce *sō'su* ソース pour sauce *sō'su o kake're·ru* ソースをかける

saucepan *na'be* 鍋

saucer 1 (for a cup) *uke'zara* 受け皿 2 small dish *kozara* 小皿

Saudi Arabia *Sauji A'rabia* サウジアラビア

Saudi Arabian (person) *Sauji Arabia' jin* サウジアラビア人 ——(attr) *Sauji A'rabia no* サウジアラビアの

sauna *sa'una* サウナ

sausage *sōsē'ji* ソーセージ

save obj *o* (v) 1 accumulate *tame'·ru* 貯める Save the old newspapers. *Furu'i shimbun o tamete o'ite kudasa'i.* 古い新聞を貯めてお

いて下さい. **2** save money (irr) *chokin-suru* 貯金する I'm saving a little each month. *Maitsuki sukoshi-zu'tsu chokin-shite iru.* 毎月少しずつ貯金している. **3** lay by *takuwae'·ru* 蓄える save one's strength *chikara' o takuwae'·ru* 力を蓄える **4** economize (irr) *ken'yaku-suru* 倹約する My son is saving his money to buy Christmas presents. *Musuko wa Kurisumasu pure'zento o kau tame' ni o-kane o ken'yaku-shite iru.* 息子はクリスマスプレゼントを買うためにお金を倹約している.; *setsuyaku-suru* 節約する We must save energy. *Ene'rugi o setsuyaku-shina'kereba nara'nai.* エネルギーを節約しなければならない. **5** rescue *tasuke'·ru* 助ける The lifeguard threw him a rope and saved him. *Kyūjo'in ga ka're ni tsuna' o na'getate tasuke'ta.* 救助員が彼に綱を投げて助けた.

saving *chokin* 貯金; *chochiku* 貯蓄

saving account *futsū yo'kin* 普通預金; (term) *teiki yo'kin* 定期預金

Savior (Chr) *Sukui'nushi* 救い主

saw *nokogi'ri* のこぎり

sawdust *ogaku'zu* おがくず

saxophone *sakiso'fon* サキソフォン

say obj *o* (v) *i·u* 言う What did that person say? *Ano' hito wa na'n to iima'shita ka?* あの人は何と言いましたか. How do you say "X" in Japanese? *"X" wa Nihon-go de dō' iima'su ka?* 「X」は日本語でどう言いますか.

saying *kotowaza* ことわざ

scab *kasabuta* かさぶた ——(idiom) form a scab *kasabuta o shōji·ru* かさぶたを生じる

scald *yakedo* やけど ——(irr) be scalded *yakedo-suru* やけどする

scale **1** (for measuring weight) *hakari'* はかり; a pair/set of scales *tembin* 天秤 **2** degree *ki'bo* 規模 on a large scale *dai-ki'bo ni* 大規模に We're planning a large-scale operation *Ko'ndo no keikaku no ki'bo wa ōki'i.* 今度の計画の規模は大きい. ——(idiom) scale down *ki'bo o kezur·u* 規模を削る We'll have to scale down the plan a bit. *Keikaku no ki'bo o suko'shi kezurana'kute wa nara'nai.* 計画の規模を少し削らなくてはならない. **3** (fish) scale *uroko'* うろこ **4** (map) scale *shukushaku* 縮尺 ——(v) climb *yojinobo'r·u* よじ登る

scallion *wakegi* わけぎ

scallop *hotate'gai* 帆立貝

scalp *tōhi* 頭皮 ——(idiom) cheat *dafuya o suru* だふ屋をする

scan (idiom) *me' o tō'su* 目を通す I scanned the manuscript. *Genkō ni me' o tō'shita.* 原稿に目を通した.

scandal *sukya'ndaru* スキャンダル

Scandinavia *Sukanjina'bia* スカンジナビア

Scandinavian (person) *Hokuō' jin* 北欧人; *Sukanjinabia'jin* ス

カンジナビア人 ——(attr) *Sukanjina'bia no* スカンジナビアの

scar *kizu-ato* 傷あと

scare obj *o* (v) *odokas·u* 脅かす Don't scare me like that! *Sō odokasana'ide kudasa'i!* そう脅かさないで下さい. ——(irr) be scared *bi'kubiku-suru* びくびくする I was scared. *Bi'kubiku-shita.* びくびくした.

scarf *sukā'fu* スカーフ; *eri'maki* 襟巻

scarlet *kurenai* 紅

scarlet fever *shōkō'netsu* しょう紅熱

scatter obj *o* (v) *baramak·u* ばらまく ——(idiom) *barabara ni suru* ばらばらにする

scene 1 in a play *shi'n* シーン; *bamen* 場面 2 setting *gemba* 現場 view the scene of an incident *ji'ken no gemba o mi'ru* 事件の現場を見る

scenery 1 view *ke'shiki* 景色 2 (for the stage) *se'tto* セット

scent 1 smell *nio'i* 臭い 2 fragrance *kaori* 香り

schedule 1 *suke'jūru* スケジュール 2 plan *keikakuhyō* 計画表 3 agenda *nittei* 日程 4 prearrangement *yotei* 予定 5 timetable *jikan-hyō* 時間表; *jikokuhyō* 時刻表 6 train schedule *ressha da'iya* 列車ダイヤ ——obj *o* (irr) *yotei-suru* 予定する

scheme *kuwadate* 企て ——obj *o* (v) *kuwadate'·ru* 企てる

schism 1 *bunretsu* 分裂 2 *fu'wa* 不和

schizophrenia *seishin bunretsushō* 精神分裂症

scholar *gakusha* 学者

scholarship 1 assistance *shōgakukin* 奨学金 2 learning *gaku'mon* 学問

school 1 elementary school *shōga'kkō* 小学校 2 junior high school; middle school *chūga'kkō* 中学校 3 night school *yakan ga'kkō* 夜間学校 4 nursery school *hoikusho* 保育所 5 preparatory school *yobikō* 予備校 6 private school *shiritsu ga'kkō* 私立学校 7 senior high school *kōtōga'kkō* 高等学校; (abbr) *kōkō* 高校 8 Sunday school; church school *Nichiyō ga'kkō* 日曜学校 9 vocational school *semmon ga'kkō* 専門学校

schooling *kyōiku* 教育

school term *gakki* 学期

school uniform *seifuku* 制服

school vacation 1 (spring) *haru ya'sumi* 春休み 2 (summer) *natsu ya'sumi* 夏休み 3 (winter) *fuyu ya'sumi* 冬休み

science 1 *ka'gaku* 科学 2 applied science *ōyō ka'gaku* 応用科学 3 medical science *i'gaku* 医学 4 natural science *shizen ka'gaku* 自然科学

science fiction *Esu-Efu;* SF; *kūsō kagaku shō'setsu* 空想科学小説

scientific *kagakuteki [na]* 科学的[な]

scientist *kaga'kusha* 科学者

scissors 1 *hasami′* はさみ 2 manicure scissors *manikyua-ba′sami* マニキュアばさみ 3 sewing scissors *tachibasami* 裁ちばさみ

sclerosis *kōkashō* 硬化症

scold obj *o* (v) *shikar·u* 叱る ——(pass) *shikarare·ru* 叱られる He was scolded by the teacher. *Ka′re wa sense′i ni shikarareta.* 彼は先生に叱られた.

scope *ha′n′i* 範囲 enlarge the scope *ha′n′i o hirogeru* 範囲を広げる This phenomenon is outside the scope of human experience. *Kono genshō wa ningen no keiken no ha′n′i-ga′i no mono′ desu.* この現象は人間の経験の範囲外のものです.

scorch (v) *koge′·ru* 焦げる ——obj *o* (v) *koga′s·u* 焦す He scorched his shirt. *Ka′re wa sha′tsu o koga′shita.* 彼はシャツを焦した.

score 1 (in a game) *suko′a* スコア 2 (on a test) *seiseki* 成績

scorn *keibetsu* 軽蔑 ——obj *o* (irr) *keibetsu-suru* 軽蔑する scorn a person *hito o keibetsu-suru* 人を軽蔑する

Scorpio *Sasori-za* さそり座

scorpion *sasori* さそり

Scot *Sukottorando′jin* スコットランド人

Scotch (whisky) *suko′tchi* スコッチ

Scotch tape *serote′pu* セロテープ

Scotland *Sukottora′ndo* スコットランド

Scottish (person) *Sukottorando′jin* スコットランド人 ——(attr) *Sukottora′ndo no* スコットランドの

scoundrel *akutō′* 悪党; *aitsu* あいつ The scoundrel took my umbrella! *Aitsu ga watashi no ka′sa o to′tta!* あいつが私の傘をとった.

scour obj *o* (v) *surimigak·u* すりみがく

scout 1 *sekkō* 斥候; *teisatsu* 偵察 2 Boy (Girl) Scout *bōi* [*gāru*] *suka′uto* ボーイ[ガール]スカウト ——obj *o* (irr) *teisatsu-suru* 偵察する

scrambled egg *sukuramburu* [*e′ggu*] スクランブル[エッグ]

scrap 1 *ku′zu* 屑; *-kuzu* 屑 paper scraps *kamiku′zu* 紙屑 Save the scraps of bread, please. *Panku′zu o to′tte oite kudasa′i.* パン屑を取っておいて下さい. 2 leftovers *nokorimono* 残り物 ——(irr) *kenka-suru* 喧嘩する My son is always scrapping. *Musuko wa i′tsu mo kenka ba′kari shite iru.* 息子はいつも喧嘩ばかりしている. ——obj *o* (irr) *haiki-suru* 廃棄する scrap old documents *furu′i shorui o haiki-suru* 古い書類を廃棄する

scrape obj *o* (v) 1 abrade *surimu′k·u* すりむく I scraped my shin. *Sune′ o surimu′ita.* すねをすりむいた. 2 (with a rough instrument) *kosuri-oto′s·u* こすり落とす scrape off paint *penki o kosuri-oto′su* ペンキをこすり落とす

scratch *kizu* 傷 ——obj *o* (v) **1** *ka'k·u* かく He scratched his head. *Ka're wa atama' o ka'ita.* 彼は頭をかいた。 **2** scratch hard *hikka'k·u* ひっかく ——(pass) *hikkakare'·ru* ひっかかれる I was scratched by the cat. *Watashi wa ne'ko ni hikkaka'reta.* 私は猫にひっかかれた。

scratch paper *zakki yō'shi* 雑記用紙; *memo yō'shi* メモ用紙

scream *himei* 悲鳴; *wamekigo'e* わめき声 ——(v) *wame'k·u* わめく She screamed out in the middle of the night. *Ka'nojo wa yonaka' ni ōgo'e de wame'ita.* 彼女は夜中に大声でわめいた。

screen 1 window screen *ami'do* 網戸 **2** screening *ami'* 網 **3** projection screen *sukuri'n* スクリーン

screw *ne'ji* ねじ

screwdriver *nejima'washi* ねじ回し

scribble *rakugaki* 落書き ——obj *o* (irr) *rakugaki-suru* 落書きする

scripture 1 *kyōten* 経典 **2** (Chr) *Se'isho* 聖書 **3** (Budd) *Butten* 仏典

scroll 1 hanging scroll *kake'jiku* 掛け軸 **2** rolled manuscript *makimono* 巻物

scrotum *innō* 陰のう

scrub (Bot) *yabu* 薮; *kamboku* 灌木 ——obj *o* (v) *kosu'r·u* 擦る I scrubbed the floor with a scrub brush. *Yuka o tawashi de go'shigoshi kosu'tta.* 床を束子でごしごし擦った。

scruff *kubisuji* 首筋

sculptor *chōkokuka* 彫刻家

sculpture *chōkoku* 彫刻

scythe *ka'ma* かま

sea *u'mi* 海; -*kai* 海 Sea of Japan *Niho'n-kai* 日本海

sea bird *umi'dori* 海鳥

sea bream *ta'i* 鯛

seafood *kaisa'mbutsu* 海産物

sea gull *kamome* 鷗

sea horse *tatsu-no-otoshigo* たつのおとしご

seal 1 (earless) *aza'rashi* あざらし **2** (eared) *otto'sei* おっとせい **3** stamp *ha'n* 判; *inkan* 印鑑 ——obj *o* (irr) *fū-suru* 封する

sea level *kaimen* 海面

sea lion *ashika* あしか

seam *nuime'* 縫い目

seaman *funa'nori* 船乗り; *sen'in* 船員

seamstress *onna shitate'shi* 女仕立師; (coll) *hariko* 針子

seaport *minato* 港 seaport town *minato' machi* 港町

search *tsuikyū* 追求 ——obj *o* (v) *sagas·u* 捜す search for a house *uchi o sagasu* 家を捜す

seashell *kaiga'ra* 貝殻

seashore *kaigan* 海岸

seasickness *funayoi* 船酔い、

season 1 (of the year) *ki'setsu* 季節 2 the four seasons *shi'ki* 四季 ——obj *o* (irr) *chō'mi-suru* 調味する

seasoning *chōmi'ryō* 調味料

seat *se'ki* 席 reserved seat *shite'i seki* 指定席 ——obj *o* (caus) *suwarase·ru* すわらせる ——(idiom) take a seat *se'ki ni tsuk·u* 席に着く

seat belt *shīto be'ruto* シートベルト

seat number *zaseki ba'ngō* 座席番号

seaweed *kaisō* 海草

second 1 (ordinal) *daini* 第二 2 (measurement of time) *byō'* 秒 fifteen seconds *jūgo'byō* 十五秒 3 second gear of a car *sekando gi'ya* セカンドギヤ; *dai-ni gi'ya* 第二ギヤ

second-class 1 *nitō [no]* 二等[の] 2 inferior *niryū [no]* 二流[の]

second day of the month *futsuka* 二日

second floor *nikai* 二階

secondhand *chūburu [no]* 中古[の] secondhand clothes *chūburu no fuku* 中古の服; *chūko-* 中古 secondhand car *chūko'sha* 中古車

second hand *byōshin* 秒針

second helping *o-ka'wari* おかわり How about a second helping? *O-ka'wari wa ika'ga desu ka?* おかわりはいかがですか。

secret *himitsu* 秘密 in secret *himitsu ni* 秘密に; *naisho* 内緒 Is it a secret? *Naisho de' su ka?* 内緒ですか。Please keep it secret. *Naisho ni shite kudasa'i.* 内緒にして下さい。

secretary 1 executive secretary *ka'nji* 幹事 2 minutes secretary *shoki* 書記 3 office secretary *se'kuretari* セクレタリー; *jimu'in* 事務員 4 private secretary *hi'sho* 秘書

secretly *himitsu ni* 秘密に; *hi'soka ni* 密かに; *kosso'ri to* こっそりと He secretly slipped a ¥5,000 bill into my pocket. *Ka're wa kosso'ri to watashi no poke'tto ni gosen'e'n-satsu o shinoba'seta.* 彼はこっそりと私のポケットに五千円札を忍ばせた。

sect *-ha* 派 the Otani sect of Pure Land Buddhism *Shinshū Ō tani-ha* 真宗大谷派

section 1 *bu'bun* 部分 2 (of an organization) *-ka* 課 3 (of a book) *-setsu* 節 4 (of a city) *ku'iki* 区域; *-ku* 区 5 (Med) *se'k-kai* 切開

secure *anzen [na]* 安全[な] ——obj *o* (v) 1 *tome·ru* 留める 2 obtain (irr) *kakutoku-suru* 獲得する

securely *shikka'ri [to]* しっかり[と] Is the house securely locked? *Ie' wa shikka'ri toji'mari-shite imasu ka?* 家はしっかり戸締まりしていますか。

securities *shōken* 証券

security 1 *anzen* 安全 2 protection *ho'go* 保護 3 (for a loan) *ta'mpo* 担保

sedative *chinse'i-zai* 鎮静剤

seduce obj *o* (irr) *yūwaku-suru* 誘惑する

see compl *ni* (v) meet *a'·u* 会う Did you see her? *Ka'nojo ni aima'shita ka?* 彼女に会いましたか. ——(pot) be able to meet *ae'·ru* 会える I wasn't able to see him on Thursday. *Mokuyō'bi ni ka·re ni ae'nakatta.* 木曜日に彼に会えなかった. ——obj *ga* (v) *mie'·ru* 見える It's so dark I can't see. *Kura'kute mie'nai.* 暗くて見えない. Can one see Mt. Fuji from Atami? *A'tami kara Fu'ji-san ga miema'su ka?* 熱海から富士山が見えますか. —— obj *o* look at *mi'·ru* 見る see a movie *e'iga o mi'ru* 映画を見る see TV *te'rebi o mi'ru* テレビを見る Did you see the exhibit? *Tenra'nkai o mima'shita ka?* 展覧会を見ましたか. ——(idiom) I haven't seen you in a long time! *Shiba'raku deshita!* しばらくでした.

seed *ta'ne* 種 ——(idiom) sow seed *ta'ne o ma'k·u* 種を播く

seedling *na'e* 苗

seek obj *o* (v) 1 look for *sagas·u* 捜す seek employment *shigoto o sagasu* 仕事を捜す 2 pursue (irr) *tsuikyū-suru* 追求する seek after profits *ri'eki o tsuikyū-suru* 利益を追求する

seem *...to mie'·ru* ...と見える She seemed to be angry; she didn't say a word. *Ka'nojo wa oko'tta to mi'ete, kuchi o kikana'-katta.* 彼女は怒ったと見えて口をきかなかった. ——(adj) *...ra-shi·i* ...らしい He seems to have returned to America. *Ka're wa Amerika ni kikoku-shita rashi'i.* 彼はアメリカに帰国したらしい. *see also* appear

see off obj *o* (v) *miokur·u* 見送る They're planning to see you off at Narita. *Ka'rera wa Na'rita de ana'ta o miokuru tsumori' desu.* 彼らは成田であなたを見送るつもりです.

segment 1 *bu'bun* 部分 2 (e.g., of an orange) *hito'fukuro* 一袋 3 (Tech) of a circle *e'n no kyūkei* 円の弓形 ——obj *o* (v) *wake'·ru* 分ける

segregation 1 *bunri* 分離 2 racial segregation *jinshu sa'betsu* 人種差別

seismology *jishi'ngaku* 地震学

seize obj *o* (v) 1 take *tora'e·ru* 捕える 2 take hold of *tsuka'm·u* 摑む *see also* arrest; catch

seldom *me'tta ni* (+ neg) めったに He's seldom late (to work). *Ka're wa me'tta ni chikoku-shina'i.* 彼はめったに遅刻しない.

select obj *o* (v) *era'b·u* 選ぶ Select the one you like. *Suki' na no o era'nde kudasa'i.* 好きなのを選んで下さい.

selection *sentaku* 選択 It was a bad selection. *Sentaku ga wa'ru-katta.* 選択が悪かった.

self *jibun* 自分

self-centered *ji'ko chūshinteki* [na] 自己中心的[な] a self-centered person *ji'ko chushinteki na hito'* 自己中心的な人

self-confidence *jishin* 自信 That person has self-confidence. *Ano' hito wa jishin ga a'ru.* あの人は自信がある.

self-conscious *hanikamiya* [no] はにかみ屋[の]; *ji-i'shiki no tsu-yo'·i* 自意識の強い, a self-conscious person *ji-i'shiki no tsuyo'i hito* 自意識の強い人 ——(idiom) *hitomae o ki ni suru* 人前を気にする I feel self-conscious dancing in Japan. *Niho'n de wa dansu o suru toki, hitomae o ki ni suru.* 日本ではダンスをする時, 人前を気にする.

self-consciousness *ji-i'shiki* 自意識

self-control *jiko yo'kusei* 自己抑制 I must practice more self-control. *Watashi wa mo'tto jiko yo'kusei o ku'nren-shinakereba nara'nai.* 私はもっと自己抑制を訓練しなければならない.

self-defense *jiei* 自衛

Self-Defense Force (J) *Jieitai* 自衛隊

self-examination *hansei* 反省; *jisei* 自省

self-explanatory *jimei* [no] 自明[の]

self-government *ji'chi* 自治

self-indulgent *wagama'ma* [na] わがまま[な]

selfish 1 *rikoteki* [na] 利己的[な] That's a selfish attitude. *Sore wa rikoteki na ta'ido desu.* それは利己的な態度です. 2 willful *waga-ma'ma* [na] わがまま[な] a selfish request *wagama'ma na yōkyu'* わがままな要求

selfishly *katte ni* 勝手に behave selfishly *katte ni furuma'u* 勝手に振舞う

self-operating *jidōteki* [na] 自動的[な] This machine is self-operating. *Kono kika'i wa jidōteki de'su.* この機械は自動的です.

self-portrait *jiga'zō* 自画像

self-respect *jiso'nshin* 自尊心 She has strong self-respect. *Ka'nojo wa jiso'nshin ga tsuyo'i.* 彼女は自尊心が強い.

self-service *serufusā'bisu* セルフサービス a self-service restaurant *serufusābisu-shiki re'sutoran* セルフサービス式レストラン

self-supporting (irr) be self-supporting *jikyū-suru* 自給する

sell (v) *ure·ru* 売れる Do you think this item will sell? *Kono shinamono wa ureru to omoima'su ka?* この品物は売れると思いますか. ——obj *o* (v) *ur·u* 売る Where do they sell that? *Do'ko de sore o utte ima'su ka?* どこでそれを売っていますか. They sold their house. *Ka'rera wa uchi o utta.* 彼らは家を売った.

semantics *imi'ron* 意味論

semen *se'ieki* 精液

semester *gakki* 学期

semi- *han-* 半 semiannual *hanto'shi ni ikka'i* 半年に一回 semi-circle *han'en* [*kei*] 半円[形]

seminar *zeminā'ru* ゼミナール; (abbr) *ze'mi* ゼミ; *se'minā* セミナー

seminary *shinga'kkō* 神学校

senate 1 (parliamentary) *jōin* 上院 2 (university) *hyōgi'kai* 評議会

senator *jōin gi'in* 上院議員

send obj *o* (v) 1 (a letter) [*tegami o*] *da's·u* [手紙を]出す 2 (a telegram) [*dempō o*] *u'ts·u* [電報を]打つ 3 (a package) [*kozu'tsumi o*] *okur·u* [小包みを]送る ——(caus) *ikase·ru* 行かせる I'll send my son to get it. *Musuko ni sore o to'ri ni ikaseru.* 息子にそれを取りに行かせる.

sender *sashidashinin* 差出人

send-off *miokuri* 見送り She received a great send-off. *Ka'nojo wa hade' na miokuri o u'keta.* 彼女は派手な見送りを受けた.

senile (attr) *mō'roku-shita* もうろくした ——(irr) be senile *mō'-roku-suru* もうろくする She is senile. *Ka'nojo wa mō'roku-shite iru.* 彼女はもうろくしている. *boke'·ru* ぼける

senior 1 high school senior *kōkō sanne'n-sei* 高校三年生 2 university senior *daigaku yone'n-sei* 大学四年生 3 one's senior (in rank) *sempai* 先輩

senior citizen *kōre'isha* 高齢者

senior high school *kōkō* 高校 see also high school

seniority 1 *nenchō* [*jun*] 年長[順]; *senyo'riti* セニョリティー The allotment of work is on the basis of seniority. *Shigoto no buntan wa senyo'riti ni motozu'ite iru.* 仕事の分担はセニョリティーに基づいている. 2 priority *senni'nken* 先任権 In my company, Mr. Yamada has seniority. *Watashi no kaisha de' wa, Yamada-san ni senni'nken ga a'ru.* 私の会社では山田さんに先任権がある.

sensation 1 feeling *kanji* 感じ a queer sensation *he'n na kanji* 変な感じ 2 aroused interest *kandō* 感動 a new sensation *atarashi'i kandō* 新しい感動

sense 1 *kankaku* 感覚 the five senses *gokan* 五感 2 common sense *jōshiki* 常識 3 good sense *ryōshiki* 良識 4 meaning *i'mi* 意味 That makes no sense. *Sore wa i'mi o nasa'nai.* それは意味をなさない.

sensible *kemmei* [*na*] 賢明[な] That's sensible. *Sore wa kemmei de'su.* それは賢明です.

sensitive *binkan* [*na*] 敏感[な] He is sensitive to the cold. *Ka're wa sa'musa ni binkan de'su.* 彼は寒さに敏感です. ——(idiom) *ki ga' tsuk·u* 気が付く She's sensitive. *Ka'nojo wa ki ga' tsuku.* 彼女は気が付く.

sentence (Gram) *bu′n* 文; *bu′nshō* 文章

sentence structure *bunkei* 文型; *kōbun* 構文

sentimental *senchime′ntaru* [*na*] センチメンタル[な]; *kanshōteki* [*na*] 感傷的[な]

separate *betsu* [*no*] 別[の] Put it in a separate box, please. *Betsu no hako ni irete kudasa′i.* 別の箱に入れて下さい. ——(v) **1** *wakare′·ru* 別れる separate into two *futa′tsu ni wakare′ru* 二つに別れる **2** part from *hanare′·ru* 離れる Don't get separated from your mother! *Okā′-san no so′ba o hanare′naide!* お母さんのそばを離れないで. **3** live apart (irr) *bekkyo-suru* 別居する ——obj *o* (v) divide *wake′·ru* 分ける The teacher separated the class into groups of five. *Sense′i wa ku′rasu o gonin-zu′tsu no gurū′pu ni wa′keta.* 先生はクラスを五人ずつのグループに分けた.

separately *betsubetsu ni* 別々に Wrap them separately, please. *Betsubetsu ni tsutsu′nde kudasai.* 別々に包んで下さい.

separation (living separately) *bekkyo* 別居

September *ku′gatsu* 九月 September 9 *ku′gatsu kokonoka′* 九月九日

septic tank *jōka′sō* 浄化槽

sequence *renzoku* 連続 a sequence of five lectures *gokai renzoku no kōen* 五回連続の講演

sergeant (military) *gu′nsō* 軍曹; (police) *ke′ibu* 警部

serial *renzoku* [*no*] 連続[の] radio/TV serial *renzoku do′rama* 連続ドラマ

serious **1** important *jūdai* [*na*] 重大[な] a serious matter *jūdai na ji′ken* 重大な事件 **2** earnest *majime* [*na*] 真面目[な] a serious person *majime na hito* 真面目な人 ——(adj) grave *omo·i* 重い a serious illness *omoi byō′ki* 重い病気 ——(idiom) Are you serious? *Honki de′su ka?* 本気ですか.

sermon **1** (Chr) *sekkyō* 説教 **2** (Budd) *se′ppō* 説法

serum *kessei* 血清 antitoxic serum *yobō ke′ssei* 予防血清

servant *shiyōnin* 使用人

serve (irr) wait tables *kyūji-suru* 給仕する ——compl *ni* (v) be in the service of *tsukae′·ru* 仕える ——obj *o* (v) **1** *da′s·u* 出す serve a meal *go′han o da′su* 御飯を出す **2** serve (coffee/tea) *ire·ru* 入れる May I serve you some green tea? *O-cha o iremashō′ ka?* お茶を入れましょうか.

service **1** *sā′bisu* サービス. service charge *sābisu′-ryō* サービス料 The service in this restaurant is good. *Kono re′sutoran wa sā′bisu ga i′i.* このレストランはサービスがいい. **2** (Chr) religious service *reihai* 礼拝

service station *gasorin suta′ndo* ガソリンスタンド

sesame *goma* 胡麻; sesame oil *goma a′bura* 胡麻油

set **1** *kumi′* 組 one set *hito′-kumi* 一組; *soroi* そろい two sets *futa-*

so'roi 二そろい **2** collection *se'tto* セット **3** hair set *se'tto* セット ——obj *o* (v) **1** arrange (irr) *yō'i-suru* 用意する set a table *tēburu o yō'i-suru* テーブルを用意する **2** join *tsug·u* 継ぐ set a bone *hone' o tsugu* 骨を継ぐ **3** adjust; regulate *awase'·ru* 合せる set a clock *tokei o awase'ru* 時計を合せる **4** place *ok·u* 置く Set this on the table, please. *Kore o tēburu no ue' ni oite kudasa'i.* これをテーブルの上に置いて下さい. ——(idiom) The sun set. *Hi ga kureta.* 日が暮れた.

settle obj *o* (v) **1** decide *kime'·ru* 決める Did you settle on the date? *Hidori o kimema'shita ka?* 日取りを決めましたか. **2** arbitrate (irr) *chūkai-suru* 仲介する

settled (decided) (v) be settled *kimar·u* 決まる It's settled. *Kimatta.* 決まった.

seven *nana'tsu* 七つ; *shichi'/na'na* 七 see also Appendix 1

seventeen *jūna'na* 十七

seventeenth 1 (ordinal) *jūnanabam-me'* 十七番目 **2** (fraction) *jūnanabun no ichi* 十七分の一

seventeenth day of the month *jūshichi'-nichi* 十七日

seventh 1 (ordinal) *nanabam-me'* [*no*] 七番目[の] **2** (fraction) *nanabun no ichi* 七分の一

seventh day of the month *nanoka* 七日

seventy *shichi'jū/nana'jū* 七十 see also Appendix 1

several 1 (things) *i'kutsuka* [*no*] いくつか[の] several problems *i'kutsuka no mondai* いくつかの問題 **2** (persons) *na'nninka* [*no*] 何人か[の] several people *na'nninka no hito* 何人かの人

severe (adj) **1** *hido'·i* ひどい a severe cold *hido'i kaze* ひどい風邪 **2** (attitude) *kibishi'·i* 厳しい a severe person *kibishi'i hito* 厳しい人

sew obj *o* (v) **1** *nu'·u* 縫う I sewed it on the sewing machine. *Mi'shin de nu'tta.* ミシンで縫った. **2** sew on *nuitsuke'·ru* 縫い付ける sew on a button *bo'tan o nuitsuke'ru* ボタンを縫い付ける

sewer *gesuikan* 下水管

sewing 1 (W) *yōsai* 洋裁 **2** (J) *wasai* 和裁

sewing machine *mi'shin* ミシン

sex 1 -*sei* 性 male *dansei* 男性 female *josei* 女性 **2** intercourse *se'kkusu* セックス; *sei kō'i* 性行為

shabby (adj) *migurushi'·i* 見苦しい

shade 1 *ka'ge* 陰 in the shade of the house *ie no ka'ge ni* 家の陰に **2** the shade of a tree *kokage* 木陰 **3** lampshade *ka'sa* かさ

shades (blinds) *buraindo* ブラインド

shadow 1 *ka'ge* 影 **2** (of a person) *kagebō'shi* 影法師

shady *hikage* [*no*] 日陰[の] a shady place *hikage no a'ru tokoro* 日陰のある所

shake (v) **1** quiver *yure'·ru* 揺れる The earth shook violently in the earthquake. *Jishin de ji'men ga hi'doku yureta.* 地震で地面がひどく揺れた. **2** shiver *furue·ru* 震える shake from cold *sa'musa de furueru* 寒さで震える shake from fear *kyōfu ni furueru* 恐怖に震える ——obj *o* (v) **1** shake gently *yuras·u* 揺らす **2** shake vigorously *fur·u* 振る shake dice *saiko'ro o furu* サイコロを振る shake one's head *atama' o furu* 頭を振る

shake hands compl *to* (irr) *a'kushu-suru* 握手する Europeans shake hands. *Yōroppa'jin wa a'kushu-suru.* ヨーロッパ人は握手する.

shallow (adj) *asa'·i* 浅い shallow river *asai kawa'* 浅い川 a shallow wound *asa'i kizu* 浅い傷 His thinking is shallow. *Ka're wa shi'ryo ga asa'i.* 彼は思慮が浅い.

shaman *majina'ishi* まじない師

shame *haji'* 恥 ——obj *o* (v) *hazukashime'·ru* 辱かしめる

shameful (adj) *hazukashi'·i* 恥ずかしい That was a shameful thing I did. *Hazukashi'i koto'o shite shimatta.* 恥ずかしい事をしてしまった.

shameless (attr) *haji shi'razu [no]* 恥知らず[の] That woman is shameless! *Ano onna' wa haji shi'razu da!* あの女は恥知らずだ.

shampoo *sha'mpū* シャンプー ——obj *o* (v) *ara·u* 洗う shampoo hair *kami' o arau* 髪を洗う ——(irr) *sha'mpū-suru* シャンプーする

shape *katachi* 形

share **1** in a company *kabu* 株 **2** one's allotment *wake'mae* 分け前 ——ind-obj *ni*, obj *o* (v) *wake'·ru* 分ける Share that with your younger brother. *Sore o otōto' ni mo wa'kete kudasa'i.* それを弟にも分けて下さい.

shark *same* 鮫

sharp (adj) *surudo'·i* 鋭い ——(attr) **1** pointed *toga'tta* とがった a sharp stick *toga'tta bō* とがった棒 a sharp nose *toga'tta hana* とがった鼻 **2** keen *yo'ku kire'ru* よく切れる a sharp knife *yo'ku kire'ru na'ifu* よく切れるナイフ **3** (flavor) *piri'tto-shita* ピリッとした **4** intelligent *atama no i'i* 頭のいい a sharp person *atama no i'i hito'* 頭のいい人 **5** (Music) *e'i-* 嬰 A sharp major *e'i-i-chō'chō* 嬰イ長調

sharpen obj *o* (v) **1** sharpen a blade *to'g·u* 研ぐ **2** sharpen to a point *kezur·u* 削る

shatter obj *o* (v) *uchikuda'k·u* 打ち砕く The child shattered the window with a baseball bat. *Kodomo ga ba'tto de mado-ga'rasu o uchikuda'ita.* 子供がバットで窓ガラスを打ち砕いた. ——(v) *kudake'·ru* 砕ける In the earthquake the mirror shattered. *Jishin de kaga'mi ga kuda'keta.* 地震で鏡が砕けた.

shave obj *o* (v) *so'r·u* 剃る Shave my beard, please. *Hige o so'tte kudasa'i.* ひげを剃って下さい. Don't shave my sideburns. *Momiage o sora'naide kudasa'i.* もみあげを剃らないで下さい.

shaver 1 razor *kamiso'ri* 剃刀 2 electric shaver *denki ka'misori* 電気剃刀

shaving cream *shēbingu kuri'mu* シェービングクリーム

she *ka'nojo* 彼女

shears 1 *hasa'mi* はさみ 2 (pinking) *pinkingu-ba'sami* ピンキングばさみ 3 (pruning) *sentei-ba'sami* せん定ばさみ

shed *mono-oki'* 物置き

shed obj *ga* (v) *nuke·ru* 抜ける shed feathers *hane ga nukeru* 羽が抜ける ——obj *o* (v) *naga's·u* 流す shed tears *na'mida o naga'su* 涙を流す

sheep *hitsuji* 羊

sheer (material) *usuji no* 薄地の

sheet 1 bed sheet *shi'tsu* シーツ 2 a sheet of paper *kami' ichima'i* 紙一枚 *see also* Appendix 1: paper

shelf *tana* 棚

shell 1 (egg) *tama'go no kara'* 卵の殻 2 (pie) *pa'i no kawa'* パイの皮 3 seashell *kaiga'ra* 貝殻

shellfish *ka'i* 貝

shelter 1 (from disaster) *hinanjo* 避難所 2 protection *ho'go* 保護 tax shelter *zeikin ho'go* 税金保護 ——obj *o* (v) *kaba'·u* 庇う The mother sheltered her child from the rain. *Okā'-san wa kodomo ga a'me ni nurenai yō' ni kaba'tte kureta.* お母さんは子供が雨に濡れないように庇ってくれた.

shepherd *hitsuji'kai* 羊飼い

sherbet *shā'betto* シャーベット

shield *ta'te* 盾

shift 1 *kōtai* 交替 This factory operates on three shifts each twenty-four hours. *Kono kōjō' wa nijūyoji'kan ni san-kō'tai de kadō-shite iru.* この工場は二十四時間を三交替で稼動している. 2 transfer *tenkan* 転換 Because of turnover in personnel, there have been some shifts in positions. *Jinji i'dō de haichi te'nkan ni natta.* 人事異動で配置転換になった. 3 (automobile) *giya shi'futo* ギヤシフト ——obj *o* (v) *kae·ru* 変える I shifted the furniture for a change in decor. *Moyōgae de ka'gu no haichi o kaeta.* 模様替えで家具の配置を変えた. ——(idiom) shift into gear *gi'ya o ire·ru* ギヤを入れる

shimmer (v) *chi'rachira hika'r·u* ちらちら光る

shin *sune* 脛; *mukō-zune* 向こう脛

shine (v) 1 (of light) *hika'r·u* 光る A light is shining. *Akari ga hika'tte iru.* 明りが光っている. 2 (of stars) *kagaya'k·u* 輝く The stars are shining. *Hoshi ga kagaya'ite iru.* 星が輝いている. 3 (of the sun) *te'r·u* 照る The sun's shining. *Hi ga te'tte iru.* 日が照っている. ——obj *o* (v) polish *migak·u* 磨く shine shoes *kutsu' o migaku* 靴を磨く shine floors *yuka o migaku* 床を磨く

shingles (herpes zoster) *taijō hō'shin* 帯状ほう疹

ship *fu'ne* 船 ——obj *o* (v) *okur·u* 送る ship baggage *ni'motsu o okuru* 荷物を送る

shipment *tsumini* 積荷 Did the shipment arrive safely? *Tsumini wa buji ni todokima'shita ka?* 積荷は無事に届きましたか.

shipping expense *u'nchin* 運賃

shipwreck **1** *nampa* 難破 **2** (remains) *chimbotsu-sen* 沈没船

shirt **1** *sha'tsu* シャツ **2** dress shirt *waishatsu* ワイシャツ **3** sport shirt *supōtsu sha'tsu* スポーツシャツ **4** undershirt *sha'tsu* シャツ

shiver (v) [*bu'ruburu*] *furue·ru* [ぶるぶる]震える

shock *shōgeki* 衝撃 He couldn't recover from the shock of his friend's death. *Ka're wa yū jin no shi' no shōgeki kara tachinaore'-nakatta.* 彼は友人の死の衝撃から立ち直れなかった. ——(irr) *kanden-suru* 感電する Don't touch that naked wire; it will shock you. *Mukidashi ::o densen ni sawatte' wa ikemase'n. Kanden-shima'su yo.* 剥き出しの電線に触ってはいけません. 感電しますよ. ——(idiom) be shocked by *sho'kku o uke'·ru* ショックを受ける I was shocked to hear the rumor that she's getting married. *Ka'nojo ga kekkon o suru to iu uwasa o kiite, sho'kku o u'keta.* 彼女が結婚をするという噂を聞いてショックを受けた.

shoe **1** *kutsu'* 靴 **2** loafers *mokashi'n-gutsu* モカシン靴 **3** oxfords *tan'-gutsu* 短靴 **4** pumps *pa'mpusu* パンプス **5** athletic shoes *undō-gutsu* 運動靴 **6** tennis shoes *tenisu shū'zu* テニスシューズ **7** high-heels *hai-hī'ru* ハイヒール

shoehorn *kutsube'ra* 靴べら

shoelace *himo* 紐; *kutsu'-himo* 靴紐

shoe polish *kutsu'-zumi* 靴墨

shoe repair shop *kutsu-na'oshi* 靴直し; *kutsu shūri-ya* 靴修理屋

shoeshine *kutsu-mi'gaki* 靴みがき

shoe store *kutsu'ya* 靴屋

shoe tree *kutsu-gata* 靴型

shoot obj *o* (v) **1** (with a gun) *u'ts·u* 撃つ **2** (with an arrow) *i'r·u* 射る **3** (with a camera) *to'r·u* 撮る shoot a picture *shashin o to'ru* 写真を撮る

shop *mise'* 店 ——(irr) *kaimono-suru* 買物する

shopping *kaimono* 買物 go shopping *kaimono ni iku* 買物に行く

shopping street *shōte'ngai* 商店街 underground shopping street *chika shōte'ngai* 地下商店街

shore **1** *kishi'* 岸 **2** seashore *kaigan* 海岸

short (adj) (length) *mijika'·i* 短い **2** (height) *hiku'·i* 低い —— (attr) short in stature *se' ga hiku'i* 背が低い Ms. Tanaka is short. *Tanaka-san wa se' ga hiku'i.* 田中さんは背が低い.

short circuit *shō'to* ショート

shortcut *chika'michi* 近道

shorten obj *o* (irr) **1** *mijika'ku-suru* 短くする Please shorten the sleeves a bit. *Sode o suko'shi mijika'ku-shite kudasa'i.* 袖を少し短くして下さい。 **2** abridge *shōryaku-suru* 省略する shorten a speech *hanashi' o shōryaku-suru* 話を省略する

shortening *shō'toningu* ショートニング

shorthand *sokki* 速記

shorts (short pants) *hanzubon* 半ズボン

short story *tampen* [*shō'setsu*] 短編 [小説]

short-tempered *ta'nki* [*na*] 短気 [な]

shortwave *ta'mpa* 短波

shot **1** hypodermic injection *chūsha* 注射 **2** gunshot *-hatsu* 発 one gunshot *ippatsu* 一発 **3** shot of whisky *shi'nguru* シングル

shotgun *sanda'njū* 散弾銃

should ...*hō' ga i'·i* ...方がいい I should have telephoned for reservations. *Denwa de yoyaku-shite o'ita hō' ga yo'katta.* 電話で予約しておいた方が良かった。 see also **ought**

shoulder (Anat) *ka'ta* 肩 ——obj *o* (v) *katsu'g·u* かつぐ

shoulder bag *shorudā ba'ggu* ショルダーバッグ

shout *donarigo'e* どなり声 ——obj *o* (v) *dona'r·u* どなる You must not shout. *Dona'tte wa ikemase'n.* どなってはいけません。

shove obj *o* (v) *os·u* 押す Don't shove! *Osana'ide kudasa'i!* 押さないで下さい。; *oshida's·u* 押し出す I was first in line, but someone shoved me aside. *Watashi wa ichiban ma'e ni narande ita' no ni, da're ka ga watashi o oshida'shita.* 私は一番前に並んでいたのに、誰かが私を押し出した。

shovel *suko'ppu* スコップ; *sha'beru* シャベル

show **1** entertainment *moyōshi-mono* 催し物; *shō'* ショー **2** display *tenji'kai* 展示会 **3** exhibit *tenra'nkai* 展覧会 **4** movie *e'iga* 映画 ——ind-obj *ni*, obj *o* (v) *mise'·ru* 見せる Show me that, please. *Sore o mi'sete kudasa'i.* それを見せて下さい。 **2** indicate *shime's·u* 示す The graph shows a 10% increase in July. *Gurafu wa shichigatsu' ni ichi'wari no zōka o shime'shite iru.* グラフは七月に一割の増加を示している。 **3** guide (irr) *anna'i-suru* 案内する Show him to the conference room. *Ka're o kaigi'shitsu ni an na'i-shite kudasa'i.* 彼を会議室に案内して下さい。 **4** instruct *osh'ie'·ru* 教える Would you please show me how to make it? *Dō' yatte tsuku'ru ka oshiete kudasaimase'n ka?* どうやって作るか教えて下さいませんか。

shower **1** brief, light rain *niwaka a'me* にわか雨 **2** bath *sha'wā* シャワー

shred *borokire* ぼろきれ

shrewd (adj) *kashiko'·i* 賢い; *nukemena'·i* 抜け目ない

shrimp *ebi* えび

shrine **1** *miya* 宮 **2** (Shinto) *ji'nja* 神社

shrink (v) *chijim·u* 縮む Will this material shrink? *Kono ki'ji wa chijimima'su ka?* この生地は縮みますか.

shuffle (cards) obj *o* (v) [*tora'mpu o*] *ki'r·u* [トランプを]切る

shut (v) *shima'r·u* 締まる The door is shut. *Do'a ga shima'tte iru.* ドアが締まっている. ——obj *o* (v) *shime'·ru* 締める Shut the door, please. *Do'a o shi'mete kudasa'i.* ドアを締めて下さい.

shut-in (attr) *neta'kiri* [*no*] 寝たきり[の]

shutter 1 *ama'do* 雨戸 2 (of a camera) *sha'ttā* シャッター

shy *uchiki* [*na*] 内気[な] a shy person *uchiki na hito* 内気な人; *hazukashigariya* 恥ずかしがりや ——(adj) *hazukashi'·i* 恥ずかしい I'm too shy to do that! *Hazuka'shikute deki'nai!* 恥ずかしくできない. ——(v) be shy *hanika'm·u* はにかむ

shyness *hanikami* はにかみ; *hazuka'shisa* 恥ずかしさ

sick *byōki* [*no*] 病気[の] a sick person *byōki no hito* 病気の人; *byōnin* 病人 be/become sick *byōki ni na'r·u* 病気になる Mr. Tanaka is sick. *Tanaka-san ga byōki ni na'tta.* 田中さんが病気になった. ——(idiom) 1 feel sick *ki'bun ga waru'·i* 気分が悪い 2 sick to one's stomach *hakike'ga suru* 吐気がする

sickly *byōjaku* [*no*] 病弱[の]

sickness *byōki* 病気; -*byō* 病 sleeping sickness *nemuri-byō* 眠り病

sick of compl *ni* (irr) *unza'ri-suru* うんざりする I'm sick of him. *Ka're ni wa unza'ri-shite iru.* 彼にはうんざりしている.

side 1 *waki'* 側 2 beside *yoko* 横; -*gawa* 側 left-side *hidari-gawa* 左側 rightside *migi-gawa* 右側 both sides *ryō-gawa* 両側 this side *kotchi-gawa* こっち側 that side *mukō-gawa* 向こう側 opposite side *hantai-gawa* 反対側 inside *uchi-gawa* 内側 outside *soto-gawa* 外側

sideburns *momiage* もみあげ

side dish *o-kazu* おかず

side street *yokochō* 横町

sidestroke *yoko-o'yogi* 横泳ぎ

sidetrack (irr) *dassen-suru* 脱線する

sidewalk *hodō* 歩道

sideways *yoko* [*ni*] 横[に]

sieve *furui* ふるい

sifter *furui* ふるい

sigh *tame'iki* ため息 ——(idiom) to sigh *tame'iki o tsuk·u* ため息をつく

sight (vision) *shikaku* 視覚

sightsee obj *o* (irr) *kembutsu-suru* 見物する

sightseeing *kankō* 観光 sightseeing bus *kankō ba'su* 観光バス

sightseer *kankō'kyaku* 観光客

sign 1 road sign *hyō'shiki* 標識 2 billboard *kamban* 看板 3 mark; symbol *shirushi* 印 4 cue *a'izu* 合図 ——obj *o* (irr) *sa'in-suru* サインする; *shomei-suru* 署名する

signal   *shingō* 信号 stop signal *teishi shi'ngō* 停止信号

signature   *sa'in* サイン; *shomei* 署名

significant   *jūdai* [*na*] 重大[な] She made a significant comment at the meeting. *Ka'nojo wa ka'igi de jūdai na hatsugen o shita.* 彼女は会議で重大な発言をした.

sign language   *shu'wa* 手話

silence   *chimmoku* 沈黙

silent   (v) be/become silent *dama'r·u* 黙る She suddenly became silent. *Ka'nojo wa totsuzen dama'tte shimatta.* 彼女は突然黙ってしまった.

silent prayer   *mokutō* 黙禱

silk   1 *ki'nu* 絹   2 raw silk *ki'ito* 生糸

silkworm   *ka'iko* 蚕

sill   *shikii* 敷居

silly   *ba'ka* ばか Don't be silly! *Ba'ka o iu na!* ばかを言うな.; *bakarashi'·i* ばからしい That's silly! *Bakarashi'·i!* ばからしい.

silver   1 (metal) *gi'n* 銀   2 flatware *na'ifu to fo'ku* ナイフとフォーク   3 silverware *ginse'ihin* 銀製品   4 coin *gi'nka* 銀貨

silver plating   *gin me'kki* 銀メッキ

similar   *onaji yō* [*na*] 同じ様[な] I want a dress with a similar design to the one that actress was wearing. *Ano joyū ga kite ita do'resu to onaji yō' na deza'in no do'resu ga hoshi'i.* あの女優が着ていたドレスと同じ様なデザインのドレスが欲しい. ——(v) resemble *nite i·ru* 似ている Seals and sea lions are similar. *Ashika to otto'sei wa nite iru.* あしかとおっとせいは似ている.

simile   *cho'kuyu* 直喩

simmer   obj *o* (v) *bu'tsubutsu niko'm·u* ぶつぶつ煮込む

simple   1 uncomplicated *kantan* [*na*] 簡単[な] a simple way *kantan na hōhō* 簡単な方法   2 plain *jimi'* [*na*] 地味[な] a simple dress *jimi'na fuku* 地味な服 ——(adj) easy *yasashi'·i* やさしい This problem is simple. *Kono mondai wa yasashi'·i.* この問題はやさしい.

simultaneous   *dōji* [*no*] 同時[の] simultaneous interpretation *dōji tsū'yaku* 同時通訳

sin   (Chr) *tsu'mi* 罪 repent of sin *tsu'mi o kuiaratame'ru* 罪を悔い改める the forgiveness of sin *tsu'mi no yurushi* 罪の許し ——(idiom) commit sin *tsu'mi o oka's·u* 罪を犯す

since   *i'rai* 以来 I haven't seen him since he returned to Japan. *Ka're ga Niho'n ni ka'ette i'rai, a'tte inai.* 彼が日本に帰って以来, 会っていない. ——(idiom) since then *sono-go* その後 I've heard nothing since then. *Sono-go, nani mo kiite ina'i.* その後, 何も聞いていない. *see also* after; because

sincere   *seijitsu* [*na*] 誠実[な] a sincere attitude *seijitsu na ta'ido* 誠実な態度

sing   obj *o* (v) 1 (humans) *uta·u* 歌う sing a song *uta' o utau* 歌を

歌う Sing for us! *Utatte kudasa'i!* 歌って下さい． **2** (birds) *nak·u*
鳴く；*saezu'r·u* さえずる

Singapore *Shingapo'ru* シンガポール

Singaporean (person) *Shingapōru' jin* シンガポール人 ──(attr)
Shingapō'ru no シンガポールの

singe (v) *koge'·ru* 焦げる Be careful not to let it singe. *Koge'nai*
yō ni chū'i-shite kudasa'i. 焦げないよう注意して下さい．

singer *ka'shu* 歌手

single 1 unmarried *hitorimono* 独り者；(masc) *dokushin [no]* 独身
[の]；(fem) *mikon [no]* 未婚[の] **2** one *hitotsu* (counter) (+
neg) 一つも I don't have a single thing to do tomorrow. *Ashita'*
wa suru koto' ga hitotsu mo na'i. 明日はすることが一つもない．I
don't have a single clean shirt. *Ki'rei na sha'tsu wa ichimai mo*
na'i. きれいなシャツは一枚もない．

single bed *shi'nguru* シングル；*shinguru be'ddo* シングルベッド

single room *shi'nguru* シングル

singular (Gram) *tansū'* 単数 ──(adj) rare *mezurashi'·i* 珍しい
She is a musician of singular skill. *Ka'nojo wa mezurashii gi'ryō o*
motta onga'kuka desu. 彼女は珍しい技量をもった音楽家です．

Sinhalese 1 (language) *Suriranka-go* スリランカ語 **2** (person)
Surira'nka iin スリランカ人 ──(attr) *Surira'nka no* スリランカ
の

sink 1 (kitchen) *nagashi'* 流し **2** (bathroom) *semmendai* 洗面台
──(v) *shizum·u* 沈む；(irr) *chimbotsu-suru* 沈没する The ship
sank. *Fu'ne ga chimbotsu-shita.* 船が沈没した．

sinner (Chr) *tsumibito* 罪人

sinus *tō'* 洞

sinus headache (sinusitis) *chikunō'shō* 蓄膿症

sip obj *o* (v) *susur·u* すする take small sips *chi'bichibi susuru* ちび
ちびする

siren *sa'iren* サイレン

sister 1 (one's younger) *imōto'* 妹 **2** (one's older) *ane* 姉 **3**
(another's younger) *imōto-san* 妹さん **4** (another's older) *o-nē'-*
san お姉さん **5** (Chr) nun *nisō* 尼僧；*shi'sutā* シスター

sister-in-law 1 (one's younger) *imōto'* 妹 **2** (one's older) *ane* 姉
3 (another's younger) *giri no imōto-san* 義理の妹さん **4** (another's
older) *giri no o-nē'-san* 義理のお姉さん

sit (v) **1** *suwar·u* 坐る Please sit down. *Dō'zo o-suwari kudasa'i.*
どうぞお坐り下さい． **2** (on a chair) *koshikake'·ru* 腰かける

site 1 *basho* 場所 This is a good site to build a house. *Koko wa*
ie' o tate'ru ni wa i'i basho de'su. ここは家を建てるにはいい場所
です． **2** historical site *shiseki* 史跡

situation *ji'tai* 事態 Trade friction between Japan and America
has become a serious situation. *Ni'chibei no bōeki ma'satsu wa*

shinkoku na ji'tai ni natta. 日米の貿易摩擦は深刻な事態になった.; *tachiba* 立場 I found myself in an embarrassing situation. *Watashi wa koma'tta tachiba' ni ita.* 私は困った立場にいた.

six *muttsu* 六つ; *roku'* 六 *see also* Appendix 1

sixteen *jūroku'* 十六

sixteenth **1** (ordinal) *jūrokubam-me'* [*no*] 十六番目[の] **2** (fraction) *jūrokubun no ichi* 十六分の一

sixteenth day of the month *jūroku-nichi* 十六日

sixth **1** (ordinal) *rokubam-me'* [*no*] 六番目[の] **2** (fraction) *rokubun no ichi* 六分の一

sixth day of the month *muika* 六日

sixty *rokujū'* 六十 *see also* Appendix 1

size **1** *ōkisa* 大きさ **2** (of clothing) *sa'izu* サイズ; small size (S) *shō'* 小; medium size (M) *chū'* 中; large size (L) *da'i* 大; extra-large (LL) *tokudai* 特大; *eru-eru sa'izu* LL サイズ

skate/skating *sukē'to* スケート ice skate/skating *sukē'to* スケート roller skate/skating *rōrā-sukē'to* ローラースケート ——(irr) *sukē'to-suru* スケートする

skating rink *sukētojō* スケート場

skeleton *ga'ikotsu* 骸骨

sketch *suke'tchi* スケッチ ——obj *o* (irr) *suke'tchi-suru* スケッチする

ski/skiing *sukī'* スキー ——(irr) *sukī' o suru* スキーをする

ski binding *shime'gu* 締め具

ski lift *ri'futo* リフト

skill *udemae* 腕前

skillet *furai-pan* フライパン

skillful **1** *jōzu'* [*na*] 上手[な] **2** dexterous *ki'yō* [*na*] 器用[な] He's skillful with his hands. *Ka're wa tesaki' ga ki'yō desu.* 彼は手先が器用です. ——(adj) *uma'·i* うまい She's a skillful tennis player. *Ka'nojo wa te'nisu ga uma'i.* 彼女はテニスがうまい.

skillfully *jōzu'ni* 上手に; *u'maku* うまく He plays the piano skillfully. *Ka're wa piano o u'maku hiku.* 彼はピアノをうまく弾く.

skin **1** (human) *hi'fu* 皮膚 skin disease *hifu-byō* 皮膚病 **2** (animal) *kawa'* 皮 ——obj *o* (v) graze *surimu'k·u* すりむく I skinned my knee. *Hiza o surimu'ita.* 膝をすりむいた. ——(idiom) skin an animal *kawa' o ha'g·u* 皮をはぐ

skin diving *sukin da'ibingu* スキンダイビング

skip obj *o* (v) *tobas·u* 飛ばす You skipped a line when you typed the manuscript. *Ana'ta wa genkō o i'pu-suru toki, ichi'gyō o tobashite shima'tta.* あなたは原稿をタイプする時, 一行を飛ばしてしまった. ——(irr) *suki'ppu-suru* スキップする The girl came skipping out of the classroom. *Onna' no ko wa suki'ppu-shina'gara,* *kyōshitsu kara de'te kita.* 女の子はスキップしながら、教室から出て来た. ——(idiom) **1** skip rope *nawato'bi o suru* 縄跳びをする **2** skip class *ju'gyō o sabo'r·u* 授業をサボる; *ku'rasu o esukē' pu-suru* クラスをエスケープする **3** skip a grade (in school) *tobi-shi'nkyū-suru* 飛び進級する He skipped from third to fifth grade. *Ka're wa sanne'n-sei kara gone'n-sei ni tobi-shi'nkyū-shita.* 彼は三年生から五年生に飛び進級した.

ski resort *sukī'jō* スキー場

skirt *sukā'to* スカート a red skirt *akai sukā'to* 赤いスカート

skull *zuga'ikotsu* 頭蓋骨

sky *so'ra* 空 blue sky *aozo'ra* 青空 The sky is clear. *So'ra ga ha'rete iru.* 空が晴れている.

skylark *hibari* 雲雀

skyscraper *mate'nrō* 摩天楼

slacks *sura'kkusu* スラックス

slander *me'iyo kison* 名誉棄損; *waru'kuchi* 悪口 ——obj *o* (irr) *hi'nan-suru* 非難する ——(idiom) *waru'kuchi o i·u* 悪口を言う

slang 1 *sura'ngu* スラング **2** colloquial language *zokugo* 俗語

slant *keisha* 傾斜 ——(irr) *keisha-suru* 傾斜する This floor slants a little. *Kono yuka wa suko'shi keisha-shite iru.* この床は少し傾斜している. ——(idiom) write with a slant *yuga'mete kak·u* 歪めて書く The reporter (under government patronage) slants the news regarding political matters in favor of the government. *Goyō-ki'sha wa se'ifu ni tsugō i'i yō ni, seiji mo'ndai o yuga'mete ka'ku.* 御用記者は政府に都合いいように, 政治問題を歪めて書く.

slave *dorei* 奴隷

sled *so'ri* そり

sleep *suimin* 睡眠 ——(v) *nemur·u* 眠る I slept well. *Yo'ku ne-mutta.* よく眠った. **2** go to bed *ne·ru* 寝る Where do the children sleep? *Kodomo wa do'ko de nema'su ka?* 子供はどこで寝ますか. ——obj *o* (caus) *nekase·ru* 寝かせる After I put the baby to sleep, I watch TV. *A'kachan o nekasete kara, te'rebi o mi'ru.* 赤ちゃんを寝かせてからテレビを見る. ——(idiom) go to bed *toko ni ha'ir·u* 床に入る

sleeping car *shinda'isha* 寝台車

sleeping pill *suimi'n-yaku* 睡眠薬

sleepwalking *muyūbyō* 夢遊病

sleepy (adj) *nemu'·i* 眠い Are you sleepy? *Nemu'i desu ka?* 眠いですか.

sleet *mizore* みぞれ

sleeve *sode* 袖 half/short sleeve *han-sode* 半袖

slender *sumā'to* [na] スマート[な] ——(adj) *hoso'·i* 細い

slice *-kire* 切れ one slice *hito'kire* 一切れ three slices *mi'-kire* 三

切れ ——obj o (v) ki'r·u 切る Please slice the bread. Pa'n o ki'tte kudasa'i. パンを切って下さい.

slide 1 (on a playground) suberi'dai 滑り台 2 transparency su-raido スライド ——(v) sube'r·u 滑る

slight suko'shi [no] 少し[の] You have a slight fever. Ana'ta wa netsu' ga suko'shi a'ru. あなたは熱が少しある. ——(pass) be slighted bujoku-sare'ru 侮辱される I felt slighted. Watashi wa bu-joku-sareta to omo'tta. 私は侮辱されたと思った.

slip (v) sube'r·u 滑る; (irr) suri'ppu-suru スリップする

slip (undergarment) su'rippu スリップ

slipper suri'ppa スリッパ

slippery (attr) tsu'rutsuru-shita つるつるした a slippery street tsu'rutsuru-shita michi つるつるした道

slobber yodare よだれ ——(idiom) to slobber yodare o tara's·u よだれをたらす

slope saka' 坂; sha'men 斜面

sloppily darashina'ku だらしなく She was dressed sloppily. Ka'nojo wa darashina'ku kitsuke o shite ita. 彼女はだらしなく着付けをしていた.

sloppy (adj) darashina'·i だらしない His desk is always sloppy. Ka're no tsukue no ue' wa i'tsumo darashina'i. 彼の机の上はいつもだらしない. ——(attr) darashi no na'i だらしのない a sloppy person darashi no na'i hito' だらしのない人

slot machine surotto mashi'n スロットマシン

Slovak 1 (language) Surobakia-go スロバキア語 2 (person) Suro-bakia'jin スロバキア人 ——(attr) Suroba'kia no スロバキアの

slow (adj) 1 oso'·i 遅い Progress is slow. Shi'mpo ga oso'i. 進歩が遅い. 2 dull nibu'·i 鈍い I'm slow to understand. Atama no kaiten ga nibu'i. 頭の回転が鈍い. 3 (vehicles; actions) noro'·i のろい a slow train noro'i de'nsha のろい電車 ——(v) be behind time okure·ru 遅れる Is this clock slow? Kono tokei wa okurete ima'su ka? この時計は遅れていますか?

slow down (idiom) supido o oto's·u スピードを落とす Slow down! Supido o oto'shite kudasa'i! スピードを落として下さい.

slowly yukku'ri [to] ゆっくり[と] Go slowly, please! Yukku'ri one-gai shima'su! ゆっくりお願いします. Please speak more slowly. Mo'tto yukku'ri hana'shite kudasa'i. もっとゆっくり話して下さい.

slum su'ramu スラム; suramu'-gai スラム街

slush yuki-doke 雪解け

sly zuruso' [na] ずるそう[な] a sly-looking person zuruso' na hito ずるそうな人 ——(adj) zuru'·i ずるい Be careful of that person; he's sly. Ano' hito ni chu'·i-shite kudasa'i. Ka're wa zuru'in desu. あの人に注意して下さい. 彼はずるいんです.

small (adj) **1** (size) *chīsa'·i* 小さい small child *chīsai kodomo* 小さい子供 These shoes are too small. *Kono kutsu' wa chīsa-sugi'ru.* この靴は小さすぎる. **2** (space) *sema'·i* 狭い, small room *sema'i heya'* 狭い部屋 My house is small. *Uchi' wa sema'i.* 家は狭い. **3** (amount) *sukuna'·i* 少ない a small number of people *ka'zu sukuna'i hito* 数少ない人

small change *kozeni* 小銭; *komaka'i o-kane* こまかいお金

smallpox *tennentō* 天然痘

small-size *kogata* [no] 小型[の] small-size car *kogata'sha* 小型車

small talk *sekenba'nashi* 世間話; *zatsudan* 雑談

smart *rikō* [na] 利口[な] smart child *rikō na kodomo* 利口な子供 This dog is smart. *Kono inu' wa rikō de'su.* この犬は利口です. ——(attr) *atama no i'·i* 頭のいい a smart person *atama no i'i hito* 頭のいい人

smash 1 *dai-hi'tto* [no] 大ヒット[の] The musical was a smash. *Sono myū'jikaru wa dai-hi'tto deshita.* そのミュージカルは大ヒットでした. **2** (sports) *kyō'da* 強打 ——obj *o* (irr) *funsai-suru* 粉砕する University students rose up to smash the old system. *Daiga'kusei wa gen-ta'isei o funsai-shiyō to tachiaga'tta.* 大学生は現体制を粉砕しようと立ち上がった. ——(pass) be smashed *kuzusare'ru* 崩される Several houses were smashed in the landslide. *Yamaku'zure de na'ngen mo no ie' ga kuzusa'reta.* 山崩れで何軒もの家が崩された.

smell 1 *nio'i* 匂い a pleasing smell *i'i nio'i* いい匂い an unpleasant smell *kusa'i nio'i* 臭い匂い a strange smell *he'n na nio'i* 変な匂い **2** (sense of) *kyūkaku* 嗅覚 ——(v) *nio'·u* 匂う The fish smells! *Sakana ga nio'u!* 魚が匂う! ——obj *o* (v) *kag·u* 嗅ぐ Smell this! *Kore o kaide goran!* これを嗅いでごらん. ——(idiom) to have an odor *nio'i ga suru* 匂いがする It smells good. *I'i nio'i ga suru.* いい匂いがする. **2** It smells (stinks)! *Kusa'i!* 臭い.

smelt *wakasagi* わかさぎ

smile *hohoemi* ほほえみ; *bishō* 微笑; *warai* 笑い a bitter smile *niga-wa'rai* 苦笑い a smiling face *warai-gao* 笑い顔 ——(v) **1** *wara·u* 笑う smile pleasantly *ni'koniko warau* にこにこ笑う Smile, please! *Waratte kudasa'i!* 笑って下さい.; *hohoe'm·u* ほほえむ **2** (irr) *ni'koniko-suru* にこにこする She's always smiling. *Ka'nojo wa i'tsumo ni'koniko-shite iru.* 彼女はいつもにこにこしている.

smoke *kemuri* 煙 Smoke billowed out of the chimney. *Kemuri ga mo'kumoku to entotsu kara de'ta.* 煙がもくもくと煙突から出た. ——(v) *kemur·u* 煙る This stove smokes badly. *Kono sutō'bu wa iya'ni kemuru.* このストーブはいやに煙る. ——obj *o* (v) [*tabako o*] *no'm·u* [たばこを]のむ; *su·u* 吸う Do you smoke? *Tabako o suima'su ka?* たばこを吸いますか.

smoky (adj) *kemu·i* 煙い、The room is smoky. *Heya' ga kemu' i.* 部屋が煙い.; (coll) *kemuta' ·i* 煙たい

smooth *name' raka* [na] なめらか[な] a smooth surface *name' raka na hyōme'n* なめらかな表面 The road was smooth. *Dō' ro wa name' raka deshita.* 道路はなめらかでした. ——(idiom) make smooth *name' raka ni suru* なめらかにする They smoothed the playing field. *Guraundo o name' raka ni shita.* グラウンドをなめらかにした.

smoothly *name' raka ni* なめらかに I hope everything goes smoothly. *Su' bete ga name' raka ni susumu yō' ni.* すべてがなめらかにすすむように.

smother (to death) obj *o* (caus) *chisso' kushi-sase·ru* 窒息死させる

snack 1 *oya' tsu* おやつ 2 a light meal *keishoku* 軽食; *karui shokuji* 軽い食事 ——(idiom) 1 eat a snack *oya' tsu o tabe' ·ru* おやつを食べる 2 (with the fingers) *tsumam·u* つまむ Snack on this! *Hito' tsu tsumande kudasa' i!* 一つつまんで下さい.

snail *katatsu' muri* かたつむり

snake *he' bi* 蛇 poisonous snake *doku he' bi* 毒蛇

snap 1 snapshot *suna' ppu* スナップ 2 fastener *ho' kku* ホック ——obj *o* (v) *pachi' n to hame' ·ru* ぱちんとはめる

sneak *tsugeguchiya* 告げ口屋 ——(irr) *ko' sokoso-suru* こそこそする

sneakers *undō' -gutsu* 運動靴

sneeze *kusha' mi* くしゃみ ——(idiom) *kusha' mi o suru* くしゃみをする

snobbish (attr) *iba' tta* いばった; *ki' za* [na] きざ[な]

snore *ibiki* いびき ——(idiom) to snore *ibiki' o ka' k·u* いびきをかく

snorkel *shunō' keru* シュノーケル

snow *yuki'* 雪 heavy snow *ōyuki* 大雪 ——(idiom) to snow *yuki' ga fu' r·u* 雪が降る Does it snow in Tokyo *Tōkyō wa yuki' ga furima' su ka?* 東京は雪が降りますか.

snowball fight *yuki ga' ssen* 雪合戦

snowflake (Tech) *seppen* 雪片; (coll) *yuki'* 雪

snowman *yuki-da' ruma* 雪だるま

snowplow *jose' tsuki* 除雪機

snowshoe *yuki' -gutsu* 雪靴

snowstorm *fu' buki* 吹雪

snow tire *sunō-ta' iya* スノータイヤ

so 1 thus *sō'* そう Do you think so? *Sō' omoima' su ka?* そう思いますか. I don't think so. *Sō' omoimase' n.* そう思いません. He said so. *Ka' re wa sō' iima' shita.* 彼はそう言いました. 2 to such an extent *sonna ni* そんなに I don't need so much. *Sonna ni irana'i.* そんなにいらない。 It's not so far. *Sonna ni tōku na'i.* そんなに遠くない。 **3** therefore *da'kara* だから; (v, past +) *kara* から I didn't have much money with me then, so I couldn't buy it. *Sono toki o-kane o amari mo'tte ina'katta kara, kaena'katta.* その時お金をあまり持っていなかったから買えなかった。

soak obj *o* (v) *hitas·u* 浸す Soak this in lukewarm water for about five minutes. *Kore o gofun-gu'rai nuru'i o-yu ni hitashite kudasa'i.* これを五分ぐらい温いお湯に浸して下さい。

soap 1 *sekken* 石鹸 face soap *keshō se'kken* 化粧石鹸 powdered soap *kona se'kken* 粉石鹸 **2** detergent *senzai* 洗剤

soapsuds *sekken no awa'* 石鹸の泡

sob (v) [*shiku' shiku to*] *nak·u* [しくしくと]泣く When he heard that his father was on his deathbed, he sobbed. *Otō'-san ga rinjū da'to kiite, ka're wa shiku'shiku to naita.* お父さんが臨終だと聞いて彼はしくしくと泣いた。

sober *shirafu* しらふ ——(idiom) to become sober *yoi o sama's·u* 酔いを覚ます; *yoi ga same'·ru* 酔いが覚める

so-called *iwa'yuru* いわゆる The so-called era of peace is nothing but a deception. *Iwa'yuru heiwa no jidai wa, maya'kashi ni sugina'i.* いわゆる平和の時代はまやかしにすぎない。

soccer *sa'kkā* サッカー

social 1 outgoing *shakōteki* [*na*] 社交的[な] a social person *shakōteki na hito'* 社交的な人 **2** (of society) *shakaiteki* [*na*] 社会的[な]; *sha'kai-* 社会 a social problem *shakai mo'ndai* 社会問題

socialism *shakaishu'gi* 社会主義

socialist *shakaishugi'sha* 社会主義者

Socialist Party *Shakai-tō* 社会党

social science *shakai ka'gaku* 社会科学

social security *shakai ho'ken* 社会保険

social work *shakai fuku'shi* 社会福祉

society 1 *sha'kai* 社会 He works hard for society. *Ka're wa sha'kai no tame' ni zenryoku o tsuku'shite iru.* 彼は社会のために全力を尽くしている。; *se'ken* 世間 Society won't permit it. *Se'ken ga yurusa'nai.* 世間が許さない。 **2** organization *kyōkai* 協会 The Asiatic Society *Ajia Kyō'kai* アジア協会; *-kai* 会 church women's society *kyōkai fuji'n-kai* 教会婦人会

sociology *shaka'igaku* 社会学

socket (electrical outlet) *ko'nsento* コンセント plug into a socket *ko'nsento ni sashikomu* コンセントに差し込む

socks *kutsu'shita* 靴下

soda 1 baking soda *jūsō* 重曹 **2** soft drink *sōda'sui* ソーダ水

sofa *so'fā* ソファー

soft 1 quiet *shi'zuka* [*na*] 静か[な] soft music *shi'zuka na o'ngaku*

静かな音楽 **2** (not hard) (adj) *yawaraka'・i* やわらかい a soft blanket *yawaraka'i mō'fu* やわらかい毛布

soft-boiled egg *hanjuku ta'mago* 半熟卵

soft drink *jū'su* ジュース

softly 1 gently *yawaraka'ku* やわらかく touch softly *yawaraka'ku sawaru* やわらかく触る; *so'yosoyo* [*to*] そよそよ[と] The wind is blowing softly. *Kaze ga so'yosoyo to fu'ite iru.* 風がそよそよと吹いている. **2** quietly *shi'zuka ni* 静かに walk softly *shi'zuka ni aru'ku* 静かに歩く

software *sofuto-ue'ā* ソフトウェアー

soggy *zubunure no* ずぶ濡れの; *mizubitashi no* 水浸しの

soil (earth) *tsuchi'* 土

soiled (adj) *kitana'・i* 汚い Is this shirt soiled? *Kono sha'tsu wa kitana'i desu ka?* このシャツは汚いですか. ——(v) be/become soiled *yogore・ru* 汚れる This napkin's soiled. *Kono na'pukin wa yogorete i'ru.* このナプキンは汚れている.

solar *ta'iyō [no]* 太陽[の]; *taiyō-* 太陽 solar heat *taiyō'-netsu* 太陽熱

solar eclipse *nisshoku* 日食

solar energy *taiyō ene'rugī* 太陽エネルギー

solar system 1 *taiyōkei* 太陽系 **2** heat *sōrā shi'sutemu* ソーラーシステム

solder *handa* はんだ ——(idiom) to solder *handa de tsunag・u* はんだでつなぐ

soldier *heitai* 兵隊

sold out *urikire* 売り切れ I'm sorry, but we're sold out. *Osore irima'su ga urikire de'su.* 恐れ入りますが売り切れです. ——(v) be sold out *urikire'・ru* 売り切れる The concert tickets are sold out. *Ko'nsāto no kippu wa uriki'rete iru.* コンサートの切符は売り切れている.

sole 1 (of the foot) *ashi no ura* 足の裏 **2** (of a shoe) *kutsu-zoko* 靴底

sole (fish) *shita-bi'rame* 舌平目

solid 1 strong *ganjō* 頑丈[な] **2** firm (adj) *kata・i* 堅い **3** sturdy (attr) *shikka'ri-shita* しっかりした

solitaire (card game) *hitori tora'mpu* 一人トランプ

solo 1 (vocal) *dokushō* 独唱 **2** (instrumental) *dokusō* 独奏

solution 1 (to a problem) *kaiketsu* 解決 **2** (Lab) *ekitai* 液体

solve obj *o* (irr) *kaiketsu-suru* 解決する It is very difficult to solve the housing shortage problem. *Jūtaku-bu'soku no mondai o kaike-tsu-suru koto' wa hijō ni ko'nnan desu.* 住宅不足の問題を解決することは非常に困難です. ——(v) be solved *toke'・ru* 解ける The problem was solved. *Mondai ga to'keta.* 問題が解けた.

some *i'kutsuka* [*no*] いくつか[の] There are some eggs in the refrigerator. *Tama'go ga i'kutsuka reizō'ko ni ha'itte iru.* 卵がいくつか冷蔵庫に入っている.; *i'kuraka [no]* いくらか[の] I have some money. *O-kane wa i'kuraka mo'tte iru.* お金はいくらか持っている.; *suko'shi [no]* 少し[の] There is some left. *Suko'shi noko'tte iru.* 少し残っている.

somebody *da'reka* だれか Somebody came to see you while you were out. *O-ru'su no toki ni, da'reka ana'ta ni a'i ni kita.* お留守の時にだれかがあなたに会いに来た.

someday *i'tsuka* いつか Someday I'd like to visit the National Museum of Western Art in Ueno. *I'tsuka Ueno no Kokuritsu Seiyō Biju'tsukan ni ikita'i to omou.* いつか上野の国立西洋美術館に行きたいと思う.

somehow **1** *na'ndaka* 何だか Somehow I feel lonely tonight. *Ko'mban wa na'ndaka sabishi'i.* 今晩は何だか寂しい. **2** *dō'nika* どうにか Somehow I've managed to survive. *Dō'nika kurashite iru.* どうにか暮らしている.; *na'ntoka* 何とか Somehow or other, things will work out, I'm sure. *Na'ntoka na'ru deshō.* 何とかなるでしょう.

someone *da'reka* だれか; (polite) *do'nataka* どなたか Is there someone here who understands German? *Do'nataka Doitsu-go no waka'ru hito wa imase'n ka?* どなたかドイツ語の分かる人はいませんか.

something *na'nika* 何か Is there something to see there? *Asoko ni na'nika mi'ru yō na mono ga arima'su ka?* あそこに何か見るようなものがありますか.

sometime *i'tsuka* いつか Please come over sometime. *I'tsuka asobi ni ki'te kudasa'i.* いつか遊びに来て下さい.

sometimes *tokidoki* 時々 Sometimes we go to the movies. *Tokidoki e'iga o mi' ni iku.* 時々映画を見に行く.

somewhat *tashō* 多少 He looked somewhat disgusted. *Ka're wa tashō fuman-sō' na kao o shita.* 彼は多少不満そうな顔をした. What she said was somewhat different from the actual situation. *Ka'nojo ga itta koto' wa ji'jitsu to wa tashō kuichiga'tte ita.* 彼女が言ったことは事実とは多少食い違っていた.

somewhere *do'koka* どこか I'd like to take a trip somewhere. *Do'koka e ryokō-shita'i.* どこかへ旅行したい. I can hear beautiful piano music coming from somewhere. *Do'koka kara ki'rei na piano no oto' ga suru.* どこかからきれいなピアノの音がする.

son **1** (one's own) *musuko* 息子; (coll) *segare* せがれ **2** (another's) *musuko-san* 息子さん

song **1** (human) *uta'* 歌 **2** (bird) *nakigo'e* 鳴き声

songwriter **1** (music) *sakkyokuka* 作曲家 **2** (lyrics) *sakushika* 作詩家

son-in-law **1** (one's own) *mu′ko* 婿 **2** (another's) *o-mu′ko-san* お婿さん

soon **1** *su′gu* [*ni*] すぐ[に] **2** right away *sassoku* 早速 **3** before long *mamo′naku* 間もなく *Ka′nojo wa mamo′naku ku′ru.* 彼女は間もなく来る。 **4** as soon as possible *dekiru dake ha′yaku* できるだけ早く Please do it as soon as possible. *Dekiru dake ha′yaku shite kudasa′i.* できるだけ早くして下さい。

soot *su′su* 煤

sophisticated (attr) *senren-sareta* 洗練された He's very sophisticated. *Ka′re wa taihen senren-sareta hito′ desu.* 彼は大変洗練された人です。

sophomore *nine′nsei* 二年生

soprano (voice) *sopurano* ソプラノ

sore *kaiyō* 潰瘍; *o-de′ki* おでき ——(adj) be sore *ita′·i* 痛い Is it sore? *Ita′i desu ka?* 痛いですか。 I have a sore throat. *No′do ga ita′i.* のどが痛い。

sorrow *kanashimi′* 悲しみ

sorrowful (v) be sorrowful *kanashi′m·u* 悲しむ

sorry (idiom) **1** feel sorry for *kawaisō′ ni omo′·u* かわいそうに思う I feel sorry for that person. *Ano′ hito o kawaisō′ ni omo′u.* あの人をかわいそうに思う。 **2** (to someone who has suffered misfortune) I'm sorry. *O-ki-no-doku-sama* [*de′su*]. お気の毒様[です]。 **3** (to the bereaved) I'm sorry. *Go-shūshō-sama de′su.* 御愁傷様です。 **4** I'm sorry (to bother you), but... *Sumimase′n ga...* すみませんが。 **5** I'm sorry to have kept you waiting. *O-machidō-sama de′shtia.* お待ち遠さまでした。 **6** I'm sorry (I have no excuse for what I did). *Mōshiwake gozaimase′n.* 申し訳ございません。 **7** I'm sorry I haven't kept in touch with you. *Go-busata shima′shita.* 御無沙汰しました。; (polite) *Go-busata itashima′shita.* 御無沙汰いたしました。 **8** I'm sorry (I apologize). *Gomen nasa′i.* 御免なさい。

sort *shu′rui* 種類; *ta′gui* 類 ——obj *o* (irr) *bunrui-suru* 分類する Sort these documents, please. *Kono shorui o bunrui-shite kudasa′i.* この書類を分類して下さい。

soul *ta′mashii* 魂; (Tech) *re′ikon* 霊魂

sound *oto′* 音 make a sound *oto′ o tate′·ru* 音を立てる I hear the sound of footsteps. *Ashi-o′to ga kikoeru.* 足音が聞こえる。

sound wave *o′npa* 音波

soup **1** (W) *sū′pu* スープ **2** (J) *o-tsu′yu* おつゆ; *suimono* 吸い物

sour (adj) *suppa′·i* すっぱい

source **1** *minamoto* 源; *moto* 元 **2** cause *gen'in* 原因 **3** place of origin *dedokoro* 出所

source material *shi′ryō* 資料

south *minami* 南 south exit *minami-guchi* 南口

South Africa *Minami A'furika* 南アフリカ

South African (person) *Minami Afurika'jin* 南アフリカ人 ——
(attr) *Minami A'furika no* 南アフリカの

South America *Minami Ame'rika* 南アメリカ

southeast *tōnan* 東南

Southeast Asia *Tōnan A'jia* 東南アジア

South Pole *Nankyoku* 南極

southwest *nansei* 南西

souvenir *o-miyage* おみやげ

sovereignty *shuken* 主権

Soviet Union *see* Union of Soviet Socialist Republics

sow obj *o* (v) *ma'k·u* 蒔く sow seed *ta'ne o ma'ku* 種を蒔く

soybean *daizu* 大豆

soybean curd *tōfu* 豆腐

soy sauce *shōyu* 醬油

spa *onsen* 温泉

space **1** empty space *kūkan* 空間 **2** interval *aida* 間 leave a space
aida o akeru 間を開ける; (Tech) *ma* 間 **3** outer space *u'chū* 宇宙
spaceman *uchū hiko'shi* 宇宙飛行士 a creature from outer space
uchū'jin 宇宙人

spaceship *uchūsen* 宇宙船

spacious (adj) *hiro'·i* 広い, a spacious room *hiro'i heya'* 広い部屋

spade **1** (suit of playing cards) *supēdo* スペード **2** (tool) *suko'ppu*
スコップ

spaghetti *supage'tti* スパゲッティ spaghetti with meat sauce *supa-
getti mīto sō'su* スパゲッティミートソース

Spain *Supe'in* スペイン

Spanish **1** (language) *Supein-go* スペイン語 **2** (person) *Supe'injin*
スペイン人 ——(attr) *Supe'in no* スペインの

spank (idiom) *o-shiri o tata'k·u* お尻を叩く

spanking *hirate-uchi* 平手打ち

spare time *hima* [*na*] 暇[な] When you have some spare time, give
me a call. *Hima na toki denwa-shite kudasa'i.* 暇な時, 電話して下
さい.

spare tire *supe'a* スペア; *supea ta'iya* スペアタイヤ

spark *hi'bana* 火花

spark plug *supāku pu'ragu* スパークプラグ

sparrow *suzume* 雀

spatula *he'ra* へら

speak ind-obj *ni*, obj *o* (v) *hana's·u* 話す Did you speak to him?
Ka're ni hanashima'shita ka? 彼に話しましたか. ——(irr) speak
up; take the floor *hatsugen-suru* 発言する

speaker **1** at a meeting *hatsuge'nsha* 発言者 **2** lecturer *kōe'nsha*

講演者 **3** loudspeaker *kakuse'iki* 拡声器　**4** stereo [*sutereo*] *supi'kā* [ステレオ]スピーカー

spear *yari* 槍

special *tokubetsu* [*na*] 特別[な] a special meeting *tokubetsu na atsumari* 特別な集まり special express (train) *tokubetsu kyū'kō* [*de'nsha*] 特別急行[電車]; (abbr) *tokkyū* 特急 special treatment *tokubetsu a'tsukai* 特別扱い

special delivery *sokutatsu* 速達 Send this letter by special delivery, please. *Kono tegami o sokutatsu ni shite kudasa'i.* この手紙を速達にして下さい.

specialist *semmonka* 専門家

specialty **1** subject of specialization *semmon* 専門 What is your specialty? *Go-semmon wa na'n desu ka?* ご専門は何ですか. **2** something one is proficient at *tokui* [*na*] 得意[な] Spanish is his specialty. *Kare wa Supein-go ga tokui de'su.* 彼はスペイン語が得意です.

species *shu'rui* 種類

spectator *kanra'nsha* 観覧者

speech **1** *o-hanashi* お話　**2** address *enzetsu* 演説　**3** lecture *kō'gi* 講義　**4** public lecture *kōen* 講演

speed **1** *ha'yasa* 速さ　**2** vehicle speed *supido* スピード; km/hr *jisoku* 時速 travel at a speed of 80 km/hr *jisoku hachiju'kkiro de hashi'ru* 時速80キロで走る　——(idiom) to speed *supido o da's·u* スピードを出す

speed limit *seigen so'kudo* 制限速度

spelling *tsuzuri'* 綴り What is the spelling? *Dō' iu tsuzuri de'su ka?* どういう綴りですか.

spend obj *o* (v) **1** spend (money) [*o-kane o*] *tsuka·u* [お金を]使う I spent all the money. *O-kane o ze'mbu tsukatte shima'tta.* お金を全部使ってしまった. **2** spend (time) [*jikan o*] *tsuiyas·u* [時間を]費やす How much time do you spend studying *kanji* each day? *Ichinichi' ni kanji no benkyō ni dono kurai jikan o tsuiyashima'su ka?* 一日に漢字の勉強にどの位時間を費やしますか.　——(v) spend the night *tomar·u* 泊る I spent the night with a friend. *Tomodachi no tokoro' ni toma'tta.* 友達のところに泊った.

sperm *se'ieki* 精液

sphere **1** globe *kyū'* 球　**2** realm; range *ha'n·i* 範囲 sphere of activity *kōdō ha'n·i* 行動範囲 That's out of my sphere. *Sore wa watashi no kankei-suru han·i'-gai desu.* それは私の関係する範囲外です.

spice *kōshi'nryō* 香辛料; *supa'isu* スパイス

spicy (adj) *kara'·i* 辛い; (attr) *piri'tto-shita* ぴりっとした a spicy flavor *piri'tto-shita aji* ぴりっとした味

spider *ku'mo* くも spider web *ku'mo no su* くもの巣

spigot *jaguchi* 蛇口

spill (v) *kobore'·ru* こぼれる It spilled! *Kobo'reta!* こぼれた.
——obj o (v) *kobo's·u* こぼす Don't spill it! *Kobosa'naide!* こぼ
さないで.

spin (v) spin around *gu'ruguru mawar·u* ぐるぐる回る ——obj o
(v) make thread/yarn *tsumu'g·u* 紡ぐ

spinach *hōre'nsō* ほうれん草

spine *sebone* 背骨

spinning *bōseki* 紡績 spinning factory *bōseki kō'jō* 紡績工場

spinning wheel *tsumugi-gu'ruma* 紡ぎ車

spirit 1 *kigen* 機嫌 She is in good spirits today. *Ka'nojo wa kyō',
kigen ga i'i.* 彼女は今日, 機嫌がいい.; *koko'ro* 心 a person of generous spirit *koko'ro no yu'taka na hito'* 心の豊かな人; *se'ishin* 精
神 patriotic spirit *aikokuteki se'ishin* 愛国的精神; *ko'njō* 根性 a
person with a lot of spirit *ko'njō no a'ru hito* 根性のある人 2 soul
ta'mashii 魂; (Tech) *re'ikon* 霊魂 3 Holy Spirit *Seirei* 聖霊

spiritual 1 *seishinteki* [*na*] 精神的[な] 2 (Music) *kokujin re'ika* 黒
人霊歌

spit *tsu'ba* つば ——loc ni (v) spit on *tsu'ba o kake'·ru* つばを
かける spit on the sidewalk *hodō ni tsu'ba o kake'ru* 歩道につば
をかける

spiteful (attr) *iji no waru'·i* 意地の悪い a spiteful person *iji no
waru'i hito'* 意地の悪い人

(in) spite of ...*no ni* ...のに He rides his motorbike, in spite of
the fact that I warned him (that it was dangerous). *Chūkoku-
shita' no ni, ka're wa ōtoba'i ni notte iru.* 忠告したのに彼はオート
バイに乗っている.

splash obj o (v) *hanechira's·u* はね散らす The children splashed
water in the swimming pool. *Kodomo wa pū'ru de mizu o ba'sha-
basha hanechira'shita.* 子供はプールで水をばしゃばしゃはね散ら
した. ——(idiom) make a splash [*hito' o*] *atto' iwase'·ru* [人を]あ
っと言わせる The new album he recorded in London made a
splash the moment it was released. *Ka're ga Ro'ndon de fukiko'n-
da shinkyoku wa hatsubai to dō'ji ni atto' iwa'seta.* 彼がロンドン
で吹き込んだ新曲は発売と同時にあっと言わせた.

splendid *rippa* [*na*] 立派[な] a splendid house *rippa na uchi'* 立派
な家

splint *soegi* 添え木

splinter *toge'* とげ

split *bunretsu* 分裂 ——obj o (v) *war·u* 割る I split the board.
I'ta o watta. 板を割った. ——(v) *ware'·ru* 割れる The board
split. *I'ta ga wareta.* 板が割れた.

spoil (v) *kusa'r·u* 腐る This fish is spoiled. *Kono sakana wa kusa'-
tte iru.* この魚は腐っている.; *wa'ruku nar·u* 悪くなる These bean

sprouts have spoiled. *Kono moyashi' wa wa'ruku natte iru.* このもやしは悪くなっている.; *dame' ni nar·u* だめになる This meat is spoiled. *Kono niku' wa dame' ni na'tte iru.* この肉はだめになっている.

spoiled (pampered) (attr) *amayakas'areta* 甘やかされた a spoiled child *amayakasa'reta ko* 甘やかされた子

sponge 1 (natural) *kaimen* 海綿 2 (man-made) *suponji* スポンジ

sponge cake *suponji kē'ki* スポンジケーキ; *kasutera* カステラ

sponsor 1 *supo'nsā* スポンサー 2 guarantor *hoshōnin* 保証人 3 backer *kōe'nsha* 後援者 ——obj *o* (irr) 1 *hoshō-suru* 保証する Because I sponsored him, he was able to get a job. *Watashi ga hoshō-shita no de, ka're wa shūshoku-de'kita.* 私が保証したので, 彼は就職できた. 2 to back *kōen-suru* 後援する PepsiCo is sponsoring Michael Jackson's concert. *Maikeru Ja'kuson no ko'nsā'to wa Pepushiko ga kōen-shite iru.* マイケル・ジャクソンのコンサートはペプシコが後援している.

spool *ito'maki* 糸巻

spoon *supū'n* スプーン; *sa'ji* 匙

spoonful *hito'saji* 一匙

sport *supō'tsu* スポーツ sport shirt *supōtsu sha'tsu* スポーツシャツ

sporting goods *supōtsu yō'hin* スポーツ用品; *undō'gu* 運動具

sports event 1 *shiai* 試合 2 (school) *undō'kai* 運動会

sportswear *supōtsu ue'a* スポーツウエア

spot (stain) *shimi* 染み

spouse *haigū'sha* 配偶者

sprain *nenza* ねんざ ——obj *o* (irr) *nenza-suru* ねんざする I sprained my ankle. *Ashi-ku'bi o nenza-shite shima'tta.* 足首をねんざしてしまった.

spray *supu'rē* スプレー ——loc *ni*, obj *o* (v) *fukikake'·ru* 吹きかける

spread (v) *hirogar'·u* 広がる The rumor spread like wildfire. *Sono uwasa wa hi' no yō ni hirogatta.* その噂は火のように広がった. ——obj *o* (v) 1 extend *hiroge·ru* 広げる spread a rumor *uwasa o hirogeru* 噂を広げる 2 lay out *shik·u* 敷く spread a futon on the floor *yuka ni futon o shiku* 床に蒲団を敷く ——(idiom) spread butter *ba'tā o nur·u* バターを塗る

sprig *kozue* 梢

spring 1 (season) *ha'ru* 春 spring vacation *haru ya'sumi* 春休み 2 (mechanism) *ba'ne* ばね 3 (water) *izumi* 泉 4 hot spring *onsen* 温泉

sprinkle *niwaka-a'me* 俄か雨 ——ind-obj *ni*, obj *o* (v) 1 *kake'·ru* かける 2 (over a large surface) *ma'k·u* まく sprinkle the lawn *shibafu ni mizu o ma′ku* 芝生に水をまく ——(v) *shito′shito fu′r·u* しとしと降る It's sprinkling. *A′me ga shito′shito fu′tte iru.* 雨がしとしと降っている.

sprinkler 1 (for the garden) *mizuma′kiki* 水まき機 2 (watering can) *jō′ro* じょうろ 3 (sprinkling vehicle for roads) *supuri′nkurā* スプリンクラー

sprout 1 *me′* 芽 a plant sprout *shoku′butsu no me′* 植物の芽 Brussels sprouts *mekya′betsu* 芽キャベツ 2 bean sprouts *moyashi* もやし

spy *supa′i* スパイ; *mittei* 密偵

square *shikaku′[no]* 四角[の]; (Math) *seihō′kei′* 正方形 ——(adj) *shikaku′·i* 四角い

squash (pumpkin) *kabocha* カボチャ

squat (v) *shagam·u* しゃがむ

squeeze obj o (v) 1 compress *tsubus·u* つぶす Don't squeeze your pimples! *Ni′kibi o tsubusana′ide!* にきびをつぶさないで. 2 hug *dakishime′·ru* 抱きしめる

squid *ik·a* いか

squint (idiom) *me′ o hosome′·ru* 目を細める

squirrel *ri′su* りす

squirt obj o (irr) *funshutsu-suru* 噴出する

Sri Lanka *Surira′nka* スリランカ

Sri Lankan see Sinhalese

stab obj o (v) *sa′s·u* 刺す ——(pass) *sasare′·ru* 刺される be stabbed with a knife *na′ifu de sasare′ru* ナイフで刺される

stability *antei* 安定

stable *umagoya* 馬小屋 ——(attr) *antei-shita* 安定した a stable government *antei-shita se′ifu* 安定した政府

stack *tsumikasane* 積み重ね; *yama′* 山 ——obj o (v) *tsum·u* 積む stack firewood *maki o tsumu* まきを積む; *tsumikasane′·ru* 積み重ねる

stadium 1 *suta′jiamu* スタジアム 2 baseball stadium *yakyūjō* 野球場

staff (personnel) *shoku′in* 職員

stage *bu′tai* 舞台 appear on stage *bu′tai ni de′ru* 舞台に出る

stagger *chidori′ashi* 千鳥足 ——(v) *yorome′k·u* よろめく; *yo′ro-yoro aru′k·u* よろよろ歩く

stain *shimi* 染み ——obj o (v) *yogos·u* 汚す

stainless steel *sute′nresu* ステンレス

stairs *kaidan* 階段

stake 1 *ku′i* 杭 2 (wager) *kake′* 賭け

stale *chi′mpu [na]* 陳腐[な] a stale joke *chi′mpu na jōdan* 陳腐な冗談 ——(attr) *kataku-na′tta* 堅くなった stale bread *kataku-na′tta pa′n* 堅くなったパン

stamp   1 *ō-in* 押印   2 postage stamp *kitte'* 切手 ——obj *o* (v) *os·u* 押す

stamp collecting   *kitte shūshū* 切手収集

stand   *da'i* 台 ——(v) *ta'ts·u* 立つ I stood for an hour. *Ichiji'kan mo ta'tte ita.* 一時間も立っていた.

standard   1 basis *kijun* 基準 standard for evaluation *ha'ndan no kijun* 判断の基準 standard of morality *dōtoku ki'jun* 道徳基準   2 conventional *hyōjun [no]* 標準[の] standard language *hyōjun-go* 標準語 standard price *hyōjun ka'kaku* 標準価格   3 flag; banner *hata'* 旗

standing committee   *jōnin ii'nkai* 常任委員会

standing room   *tachimi'seki* 立見席

stand up   (v) *tachiaga'r·u* 立ち上がる He stood up and left the room. *Ka're wa tachiaga'tte heya' o de'ta.* 彼は立ち上がって部屋を出た.

staple   1 (food) *shushoku* 主食   2 staple product *tokusa'mbutsu* 特産物   3 (for stapling machine) *ha'ri* 針

stapler   *ho'tchikisu* ホッチキス

star   1 (celestial) *hoshi* 星   2 (entertainer) *sutā'* スター

starch   *nori'* 糊; *sutā'chi* スターチ

stare at   obj *o* (v) *mitsume·ru* 見つめる She stared at me. *Ka'nojo wa watashi no koto' o jitto mitsu'mete ita.* 彼女は私のことをじっと見つめていた.; *ji'rojiro mi'·ru* じろじろ見る Don't stare! *Ji'rojiro mi'te wa dame' desu yo!* じろじろ見てはだめですよ.

starfish   *hitode* 海星

stark-naked   *suppa'daka [no]* すっ裸[の]

start   1 (v) begin *hajimar·u* 始まる What time does the movie start? *E'iga wa na'nji ni hajimarima'su ka?* 映画は何時に始まりますか. ——obj *o* (v) *hajime·ru* 始める I started studying flower arranging. *Ike'bana no keiko o hajimeta.* 生け花の稽古を始めた. When shall we start it? *I'tsu sore o hajimemashō' ka?* いつそれを始めましょうか.   2 set out (irr) *shuppatsu-suru* 出発する When do you start on (on your trip)? *I'tsu [ryokō ni] shuppatsu-shima'su ka?* いつ[旅行に]出発しますか.; (v) *ta'ts·u* 立つ We start for Europe on July 1. *Wata'shitachi wa shichi'gatsu tsuitachi' ni Yōro'ppa e ta'tsu.* 私たちは七月一日にヨーロッパへ立つ.

starter (switch)   *sui'tchi* スイッチ

startled   (v) be/become startled *odoro'k·u* 驚く I was startled by a loud noise in the middle of the night. *Yonaka' ni ō'ki na oto' ga shite, odoro'ita.* 夜中に大きな音がして驚いた.; (irr) *doki'tto-suru* どきっとする I was really startled when I heard that. *Sore o kiita toki, hontō ni doki'tto-shita.* それを聞いた時本当にどきっとした.

start to (do)   -*das·u* 出す The car started to move. *Kuruma ga ugoki-da'shita.* 車が動き出した.; -*hajime·ru* 始める When are you going to start to make it? *I'tsu tsukuri-hajimema'su ka?* いつ作り始めますか.

starve (v) **1** *ue'·ru* 飢える **2** (irr) starve to death *uejini-suru* 飢え死にする

state **1** (of a nation) *-shū* 州 the state of Texas *Tekisa'su-shū* テキサス州 **2** nation *ko'kka* 国家 **3** condition *jōtai* 状態 **4** circumstances *[ji'ken no] jōkyō* [事件の]状況 **5** natural state *ari-no-ma-ma'* ありのまま ——obj *o* (v) *nobe'·ru* 述べる state one's position *jibun no tachiba' o nobe'ru* 自分の立場を述べる

stately (attr) *dōdō' to shita* 堂々とした a stately attitude *dōdō to shita ta'ido* 堂々とした態度

statement **1** announcement; proclamation *seimei* 声明 an official statement *kōshiki se'imei* 公式声明 **2** (Leg) *chinjutsu* 陳述 a sworn statement *sensei chi'njutsu* 宣誓陳述 **3** financial statement *kessansho* 決算書 **4** bank statement *tori'hiki meisaisho* 取引明細書

stateroom (on a ship) *senshitsu* 船室

static **1** (radio) *zatsuon* 雑音 **2** static electricity *seide'nki* 静電気

station **1** train *e'ki* 駅; *-eki* 駅 Yokohama Station *Yokohama'-eki* 横浜駅 **2** bus *basu tā'minaru* バスターミナル **3** radio *hōsō'kyoku* 放送局 **4** gasoline *[gasorin] suta'ndo* [ガソリン]スタンド

stationery **1** *binsen* 便せん **2** stationery and office supplies (store) *bumbō'gu [ten]* 文房具[店]

stationmaster *ekichō* 駅長

statistics *tōkei* 統計

statue **1** *zō'* 像 **2** (of wood) *mokuzō* 木像 **3** (of bronze) *dōzō* 銅像

status *mi'bun* 身分 a person of low status *mi'bun no hiku'i hito'* 身分の低い人

stay loc *ni* (v) *tomar·u* 泊まる Where did you stay in Kyoto? *Kyō'to de wa do'ko ni tomarima'shita ka?* 京都ではどこに泊りましたか.

steak *sutē'ki* ステーキ

steal obj *o* (v) *to'r·u* 取る; *nusu'm·u* 盗む It is not good to steal others' things. *Hito no mono' o nusu'mu no wa yoku na'i.* 人の物を盗むのはよくない. ——(pass) *torare'·ru* 取られる My watch was stolen at the public bath. *Se'ntō de tokei o tora'reta.* 銭湯で時計を取られた.

steam *yu'ge* 湯気; *jō'ki* 蒸気

steam iron *suchimu a'iron* スチームアイロン

steam locomotive *jōki kika'nsha* 蒸気機関車; SL *esue'ru* エスエル

steamship *kisen* 汽船

steel *kōtetsu* 鋼鉄

steel wool *suchīru ūru [ta'washi]* スチールウール[たわし]

steep *kyū* [*na*] 急[な] a steep incline *kyū na saka'* 急な坂

steeple *tō'* 塔

steer (idiom) 1 steer a ship *ka'ji o to'r·u* 舵を取る 2 steer a car *handoru o to'r·u* ハンドルを取る

steering wheel *handoru* ハンドル

stem *kuki'* 茎

stencil *sute'nshiru* ステンシル; *genshi* 原紙

step 1 (on a stairway) *da'n* 段 2 a stage in a process *dankai* 段階 3 a measure toward a solution *shu'dan* 手段 take steps *shu'dan o to'ru* 手段をとる 4 a pace; a stride *ashi'* 足 5 one footstep *i'ppo* 一歩

stepbrother 1 (one's own, younger) *giri no otōto'* 義理の弟 2 (one's own, older) *giri no a'ni* 義理の兄 3 (another's, younger) *giri no otōto'-san* 義理の弟さん 4 (another's, older) *giri no onī-san* 義理のお兄さん

stepchild (one's own; another's) *giri no kodomo* 義理の子供

stepdaughter 1 (one's own) *giri no musume* 義理の娘 2 (another's) *giri no ojō'-san* 義理のお嬢さん

step down loc *o* (v) *ori'·ru* 降りる step down from a platform *dan kara ori'ru* 段から降りる ——(irr) leave a position *kōkaku-suru* 降格する

stepfather 1 (one's own) *giri no chi'chi* 義理の父; (address) *otō'-san* お父さん 2 (another's) *giri no otō'-san* 義理のお父さん

stepladder *kyatatsu* 脚立

stepmother 1 (one's own) *giri no ha'ha* 義理の母; (address) *okā'-san* お母さん 2 (another's) *giri no okā'-san* 義理のお母さん

step on obj *o* (v) *fum·u* 踏む I stepped on the cat's tail. *Ne'ko no shippo' o funda.* 猫のしっぽを踏んだ.

stepsister 1 (one's own, younger) *giri no imōto* 義理の妹 2 (one's own, older) *giri no ane* 義理の姉 3 (another's, younger) *giri no imōto-san* 義理の妹さん 4 (another's, older) *giri no onē'-san* 義理のお姉さん

stepson 1 (one's own) *giri no musuko* 義理の息子 2 (another's) *giri no musuko-san* 義理の息子さん

stereo *sutereo* ステレオ car stereo *kā-sute'reo* カーステレオ

stereotype *tenkeiteki* [*na*] 典型的[な]

sterile *mukin* [*no*] 無菌[の] a sterile (operating) room *muki'n-shitsu* 無菌室

sterilize obj *o* (irr) 1 *sakkin-suru* 殺菌する 2 make infertile *dan-shu-suru* 断種する ——(idiom) *funin ni suru* 不妊にする

sterling silver *jungin* 純銀

stern 1 *genkaku na* 厳格な 2 (of a boat) *se'mbi* 船尾

stethoscope *chōshi'nki* 聴診器

stew *shichū'* シチュー ——obj *o* (v) *ni·ru* 煮る

stewardess *suchuwā'desu* スチュワーデス *see also* flight attendant
stick (v) *tsuk·u'* 付く Japanese stamps don't stick very well. *Nihon no kitte wa yoku tsuka'nai.* 日本の切手はよく付かない.
——obj *o* (v) *har·u* 貼る Stick the revenue stamp on here. *Shūnyū i'nshi o koko ni hatte kudasa'i.* 収入印紙をここに貼って下さい.
stick (pole) *bō* 棒
sticky (irr) be sticky *ne'baneba-suru* ねばねばする This candy is sticky. *Kono ame wa ne'baneba-shite iru.* この飴はねばねばしている.
stiff (adj) *kata·i* 堅い Beat the batter until it becomes stiff. *Ki'ji ga kataku na'ru made, kakima'zete kudasa'i.* 生地が堅くなるまで, かき混ぜて下さい.
stiff shoulders *katako'ri* 肩こり
still (quiet) *shi'zuka [na]* 静か[な] a still sea *shi'zuka na u'mi* 静かな海 ——(idiom) be still *shi'zuka ni suru* 静かにする Children can't be still for five minutes. *Kodomo wa gofu'nkan mo shi'zuka ni shite irare'nai.* 子供は五分間も静かにしていられない.
still (yet) *ma'da* まだ I'm still single. *Ma'da hito'ri desu.* まだ一人です.
stillbirth *shi'zan* 死産
stilts *take-uma* 竹馬
stimulant (Med) *kakuse'i-zai* 覚せい剤
stimulate obj *o* (irr) *shigeki-suru* 刺激する Caffeine stimulates the heart. *Kafe'in wa shinzō o shigeki-suru.* カフェインは心臓を刺激する.
sting (v) *shimi·ru* しみる Does it sting? *Shimima'su ka?* しみますか. ——obj *o* (v) *sa's·u* 刺す ——(pass) *sasare'·ru* 刺される I was stung by a wasp. *Watashi wa kuma'nbachi ni sasa'reta.* 私は熊ん蜂に刺された.
stingray *aka'ei* 赤えい
stingy *ke'chi [na]* けち[な] a stingy person *kechi'mbō* けちんぼう
stink *akushū* 悪臭 ——(idiom) to stink *akushū o hana'ts·u* 悪臭を放つ
stir obj *o* (v) *maze'·ru* 混ぜる Stir slowly. *Yukku'ri ma'zete kudasa'i.* ゆっくり混ぜて下さい.; *kakimawa's·u* かき回す stir one's coffee *kōhi' o kakimawa'su* コーヒーをかき回す
stir-fry obj *o* (v) *itame'·ru* 炒める
stirrup *abumi* 鐙
stitch *ha'ri* 針 one stitch *hito'-hari* 一針 ——obj *o* (v) *nu'·u* 縫う
stock (for cooking) *dashi'* だし
stock (holdings) *kabu* 株 common stock *futsū kabu* 普通株 preferred stock *yūse'n kabu* 優先株
stockbroker *kabu no nakagainin* 株の仲買人
stock exchange *shōken torihikijo* 証券取引所

stock market *kabushiki shi'jō* 株式市場

stocking *kutsu'shita* 靴下 a pair of stockings *kutsu'shita issoku* 靴下一足

stoic *sutoashugi'sha* ストア主義者; *kin'yokushugi'sha* 禁欲主義者 ──(attr) *kin'yokuteki* [na] 禁欲的[な]

stoicism *sutoashu'gi* ストア主義; *kin'yokushu'gi* 禁欲主義

stomach 1 *onaka* おなか I have a stomachache. *Onaka ga ita'i.* おなかが痛い. My stomach's upset. *Onaka o kowa'shita.* おなかをこわした.; (coll) *hara'* 腹 He has a protruding stomach. *Ka're wa hara' ga de'te iru.* 彼は腹が出ている. 2 (Anat) *i* 胃; *ibu'kuro* 胃袋

stone *ishi'* 石 stone wall *ishi-bei* 石塀

stone lantern *ishi-dō'rō* 石灯籠

stop 1 bus stop *teiryū'jo* 停留所; *basu-tei* バス停 2 momentary stop *ichiji te'ishi* 一時停止 ──(v) 1 halt *tomar·u* 止まる The bus stops near my house. *Watashi no uchi no chika'ku ni ba'su ga tomaru.* 私の家の近くにバスが止まる. ──obj *o* (v) 1 *tome·ru* 止める Stop a taxi for me, please. *Ta'kushi o tomete kudasa'i.* タクシーを止めて下さい. 2 cease *yam·u* やむ It has stopped raining. *A'me ga yanda.* 雨がやんだ. ──obj *o* (v) *yame·ru* やめる Stop it! *Yamete kudasa'i!* やめて下さい.

stop by loc *ni* (v) *yor·u* 寄る I also stopped by the department store on my way home. *Kaeri'michi ni depa'to ni mo yotta.* 帰り道にデパートにも寄った; *tachiyoru* 立ち寄る.

Stop it! *Yoshinasa'i!* よしなさい.; *Yamenasa'i!* やめなさい.

stoplight *teishi shi'ngō* 停止信号

stop over loc *de* (v) *sugo's·u* 過ごす We stopped over in Los Angeles for two days and a night. *Ippaku fu'tsuka Ro'su de sugo'shita.* 一泊二日ロスで過ごした.

stopper *se'n* 栓

storage battery *chikude'nchi* 蓄電池

store (shop) *mise'* 店

storehouse *sō'ko* 倉庫

storeroom *chozō'shitsu* 貯蔵室

stork *kōno'tori* こうのとり

storm 1 *a'rashi* 嵐 2 snowstorm *fu'buki* 吹雪 3 thunderstorm *ra'iu* 雷雨 4 windstorm *bōfū* 暴風

story (floor) 1 *-kai* 階 two-story house *nikai-date no ie'* 二階建の家 2 one-story house *hiraya* 平屋

story (tale) *o-hanashi* お話

stove 1 range *re'nji* レンジ 2 heater *sutō'bu* ストーブ 3 hot plate *ko'nro* こんろ

straddle compl *ni* (v) *mataga'r·u* またがる straddle a horse *uma' ni mataga'ru* 馬にまたがる

straight *massu'gu [na]* まっすぐ[な] straight hair *massu'gu na kami'* まっすぐな髪 ——(adv) *massu'gu [ni]* まっすぐ[に] Go straight, please! *Massu'gu itte kudasa'i!* まっすぐ行って下さい.

straight pin *machi-ba'ri* 待ち針

strain *kinchō* 緊張 mental strain *se'ishin no kinchō* 精神の緊張 ——(idiom) 1 overextend *mu'ri o suru* 無理をする Don't strain yourself. *Mu'ri o shina'ide.* 無理をしないで. 2 strain one's eyes to see *me'o mihar·u* 目を見張る 3 strain one's ears to hear *mimi o suma's·u* 耳をすます *see also* stress

strained (attr) *hatta* 張った; (coll) *tsuppa'tta* つっぱった ——(v) be/become strained *tsuppa'r·u* つっぱる You have strained a muscle. *Ana'ta wa ki'nniku ga tsuppa'tte iru.* あなたは筋肉がつっぱっている.

strainer *uragoshi* 裏ごし

strange 1 weird *he'n [na]* 変[な] a strange person *he'n na hito'* 変な人 2 mysterious *fushigi [na]* 不思議[な] a strange happening *fushigi na deki'goto* 不思議な出来事 ——(adj) *okashi'·i* おかしい That's strange! I'm sure I had my wallet a minute ago! *Okashi'i! Ta'shika, sa'kki, saifu o mo'tte ita no ni!* おかしい. 確か, さっき財布を持っていたのに.

stranger *tanin* 他人 total stranger *a'ka no tanin* 赤の他人; *shiranai hito'* 知らない人

strangle *obj o* (v) [*kubi o*] *shime'·ru* [首を]絞める strangle someone *hito no kubi o shime'ru* 人の首を絞める ——(v) *muse·ru* 咽せる

strap 1 *himo* 紐 leather strap *kawahimo* 皮紐 cloth strap (on clothing) *tsurihimo* つり紐 2 (for holding onto) *tsurikawa* つり皮

stratosphere *seisō'ken* 成層圏

straw 1 *wa'ra* わら 2 drinking straw *suto'rō* ストロー

strawberry *ichigo* いちご

straw mat 1 (finished) *tatami* 畳 2 (rough) *mushiro'* むしろ

stream 1 *nagare'* 流れ 2 small river *ogawa* 小川

street 1 *michi* 道 2 city street *tōri'* 通り

street corner [*machi*]*kado* [街]角

strength 1 power *chikara'* 力 have strength *chikara' ga a'ru* 力がある have no strength *chikara' ga na'i* 力がない 2 intensity *tsu'-yosa* 強さ

strengthen *obj o* (v) *tsuyome'·ru* 強める strengthen relations *kankei o tsuyome'ru* 関係を強める

stress 1 *kyōchō* 強調 2 psychological tension *suto'resu* ストレス

stretch *nobi'·ru* 伸びる A knit dress stretches. *Ni'tto wa nobi'·ru.* ニットは伸びる. ——*obj o* (v) *noba's·u* 伸ばす Can you stretch this? *Kore o noba'su koto' ga dekima'su ka?* これを伸ばすことができますか.

stretcher *ta′nka* 担架

strict (adj) *kibishi′·i* 厳しい a strict teacher *kibishi′i sense′i* 厳しい先生

strike 1 *de′mo* デモ 2 refusal to work *suto′[ra′iki]* スト[ライキ] 3 (baseball) *sutora′iku* ストライク ——obj *o* (v) 1 *tata′k·u* 叩く 2 hit *u′ts·u* 打つ 3 hit with the fist *nagu′r·u* 殴る 4 hit hard with the fist *bunnagu′r·u* ぶんなぐる 5 hit on/against *atar·u* 当たる 6 bump into *butsukar·u* ぶつかる

string *himo* 紐

string beans *sayai′ngen* さやいんげん

stripe *shima′* 縞; *shimamo′yō* 縞模様

striptease *sutori′ppu* ストリップ

strive (irr) *do′ryoku-suru* 努力する

stroke (cerebral apoplexy) *nō′kketsu* 脳溢血 suffer a stroke *noi′k-ketsu o oko′su* 脳溢血を起こす

stroll loc *o* (v) *bu′rabura aru′k·u* ぶらぶら歩く

stroller *ubagu′ruma* うば車

strong *jōbu* [na] 丈夫[な] a strong, healthy boy *jōbu na otoko′ no ko* 丈夫な男の子 This material is strong. *Kono ki′ji wa jōbu de′su.* この生地は丈夫です。 ——(adj) 1 *tsuyo′·i* 強い a strong girl *tsuyo′i onna′no ko* 強い女の子 strong paper *tsuyo′i kami* 強い紙 2 *ko′·i* 濃い、strong coffee *ko′i kōhī* 濃いコーヒー

structure 1 *kōzō* 構造 2 building *tatemo′no* 建物

struggle *tōsō* 闘争

stubborn *gōjō* [na] 強情[な]; *katakuna* [na] かたくな[な] Don't be so stubborn! *Sonna ni katakuna ni na′ru na!* そんなにかたくなになるな。

student 1 (university; high school) *gakusei* 学生 2 (high school) *kōkō′sei* 高校生 3 (junior high school) *chūga′kusei* 中学生 4 (elementary school) *shōga′kusei* 小学生 5 (university) *daiga′kusei* 大学生 6 (graduate school) *daigakui′nsei* 大学院生 7 (foreign) *ryūga′kusei* 留学生 8 -year student -*nensei* 年生 first-year student *ichine′nsei* 一年生

study 1 *benkyō* 勉強 2 (room) *benkyō-beya* 勉強部屋; *shosai* 書斎 ——obj *o* (irr) 1 *benkyō-suru* 勉強する 2 study abroad *ryūgaku-suru* 留学する

stupid *ba′ka* [na] ばか[な] Stupid! *Ba′ka!* ばか。 That's stupid! *Baka-rashi′i!* ばからしい。

sturdy *ganjō* [na] 頑丈[な]

stutter (v) *domo′r·u* 吃る

stutterer *kitsuo′nsha* 吃音者

sty (infection on the eyelid) *monomo′rai* ものもらい

style 1 fashion; cut *suta′iru* スタイル 2 manner -*fū* [no] 風[の]

American style *Amerika-fū* アメリカ風 **3** of writing *buntai* 文体

stylish *sumā'to* [na] スマート[な] She's very stylish. *Ka'nojo wa totemo sumā'to desu.* 彼女はとてもスマートです.

subconscious *senzai i'shiki* [no] 潜在意識[の] ——(idiom) be subconscious *bon'ya'ri to i'shiki-shite i·ru* ぼんやりと意識している

subject 1 (academic) *kamoku* 科目 **2** (of a conversation) *wadai* 話題 **3** (of a discussion) *gidai* 議題 **4** (of a theme/article) *da'i dai* 題 **5** (of research) *taishō* 対象 **6** (Gram) *shu'go* 主語

subjective *shukanteki* [na] 主観的[な] subjective judgment *shukanteki ha'ndan* 主観的判断

submarine *sensuikan* 潜水艦

submit ind-obj *ni*, obj *o* (v) **1** (irr) *teishutsu-suru* 提出する **2** (for discussion) *kake'·ru* かける He submitted a sales plan to the meeting. *Ka're wa hambai ke'ikaku o kaigi ni ka'keta.* 彼は販売計画を会議にかけた. **3** (for decision) (irr) *teian-suru* 提案する

subscription 1 *kōdo'kushi* 購読紙 **2** reservation *kōdoku yo'yaku* 購読予約

subsidy *ho'jo* 補助

substitute *kawari* [ni] 代わり[に] Is it OK to use margarine as a substitute for butter? *Ba'tā no kawari ni ma'garin o tsukatte mo i'i desu ka?* バターの代わりにマーガリンを使ってもいいですか. ——compl *ni* (v) *kawar·u* 代わる

subtle *kōmyō* [na] 巧妙[な]; *bimyō* [na] 微妙[な] a subtle influence *bimyō na chikara* 微妙な力

subtract obj *o* (v) *hik·u* 引く subtract 5 from 8 *hachi ka'ra go' o hiku* 8から5を引く

subtraction *hiki'zan* 引き算

suburb *kō'gai* 郊外

subway *chikatetsu* 地下鉄 subway station *chikatetsu no e'ki* 地下鉄の駅

succeed compl *ni* (irr) *seikō-suru* 成功する succeed in business *shō'bai ni seikō-suru* 商売に成功する

success *seikō* 成功 a great success *dai-se'ikō* 大成功

successful (attr) *seikō-shita* 成功した a successful person *seikō-shita hito* 成功した人

such 1 to such an extent *sonna ni* そんなに; *konna ni* こんなに I didn't realize it would be such a task! *Konna ni muzukashi'i to wa omowa'nakatta!* こんなに難しいとは思わなかった.; *kō iu* こういう; *sō iu* そういう You can rely on such a person. *Sō iu hito' wa shinrai-deki'ru.* そういう人は信頼できる. **2** etc. *na'do* など That store has typewriters and office supplies and such. *Ano mise' ni wa taipura'itā ya bumbō'gu nado ga oite arima'su.* あの店にはタイプライターや文房具などが置いてあります.

suck obj *o* (v) *su·u* 吸う suck in one's breath *i'ki o suu* 息を吸う

sucker (lollipop) *bōtsuki'-ame* 棒つき飴

sudden *kyū* [*na*] 急[な] sudden business *kyū na yōji* 急な用事 It was such sudden notice, I didn't have time to prepare. *Sono hanashi' ga amari ni' mo kyū da'tta no de, nani mo yō'i deki'na-katta.* その話があまりにも急だったので, 何も用意できなかった.

suddenly *kyū ni* 急に It was decided suddenly. *Kyū ni kimatta.* 急に決まった.; *totsuzen* 突然 He suddenly became angry. *Ka're wa totsuzen okorida'shita.* 彼は突然怒り出した.

sue obj *o* (v) *utta'e·ru* 訴える; (irr) *ko'kuso-suru* 告訴する ——(idiom) *soshō o oko'·su* 訴訟をおこす

suede *suēdo* スエード

suffer (v) *kurushi'm·u* 苦しむ; *naya'm·u* 悩む

sufficient *jūbu'n* [*na*] 十分[な] sufficient consideration *jūbu'n na kō'ryo* 十分な考慮 Is this sufficient? *Kore de jūbu'n desu ka?* これで十分ですか. ——(v) be sufficient *tari·ru* 足りる It wasn't suffi-cient. *Sore de tarina'katta.* それで足りなかった.

sufficiently *jūbu'n ni* 十分に I wasn't able to explain it sufficiently. *Jūbu'n ni setsumei deki'nakatta.* 十分に説明できなかった.

suffocate (irr) *chissoku-suru* 窒息する ——(caus) *chissoku-saseru* 窒息させる

sugar 1 *satō'* 砂糖 2 granulated *guranyūtō* グラニュー糖 3 brown *akaza'tō* 赤砂糖 4 (unrefined) *kuroza'tō* 黒砂糖 5 pow-dered *konaza'tō* 粉砂糖 6 sugar crystals *zarame* ざらめ

suggest obj *o* (irr) *teian-suru* 提案する

suggestion *teian* 提案

suicide *jisatsu* 自殺 attempted suicide *jisatsu mi'sui* 自殺未遂 ——(irr) commit suicide *jisatsu-suru* 自殺する

suit 1 set of clothes *sū'tsu* スーツ 2 lawsuit *soshō* 訴訟 ——compl *ni* (v) be/become suitable to *nia'·u* 似合う That color suits you. *Sono iro' wa ana'ta ni yo'ku nia'u.* その色はあなたによく似合う.

suitable (adj) *fusawashi'·i* ふさわしい It's good she found a suit-able job. *Ka'nojo ni fusawashi'i shigoto ga mitsukatte, yo'katta.* 彼女にふさわしい仕事が見つかってよかった.

suitcase *tora'nku* トランク; *sūtsukē'su* スーツケース

suit coat *sū'tsu no uwagi* スーツの上着

sultry (adj) *mushiatsu'·i* 蒸し暑い

sum *gōkei* 合計

summarize obj *o* (v) *matome·ru* まとめる To summarize... *Mato-mema'su to...* まとめますと...

summary (digest) *gairyaku* 概略

summer *natsu'* 夏

summit *chōjō'* 頂上

summit conference *shunō ka'idan* 首脳会談

sun 1 *hi* 日 The sun is shining. *Hi ga te'tte iru.* 日が照っている.; *ta'iyō* 太陽 The sun rises in the east and sets in the west. *Ta'iyō wa higashi kara nobori, nishi ni shizu'mu.* 太陽は東から昇り西に沈む. 2 morning sun *a'sahi* 朝日 3 setting sun *yūhi* 夕日

sunbathing *hinata bo'kko* 日なたぼっこ; *nikkō'-yoku* 日光浴

sunburn *hiyake* 日焼け

sundae [*aisu*]*kurimu sa'ndē* [アイス]クリームサンデー

Sunday *nichiyō'bi* 日曜日

Sunday School *nichiyō ga'kkō* 日曜学校

sunflower *hima'wari* ひまわり

sunglasses *sangu'rasu* サングラス

sunlamp *taiyōtō* 太陽灯

sunlight *hizashi* 日射し

sunny *yōki na* 陽気な ——(adj) *akaru·i* 明るい, a sunny disposition *akarui kishitsu* 明るい気質 ——(v) be/become sunny *hare'·ru* 晴れる Tomorrow will be sunny. *Ashita' wa hare'ru deshō.* 明日は晴れるでしょう.

sunrise *hinode* 日の出

sunset *hinoiri* 日の入り

sunshine *ni'kkō* 日光; *hinata* 日なた

sunshiny (attr) *hiatari no i'·i* 日当たりのいい, a sunshiny room *hiatari no i'i heya'* 日当たりのいい部屋

sunstroke *nisshabyō* 日射病

suntan *hiyake* 日焼け suntan oil *hiyake-yō o'iru* 日焼け用オイル

superb (adj) *sugo'·i* すごい; *mi'goto na* 見事な

superior (one's superior) *meue no hito'* 目上の人; *sempai* 先輩 ——(attr) *sugu'reta* 勝れた

superiority complex *yūetsu'kan* 優越感

supermarket *sūpāmā'ketto* スーパーマーケット; (abbr) *sū'pā* スーパー

supernatural *chō'shizenteki* [na] 超自然的[な]

superstition *meishin* 迷信·

superstitious *meishinteki* [na] 迷信的[な] ——(adj) *meishin-buka'·i* 迷信深い

supervise obj *o* (irr) *kantoku-suru* 監督する

supervision *kantoku* 監督

supper *bango'han* 晩御飯; *yūshoku* 夕食

supplement *tsuika* 追加 ——obj *o* (v) *tsuika-suru* 追加する; *ogina'·u* 補う Please supplement my explanation where it isn't sufficient. *Setsumei no tarinai tokoro' o ogina'tte kudasa'i.* 説明の足りないところを補って下さい.

supplies *hokyū* 補給; *yōhin* 用品

supply *kyōkyū* 供給 supply and demand *juyō to kyōkyū* 需要と供給 ——ind-obj *ni*, obj *o* (irr) *kyōkyū-suru* 供給する

support *shi'ji* 支持 ——obj *o* (irr) *shi'ji-suru* 支持する

supporter (elastic) *sapō'tā* サポーター

suppose *mo'shi...(v)-tara* もし...たら Suppose I should win the lottery, I wonder what I'll use the prize money for. *Mo'shi watashi ga takaraku'ji ni atatta'ra, sono shōkin o na'ni ni tsukau kashira.* もし私が宝くじに当たったら,その賞金を何に使うかしら.

suppression 1 repression *yokusei* 抑制 2 concealment *intoku* 隠匿

Supreme Court *Saikō Saibansho* 最高裁判所

sure *ta'shika* 確か[な/に] I'm sure I saw it. *Ta'shika ni sore o mi'ta.* 確かにそれを見た.; *kitto* きっと I'm sure he'll come. *Ka're wa kitto ku'ru.* 彼はきっと来る.

Sure! (Certainly!) *Mochi'ron!* もちろん.

surf *yose-nami* 寄せ波

surface *hyōme'n* 表面

surfboard *sāfubō'do* サーフボード

surfing *sā'fin* サーフィン; *naminori* 波乗り

surgeon *geka'-i* 外科医

surgery department of surgery *geka* 外科 ——(irr) perform/have surgery *shu'jutsu-suru* 手術する

surname *myō'ji* 名字; *sei* 姓

surplus 1 superabundance *yobun* 余分 2 surplus funds *jōyokin* 剰余金

surprise *igai* 意外 It was a surprise. *Igai de'shita.* 意外でした. ——obj *o* (v) *odoroka's•u* 驚かす

surprised (v) be surprised *odoro'k•u* 驚く I was surprised. *Odoro'-ita.* 驚いた.; (irr) *bikku'ri-suru* びっくりする Don't be surprised. *Bikku'ri-shina'ide.* びっくりしないで.

surrender comp *ni* (irr) *kōsan-suru* 降参する

surroundings *a'tari* あたり

survey *chō'sa* 調査 ——obj *o* (irr) *chō'sa-suru* 調査する

survival *ikinokori* 生き残り; *seizon* 生存 ——(idiom) survival kit *sabaibaru ki'tto* サバイバルキット

survive (v) 1 *tasuka'r•u* 助かる He was underwater five minutes but survived. *Ka're wa gofu'nkan mo kaichū ni shizunde ita' ga tasuka'tta.* 彼は五分間も海中に沈んでいたが助かった. 2 overcome *kirinuke'•ru* 切り抜ける The villagers survived the tidal wave. *Murabito-ta'chi wa tsunami o kirinuketa.* 村人たちは津波を切り抜けた.

suspicion *utagai* 疑い

swallow obj *o* (v) *no'm•u* 飲む swallow a pill *jōzai o no'mu* 錠剤を飲む; *nomikom•u* 飲みこむ

swallow (bird) *tsubame* 燕

swamp *numa'* 沼

swan *hakuchō* 白鳥

swanky (attr) *shareta* しゃれた a swanky place *shareta tokoro'* しゃれた所

swatter fly swatter *hae-ta'taki* はえたたき

sway (v) *yure·ru* 揺れる The train swayed. *Densha ga yureta.* 電車が揺れた.

swear (vow) ind-obj *ni*, obj *o* (v) *chika·u* 誓う

sweat *a'se* 汗 cold sweat *hiya-a'se* 冷や汗 ——(idiom) perspire *a'se o ka'k·u* 汗をかく

sweater *sē'tā* セーター

Swede *Suēde'njin* スウェーデン人

Sweden *Suē'den* スウェーデン

Swedish (language) *Suēden-go* スウェーデン語 ——(attr) *Suē'den no* スウェーデンの

sweep obj *o* (v) *ha'k·u* 掃く

sweet (adj) 1 (taste) *ama·i* 甘い This is too sweet. *Kore wa amasugi'ru.* これは甘すぎる. 2 gentle *yasashi'·i* 優しい a sweet person *yasashi'i hito* 優しい人

sweetheart *koibito* 恋人

sweet pea *suito'pī* スイートピー

sweet potato *satsumaimo* さつま芋

sweet roll *kashi-pan* 菓子パン; *suito rō'ru* スイートロール

sweets *o-ka'shi* お菓子

swell (v) *hare·ru* 腫れる It's swollen here. *Koko ga harete iru.* ここが腫れている.; *muku'm·u* むくむ

swim loc *de* (v) 1 *oyo'g·u* 泳ぐ swim in a swimming pool *pūru de oyo'gu* プールで泳ぐ 2 (underwater) *mogu'r·u* 潜る

swimsuit *mizugi* 水着

swindler *sagi'shi* 詐欺師

swing (for children) *bu'ranko* ぶらんこ ——(v) *burasaga'·ru* ぶらさがる

swinging door 1 *jizai do'a* 自在ドア 2 revolving door *kaiten do'a* 回転ドア

Swiss (person) *Suisu'jin* スイス人 ——(attr) *Sui'su no* スイスの

switch *sui'tchi* スイッチ ——compl *ni*, obj *o* (v) to change *kirika'e·ru* 切り替える ——(idiom) to switch on *sui'tchi o ire·ru* スイッチを入れる

Switzerland *Sui'su* スイス

sword *katana'* 刀

swordfish *meka'jiki* めかじき

syllable *onsetsu* 音節

symbol *shi'mboru* シンボル; *shōchō* 象徴

symmetrical (attr) *taishō no* 対称の; *kinsei no to'reta* 均整のとれた a symmetrical design *kinsei no to'reta deza'in* 均整のとれたデザイン

sympathize comp *to* (irr) *dōjō-suru* 同情する
sympathy *dōjō* 同情
symphony *kōkyō'kyoku* 交響曲
symphony orchestra *kangen ga'kudan* 管弦楽団; *kōkyō ga'kudan* 交響楽団
symptom *chōkō* 兆候
synagogue *Yudayajin shū'kai* ユダヤ人集会; *Yudaya kyō'kai* ユダヤ教会
synonym *dō'gigo* 同義語
synthesis *sōgō* 総合
syphilis *bai'doku* 梅毒
Syrian (person) *Shiria'jin* シリア人 ——(attr) *Shiria'jin no* シリア人の
syringe 1 *senjō'ki* 洗浄器 2 hypodermic needle *chūsha'ki* 注射器
syrup *shi'roppu* シロップ
system *taikei* 体系; *se'ido* 制度
systematic 1 methodical *soshikiteki* [*na*] 組織的[な] 2 regular *kisokuteki* [*na*] 規則的[な] 3 planned *keikakuteki* [*na*] 計画的[な]

T

tab (bill) *dempyō* 伝票; *kanjō'* 勘定 My tab, please. *Kanjō' o onegai-shima'su.* 勘定をお願いします.
table 1 *tēburu* テーブル end table *saido tē'buru* サイドテーブル 2 dining table *shokutaku* 食卓
tablecloth *tēburu'-kake* テーブル掛け
table lamp *takujō suta'ndo* 卓上スタンド
tablespoon *ōsaji* 大匙 Add one tablespoon of sugar. *Satō' o ōsaji i'ppai irete kudasa'i.* 砂糖を大匙一杯入れて下さい.
table tennis *takkyū* 卓球; *pi'npon* ピンポン
tablet 1 pill *jōzai* 錠剤 2 pad of writing paper *nō'to* ノート
taboo *tabū'* タブー
tack 1 short nail *byō'* 鋲 2 thumbtack *gabyō* 画鋲
tactful (attr) *kiten no kiku'* 機転のきく; *josai na'i* 如才ない
tadpole *otamaja'kushi* おたまじゃくし
tag 1 label *retteru* レッテル 2 name tag *nafuda* 名札 3 baggage identification tag *ni'fuda* 荷札
tail *shippo'* しっぽ ——obj *o* (v) [*a' to o*] *tsuke'·ru* [後を]付ける
tails (formal wear) *embi' fuku* 燕尾服
tailor *yō fukuya-san* 洋服屋さん tailor shop *yō fukuya* 洋服屋
tailoring *shitate* 仕立て
Taiwan *Taiwa'n* 台湾

Taiwanese (person) *Taiwa'njin* 台湾人 ——(attr) *Taiwa'n no* 台湾の

take (v) require *kaka'r·u* かかる It takes about fifteen minutes (to go) from here. *Koko kara jūgofun gu'rai kaka'ru.* ここから十五分ぐらいかかる. ——obj *o* (v) 1 *to'r·u* 取る Take one sheet of paper, please. *Kami' o ichi'mai to'tte kudasa'i.* 紙を一枚取って下さい. 2 carry *motte ik·u* 持って行く Take this into the living room, please. *Kore o kyakuma ni motte i'tte kudasa'i.* これを客間に持って行って下さい. 3 receive; be given *uke'·ru* 受ける take an exam *shike'n o uke'ru* 試験を受ける She took my advice and went to see a doctor. *Ka'nojo wa watashi no chūkoku o u'kete isha ni itta.* 彼女は私の忠告を受けて，医者に行った. 4 take (a photograph) [*shashin o*] *to'r·u* [写真を]撮る 5 (medicine) [*kusuri o*] *no'm·u* [薬を]飲む

take care comp *ni* (irr) *chū'i-suru* 注意する Take care not to lose your train pass. *Te'iki o nakusanai yō' ni chū'i-shite kudasa'i.* 定期をなくさないように注意して下さい. ——(idiom) 1 *ki o tsuke'·ru* 気を付ける

Take care! *Ki o tsu'kete!* 気を付けて. 2 (when one is sick) Take care! *O-daiji ni!* お大事に. see also **care**

take down obj *o* (v) *oro's·u* 降ろす take down a book from the shelf *ho'n o ho'ndana kara oro'su* 本を本棚から降ろす

take-home pay *tedori* [*kyū'ryō*] 手取り[給料]

take into account *kanjō' ni ire'·ru* 勘定に入れる I didn't take that into account. *Sore o kanjō' ni irena'katta.* それを勘定に入れなかった.

takeoff (airplane) *ririku* 離陸

take off (clothing) 1 obj *o* (v) *nu'g·u* 脱ぐ Take off your overcoat. *Ō'bā o nu'ide kudasa'i.* オーバーを脱いで下さい. People take off their shoes when entering a Japanese house. *Nihon no ie'ni ha'iru toki wa, kutsu' o nu'ide agaru.* 日本の家に入る時は，靴を脱いで上がる. 2 (plane) (irr) *ririku-suru* 離陸する

take out obj *o* (v) 1 *mochidas'·u* 持ち出す Take this chair out to the yard. *Kono isu o niwa e mochida'shite kudasa'i.* この椅子を庭へ持ち出して下さい.; *da's·u* 出す take out the garbage *gomi' o da'su* ごみを出す 2 omit (irr) *shōryaku-suru* 省略する 3 extract *nuk·u* 抜く The dentist took out two wisdom teeth. *Ha'isha wa oyashi'razu o ni'hon nuita.* 歯医者は親知らずを二本抜いた.

take-out food 1 *mochikaeri ryō'ri* 持ち帰り料理 2 home delivery *demae ryō'ri* 出前料理

take sick *byōki ni na'r·u* 病気になる

take turns obj *o* (irr) *kōtai-suru* 交代する ——(caus) *kōtai-sase'·ru* 交代させる have (baseball) pitchers take turns *tō'shu o kōtai-saseru* 投手を交代させる ——(adv) *kōtai de* 交代で We took turns driving. *Kōtai de unten-shita.* 交代で運転した.; *kawaribanko ni* かわりばんこに take turns keeping watch *kawariba'nko ni mihari o suru* かわりばんこに見張りをする

take up (discuss)   obj *o* (v) *toriage'ru* 取り上げる There is no time to take that problem up today. *Kyō' wa sono mondai o toriage'ru jikan ga na'i.* 今日はその問題を取り上げる時間がない.

tale   1 *monoga'tari* 物語   2 fairy tale *otogiba'nashi* おとぎ話   3 folk tale *minwa* 民話   4 tall tale *tsukuri-ba'nashi* 作り話

talent   *sainō* 才能 a person with talent *sainō no a'ru hito* 才能のある人

talisman   *o-mamori* おまもり

talk   1 *hanashi'* 話   2 chit-chat *o-sha'beri* おしゃべり   3 formal talk; lecture *kōen* 講演   ——comp *to,* ind-obj *ni,* obj *o* (v) *hana's·u* 話す Did you talk to him about that? *Ka're ni sono koto o hanashima'shita ka?* 彼にそのことを話しましたか.

talkative person   *o-sha'beri* おしゃべり

talk to oneself (idiom) *hitorigoto o i·u* 独り言を言う

tall (adj) *taka'·i* 高い, a tall building *takai tatemono* 高い建物   ——(attr) tall in stature *se' ga taka'·i* 背が高い She's tall. *Ka'nojo wa se' ga taka'i.* 彼女は背が高い.

tambourine   *ta'mbarin* タンバリン

tame (adj) *otonashi'·i* おとなしい Is this horse tame? *Kono uma' wa otonashi'i desu ka?* この馬はおとなしいですか.   ——(attr) domesticated *kainarasa'reta* 飼い慣らされた; *hitonare-shita* 人慣れした a tame bird *hitonare-shita tori* 人慣れした鳥   ——obj *o* (v) *nara's·u* 慣らす tame a horse *uma' o nara'su* 馬を慣らす

tamper   obj *o* (v) *iji'r·u* いじる Don't tamper with this! *Kore o iji'tte wa ikenai!* これをいじってはいけない.

tampon   *ta'mpon* タンポン

tan   1 (color) *usu-chairo* 薄茶色   2 suntan *hiyake* 日焼け   —— obj *o* (v) tan (in the sun) [*hi ni*] *yake·ru* [日に]焼ける   ——obj *o* (v) tan (a hide) [*kawa'* de] *name's·u* [皮を]なめす

tangerine (J) *mi'kan* みかん

tangible   1 *yūkei* [*no*] 有形[の] tangible assets *yūkei shi'san* 有形資産   2 real *jisshitsuteki* [*na*] 実質的[な] tangible proof *jisshitsuteki na shōko* 実質的な証拠   3 concrete *gutaiteki* [*na*] 具体的[な]   4 (having material form) *te' de sawaru koto' ga deki·ru* 手で触ることができる a tangible substance *te' de sawaru koto' ga deki'ru busshitsu* 手で触ることができる物質

tank   1 (storage) *ta'nku* タンク   2 (combat) *se'nsha* 戦車

tantrum   *kanshaku* かんしゃく have a tantrum *kanshaku o oko'su* かんしゃくを起こす

tap   water faucet *ko'kku* コック; *jaguchi* 蛇口; *se'n* 栓   ——obj *o* (v)   1 *tata'k·u* 叩く tap on the door *to o tata'ku* 戸を叩く   2 tap (a telephone line) (irr) [*denwa o*] *tōchō-suru* [電話を] 盗聴する

tape 1 *tē̆'pu* テープ 2 adhesive tape *bansōkō* ばんそうこう 3 friction tape *zetsuen tē̆'pu* 絶縁テープ 4 packaging tape *hōsō-yō tē̆'pu* 包装用テープ 5 recording tape *rokuon tē̆'pu* 録音テープ 6 Scotch tape *sero tē̆'pu* セロテープ ——obj *o* (irr) *rokuon-suru* 録音する I taped the professor's lecture. *Kyōju no kō̆'gi o rokuon-shita.* 教授の講義を録音した.

tape measure *makijaku* 巻き尺; *mĕ'jā* メジャー

tape recorder *tēpu rekō̆'dā* テープレコーダー

tar *tā̆'ru* タール ——(idiom) paint with tar *tā̆'ru o nur·u* タールを塗る

tardy (irr) be tardy *chikoku-suru* 遅刻する I was tardy for school. *Gakkō ni chikoku-shita.* 学校に遅刻した.

target 1 *mato* 的 2 goal *mĕ'ate* 目当

tarnish (v) 1 discolor (irr) *henshoku-suru* 変色する This metal won't tarnish. *Kono kĭ'nzoku wa henshoku-shina'i.* この金属は変色しない. 2 lose luster *kumŏ'r·u* 曇る

tart (adj) *suppă'·i* すっぱい It's a bit tart. *Sukŏ'shi suppă'i.* 少しすっぱい.

task *shigoto* 仕事

tassel *fusa* 房

taste 1 *aji* 味 sweet taste *amai aji* 甘い味 bitter taste *nigă'i aji* 苦い味 2 (sense of) *mikaku* 味覚 ——obj *o* (v) *ajiwă'·u* 味わう Taste this. *Kore o ajiwă'tte mite kudasă'i.* これを味わって見て下さい. ——(idiom) 1 have a taste *aji ga suru* 味がする What does it taste like? *Dŏ'nna aji ga shimă'su ka?* どんな味がしますか. 2 predilection *shŭ'mi* 趣味 good taste *shŭ'mi ga ĭ'·i* 趣味がいい He has good taste in ties. *Kă're wa nĕ'kutai no shŭ'mi ga ĭ'·i.* 彼はネクタイの趣味がいい. bad taste *shŭ'mi ga warŭ'·i* 趣味が悪い She has bad taste in clothing. *Kă'nojo wa fukusō no shŭ'mi ga warŭ'i.* 彼女は服装の趣味が悪い. matter of taste *shŭ'mi no mondai* 趣味の問題

tasteful *fū̆'ga [na]* 風雅[な] a tasteful house *fū̆'ga na kă'oku* 風雅な家屋

tasteless (adj) *ajikenă'·i* 味けない ——(attr) *aji no nă'·i* 味のない

tasty (adj) *oishĭ·i* おいしい

tattoo *irezumi* 刺青

Taurus *Oushi-za* 牡牛座

tax 1 *zeikin* 税金 pay taxes *zeikin o osamĕ'r·u* 税金を納める 2 -*zei* business tax *eigyō̆'zei* 営業税; municipal tax *shimĭ'nzei* 市民税; income tax *shotokŭ'zei* 所得税; ward tax *kumĭ'nzei* 区民税 ——(irr) *kazei-suru* 課税する ——(idiom) levy a tax *zeikin o kakĕ'r·u* 税金をかける

taxation *kazei* 課税

tax-free *menzei [no]* 免税[の] Is this tax-free? *Kore wa menzei de′su ka?* これは免税ですか.

taxi *ta′kushī* タクシー flag a taxi *ta′kushī o hirou* タクシーを拾う take a taxi *ta′kushī ni noru* タクシーに乗る

taxi driver *ta′kushī no unte′nshu* タクシーの運転手

tax office *zeimusho* 税務署

tea **1** *ocha* お茶 **2** (black) *kōcha* 紅茶 **3** (green) *ryokucha* 緑茶 **4** (iced) *a′isu-tī* アイスティー

tea bag *tī ba′ggu* ティーバッグ

teach ind-obj *ni*, obj *o* (v) *oshie·ru* 教える Would you teach me Japanese, please? *Nihon-go o oshiete kudasaimase′n ka?* 日本語を教えて下さいませんか. I teach English to children. *Watashi wa kodomo ni Ei-go o oshiete iru.* 私は子供に英語を教えている. ── obj *o* (v) be taught *osowa r·u* 教わる I was taught Japanese by a noted teacher. *Watashi wa yūmei na sense′i ni Nihon-go o osowa′tta.* 私は有名な先生に日本語を教わった.

teacher *sense′i* 先生 That person is my teacher. *Ano′ hito wa watashi no nose′i desu.* あの人は私の先生です; *kyo′shi* 教師 I am a teacher. *Watashi wa kyo′shi desu.* 私は教師です.

teacup **1** (J) *chawan* 茶碗; *yunomi* 湯のみ **2** (W) *kōcha-ja′wan* 紅茶茶碗

teak *chī′ku* チーク

teakettle *yakan* やかん; *yuwa′kashi* 湯沸かし

team *chī′mu* チーム baseball team *yakyū chi′mu* 野球チーム

teapot **1** (J) *kyūsu* 急須 **2** (W) *tīpo′tto* ティーポット

tear (drop) *na′mida* 涙 shed tears *na′mida o naga′su* 涙を流す

tear (rip) (v) *yabure′·ru* 破れる The bag tore. *Fukuro′ ga yabu′reta.* 袋が破れた. ──obj *o* (v) *yabu′r·u* 破る I tore my shirt. *Sha′tsu o yabu′tta.* シャツを破った.; (coll) *yabu′k·u* 破く Don't tear it! *Yabu′ite wa ike′nai!* 破いてはいけない.

tease obj *o* (v) *karaka′·u* からかう Don't tease me! *Karakawa′-naide kudasa′i!* からかわないで下さい.

teapoon *kosaji* 小匙

technical **1** *gijutsuteki [na]* 技術的[な] This is a technical problem. *Kore wa gijutsuteki na mondai de′su.* これは技術的な問題です. **2** specialized *semmon [no]* 専門[の] a technical term *semmon yō′go* 専門用語

technician *semmonka* 専門家

technique *te′kunikku* テクニック

technology **1** *gi′jutsu* 技術 industrial technology *kōgyō gi′jutsu* 工業技術 scientific technology *kagaku gi′jutsu* 科学技術 **2** high technology (high-tech) *kōdo gi′jutsu* 高度技術; *haiteku* ハイテク

tedious *taikutsu [na]* 退屈[な] a tedious job *taikutsu na shigoto* 退屈な仕事

tee   *tī* ティー

teenager   *jū′dai no hito* 十代の人；*tīn-ē′jā* ティーンエージャー

teeth   **1** *ha′* 歯   **2** false teeth *ireba* 入れ歯

teethe   (idiom) *ha′ ga hae′·ru* 歯が生える Baby's teething. *A′ka-chan ni ha′ ga ha′ete kita.* 赤ちゃんに歯が生えてきた.

telegram   *dempō* 電報 send a telegram *dempō o u′tsu* 電報を打つ

telegraph office   *denshi′nkyoku* 電信局

telephone   *denwa* 電話 public telephone *kōshū de′nwa*   公衆電話
—— (irr) *denwa-suru* 電話する Telephone me tomorrow. *Ashita denwa-shite kudasa′i.* 明日電話して下さい. ——(idiom)   **1** call on the telephone *denwa o kake′·ru* 電話をかける I telephoned, but she wasn't home. *Denwa o kakema′shita ga, ka′nojo wa o-ru′su deshita.* 電話をかけましたが、彼女はお留守でした.   **2** Telephone (call for you)! *O-de′nwa desu!* お電話です.   **3** place a (telephone) call *denwa o ire·ru* 電話を入れる Telephone and confirm it. *Denwa o irete, kakunin-shite kudasa′i.* 電話を入れて確認して下さい.

telephone bill   *denwa ryōkin-hyō* 電話料金表

telephone book   *denwa-chō* 電話帳

telephone booth   *denwa bo′kkusu* 電話ボックス

telephone company   *denwakyoku* 電話局

telephone directory   *denwachō* 電話帳

telephone number   *denwa ba′ngō* 電話番号

telephone operator   *kōka′nshu* 交換手

telephone receiver   *juwa′ki* 受話器 pick up the receiver *juwa′ki o hazusu* 受話器を外す hang up the receiver *juwaki o oku* 受話器を置く

telephone switchboard   *kōkandai* 交換台

telephoto lens   *bōen re′nzu* 望遠レンズ

telescope   *bōenkyō* 望遠鏡

teletype   *see* telex

television   *te′rebi* テレビ watch television *te′rebi o mi′ru* テレビを見る

television announcer   *terebi ana′unsā* テレビアナウンサー

television channel   *channeru* チャンネル

television commercial   *komā′sharu* コマーシャル

telex   *tere′kkusu* テレックス

tell   ind-obj *ni*, o (v)   **1** *i·u* 言う tell a joke *jōda′n o iu* 冗談を言う Don't tell anyone! *Dare ni mo iwana′i de!* 誰にも言わないで!   **2** inform *shirase·ru* 知らせる He told me the result of the voting. *Ka′re wa watashi ni tōhyō no kekka o shira′seta.* 彼は私に投票の結果を知らせた.

teller   *suitō-ga′kari* 出納係

temper   *kanshaku* かんしゃく lose one's temper *kanshaku o oko′su*

かんしゃくを起こす ——(attr) **1** bad-tempered *iji no waru'i* 意地の悪い **2** quick-tempered *okorippo'i* 怒りっぽい

temperate (climate) *onwa* [na] 温和[な]

temperature 1 *o'ndo* 温度 high (atmospheric) temperature *o'ndo no taka'i* 温度の高い **2** body temperature *ta'ion* 体温 **3** fever *netsu'* 熱 The baby has a temperature. *A'kachan wa netsu' ga aru.* 赤ちゃんは熱がある.

temple 1 (Budd) *tera* 寺; (Tech) *ji'in* 寺院; *-ji* 寺 Jindai Temple *Ji'ndai-ji* 深大寺 **2** non-Buddhist temple *shinden* 神殿

temporary 1 *rinji* [no] 臨時[の] a temporary teacher *rinji no kō'shi* 臨時の講師; *kari* [no] 仮[の] a temporary office *kari jimu'sho* 仮事務所 a temporary operator's license *kari me'nkyo* 仮免許 **2** makeshift *tōza* [no] 当座[の] a temporary job *tōza no shigoto* 当座の仕事

tempt obj *o* (irr) *yūwaku-suru* 誘惑する tempt a person with money *hito o o-kane de yūwaku-suru* 人をお金で誘惑する ——(pass) be tempted *yūwaku-sare·ru* 誘惑される

temptation *yūwaku* 誘惑 overcome temptation *yūwaku o koku-fuku-suru* 誘惑を克服する

ten *tō'* 十; *jū'* 十 *see also* Appendix 1

tenacious (adj) *shibuto'·i* しぶとい

tenant *shakuyanin* 借家人

tendency *keikō* 傾向 She has a tendency to drink too much. *Ka'nojo wa nomi-sugi'ru keikō ga a'ru.* 彼女は飲みすぎる傾向がある. ——(idiom) *-gachi* がち My watch has a tendency to gain. *Watashi no tokei wa susumi-gachi de'su.* 私の時計は進みがちです.

tender (adj) **1** *yawaraka'·i* 柔らかい tender meat *yawaraka'i niku'* 柔らかい肉 **2** affectionate *yasashi·i* 優しい a tenderhearted person *kokoro no yasashii hito'* 心の優しい人 **3** painful (adj) *ita·i* 痛い a tender spot *ita'i tokoro* 痛い所

tenderness *yasashisa* 優しさ

tendon *su'ji* 筋; *ke'n* 腱

tend to (idiom) **1** mind; look after *sewa o suru* 世話をする tend to a patient *kanja no sewa' o suru* 患者の世話をする; *mendō' o mi'·ru* 面倒を見る Would you tend to the children while I'm away? *Ru'su no aida, kodomo no mendō' o mite kuremase'n ka?* 留守の間, 子供の面倒を見てくれませんか. **2** see to; take care of obj *o* (v) *yatte ok·u* やっておく I'll tend to the matter right away. *Su'gu ni sono koto' o yatte okima'su.* すぐにその事をやっておきます. *see also* tendency

tennis *te'nisu* テニス play tennis *te'nisu o suru* テニスをする

tennis ball *tenisu bō'ru* テニスボール

tennis court *te'nisu kō'to* テニスコート

tennis match *te'nisu no shiai* テニスの試合

tennis racket *tenisu rake′tto* テニスラケット

tennis shoes *tenisu shū′zu* テニスシューズ

tenor (voice) *tenō′ru* テノール; *te′nā* テナー

tense compl *ni* (irr) *kinchō-suru* 緊張する The more I think about it the more tense I become. *Kanga′ereba kanga′eru hodo kinchō-shite shima′u.* 考えれば考える程緊張してしまう. ——(attr) *kinchō-shita* 緊張した a tense atmosphere *kinchō-shita fun′i′ki* 緊張した雰囲気

tense (Gram) *jisei* 時制

tension 1 strain *kinchō* 緊張 2 stress *suto′resu* ストレス 3 (Physics) *chō′ryoku* 張力 surface tension *hyōmen chō′ryoku* 表面張力

tent *te′nto* テント

tentative *ichijiteki* [*na*] 一時的[な] tentative measure *ichijiteki na shu′dan* 一時的な手段

tenth 1 (ordinal) *jūbam-me′* [*no*] 十番目[の] 2 (fraction) *jūbun no ichi* 十分の一

tenth day of the month *tōka* 十日

ten thousand *ichima′n* 一万 ten-thousand yen bill *ichiman-e′n satsu* 一万円札

tepid (adj) *nama-nuru′·i* 生温い

term 1 period *ki′kan* 期間 2 school term *gakki* 学期 3 term of office/duty *ni′nki* 任期

terminal 1 (airline) *ea tā′minaru* エアターミナル 2 (bus) *basu tā′minaru* バスターミナル 3 (railroad station) *shūchaku′-eki* 終着駅 4 (Elec; computer) *tā′minaru* ターミナル; *ta′nshi* 端子 5 (last stage) *makki-* 末期 terminal cancer *makki′-gan* 末期癌

termite *shiro-ari* 白蟻

terms *jōke′n* 条件 accept terms *jōke′n ni ōjiru* 条件に応じる

terrible (adj) *monosugo′·i* ものすごい a terrible noise *monosugo′i oto′* ものすごい音; *osoroshi′·i* 恐ろしい War is terrible. *Sensō wa osoroshi′i.* 戦争は恐ろしい.

terrific (attr) *ta′ishita* 大した He is a terrific man! *Ka′re wa ta′ishita ji′mbutsu desu!* 彼は大した人物です. ——(idiom) That's terrific! *Sugo′i!* 凄い.

terrify (irr) *gyōten-suru* 仰天する When I heard that news, I was terrified. *Sono nyū′su o kiite, gyōten-shita.* そのニュースを聞いて, 仰天した. ——(caus) *gyōten-sase·ru* 仰天させる

territory 1 domain *ryōiki* 領域 sales territory *hambai ryō′iki* 販売領域 2 dominion *ryō′do* 領土 3 sphere of influence *nawabari* 縄張り

terror *kyōfu* 恐怖

terrorism *terori′zumu* テロリズム

test 1 *te′suto* テスト IQ test *chinō te′suto* 知能テスト 2 examination *shike′n* 試験 ——obj *o* (v) *tame′s·u* 試す Test the tempera-

ture of the water. *O-yu no o'ndo o tame'shite mite kudasa'i.* お湯
の温度を試してみて下さい. ——(idiom) give a test *shike'n o
suru* 試験をする I'm going to give a test on Friday. *Kin'yō'bi ni
shike'n o suru.* 金曜日に試験をする.

testament **1** will *yuigonjō* 遺言状 **2** New Testament *Shin'yaku
Se'isho* 新約聖書 **3** Old Testament *Kyūyaku Se'isho* 旧約聖書

testicles (Tech) *kōgan* 睾丸; (coll) *kinta'ma* 金玉

testify obj o (irr) *shōge'n-suru* 証言する

testimony **1** (Leg) *shōgen* 証言 **2** (Chr) *akashi* 証し

test tube *shikenkan* 試験管

tetanus *hashōfū* 破傷風

text **1** main text *ho'mbun/hommon* 本文 **2** original text *gembun*
原文 **3** topic *rondai* 論題

textbook *kyōka'sho* 教科書; *teki'suto* テキスト

textiles *se'ni* 繊維; *orimo'no* 織物

texture *kime* きめ material of rough texture *kime no arai ki'ji* き
めの粗い生地

Thai **1** (language) *Tai-go* タイ語 **2** (person) *Tai'jin* タイ人 ——
(attr) *Ta'i no* タイの

Thailand *Ta'i* タイ

than *yori...[no] hō* より...[の]方 This is cheaper than that. *Sore
yo'ri kore no hō' ga yasu'i.* それよりこれの方が安い.

thank (idiom) *o-rei o i·u* お礼を言う I don't know how to thank
you. *Na'n to o-rei o itte i'i ka wakarimase'n.* 何とお礼を言ってい
いか分かりません.

Thanksgiving Day *Kansha'sai* 感謝祭

thanks to... *[no] o-kage de...* [の]おかげで Thanks to her I suc-
ceeded. *Ka'nojo no o-kage de seikō-shita.* 彼女のおかげで成功した.

Thank you. **1** (plain) *Ari'gatō.* ありがとう.; (polite) *Ari'gatō gozaima'su.* ありがとうございます. **2** Thank you very much. *Dō'mo
[ari'gatō gozaima'su]* どうも [ありがとうございます] **3** Thank
you (for service in the course of duty). *Goku'rōsama.* ごくろうさ
ま. **4** Thank you (I'm sorry to have troubled you). *Sumimase'n.*
すみません. **5** Thank you (I am obliged to you). *Oso're-irimasu.*
恐れ入ります. **6** Thank you (for doing that for me). *O-sewa-sama
de'shita.* お世話様でした.

that **1** (referent that is near listener) *sore* それ Give me that,
please. *Sore o kudasa'i.* それを下さい.; (designating a person or
thing near listener) *sono* その Give me that pencil, please. *Sono
empitsu o kudasa'i.* その鉛筆を下さい. **2** (referent that is far from
speaker and listener) *are* あれ What is that? *Are wa na'n desu ka?*
あれは何ですか.; (designating a person or thing far from speaker
and listener) *ano* あの What is that tall building? *Ano taka'i tate-
mo'no wa na'n desu ka?* あの高い建物は何ですか.

thatch roof *kayabuki ya'ne* かやぶき屋根

that is (to say) *tsu'mari* つまり That is (in short), Friday is not convenient, is it? *Tsu'mari, kin'yō'bi wa tsugō ga waru'i desu, ne?* つまり、金曜日は都合が悪いですね.

that kind of 1 (designating a person or thing known to the speaker but not to the listener) *sonna* そんな I dislike that kind of person. *Sonna hito' wa kirai de'su.* そんな人は嫌いです. 2 (designating a person or thing known by both speaker and listener) *anna* あんな You should not have anything to do with that kind of person. *Anna hito' o aite' ni shinai hō' ga i'i.* あんな人を相手にしない方がいい.

that way 1 (direction) *atchi* あっち; *achira* あちら It's that way. *Achira de'su.* あちらです. 2 (manner) *sō* そう Do it that way. *Sō shi-nasa'i.* そうしなさい.

thaw (v) *toke'•ru* 溶ける The ice on the pond thaws in March. *Ike no kōri wa sa'ngatsu ni wa toke'ru.* 池の氷は三月には溶ける. ——obj *o* (v) *toka's•u* 溶かす Let's thaw the frozen meat. *Reitō-shita niku' o tokashimashō'.* 冷凍した肉を溶かしましょう.

the *see* that

theater 1 drama *ge'ki* 劇; *shibai* 芝居; (Tech) *gikyoku* 戯曲 2 playhouse *gekijō* 劇場 3 movie theater *eiga'kan* 映画館

theft *tōnan* 盗難 a theft case *tōnan ji'ken* 盗難事件

their (fem) *ka'nojo-tachi no* 彼女たちの; (masc/fem) *ka'rera no* 彼らの their problem *karera no mondai* 彼らの問題; (other) -*tachi no* たちの

them (fem) *ka'nojo-tachi* 彼女たち; (masc) *ka'rera* 彼ら Did you invite them? *Ka'rera o shōtai-shimashita ka?* 彼らを招待しましたか.; (other) -*tachi* たち

theme 1 subject *shudai* 主題 2 basic point *shu'shi* 趣旨

themselves (fem) *kanojo-tachi ji'shin* 彼女たち自身; (masc/fem) *karera ji'shin* 彼ら自身

then 1 at that time *sono to'ki* その時 I didn't know it then. *Sono to'ki wa shira'nakatta.* その時は知らなかった. 2 (next) *soshite* そして; *sore kara* それから Then what did you do? *Sore kara na'ni o shima'shita ka?* それから何をしましたか. 3 accordingly *soko de* そこで Then I decided to go home. *Soko de uchi ni ka'eru koto' ni shita.* そこで家に帰ることにした.; *suruto* すると Then, do you plan to give it up? *Suruto, yameru tsumori de'su ka?* すると、やめるつもりですか.

the n-th time -*dome'* 度目 the third time *sandome* 三度目

theological *shingakuteki* [*na*] 神学的[な]; *shingaku* [*no*] 神学[の] theological school *shinga'kkō* 神学校

theology *shingaku* 神学

theorem (Math) *te′iri* 定理
theoretical *rironteki* [*na*] 理論的[な]; *riron-* 理論 theoretical physics *riron butsuri′gaku* 理論物理学
theory *ri′ron* 理論
therapeutic *chiryō* [*gaku*] [*no*] 治療[学] [の] therapeutic method *chiryō-hō* 治療法
therapy *chiryō* 治療; *-ryōhō* 療法 electrotherapy *denki ryo′hō* 電気療法
there **1** (near listener) *soko* そこ **2** (far from speaker and listener) *asoko* あそこ **3** over there *mukō* 向こう
therefore (polite) *de′su kara* ですから; (plain) *da′kara* だから The argument is weak; therefore, it is unconvincing. *Ro′nshi ga yowa′i. Da′kara settoku′ryoku ga na′i.* 論旨が弱い。だから説得力がない。
thermodynamics *netsuriki′gaku* 熱力学
thermometer **1** *ondokei* 温度計 **2** (clinical) *taionkei* 体温計
thermonuclear *nekkaku* [*no*] 熱核[の] thermonuclear explosion *nekkaku ba′kuhatsu* 熱核爆発
thermos *mahō′bin* 魔法びん; *po′tto* ポット
thermostat *sāmosuta′tto* サーモスタット
thesaurus *ruigo ji′ten* 類語辞典
these *kore′ra* これら These are examples. *Kore′ra ga re′i desu.* これらが例です。; *kono* この these books *kono ho′n* この本
thesis *rombun* 論文 doctoral thesis *hakushi ro′mbun* 博士論文
they (fem) *ka′nojo-tachi* 彼女たち; (masc/masc-fem) *ka′rera* 彼ら; (other) *-tachi* たち
thick (adj) **1** *futo′·i* 太い thick tree trunk *futo′i mi′ki* 太い幹 **2** *atsu· i* 厚い thick book *atsui ho′n* 厚い本 **3** *ko′·i* 濃い
thick hair *ko′i kami-no′-ke* 濃い髪の毛 ——(attr) dense *shigetta* 茂った a thick forest *shigetta hayashi* 茂った林
thicket *yabu* やぶ bamboo thicket *take yabu* 竹やぶ
thickness (density) *atsusa* 厚さ; *fu′tosa* 太さ; *ko′sa* 濃さ
thief *dorobō* どろぼう
thigh (human) *futomomo* 太股; (chicken) *mo′mo* 股
thimble *yubinuki* 指ぬき
thin (adj) **1** *hoso′· i* 細い thin legs *hoso′i ashi′* 細い足 a thin person *hoso′i hito* 細い人 **2** *usu·i* 薄い thin book *usui ho′n* 薄い本 thin color *usui iro′* 薄い色 ——(v) be/become thin *yase·ru* やせる You've become thin, haven't you? *Yasema′shita, ne.* やせましたね。 ——obj *o* (v) dilute *usume·ru* 薄める ——(attr) slender *yaseta* やせた a thin person *yaseta hito′* やせた人
thing **1** (material) *mono* 物 What kind of thing are you looking for? *Do′nna mono′ o sagashite ima′su ka?* どんな物を探していま

すか． **2** (event) *koto'* 事 I don't have a thing to do this weekend. *Kono shūmatsu ni, suru koto' ga nani mo na'i.* この週末に，する事が何もない．

think obj *o* (v) **1** form an idea *omoi'tsuk·u* 思いつく No one thought of asking her advice. *Dare mo ka'nojo ni sōdan-suru koto' o omoitsuka'nakatta.* だれも彼女に相談することを思いつかなかった． **2** consider; deliberate *kanga'e·ru* 考える I'll think about it. *Kanga'ete oku.* 考えておく． I don't know what that person's thinking. *Ano' hito no kanga'ete iru koto' wa wakara'nai.* あの人の考えていることは分からない． **3** conceive; surmise *omo'·u* 思う What do you think? *Dō' omoima'su ka?* どう思いますか． I don't think so. *Sō omowa'nai.* そう思わない． **4** recall *omoida's·u* 思い出す I can't think of the restaurant's name right now. *I'ma sono re'sutoran no namae o omoida'su koto' wa deki'nai.* 今，そのレストランの名前を思い出すことはできない．

thinner (for paint) *shi'nnā* シンナー

third **1** (ordinal) *sambam-me'* [*no*] 三番目[の] **2** (fraction) *sambun no ichi* 三分の一 **3** third gear *dai-san gi'ya* 第三ギヤ

third day of the month *mikka* 三日

third-degree burn *omoi yakedo* 重い火傷

thirsty (idiom) (lit., throat is dry) *no'do ga kawa'k·u* のどがかわく I'm thirsty! *No'do ga kawa'ita!* のどがかわいた．

thirteen *jū'san* 十三 thirteen years old *jūsa'n-sai* 十三歳

thirteenth **1** (ordinal) *da'i-jūsan* [*no*] 第十三[の] **2** (fraction) *jū-san-bun no ichi* 十三分の一 **3** (of the month) *jūsa'n-nichi* 十三日

thirtieth day of the month *sanjū'-nichi* 三十日

thirty *sa'njū* 三十

this **1** *kore* これ How much is this? *Kore wa i'kura desu ka?* これはいくらですか． **2** this (one) *kono* この this book *kono ho'n* この本

this kind of *konna* こんな I want this kind of desk. *Konna tsukue ga hoshi'i.* こんな机が欲しい．

thistle *azami* あざみ

this way **1** (direction) *kotchi* こっち; *kochira* こちら Come this way, please. *Kochira ni ira'shite kudasa'i.* こちらにいらして下さい． **2** (manner) *kō* こう Do it this way. *Kō shi-nasa'i.* こうしなさい．

thorn *toge'* とげ

thorough *tetteiteki* [*na*] 徹底的[な] a thorough survey *tetteiteki na chō'sa* 徹底的な調査

thoroughly *tetteiteki ni* 徹底的に We investigated thoroughly. *Wata'shi-tachi wa tetteiteki ni shira'beta.* 私たちは徹底的に調べた．

those **1** (things near listener) *sore'ra* それら；(things distant from speaker and listener) *are'ra* あれら **2** (persons or things near listener) *sono* その those books *sono ho'n* その本; (persons or things distant from speaker and listener) *ano* あの those people *ano'hito* [*-tachi*] あの人[たち]

thought   **1** *shisō* 思想   **2** power of thought *shikō'ryoku* 思考力   **3** an idea *kanga'e* 考え   **4** *omo'i* 思い be lost in thought *omo'i ni fuke'ru* 思いにふける

thoughtful (considerate) *omoiyari no a'ru* 思いやりのある She is a thoughtful person. *Ka'nojo wa omoiyari no a'ru hito desu.* 彼女は思いやりのある人です. ——(idiom) Thank you, that was very thoughtful of you. *Go-shi'nsetsu ni, ari'gatō gozaima'su.* 御親切にありがとうございます.

thoughtless (attr) *omoiyari no na'i* 思いやりのない; *ha'iryo o kaku* 配慮を欠く

thousand *se'n* 千 a thousand-yen bill *sen-e'n satsu* 千円礼 ten thousand *ichima'n* 一万

thread *i'to* 糸 ——(idiom) thread a needle *ha'ri ni i'to o tō's·u* 針に糸を通す

threat *kyōhaku* 脅迫

threaten obj *o* (v) *obiyaka's·u* 脅かす; (irr) *kyōhaku-suru* 脅迫する

three *mittsu* 三つ; *san* 三 see also Appendix 1

three-dimensional *rittai* [*teki na*] 立体[的な]; *sanji'gen* [*no*] 三次元[の]

three-quarter *yombun no san* 四分の三

threshold *shiki-i* 敷居

thrifty *setsuyakuteki* [*na*] 節約的[な] ——(irr) be thrifty *setsuya-ku-suru* 節約する

thrill *senritsu* 戦慄; *su'riru* スリル It is a novel filled with thrills and suspense. *Sore wa su'riru to sa'spensu ni afu'reta shōsetsu de'su.* それはスリルとサスペンスにあふれた小説です. ——(caus) *zo'kuzoku-sase·ru* ぞくぞくさせる

thriving *sakan* [*na*] 盛ん[な] a thriving industry *sakan na kō'gyō* 盛んな工業 Industry is thriving in Japan. *Niho'n wa kō'gyō ga sakan de'su.* 日本は工業が盛んです. ——(irr) be thriving *ha'njō-suru* 繁盛する Business is thriving. *Shō'bai ga ha'njō-shite iru.* 商売が繁盛している.

throat *no'do* のど I have a sore throat. *No'do ga ita'i.* のどが痛い.

throb (irr) *zuki'nzukin-suru* ずきんずきんする My head's throbbing. *Ata'ma ga zuki'nzukin-suru.* 頭がずきんずきんする.

throne *ō'za* 王座

through (v) be finished *su'm·u* 済む Are you through with dinner? *Go'han ga sumima'shita ka?* 御飯が済みましたか. ——(idiom) **1** through the window *ma'do kara* 窓から I saw it through the window. *Ma'do kara sore o mi'ta.* 窓からそれを見た. **2** by way of ...*o tō' shite* ...を通して I made the request through my friend. *Tomodachi o tō' shite, sono koto' o-negai-shita.* 友達を通してそのことをお願いした.; ...*o tōtte* ...を通って We're going through Russia to Europe. *Sobie' to o tōtte Yōro' ppa ni iku.* ソビエトを通ってヨーロッパに行く. **3** from beginning to end ...*o tō' shite* ...を通して through the year *ichi' nen o tō' shite* 一年を通して; -*chū* [-*jū*] 中 through the day *ichinichi-jū* 一日中

throughout -*chū* [-*jū*] 中 throughout the year *ichinen-jū* 一年中

throw obj *o* (v) **1** hurl *nage' ·ru* 投げる Throw the ball! *Bōru o na' gete kudasa' i!* ボールを投げて下さい. **2** throw at *butsuke·ru* ぶつける I threw a stick at the dog. *Inu' ni bō o butsuketa.* 犬に棒をぶつけた. **3** throw away *sute·ru* 捨てる Throw this away. *Kore o sutete kudasa' i.* これを捨てて下さい.

thud *doshi' n* [*to*] どしん[と] It fell to the ground with a thud. *Doshi' n to ji' men ni ochita.* どしんと地面に落ちた.

thumb [*te' no*] *oya-yubi* [手の]親指

thumbtack *gabyō* 画鋲

thump *pata' n* [*to*] ばたん[と] The book fell to the floor with a thump. *Ho' n wa yuka no ue' ni pata' n to ochita.* 本は床の上にばたんと落ちた.

thunder *kaminari* 雷

thunderclap *rakurai* 落雷

thunderstorm *ra' iu* 雷雨

Thursday *mokuyō' bi* 木曜日 every week on Thursday *maishū mokuyō' bi ni* 毎週木曜日に

thus *sō'* そう; *kono yō' ni* このように; *kō iu fu' ni* こういうふうに

thyroid gland *kōjōsen* 甲状腺

Tibet *Chibe' tto* チベット

Tibetan 1 (language) *Chibetto-go* チベット語 **2** (person) *Chibetto' jin* チベット人 ——(attr) *Chibetto no* チベットの

tick (insect) *dani* だに

tick (sound) *ka' chikachi* かちかち ——(idiom) make a ticking sound *ka' chikachi oto' o tate' ·ru* かちかち音を立てる The clock was ticking. *Tokei wa ka' chikachi oto' o ta' tete ita.* 時計はかちかち音を立てていた.

ticket 1 *kippu* 切符; *ke' n* 券 express (train) ticket *kyūkō' -ken* 急行券 special express (train) ticket *tokkyū' -ken* 特急券 one-way ticket *katamichi* [*ki' ppu*] 片道[切符] round-trip ticket *ōfuku* [*ki' ppu*] 往復[切符] reserved seat ticket *zaseki shite' i-ken* 座席指定券 **2** theater ticket *ke' n* 券; *nyūjō' -ken* 入場券 **3** traffic ticket *kōtsū ihan ki' ppu* 交通違反切符

ticket window *mado' guchi* 窓口

tickle (adj) it tickles *kusugutta' ·i* くすぐったい ——obj *o* (v) *kusugur·u* くすぐる

tide   1 *shio'* 潮 with the tide *shio' ni notte* 潮に乗って   2 flood tide *manchō* 満潮   3 ebb tide *kanchō* 干潮

tidy   (attr) *kichi'nto-shita* きちんとした a tidy room *kichi'nto-shita heya'* きちんとした部屋 ——obj *o* (irr) *kichi'nto-suru* きちんとする Tidy your room. *Heya'o kichi'nto-shinasa'i.* 部屋をきちんとしなさい.

tie   necktie *ne'kutai* ネクタイ ——obj *o* (v)   1 bind *shiba'r·u* 縛る Tie up the old newspapers, please. *Furu-shi'mbun o shiba'tte oite kudasa'i.* 古新聞を縛っておいて下さい.   2 secure *musub·u* 結ぶ Tie the string on the package well. *Koni'motsu no himo o shikka'ri musunde kudasa'i.* 小荷物の紐をしっかり結んで下さい. 3 fasten *shime'·ru* しめる tie a necktie *ne'kutai o shime'·ru* ネクタイをしめる   4 tether *tsunag·u* つなぐ I tied the boat to the pier. *Bō'to o sambashi ni tsunaida.* ボートを桟橋につないだ.

tiger   *tora* 虎

tight   tight fitting *kyu'kutsu* [*na*] 窮屈[な] ——(adj) *kitsu'·i* きつい These shoes are a bit tight. *Kono kutsu'wa suko'shi kitsu'i.* この靴は少しきつい. ——(attr)   1 packed *tsuma'tta* つまった a tight schedule *tsuma'tta suke'jūru* つまったスケジュール   2 stingy *ke'chi* [*na*] けち[な]

tighten   obj *o* (irr) *kataku-suru* 堅くなる; (v) *shime'·ru* 締める tighten a bolt *boruto o shime'ru* ボルトを締める

tights   *ta'itsu* タイツ

tile   1 floor tile *ta'iru* タイル   2 roof tile *kawara* 瓦

till then   *see* until

tilt   obj *o* (v) *katamuke'·ru* 傾ける

timber   *zaimoku* 材木

time   1 *jikan* 時間 Do you have time to go with me? *Issho ni iku jikan ga arima'su ka?* 一緒に行く時間がありますか. Time's up! *Jikan de'su!* 時間です.   2 what time (?) *na'nji* 何時 What time is it (now)? *[I'ma] na'nji desu ka?* [今] 何時ですか.   3 occasion *toki* 時 that time *sono to'ki* その時 the time when I was little *chīsa'i toki* 小さい時   4 interval *aida* 間 a short time *mijika'i aida* 短い間; *shiba'raku no aida* しばらくの間   5 the first time *haji'mete* 初めて Is this your first time to visit Japan? *Niho'n wa haji'mete desu ka?* 日本は初めてですか.   6 the last time *sa'igo* 最後   7 next time *tsugi ni* 次に; *ko'ndo* 今度   8 at the same time *dōji ni* 同時に ——(idiom)   1 to time (something) *jikan o haka'r·u* 時間を計る   2 to take (require) time *jikan ga kaka'r·u* 時間がかかる   3 to kill time *jikan o tsubu's·u* 時間をつぶす   4 be on time *ma ni a'·u* 間に合う Will we be on time? *Ma ni aima'su ka?* 間に合いますか.   5 Take your time! *Dō'zo go-yukku'ri!* どうぞごゆっくり.   6 a waste of time *jikan no rōhi* 時間の浪費

time (rhythm)   *hyōshi'* 拍子

timeclock   *taimu rekō′dā* タイムレコーダー

time deposit   *teiki yo′kin* 定期預金

time-out   *ta′imu* タイム

times   1 olden times *mukashi* 昔   2 era *jidai* 時代; *-dai* 代 ancient times *ko′dai* 古代 modern times *ge′ndai* 現代

timetable   *jikokuhyō* 時刻表

time zone   *jikan-tai* 時間帯

timid   *okubyō′ [na]* 憶病[な]; *uchiki [na]* 内気[な] ——(v) be timid *hanika′m·u* はにかむ Don't be timid! *Hanikama′naide!* はにかまないで.

tin   1 *su′zu* 錫   2 tin plate *buriki* ブリキ   3 tin roof *totan yane* トタン屋根

tinfoil   *ho′iru* ホイル

tiny   1 (size) *chī′sa [na]* 小さ[な]   2 (amount) *hon no cho′tto* ほんのちょっと ——(adj) (space) *sema′·i* 狭い

tip   1 (gratuity) *chi′ppu* チップ   2 (end) *saki* 先

tipsy   (attr) *chidori′ashi no* 千鳥足の

tiptoe   (idiom) to walk on toptoe *tsumasaki de aru′k·u* 爪先で歩く

tire   (for a vehicle)   1 *taiya* タイヤ   2 flat tire *panku* パンク   3 spare tire *supea ta′iya* スペアタイヤ

tired   (v) be/become tired *tsukare′·ru* 疲れる I'm tired! *Tsuka′re-ta!* 疲れた.

tire of   compl *ni* (v) *aki′·ru* 飽きる I'm tired of studying. *Benkyō ni a′kite shimatta.* 勉強に飽きてしまった.

tissue paper   *chirigami* ちり紙; *ti′sshu* ティッシュ

title   (book, etc.)   *daimoku* 題目; *da′i* 題 the title of a book *ho′n no da′i* 本の題

to   1 ... *ni* ... に I'm going to Tokyo. *Tōkyō ni iku.* 東京に行く.; ... *e* ... へ Last summer I traveled to Hokkaido. *Kyo′nen no natsu, Hokka′idō e ryokō-shita.* 去年の夏北海道へ旅行した.; *ma′de* ... まで How many minutes is it from Tokyo to Yokohama? *Tōkyō kara Yokohama ma′de na′mpun kakarima′su ka?* 東京から横浜まで何分かかりますか.   2 (with the indirect object of the verb) ... *ni* ... に I sent the package to mother by seamail. *Funabin de kozu′tsumi o okā′-san ni okutta.* 船便で小包をお母さんに送った.   3 (in the opinion of) ... *ni totte* ... にとって You're important to me. *Watashi ni to′tte ana′ta wa ta′isetsu na hito desu.* 私にとってあなたは大切な人です.   4 (for the purpose of) ... *ni* ... に go to buy *kai ni iku* 買いに行く Please come to visit. *Asobi ni ki′te kudasa′i.* 遊びに来て下さい.; ... *[no] tame′ ni* ... [の]ために I jog in the morning to lose weight. *Yaseru tame′ni, a′sa jogingu o suru.* やせるために朝ジョギングをする.

toad   *gama-ga′eru* がまがえる

toast   *tōsuto* トースト a piece of toast *tōsuto ichi′mai* トースト

1枚 make toast *tōsuto o yaku* トーストを焼く ——obj *o* (v) *yak·u*
焼く toast bread *pa'n o yaku* パンを焼く

toaster   *tō'sutā* トースター

tobacco   *tabako* たばこ pipe tobacco *paipu-ta'bako* パイプたばこ

today   **1** *kyō'* 今日   **2** these days *konogoro* このごろ; *ko'nnichi* 今日   **3** the present *ge'nzai* 現在

toe   *ashi' no yubi* 足の指; *tsumasaki* 爪先

toenail   *ashi' no tsume* 足の爪

together   ...*to* ...*to*; ...[*to*] *issho* [*ni*] ...[と]一緒[に] We went to Kamakura together. *Wata'shi-tachi wa issho ni Kamakura ni itta.* 私たちは一緒に鎌倉に行った.

toilet   **1** *to'ire* トイレ; *o-tea'rai* お手洗い   **2** (public) *kōshū be'njo* 公衆便所   **3** (Western-style) *yōshiki be'njo* 洋式便所

toilet articles   *semmen yō'gu* 洗面用具

toilet paper   *toiretto pē'pā* トイレットペーパー

token   *shirushi* しるし This is just a token of my appreciation. *Kore wa hon no o-shirushi de'su.* これはほんのおしるしです.

tolerate   obj *o* (v) *tae'·ru* 耐える ——comp *ni* (irr) *ga'man-suru* 我慢する ——(pot) *ga'man-deki·ru* 我慢できる I can't tolerate that person. *Ano' hito ni ga'man-deki·nai.* あの人に我慢できない.

toll road   *yūryō dō'ro* 有料道路

tomato   *to'mato* トマト tomato juice *tomato jū'su* トマトジュース

tomb   *haka'* 墓; ancient tomb *kofun* 古墳

tombstone   *hakaishi* 墓石

tomorrow   *ashita'* 明日; *asu'* あす; *myō'nichi* 明日

ton   *to'n* トン one ton *i'tton* 1トン

tone   *onchō* 音調

tongs   *-basami* ばさみ ice tongs *kōri-ba'sami* 氷ばさみ fire tongs *hi-ba'sami* 火ばさみ

tongue   **1** *shita'* 舌   **2** (meat) *ta'n* タン

tongue-tied   (attr) *shita-ta'razu* [*no*] 舌足らず[の]

tongue twister   *hayakuchi ko'toba* 早口ことば

tonight   *ko'mban* 今晩; *ko'n'ya* 今夜

tonsillectomy   *hentōsen tekishutsu* 扁桃腺摘出

tonsillitis   *hentōsen-en* 扁桃腺炎

tonsils   *hentōsen* 扁桃腺

too   **1** also ...*mo* ...も I want this too. *Kore mo hoshi'i.* これも欲しい.   **2** overly *amari* あまり Don't be too late! *Amari osoku nara'nai yō ni!* あまり遅くならないように. ; *-sugi'·ru* すぎる too big *ōki-sugi'·ru* 大きすぎる I ate too much. *Tabe-su'gita.* 食べすぎた.

tool   *dōgu* 道具

toolbox   *dōgu'-bako* 道具箱

tooth   *ha'* 歯

toothache (idiom) (lit., tooth hurts) *ha′ ga ita′i* 歯が痛い, I have a toothache! *Ha′ ga ita′i!* 歯が痛い.

toothbrush *habu′rashi* 歯ブラシ

toothpaste *hami′gaki* 歯みがき

toothpick *yōji* ようじ; *tsumayō′ji* つまようじ

tooth powder *hamigaki′ko* 歯みがき粉

top **1** (toy) *ko′ma* こま **2** the highest part of a thing *teppe′n* てっぺん **3** zenith *chōjō* 頂上 **4** the top of ... [*no*] *ue′* ... [の]上 the top of the table *tēburu no ue′* テーブルの上 ——obj *o* (v) exceed *uwamawa′r·u* 上回る top the cost *ko′suto o uwamawa′ru ri′eki* コストを上回る利益; (irr) *toppa-suru* 突破する The population of Japan has topped 100 million. *Nihon no jinkō wa ichi′-oku o toppa-shita.* 日本の人口は一億を突破した.

topic **1** study subject; theme *tē′ma* テーマ **2** subject of a conversation *wadai* 話題 Let's change the topic. *Wadai o kaemashō′.* 話題を変えましょう.

torch *ta′imatsu* たいまつ *see also* flashlight

tornado *tatsumaki* 竜巻

torpedo *suirai* 水雷; *gyorai* 魚雷

torso *dō′* 胴

tortoise *ka′me* 亀

tortoise shell *bekkō* べっ甲

torture *gōmon* 拷問 ——obj *o* (irr) *gōmon-suru* 拷問する The police tortured the prisoner until he confessed. *Keisatsu wa ha′-kujō-suru made shūjin o gōmon-shita.* 警察は白状するまで囚人を拷問した.

toss obj *o* (v) *nage′r·u* 投げる Toss me the ball. *Bōru o na′gete kudasa′i.* ボールを投げて下さい.

total **1** amount *gōkei* 合計 total amount of money *gōkei ki′ngaku* 合計金額; *sōgaku* 総額 What is the total? *Gōkei de i′kura desu ka?* 合計でいくらですか. There is a total of 1,000 books. *Ho′n wa gōkei se′n-satsu a′ru.* 本は合計千冊ある. **2** number *ze′mbu* [*de*] 全部[で] What is the total number of people? *Ze′mbu de na′nnin desu ka?* 全部で何人ですか. **3** net *shō′mi* 正味 The test will take a total of two and a half hours. *Shike′n wa shō′mi nijikan-ha′n kaka′ru.* 試験は正味二時間半かかる. ——(attr) **1** *a′ka no* 赤の total stranger *a′ka no tanin* 赤の他人 **2** *zen-* 全 total loss *zenson* 全損 total defeat *zempai* 全敗

totalitarian *zentaishu′gi* [*no*] 全体主義[の] totalitarian government *zentaishugi se′ifu* 全体主義政府

totally *zemmenteki ni* 全面的に That text should be totally revised. *Ano teki′suto wa zemmenteki ni kaitei-shita hō′ ga i′i.* あのテキストは全面的に改訂した方がいい.

touch **1** (sense of) *shokkaku* 触覚 **2** contact *sesshoku* 接触 ——

comp *ni* (irr) **1** make contact *sesshoku-suru* 接触する The wires are not touching. *Se'n wa sesshoku-shite ina'i.* 線は接触していない。 **2** get in touch *renraku-suru* 連絡する Get in touch with Mr. Tanaka, please. *Tanaka-san ni renraku-shite kudasa'i.* 田中さんに連絡して下さい。 ——obj *o* (v) **1** make contact with *fure·ru* 触れる Don't touch! *Te' o fureru na!* 手を触れるな。; *Te' o furena'i de!* 手を触れないで。 In her speech she didn't touch on that point. *Ka'nojo wa o-hanashi de' wa sono ten ni fure'nakatta.* 彼女はお話ではその点に触れなかった。 **2** feel *sawar·u* 触る Try touching the braille with your fingers. *Kono tenji o yubi' de sawatte mi'te kudasa'i.* この点字を指で触ってみて下さい。

tough strong; durable *jōbu* [*na*] 丈夫[な] tough fiber *jōbu na se'n'i* 丈夫な繊維 tough material *jōbu na zairyo'* 丈夫な材料 ——(adj) **1** hard to cut *kata·i* 堅い This meat is tough. *Kono niku' wa katai.* この肉は堅い。 **2** *nebarizuyo'·i* 粘り強い He's tough; he never gives up. *Ka're wa nebarizuyo'i node, kesshite akirame'nai.* 彼は粘り強いので、けっして諦めない。

toupee *bubun ka'tsura* 部分かつら; *tsū' pe* ツーペ

tour **1** *ryokō* 旅行; *tsu'ā* ツアー **2** group tour *dantai ryo'kō* 団体旅行 **3** guided tour *gaido-tsuki ka'nkō* ガイド付き観光 ——(irr) *ryokō-suru* 旅行する

tourist *kankō'-kyaku* 観光客

tournament *shiai* 試合; *tō'namento* トーナメント

tow obj *o* (v) *hippa'r·u* 引っ張る tow a car *kuruma o hippa'ru* 車を引っ張る

toward *...no hō'* [*e*] ...の方[へ] She walked toward the river. *Ka'nojo wa kawa no hō' e aru'ite itta.* 彼女は川の方へ歩いて行った。

towel **1** *ta'oru* タオル; (J) *tenugui* 手拭い **2** dish towel *fuki'n* 布巾 **3** *pēpā ta'oru* ペーパータオル

tower *tō'* 塔

town *machi'* 町

town hall *shiya'kusho* 市役所

tow truck *rekkā'sha* レッカー車; *ken'i'nsha* 牽引車

toxic *doku* [*no*] 毒[の]

toy *omo'cha* おもちゃ toy shop *omochaya* おもちゃ屋

trace *a'to* 跡 It left no trace. *A'to ga nokorana'katta.* 跡が残らなかった。 ——(idiom) to trace *shikiutsushi ni suru* 敷き写しにする; *torē'su-suru* トレースする

track **1** horse-racing track *keibajō* 競馬場 **2** railroad track *senro* 線路 **3** running track *tora'kku* トラック see also race track

track number (train) *-bansen* 番線 What is the track number for the Osaka train? *Ōsaka-yuki wa nambansen de' su ka?* 大阪行きは何番線ですか。

tractor *tora'kutā* トラクター
trade 1 commerce *tori'hiki* 取引| 2 international trade *bōeki* 貿易 trade policy *bōeki se'isaku* 貿易政策 trade friction *bōeki ma'satsu* 貿易摩擦 trade dispute *bōeki ro'nsō* 貿易論争 3 occupation *shoku* 職 ——obj *o*, comp *to* (irr) *kōkan-suru* 交換する I traded our son's desk for Mrs. Tanaka's baby crib. *Watashi wa musuko no tsukue' o Tanaka-san no bebī-be'ddo to kōka'n-shita.* 私は息子の机を田中さんのベビーベッドと交換した.
trademark *shōhyō* 商標
trader *shō'nin* 商人
trade union *rōdō kumi'ai* 労働組合
tradition *dentō* 伝統
traditional *dentōteki* [na] 伝統的[な]
traffic 1 *kōtsū* 交通 traffic accident *kōtsū ji'ko* 交通事故 2 bumper-to-bumper traffic *noronoro u'nten* のろのろ運転 3 one-way traffic *ippō tsu'kō* 一方通行
traffic circle *rō'tari* ロータリー
traffic jam *kōtsū jū'tai* 交通渋滞
traffic signal *shingō* 信号; *kōtsū shi'ngō* 交通信号
traffic ticket *kōtsū ihan ki'ppu* 交通違反切符
tragedy *hi'geki* 悲劇; (theater) *hi'geki* 悲劇
trail (path) *michi* 道; *komichi* 小道
trailer *torē'rā* トレーラー
train 1 (electric) *densha* 電車 2 (commuter) *tsūkin de'nsha* 通勤電車 3 (express) *kyūkō de'nsha* 急行電車 4 (special express) *tokkyū de'nsha* 特急電車 5 (freight) *kamotsu re'ssha* 貨物列車 6 (local) *futsū re'ssha* 普通列車 7 (locomotive; long distance) *kisha'* 汽車 8 (superexpress; Bullet) *shinka'nsen* 新幹線
train obj *o* (irr) *ku'nren-suru* 訓練する
train conductor *shashō* 車掌
training *ku'nren* 訓練
traitor *hangya'kusha* 反逆者
trampoline *tora'mporin* トランポリン
trance *kōkotsu jō'tai* 恍惚状態
tranquilizer *torankira'izā* トランキライザー; *chinse'izai* 鎮静剤
transaction *tori'hiki* 取引
transfer obj *o* (v) 1 (property) (irr) *jō'to-suru* 譲渡する 2 (to a new post/job) (irr) *tennin-suru* 転任する 3 (to a new school) (irr) *tenkō-suru* 転校する 4 (from one vehicle to another) *norika'e·ru* 乗り換える
transformation *henkei* 変形
transformational grammer *henkei bu'mpō* 変形文法
transistor radio *tranjisutā ra'jio* トランジスターラジオ
translate obj *o* (v) 1 *yaku's·u* 訳す Please translate (it) into

English. *Ei-go ni yaku′shite kudasa′i.* 英語に訳して下さい. **2**
interpret (irr) *tsū′yaku-suru* 通訳する *see also* interpret

translation **1** (of writing) *hon′yaku* 翻訳 **2** (of speech) *tsū′yaku*
通訳

translator **1** (of writing) *hon′ya′kusha* 翻訳者 **2** (of speech)
tsū′yaku 通訳

transmission (vehicle) **1** automatic *jidō he′nsoku* 自動変速 **2** standard *hyōjun he′nsoku* 標準変速

transmit (v) *tsutawar·u* 伝わる This has been transmitted from
generation to generation. *Kore wa da′idai ie′ ni tsutawatte iru.* これは代々家に伝わっている. ——obj *o* (v) *tsutae·ru* 伝える Iron
transmits heat. *Tetsu wa netsu′ o tsutaeru.* 鉄は熱を伝える.

transparent *tōmei* [*na*] 透明[な]

transplant obj *o* (irr) *ishoku-suru* 移植する

transport obj *o* (v) **1** haul *hakob·u* 運ぶ I had the piano transported by a moving company. *Piano wa unsōya ni hakonde mora′tta.*
ピアノは運送屋に運んでもらった. **2** carry (irr) *yusō-suru* 輸送する A train transports passengers and cargo. *Kisha′ wa hito to
ka′motsu o yusō-suru.* 汽車は人と貨物を輸送する.

transportation *yusō* 輸送

trap *wa′na* わな ——(idiom) to trap *wa′na de to′r·u* わなで捕る

trash *gomi′* ごみ trash can *gomi-bako* ごみ箱

travel *ryokō* 旅行 ——(irr) *ryokō-suru* 旅行する

travel agency *ryokō dairi′-ten* 旅行代理店

traveler's aid (station) *ryokō′sha engojo* 旅行者援護所

traveler's check *ryokō* [*yō*] *kogi′tte* 旅行[用] 小切手

tray [*o-*]*bon* [お]盆

treason *hangyaku* 反逆; (Leg) *taigyaku′zai* 大逆罪

treasure *takaramono* 宝物

treasury department *zaimu′shō* 財務省

treat *gochisō* ごちそう ——obj *o* (v) **1** *toriatsuka·u* 取り扱う
These are breakable, so treat them gently. *Kore wa waremono
desu kara, te′inei ni toriatsukatte kudasa′i.* これは割れ物ですから
丁寧に取り扱って下さい. **2** *ogor·u* おごる I'll treat you! *Ogotte
agema′su!* おごって上げます.

treatment **1** *toriatsukai* 取り扱い, treatment of people *hito no
toriatsukai* 人の取り扱い, **2** medical treatment *chiryō* [*hō*] 治療
[法]

treaty *jōyaku* 条約 peace treaty *heiwa jō′yaku* 平和条約

tree *ki′* 木 trees *ki′gi* 木々

trellis *kōshidana* 格子棚

tremble (v) **1** quaver *yure·ru* 揺れる **2** shiver *furue·ru* 震える

tremor *shindō* 震動

trench coat *torenchi kō′to* トレンチコート

trend *keikō* 傾向

trespass loc *ni* (irr) *shinnyū-suru* 侵入する ——(idiom) No trespassing! *Tachi-iri kinshi!* 立ち入り禁止

trial **1** (judicial assembly) *sa'iban* 裁判 **2** (ordeal) *shi'ren* 試練

triangle *sanka'kukei* 三角形

triangular *sa'nkaku* [*no*] 三角[の]

tribe *shu'zoku* 種族

trick *tori'kku* トリック; (magic) *te'jina* 手品 ——obj *o* (v) *dama's·u* だます

tricycle *sanri'nsha* 三輪車

trigger *hikigane* 引き金

trigonometry *sankaku-hō* 三角法

trillion *-chō* 兆 one trillion *i'tchō* 一兆

trim obj *o* (v) *kariko'm·u* 刈り込む trim a hedge *ikegaki o kariko'm·u* 生け垣を刈り込む ——(idiom) I'd like just a trim, please. *Karuku ka'tte kudasa'i.* 軽く刈って下さい.

Trinity (Chr) *Sa'mmi-ittai* 三位一体

trio **1** (instrumental) *sanjū'sō* 三重奏 **2** (vocal) *sanjū'shō* 三重唱

trip *ryokō* 旅行 ——(v) *tsumazuk·u* つまずく

triplets *mitsugo* 三つ子

triumphantly *tokui-gao de* 得意顔で

trivial (adj) *kudarana·i* くだらない; *tsumara'na·i* つまらない

trombone *torombō'n* トロンボーン

troops *gu'n* 軍 Israeli troops *Isuraeru' gun* イスラエル軍; *gu'ntai* 軍隊

tropical *nettai* [*no*] 熱帯[の]

tropical fish *netta'igyo* 熱帯魚

Tropic of Cancer *Kita Kaiki-sen* 北回帰線

Tropic of Capricorn *Minami Kaiki-sen* 南回帰線

tropics *nettai* 熱帯

trouble **1** *mendō'* 面倒 **2** burden *tesū'* 手数; *me'iwaku* 迷惑 **3** problem *tora'buru* トラブル **4** worry *shimpai* 心配

troublesome *mendō'* [*na*] 面倒[な]; *ya'kkai* [*na*] やっかい[な] ——(adj) *mendōkusa·i* めんどうくさい a troublesome procedure *mendōkusa'i tetsu'zuki* めんどうくさい手続き

trousers *zu'bon* ズボン two pairs of trousers *zu'bon ni'hon* ズボン二本

trousseau *yomeiri i'shō* 嫁入り衣裳

trout *masu'* 鱒 rainbow trout *niji masu* 虹鱒

truck **1** *tora'kku* トラック **2** delivery truck *umpa'nsha* 運搬車 **3** dump truck *da'mpukā* ダンプカー **4** tow truck *ken'i'nsha* 牽引車

truck driver *tora'kku no unte'nshu* トラックの運転手

true *shi'njitsu* [*no*] 真実[の]; *hontō* [*no*] 本当[の]

truly *hontō ni* 本当に

trump (card) *kiri'fuda* 切り札

trumpet *torampe'tto* トランペット

trunk 1 *tora'nku* トランク 2 elephant's trunk *zō no hana* 象の鼻 3 tree trunk *mi'ki* 幹 4 (Anat) *dō* 胴

trust 1 faith; reliance *shinrai* 信頼 2 belief; confidence *shin'yō* 信用 3 (Leg) *shintaku* 信託 an investment trust *tōshi shi'ntaku* 投資信託 ——obj *o* (irr) 1 rely on *shinrai-suru* 信頼する 2 have confidence in *shin'yō-suru* 信用する

trustworthy (attr) *shinrai-deki'ru* 信頼できる a trustworthy person *shinrai-deki'ru hito* 信頼できる人

truth *shi'njitsu* 真実 tell the truth *shi'njitsu o iu* 真実を言う

truthful *shi'njitsu no* 真実の ——(idiom) not lying *u'so no na'i* うそのない

try obj *o* (v) *kokoromi'·ru* 試みる We tried a new method. *Atarashi'i hōhō o kokoro'mita.* 新しい方法を試みた. ——(idiom) 1 (try and see) ...*mi'·ru* みる Try this dress on. *Kono fuku' o kite mi'te kudasa'i.* この服を着てみて下さい. 2 (attempt) *-yō to suru* ようとする I tried to contact him, but... *Ka're ni renraku-shiyō' to shima'shita ga...* 彼に連絡しようとしましたが... I tried to give up cigarettes, but... *Tabako o yameyō' to shima'shita ga ...* たばこをやめようとしましたが...

trying (adj) *tsura·i* つらい I had a trying day yesterday. *Kinō' wa tsura'katta.* 昨日はつらかった.

T-shirt *Ti-sha'tsu* ティーシャツ

tub 1 bathtub *furo-o'ke* 風呂桶 2 washtub *tarai* たらい

tube 1 (for tire) *chū'bu* チューブ 2 pipe *ku'da* 管 3 vacuum tube *shinkūkan* 真空管

tuberculosis *kekkaku* 結核 tuberculosis of the lungs *hai ke'kkaku* 肺結核

Tuesday *kayō'bi* 火曜日

tugboat *tagubō'to* タグボート

tuition *jugyō'ryō* 授業料

tulip *chū'rippu* チューリップ

tumble (v) *korogar·u* 転がる; *korogemawa'r·u* ころげ回る The kittens tumbled across the floor. *Kone'ko ga yuka no ue' o korogemawa'tta.* 子猫が床の上をころげ回った.

tumor *haremono* 腫れ物; (Tech) *shuyō* 腫瘍

tuna *maguro* 鮪

tune 1 song *kyoku* 曲 a dance tune *da'nsu kyoku* ダンス曲 2 melody *fushi'* 節 set words to a tune *fushi' ni uta' o awase'ru* 節に歌を合わせる ——obj *o* (irr) *chōritsu-suru* 調律する ——(idiom) 1 out of tune *oto' ga kurut'te iru* 音が狂っている 2 in tune *oto' ga a'tte iru* 音が合っている

tune-up *chūn a′ppu* チューンアップ; *chōsei-suru* 調整する

tunnel *tonneru* トンネル

turkey *shichimenchō* 七面鳥

Turkey *To′ruko* トルコ

Turkish **1** (language) *Toruko-go* トルコ語 **2** (person) *Toruko′jin* トルコ人 ——(attr) *To′ruko no* トルコの

turn (v) *mawar·u* 回る This doesn't turn. *Kore wa mawarana′i.* これは回らない; (irr) *kaiten-suru* 回転する The earth turns on its axis. *Chikyū wa jiku′ o chūshin to shite kaiten-suru.* 地球は軸を中心として回転する. ——loc *o* (v) turn; bend *magar·u* 曲がる Turn right! *Migi ni magatte kudasa′i!* 右に曲がって下さい. Turn at that corner! *Sono ka′do o magatte kudasa′i!* その角を曲がって下さい. ——obj *o* (v) *mawas·u* 回す Turn the doorknob. *Totte′ o mawashite kudasa′i.* 把手を回して下さい.

turn around (idiom) *ushiro o muk·u* 後ろを向く Turn around, please. *Ushiro o muite kudasa′i.* 後ろを向いて下さい.

turn back loc *o* (v) *modo′r·u* 戻る ——obj *o* (v) return (something) to its original position *modo′s·u* 戻す

turn (in order) *jumban* 順番; *ba′n* 番 It's your turn. *Ana′ta no ba′n desu.* あなたの番です.

turnip *kabu* かぶ; *kabura* かぶら

turn off obj *o* (v) **1** stop a flow *tome·ru* 止める Turn off the water, please. *Mizu o tomete kudasa′i.* 水を止めて下さい. **2** close a valve *shime′·ru* 閉める Turn off the faucet, please. *Ko′kku o shi′mete kudasa′i.* コックを閉めて下さい. **3** switch off *kes·u* 消す Turn off the light! *De′nki o keshite!* 電気を消して.

turn on obj *o* (v) **1** open a valve *ake·ru* 開ける Turn on the faucet, please. *Ko′kku o akete kudasa′i.* コックを開けて下さい. **2** switch on *tsuke′·ru* 付ける Turn on the light! *De′nki o tsu′kete!* 電気を付けて.

turn over (v) *hikkuri-ka′er·u* ひっくり返る The boat turned over. *Bō′to ga hikkuri-ka′etta.* ボートがひっくり返った. ——obj *o* (v) *hikkuri-ka′es·u* ひっくり返す When the top side is brown, turn it over. *Ue ga chairoku yaketa′ra, hikkuri-ka′eshite kudasa′i.* 上が茶色く焼けたら, ひっくり返して下さい.

turns obj *o* (irr) take turns *kawariba′nko-suru* かわりばんこする; *kōtai-suru* 交替する ——(adv) by turns *jumban ni* 順番に

turn signal *hōkō shiji′ki* 方向指示器

turpentine **1** *terebi′n'yu* テレビン油 **2** gum turpentine *matsu yani* 松やに

turtle *ka′me* 亀

turtleneck *tātoru-ne′kku* タートルネック

tutor *katei kyō′shi* 家庭教師

tuxedo *takishi′do* タキシード

TV *te'rebi* テレビ

tweed *tsuido* ツィード

tweezers *kenuki* 毛抜き

twelfth 1 (ordinal) *da'i-jūni'* [*no*] 第十二[の] 2 (fraction) *jūni-bun no ichi* 十二分の一

twelfth day of the month *jūni-nichi* 十二日

twelve *jūni* 十二 see also Appendix 1

twentieth day of the month *hatsuka* 二十日

twenty 1 *ni'jū* 二十 2 twenty years old *ha'tachi* 二十歳

twice 1 *nido* 二度 2 (Math) *nibai* 二倍

twilight *tasogare* たそがれ; *yūgata* 夕方

twin beds *tsuin be'ddo* ツインベッド

twinkle (v) *ki'rakira kagaya'k·u* きらきら輝く

twins *futago* 双子

twist obj *o* (v) *neji'r·u* ねじる

two *futa'tsu* 二つ; *ni* 二 see also Appendix 1

two-dimensional *niji'gen* [*no*] 二次元[の]

type 1 variety *shu'rui* 種類 2 manner *-fū* [*na*] 風[な] a thing of that type *ā itta fū' na mono* ああいった風な物 ——(idiom) type-write *ta'ipu o u'ts·u* タイプを打つ

type (font) *katsuji* 活字

typewriter *taipura'itā* タイプライター typewriter ribbon *taipurai-tā-yō ri'bon* タイプライター用リボン

typhoon *taifū'* 台風

typhus *hasshin chi'fusu* 発疹チフス

typical *tenkeiteki* [*na*] 典型的[な] a typical tourist *tenkeiteki na ryokō'sha* 典型的な旅行者

typing paper *taipu yō'shi* タイプ用紙

tyranny *bōgyaku* 暴虐

tyrant *bō'kun* 暴君

U

Uganda *Uga'nda* ウガンダ

Ugandan (person) *Uganda'jin* ウガンダ人 ——(attr) *Uga'nda no* ウガンダの

ugly (adj) *miniku'·i* 醜い an ugly face *miniku'i kao* 醜い顔

ukulele *ukurere* ウクレレ

ulcer *kaiyō* 潰瘍 stomach ulcer *ika'iyō* 胃潰瘍

ultimate 1 last *sa'igo* [*no*] 最後[の] the ultimate measure *sa'igo no shu'dan* 最後の手段 2 maximum *kyūkyoku* [*no*] 究極[の]

ultimately *kekkyoku* 結局 Ultimately the following conclusion

was reached. *Kekkyoku tsugi' no yō' na kekka ni na'tta.* 結局次の
ような結果になった.

ultraviolet rays *shigaisen* 紫外線

umbilical cord *heso no o'* へその緒

umbrella 1 (J) *ka'sa* 傘 2 (W) *kō'mori* こうもり; (coll) *ka'sa* 傘

umbrella stand *kasa'-tate* 傘立て

unable to (do) *...koto' ga deki'nai* ...ことができない I'm unable
to go tomorrow. *Ashita iku koto' ga deki'nai.* 明日行くことがで
きない. I'm unable to to read Japanese. *Nihon-go o yo'mu koto'
ga deki'nai.* 日本語を読むことができない.

unaccompanied baggage *betsubin no ni'motsu* 別便の荷物

unaffected (sincere) (attr) *kidoranai* 気取らない an unaffected person *kidoranai hito'* 気取らない人

unanimous *manjō i'tchi [no]* 満場一致[の]

unassuming (attr) *kidoranai* 気取らない an unassuming manner
kidoranai ta'ido 気取らない態度

unattractive (adj) *miniku'·i* 醜い

unavoidable (adj) *yamu-o-e'na·i* やむをえない something unavoidable *yamu-o-e'nai koto'* やむをえない事 It was unavoidable.
Yamu-o-e'nakatta. やむをえなかった.

unaware (adj) *kizuka'na·i* 気付かない He was unaware of his
mistake. *Ka're wa jibun no machiga'i ni kizuka'nakatta.* 彼は自分
の間違いに気付かなかった.

unbearable (adj) *taerarena'·i* 耐えられない It was unbearable!
Taerarena'katta! 耐えられなかった.

unbelievable (adj) be unbelievable *shinjirare'na·i* 信じられない
That's unbelievable! *Sore wa shinjirare'nai koto' desu!* それは信
じられないことです.

unbiased *kōhei [na]* 公平[な] an unbiased opinion *kōhei na i'ken*
公平な意見

unbounded *mugen [no]* 無限[の] unbounded love *mugen no a'i* 無
限の愛

unbutton (idiom) 1 *bo'tan o hazus·u* ボタンを外す 2 be/become
unbuttoned *bo'tan ga hazure·ru* ボタンが外れる It came unbuttoned. *Bo'tan ga hazureta.* ボタンが外れた.

uncanny *fushigi [na]* 不思議[な]

uncertain *futa'shika [na]* 不確か[な] The outcome is uncertain.
Kekka ga futa'shika desu. 結果が不確かです. ——(adj) *obotsukana'·i* おぼつかない I feel uncertain about my future. *Watashi no
shō'rai wa obotsukana'i.* 私の将来はおぼつかない. ——(attr) not
clear *hakki'ri-shinai* はっきりしない an uncertain attitude *hakki'-
ri-shinai ta'ido* はっきりしない態度

uncertainty *fuka'kujitsusa* 不確実さ

uncle 1 (one's own) *oji* おじ 2 (another) *oji-san* おじさん

uncomfortable (attr) *kokochi waru'i* 心地悪い、an uncomfortable chair *kokochi waru'i isu* 心地悪い椅子 ;-*nikui* にくい、uncomfortable shoes *haki-niku'i kutsu'* 履きにくい靴

uncommon *mare* [*na*] 希[な] Such success is uncommon. *Konna ni u'maku iku koto' wa mare de'su.* こんなにうまくいくことは希です.

unconscious 1 *i'shiki fumei* 意識不明 The patient is unconscious. *Kanja wa i'shiki fumei de'su.* 患者は意識不明です. 2 incognizant *mui'shiki* [*no*] 無意識[の] an unconscious act *mui'shiki no kōdō* 無意識の行動 ——(idiom) be unconscious (lose consciousness) *ki o ushina·u* 気を失う

unconsciously *omo'wazu* 思わず I did it unconsciously. *Omo'wazu yatte shimatta.* 思わずやってしまった.

uncooked *na'ma* [*no*] 生[の]

uncover (idiom) *futa o ake·ru* ふたを開ける

undecided *mitei* [*no*] 未定[の] The date is undecided. *Hinichi wa mitei de'su.* 日にちは未定です.

under 1 ...*no shita* [*ni*] ...の下[に] under the roof *ya'ne no shita* 屋根の下 The cat is under the table. *Ne'ko wa tēburu no shita' ni iru.* 猫はテーブルの下にいる. 2 ...*no moto ni* ...の下に She wrote her master's thesis under Prof. Tanaka. *Ka'nojo wa shūshi ro'mbun o Tanaka kyō'ju no moto' ni ka'ita.* 彼女は修士論文を田中教授の下に書いた.

underarm *waki'-no-shita* わきの下

underclothes *shitagi* 下着

underdeveloped 1 underexploited *teika'ihatsu* [*no*] 低開発[の] 2 immature *mijuku* [*na*] 未熟[な]

underdog *make-inu* 負け犬 *haibo'kusha* 敗北者

underdone *nama-yake* [*no*] 生焼け[の] The meat is underdone. *Niku' wa nama-yake de'su.* 肉は生焼けです.

undergraduate 1 (student) *daiga'kusei* 大学生 2 (division) *gaku-bu* 学部

underground *chika'* 地下 see also subway

underground passage *chika'dō* 地下道

underline *kasen* 下線 ——(idiom) to underline *kasen o hik·u* 下線を引く

underneath ...[*no*] *shita ni* ...[の]下に Your socks are underneath your shirts in the drawer. *Ana'ta no kutsu'shita wa hikidashi no na'ka no sha'tsu no shita' ni a'ru.* あなたの靴下は引き出しの中のシャツの下にある.

underpants *pa'ntsu* パンツ two pairs of underpants *pa'ntsu ni'mai* パンツ二枚

underpass *chika'dō* 地下道 go through the underpass *chika'dō o tō'ru* 地下道を通る

undershirt *sha′tsu* シャツ

undershorts *pa′ntsu* パンツ three pairs of undershorts *pa′ntsu sa′mmai* パンツ三枚

understand obj *ga* (v) *waka′r·u* 分かる Did you understand? *Wakarima′shita ka?* 分かりましたか。 ——obj *o* (irr) *ri′kai-suru* 理解する He understands music. *Ka′re wa o′ngaku o ri′kai-shite iru.* 彼は音楽を理解している。

understanding *ryōkai* 了解 We'll have to have her understanding on this. *Kono mondai ni tsu′ite ka′nojo no ryōkai o motome′na-kereba nara′nai.* この問題について彼女の了解を求めなければならない。 ——(attr) *ri′kai no a′ru* 理解のある an understanding person *ri′kai no a′ru hito* 理解のある人

undertaker *sōgiya* 葬儀屋

undertaking (enterprise) *kikaku* 企画 This is a difficult undertaking. *Kore wa muzukashi′i kikaku de′su.* これは難しい企画です。

undertow *kaeshinami* 返し波

underwater *suichū* 水中

underwear *shitagi* 下着

underweight *mekata-bu′soku* 目方不足 ——(v) **1** be underweight *yase-sugi′·ru* やせすぎる **2** be too thin *hoso-sugi′·ru* 細すぎる He's underweight. *Ka′re wa hoso-sugi′ru.* 彼は細すぎる。

undress *fuku′ o nu′g·u* 服を脱ぐ She undressed. *Ka′nojo wa fuku′ o nu′ida.* 彼女は服を脱いだ。

uneasy *fuan* [*na*] 不安[な] I feel uneasy coming home alone late at night. *Yo′ru osoku hito′ri de uchi′ ni ka′eru no wa fuan de′su.* 夜遅く一人で家に帰るのは不安です。

unemployed *shitsugyō* [*no*] 失業[の] unemployed person *shitsugyō′-sha* 失業者

unemployment *shitsugyō* 失業 unemployment insurance *shitsugyō ho′ken* 失業保険

unequal *fubyō′dō* [*na*] 不平等[な]

uneven *dekoboko* [*no*] でこぼこ[の] ——(irr) be uneven *de′koboko-suru* でこぼこする The floor is uneven. *Yuka wa de′koboko-shite iru.* 床はでこぼこしている。

unexpected (attr) *omoigakena′i* 思いがけない an unexpected guest *omoigakena′i kyaku* 思いがけない客

unexpectedly *totsuzen* 突然 Excuse me for dropping in unexpectedly. *Totsuzen o-ukagai-shite shitsu′rei-shima′shita.* 突然お伺いして失礼しました。

unfair *fukō′hei* [*na*] 不公平[な] unfair treatment *fukō′hei na toria-tsukai* 不公平な取り扱い

unfairness *fukō′hei* 不公平; *futō* 不当

unfamiliar (attr) **1** *najimi no na′i* なじみのない; *mishiranu* 見知らぬ an unfamiliar person *mishiranu hito′* 見知らぬ人 **2** unaccustomed *fu'nare* [*na*] 不慣れ[な] unfamiliar work *fu'nare na shigoto* 不慣れな仕事

unfinished *mika'nsei* [*no*] 未完成[の]

unfortunate *fukō'* [*na*] 不幸[な]; *fushia'wase* [*na*] 不幸せ[な]

unfortunately *ainiku* あいにく Unfortunately, I have a previous engagement. *Ainiku, sen'yaku ga a'tte...* あいにく先約があって...

unfriendly (adj) *aisō'no na'·i* 愛想のない

ungrateful (attr) *on-shi'razu no* 恩知らずの

unhappy *fushia'wase* [*na*] 不幸せ[な]

unhealthy *fuke'nkō* [*na*] 不健康[な]

unification *tōitsu* 統一

uniform (clothing) *seifuku* 制服

unimportant (idiom) *jūyō de na'·i* 重要でない; *ta'ishita koto' de na'·i* 大した事でない

unintentionally *omo'wazu* 思わず Unintentionally I mentioned it. *Omo'wazu kuchi o subera'sete shimatta.* 思わず口をすべらせてしまった。

uninteresting (adj) *tsumara'na·i* つまらない an uninteresting book *tsumara'nai ho'n* つまらない本

union **1** *rengō* 連合 **2** federation *remmei* 連盟 **3** cooperative *ku'miai* 組合 labor union *rōdō ku'miai* 労働組合

Union of Soviet Socialist Republics (USSR) *Sobieto Shakaishugi Kyōwa-koku Re'mpō* ソビエト社会主義共和国連邦; (abbr) *So'ren* ソ連

unique **1** *yuni'ku* [*na*] ユニーク[な] **2** peculiar *dokutoku* [*no*] 独特 [の]

unit *ta'n·i* 単位 three academic units *san ta'n·i* 三単位

unite (irr) *ketsugō-suru* 結合する; *danketsu-suru* 団結する

United Kingdom *Rengō Ō'koku* 連合王国; (coll) *Eikoku* 英国

United Nations *Kokusai Re'ngō* 国際連合; (abbr) *Kokuren* 国連

United States of America (USA) *Amerika Gasshū'koku* アメリカ合衆国; (abbr) *Amerika* アメリカ

universe *u'chū* 宇宙

university *daigaku* 大学

unjust *fusei* [*na*] 不正[な]

unkind *fushi'nsetsu* [*na*] 不親切[な]

unknown (attr) **1** *shirarete inai* 知られていない **2** *na no na'i* 名のない an unknown author *na no na'i sakka* 名のない作家

unlawful *fuhō* [*na*] 不法[な]

unless *...nakereba...* なければ Unless we receive an answer by tomorrow, we'll have to make an overseas phone call. *Ashita ma'de ni henji ga na'kereba, kokusai de'nwa o shina'kereba nara'nai.* 明日までに返事がなければ国際電話をしなければならない。

unlike compl *ni/to* (v) be unlike *kotona'r·u* 異なる ——(idiom)

-rashiku nai らしくない It's unlike him to be late for an appointment. *Yakusoku ni okureru na'nte, kare-ra'shiku nai.* 約束に遅れるなんて, 彼らしくない.

unlimited *muse'igen* [no] 無制限[の]

unlock (idiom) to unlock *kagi' o ake·ru* 鍵を開ける

unlucky (idiom) *u'n ga waru'·i* 運が悪い I was unlucky. *U'n ga wa'rukatta.* 運が悪かった.

unmarried 1 *dokushin* [no] 独身[の] 2 unmarried woman *mikon no josei* 未婚の女性 3 unmarried man/woman *dokushi'nsha* 独身者

unnatural *fushi'zen* [na] 不自然[な]

unnecessary *fuyō* [na] 不要[な]

unpleasant *fuyu'kai* [na] 不愉快[な]

unplug (idiom) *se'n o nuk·u* 栓を抜く Unplug the iron, please. *Airon no sashikomi o nuite kudasa'i.* アイロンの差込を抜いて下さい.

unpopular (attr) *ninki no na'i* 人気のない

unreasonable 1 *mu'ri* [na] 無理[な] an unreasonable demand *mu'ri na yōkyū* 無理な要求; *fugō'ri* [na] 不合理[な] an unreasonable theory *fugō'ri na setsu* 不合理な説 ——(idiom) *mu'ri o i·u* 無理を言う Don't be unreasonable! *Mu'ri o iwana'ide!* 無理を言わないで.

unreasonably *mu'ri ni* 無理に; *ba'ka ni* ばかに The price is unreasonably high. *Nedan wa ba'ka ni taka'i.* 値段はばかに高い.

unsafe (adj) *abuna'·i* 危い

unsanitary *fue'isei* [na] 不衛生[な] unsanitary living conditions *fue'isei na seikatsu jō'tai* 不衛生な生活状態

unsatisfactory *fumanzoku* [na] 不満足[な] The results were unsatisfactory. *Kekka wa fuma'nzoku deshita.* 結果は不満足でした.

unsavory (unpalatable) (adj) *mazu'·i* まずい

unsightly *meza'wari* [na] 目障り[な]

unskillful *heta'* [na] 下手[な] an unskillful way of doing (something) *heta' na yarikata* 下手なやり方

unskillfully *heta' ni* 下手に

unsteadily *fua'ntei ni* 不安定に

unsuccessful *fuse'ikō* [na] 不成功[な]

untidy (attr) *chirakashita* 散らかした

untie obj *o* (v) *to'k·u* 解く I can't untie this knot. *Kono musubime o dō shite' mo to'ku koto ga deki'nai.* この結び目をどうしても解くことができない.; *hodo'k·u* ほどく untie a package *tsutsu'mi o hodo'ku* 包みをほどく

until *ma'de* まで until tomorrow *ashita ma'de* 明日まで

unusual (adj) *mezurashi'·i* 珍しい This netsuke is unusual. *Kono netsuke wa mezurashi'i.* この根付は珍しい. ——(attr) *kawatta* 変わった an unusual angle *kawatta ka'kudo* 変わった角度

unwilling (idiom) *ki ga mukana·i* 気が向かない He was unwilling to do it. *Ka're wa sore o suru' no wa ki ga mukana'katta.* 彼はそれをするのは気が向かなかった。

unworthy (attr) *ka'chi no na'i* 価値のない

up *ue* 上 go up *ue ni iku* 上に行く

upbringing *sodachi'* 育ち; *shitsuke* 仕付け

upkeep *iji* 維持 upkeep expense *iji'hi* 維持費

upper berth *jōdan* 上段

Upper House *jōin* 上院; (J) House of Councillors *Sangi'-in* 参議院

uprising *hanran* 反乱

upset obj *o* (v) *hikkurika'es·u* 引っくり返す upset a boat *fu'ne o hikkurika'esu* 船を引っくり返す ——(idiom) **1** be upset *ki ga tentō-suru* 気が転倒する She was upset by the incident. *Ka'nojo wa sono jiken de ki ga tentō-shita.* 彼女はその事件で気が転倒した。 **2** have an upset stomach *onaka no guai ga waru'i* おなかの具合が悪い He had an upset stomach. *Ka're wa onaka no guai ga wa'rukatta.* 彼はおなかの具合が悪かった。

upside down *sakasama* さかさま; *sakasa* さかさ

upstairs *nikai* 二階

upstream *kawakami* [*ni*] 川上[に]

up-to-date *saishin* [*no*] 最新[の]

uranium *uranyūmu* ウラニウム

Uranus (planet) *Tennōsei* 天王星

urban *to'shi* [*no*] 都市[の] urban population *toshi ji'nkō* 都市人口

Urdu *Urudū-go* ウルドゥー語

urge obj *o* (v) *susume'·ru* 勧める ——(idiom) get the urge *ki ga muk·u* 気が向く When one gets the urge... *Ki ga muita'ra...* 気が向いたら...

urgent *kinkyū* [*no*] 緊急[の]

urinate (irr) *shōbe'n-suru* 小便する; (coll) *o-shi'kko-suru* おしっこする

urine *nyō'* 尿; (coll) *o-shi'kko* おしっこ

Uruguay *Uru'guai* ウルグアイ

Uruguayan (person) *Urugua'ijin* ウルグアイ人 ——(attr) *Uru'guai no* ウルグアイの

us *wata'shi-tachi* 私たち

use obj *o* (v) **1** *tsuka·u* 使う Are you using your typewriter today? *Kyō wa taipura'itā o tsukatte ima'su ka?* 今日はタイプライターを使っていますか. **2** utilize (irr) *riyō-suru* 利用する **3** make use of *mochii'·ru* 用いる

used car *chūko'sha* 中古車

used to 1 *...mono' desu...* ものです When I was a child, my mother used to read to me every night. *Kodomo no ko'ro, okā'san wa* *maiban ho'n o yo'nde kureta mono' desu.* 子供の頃お母さんは毎晩本を読んでくれたものです. **2** (habit) to be used to *na'rete ir·u* 慣れている I'm not used to such low ceilings. *Konna hiku'i tenjō ni na'rete inai.* こんな低い天井に慣れていない.

useful (idiom) *yaku' ni tats·u* 役に立つ This is very useful. *Kore wa taihen yaku' ni tatsu.* これは大変役に立つ.

useless 1 *dame'* [*na*] だめ[な] **2** futile *muda* [*na*] 無駄[な] —— (idiom) *yaku' ni tata'nai* 役に立たない This map is useless. *Kono chi'zu wa yaku' ni tata'nai.* この地図は役に立たない.

usual *futsū* [*no*] 普通[の]

usually 1 *taitei* 大抵 I usually drive to work. *Taitei kuruma de shukkin-suru.* 大抵車で出勤する. **2** ordinarily *futsū* 普通 Companies usually take Sundays off. *Nichiyō'bi wa kaisha wa futsū yasumi' desu.* 日曜日は会社は普通休みです.

utensil (kitchen) *daidokoro yō'hin* 台所用品; (household) *katei yō'hin* 家庭用品

uterus *shikyū* 子宮

utilities *kōnetsu* 光熱 utility expenses *konetsu'hi* 光熱費

utilize obj *o* (irr) *riyō-suru* 利用する

U-turn *yūtā'n* ユーターン

V

vacancy 1 room *akishitsu* 空き室; *akibeya* 空き部屋 **2** job opening *ketsuin* 欠員; *kuchi* 口 **3** position opening *kūseki* 空席

vacant (idiom) be vacant *aite i·ru* あいている Is this seat vacant? *Kono se'ki wa aite ima'su ka?* この席はあいていますか.

vacant lot *akichi* 空き地

vacation *yasumi'* 休み summer vacation *natsu-ya'sumi* 夏休み; *ba'kansu* バカンス; *kyūka* 休暇

vaccination *yobō chū'sha* 予防注射

vaccine *wa'kuchin* ワクチン

vacuum cleaner *denki sōji'ki* 電気掃除機

vacuum tube *shinkūkan* 真空管

vagina (Anat) *chitsu* 腟

vague *aimai* [*na*] あいまい [な] a vague answer *aimai na henji'* あいまいな返事

valley *tani'* 谷

valuable 1 important *taisetsu* [*na*] 大切[な] Nothing is as valuable as time. *Jikan hodo taisetsu na mono' wa na'i.* 時間ほど大切なものはない. **2** precious *kichō* [*na*] 貴重[な] It was a valuable

experience for me. *Watashi ni to'tte kichō na keiken de'shita.* 私
にとって貴重な経験でした.

valuables *kichōhin* 貴重品

value 1 merit *ka'chi* 価値 2 worth *neuchi* 値打ち of no value
neuchi no na'i 値打ちのない

vanilla *ba'nira* バニラ vanilla ice cream *banira aisukuri'mu* バニ
ラアイスクリーム

vanish (v) 1 disappear *kie·ru* 消える He vanished into the dark.
Ka're no sugata wa yami no na'ka ni kieta. 彼の姿は闇の中に消え
た. 2 go out of sight *mie'naku nar·u* 見えなくなる

vapor *yu'ge* 湯気; *jō'ki* 蒸気

varicose veins *jōmyaku'ryū* 静脈瘤

variety *shu'rui* 種類 ——*iroiro na* 色々な That department
store has a variety of foreign goods. *Sono depa'to ni wa iroiro
na gaikoku se'ihin ga a'ru.* そのデパートには色々な外国製品が
ある.

various *iroiro [na]* 色々[な] We've lived in various places. *Iroiro
na tokoro' ni sunda.* 色々な所に住んだ.

varnish *wa'nisu* ワニス; *ni'su* ニス

vase *kabin* 花瓶

vaseline *waserin* ワセリン

veal *bi'ru* ヴィール; *koushi no niku* 子牛の肉

vegetable *yasai* 野菜 vegetable garden *yasai-ba'take* 野菜畑

vegetable store *yaoya* 八百屋

vegetarian *saishokushugi'sha* 菜食主義者

vehicle *norimono* 乗り物

vein (Anat) *jōmyaku* 静脈

velvet *birōdo* ビロード

vending machine *jidō hamba'i-ki* 自動販売機

venereal disease *seibyō* 性病; *seikō'i kansenshō* 性行為感染症

venetian blind *buraindo* ブラインド

Venezuela *Benezue'ra* ベネズエラ

Venezuelan (person) *Benezuera'jin* ベネズエラ人 ——(attr) *Benezue'ra no* ベネズエラの

vent *tsūkikō* 通気口

Venus (planet) *Kinsei* 金星

verb (Gram) *dōshi* 動詞

verbatim *moji-dō'ri* 文字通り

verification *shōmei* 証明

verse *shi'ika* 詩歌

vertical *ta'te [no]* 縦[の] a vertical line *ta'te no se'n* 縦の線

vertically *ta'te ni* 縦に Arrange them vertically, please. *Ta'te ni
narabete kudasa'i.* 縦に並べて下さい.

very 1 (attr) *taihen* 大変 She is very pretty. *Ka'nojo wa taihen* *ki'rei desu.* 彼女は大変きれいです。; *totemo* とても I'm very busy right now. *I'ma watashi wa totemo isogashi'i.* 今私はとても忙しい。 **2** (neg) not very *amari* (+ neg) あまり The movie wasn't very good. *E'iga wa amari yo'ku na'katta.* 映画はあまりよくなかった。

vessel 1 *yō'ki* 容器; *iremono* 入れ物 **2** (ship) *fu'ne* 船

vest *chokki* チョッキ; *be'suto* ベスト

vestibule *ge'nkan* 玄関

veterinarian *jū'i* 獣医

vibration *shindō* 振動

vice 1 (immorality) *fudō'toku* 不道徳 **2** (foible) *kette'n* 欠点

vice president 1 (of a country) *fuku-daitō'ryō* 副大統領 **2** (of a company) *fuku-sha'chō* 副社長 **3** (of a bank) *fuku-tō'dori* 副頭取 **4** (of an association) *fuku-ka'ichō* 副会長

vicinity 1 *ki'njo* 近所 He lives in the vicinity. *Ka're wa ki'njo ni su'nde iru.* 彼は近所に住んでいる。 **2** in the vicinity of... *[no] fukin...* [の]付近 There's no hospital in the vicinity of my house. *Uchi no fuki'n ni wa byōin ga na'i.* 家の付近には病院がない。

victim *higa'isha* 被害者; *gise'isha* 犠牲者

victory *shō'ri* 勝利 gain a victory *shō'ri o e'ru* 勝利を得る

videotape *bideo tē'pu* ビデオテープ

videotape recorder *bideo tēpu rekō'dā* ビデオテープレコーダー; (abbr) *bitia'ru* VTR

Vietnam *Betonamu* ベトナム

Vietnamese 1 (language) *Betonamu-go* ベトナム語 **2** (person) *Betonamu'jin* ベトナム人 ——(attr) *Betonamu no* ベトナムの

view *ke'shiki* 景色 The view here is magnificent. *Koko no ke'shiki wa subarashi'i.* ここの景色はすばらしい。 ——(obj *o* (v) *naga-me-ru* 眺める

villa *bessō'* 別荘

village *mura'* 村; *-son* 村 farm village *nō-son* 農村

villain *akunin* 悪人

vim *ge'nki* 元気 She's full of vim. *Ka'nojo wa ge'nki ippai de'su.* 彼女は元気いっぱいです。 ——(idiom) vim and vigor *ge'nki ha-tsura'tsu* 元気はつらつ

vine 1 *tsuru'* つる **2** grapevine *budō no ki'* ぶどうの木

vinegar *su* 酢

violation *ihan* 違反 speed-limit violation *supīdo i'han* スピード違反 traffic violation *kōtsū i'han* 交通違反

violence *bō'ryoku* 暴力; *bōkō* 暴行

violent *rambō na* 乱暴な a violent act *rambō na kō'i* 乱暴な行為 ——(adj) *hageshi'i* 激しい a violent storm *hageshi'i a'rashi* 激しい嵐

violet 1 (flower) *sumire* すみれ **2** (color) *sumire-iro* すみれ色

violin *baiorin* バイオリン
violinist *baiorin ensō'sha* バイオリン演奏者
viper *mamushi* まむし
virgin **1** (female) *kimu'sume* 生娘; *sho'jo* 処女; *bā'jin* バージン **2** (male) *dōtei* 童貞
Virgo *Otome-za* 乙女座
virus *ui'rusu* ウイルス
visa *bi'za* ビザ; *sashō* 査証
vise *manriki* 万力
visible obj *ga* (v) be visible *mie'·ru* 見える Is Mt. Fuji visible from here? *Koko kara Fu'ji-san ga miema'su ka?* ここから富士山が見えますか。 Germs are not visible to the naked eye. *Baikin wa nikugan de wa mie'nai.* ばい菌は肉眼では見えない。
vision **1** *shi'ryoku* 視力 I have good vision. *Watashi wa shi'ryoku ga i'i.* 私は視力がいい。 **2** (foresight) *senken* 先見 a man of vision *senken no me'i no a'ru hito* 先見の明のある人 **3** (illusion) *maboroshi* 幻
visit **1** *hōmon* 訪問 **2** (someone sick) *o-mimai* お見舞い **3** doctor's visit (house call) *ōshin* 往診 ——obj *o* (irr) *hōmon-suru* 訪問する call on a teacher at his/her home *o-taku ni sense'i o hōmon-suru* お宅に先生を訪問する ——(idiom) **1** visit someone sick *mimai ni ik·u* 見舞いに行く **2** visit a friend *asobi ni ik·u* 遊びに行く On Saturday I visited a friend in Kamakura. *Doyō'bi wa, Kamakura no tomodachi no uchi' ni asobi ni itta.* 土曜日は鎌倉の友達の家に遊びに行った。
visiting card *meishi* 名刺
visitor *raikyaku* 来客; *hōmo'nsha* 訪問者
vitamin *bita'min* ビタミン
vocabulary *go'i* 語彙 He has a large vocabulary. *Ka're wa go'i ga hō'fu da de'su.* 彼は語彙が豊富です。
vocal cords *seitai* 声帯
vocalist *ka'shu* 歌手
vodka *uo'kka* ウオッカ
voice *ko'e* 声 She has a good voice. *Ka'nojo wa ko'e ga i'i.* 彼女は声がいい。
volcano *ka'zan* 火山 volcanic eruption *ka'zan no funka* 火山の噴火
volleyball *barēbō'ru* バレーボール play volleyball *barēbō'ru o suru* バレーボールをする
volt *boruto* ボルト 100 volts *hyaku bo'ruto* 100 ボルト
volume **1** (book) *ho'n* 本; *-satsu* 冊 one volume *issatsu* 一冊 two volumes *ni'satsu* 二冊 **2** (amount) *kasa* かさ; *yōseki* 容積 **3** (loudness) *onryō* 音量 Please turn down the volume. *Onryō o sa'gete kudasa'i.* 音量を下げて下さい。

voluntarily *jihatsuteki ni* 自発的に resign voluntarily *jihatsuteki ni jishoku-suru* 自発的に辞職する; *susunde* すすんで accept voluntarily *susunde hikiuke'ru* すすんで引き受ける

volunteer *yū'shi [no hito']* 有志[の人]; *kibō'sha* 希望者

vomit 1 obj *o* (v) *ha'k·u* 吐く My son vomited during the night. *Musuko wa yonaka' ni hakima'shita.* 息子は夜中に吐きました. 2 throw up *modo's·u* 戻す ——(idiom) nausea *hakike' ga suru* 吐き気がする Do you feel like vomiting? *Hakike' ga shima'su ka?* 吐き気がしますか?

vote *tōhyō* 投票 ——comp *ni* (irr) vote for *tōhyō-suru* 投票する

voting *tōhyō* 投票

vowel (Gram) *boin* 母音

vows *chikai* 誓い

vulgar *gehi'n [na]* 下品[な]

vulture *hagewashi* 禿鷲

W

waffle *wa'ffuru* ワッフル

wag obj *o* (v) *fur·u* 振る The dog wagged his tail. *Inu' wa shippo' o futta.* 犬はしっぽを振った.

wage (pay) *chi'ngin* 賃金 standard wage *kihon chi'ngin* 基本賃金

wagon 1 *nigu'ruma* 荷車 2 (horse-drawn) *ba'sha* 馬車

waist *uesuto* ウェスト; *koshi-ma'wari* 腰回り

wait obj *o* *ma'ts·u* 待つ Wait a moment, please. *Cho'tto ma'tte kudasa'i.* ちょっと待って下さい.; (impatiently) *machikane·ru* 待ちかねる The children can hardly wait for summer vacation. *Kodomo'tachi wa natsu-ya'sumi o machikanete iru.* 子供たちは夏休みを待ちかねている.

waiter *ue'tā* ウエーター

waiting room *machia'i-shitsu* 待合室

waitress *ue'toresu* ウエートレス

wake *o-tsu'ya* お通夜

wake obj *o* (v) cause to wake *oko's·u* 起こす Wake me at 7:00, please. *Shichi'ji ni oko'shite kudasa'i.* 七時に起こして下さい. ——(v) wake up *oki'·ru* 起きる I woke at 7:00. *Shichi'ji ni o'kita.* 七時に起きた. ——(idiom) 1 cause to wake *me' o sama's·u* 目を覚ます 2 wake up *me' ga same'·ru* 目が覚める

walk 1 stroll *sampo* 散歩 2 sidewalk *hodō* 歩道 ——loc *o* (v) 1 *aru'k·u* 歩く I walk to the station for exercise. *Undō-ga'tera, e'ki made aru'ku koto ni shite iru.* 運動がてら、駅まで歩くことにしている. 2 stroll (irr) *sampo-suru* 散歩する Let's walk in the park.

Kōen de sampo-shimashō'. 公園で散歩しましょう. ——(pot) *aruke·ru* 歩ける Is the child already able to walk? *Kodomo wa mō' arukema'su ka?* 子供はもう歩けますか.

walking stick   *sute'kki* ステッキ; *tsu'e* 杖

wall   **1** (building) *kabe* 壁   **2** (garden) *hei* 塀   **3** (brick) *renga'-bei* れんが塀

wallet   *saifu* 財布; *satsu-ire* 札入れ

wallpaper   *kabe-gami* 壁紙

walnut   *kurumi* くるみ

walrus   *seiuchi* せいうち

waltz   *wa'rutsu* ワルツ

wander   loc *o* (v) **1** *samayo'·u* さまよう wander around in the desert *sabaku o samayo'u* 砂漠をさまよう   **2** loiter; hang out *urotsuk·u* うろつく Where were you wandering around last night after midnight? *Saku'ban, mayona'ka ni do'ko o urotsuite ima'shita ka?* 昨晩真夜中にどこをうろついていましたか.

want   need *ketsubō* 欠乏 ——(adj) desire [ga] *hoshii'·i* [が]欲しい I want a new camera. *Atarashi'i ka'mera ga hoshi'i.* 新しいカメラが欲しい. ——obj *ga* (v) *ir·u* 要る Do you want milk? *Mi'ruku ga irima'su ka?* ミルクが要りますか.

wanting   *fusoku* 不足 [no] This manuscript is wanting three pages. *Kono genkō wa sam-pē'ji fusoku de'su.* この原稿は3ページ不足です. ——(v) be lacking *kakete ir·u* 欠けている

want to (do something)   (adj) *-ta·i* たい This winter I want to go to Sapporo. *Kotoshi no fuyu' wa Sapporo ni ikita'i.* 今年の冬は札幌に行きたい. see also desiderative verb forms, tables 1–3, pp. xxi–xxxv.

war   *sensō* 戦争 ——comp *to* (irr) *sensō-suru* 戦争する fight a war with the enemy *teki to sensō-suru* 敵と戦争する

ward   **1** city ward *-ku* 区 Minato Ward *Minato'-ku* 港区   **2** hospital ward *-ka* 科 maternity ward *sanfujin-ka* 産婦人科

ward office   *kuya'kusho* 区役所

warehouse   *sō'ko* 倉庫

wares   *shinamono* 品物

warm   (adj) *atataka'·i* 暖かい a warm room *atataka'i heya'* 暖かい部屋

warmth   *atataka'sa* 暖かさ

warn   obj *o* (irr) *keikoku-suru* 警告する

warning   *keikoku* 警告

warship   *gunkan* 軍艦

wart   *i'bo* いぼ

wash   obj *o* (v) **1** *ara·u* 洗う wash hands *te' o arau* 手を洗う wash dishes *sara o arau* 皿を洗う   **2** launder (irr) *sentaku-suru* 洗濯す

る; wash in cold water (irr) *mizua′rai-suru* 水洗いする Don't wash in water. *Mizua′rai-shina′ide kudasa′i.* 水洗いしないで下さい.

wash-and-wear   *nō-a′iron* ノーアイロン

wash basin   *semmendai* 洗面台

washboard   *sentaku-i′ta* 洗濯板

washer   *see* washing machine

washer (used with a bolt)   *wa′sshā* ワッシャー

washing   *sentaku* 洗濯; *sentakumono* 洗濯物

washing machine   *sentakuki/sentakki* 洗濯機

washroom   *see* lavatory; toilet

washtub   *tarai* たらい

wasp   *kumanbachi* 熊ん蜂; *suzume′bachi* 雀蜂

waste   *gomi* ごみ ——obj *o* (irr) *rōhi-suru* 浪費する ——(idiom) **1** waste (something) *muda ni suru* 無駄にする Don't waste it! *Muda ni shinai yō′ ni!* 無駄にしないように. **2** a waste of time *jikan no rōhi* 時間の浪費

wastebasket   *kuzuka′go* 屑かご

wasteful   *muda* [*na*] 無駄[な] a wasteful enterprise *muda na sa′gyō* 無駄な作業 ——(adj) *mottaina′i* もったいない It's wasteful if you don't eat it all. *Ta′bete shimawanai to, mottaina′i.* 食べてしまわないともったいない. ——(idiom) a wasteful person *rōhi-guse no a′ru hito* 浪費癖のある人

wasteland   *arechi* 荒れ地

wastepaper   *kamiku′zu* 紙くず

watch   obj *o* (v) *mimamor·u* 見守る watch the development *shinten o mimamoru* 進展を見守る; *mi′·ru* 見る Watch! *Mi′te goran!* 見てごらん. ——(idiom) **1** keep watch over *ba′n o suru* 番をする Our dog watches over our house faithfully. *Uchi no inu′ wa yo′ku ba′n o shite kureru.* 家の犬はよく番をしてくれる.

watch (timepiece)   *tokei* 時計 wristwatch *ude-do′kei* 腕時計

watchdog   *banken* 番犬

watchman   *keibi′-in* 警備員

Watch out!   *Abuna′i!* 危い.

watch repairman   *tokei shūri′kō* 時計修理工

Watch your step.   *Ashimo′to ni chū′i-shite kudasa′i.* 足下に注意して下さい.

water   **1** *mizu* 水   **2** chilled water *tsumetai mizu* 冷たい水; *o-hi′ya* お冷   **3** drinking water *nomi′-mizu* 飲み水; *inryō′ sui* 飲料水   **4** hot water *oyu* お湯   **5** rainwater *ama′mizu* 雨水   **6** saltwater *shio′mizu* 塩水   **7** a glass of water *mizu i′ppai* 水一杯 ——(idiom) **1** water (something) *mizu o yar·u* 水をやる Please water the plants. *Ueki ni mizu o yatte kudasa′i.* 植木に水をやって下さい.   **2** water a large area *mizu o ma′k·u* 水をまく

watercolor   **1** *suisai* 水彩   **2** watercolor painting *suisaiga* 水彩画   **3** watercolor paint *mizu e'nogu* 水絵の具

waterfall   *taki* 滝

waterfront   (river) *kashi-dō'ri* 河岸通り; (ocean) *kaigan-dō'ri* 海岸通り

watering can   *jō'ro* じょうろ

water level   *su'i-i* 水位

waterlily   *su'iren* 水蓮

watermelon   *suika* すいか

water pistol   *mizu-de'ppō* 水鉄砲

water power   *su'iryoku* 水力

waterproof   *bōsui* [no] 防水[の]   ——obj *o* (irr) *bōsuika'kō-suru* 防水加工する Is this waterproof? *Kore wa bōsuika'kō-shite arima'su ka?* これは防水加工してありますか.

water softener   *kōsui chūwa'-zai* 硬水中和剤

water stoppage   *dansui* 断水

water supply   *kyūsui* 給水

water wheel   *su'isha* 水車

waterworks   *suidō* 水道 waterworks department *suidō'kyoku* 水道局

watery   (adj) *mizuppo'·i* 水っぽい

watt   *wa'tto* ワット sixty watts *rokujū wa'tto* 60ワット

wave   *nami'* 波 ride the waves *nami' ni noru* 波に乗る

wave   obj *o* (v) *fur·u* 振る wave the hand *te' o furu* 手を振る wave a handkerchief *hanka'chi o furu* ハンカチを振る

waver   obj *o* (v) *tamera'·u* ためらう waver in one's judgment *ha'ndan o tamera'u* 判断をためらう

wax   **1** (for polishing) *wa'kkusu* ワックス   **2** candle wax *rō'* ろう

wax paper   *rō'gami* ろう紙

way   **1** manner *hōhō* 方法 in this way *kono hōhō de* この方法で   **2** direction *hōkō* 方向   **3** way of (doing something) *-kata* 方 way of doing *shikata* 仕方; *yarikata* やり方 way of making *tsukurikata* 作り方 way of opening *akekata* 開け方   **4** out of the way *he'mpi* [na] へんぴ[な]   ——(adv)   **1** on the way *tochū de* 途中で On the way, stop by the meat market. *Tochū de, niku' ya ni yotte kudasa'i.* 途中で肉屋に寄って下さい.   **2** on the way home *kaeri'-michi ni* 帰り道に   **3** this way (in this direction) *kotchi e* こっちへ; *kochira e* こちらへ   **4** this way (in this manner) *kō* こう   **5** which way *do'tchi* どっち; *do'chira* どちら   ——(idiom)   **1** show the way (irr) *anna'i-suru* 案内する Will you show me the way? *Anna'i-shite kudasaima'su ka?* 案内して下さいますか.   **2** Get out of the way! *Doite kudasa'i!* どいて下さい.   **3** I've lost my way. *Michi ni mayo'tte shimatta.* 道に迷ってしまった.

we   *wata'shi-tachi* 私たち; (masc, plain) *bo'ku-tachi* 僕たち

weak (adj) **1** *yowa'·i* 弱い This thread is weak. *Kono i'to wa yowa'i.* この糸は弱い。 He is weak in character. *Ka're wa ko'njō ga yowa'i.* 彼は根性が弱い。; *kayowa'·i* か弱い a weak woman *kayowa'i josei* か弱い女性 **2** diluted *usu·i* 薄い weak (black) tea *usui kōcha* 薄い紅茶

weaken obj *o* (v) **1** dilute *usume·ru* 薄める weaken a solution with water *yō'eki o mizu de usumeru* 溶液を水で薄める; (irr) *usuku-suru* 薄くする **2** attenuate *yowame'·ru* 弱める weaken one's health *karada o yowame'ru* 体を弱める

weakness *yo'wasa* 弱さ; *jakute'n* 弱点 take advantage of another's weakness *hito no jakute'n ni tsukekomu* 人の弱点につけこむ ——(idiom) have a weakness (special fondness) for *da'isuki* 大好き I have a weakness for plays. *Watashi wa shibai ga da'isuki desu.* 私は芝居が大好きです。

wealthy *kanemo'chi [no]* 金持ち[の] That person is wealthy. *Ano' hito wa kanemo'chi desu.* あの人は金持ちです。

weapon *bu'ki* 武器

wear **1** obj *o* (v) (clothing) *ki·ru* 着る; (eyeglasses) *kake'·ru* かける; (a hat) *kabu'r·u* かぶる; (pants/skirt/shoes) *hak·u* はく **2** (v) be worn out *surihe'r·u* すり減る These shoes are worn out. *Kono kutsu' wa surihe'tte iru.* この靴はすり減っている。

wearing apparel *i'fuku* 衣服; *i'rui* 衣類; *kiru mono* 着る物

weary (v) **1** be weary *tsukare'·ru* 疲れる **2** be tired of *aki'·ru* 飽きる

weather *te'nki* 天気 good weather *i'i te'nki* いい天気 bad weather *waru'i te'nki* 悪い天気 ——(idiom) be/become good weather *te'nki ni na'r·u* 天気になる It'll probably be good weather tomorrow. *Ashita' wa te'nki ni na'ru deshō.* 明日は天気になるでしょう。

weather forecast *tenki yo'hō* 天気予報

weather stripping *sukima te̋'pu* 隙間テープ; *mebari te̋'pu* 目貼りテープ

weave obj *o* (v) *o'r·u* 織る

web (spider's) *ku'mo no su* くもの巣

wedding *kekkon* 結婚 wedding anniversary *kekkon kine'mbi* 結婚記念日 wedding ceremony *kekko'n-shiki* 結婚式

wedge *kusabi* 楔 ——(idiom) to wedge *kusabi de shime'·ru* 楔で締める

Wednesday *suiyō'bi* 水曜日

weed *zassō* 雑草 ——(idiom) pull weeds *zassō o nuk·u* 雑草をぬく

week **1** *shū'* 週 **2** all week *isshū'kan tō'shite* 一週間通して **3** every week *maishū* 毎週 **4** once a week *isshū'kan ni ikka'* 一週間に一回 **5** week before last *sensenshū* 先々週 **6** last week *senshū* 先週

先週 **7** this week *konshū* 今週   **8** next week *raishū* 来週   **9** week after next *saraishū* さ来週   **10** one week *isshū'kan* 一週間

weekday   *heijitsu* 平日

weekend   *shūmatsu* 週末

weekly   *maishū* 毎週

weekly magazine   *shūka'nshi* 週刊誌

weep (v) **1** cry *nak·u* 泣く She wept. *Ka'nojo wa naite shimatta.* 彼女は泣いてしまった.   **2** break down *nakifu's·u* 泣き伏す He wept at the sad news. *Ka're wa hihō o kiite, nakifu'shita.* 彼は悲報を聞いて、泣き伏した.   ——(idiom) shed tears *na'mida o naga's·u* 涙を流す

weigh obj *o* (v) [*mekata o*] *haka'r·u* [目方を]量る   ——(idiom) How much do you weigh? *Taijū wa dono gurai arima'su ka?* 体重はどのぐらいありますか.

weight **1** *mekata* 目方; *omosa* 重さ   **2** (body) *taijū* 体重   **3** (cargo) *jūryō'* 重量

weird (attr) *kimi no waru'i* 気味の悪い, a weird movie *kimi no waru'i e'iga* 気味の悪い映画

welcome obj *o* (irr) *kangei-suru* 歓迎する   ——(idiom) **1** Welcome! *Yo'ku irasshaima'shita!* よくいらっしゃいました.   **2** Welcome home! *Okaeri-nasa'i!* お帰りなさい.   **3** You're welcome. *Dō' itashimashite.* どういたしまして.

welfare **1** *fuku'shi* 福祉 social welfare *shakai fuku'shi* 社会福祉   **2** well-being *a'mpi* 安否 I'm concerned about my parents' welfare. *Watashi wa ryō'shin no a'mpi ga shimpai de'su.* 私は両親の安否が心配です.

well (adv) *yo'ku* よく You did well. *Yo'ku dekima'shita.* よくできました.

well (for water) *i'do* 井戸

well (healthy) *ge'nki* [na] 元気[な] Is your mother well? *Okā'-san wa o-ge'nki desu ka?* お母さんはお元気ですか.   ——(idiom) get well *ge'nki ni na'r·u* 元気になる

well-behaved (attr) *gyōgi no i'·i* 行儀のいい

well-known *yūmei* [na] 有名[な] a well-known composer *yūmei na sakkyokuka* 有名な作曲家

Welsh **1** (language) *Uēruzu-go* ウェールズ語   **2** (person) *Uēruzu'-jin* ウェールズ人   ——(attr) *Uē'ruzu no* ウェールズの

west **1** *nishi* 西 west exit *nishi-guchi* 西口   **2** the West; the Occident *Se'iyō* 西洋

Westerner *Seiyō'jin* 西洋人

wet (v) be/become wet *nure·ru* 濡れるThis towel is wet. *Kono ta'oru wa nurete iru.* このタオルは濡れている.   ——obj *o* (v) dampen *nuras·u* 濡らす Wet this cloth, please. *Kono fuki'n o nura-*

shite kudasa'i. この布巾を濡らして下さい. ——(idiom) soaking wet *bishobisho* びしょびしょ

wet suit   *uetto-sū'tsu* ウエットスーツ

whale   *kujira* 鯨

wharf   *hatoba* 波止場

what   *na'ni* 何; *na'n* 何 What is this? *Kore wa na'n desu ka?* これは何ですか.

what day   *na'nnichi* 何日

what day of the week   *nan'yō'bi* 何曜日

What did you buy?   *Na'ni o kaima'shita ka?* 何を買いましたか.

What did you say?   *Na'ni?* 何.

What happened?   *Dō' shimashita ka?* どうしましたか.

What is it?   *Na'n desu ka?* 何ですか.

what month   *na'ngatsu* 何月

what time   *na'nji* 何時 What time is it now? *I'ma na'nji desu ka?* 今何時ですか.

what year   *na'nnen* 何年 What year were you born? *Na'nnen ni umarema'shita ka?* 何年に生れましたか.

wheat   *komugi* 小麦 wheat flour *komugiko* 小麦粉

wheel   **1** *wa'* 輪; *kuruma* 車   **2** steering wheel *handoru'* ハンドル

wheelchair   *kuruma'-isu* 車椅子

when   *i'tsu* いつ When did you come to Japan? *I'tsu Niho'n ni kima'shita ka?* いつ日本に来ましたか.

when   ...*to* ...と When spring comes, the flowers bloom. *Ha'ru ni naru to, hana' ga saku.* 春になると花が咲く.

where   *do'ko* どこ Where is the toilet? *To'ire wa do'ko desu ka?* トイレはどこですか. Where is a telephone? *Denwa wa do'ko ni arima'su ka?* 電話はどこにありますか. Where did you buy that? *Sore o do'ko de kaima'shita ka?* それをどこで買いましたか.

whether   ...*ka dō' ka* ...かどうか I don't know whether or not we're going. *Iku ka dō' ka wakarimase'n.* 行くかどうか分りません.

which   **1** (of several) *do're* どれ Which is yours? *Do're ga ana'ta no desu ka?* どれがあなたのですか.   **2** (of two) *do'tchi* どっち; *do'chira* どちら Which do you want? *Do'chira ga irima'su ka?* どちらが要りますか.   **3** *do'no* どの which book *do'no ho'n* どの本

which direction   *do'tchi* どっち; *do'chira* どちら Which direction is the post office? *Yūbi'nkyoku wa do'chira desu ka?* 郵便局はどちらですか.

whichever   **1** (of several) *do're [de]mo* どれ[で]も   **2** (of two) *do'tchi [de]mo* どっち[で]も; *do'chira [de]mo* どちら[で]も

while   **1** (during the time interval of) ...*[no] aida* ...[の]間 Don't go into your brother's room while he's studying. *O-ni'-san ga* *benkyō-shite iru aida, ka're no heya' ni haira'naide!* お兄さんが勉強している間，彼の部屋に入らないで.; ...[*no*] *uchi* [*ni*] ...[*の*] うち[に] I must go home while the trains are still running. *Densha ga ugo'ite iru uchi ni kaera'nakereba nara'nai.* 電車が動いているうちに帰らなければならない. **2** (at the same time) ...*nagara* ...ながら Don't smoke while you're walking. *Arukina'gara tabako o su'u no wa yamete kudasa'i.* 歩きながらたばこを吸うのはやめて下さい. **3** for a while *shiba'raku* しばらく I waited for a while, but he never came. *Shiba'raku machima'shita ga, ka're wa tō'tō ko'nakatta.* しばらく待ちましたが彼はとうとう来なかった.

whip *mu'chi* むち ——(idiom) to whip *mu'chi de tata'k·u* むちで叩く

whipped cream *hoippu kuri'mu* ホイップクリーム

whirlpool *uzu'maki* 渦巻き

whisk broom *yōfuku bu'rashi* 洋服ブラシ

whiskers 1 *hige* 髭 **2** (on the chin) *ago'hige* あご髭 **3** mustache *kuchihige* 口髭

whisky 1 *ui'sukī* ウイスキー **2** whisky and water *mizuwari* 水割り

whisper *sasayaki'* ささやき ——obj *o* (v) *sasaya'k·u* ささやく

whistle *fue* 笛 blow a whistle *fue o fuku* 笛を吹く ——(idiom) to whistle with the mouth *kuchibue o fuku* 口笛を吹く

white 1 *shi'ro* 白 ——(adj) *shiro'·i* 白い **2** egg white *shiromi* 白身

who *da're* だれ Who was that? *Ano' hito wa da're deshita ka?* あの人はだれでしたか.; (polite) *do'nata* どなた Who is it? *Do'nata desu ka?* どなたですか.

whole 1 *zentai* [*no*] 全体[の] The rumor spread through the whole town. *Uwasa wa machi' zentai ni hiroga'tta.* うわさは町全体に広がった. **2** (undivided) *maru-* 丸 eat something whole *marugoto tabe'ru* 丸ごと食べる; *ichi-*...*-bun no* 一...分の a whole chicken *ichiwa-bun no niwatori* 一羽分の鶏

wholesale *oroshi'* 卸 I bought this wholesale. *Kore wa oroshi' de kaima'shita.* これは卸で買いました.

wholesaler *ton'ya* 問屋

wholesale store *oroshido'n'ya* 卸問屋; *ton'ya* 問屋

whole-wheat bread *kuro-pan* 黒パン; *hōru-hoitto no pan* ホールホイットのパン

whore *baishu'nfu* 売春婦

whose *da're no* だれの Whose coat is this? *Kore wa da're no o'bā desu ka?* これはだれのオーバーですか.; (polite) *do'nata no* どなたの

why *dō'shite* どうして; *na'ze* なぜ Why didn't you go? *Na'ze ikana'kattan desu ka?* なぜ行かなかったんですか.

wick *shi'n* 芯

wicked (adj) *waru'·i* 悪い; *aku-* 悪 a wicked person *akunin* 悪人

wide (adj) *hiro'·i* 広い a wide street *hiro'i dō'ro* 広い道路

widen (v) *hirogar·u* 広がる ——obj *o* (v) *hiroge·ru* 広げる; (irr) *hi'roku-suru* 広くする widen a road *dō'ro o hi'roku-suru* 道路を広くする

widow *mibō'jin* 未亡人

widower *otoko ya'mome* 男やもめ

width *hi'rosa* 広さ; *haba* 幅 Measure the width, please. *Haba o haka'tte kudas'ai.* 幅を測って下さい.

wife **1** (one's own) *ka'nai* 家内; *tsu'ma* 妻; *nyō'bō* 女房 **2** (another) *o'ku-san* 奥さん

wig *katsura* かつら

wild **1** *yasei* [no] 野性[の] **2** wild animal *yajū* 野獣 **3** wild flowers *yasō* 野草

will **1** testament *yuigon* 遺言 **2** intention *i'shi* 意志 That person has a strong will. *Ano' hito wa i'shi ga tsuyo'i.* あの人は意志が強い. **3** (Chr) the will of God *Ka'mi no mimune* 神の御旨

will (v + -*masu*) I will go later. *A'to de ikima'su.* 後で行きます.

willing (idiom) ...*ki ga a'r·u* ...気がある Are you willing to do it? *Yaru ki ga arima'su ka?* やる気がありますか.

willingly (attr) *yoroko'nde* 喜んで She accepted willingly. *Ka'nojo wa yoroko'nde hikiukete kudasaima'shita.* 彼女は喜んで引き受けて下さいました.

willow *yanagi* 柳

wilt (v) *shiore·ru* しおれる The rose wilted. *Bara ga shioreta.* ばらがしおれた.

win compl *ni* (v) **1** (in a game) *ka'ts·u* 勝つ **2** (in an election) (irr) *tōsen-suru* 当選する

wind *kaze* 風 A strong wind was blowing. *Tsuyo'i kaze ga fu'ite ita.* 強い風が吹いていた.

wind obj *o* (v) *mak·u* 巻く wind a watch *tokei o maku* 時計を巻く

winding (attr) *magarikune'tta* 曲がりくねった a winding road *magarikune'tta michi* 曲がりくねった道

windmill *fū'sha* 風車

window **1** *ma'do* 窓 **2** show window *shō ui'ndō* ショーウインドー **3** storm (double) windows *nijū ma'do* 二重窓 **4** ticket window *mado'-guchi* 窓口

windpipe *nodobue* のど笛

windshield *furonto ga'rasu* フロントガラス

windshild wiper *wa'ipā* ワイパー

windstorm *bōfū* 暴風

windy (idiom) *kaze ga tsuyo'·i* 風が強い a windy hill *kaze ga* *tsuyo'i oka* 風が強い丘 It's windy today. *Kyō' wa kaze ga tsuyo'i.* 今日は風が強い.

wine   *budō'shu* ぶどう酒; *wa'in* ワイン

wing   **1** *tsubasa* 翼   **2** (of an insect) *hane* 羽   **3** (politics) *-yoku* 翼 left wing *sa'-yoku* 左翼 right wing *u'-yoku* 右翼

wink   *meku'base* 目くばせ; *ui'nku* ウインク ——obj *o* (irr) *ma-ba'taki-suru* まばたきする

winner   *shōri'sha* 勝利者

winter   *fuyu'* 冬

wipe   obj *o* (v) **1** *fuk·u* 拭く wipe (one's) nose *hana o fuku* 鼻を拭く Wipe the dishes, please. *O-sara o fuite kudasa'i.* お皿を拭いて下さい.   **2** wipe dry *nugu'·u* ぬぐう He wiped his tears with a handkerchief. *Ka're wa na'mida o hanka'chi de nugu'tta.* 彼は涙をハンカチでぬぐった.

wire   **1** *harigane* 針金   **2** telegram *dempō* 電報 ——(idiom) send a telegram *dempō o u'ts·u* 電報を打つ

wisdom   *chie'* 知恵 a person with wisdom *chie no a'ru hito* 知恵のある人

wisdom tooth   *oyashira'zu [no ha']* 親知らず[の歯]

wise   *kemmei* [*na*] 賢明[な] a wise plan *kemmei na a'n* 賢明な案 ——(adj) *kashiko'·i* 賢い a wise person *kashiko'i hito* 賢い人

wish   **1** *nega'i* 願い, My wish came true. *Watashi no nega'i ga kana'tta.* 私の願いがかなった.   **2** hope *kibō* 希望 ——obj *o* (v) *nega'·u* 願う I wish from the bottom of my heart that he would come. *Ka're no arawa're'ru koto' o koko'ro kara negaima'·su.* 彼の現れることを心から願います.

wisteria   *fuji* 藤

wit   *kichi'* 機知 This work is filled with wit and humor. *Kono sakuhin wa kichi o yū'moa ni afu'rete iru.* この作品は機知とユーモアにあふれている.

witch   *ma'jo* 魔女

with   **1** by means of ...*de* ...で I cut the cloth for the dress with pinking shears. *Yōfuku no ki'ji o pinkingu-ba'sami de kitta.* 洋服の生地をピンキングばさみで切った.   **2** accompanied by ...*to* [*issho ni*] ...と[一緒に] I went to Kyoto with a friend. *Tomodachi to issho ni Kyō'to ni itta.* 友達と一緒に京都に行った.

withdraw   obj *o* (v) **1** *hikiage'·ru* 引き上げる; (irr) *te'kkai-suru* 撤回する   **2** withdraw (money) [*o-kane o*] *oro's·u* [お金を]おろす

withdrawal   **1** (bank) *hikidashi* 引き出し   **2** (cancellation) *tekkai* 撤回

withered   (attr) *kareta* 枯れた; *kare-* 枯れ a withered branch *kare-eda* 枯れ枝

withholding tax   *gensen chōshū'-zei* 源泉徴収税

without *na′shi ni*/*de* なしに/で You can't go there without a car. *Kuruma na′shi de iku koto′ wa deki′nai.* 車なしで行くことはできない.; *...-naide* ...ないで She went to bed without eating. *Ka′nojo wa tabe′naide nema′shita.* 彼女は食べないで寝ました.; *-zu ni* ずに without saying *iwazu ni* 言わずに

without fail *kanarazu* 必ず I'll be there without fail. *Kanarazu iku.* 必ず行く

witness *shōnin* 証人 ——ind-obj *ni*, obj *o* (irr) *shōge′n-suru* 証言する; *mokugeki-suru* 目撃する I witnessed the accident. *Watashi wa sono ji′ken o mokugeki-shita.* 私はその事件を目撃した.

wolf *ō′kami* 狼

woman *onna′no hito* 女の人; *josei* 女性

womb *shikyū* 子宮

wonder (fem) *...[no] kashira* ...[の]かしら I wonder where I put it. *Sore o do′ko ni oita′ no kashira?* それをどこに置いたのかしら.; (masc) *...ka na* ...かな I wonder if he forgot. *Ka′re wa wasureta′ ka na.* 彼は忘れたかな. ——(idiom) *fushigi ni omo′·u* 不思議に思う wonder at the laws of nature *shizen no se′tsuri o fushigi ni omo′u* 自然の摂理を不思議に思う

wonderful *suteki* [*na*] すてき[な] a wonderful meal *suteki na gochisō* すてきな御馳走 ——(adj) 1 remarkable *subarashi·i* 素晴らしい wonderful weather *subarashi′i te′nki* 素晴らしい天気 2 extraordinary *sugo′·i* 凄い He is a man of wonderful ability. *Ka′re wa sugo′i udeme de′su.* 彼は凄い腕前です.

wood 1 lumber *moku′zai* 木材; *ki′* 木 Is it made of wood? *Ki′ de de′kite ima′su ka?* 木でできていますか. 2 firewood *maki* 薪

woodblock *mokuhan* 木版 woodblock print *mokuhan-ga* 木版画

wooden (attr) 1 *ki′ no* 木の wooden box *ki′ no hako* 木の箱 2 *moku-* 木 wooden statue *mokuzō* 木像 3 made of wood *mokuzō* [*no*] 木造[の] timber-frame house *mokuzō ka′oku* 木造家屋; *mokusei* [*no*] 木製[の] wooden furniture *mokusei ka′gu* 木製家具

woodpecker *kitsu′tsuki* きつつき

woods *mori* 森

woodwork (woodcraft) *mokuse′ihin* 木製品

wool 1 *yōmō* 羊毛 2 wool fabric *ū′ru* ウール 3 pure (100%) wool *jummō* 純毛

word 1 *kotoba′* 言葉; *tango* 単語 2 a written word *ji′* 字 ——(idiom) 1 be as good as one's word *yakusoku o mamo′r·u* 約束を守る 2 I give you my word for it. *Sore o hoshō-shima′su.* それを保証します.

word processor *wādo-purose′ssā* ワードプロセッサー; (abbr) *wā-puro* ワープロ

work *shigoto* 仕事; *hataraki* 働き ——loc *de* (v) *hatarak·u* 働く I work at home. *Uchi de hatara′ku.* 家で働く. ——loc *ni* (v)

work for; be employed by *tsutome'·ru* 勤める Where do you work? *Do'ko ni tsuto'mete imasu ka?* どこに勤めていますか. ――
(idiom) *shigoto o suru* 仕事をする

worker   *rōdō'sha* 労働者

workout   *undō* 運動; *renshū* 練習

workshop   **1** *shigoto-ba* 仕事場   **2** work-study group *kenkyū gurū'pu* 研究グループ

workweek   *isshū'kan no kimmu'-bi* 一週間の勤務日

world   **1** *se'kai* 世界 The world's become smaller. *Se'kai ga se'maku natte kita.* 世界が狭くなってきた.   **2** (public) *se'ken* 世間 know the world *se'ken o shiru* 世間を知る   **3** the earth *chikyū* 地球

worldly   *sezokuteki* [*na*] 世俗的な[な]

World War   *sekai se'nsō* 世界戦争 World War I *Dai-ichi'ji Sekai Ta'isen* 第一次世界大戦 World War II *Dai-ni'ji Sekai Ta'isen* 第二次世界大戦

worm   **1** *mushi* 虫   **2** roundworm *kaichū* 回虫   **3** earthworm *mimizu* みみず

worn-out   (irr) be/become worn-out *gutta'ri-suru* ぐったりする; (v) *tsukareki'r·u* 疲れきる I'm worn-out! *Tsukareki'tte shimatta!* 疲れきってしまった.

worry   *shimpai* 心配 I'm sorry to have caused you worry. *Go-shimpai o o-kake shite, sumimase'n deshita.* 御心配をおかけしてすみませんでした. ――obj *o* (irr) *shimpai-suru* 心配する Don't worry! *Shimpai-shina'ide kudasa'i!* 心配しないで下さい. ――(idiom) *ki ni suru* 気にする I don't worry about such things. *Sonna koto' wa ki ni shina'i.* そんなことは気にしない.

worse   (adj) *mo'tto waru'·i* もっと悪い My cold's much worse. *Kaze wa mo'tto wa'ruku natta.* 風邪はもっと悪くなった.

worship   *reihai* 礼拝 ――obj *o* (irr) *sūhai-suru* 崇拝する; *reihai-suru* 礼拝する worship God *Ka'mi o reihai-suru* 神を礼拝する

worship service   *reihai* 礼拝

worth   *ka'chi* 価値 ――(idiom) How much is this worth? *Nedan wa i'kura desu ka?* 値段はいくらですか.

worthless   (attr) **1** useless *yaku' ni tatana'i* 役に立たない   **2** valueless *ka'chi no na'i* 価値のない

wound   *kega'* 怪我 ――(idiom) **1** be wounded *kega' o suru* 怪我をする   **2** inflict a wound *kega' o sase·ru* 怪我をさせる

wrap   obj *o* (v) *tsutsu'm·u* 包む Wrap this in paper, please. *Kore o kami' ni tsutsu'nde kudasa'i.* これを紙に包んで下さい. ――(idiom) wrap around *gu'ruguru mak·u* ぐるぐる巻く I wrapped tape around the hose to keep it from leaking. *Mizu ga morana'i yō ni hō'su ni te'pu o gu'ruguru maita.* 水が漏らないようにホースにテープをぐるぐる巻いた.

wrapping paper *tsutsumi'-gami* 包み紙

wreck 1 accident *ji'ko* 事故 2 collision *shōtotsu* 衝突 3 ship-wreck *nampa* 難破 4 plane crash *tsuiraku* 墜落

wrench *supa'nā* スパナー monkey wrench *monkī-supa'nā* モンキースパナー

wrestling *re'suringu* レスリング

wring obj *o* (v) *shibo'r·u* 絞る wring out the washing *sentakumono o shibo'ru* 洗濯物を絞る

wringer 1 *shibori'ki* 絞り機 2 (on a spin-dry washer) *dassu'iki* 脱水機

wrinkle *shiwa* しわ

wrinkled (attr) *shiwa-da'rake* [*no*] しわだらけ[の]

wrist *te'kubi* 手首

wristwatch *ude-do'kei* 腕時計

write ind-obj *ni*, obj *o* (v) *ka'k·u* 書く write a letter *tegami o ka'ku* 手紙を書く write by hand *te' de ka'ku* 手で書く

writer *sakka* 作家

writing 1 *bu'nshō* 文章 2 composition *sakubun* 作文 see also handwriting

wrong (attr) *machiga'tta* 間違った the wrong method *machiga'tta hōhō* 間違った方法 ——(v) be wrong *machiga'u* 間違う Isn't that wrong? *Machiga'tte imase'n ka?* 間違っていませんか.

wrong number (telephone) *bangō-chiga'i* 番号違い

X

Xerox *zero'kkusu* ゼロックス

x-ray *rentogen* レントゲン I had a chest x-ray. *Mune no rentogen o torima'shita.* 胸のレントゲンをとりました.; *ekkusu-sen* X 線

xylophone *mokkin* 木琴

Y

yacht *yo'tto* ヨット

yard (plot) *niwa* 庭 backyard *ura-niwa* 裏庭

yard (measurement) *yā'do* ヤード

yarn *keito* 毛糸 a ball of yarn *keito hito'-maki* 毛糸一巻

yawn *akubi* あくび ——(idiom) to yawn *akubi o suru* あくびをする

year 1 *toshi* 年; *ne'n* 年 2 all year *ne'n-jū* 年中 3 every year *maitoshi* 毎年   **4** once a year *ne'n ni ichido* 年に一度   **5** year before last *oto'toshi* おと年   **6** last year *kyo'nen* 去年   **7** this year *kotoshi* 今年   **8** next year *rainen* 来年   **9** year after next *sarainen* さ来年   **10** one year *ichi'nen* 一年

year (period) *ne'ndo* 年度 the current year *honne'ndo* 本年度

yearly *mainen* [*no*] 毎年[の]

years old *-sai* 才[歳] eleven years old *jūi'ssai* 11才

yeast *i'suto* イースト

yell *sakebi* 叫び; *sakebigo'e* 叫び声 ——obj *o* (v) *sake'b·u* 叫ぶ

yellow *ki* [*iro*] 黄[色] ——(adj) *kiiro·i* 黄色い

yen (currency) *e'n* 円 ¥ 1,000 *sen-en* 千円 ¥ 5,000 *gosen-en* 五千円 ¥ 10,000 *ichiman-en* 一万円

yes **1** (plain) *ha'i* はい; (polite) *ē* ええ   **2** (That's right./I agree.) *So' desu.* そうです.

yesterday *kinō* 昨日

yet *ma'da* (+ neg) まだ I haven't finished yet. *Ma'da owarana'i.* まだ終わらない. I haven't seen Kabuki yet. *Ma'da Kabuki o mi'te inai.* まだ歌舞伎を見ていない.

yield obj *o* (v) *yuzur·u* 譲る He yielded his seat to an elderly person. *Ka're wa toshiyo'ri ni se'ki o yuzutta.* 彼は年寄りに席を譲った.

yoga *yo'ga* ヨガ

yogurt *yōgu'ruto* ヨーグルト

yoke *kubiki* くびき

yolk *kimi* 黄身

you **1** *ana'ta* あなた; (familiar) *kimi* 君   **2** (plural) *anata'-gata* あなた方; (familiar) *kimi'-tachi* 君たち

young (adj) *waka'·i* 若い

your *ana'ta no* あなたの

yourself *anata ji'shin* あなた自身

yourselves *jibu'n-tachi* 自分たち; *anata-gata ji'shin* あなた方自身

youth **1** *seishun* 青春   **2** a youth *seinen* 青年

youthful (adj) *wakawakashi'·i* 若々しい

youth hostel *yūsu-ho'suteru* ユースホステル

Yugoslavia *Yūgosura'bia* ユーゴスラビア

Yugoslavian (person) *Yūgosurabia'jin* ユーゴスラビア人 ——(attr) *Yugosura'bia no* ユーゴスラビアの

Z

zeal *netsujō* 熱情

zebra *shima-uma* しま馬

zero *ze'ro* ゼロ

zigzag *jiguzagu* ジグザグ

zinc *aen* 亜鉛

zip code (U.S.) *yūbin ba'ngō* 郵便番号

zipper 1 *cha'kku* チャック；*ji'ppā* ジッパー 2 fastener *fa'sunā* ファスナー

zodiac *jūni'kyū* 十二宮

zone 1 *chi'tai* 地帯 residential zone *jūtaku chi'tai* 住宅地帯 safety zone *anzen chi'tai* 安全地帯 2 earth zones *-tai* 帯 Torrid Zone *nettai* 熱帯 Frigid Zone *kantai* 寒帯 Temperate Zone *ontai* 温帯

zoo *dōbutsu'en* 動物園

zoology *dobutsu'gaku* 動物学

zoom lens *zūmu re'nzu* ズームレンズ

Appendices

Appendix 1
Classifiers

As mentioned on page xii, there are systems for counting things in Japanese: (1) native Japanese numerals (for quantities of up to ten) supplemented by Chinese-derived numerals (for quantities of more than ten) and (2) counters, a Japanese or Chinese-derived numeral plus a classifier.

Many things may be counted with the two numeral systems. Still others traditionally have classifiers associated with them. For instance, the classifier for cylindrical things such as pencils or cans of beer is *hon*. Sheets of paper, slices of bread, and shirts—all thin and flat things—are counted with the classifier *mai*. Animate things, such as people, dogs, cats, horses, birds, and so on, are always counted with a numeral plus classifier.

The principal classifiers in use today are given in the following table. If you cannot find the appropriate classifier, count with the native Japanese numeral system up to ten, and the Chinese-derived numeral system beyond; for quantities of up to ten, native Japanese numerals are provided at the very top of the table.

When used in a sentence, the counter normally follows the thing one is counting; for example, There are three children. *Kodomo ga* (children) *sannin* (three persons) *imasu* (are). When the counter is used alone as a noun, it is not followed by a particle; for example, Give me one sheet [of paper]. *Ichimai* (one sheet [of paper]) *kudasai* (please).

Classifiers

Classifier	1	2	3	4
Japanese numerals	hito'tsu	futa'tsu	mittsu	yottsu
animals -*hiki* (small, 4-legged; fish)	ippiki	nihiki	sa'mbiki	yo'nhiki
birds -*wa*	ichi'wa	ni'wa	sa'nwa	yo'nwa
books -*satsu*	issatsu	ni'satsu	sa'nsatsu	yo'nsatsu
bunches -*taba*	hito'taba	futa'taba	mi'taba	yo'ntaba
days -*nichi*	ichinichi	futsuka	mikka	yokka
dishes -*sara*	hito'sara	futa'sara	mi'sara	yo'nsara
fruit -*ko*	i'kko	ni'ko	sa'nko	yo'nko
glassfuls -*hai*	i'ppai	ni'hai	sa'mbai	yo'nhai
hours -*jikan*	ichiji'kan	niji'kan	sanji'kan	yoji'kan
houses -*ken*	i'kken	ni'ken	sa'nken	yo'nken
machines -*dai*	ichi'dai	ni'dai	sa'ndai	yo'ndai
minutes -*fun*	i'ppun	ni'fun	sa'mpun	yo'nfun
months -*kagetsu*	ikka'getsu	nika'getsu	sanka'getsu	yonka'-getsu
pairs -*soku* (of shoes)	issoku	ni'soku	sa'nzoku	yo'nsoku
pencils -*hon*	i'ppon	ni'hon	sa'mbon	yo'nhon
people -*nin*	hito'ri	futari	sanni'n	yoni'n
sheets -*mai* (of paper)	ichi'mai	ni'mai	sa'mmai	yo'mmai
stories -*kai* (of a building)	ikkai	nikai	sangai	yonkai
times -*do*	ichido	nido	sando	yondo
years -*nen*	ichi'nen	ni'nen	sannen	yonen

Classifiers

5	6	7	8	9	10
itsu'tsu	muttsu	nana'tsu	yattsu	koko'no-tsu	tō
go'hiki	roppiki	nana'hiki	happiki	kyū'hiki	juppiki
go'wa	roku'wa	nana'wa	hachi'wa	kyū'wa	jū'wa
gosatsu	roku'satsu	nana'satsu	hassatsu	kyū'satsu	jussatsu
go'taba	rokuta'ba	nana'taba	hachita'ba	kyū'taba	jutta'ba
itsuka	muika	nanoka	yōka	kokonoka	tōka
go'sara	rokusa'ra	nana'sara	hachisa'ra	kyū'sara	ju'ssara
go'ko	ro'kko	nana'ko	ha'chiko	kyū'ko	ju'kko
gohai	ro'ppai	nana'hai	hachi'hai	kyū'hai	ju'ppai
goji'kan	rokuji'kan	nanaji'kan	hachiji'kan	kuji'kan	jūji'kan
goken	ro'kken	nana'ken	hakken	kyū'ken	ju'kken
godai	roku'dai	nana'dai	hachi'dai	kyū'dai	jū'dai
gofun	ro'ppun	nana'fun	hachi'fun	kyū'fun	ju'ppun
goka'-getsu	rokka'-getsu	nanaka'-getsu	hakka'-getsu	kyūka'-getsu	jukka'-getsu
go'soku	rokusoku	nana'soku	hasso'ku	kyū'soku	jussoku
gohon	ro'ppon	nana'hon	hachi'hon	kyū'hon	ju'ppon
goni'n	roku'nin	nana'nin	hachi'nin	kyū'nin	jū'nin
gomai	roku'mai	nana'mai	hachi'mai	kyū'mai	jū'mai
gokai	rokkai	nanakai	hachikai	kyūkai	jukkai
godo	rokudo	nanado	hachido	kyūdo	jūdo
gonen	roku'nen	nana'nen	hachi'nen	kyū'nen	jū'nen

Appendix 2
Date Conversion Table, 1868–1991

Year	Era	Year	Era	Year	Era	Year	Era
1868	Meiji 1	1900	33	1930	5	1962	37
1869	2	1901	34	1931	6	1963	38
1870	3	1902	35	1932	7	1964	39
1871	4	1903	36	1933	8	1965	40
1872	5	1904	37	1934	9	1966	41
1873	6	1905	38	1935	10	1967	42
1874	7	1906	39	1936	11	1968	43
1875	8	1907	40	1937	12	1969	44
1876	9	1908	41	1938	13	1970	45
1877	10	1909	42	1939	14	1971	46
1878	11	1910	43	1940	15	1972	47
1879	12	1911	44	1941	16	1973	48
1880	13	1912	45	1942	17	1974	49
1881	14	1912	Taishō 1	1943	18	1975	50
1882	15	1913	2	1944	19	1976	51
1883	16	1914	3	1945	20	1977	52
1884	17	1915	4	1946	21	1978	53
1885	18	1916	5	1947	22	1979	54
1886	19	1917	6	1948	23	1980	55
1887	20	1918	7	1949	24	1981	56
1888	21	1919	8	1950	25	1982	57
1889	22	1920	9	1951	26	1983	58
1890	23	1921	10	1952	27	1984	59
1891	24	1922	11	1953	28	1985	60
1892	25	1923	12	1954	29	1986	61
1893	26	1924	13	1955	30	1987	62
1894	27	1925	14	1956	31	1988	63
1895	28	1926	15	1957	32	1989	64
1896	29	1926	Shōwa 1	1958	33	1989	Heisei 1
1897	30	1927	2	1959	34	1990	2
1898	31	1928	3	1960	35	1991	3
1899	32	1929	4	1961	36		